BUILDING
Integrated Office
Applications

D1537166

BUILDING
Integrated Office
Applications

Written by Gordon Padwick

with

Lisa A. Bucki	*William J. Orvis*
Kim Demers	*Rod Paddock*
Bob Dover	*Rama Ramachandran*
Dr. David Fullerton	*Patrice-Anne Rutledge*
Stuart Kippelman	*Ron Talmage*
John Lacher	*Diane Tinney*

que ®

Building Integrated Office Applications

Copyright© 1996 by Que® Corporation.

Library of Congress Catalog No.: 95-73257

ISBN: 0-7897-0609-1

98 97 96   6 5 4 3 2 1

Interpretation of the printing code: the rightmost double-digit number is the year of the book's printing; the rightmost single-digit number, the number of the book's printing. For example, a printing code of 96-1 shows that the first printing of the book occurred in 1996.

Screen reproductions in this book were created using Collage Plus from Inner Media, Inc., Hollis, NH.

Composed in *Stone Serif* and *MCPdigital* by Que Corporation.

Credits

To Kathy

About the Authors

Gordon Padwick is employed by an engineering consulting company as a senior programmer/analyst where he is primarily responsible for developing integrated applications based on Microsoft's Office suite. Padwick has long experience with mini-computers and personal computers. He has worked with Windows and Windows applications since Microsoft introduced the first version of Windows in 1987.

Previously, Padwick was an independent consultant who specialized in Windows applications. He has contributed to many books about word processing, spreadsheets, databases, graphics, desktop publishing, and presentation software. In addition, he has presented training classes, provided computer applications support, and written custom programs.

Padwick is a graduate of London Univeristy, and has completed postgraduate studies in computer science and communciations. He currently lives in southern California.

Bob Dover, a senior programmer/analyst with SYS, Inc., has ten years programming experience. He is currently involved with creating database applications, primarily using Visual Basic and Access, though his applications have done everything from controlling major machinery, to helping teach elementary school children to add and subtract. Bob has been very active in the online community, and since early 1995, has been the leader of America Online's PC Development Forum.

In 1994, Bob helped to found the Visual Developers Group, an international, non-profit organization for Visual Basic developers, and is now serving as the group's president. He can be reached online at **bobd@vcnet.com**, at screen name **PC BobD** on America Online, or on CompuServe at address **73302,1357**.

Diane Tinney is proprietor of The Software Professional, a business that provides education, development support, and consulting on a variety of Windows 3.x, Windows 95, and Windows NT applications. Diane specializes in the integration of Windows products and, specifically, database design and implementation. Diane is the author of Que's *Paradox for Windows Programming By Example,* and is a contributing author to Que's *Killer dBASE 5.0 for Windows, Using Microsoft Office for Windows, Using Paradox for Windows, Using Microsoft Office 95,* and *Installing and Configuring Windows 95.* You can reach Diane via the Internet at **Dtinney@warwick.net**.

Rod Paddock lives in Seattle, WA with his wife Maria, cat Sylvester, turtle Harriet, horse Candy, and five fish (whose names have been withheld to protect the innocent). Rod is president and founder of Dash Point Software, Inc. DPSI is based in Seattle, WA, specializing in FoxPro, Visual Basic, and Microsoft Access database development. Rod's clients include SBT Accounting, the U.S. Coast Guard, HO Sports, Pinnacle Publishing, Intel, and Azalea Software. Rod was a featured speaker at the 1995

FoxPro Developers Conference, and the 1995 FoxTeach and VBTeach conferences. Rod writes for several database publications including *Data Based Advisor*, *Foxtalk*, and *dBASE Advisor*, his work is featured in *Using Visual FoxPro,* Special Edition from Que.

Patrice-Anne Rutledge is a computer journalist and database developer from the San Francisco Bay area. She is the author of seven computer books, including *Using Microsoft Office for Windows 95*, *Using Visual FoxPro 3*, *Using PerfectOffice 3*, and *Using Paradox 5 for Windows,* all published by Que. Patrice discovered computers while pursuing her original career as a translator and was quickly hooked. She holds a degree from the University of California and has been developing applications with Microsoft Office for three years.

William J. Orvis is an electronics engineer at the University of California's Lawrence Livermore National Laboratory where he is involved in the large-scale numerical modeling of solid-state materials and devices. He is also a member of the Computer Incident Advisory Capability (CIAC), the Department of Energy's response team for computer intrusion incidents and virus infections. Orvis received both B.S. and M.S. degrees in physics and astronomy from the University of Denver in Colorado, where he studied numerical modeling of the dynamics of orbiting bodies such as asteroids and comets. He is the author of *1-2-3 for Scientists and Engineers* (Sybex, 1987; 2nd ed., 1991), *Excel 4 for Scientists and Engineers* (Sybex, 1993), *The Excel Instant Reference* (Sybex, 1989), *ABC's of GW-BASIC* (Sybex, 1990), *Do-It-Yourself Visual Basic for Windows* (Sams, 1992; 2nd ed., 1993), *Do-It-Yourself Visual Basic for MS-DOS* (Sams, 1992), *Visual Basic for Applications By Example* (Que, 1994), *Develop a Professional Visual Basic Application in 14 Days* (Que, 1995), and *Electrical Overstress Protection for Electronic Devices* (Noyes Data Corporation, 1986). His books have been translated into Japanese, Greek, Italian, Chinese, Spanish, and Portugese. He has written for the *Computers in Physics* journal and the *IEEE Circuits Devices* magazine.

John Lacher is an Excel trainer consultant who provides services via e-mail and data conferencing to companies around the world. He has been awarded "Most Valued Professional" status by Microsoft for his contributions to the CompuServe Excel forum. He is a Certified Public Accountant and has an MBA from the University of Akron. He can be reached at **73447.2431@compuserve.com** and is the publisher of John Lacher's Excel Help Page (**http://home.navisoft.com/excelhelp**).

Ron Talmage is director of New Product Development with IntegraTRAK, a Seattle firm specializing in telemanagement software. He has over fifteen years experience in software design and programming, including eight years of teaching computing at the college level. He is currently involved in the team development of VBA, Visual FoxPro, and SQL Server applications. Ron is active in local database SIGs and a board member of the Washington Software Assocation's Northwest Developers Conference. He can be reached at **70274,1244** on CompuServe.

Kim Demers is a Microsoft Certified Product Specialist for both Word and Excel. Through her company, Demtech & Associates, Kim provides MS Office customization, integration, and support services to a number of corporations. In addition, Kim is a training associate for The Skill Set Inc., teaching Supporting MS Office and Supporting Windows courses.

Stuart Kippelman and his wife live in central New Jersey. Stuart is a Project Manager for a major pharmaceutical company. He has been involved with the evaluation, design, and implementation of computer software and hardware since 1985. Stuart owns a consulting company designing networks, multimedia kiosks, presentations and computer animations. In 1991, he was voted into Who's Who In US Executives for aiding in the successful establishment of two public access television stations. He works closely with Microsoft, testing and evaluating many pre-release products. You can contact Stuart at **73073,2251** on CompuServe or **73073.2251@compuserve. com** on the Internet.

Rama Ramachandran is a senior consultant with TechWorks International, a Westport, Connecticut-based Microsoft Solution Provider Partner. He specializes in the design and development of custom GUI-based stand-alone, network, and client/ server database systems. He has been developing database systems on Windows, Windows NT, and Windows 95 using Visual Basic, Access, FoxPro, and PowerBuilder. Rama has contributed numerous articles in *VBPJ* and is the coauthor of Que's *Visual Basic Expert Solutions* and *VBPJ Guide to VB4*. Rama lives in Stamford, Connecticut with his wife, Beena, and their son, Ashish. Reach him at Internet: **73313.3030@compuserve.com**.

Lisa Bucki has been involved in the computer book business for more than five years. In addition to Que's *Guide to WordPerfect Presentations 3.0 for Windows*, she wrote the *10 Minute Guide to Harvard Graphics*, the *10 Minute Guide to Harvard Graphics for Windows*, and the *One Minute Reference to Windows 3.1*. She coauthored Que's *The Big Basics Book of PCs* and *The Big Basics Book of Excel for Windows 95*. She has contributed chapters dealing with presentation graphics and multimedia for other books, as well as spearheading or developing more than 100 titles during her association with Macmillan. Bucki resides in Fishers, Indiana.

Dr. David Fullerton has over 25 years experience in developing computer solutions for business problems, including many years of mainframe database management and application development. He left the corporate MIS world in 1991, where he was director of applications for NBC, and worked as an independent consultant focusing on Windows development integrating Visual Basic, Access, Excel, and Word using ODBC to access mainframe and server databases. David has been a Visual Basic beta tester from release 1.0. One application he developed in Visual Basic was a finalist in the first Windows World Open. He is a Microsoft Certified Professional in Windows 3.1, Visual Basic, Access, and Word and is MES certified as an instructor in Visual Basic. Additionally, he has instructed many PC and Management courses, and most recently developed a course in Access Basic. He has had several articles and reviews published in *Visual Basic Programmers Journal* and *Data Based Advisor*. David has a Ph.D. in Theoretical Chemistry from Georgia Tech University, where he also served as an instructor.

Acknowledgments

I offer my grateful thanks to the many people and organizations who have contributed to this book.

Primarily, my thanks go to the team of talented and knowledgable authors who have contributed so much to the book. Despite a very tight schedule and many other commitments, they have all done an excellent job in providing interesting and useful insights into the processes of creating integrated applications.

My thanks also go to Elizabeth South and Tom Barich, Que Acquisitions Editors, for their invaluable help in smoothing the way, providing contacts, and keeping me on track. Among the many Que people who have made this book possible are Jan Snyder (Developer) and Lorna Gentry (Product Development Specialists), Lisa Gebken and Julie McNamee (Production Editors), and Greg Dew, Karl Kemerait, and Robert Bogue (Technical Editors). Thanks to all for a job well done.

Among numerous other people who have helped me get this book into your hands are representatives of several software companies who have provided software and information. These include Nancy and Neil Rosenberg of Inner Media for providing Collage Complete, the application used to capture the screen images printed throughout the book; Michael Bellefeuille of Corel Corporation for providing CorelDRAW! and putting me in touch with Corel's technical support team; and Christine Hansen of Visio Corporation for providing Visio and valuable technical information about it.

As always, I'm grateful to my wife, Kathy, who has uncomplainingly put up with seeing the back of my head during the many evening and weekend hours I have been working on this book. Her support and encouragement have made it possible for me to complete this book almost according to schedule.

We'd Like to Hear from You!

As part of our continuing effort to produce books of the highest possible quality, Que would like to hear your comments. To stay competitive, we *really* want you, as a computer book reader and user, to let us know what you like or dislike most about this book or other Que products.

You can mail comments, ideas, or suggestions for improving future editions to the address below, or send us a fax at (317) 581-4663. For the online inclined, Macmillan Computer Publishing has a forum on CompuServe (type **GO QUEBOOKS** at any prompt) through which our staff and authors are available for questions and comments. The address of our Internet site is **http://www.mcp.com** (World Wide Web).

In addition to exploring our forum, please feel free to contact me personally to discuss your opinions of this book: I'm at **75703,3251** on CompuServe, and **lgentry@que.mcp.com** on the Internet.

Thanks in advance—your comments will help us to continue publishing the best books available on computer topics in today's market.

Lorna Gentry
Senior Product Development Specialist
Que Corporation
201 W. 103rd Street
Indianapolis, Indiana 46290
USA

Contents at a Glance

Introducing Integrated Applications

Basic Office Integration

Advanced Integration

Contents

IV Optimizing Integration   433

18 Designing the User Interface   435

22 Working in a Multimedia Environment   535

Introduction

Walk into your local software store, get your Office for Windows 95 Upgrade, and install it on your computer. All of a sudden you have everything you need to create all sorts of exciting applications that combine the capabilities of Word, Excel, Access, and PowerPoint, right? Well, not quite. What's missing is a lot of know-how. That's where *Building Integrated Office Applications* comes in.

Some things are simple and almost intuitive. If you have any experience with Windows applications, you won't run into any trouble if all you want to do is copy something from one document into the Clipboard and then paste from the Clipboard into another document. But, if that's all you want to do, you don't need this book.

Gaining full benefit from all the facilities in Office for combining the power of individual applications is definitely not intuitive. Suppose you have data in an Access database and you want to use that data as the basis of some statistical calculations using Excel's Analysis Pak. You then want to call on Project to create a Gantt chart, and then you want to combine the statistics and chart in a report formatted by Word. All that is possible when you take advantage of the OLE Automation facilities built into Windows 95 and applications available for the Windows 95 environment. This book prepares you to handle requirements of this type.

Notice that the scenario just described brings in Project, an application that is compatible with Office applications, but not part of the Office package. As you read this book, you'll discover that you are not limited to using only the major applications in Office. You'll learn about using the many mini-applications Microsoft includes with Office, Graph, and WordArt, for example, other applications from Microsoft, such as Project, and applications from independent suppliers, such as Visio.

We're only at the beginning of the era of integrated applications. Consequently, the range of applications from which you can choose is somewhat limited. However, more and more software developers are providing integration capabilities. Look for labels such as "Office Compatible" and "Supports OLE Automation" on software boxes to find those that might offer the integration support you need. You'll find examples of using applications other than those in Office described in this book. Though these examples might not always explicitly refer to the applications you plan to use, they establish the principles you can use to develop your own integrated applications.

What is an Integrated Office Application?

Strictly speaking, an integrated office application is an application that uses components of two or more of the applications in the Office package. For example, a Word document that contains a chart created by Excel is an integrated application. In the broader sense used in this book, an integrated Office application is an application that uses one or more components of the Office package and may use components of other compatible applications. In this sense, a Word document that contains a Gantt chart created by Project or a graphic created by Visio is an integrated Office application.

This book goes somewhat beyond using applications that integrate components of Office and other applications. It introduces the concepts of using the Access Basic programming language as a foundation for integrated applications and of basing integrated applications on the Visual Basic programming environment.

Object Linking and Embedding (OLE) is the glue that holds integrated applications together. OLE is a specification that was originally created by a team of software developers from Aldus, Lotus, Microsoft, and WordPerfect, starting in 1989. The first products to fully support the first version of the OLE specification were Lotus Notes and Microsoft Excel, both released in 1991. Since then, many other software companies have released products that adhere to some or all of the early OLE specifications.

In subsequent years Microsoft began working with some 150 software suppliers to develop an enhanced version of OLE, originally known as OLE 2, but now known simply as OLE. Products complying with this new specification began to appear in 1993.

The formal OLE specification consists of 359 pages, most of it highly technical and detailed. As a builder of integrated applications, you don't have to concern yourself with the details of this specification. What you do need to know is that the OLE specification is, in fact, a set of specifications, each of which defines how a certain facility should work. There are individual specifications, for example, that define how drag-and-drop, in-place editing, and so on, should work.

Few, if any, applications fully comply with every aspect of the overall OLE specification. Many applications are, what is called, *OLE-aware*, *OLE-compliant*, or *OLE-compatible*. These phrases mean that an application offers some of the facilities covered by the OLE specification and that it does so in the manner described by the specification.

The bottom-line is you should not assume that, just because an application has OLE on its label, you can use it in the ways described in this book. You should dig deeper into which elements of OLE the application supports before making any assumptions about how an application or its components can be used as part of an integrated application. As you read this book, you'll gain insight into how you can, and how you can't, use the applications in the Office suite to build integrated applications.

Who Should Read This Book

You will gain a lot of useful knowledge from this book if you want to build applications that combine the facilities in two or more of the applications in the Office suite. You don't really need this book if you're content to occasionally copy something from a document into the Clipboard and then paste from the Clipboard into another document. You do need this book if your ideas about integration are even a little more sophisticated than that.

This book is primarily intended for readers who want to develop integrated Office applications for their own use, for use within a workgroup, or even for larger numbers of users. Although the book provides information that will help you give your applications a professional look and feel, it is not intended for developers who expect to see their work in shrink-wrapped boxes on retail shelves.

The book assumes you have a good working knowledge of Windows 95 and of at least one of the principal components of the Office for Windows 95 Professional Package: Access, Excel, PowerPoint, and Word. Of course, if your primary interests are word processing and spreadsheets, you don't need to know anything about Access. However, if you do intend to incorporate databases, you won't get very far if you haven't already developed a working knowledge of Access.

It's usually a good idea to use the simplest possible methods that are capable of achieving the desired results. Following this principle, you'll find you can create powerful integrated applications by using interactive methods, without resorting to programming. Don't think you have to become a skilled programmer before you can begin to take advantage of integration techniques.

There are many times, though, when interactive methods are not enough. That's where you need to venture into Basic programming. You'll find three flavors of Basic programming covered in this book: Visual Basic, Visual Basic for Applications, and WordBasic. The book assumes you have a little previous experience with programming and, based on that, provides a thorough understanding of how to start using these languages.

What You'll Learn in This Book

You'll learn how to build integrated Office applications, applications that combine the capabilities of the applications in the Office for Windows 95 Professional suite, and also applications that are compatible.

Here's a brief, chapter-by-chapter summary of what you can expect to learn.

Part I: Introducing Integrated Applications

Chapter 1, "Why Build Integrated Applications," sets the stage for the book by describing what integration is all about, and shows some of the benefits you can gain by building integrated applications.

Chapter 2, "Windows and Office Capabilities," gives you a fast insight into the capabilities of Office applications, with special emphasis on how each can contribute to integrated applications.

Chapter 3, "Integration Basics," helps you understand some of the OLE concepts that are the basis of integration. The chapter brings you up to speed on Dynamic Data Exchange (DDE)—the forerunner of OLE, Object Linking and Embedding (OLE)—and Open Database Connectivity (ODBC), an industry-standard method of accessing data stored in many different types of computers.

Chapter 4, "Visual Basic and Visual Basic for Applications," assumes you have a little previous knowledge of programming. From that, it leads you through the essentials of Visual Basic, Visual Basic for Applications, and WordBasic, preparing you for more detailed information about using programming to achieve integration in subsequent chapters.

Chapter 5, "Programming Application Integration," shows how you can use your knowledge of integration principles gained in Chapter 3 and programming gained in Chapter 4 to make integration work. The chapter includes specific examples involving DDE, OLE, and ODBC.

Part II: Basic Office Integration

Chapter 6, "Creating an Integrated Application with Word and Excel," illustrates some of the benefits of using Word and Excel together. It describes in detail how to use a list of names and addresses in an Excel worksheet in order to create form letters in Word, including how to create WordBasic macros to customize the integrated application.

Chapter 7, "Creating an Integrated Application with Word and Access," shows how to use an Access database as the basis of a form letter in Word instead of using a list of names and addresses in Excel. The chapter shows how to publish various types of data from Access databases as Word documents, and how to bring data from Word documents into Access tables, forms, and reports.

Chapter 8, "Creating an Integrated Application with Access and Excel," recognizes that Access and Excel have some overlapping capabilities, but each has its own specific strengths. This chapter shows you how to start creating documents that take optimum advantage of what each of these applications has to offer. You learn how to use data from Access in Excel worksheets, and how to use data from Excel worksheets in Access.

Part III: Advanced Integration

Chapter 9, "Building an Integrated Application," takes you behind the scenes of creating an integrated application. The chapter leads you through the process of analyzing a user's needs, and planning an integration project. In addition to integrating Access, Excel, and Word, this chapter also involves communication by way of the Internet.

Chapter 10, "Automating Office Integration with Word," looks at Word in detail as a component of integrated applications. It shows how Word can be used as the source of data used in other applications. The chapter shows how Word can use data in other applications, and also how other applications can send WordBasic code that controls Word's actions.

Chapter 11, "Automating Office Integration with Excel," gives you a detailed look into the structure of Excel and explores the hundreds of Excel objects you can control with Visual Basic code within Excel itself, and also by Visual Basic code that's part of other applications. You also learn how to control other applications by Visual Basic code within Excel.

Chapter 12, "Automating Office Integration with Access," shows you that an Access form is often a good starting point for an integrated application. You'll gain introductory information about how to control Access by Visual Basic code, and also how you can use Visual Basic code in Access to control other applications.

Chapter 13, "Automating Office Integration with PowerPoint," recognizes that PowerPoint by itself is a versatile tool for creating presentations. However, the techniques described in this chapter show you how to make PowerPoint even more versatile by integrating it with other Office applications.

In Chapter 14, "Integrating Schedule+ and E-Mail with Other Office Applications," you learn how to add automation features to Schedule+ (the stand-alone application that let's you organize your time) by integrating it with other applications. You also learn how you can enhance your integrated applications by incorporating e-mail capabilities.

Chapter 15, "Integrating Project with Office Applications," broadens your scope by showing how you can use Project, an application that's not part of Office, with Office applications. Among other techniques, you learn how to use Project data and charts in other applications, and how to use data from other applications as the basis for Project charts.

Chapter 16, "Working with Office Compatible Applications," broadens your scope even further, by showing how you can use components in applications from several suppliers other than Microsoft to enhance your integrated applications.

In Chapter 17, "Controlling Office Applications with Visual Basic," we progress beyond integrating separate applications to controlling them all with the Visual Basic programming language. The chapter explains the capabilities available in the Standard, Professional, and Enterprise editions of Visual Basic, and suggests how you can use them to create top-rate integrated applications.

Part IV: Optimizing Integration

Chapter 18, "Designing the User Interface," shows you that a successful integrated application is one that does what users need and is easy to work with. This chapter draws your attention to many often-ignored considerations about designing an application that people enjoy using. It shows you how to design a professional-quality user interface.

In Chapter 19, "Handling the Unexpected," you learn how to handle questions like: What if a user hits a key other than those you intended? What if a user tries to save a file on a disk, but the disk is full? What if a user tries to print a document but the printer is busy printing somebody else's document? These and many more problems occur in the real world. Learn in this chapter how to create an integrated application that copes kindly with problem situations.

In Chapter 20, "Creating Custom Menus, Toolbars, and Shortcut Bars," you learn that every integrated application should provide users with menus, toolbars, and shortcut bars that are relevant to the integrated application, not those provided by the underlying applications. This chapter shows how to replace standard menus and toolbars with those that provide access to what users need to do.

In Chapter 21, "Providing Help for Users," you learn that users should be able to click the Help button on the menu bar and get help that's specific to your integrated application, not help for the underlying Word, Excel, or whatever. Here you learn how to replace standard Help information with help you provide.

Chapter 22, "Working in a Multimedia Environment," shows how you can create compelling custom applications by providing more than just text and charts on the screen. This chapter shows you how to communicate more effectively by incorporating sound, animation, and videos into your applications.

In Chapter 23, "Using Windows APIs," we recognize that sometimes you run up against the proverbial brick wall. There's just no way to achieve what you want to do. Very often, the way to solve this problem is to use a function that's built into Windows—what's known as an API. Here you gain an introduction to how you can draw on many of the functions that are the basic components of Windows.

Part V: Appendixes

The four appendixes (including the glossary) at the back of the book provide extra help for you.

Appendix A, "Office 95 Compatible Products," provides information about software products that are compatible with the applications in the Office package. Some of these carry the Office for Windows 95 Compatible label. Others are in some ways compatible with Office applications, but are not labeled as such. Here you gain an understanding about what *compatible* means in this context. The appendix contains some examples of products that are labeled as Office compatible.

Appendix B, "Office Resources," is a list of various resources you may wish to consult for additional information and tools you can use in your Office integration projects.

Appendix C, "Glossary," recognizes that as you read this book, you will probably find words and phrases you don't fully understand. When this happens, look in the glossary for a brief description of what the word means *as it is used in this book*. Our intention in including a glossary is not to provide an authoritative definition of words and phrases; rather, it is to help you understand what we mean by them. In this fast-moving computer world, words come into use and rapidly spread without any real agreement about what they mean. What we mean by *object* is probably different from what you mean, and is certainly different from what people who have written doctoral theses mean. However, we offer our definitions with the simple purpose of helping you get as much as possible out of this book.

In Appendix D, "What's on the CD," you'll find a brief description of the many utilities, demonstration applications, and information files on the CD-ROM that accompanies this book.

Final Comment

As lead author of this book, I offer my sincere thanks to the contributing authors, editors, and production people who've made this book possible. In anticipation, I also offer my thanks to the readers for their interest in the subject.

Readers: I hope there are enough of you that Que asks me to prepare a second edition. I hope, too, that you'll send me comments about this book so that the second edition will serve you better than the first. Send comments to me by way of Que or, if you prefer, to my CompuServe address (**71760,25**).

I hope you enjoy and benefit from this book.

Gordon Padwick

March 1996

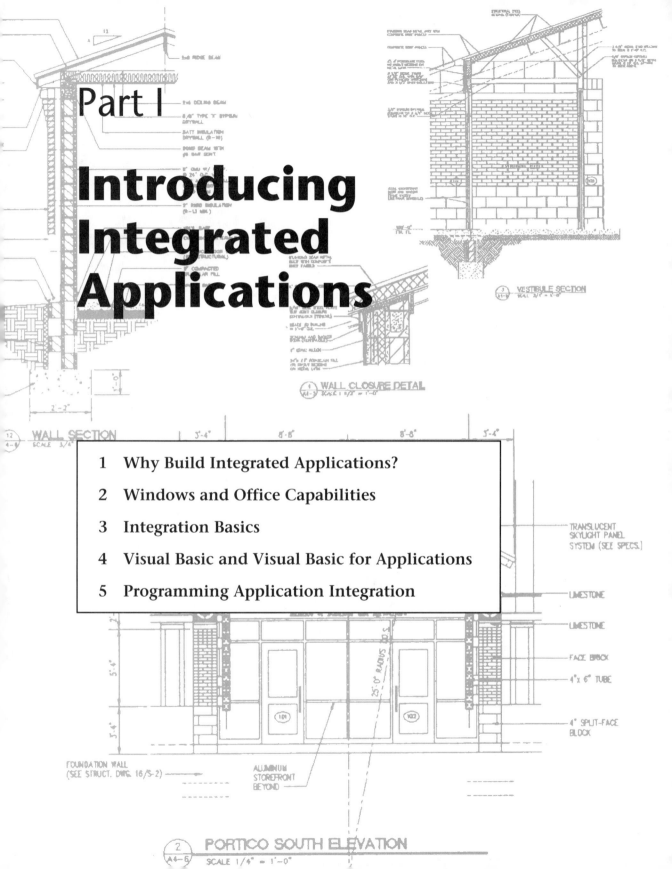

Part I

Introducing
Integrated
Applications

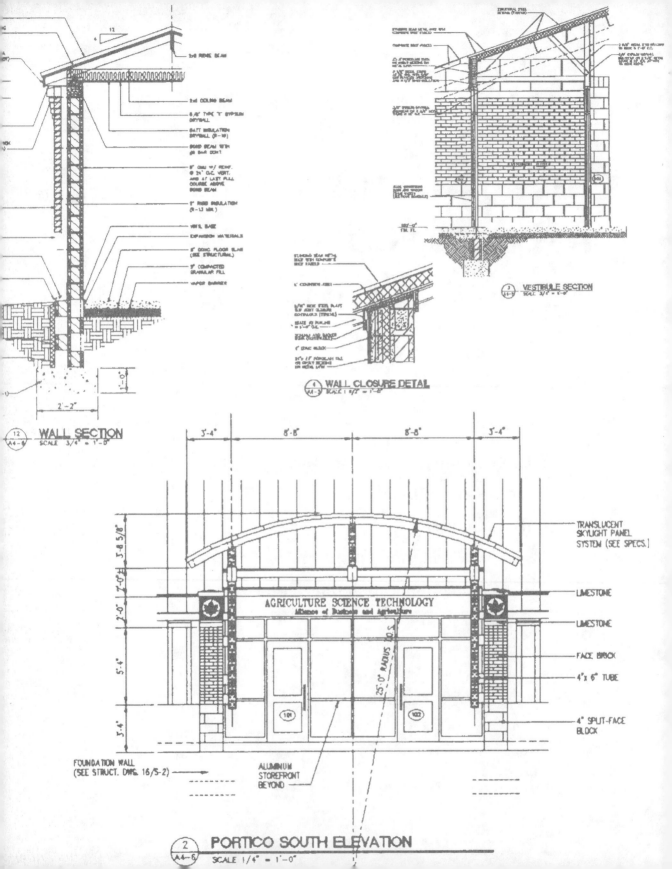

CHAPTER 1

Why Build Integrated Applications?

Whether you're a seasoned programmer or a newcomer to the field of application development, the process of integrating software products can be both fun and frustrating. If you've only experienced the fun of integration, you are indeed fortunate. If you're anything like me though, you've probably had a very healthy dose of frustration as well. Just a few short years ago, integrating applications was a cumbersome ordeal.

Thankfully, those times have changed. Windows 95 and Office 95 have provided us with integration tools that are powerful and easier to use. What's more, both the tools and techniques of integration are better documented by way of online help and books such as this one. But make no mistake—integrating applications successfully is not an effortless task. This book aims to help you better apply your development efforts so you can achieve professional results in a reasonable time frame. I'll start off here by introducing you to integration with Windows 95 and Office 95.

In this chapter you learn about

- The definition and scope of integration
- How integration benefits corporations, IS departments, users, and developers
- The tools used in integrated applications
- Hints on planning and designing integrated applications
- The future of integration

What is Integration?

Integration enables computer users to optimize information. By integrating desktop applications like those in Office, developers provide information to end users in the way those users like to see it and want to use it, rather than in the way a single application can present the information.·

According to Microsoft, an integrated solution is a "customized desktop application designed for a specific purpose," and is created by using "two or more existing applications that behave in such a way as to seem like a single application" (see fig. 1.1). The environment created through this type of development is known as *document-centric*, or *container-centric*. In a container-centric environment, *objects* (functionality, features, or data) belonging to various applications are placed in a container document (for example, a Word document) without users having to concern themselves with the applications that are the sources of those objects. In other words, integration enables users to concentrate on working with the data instead of with a variety of applications.

Fig. 1.1

Regardless of the type or number of pieces, the resulting integrated application should always appear "seamless."

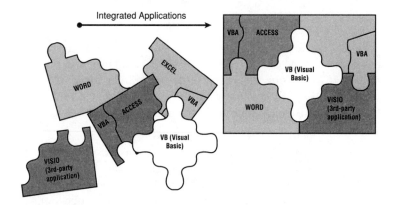

At the most basic level, embedding an Excel pie chart into a Word document is integration. At the most advanced level, a container can get database information, analyze it, plot it, report it, present it, and route it to users (internally and globally) with or without any user interaction (beyond perhaps the click of a macro or toolbar button).

Building an integrated application can be much like building a car. First, put in an engine (Windows), add the parts that make it operational (components of integration like OLE and ODBC), and then wrap the whole thing up with a great body (Office). If developers do it right, the driver gets a vehicle that not only runs faster and with greater comfort and dependability, but it also gets great gas mileage!

In a very real sense, developers must become "idea managers." As creators of integrated solutions, developers must learn to think both in terms of the corporate "big picture" and technical logistics. Many industries already recognize this and have decentralized Information Services (IS) groups so that the IS resources (people and technology) are now merged with individual business units. Developers have to become a true member of the business process in order to understand what a company really does and how the company really does it. If you build an application that doesn't process information correctly, for example, you'll be interrupting your group's ability to do business rather than enhancing your group's effectiveness. Thus, a solid business perspective is crucial in the development of any business system, integrated or otherwise.

The Power of Integration...
Everybody Wins

An integrated solution either solves a problem or answers some need and, when well-designed, it will benefit those who use it, those who paid for it, and those who created it!

Corporations increasingly rely on custom integrated solutions to speed product development, better serve customers, and more effectively manage the bottom line. Corporations see the following benefits from integrated solutions:

- Information gets to those who need it faster, and that enables a more efficient decision-making environment.

- Information can be presented more meaningfully and in a more flexible manner.

- Fewer errors occur because data is accessed directly from its source rather than reentered in multiple documents.

- Employees have more time to focus on productive tasks rather than creating and formatting documents. Companies particularly don't want technicians and managerial professionals to spend time composing documents.

IS departments with slim staffs increasingly face the challenge of helping users in non-computer-oriented jobs access new and changing technology. Integrated applications and the integration tools offered in Windows 95 and Office 95, offer the following benefits to IS departments and developers:

- Developers' knowledge of any Basic language eases the transition to using Visual Basic and Visual Basic for Applications.

- It takes far less time to create customized solutions, because developers can use hundreds of programmable OLE objects (functions and features, for example) that already exist in desktop applications.

- IS can develop solutions "custom-fit" to meet specific needs of individuals or workgroups as opposed to "one-size-fits-all" applications.

- Office components have been specifically designed to work together, enabling developers to create data exchange systems that are automatic, dynamic, and transparent.

- Because objects provide greater precision and control in the programming, custom applications require less testing.

- With properly-trained staff members, development time can be reduced.

- Because custom integrated applications generally use tools that are already familiar to end users, support and training requirements decline.

- Overhead may be reduced if fewer staff members are required for the same amount of development.

Of course, a key reason for creating integrated applications is to make life easier for end users. End users working with custom, integrated applications can:

- Access corporate data more easily and quickly.
- Manipulate and analyze the information received.
- Take advantage of an application's features (when they are included in an integrated solution) without having to actually understand the fine points of those features.

What's Under the Hood? The Tools of Integration

The technologies that enable integration are:

- Object Linking and Embedding (OLE)
- OLE Automation
- Visual Basic for Applications (VBA)
- Open Database Connectivity (ODBC)

OLE, OLE Automation, and VBA act to extend the functionality within and between desktop applications. VBA, ODBC, and all the tools described in the "Available Technology for Extending Integrated Applications" section later in this chapter act to extend functionality between desktop applications and the entire enterprise. OLE Automation, VBA, and ODBC (singly and together) are key in forming the "power train" of the integrated vehicle you are building.

The next few sections will be easier to understand if you're comfortable with the acronym *API*, because it's an essential specification used by many of the tools I'm about to describe (such as ODBC). *Application Programming Interface* (*API*) is a collection of code developed by Microsoft that provides a standard system-level interface for programmers. The API architecture is completely open and both vendor- and device-independent. Its various flavors (for example, MAPI) can provide a gateway between the developer's application and devices such as messaging, communication, and network systems.

Object Linking and Embedding

As an open, published, and widely supported standard, OLE defines the manner in which applications deal with objects (their own and those of other applications). Any application that complies with all or part of this specification can share objects with other applications.

OLE uses the concept of *presentation* and *native data*. Presentation data is the data required to display a graphical representation of an object on a display device. Native data, on the other hand, is all of the object data, in addition to the information required to edit that data. Figure 1.2 demonstrates the difference between native data (embedding) and presentation data (linking) within a container.

Double-clicking embed-
ded objects such as
Sound or Video clips will
"activate" those objects
rather than initiate
Visual Editing mode.

Both linked and embedded objects can be displayed
either as icons or data. If the selected object is, for example, a large range in a worksheet, and if it is embedded as a data display, the image may be cropped due to
a size restriction imposed by Windows. In this case, it is
more advantageous to embed the object as an icon instead.

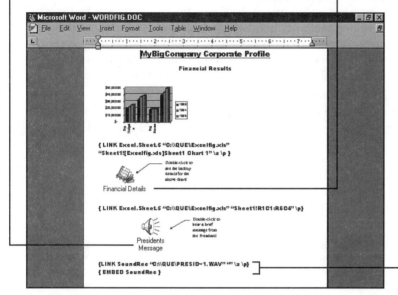

Fig. 1.2

*While both linking and
embedding may result in
identical displays for the
user, their underlying
presentation data is quite
distinct.*

Notice the difference
between the Presenta-
tion data included for
embedded versus
linked objects.

In figure 1.2, because the container already owns the data for the sound object, it
merely needs to know the application that created the sound object (for Presentation).
The container does not own the data for the financial details object, so it requires the
necessary native information for finding that object in order to edit it.

NOTE OLE drastically affects the size of a file. The document in figure 1.2, for example, is a
single-page document that's more than 1M in size.

The main specifications of OLE are linking, embedding, visual editing, nested objects,
and drag-and-drop. Applications that are OLE-compliant may implement one or
many of the specifications to varying degrees:

■ *Linking an object.* This places only Presentation data (as either an icon or a data
   display) and a pointer to the source file for that object inside the container
   document, thus reducing the size of the container document. It enables automatic or dynamic updating of object data (in single or multiple containers)
   when the data in the source object changes. As a result, linking is a reliable tool
   for summary reports that are updated regularly. On the downside, distribution
   of the container document may be limited, because users of that container

document must have access to both the object source file and the source application in order to edit the object (without the source file, they can still print and view the object as long as the source application is available). In addition, if the source file is moved or deleted, the link will be broken.

■ *Embedding an object.* This places both presentation and native data inside the container document, thereby increasing the size of the container file. Unlike linking, with embedding the container document can be distributed to any user because there is no pointer to a source file. Embedding may not be the appropriate tool for placing an object in multiple containers if that object is subject to changes (each instance of the object must be updated manually).

■ *Visual editing (or in-place editing).* This is available for most embedded objects but not linked objects. When a user double-clicks the embedded object, some of the container program's menus and toolbars are temporarily replaced by those of the application used to create the object (see fig. 1.3). When the user clicks outside the object, focus and control is returned to the container application. Objects such as sound or video are "activated" (they play) rather than opened for editing via the double-click event. A double-click on a linked object will cause the source application for that object to be launched. Visual editing is a fairly, new specification, and not all applications have implemented it.

The container application maintains control over the File and Window menu items, while the server (or Source) application assumes control over the remainder (including Help) until editing is complete.

All of the container's toolbars (including any custom toolbars) are temporarily replaced by those of the server.

Fig. 1.3

After double-clicking the Excel worksheet data embedded in this Word document, visual editing replaced most of the container application's menu and toolbar items with those of the server application (Excel), while maintaining the impression that the container application (Word) is still active.

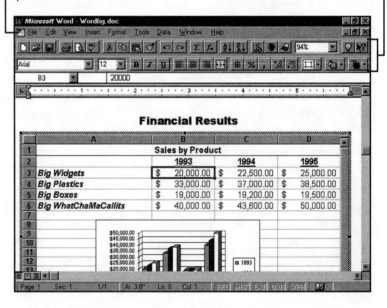

■ *Both linked and embedded objects can be nested.* That is, an object can be placed inside another object and both can be placed inside a container. In figure 1.4, an Excel chart has been embedded in an Excel worksheet which itself has been embedded in a Word document (you could have linked these objects in the same manner). Nested objects can be dragged out of their original containers and moved to other containers.

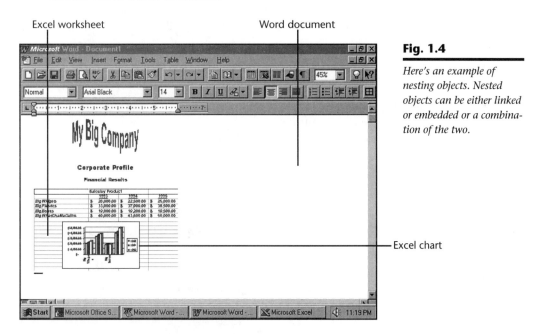

Excel worksheet   Word document

Excel chart

Fig. 1.4

Here's an example of nesting objects. Nested objects can be either linked or embedded or a combination of the two.

■ *Drag and drop.* With the drag-and-drop specification, users can click once on an object, and, holding down their left mouse button, drag that object and drop it onto a new container document (in the same or another application). The default result of a drag-and-drop procedure is an embedded object. Some third-party applications (such as Visio) allow "linking" a drag-and-drop object by pressing the Alt key during this procedure. It should be noted that the Office applications do not support this linking capability.

By understanding the impact of OLE decisions at the user level, developers can create applications that handle those decisions programmatically rather than leaving them to the users who may not understand the implications of linking and embedding. For more about linking and embedding issues, see Chapter 3, "Integration Basics."

OLE Automation

OLE Automation, while being a part of the OLE specification, is a completely separate tool from OLE.

OLE Automation is a method of communication that allows access to another application's functionality or features (made available as "objects") in a way that is generally transparent to the user and doesn't require any user interaction. OLE Automation involves a procedure much like the "handshaking" that occurs between two modems, and uses the concepts of *containers* and *servers*. A container is an application that, through its underlying language (such as VBA), can exploit or control another application's objects. It's sometimes called a *controller*. A server application will expose (or make available) its objects so they can be controlled by the container (controller).

The Office 95 applications that function as both containers and servers are Access, Excel, and Project 4.1 (while not an Office application, Project deserves mention here because it's commonly used in integrated solutions).

Office applications or components that provide strictly a server role are Schedule+, Word, Office Binder, the Document Property Object Library (a collection of objects that allow programmers to customize or exploit document statistics information), and PowerPoint.

Figure 1.5 graphically demonstrates the behavior of the server and container components of Office.

Fig. 1.5

The circled components expose one or more objects and can only be driven by the boxed components. The boxed components drive or can be driven by other boxed components.

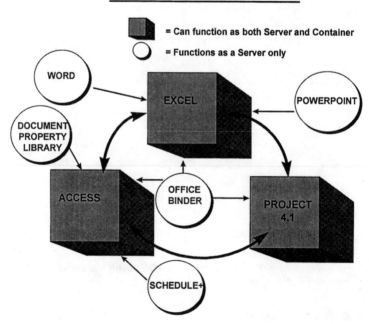

OLE Servers & Containers

= Can function as both Server and Container

= Functions as a Server only

WORD

DOCUMENT PROPERTY LIBRARY

EXCEL

POWERPOINT

ACCESS

OFFICE BINDER

PROJECT 4.1

SCHEDULE+

A description of OLE Automation is not complete without some mention of Dynamic Data Exchange (DDE). This technology was the forerunner of OLE Automation. While generally hard to use and unreliable, it remains in use in situations where there is no better method of communication (such as when neither application can operate as a container). Chapter 3 sheds more light on working with DDE connections.

BASICally Speaking

Microsoft offers a complete family of BASICs that you use to create integrated Windows 95 applications:

- *Visual Basic (VB)*. A stand-alone programming environment commonly used in developing integrated solutions that run from a stand-alone executable (EXE) file. Without the requirement of a "front-end" application in order to run, it's usually the best tool for integrating applications that are not Office-specific.

- *Visual Basic for Applications (VBA)*. A subset of Visual Basic. It's not a stand-alone programming environment, and can only be accessed from the applications with which it's included. In Excel, for example, all recorded macros are by default translated into VBA. VBA is targeted as the core programming language for all the Office applications (currently VBA is available in Access, Excel, and Project version 4.1).

NOTE Two features of VBA give it an advantage over more traditional programming languages like C. Its commands are more easily read because the syntax follows an English language structure. It also uses an object-centric syntax which makes it more practical for today's object-oriented environment. Both of these features combined promote a faster development cycle.

- *Access Basic*. The programming language for versions of Access up to 2.0. Access now uses VBA but continues to support the use of Access Basic.

- *WordBasic*. The programming language for Word. It differs from the other Basics in that its syntax is not object-centric. WordBasic syntax imitates Word's menu commands, as opposed to Excel's VBA, which uses the methods and properties of objects. The WordBasic language is currently the only object that Word exposes to other applications and thus is the only way that another application can use any of Word's functionality or features. It's not known yet whether WordBasic will be replaced by VBA in future versions of Word.

ODBC

The Open Database Connectivity (ODBC) specification developed by Microsoft (together with other database manufacturers) provides a standard method to access databases, thereby simplifying the connection process. See "Extending Integration Beyond Office" in Chapter 3 and "Exchanging Data Using ODBC" in Chapter 5 for more about ODBC.

ODBC provides three main benefits to the development environment:

- Simplifies application development when data access is required.
- Protects applications and users from underlying network and database modifications.
- Promotes the use of the SQL standard.

ODBC operates by defining an API that all ODBC-compliant applications use to talk to various data sources through Database Management System (DBMS)-specific drivers (implemented as Dynamic Link Libraries, or DLLs), as shown in figure 1.6.

Fig. 1.6

This diagram shows the basic architecture of ODBC. The "application" can be any application that supports ODBC. The actual ODBC drivers used will differ according to the database being accessed.

ODBC Architecture

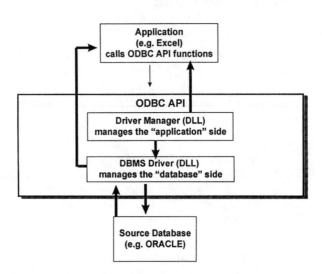

ODBC forms the database component of the *Windows Open Services Architecture* (*WOSA*). Other components of this architecture include messaging (MAPI) and telephony (TAPI). WOSA provides a single system-level interface through which front-end applications can connect to back-end services in a vendor-independent manner. By making these interfaces available to all applications, WOSA provides the framework for accessing data and resources across distributed networks. Microsoft's BackOffice is an excellent example of an integration specification that employs WOSA.

Available Technology for Extending Integrated Applications

Much of the technology discussed in this section isn't new but is included due to its increasing importance to integration now and in the future:

- *The Messaging API (MAPI).* Enables applications to "hook" into such messaging services as e-mail, schedulers, personal information managers (PIMs), bulletin boards, and online services using a standard set of protocols. Any MAPI-aware application (including all the Office 95 applications) can call upon the MAPI services. MAPI will continue to gain strategic importance for the future of integration, especially with the increased focus on the Internet for corporate use.

- *The Telephony API (TAPI).* Like MAPI, this is an open, vendor-independent API that quite simply enables communications between computers and telephone services. While it's not used to a great extent at this time, you should know what its capabilities are. Any TAPI-enabled applications such as Excel, Access, and Word can take advantage of TAPI services. For example, phone numbers located within a worksheet can be automatically dialed through the existing telephone system when TAPI is used through VB or, to a lesser extent, VBA (which uses a subset of TAPI called *Simple TAPI*). TAPI is both voice- and data-transmission enabled.

The User as an Integration Tool

Users are critical to the success of application solutions in a number of ways. They may have in-depth knowledge of the software product and can provide information about shortcuts or behavioral quirks developers aren't aware of. More importantly, though, is their input and feedback with regard to the processes used in an integrated solution. The applications you develop must function perfectly: performing calculations correctly, retrieving the right information from a database, displaying the right table. If the application doesn't function correctly, it will create (rather than solve) a business problem. Because integrated solutions are always "user-driven," it's important that users be allowed to remain as much as possible in the driver's seat to help you ensure that the integrated application really is a solution. By working with users as you develop applications, you're assured that the final product is one users can and will take advantage of.

New Office Features for Integration

A number of new features added to Office 95 strengthen its positioning for integrating the desktop with local networks, wide area networks, and information services. These features include but aren't limited to:

- *Office Binder.* Provides a common file type (ODB) for storing Office documents created with different applications in a single file and in a single location (see fig. 1.7). Word, Excel, and PowerPoint all support this technology (neither Access nor Project 4.1 support Binder at this time).

  With Office Binder, you can store documents created in any binder-enabled application in a single location. These are known as *sections* and are displayed as icons on the left side of the screen. See Chapter 2, "Windows and Office Capabilities," to learn more about the Binder.

Fig. 1.7

Clicking the icon representing the Binder section activates the appropriate application, displaying the data for that section on-screen.

Binder sections—

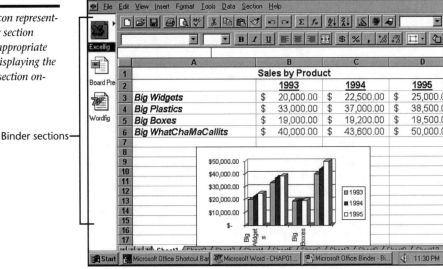

- *Full messaging integration.* This capability with the Exchange client is available with Word, Excel, and Access. For more on this, see Chapter 2, "Windows and Office Capabilities."

- *File Properties exposure.* All Office applications expose their File Properties to OLE Automation containers for solutions that require document management.

- *Shared Lists (Excel and Access).* Provide support for multiuser environments.

Adding Other Options...How Compatible is "Compatible"?

The popularity of integration has resulted in an increased demand for third-party applications that can be included in integrated solutions. Current and future third-party applications may offer different levels of compatibility with Office, and it's important to understand this when considering these products.

Any product that has `Office 95 Compatible` clearly marked on its packaging has been tested through the Microsoft Compatibility Program. The Compatibility Program tests both stand-alone applications and host applications ("mini-applications"). (Host applications like Microsoft Graph must be launched from within another application.)

NOTE   For more information on compatibility, see Chapter 16, "Working with Office Compatible Applications." For a list of products which carry the Office 95 Compatible logo, see Appendix A, "Office 95 Compatible Products."

Generally, the Compatibility Program tests only for standardized controls and menus that closely resemble those of Microsoft's applications (which themselves have become more standard in their interfaces). It's quite possible that while a product displays the Compatible logo, it may not be either an OLE Automation container or server. By the same token, products that do not display the logo may in fact be compatible in that they are either containers or servers. Their controls and menus may not follow the Microsoft Compatibility guidelines, or the vendor may simply have chosen not to participate in the program (this may not matter to you if you're merely borrowing functionality from that application).

Depending on the extent of your requirements, you would be wise to investigate the level of compatibility provided before choosing a particular product, regardless of the label affixed to the packaging.

Possible Negative Impacts of Integration and How To Avoid Them

Virtually every piece of software installed on a computer will affect the resources of that computer in some way. This is especially true of integrated applications, which can cause both memory and performance problems. Being aware of areas where that impact may be negative enables developers to prevent or minimize system burdens caused by custom applications. Some barriers to be aware of include:

- *Disk space.* Due mainly to the many graphical objects contained in many of them, integrated applications can consume anywhere from 100K to more than 2M of disk space. While most computers today can handle this requirement, remember that the larger the file, the longer it will take to load over networks. One way to minimize file size is to link rather than embed objects wherever possible.

- *Performance.* Visual Basic is an interpretive language, meaning it requires an interpreter to translate instructions for the computer. Not only does the interpreter use up disk space (the interpreter for VB, VBRUN.DLL, uses 400K), but the interpretation process itself can reduce the performance of the application. Efficient use of code (for example, running VBA directly from Access rather than calling it from another container) can go a long way towards eliminating any downside resulting from the interpretive requirements.

- *Memory.* Even with the improved memory management of Windows 95, system resources can still become an issue in any multitasking environment. While the integrated application itself may not eat up resources, it's difficult to know how many other programs users might have open when running the integrated application. Developers should also be aware that in-place editing can also affect system resources because it employs the USER.EXE file (a core file with a 64K storage heap limit). While many objects in this file have been moved to a 32-bit area in Windows 95, it can still become full. With Windows API functions (such as CheckResources()), developers can programmatically check the available system resources and prevent any "hanging" that may occur. You might also want to consider avoiding linking or embedding objects unless absolutely necessary. For example, if you want to copy Access data into Word, use the ODBC features from Word rather than pasting the data.

How To Avoid Building a Corporate "Edsel"

This section provides some helpful hints and advice gained from the experiences of those who have gone before you. Keep these points in mind when creating your own solutions so that your application will actually be used rather than becoming a "collector's item" like the Edsel.

Skills Required for Integration Team Members

Developers must understand the day-to-day business processes of the organization they work for by becoming involved in those processes either directly or through the users. They must also understand the mission and/or goals of that organization so that any integrated solutions created will align with those goals. Developers must know the software they are programming for and with. This way, there is greater likelihood that the appropriate application(s) will be selected and the development process will progress more smoothly. No matter how great your programming skills, you will be unable to make up for a poorly chosen application.

Developers must also make the switch from reactive to proactive development. By involving themselves in daily company operations, developers become well-placed to discover areas where integrated solutions can be applied.

Planning and Design (Measure Twice and Then Cut)

Proper planning and design in any project (be it woodworking, car building, or application integration) always results in an easier process and usually results in a better end result.

You should follow one or more of these planning recommendations, depending on the complexity of your integrated application:

- *Understand the potential of your application.* Know what can and can't be accomplished, keeping in mind any future possibilities where the system can be extended for more functionality.

■ *A well-designed integrated solution—as well as the features it contains—always has a clear purpose.* Which features or functions are "must haves" and which are "like to haves"? Do these features help to achieve the defined goals? Does the purpose of the application meet the requirements of both the corporation and the intended users?

■ *Make sure you're using the right tool for the job.* With all of the methods and tools available, it's easy to select the wrong product. Understand both the capabilities and limitations of the applications you intend to use.

■ *Prepare a prototype of the application and let some end users review it.* User feedback with regard to order of procedure and interface appearance is especially important at this stage. It's easier to make changes in these two areas now, rather than later when programming code has been added.

■ *Examine the architecture of your application.* You need to ensure that the architecture is workable and to foresee any impact the application may have on such things as system resources.

■ *Gather a well-rounded test group of users with varying skill levels.* Be certain that your test group is clear on what they're testing for. Ensure thorough and constructive feedback by preparing detailed checklists and by providing deadlines for the testing procedure. More importantly, listen to the users. Their satisfaction is critical.

Most of us at some point have been exposed with user interfaces that are too busy, or have too many loud colors. Sometimes you can't put your finger on what exactly is wrong with this picture, but you know the screen irritates you. That's because the designer didn't follow the most basic rule of UI (user interface) design—"Keep It Simple!" Some hints for achieving this end include:

■ *Keep the user interface as plain as possible with a minimal number of well-identified buttons and one or no menus.* If the user will be prevented from accessing the built-in menus or toolbars of the Office application while your application is running, remove those as well. If a feature doesn't contribute directly to the requirements of the application, don't include it.

■ *The interface should emulate what the users are already comfortable with.* They will expect certain features to be located in certain areas of the screen. For example, if you're providing a specific Help file for your application, always place the Help menu item at the far-right end of the window menu bar.

■ *The application must be easy to use with little or no documentation.* One of the aims of an integrated application is to reduce the support and training burden, and following this rule will help ensure that aim.

■ *Remember that some people prefer viewing graphical data and some prefer numerical data.* Whenever possible, provide both options.

- *Where it is available, use features or functionality that already exist without programming.* For example, rather than programming an Excel database to extract particular records, simply use either AutoFilter or Advanced AutoFilter.

- *To optimize performance and otherwise protect an application from being corrupted in some way, prevent users from directly interacting with the underlying software.* For example, Excel's Programmable Protection Mode enables developers using VBA to customize the protection of the workbooks or worksheets so as to prevent users from using Excel's features while at the same time allowing full programmable control of those same features.

The Future of Integration

It doesn't take any magic to predict that integration is headed for the Internet. Many of the new Office 95 features (such as integration with the Exchange client) have been provided in preparation for that shift.

In the latter part of 1995, a number of Microsoft announcements explicitly confirmed this strategy. While Microsoft isn't the only player in this game, it would be unwise for us to disregard strategic announcements such as the following:

- The November 13, 1995 issue of *PC Week* reported that Microsoft intends to provide a software and business development kit for its Internet server (code-named "Gibraltar" at the time this book was written). Gibraltar will have a connector to the Microsoft Exchange Server.

- In his fall 1995 Comdex keynote speech, Bill Gates outlined the "office of the future" in which users can simultaneously edit documents in Word and share Excel worksheets linked to other information sources over the Internet.

- In December, 1995, Microsoft introduced Visual Basic Script, which is an Internet scripting language that is a 100 percent compatible subset of VB and is upwardly compatible with VBA. Microsoft's announcement stated the following:

    This fast, cross-platform subset of Visual Basic will be provided as part of the Microsoft Internet platform, and will be licensed at no cost to application, browser and tool vendors creating Internet solutions...Developers will also be able to use either Visual Basic Script or Visual Basic 4.0 to extend Microsoft Internet Information Server (formerly code-named Gibraltar). This approach allows developers to provide business object extensions to World Wide Web applications, and facilitates their integration into existing corporate systems.

- Future versions of OLE are expected to have greater cross-platform capability. To that end, Visual Basic 4.0 (the Enterprise Edition) now supports multiple network protocols (such as TCP/IP and IPX). More importantly, Microsoft has signed an agreement with a software company to place the OLE APIs on UNIX and other major platforms, presumably by 1997.

The Internet provides opportunities attractive to both large and small corporations. Greater access to potential revenues generated by operating within the Internet will force companies to improve their competitiveness. As a result, the benefits to the corporation through integration (as described in this chapter) will be felt more keenly. Increased pressure on IS departments to respond quickly to Internet developments will in turn expand the need for integrated solutions.

From Here...

This book provides you with the information you need to create both simple and complex integrated solutions. If you're new to Office 95 or to integration programming in general, the following chapters will provide you with a "leg up" to the next levels:

- Chapter 2, "Windows and Office Capabilities," gives in-depth information about what Windows and Office can do.

- Chapter 3, "Integration Basics," teaches you more about the technologies of integration.

- Chapter 4, "Visual Basic and Visual Basic for Applications," is a good source to read if you're interested in finding out more about VB and VBA.

- Chapter 16, "Working with Office Compatible Applications," provides information if you'd like to learn more about application compatibility.

CHAPTER 2

Windows and Office Capabilities

Unlike working in a pure programming language environment, when you create integrated Office applications you need to know and take advantage of built-in Windows and Office application features. The better you know Windows and the individual Office applications, the easier it will be to create truly integrated Office applications. Moreover, the better you understand the built-in features, the more robust your own application will be. This chapter first explores the integration features built into Windows, and then covers those featured in Office.

In this chapter, you learn how to

- Review exchange capabilities (fax and e-mail)
- Identify the key features of each Office application
- Integrate features of each Office application
- Explore the data sharing features of each Office application
- Review the shared utilities and add-ons
- Identify the Binder capabilities

Exploring Windows 95 Integration Features

Although you may be an accomplished user of Windows 95, it behooves us to review the key features in Windows 95 that can be exploited to build better integrated Office applications. The key integration features are:

- Microsoft Exchange
- Microsoft Mail
- Microsoft Fax

All three applications ship with Windows 95 and allow users to send Word documents, Excel spreadsheets, and PowerPoint presentations to others within and outside the organization via fax or e-mail. The mail application even allows you to specify Word as your e-mail editor, giving you all the power of Word to compose and view messages.

Exploring Microsoft Exchange

Exchange (see fig. 2.1) is an e-mail and fax tool. Some refer to it as the *Universal Inbox*, because you can set up Exchange to hold and manage e-mail and faxes from a variety of sources. The sources are called *mail delivery services*. Supported mail delivery services include Mail (over your local area network), CompuServe, the Internet (if you have Microsoft Plus!), Fax, and The Microsoft Network (MSN).

Fig. 2.1

The Exchange Inbox allows you to manage e-mail and faxes from one location and view mail in Word by double-clicking an inbox item.

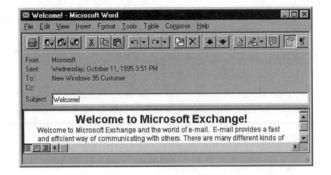

In addition to allowing you to send, receive, store, and view e-mail and faxes, Exchange allows you to include files, documents, and OLE objects in your messages. This is an important element which you should consider linking into for your integrated Office application. Instead of building your own bridging routine to share data between departments in a company, or between non-Office applications and your Office-based application, consider using Exchange as a method of sharing data.

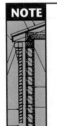

> **NOTE**
>
> Windows 95 comes with the complete workgroup version of Mail Server. This is the same Mail postoffice created by Windows for Workgroups 3.11. Thus, Windows for Workgroups users and Windows 95 users can share the same postoffice.
>
> Also note that Exchange creates a configuration file called EXCHNG32.INI (settings *not* kept in the Registry database) and will use MSMAIL.INI for backward compatibility. Be prepared to use and back up these files as necessary if you're using them in your integrated Office application.

Other key features in Exchange include:

- Universal address book
- Multiple Exchange profiles (configurations)

- Remote access and remote header preview
- MIME and UUEncode Internet file formats

Although Exchange provides many handy features, you'll find it lacks many features that you and your users may be accustomed to from using other e-mail and fax applications. The most glaring omissions are the following features:

- No capability to save messages that come from the MSN bulletin boards, CompuServe forums, or Internet newsgroups.
- No capability to convert Group 3 type faxes into editable documents or annotate faxes (no OCR support).
- No message filtering.
- No spell checker (unless you have a 32-bit word processor with a spell checker such as Word).
- Limited to one e-mail address per address-book entry.
- No automated signatures.

If your users require these features, you may need to automate these features for yourself using VB4 or link to another non-Office application.

NOTE

You can't install the MSN or Fax unless Exchange is already installed, or installed at the same time. If you uninstall Exchange, the MSN and Fax are automatically uninstalled, also.

Furthermore, in order to install Mail, you must have a shared postoffice setup and know its location.

Exploring Microsoft Mail

Before you create a profile that includes the Mail delivery service, you need to have the name and location of your workgroup's shared Mail postoffice, or you need to create a postoffice. All users in a workgroup should use the same postoffice. You should not have more than one postoffice in a workgroup.

To create a Mail postoffice, follow these steps:

1. Choose Start.
2. Choose Settings, Control Panel.
3. Double-click the Microsoft Mail Postoffice icon.
4. Follow the wizard prompts to specify the location of the postoffice and the postoffice administrator, and set various postoffice options.
5. Be sure to share the postoffice folder with the others in your workgroup.

NOTE For more information on sharing the postoffice folder, and working with the postoffice in general, see Que's *Special Edition Using Windows 95*.

Once the postoffice is set up, you can install Mail and set up user profiles. Your integrated Office application can exploit the Mail feature by providing standard communications templates, distribution lists, and even automatically invoking Mail behind the scenes for the user. If you have a situation where some users are remote, you should plan for your application to access the remote services built into Windows 95.

TIP Consider automating mail sending and retrieval for your remote users. Perform an automatic send/receive on a time schedule in the background.

To create a remote access profile for Mail, follow these steps:

1. Open the Control Panel.
2. Choose the Mail and Fax icon.
3. Click the Show Profiles button.
4. Select a profile that contains the Mail delivery service.
5. Select the Mail Information service.
6. Click the Properties button.
7. Select the Connections tab.
8. Select Automatically Sense LAN or Remote.
9. Specify the options and settings as needed on the Remote Configuration, Remote Sessions, and Dial-Up Network pages.
10. If you want to specify a schedule for checking mail, select the Remote Sessions tab and click the Schedule Item Delivery button and complete the dialog box.

Exploring Microsoft Fax

Using Microsoft Fax, you can send, print, receive, and view faxes. You can even have Fax retrieve documents from Fax-On-Demand systems. Faxes that you compose in Exchange or by using the Fax Wizard are messages. Faxes printed from Windows applications are handled as attachments to messages. The messages are stored in Exchange in the message store. You can view the stored faxes by double-clicking the attachment symbols.

NOTE The *message store* is an OLE container that can store many different types of files and objects. To the message store, a fax is just another kind of document.

Fax does not support Optical Character Recognition (OCR). Therefore, you cannot edit a Group 3 fax. You can however, send editable files through Fax with binary file transfer (BFT) to someone else who has Fax. For example, you can send an Excel spreadsheet as a fax to someone who has Fax, and that person can edit the spreadsheet in Excel.

To specify the fax message format, follow these steps:

1. Open your inbox.
2. Choose a profile that has Fax as a mail delivery service.
3. Choose <u>C</u>ompose, <u>N</u>ew Message.
4. Choose <u>F</u>ile, <u>S</u>end Options.
5. Select the desired message format: <u>E</u>ditable if Possible, E<u>d</u>itable Only, or <u>N</u>ot Editable.
6. Choose OK.

Fax also supports the sharing of a fax/modem on a network. Or, you can connect to a shared fax/modem server. In both cases, you need to create an Exchange profile on the user's computer to provide access to the shared fax/modem. And, the hardware item needs to be shared with the appropriate privileges and rights for the users.

Exploring Office 95 Integration Features

The primary design goal of Office 95 was to create a suite of core Office applications that have a common user interface and share resources, data, and automation tools with each other. Office 95 is rich with integration features. In this section, you tour the key integration features that should be considered when you build your integrated Office application.

The standard edition of Office 95 includes the following core applications:

- Word for Windows 95
- Excel for Windows 95
- PowerPoint for Windows 95
- Schedule+ for Windows 95
- Office Shortcut Bar
- Binder

The professional edition of Office 95 adds Access for Windows 95 to this list. If you've used prior versions of Office, the first feature you notice is the consistency of the user interface with Windows 95. Menus, toolbars, windows, and dialog boxes are consistent with Windows 95 in functionality and appearance. You will also notice improved consistency across the Office applications.

All Office applications support Object Linking and Embedding (OLE), Dynamic Data Exchange (DDE), and the Clipboard (copy, cut, and paste). In addition, drag-and-drop functionality has been expanded to allow you to drag-and-drop spreadsheets (or ranges), pictures, and charts. Office applications share data effortlessly. For example, a table copied from Excel to Word retains all the fonts and formats set in Excel. Linked documents automatically update when source documents change. Embedded documents provide access to the source application while storing the data in the target application. Workgroup integration with Exchange provides mail and fax capabilities from within Office applications.

Help now works the same in all Office applications, although each application has its own Help topics. And a new Find feature allows you to search for text not just in the help topic titles, but within the help file text. The Help Answer Wizard allows you to ask questions of the Help system. When you build the Help files for your integrated Office application, consider providing these features to your users.

If you purchased Office 95 on CD-ROM, you can access the *Getting Results Book* and the *Office Compatible* program. The Office 95 CD must be in the drive to launch these features. The *Getting Results Book* provides documentation and examples on efficient ways to accomplish tasks in Office 95. The *Office Compatible* program provides information and some demonstrations on products that are compatible with Office 95. As a developer of integrated Office applications, you will find these tools helpful to yourself and your users.

The Office Shortcut Bar runs as a stand-alone application that contains multiple toolbars. By default, the Shortcut Bar remains visible on the right side of the screen as you work, providing instant access to files and programs. You can use the standard toolbars that come with Office, or create your own custom toolbars. The buttons on the toolbars launch applications and/or open files. Consider creating a custom toolbar on the Office Shortcut Bar for your integrated Office application to provide users with instant access to your programs and their files.

Microsoft Binder is an OLE application that allows users to keep documents from various Office applications together in one file for easy access. Just like a metal binder clip holds papers together for you, Binder holds your Office documents together. Binder allows you to organize work by project, instead of by application. For example, a budgeting project may involve documents in Word, spreadsheets from Excel, and a PowerPoint presentation. Rather than flipping between Word, Excel, and PowerPoint applications to work on the project, you simply open Binder. Binder uses OLE to change menus and toolbars to each application as you work on the documents.

Figure 2.2 shows the Binder application with Binder 1 open. Binder 1 contains various Word, Excel, and PowerPoint documents (see the icon list on left panel). The menu and toolbars reflect the document type currently being worked on, a Word document. The only addition to the standard Word menu is a menu item named Section, which allows the user to manage the sections within a Binder document. As you plan your integrated Office application, consider the Binder application and how it might lend functionality to your application.

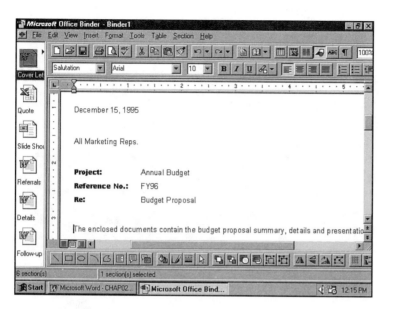

Fig. 2.2

Microsoft Office Binder provides a centralized document storage and workspace area, while giving access to server application features.

By default, Office 95 installs the Find Fast application and adds two menu choices—Find Fast Indexer and Fast Start—to the STARTUP folder (choose Start, Programs, Startup). Find Fast speeds up file searches in the Open dialog box. Find Fast creates an index of the contents of Office documents on all local drives. The indexes are automatically updated in the background while you work. You can create a Find Fast index for the contents of documents located in a specific folder, drive, or network share. The Find Fast application can be accessed from the Windows Control Panel. Be sure your integrated Office application takes advantage of Fast Start and Find Fast to speed your users' access time.

The AutoCorrect feature (corrects typing errors as you type) can be found in Word, Excel, PowerPoint, and Access. Aside from basic spelling corrections, you can customize AutoCorrect to replace text typed with other text or symbols. To display the AutoCorrect dialog box choose Tools, AutoCorrect. The replace text items are shared across Office applications. You may wish to automate data entry for users of your Office application by adding commonly typed data elements (such as replacing department codes typed with the less cryptic full departmental title).

Word and Excel provide a TipWizard feature which watches what you do. When TipWizard has a suggestion on how to make a task easier, the TipWizard light bulb button lights up. Users click the light bulb to view the quick tip. In your custom Office application, you might consider providing users with tips on how to better use features in your application.

Integrating Word

Word for Windows 95 provides many features that make your job of creating an integrated Office application easier. The templates feature allows you to create standard templates for users of your application to use when they create new documents. Within those templates you can set up standard styles and automate routine tasks. By placing your custom templates in the Office folder named TEMPLATES, users will see your custom template on the General tab of the New dialog box (see fig. 2.3). To create a new tab in the New dialog box, add a new folder to OFFICE95\TEMPLATES. To display your template on one of the existing tabs, copy your template to the corresponding folder within the OFFICE95\TEMPLATES folder.

Fig. 2.3

The custom QUE95.DOT template appears on the General tab of the New dialog box.

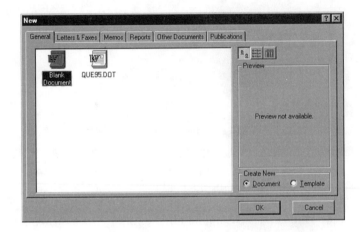

You can load global templates by choosing File, Templates in Word. This displays the Templates and Addins dialog box from which you can manage custom templates and add in applications for your integrated Office application. Unlike local templates, global templates allow you to use the macros, AutoText entries, and custom toolbar, menu, and shortcut key settings stored in a global template while you work with any document, not just documents based on that template. For example, the Normal template is a global template. Customized items you store in the Normal template are available to all documents. As you plan your integrated Office application, consider providing (and automatically loading) your own custom global template.

TIP

As part of your application exit routine, be sure to unload custom global templates to conserve system resources. Restore the normal template or other standard global template so users are returned to their normal operating environment.

The following is a list of features you may find helpful:

- *Add-ins and templates.* Unloaded when you close Word, if you loaded them by using the Templates command. To load an add-in or template each time you start Word, copy the add-in or template to the Startup file location you specified on the Tools, Options File Locations tab.

- *Automatic Spell Checking.* Identifies misspelled words as soon as they are typed by displaying a wavy line beneath the word. Users right-click the word to view a list of spelling options. If your integrated Office application relies heavily on technical terms specific to that industry, you should consider adding those terms to the dictionary to speed your user's work. You can even create custom dictionaries.

- *Enhanced AutoFormat feature.* Applies formats for borders, headings, fractions, and lists as users type. This feature may interfere with your custom application, styles, and templates. To disable this feature, choose Tools, Options and then the AutoFormat tab. Deselect any AutoFormat features which interfere with your application.

- *Highlighter.* Acts as a color marker to accentuate text in a document. Users click the Highlighter button and select a highlighter color, and then mark text as needed. The highlighting can be saved with a document and will travel via Exchange fax or e-mail. This is a handy tool that users quickly become accustomed to having. Consider providing it in your custom toolbars.

- *Address Book.* Gives users instant access to address books maintained in Schedule+ and Exchange (see fig. 2.4). Users can also define new address books from within Word. Address Book allows users to insert contact information for envelopes, labels, mail merges, and documents. For your integrated Office application, you should consider providing users with a standard custom address book.

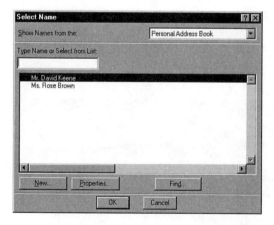

Fig. 2.4

The Address Book manages names and addresses for you.

- *Macros.* The programming language in Word is WordBasic. The easiest way to learn WordBasic is to record macros to perform routine tasks, and then view the recorded macro WordBasic commands. Macros can be assigned to a toolbar button, menu item, or shortcut keys. WordBasic provides many additional programming commands which can't be recorded. Although different than VBA, the programming language in Excel and Access, WordBasic provides many similar commands and functions.

Integrating Excel

Next to the word processor application, the spreadsheet application is probably the most used application in an office. Excel will probably play a big part in building your integrated Office application. Connectivity between Excel and the other Office applications is seamless. You can drag part of a document onto an Excel spreadsheet or drag part of an Excel spreadsheet into a PowerPoint presentation without losing formats and styles set up in the host-required application.

Integration with Access allows users to move data from Excel into an Access table. Users can drag and drop an Excel spreadsheet, or range into an Access database. Access displays a Table Analyzer Wizard to guide the user through moving data into an existing Access table, or creating a new Access table.

Users can also use Access forms to enter data into Excel spreadsheets. When it comes to creating reports on Excel data, you may consider using Access to prepare the reports. The Access report writer provides you with many built-in features which would be cumbersome to accomplish exclusively within Excel.

Here is a list of features you should be aware of:

- *AccessLinks*. Comes with Excel. In order to use AccessLinks, Access must be installed. AccessLinks adds the following choices to the Excel Data menu: Access Form, Access Report, and Convert To Access. Figure 2.5 shows how Access links can be used to create an Access form from within Excel.

TIP

If the AccessLinks commands don't appear on your data menu, you need to install the AccessLinks Add-In program.

Fig. 2.5

To create a new form using the Access Links feature in Excel, you need to identify the target database and whether your list has a header row.

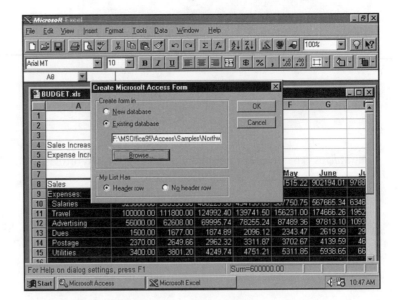

- *Access Wizard.* To create a new Access form or report from within Excel, choose Data, Access Forms or Access Reports. The applicable Access Wizard guides you through building a data entry form or report for an Excel list. The wizard places a Form or Report button on the worksheet (as applicable) to provide you with quick access to the Form or Report. The Data, Convert To Access command acts the same as dragging and dropping a spreadsheet or range onto a database. In your integrated Office application, determine the best place to store data and the best tool to use for creating forms and reports—Excel and/or Access. Then automate the integration for the users taking advantage of the built-in integration inherent in these Office applications.

- *Excel Template Wizard with Data Tracking.* Allows you to turn existing spreadsheets into forms and capture the fill-ins into a separate database. The Template Wizard helps you link the cells in the template to fields in a database or an Excel list. To launch the Template Wizard, choose Data, Template Wizard. Consider creating Excel templates linked to databases in cases where data must reside in a central location in one form, but your users need the alternative view. If the Template Wizard command doesn't appear on your data menu, you need to install the Template Wizard with the Data Tracking Add-In program.

- *Multiple users.* Multiple users can share and edit the same Excel worksheet. Excel allows multiple users to have the same sheet open concurrently. If two users try to edit the same cell, Excel automatically resolves the conflict. When designing your integrated Office application, consider whether users need to share lists of data and build the necessary features.

NOTE

Excel for Windows 95 does not provide record-locking or transaction tracking.

Also, in a shared list, users can enter data, sort data, and insert rows and columns, but users can't change cell formatting or save formulas.

To allow multiuser editing of an Excel workbook, follow these steps:

1. Choose File, Shared Lists.
2. Select the Editing tab.
3. Check the Allow Multi-User Editing checkbox.
4. Save the file on a shared network resource, such as a server or shared folder.
5. When prompted, enter your name so that the Shared Lists program can identify you to other users sharing this worksheet.

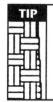

TIP

When multiuser editing an Excel workbook, click the Save button to save your changes and view other users' changes.

To see a list of other users working on a shared Excel workbook, choose File, Shared Lists and select the Status tab.

■ *AutoComplete and Pick Lists*. These features allow users to automatically complete an entry. Users can create an entry based on previous entries by typing in just the first few letters. For example, while entering data for a list of products, if you already typed the product name **Desk**, typing **De** prompts AutoComplete to fill in the **sk** for you. By right-clicking the cell and choosing Pick from List, users can select from a list of previous entries. In list-based worksheets where data repeats across rows, AutoComplete and Pick Lists can make your integrated Office application more polished and speed up data entry tasks.

■ *Cell tips*. These tips appear when you pause the mouse over a cell with a note. Use cell tips to provide interactive assistance to your users. You can describe the type of data to be entered, the actions that a button takes, or remind users of important tasks required.

■ *AutoFilter with Top 10*. This feature allows users to see the highest or lowest items in a list. Users appreciate filtering tools that allow them to find data that meets specific criteria. If your integrated Office application supports analysis of data from Excel or Access, consider providing access to AutoFilter tools.

■ *AutoCalculate*. This feature performs common math computations on the currently selected range of cells and displays the result on the right side of the status bar. Instead of scrambling for a calculator on their desk to perform a side calculation, users just select the range and view the answer. AutoCalculate can perform the following calculations: sum, minimum, maximum, count, average, and count nums. If your Office application users frequently perform these calculations, consider allowing them to use this feature (the status bar must be visible and selectable).

■ *Data Map*. This feature geographically represents your data (see fig. 2.6). The mapping feature is an OLE-based tool which uses the MapInfo application to sense geographic data in your worksheet and allows you to graph it against a map of that data. Excel comes with several maps for the U.S., Canada, Mexico, UK, Europe, North America, and the world by country. If your custom Office application deals with geographic data in Word, Excel, or Access, consider using the Excel Data Map feature.

NOTE In order to use the Map feature, the Map program must be installed. Run Setup to Add/Remove programs. Select Microsoft Excel and use Change Option to select Microsoft Data Map.

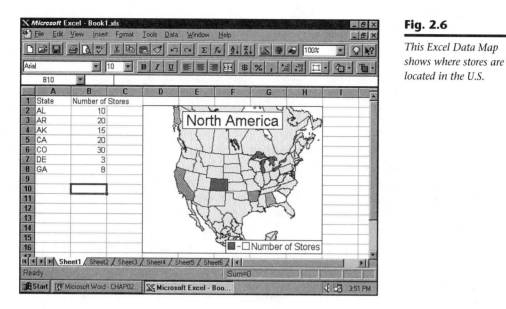

Fig. 2.6

This Excel Data Map shows where stores are located in the U.S.

Integrating Access

Access rounds out the core Office applications by providing users with a relational database management tool. Access 95 provides you with many tools that assist you in creating an integrated Office application. A major component new to Access is the VBA programming language. Access Basic has been replaced by VBA. Having a common programming language between Excel and Access streamlines your programs and allows you to share common code. VBA is also part of VB4 now, which provides you with even greater programming power. Access VBA supports most of the Access Basic commands for backward compatibility.

You should know about the following features:

■ *Access Database Wizard.* This wizard creates an entire database complete with predesigned tables, queries, forms, and reports. Review the predesigned databases to get ideas on creating your own Access database. You may even find that Access comes with a database template that you can use and tailor to your specific needs.

■ *Database Splitter Wizard.* This feature allows you to keep data on a server and the forms, queries, and reports on client computers. If you anticipate that users will frequently share a database over a network, you might find the Database Splitter feature helpful. Basically, the Database Splitter divides a database into two sections:

A back end that resides in a shared folder and contains just the tables.

A front end that resides at end-user computers and contains all other database objects (forms, reports, and queries).

The benefits include faster processing (cuts down on network traffic—only the data moves across the network), and end-users customize to meet specific data entry, analysis, and reporting needs—without affecting everyone using the data. To split a database, open the database, choose Tools, Analyze, Table, and follow the wizard prompts. If your integrated Office application includes an Access database which will be accessed over a network, you should consider using the Database Splitter feature.

■ *Performance Analyzer.* This feature reviews your database and makes suggestions on how to increase the performance of your database. The Performance Analyzer (see fig. 2.7) automatically makes changes for you and provides you with a list of other suggested improvements for your consideration. To run the Performance Analyzer, open the database and choose Tools, Analyze, Performance. Consider using the Performance Analyzer periodically to fine-tune the Access database portion of your integrated Office application.

Fig. 2.7

The Performance Analyzer allows you to specify the object type and object name(s) to be analyzed.

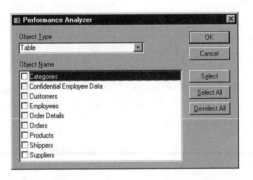

■ *Database Startup properties.* These properties allow you to control how the database opens. For example, you can specify a form to be displayed, which toolbars and menus appear, and whether to display the status bar. To set Startup properties interactively, choose Tools, Startup (see fig. 2.8). Be sure to lock users out of your application's Startup dialog box.

All Startup properties can also be set through code. In addition, note that the Startup properties take the place of many tasks previously performed in the AutoExec macro. Verify that your application's AutoExec macro doesn't undo or replicate the Startup properties that you set.

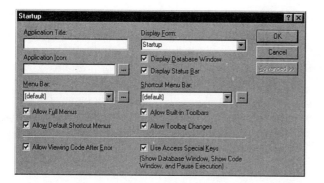

Fig. 2.8

Specify Startup properties for the currently open dialog box using the Startup dialog box in Access.

■ *Database Replicator.* This feature allows users to update data from different copies of the database. Based on the Windows 95 Briefcase feature, the Database Replicator makes a copy of your database (called a *replica*) and places it in your Briefcase. You can make changes to the Briefcase replica while you are away from the office (for example, on your home or laptop computer). When you return to the office, you can use the Update Briefcase commands to merge the changes with any changes made to the replicated copy on the desktop. Access synchronizes the two versions of the same database and keeps both current for you. To replicate a database, drag the database to the Briefcase icon on the desktop. Or, in Access, choose Tools, Replication, Create Replica. Consider providing the database Replicator feature in your Office application for mobile users and users with laptops.

■ *ControlTip property.* Similar to the CellTips feature in Excel, the Access ControlTip property can be used to display a pop-up message when the user moves the mouse pointer over a control in an Access form. Use ControlTips to describe the type of data to be entered, the actions that a control performs, or to remind users of important tasks required.

> **TIP**
> Use background pictures to add a logo or other scanned object to the background of forms and reports.

■ *Filter by Form and Filter by Selection.* The Filter by Form feature allows users to type or choose from a pull-down list of existing information in a field. The Filter by Selection feature shows only records which match the field in which the cursor currently resides. Consider using these built-in filter features rather than building your own filter feature.

■ *PivotTable Wizard.* This feature helps users create a control on a form that summarizes large amounts of data using a user-specified format and calculation method. A PivotTable is like a crosstab query, but you can switch the row and column headings dynamically to see a different view of the data. In order to use PivotTable, you need to have Excel installed. Consider using PivotTable in your integrated Office application to simplify the analysis of complex data.

■ *LookUp Wizard.* This feature helps users create a list on a form that looks up values from another table. To run the wizard in Table Design view, specify Lookup Wizard as the data type for the field. (Or in Datasheet view, choose Insert, Lookup.) When you add that field to a form, Access automatically creates a list box or combo box (depending on which control you select in the wizard) with the appropriate properties set for you. Consider providing users with Lookup lists to speed their data entry work and minimize the data repetition in your database.

Integrating PowerPoint

Having the right documents, spreadsheets and data helps, but putting it all together in a convincing way is where office workers turn to PowerPoint. A picture is worth a thousand words and a good presentation is often worth a raise. Your integrated Office application should provide access to presentation files and facilitate the process of creating, editing, packaging, and delivering a PowerPoint presentation. Fortunately, PowerPoint automates most of this for you.

 NOTE Although PowerPoint does not have its own programming language, you can use VB4 to enhance PowerPoint and perform some basic integration programming.

Here are some features you should know about:

■ *PowerPoint Style Checker.* This feature looks for mistakes such as inconsistent punctuation or material outside the slide margins. Style checker reviews your work and suggests better design solutions. For example, if you have too many bullets on a single slide, Style Checker lets you know.

■ *AutoClipArt.* This feature assists you in finding the right clip art to convey a key concept. Before using AutoClipArt for the first time, you need to import the clip art into your ClipArt Gallery.

■ *Animation toolbar.* This new toolbar provides easy access to Animation tools. Using the Animation toolbar, you can set up builds for text and objects in the slide show. By setting Animation options, you can control how objects and text builds on your slide. In addition, the PowerPoint Multimedia CD which ships with PowerPoint and the CD version of Office 95 contains a collection of multimedia clips. The CD's Help feature assists you in finding and using the various sound, movie, music, and animation clips.

■ *Presentation Conferencing.* This feature of PowerPoint for Windows 95 lets a user run a presentation for selected computers over a network, freeing participants from having to attend a presentation in one location. The presentation conference feature also allows quick reviews of a presentation still being edited.

- *Presentation Conference Wizard.* This wizard helps users set up and run the networked slide show. To set up a networked slide show, you must know the identifying name or number for each participant's computer. Once the show is running, the presenter has access to all PowerPoint tools and information, such as the Control Panel, Slide Navigator, Slide Meter, and Meeting Minder. Participants sign on for the presentation conference using the Presentation Conference Wizard. They can write and draw on the slides with the pen, which is visible to all participants.

- *Full support of OLE.* OLE allows you to drag and drop documents from Word, spreadsheets from Excel, and database information from Access into a presentation. For example, users can start with a draft outline in Word, open it in PowerPoint, apply a PowerPoint style, and polish with graphics and special effects as needed.

- *Pack and Go Wizard.* This wizard helps you assemble the various parts of a presentation and copy it to disks or another computer for you to take with you on the road. To pack up a slide show, choose File, Pack and Go. Follow the on-screen prompts and instructions to pack up your presentation.

NOTE To show the presentation on a PC that doesn't have PowerPoint, tell Pack and Go to include the PowerPoint Viewer.

Note that the PowerPoint Viewer only works on Windows 95 and Windows NT PCs. To view with Windows 3.x, use the Viewer disk included with PowerPoint 95.

Integrating Schedule+

The Schedule+ application included in Office 95 closely resembles the Schedule+ application previously released in Windows NT and Windows for Workgroups. Schedule+ allows you to create appointments, write to-do lists, and set up meetings with others in your workgroup using the Meeting Wizard. Schedule+ provides tools such as the "Seven Habits of Highly Effective People" to help you set and manage work and personal goals.

The key features in Schedule+ which may impact your integrated Office application design include the following:

- Creating a mailing list for use by the Word Address Book feature
- Transferring information to Excel and Project
- Exporting data to a Sharp Wizard or Timex Data link
- Providing a link to Schedule+ to set up and track meetings within a group

Sharing Files and Folders

The Office applications share files, programs, and folders whenever possible. This cuts down on repetition and reduces the amount of hard disk space Office needs. As a developer of integrated Office applications, you should be aware of these common areas and exploit them whenever possible in your application.

Some of the shared utilities and programs we have already discussed include ClipArt Gallery, Data Map, and VBA. A few that I haven't mentioned yet include WordArt, Equation Editor, and Graph, which create objects that you insert, or embed, into a document. These applications all use OLE to share information between applications. If you selected the Typical setup option when you installed Word or PowerPoint, then you installed Graph. If you would also like to install WordArt and Equation Editor, run Setup again. Click Add/Remove, and then select Office Tools. To verify that the applications were installed, click Object on the Insert menu. All of the installed applications are listed under Object Type.

Other programs such as Organization Chart, Query, and filters (for text and graphic files), are installed by default, ready for your use.

From Here...

This chapter explored the integration features of Windows 95 and Office 95. You examined Microsoft's Exchange, Mail, and Fax applications that come with Windows 95. Then you identified the key integration features in each Office 95 application. You learned how the Office applications share data and reviewed the shared utilities and add-ons. You also explored Binder and reviewed its capabilities.

If you would like to learn more about the integration features in Office 95, you can find more information on related topics in the following chapters:

- Chapter 3, "Integration Basics," provides you with basic information you need before you design your integrated Office application.
- Chapter 4, "Visual Basic and Visual Basic for Applications," shows you how to create a fully integrated application that can be accomplished through Visual Basic and Visual Basic for Applications.
- Chapter 6, "Creating an Integrated Application with Word and Excel," teaches you how to spend time up front to design your integrated application.

CHAPTER 3

Integration Basics

The introduction of Windows 95 brought with it a new way of looking at the way you work with your computer. In the past, Windows and the applications you worked with were the focus of your efforts. When you wanted to produce a letter, for example, you started your word processor. To work with numbers, you used a spreadsheet application. Databases were used to keep track of ordered information. Now, with Windows 95, the focus of your work is on the documents you create.

Office 95 emphasizes this new document-centric approach to computing by presenting your document as central to your efforts, and its applications as the tools you use to create them. This is most evident in the way Office integrates the applications it includes. With Office integration, you don't have to create separate documents when you need to include text, tables, and data in your projects. Now, a single document can contain all the information you need to present, and you can work with this information using the tools best suited for it. You can use Word, Excel, Access, and PowerPoint to work on the same document, without ever having to leave the document.

The idea of selling complementing applications together is not a new one. Since the early days of the IBM PC and compatibles, software vendors have offered bundled applications for an attractive price. These early ensembles, however, rarely were designed to work together or to offer a consistent interface. When Windows application suites were introduced, software bundles took on a new purpose. These suites grouped the best applications a vendor had to offer. They shared a common look and feel, and, using the Windows Clipboard, you could easily copy and paste information between them.

While the ability to copy and paste simplified the transfer of information between applications, once you copied the data, you had to update it in both applications separately. *Dynamic Data Exchange* (*DDE*) brought simple integration to Windows software by allowing you to link one document with information saved in another. This allows you to change the information once, and have it updated in any document linked to that information.

DDE could not provide the level of integration Office 95 offers. To accomplish this, Office uses *Object Linking and Embedding (OLE)*. OLE is a standard by which a Windows application can provide other applications with the functionality it was designed with. OLE is the technology that allows you to work on a single document with any of the Office applications. With OLE, true document integration has become a reality.

In this chapter, you learn how to

- Use DDE and OLE to integrate Office applications
- Recognize when to use DDE and when to use OLE
- Implement integration interactively
- Insert Office documents into other Office applications
- Integrate Office documents using Visual Basic
- Extend integration to outside applications using custom controls, SQL, and ODBC

Working with Dynamic Data Exchange (DDE)

Many Windows applications support DDE, a Windows-based standard by which applications can share information. DDE allows information created in a source application to be automatically updated in a destination application. This means that a proposal you create in a word processor can use the data produced in a spreadsheet, and whenever you make changes to the data in the spreadsheet, linked information in the proposal is updated also.

NOTE When describing DDE, this chapter refers to the application and document that supplies linked data as the source application and source document. The application and document that point to and display the linked data are referred to as the *destination application* and the *destination document*.

DDE has largely been replaced by OLE. By using OLE, you can link documents much the same as with DDE. When you use OLE in this fashion, you create a link between a source and a destination document. When you update the information in the source document, the information in the destination document is updated as well. OLE, however, includes a much more powerful function called *embedding*. The DDE functionality in Office 95 is provided for compatibility with applications that do not yet support OLE. You can learn more about using OLE to link and embed information in "Working with Object Linking and Embedding (OLE)" later in this chapter.

Linking Information Interactively in Word

In Word, you use *fields* that describe the link. Word fields are special instructions you include in your documents that Word replaces with the information that the fields describe. For linking with DDE, you use the DDE and DDEAuto fields. The difference between these two fields is the method by which the linked data is updated. With the DDE field, you must manually update the link when you want to refresh the information it is linked to. The DDEAuto link continuously updates the link whenever the destination document is open.

 TIP

You can update the information in a selected field by using the keyboard shortcut F9. Use Shift+F9 to switch between viewing field codes and field results.

Because DDE has been replaced by OLE, a newer integration standard, Word no longer inserts the DDE and DDEAuto fields from the Insert Field dialog box. Compatibility with the DDE fields is still maintained, however, for applications that do not yet support OLE.

To implement a DDE or DDEAuto link in Word, you need to insert a Link field, and manually change it to a DDE or DDEAuto field. To do this, follow these steps:

1. Choose <u>I</u>nsert, Fi<u>e</u>ld. The Insert Field dialog box appears, as shown in figure 3.1.

2. In the <u>C</u>ategories list, click Links and References. The Field <u>N</u>ames list contents will change to show fields that apply to the Links and References category.

3. In the Field <u>N</u>ames list, click Link. The Field Codes text box changes to read LINK. You need to add field codes for the DDE link into this text box.

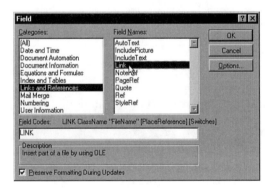

Fig. 3.1

In Word's Insert Field dialog box, you select fields to insert in your document.

4. In the <u>F</u>ield Codes text box, immediately after LINK, enter a space followed by the name of the application you want to link to, followed by another space, and the path and file name of the document you want to link to. Use a double

backslash (\\) to separate folder names in the path. Word interprets a single backslash in a field as the beginning of a *switch*, which are options you can use to customize a field. For example, to specify a document named THIS DOCUMENT.DOC, located in your MY DOCUMENTS folder, type

C:\\My Documents\\This Document.doc

5. Choose OK or press Enter. A Link field is inserted into your document. You need to manually change this to a DDE or DDEAuto field. Steps 6 and 7 explain how to do this.

6. Click the newly inserted field in your document. If an error message appears, press Shift+F9 to display the field codes.

7. Change the field name LINK in the field to read DDE or DDEAuto.

A DDEAuto field automatically updates when the source document changes. If you use a DDE field, however, the information the field is linked to will only be updated when you explicitly update the link. If you are linking to data that changes often, and you want your document to always reflect the latest changes, you'll want to use a DDEAuto link. On the other hand, if you only want to update your data—say, once a month for a sales report—use a DDE link, and manually update the data when you need updated information.

You can manually update links by choosing Edit, Links. You can also use the Edit Links dialog box to make changes to your links when, for example, the name of the source document changes.

To edit links, follow these steps:

TIP
You can also update a link by clicking the field with the right mouse button, and choosing Update Field from the shortcut menu.

1. Choose Edit, Links. The Links dialog box appears, as shown in figure 3.2.

2. To update the link, choose Update Now.

   To change the name or path of the source document, choose Change Source.

Caution

Do not change the Update Automatic/Manual options in the Links dialog box when using a DDE or DDEAuto field. Doing so will change the field to a Link field.

3. Choose OK.

Fig. 3.2

*To update a field, choose
Update Now in the Link
dialog box.*

Linking Information with WordBasic

Word, Excel, and Access include a macro programming language. *Macros* are a series
of instructions you write to automate the tasks you use an application for. Word also
allows you to create and maintain a DDE link to its macro programming language
WordBasic. With Excel and Access, you use Visual Basic for Applications (VBA).
This is referred to as linking *programmatically*.

With WordBasic, you have two ways of creating DDE links programmatically. If you
don't need to maintain a link in your document, but only want to link to another
document temporarily, you can use WordBasic's DDE functions. This is useful for
displaying information that may not be needed in future Word sessions. By using
WordBasic's Field functions, you can also insert permanent links into your document
much the same as choosing Insert, Field in Word. The following WordBasic procedure
shows how to create a temporary link to an Excel worksheet and display the value of a
cell in a Word message box:

```
Sub MAIN

    ' start Excel, and load the samples workbook
    If AppIsRunning("Microsoft Excel") = 0 Then
        Shell "c:\msoffice\excel\excel.exe \examples\samples.xls"
        AppActivate "Microsoft Word", 1
    End If

    ' open a DDE link to Excel
    intChannel = DDEInitiate("Excel", "Contents")
    ' get the value of the cell
    strCellVal$ = DDERequest$(intChannel, "R2C6")
    ' display the cell value
    MsgBox strCellVal$

    ' terminate the link
    DDETerminate intChannel

End Sub
```

This procedure produces the message shown in figure 3.3. It uses a direct DDE link
to display information in cell F2 of the Contents worksheet in the Excel sample

worksheet. Using DDE in this fashion does not create a permanent link that remains with your Word document. The link exists only while the macro is running. You can learn more about WordBasic in Chapter 4, "Visual Basic and Visual Basic for Applications."

Fig. 3.3

Running the macro shown previously produces this message.

To create a permanent link programmatically in Word, you need to use WordBasic's InsertField function. InsertField creates a field in your document that initiates and maintains a DDE link to a source document. Once you create this field, you can manipulate it just as you would any other field. This WordBasic statement shows how to create a DDEAuto field:

```
InsertField .Field = "DDEAUTO " & Chr$(34) & "Microsoft Excel" & Chr$(34)
➥& " " & "c:\msoffice\excel\examples\samples.xls" & Chr$(34)
➥& " " & chr$(34) & "Contents:R2C6"
```

This code inserts a DDEAuto link at the current cursor position in your document. When you switch to viewing field results, the contents of cell F2 in the C:\ MSOFFICE\EXCEL\EXAMPLES\SAMPLES.XLS workbook appears in place of the field. Because a DDEAuto field was used, this link updates automatically. You can also use this method to insert a DDE link, creating a manual link in your document.

Linking Information with Access and Excel Using Visual Basic for Applications

Access and Excel use a common macro language, Visual Basic for Application. VBA is derived from BASIC, and offers the power of a true programming language. VBA includes functions for linking documents using DDE. By using the DDE functions in VBA, you can create links between Excel or Access and any application that supports DDE. Table 3.1 lists the DDE methods available in VBA.

Table 3.1 DDE Functions in VBA	
Method	**Task**
DDEInitiate	Starting DDE
DDERequest	Getting text from another application
DDEPoke	Sending text to another application
DDEExecute	Carrying out a command in another application
DDETerminate	Ending DDE

VBA uses objects and their methods to accomplish tasks. A *method* is an action that an object can do. To invoke a method in VBA, you simply reference the object and method, and supply any information it requires. You can find information on using VBA in Chapter 4, "Visual Basic and Visual Basic for Applications."

The following VBA code segment shows how to create a DDE link:

```
' open a DDE link to Word's System topic
intChannel = Application.DDEInitiate(app:="WinWord", topic:="System")
' get a list of open documents
ReturnList = Application.DDERequest(intChannel, "Topics")
' list each document in the first row of Sheet1
For intCount = LBound(returnList) To UBound(ReturnList)
Worksheets("Sheet1").Cells(i, 1).Formula = ReturnList(intCount)
Next intCount
' close the DDE link
Application.DDETerminate intChannel
```

Working with Object Linking and Embedding (OLE)

OLE integrates two applications: a server application and a container application. An OLE *server* is an object that exposes all or part of its attributes. This enables other applications to access the collections, methods, and properties contained in the server object. The application and document that you embed these objects into are referred to as OLE *containers*. Access, Excel, Word, and PowerPoint are all OLE servers, and can be OLE containers. Each allows other applications to access and manipulate the attributes contained within the classes it exposes.

When you embed all or part of a document from an Office application, that application becomes a server. When you edit the embedded document, the server application essentially takes over, replacing the interface of the container application. It appears as if you are working within the server application itself, even though you are still in the container application.

NOTE When describing OLE, this chapter uses the terms source and server to describe the document, application, or object that supplies information and functions to another, and the terms *container* and *destination* to describe the documents and applications that use the information and functions. In previous versions of OLE, *container documents* were often referred to as client documents. While this is no longer the case, you may occasionally find references to this term.

An OLE server's classes are generally contained in an object library. An *object library* is a special *dynamic link library* (*DLL*) that defines the objects an OLE server exposes. Many OLE servers support *in-place activation*, a feature that allows you to work with an object using the server's interface. When you invoke in-place activation by double-clicking on the object, the object library for the embedded object activates, providing the functionality that you see when editing the embedded object. Not all object libraries behave in this fashion, however. Many of the object libraries you use have no visible interface at all, providing only behind-the-scenes functionality. You can learn more about embedding and in-place activation in "Embedding Information" later in this chapter.

Another special type of object library is an *OLE custom control* (*OCX*), which is used by component-based programming languages, such as Visual Basic. In Windows programming terminology, a *control* is any item that can be placed in a window to provide the user with information, or accept input from the user. Examples of standard controls include buttons, menus, labels, edit boxes, and list boxes. A *custom control* is a control developed to provide functionality not found in the standard Windows controls. See "Understanding Custom Controls" later in this chapter for more information on OCXs.

 NOTE You can use many different programming languages to access OLE objects using OLE Automation. This book focuses on and uses examples for Visual Basic for Applications, the macro language for Access and Excel.

Understanding Objects

OLE is based on *object technology*, the idea that the items you work with have attributes that define the item itself and what it does. These attributes are called properties, methods, and collections. *Properties* refers to the information contained in the object that describes the object. *Methods* are actions that the object can perform. A *collection* is a group of objects contained by another object. An object also has a *class* attribute. An object's class describes what type of object it is. All objects of a particular class share the same properties, methods, and collections.

One reason object technology is well-suited for computing is that once you understand object concepts, it's simple to apply this understanding to all objects. Objects that are of the same class share the same structure. Object technology makes it easy to transfer information between documents, because all the object's properties, methods, and collections are contained within the object, and are transferred with it.

To illustrate object technology, compare it to a car. Like OLE objects, a car has properties that describe it. Among these properties are the car's model, color, and style. A car also has methods, such as accelerate, decelerate, and park. Finally, a car has collections, such as collections of wheels, seats, and doors. Each of these concepts is described further in the following sections.

Setting Properties. Properties contain information that describe the object they refer to. The automobile example in the previous section listed some properties you would find in an automobile object. In an OLE object, properties can contain many types of information, such as text, numbers, or True/False, and may be limited to a choice of particular values, called *enumerated values*. The type of information contained in a property depends on the property itself. For example, an object's Name property contains text, while its Width property contains a number. A visible property is limited to settings of True or False.

Depending on the object, not all properties are accessible at all times. Properties whose values you can get and set are called *read/write properties*. Properties whose values you can get, but not set, are referred to as *read only*. *Write-only properties* are those that have values you can set, but not get. Because one of the most important attributes of a property is the capability to act upon them as they change, there are very few write-only properties.

Using Methods. *Methods* are the actions that an object can perform. Methods vary from object to object, even when the method name is the same. This is because each class defines its methods to apply to the object itself. Some methods simply perform the action they are designed to do. Others return values or objects that you can then use in subsequent OLE functions.

As an example, many objects contain a SaveAs method. Generally, this method saves the document the object refers to. Of course, a Word document needs to be saved in a different format than an Excel document, so the actions these objects' SaveAs methods perform are not exactly the same. However, because each object contains its own SaveAs method, you don't need to worry about this. Simply invoke the object's SaveAs method, and the object handles the rest.

Accessing Collections. *Object collections* allow the object to contain other objects. Almost exclusively, these collections contain objects that are of a different class than the parent class. Each item in a collection is an object in its own right, having its own properties, methods, and collections. Almost all the objects you will use are members of another object's collections.

Using Object Models. An *object model* is a graphical representation of an object's class structure. Object models are useful in quickly identifying the attributes of an object class, and how these attributes relate to each other. Object models are often represented by a tree, with the object class at the top of the tree, and properties, methods, and collections as branches. Figure 3.4 shows an object model for the automobile object.

Each bar, called a *node*, represents an object class or one of its attributes. As you can see, the bar labeled Automobile, which represents the base object class, lies at the top of the tree. This bar is referred to as the *root node*. Note how it is wide enough to cover all of its subordinate collections, methods, and properties. You'll also notice that the width of the object in each collection extends to cover each of their respective methods and properties. This helps to emphasize the fact that each object's collections, properties, and methods are contained within the object. Individual attributes are connected to the root node with lines called *branches*. These lines show the relationship between the root node and the attribute.

Fig. 3.4

An object model for the hypothetical automobile object class might look like this.

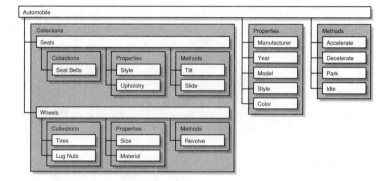

This is not the only type of object model you'll see, though most conform to the same concept. When creating object models, it's not necessary for you to show all details for every level of the tree. In fact, most object models only show the types of objects contained in their collections, and not the attributes of each object in these collections. The structure for these objects is shown in separate object models for the class of these objects.

Another common type of object model follows the same tree format, but does not show properties and methods for each object class. This type of model is used to show how objects fit together. Because all Office applications support OLE, object models can be applied to them. Figure 3.5 demonstrates this by showing the object model for Excel.

Fig. 3.5

This object model shows how the objects exposed by Excel fit together.

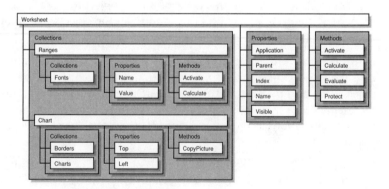

Programming with OLE Automation

You can programmatically work with OLE objects using OLE Automation. OLE Automation is a standard method by which OLE objects present their attributes, allowing you to use a common programming style to access the methods, properties, and collections contained in the object. Not all objects support OLE Automation, and consequently are not programmable. You can still link and embed nonprogrammable objects, but you can't manipulate them programmatically. On the other hand, some objects support OLE Automation but can't be linked or embedded interactively. OCXs are an example of this.

By using OLE Automation, you can create a new instance of an OLE object, and change and read its properties, manipulate the objects in its collections, and invoke its methods. In Visual Basic, you can access an object's attributes using a *dot separator*. A dot separator is a period used to separate an object's name from references to its properties, methods, and collections. For example, to access an object's property, you would use the `Object.Property` syntax; to invoke a method, you would use `Object.Method`. Accessing an object in a collection is similar, except that you need to specify which object in the collection you are addressing. You do this by enclosing an item number or key in parentheses immediately after the collection name, such as `Object.Collection(1)`. Sometimes, a collection may be designed to contain only a single object. When this is the case, you can generally leave off the item number and parentheses. For more information on using OLE Automation to control objects, see Chapter 4, "Visual Basic and Visual Basic for Applications."

Linking Information with OLE

When you link information, you are storing a pointer to the information, and a representation of the information in your document. The pointer allows the link to be updated when the information in the source document has changed. You may notice the size of your document grows quite a bit as you link information with OLE. This is because, unlike DDE, OLE stores a copy of the information as well as the link in your document. This copy of the information is called *presentation data*, and is a representation of the information as the destination document sees it. The information in the originating document is referred to as *native data*.

Linking information with OLE still requires that you work with the information in the document you originally created it in. The major benefit of linking with OLE is that the same information can be in many documents, but changes only need to be made in one. Though you can generally accomplish the same thing using DDE, using OLE should be your first choice. Why? Primarily because DDE may not be available in future versions of your applications. "Choosing Between OLE and DDE" later in this chapter lists some cases which help you decide when it's best to use DDE or OLE for a particular application.

Embedding Information

When you embed information, you create a copy of an object, rather than a link to information provided by that object. An object can be anything you create in an OLE-compliant application, such as formatted text in Word, a worksheet in Excel, or a table in Access. OLE provides developers two ways to allow you to edit embedded objects:

- In many applications, editing an embedded object will open the source application, with the object opened in it.

- In other applications, editing an object causes the object's source application to replace the container application's menus and some of its toolbars with its own. This type of editing is referred to as *in-place activation*.

Embedding information with OLE actually places an editable object in your document. This object includes all the information that pertains to it, and all the functions it can perform. If the embedded object supports in-place activation, you won't have to leave the application you used to create your document to edit the object. By double-clicking the embedded object or information in your document, the container application changes to include the menus and toolbars necessary to work with the object.

 TIP

To edit an object, double-click it while editing the container document.

With in-place activation, it appears as if you've never left the original application. In fact, you really don't. Instead of starting the application that the information is edited in, the container application allows the server application's interface to take over its own. In effect, the container application becomes the server application. Figures 3.6 and 3.7 show how in-place activation appears before and after activating an embedded object.

Some objects don't support in-place activation. These objects still allow you to edit them by double-clicking, but the server application is launched with the object loaded. In this case, you have two applications running: the original container application, and the server application that the object was created in.

Choosing Between DDE and OLE

OLE has replaced DDE as the primary tool for linking information. However, there are still situations in which DDE is appropriate . Because OLE stores much more information in the container document, the file can grow quite large. Also, because OLE is a much more complex and powerful standard, speed can be reduced significantly. You should use DDE when:

- The source or destination application does not support OLE.

- OLE makes the document size unmanageable.
- The same tasks can be accomplished with DDE and OLE, but the DDE method is faster.

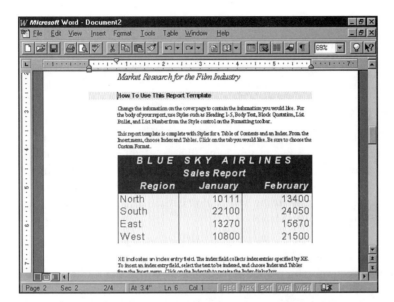

Fig. 3.6

Double-clicking an embedded Excel worksheet object activates OLE's in-place activation.

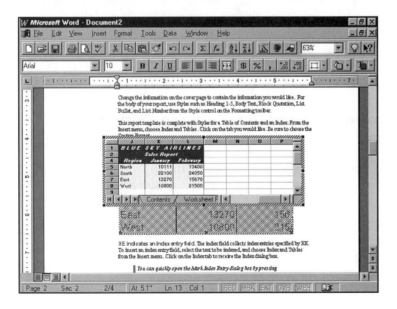

Fig. 3.7

With in-place activation, a server application's interface replaces the container application's interface.

Because DDE is an older standard, OLE should be used in most circumstances. OLE is a standard that will be available for the foreseeable future. As more applications become OLE-compliant, DDE will become less available. When you have a choice between DDE and OLE, use OLE when:

- You want your documents to be compatible with future versions of applications.
- You want to take advantage of the embedding capabilities of OLE.
- You want to access the properties, methods, and collections of objects.

Using Integration

Perhaps the way you used to work with documents is best described with an old adage: when all you have is a hammer, everything looks like a nail. Of course, if what you really need to do is cut a piece of wood in two, you want to use a saw. A hammer may do the job by breaking the piece in two, but the results would be less than satisfactory. The same idea applies to computing and could be restated: if all you have is a word processor, everything looks like a letter.

The idea behind document integration is that you should be using the tools that best fit each portion of your document. You may be writing a letter to show the effect of several different sales campaigns, which includes a table that shows the results of each campaign. To write the body of the letter, a word processor would be the tool of choice. To create the table—which will include some numbers, and perhaps a chart— a spreadsheet is the tool to use. Document integration allows you to use both.

The methods used for interactively linking and embedding OLE information vary between applications, but most allow some basic techniques. Among these are cutting and pasting information, dragging and dropping information, and inserting data and documents.

Cutting and Pasting Information Between Documents

Cutting and pasting information between documents has been an option since the early days of Windows. Prior to integration techniques, however, this information was static. To update this information, you had to either use the application you pasted the information into, or edit it in the original application and repeat the cut and paste.

When you cut and paste information between OLE-compliant applications, Office now allows you to paste a link to the original document. With this link in place, you can edit the original document, and the changes are automatically reflected in the document you pasted the information to.

TIP

Before cutting and pasting information between documents, you must have both the source and destination applications running, and the proper documents open in both.

TIP

When cutting and pasting information, it's helpful to know the Windows keyboard shortcuts for common editing functions. Ctrl+X cuts the selected information, placing a copy in the Clipboard. Ctrl+C copies the selected information to the Clipboard. Ctrl+V pastes the information in the Clipboard to the current insertion point. You can also use the Windows 95 shortcut menus to copy and paste. To do so, click the selected information with the right mouse button, and a shortcut menu appears.

To cut and paste information and create a link between the source and destination documents, follow these steps:

1. Select the information you want to link in the source document.

2. Choose Edit, Copy, or press Ctrl+C.

3. Switch to the destination application by selecting it from the Windows taskbar, or pressing Alt+Tab. Position the cursor where you want to paste the information.

4. Choose Edit, Paste Special. The Paste Special dialog box appears, as shown in figure 3.8.

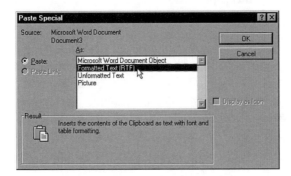

Fig. 3.8

Depending on the source application, you may be presented with several paste format options.

5. Select a format from the As list.

6. If you want to have the linked information shown as an icon in the destination document, select the Display as Icon check box.

7. Choose Paste Link.

8. Click OK, or press Enter.

When the Paste Special dialog box appears, you see options for the types of information you can paste in the <u>A</u>s list. There will almost always be at least two options:

- *Paste the information as an object.* Selecting this option embeds a copy of the information in your destination document.

- *Paste the information as a picture.* This option pastes the information as a snapshot of the information, and stores it as a picture which can be manipulated as a single item.

Pasting objects as a picture can be helpful if you are concerned about document size. This is because a picture of the information can generally be shown with less information than the data it represents. This is a problem, however, if you need to edit the data, because the picture won't contain the actual data, and can only be edited with a bitmap editor, such as Windows 95's Paintbrush application.

Dragging and Dropping Between Documents

When you have both the source application and destination application running, linking information is as simple as dragging and dropping it from one to the other.

To link information using drag and drop, follow these steps:

1. Select the information you want to link in the source document.
2. Position the cursor over the selected information, and press and hold the left mouse button.
3. Drag the cursor to the destination application, and position it where you want to paste the information.

   If the destination application is not visible, drag the cursor to the Windows taskbar. When the taskbar appears, position the cursor over the item that represents your destination document, and hold it there. The destination application appears, and you can drag the cursor to it.
4. Release the mouse button. Depending on the source application, you may be presented with several paste format options.
5. Select a format from the <u>A</u>s list.
6. If you want to have the linked information shown as an icon in the destination document, select the Display as Icon check box.
7. Choose Paste Link.
8. Click OK, or press Enter.

Inserting Information into a Document

Another method of creating links is to insert an entire document or object into your current document. If you want to use all of a file rather than just a portion of it, you can save the time necessary to select the source information before inserting it. If you select to insert a file, you can also choose to link it to the original document.

To insert a file into a Word document at the current insertion point:

1. Choose Insert, File. The Insert File dialog box appears, as shown in figure 3.9.

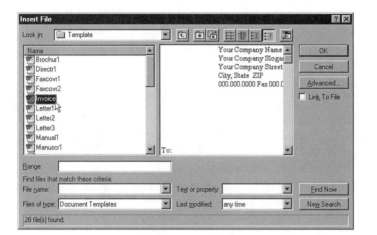

Fig. 3.9

You select an entire file to insert from the Insert File dialog box.

2. Select the file you want to insert.

3. Select the Link to File check box.

4. Click OK.

You can also insert objects into Word, Excel, Access, and PowerPoint. Inserting an object allows you to embed OLE objects into your document. Depending on the object, you may have many of the OLE standard functions for objects available, including in-place activation.

To insert an object, follow these steps:

1. Choose Insert, Object. The Object dialog box appears, as shown in figure 3.10.

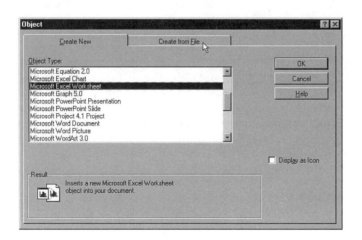

Fig. 3.10

The Object dialog box allows you to create an object from an existing file.

2. Select the type of object you want to insert. If you want to create an object from an existing file, click on the Create from File tab. Enter a file name in the File Name box, or select a file by clicking Browse.

3. If you are creating the object from a file, select the Link to File check box.

4. Click OK.

Using Mail Merge

Using the mail merge feature in Word demonstrates a specific application of linking information between documents. Mail merge allows you to maintain a database of information about people, companies, and addresses with a tool that is well-suited for that application, such as Access or Excel, and maintain a mailing document, such as a form letter in Word. By merging the two documents, you can create individualized copies of the Word document for mass mailing.

To create a mail merge document in Word, you insert fields into your document that correspond to the information you need to individualize each copy, such as names, companies, and addresses. These fields will be linked to a source for the data that includes fields that match those you insert into your Word document. When you update these fields, Word creates multiple copies of the document, each with the information for each mailing. Word includes a Mail Merge Helper to help you with the process of creating a mail merge document.

Extending Integration Beyond Office

While much of your integration tasks will occur between Office applications, you can add power and functionality to your projects by using tools that are not a part of the Office suite. Some of these tools may be included in your Office software, such as selected custom controls and Open Database Connectivity (ODBC) drivers. Others, such as Dynamic Link Libraries (DLLs), may need to be purchased separately. A *DLL* is a special Windows file that runs behind the scenes, providing functionality to Windows applications. A special set of DLLs, called *the Windows Application Interface (API)*, is included with every copy of Windows 95, and in fact makes up the core of Windows 95 itself.

There is also a large number of OLE-compliant applications available, some of which adhere to standards that make them especially suited for integrating with Office. Microsoft Project is one such application. Visio is another application that complies with the Office 95 Compatible standards defined by Microsoft and is OLE-compliant. You can find additional information on these and other selected applications in Appendix A, "Office 95 Compatible Products."

> **Caution**
>
> Not all applications designated as "Office Compatible" are fully OLE-compliant. You should check with the publisher of products you are considering to determine what OLE capabilities they have.

Integrating with applications that are not a part of the Office suite works much like integrating within Office. You can generally link and embed documents created by these applications, and some support OLE Automation and in-place activation. Oftentimes, the objects an application exposes may not be well-documented. Office includes a mini-application, Object Browser, that you can use to get information on the objects an application exposes. To learn about Object Browser, and how you can use it to help you implement objects in your applications, refer to Chapter 11, "Automating Office Integration with Excel."

Working with Custom Controls

In 1991, Microsoft introduced Visual Basic, as a stand-alone, general purpose Windows programming language. Visual Basic is unique in the way you use it to design a Windows-based user interface by drawing windows and the controls they contain interactively. Visual Basic includes a unique feature: the capability to add functionality to your applications with custom controls. *Custom controls* are specialized DLLs that provide information which defines new controls for applications you design. The custom control interface was designed with the concept of "Don't reinvent the wheel" in mind. With custom controls, you can add prepackaged, pretested functionality to your project with a click of the mouse.

A custom control not only defines the functionality of a new control class, but also provides an interface for implementing that functionality when using the Visual Basic programming environment. Properties can be set via a Properties window, and changes to the visual properties of the control are generally updated instantly. The inclusion of custom controls is probably the single biggest reason for the popularity of Visual Basic, because it allows programmers to implement a great deal of functionality in their applications with little effort.

Using Visual Basic Extensions (VBXs). Originally, Visual Basic was strictly for 16-bit systems such as Windows 3.1. The custom controls specifications for the first version of Visual Basic were also designed for 16-bit systems, and were very closely tied to the Visual Basic language. This made these first custom controls, called *Visual Basic Extensions* (VBXs) very difficult to use in other environments, and poorly suited for the dawn of 32-bit Windows, which was introduced with Windows NT and later Windows 95.

Despite their shortcomings, VBXs were widely regarded as one of the best aspects of Visual Basic. Because they gave programmers the ability to add complex features to their applications in a short amount of time, many VBXs found a willing customer base ready to buy them. Eventually, other programming languages implemented VBX support. Unfortunately, because VBXs weren't very suitable to other languages and operating environments, implementation in these other languages met with limited success. As a cure, Microsoft introduced a new specification for custom controls, now called *Object Control Extension*, or *OCXs*.

Using OCXs. OCXs fulfill the promise that VBXs couldn't quite live up to. OCXs are custom controls based on object technology, and have a foundation in OLE. With an OCX and OLE Automation, you can add the functionality that previous custom controls had to offer, but in an object-based manner. Like other OLE objects, OCXs contain properties, methods, and collections. They also include an interface that lets you interactively set their properties when you design applications with them.

The OCX standard has also been designed with both 16-bit and 32-bit operating systems in mind, so OCXs are equally applicable to Windows 3.x, Windows 95, and Windows NT. In addition, the OCX standard has been designed so that OCXs will be usable in languages and applications beyond Visual Basic. Because OCXs adhere to the OLE Automation standards, when you create applications using OCXs, you can access their attributes using standard OLE Automation syntax.

Using an OCX in your applications is simple; all you need to do is add a reference in your project to it. How you actually do this depends on the programming language or application you are using, and is described in Chapter 17, "Controlling Office Applications with Visual Basic." For more information on implementing OCXs, see Chapter 4, "Visual Basic and Visual Basic for Applications."

Understanding ODBC

Open Database Connectivity, or *ODBC,* is a database standard created by Microsoft to deal with the differences among database connection and access. Connection to and manipulation of one particular database application can vary greatly from another. Creating applications to interact directly with incompatible database systems requires that separate interfaces be designed, each developed to interact with a particular database. ODBC creates a middle layer that allows applications you develop for use with differing databases to use a common interface.

ODBC supports most major databases and many types of computers. When you set up ODBC to work with a particular database, that database is referred to as an *ODBC database.* You set up an ODBC database using the ODBC Administrator, which is included with Windows 95. To set up an ODBC database, you tell the ODBC Administrator where to find the database, what type of database system it was designed in, and certain connection properties, such as a user name and password. Once the ODBC database has been set up, it's available to all applications.

Integrating with Structured Query Language (SQL)

Structured Query Language, commonly known as *SQL* and often pronounced "sequel," is a standardized database querying language. With SQL, you can create, edit, and remove database components such as tables and queries. Most database systems today support SQL, though they generally implement it with additions specific to the system.

You use SQL by sending a series of commands to a database that describes what you want to happen to the database. Some commands are designed to return to you a group of records in one or more tables in a database, which you can manipulate from your application. The following is an example of an SQL statement that returns the last name from a Customer table when the customers live in California:

```
SELECT Customer.LastName FROM Customer WHERE Customer.State = "CA"
```

Using Dynamic Link Libraries (DLLs)

A *Dynamic Link Library*, or *DLL*, is a special type of executable file used by Windows applications. DLLs are often used to provide core functionality for applications. Functions that have been traditionally programmed into an application's executable file in the past can now be placed in a DLL. Two major benefits exist for applications using DLLs:

■ *There only needs to be one instance of the DLL in use at a time.* If three of your applications use the same DLL, for example, there only needs to be a single copy of the DLL running, even if you run all three applications at the same time. This can result in a large reduction of resource usage, allowing you to run more applications at one time.

■ *DLLs aren't loaded into memory until they are needed.* By doing this, resources that will be used by the DLL aren't used until the DLL is needed, further reducing resource consumption.

Like objects, DLLs expose some of their functionality. You can take advantage of this by accessing these exposed functions directly. When working with Visual Basic, you can access a DLL's functions by declaring the function, which tells your application what DLL the function is in, what parameters the DLL expects to receive, and what type of value the DLL function will return, if any. Once the DLL function has been declared, you can call it from within Visual Basic as you would any other function.

Using the Windows API

The core of Windows 95 itself is made up of several DLLs. These DLLs together, and the methods by which you use them to create applications, are called the Windows Application Programming Interface (API). Table 3.2 lists the Windows API DLLs and what their primary purposes are.

Table 3.2   The Windows 95 API DLLs

File Name	Primary Function
KERNEL32.EXE	Provides basic operating functions, such as memory and resource management, and task management.
USER32.DLL	Provides window functionality, such as functions for messaging between windows, menus, and pointers.
GDI32.EXE	Provides graphics capabilities, such as drawings, bitmaps and metafiles, and fonts.

You can use the API to tap into the full power of the Windows 95 operating system. Almost every function in the API DLLs are available to Visual Basic. You declare and use API functions as you would any other DLL function. Refer to Chapter 23, "Using Windows APIs," for additional information on using API functions.

From Here...

This chapter has introduced you to Office integration and the concept of objects. You learned the fundamentals of how Office applications work together, and what tools they provide for making integration work for you. Refer to the following chapters to learn more about integration and objects and how to implement them in your own applications:

- Chapter 4, "Visual Basic and Visual Basic for Applications," teaches you how to use Visual Basic with OLE Automation.

- Chapter 5, "Programming Application Integration," shows you how to apply Visual Basic to integrated application projects.

- Chapter 16, "Working with Office Compatible Applications," introduces you to other applications that are compatible with Office.

- Chapter 17, "Controlling Office Applications with Visual Basic," shows you how to use Visual Basic to manipulate and maintain documents created with Office.

- Chapter 23, "Using Windows APIs," guides you through declaring and implementing Windows 95 API calls, and provides examples of useful API functions.

Visual Basic and Visual Basic for Applications

The linking and embedding capabilities of Office applications allow you to create robust compound documents that combine text, tables, formulas, and graphics. You no longer need to limit yourself to a single tool for your documents, since many applications can be used to edit a document. The interactive embedding techniques discussed in Chapter 3, "Integration Basics," work great for producing single documents with multiple tools. But often, you may need to create custom documents that automate your work.

For example, you may have the task of producing a daily report that shows sales information for various regions, salespersons, and customers. Customer and salesperson information is maintained in an Access database. Sales figures are calculated in an Excel workbook. The report needs to be produced in Word. Even with Word's powerful template feature, creating a new document each day could be a time-consuming task. This is where the power of Visual Basic can help.

In this chapter, you learn to

- Recognize how Visual Basic works with OLE
- Create macros and applications using Visual Basic
- Use Visual Basic to automate common tasks
- Manipulate OLE objects using OLE Automation
- Create custom Office applications

NOTE Visual Basic and Visual Basic for Applications are very closely related. In fact, their syntax and language structure are identical, and they differ only in the methods by which you create the application you build with them. This chapter often uses the term Visual Basic to refer to both. In cases where implementation of the two differs, the differences are outlined. Also, while there is a version of Visual Basic for the DOS operating system, Visual Basic for DOS is not discussed here, and most of this chapter can't be applied to it.

Learning About Visual Basic

Visual Basic, introduced in May, 1991, defined a new model for programming Windows applications. Prior to Visual Basic, programming Windows applications required you to master the Windows Software Development Kit (SDK), which is a set of programming tools provided by Microsoft for tapping into the power of the Windows environment. Creating Windows applications was often a tedious, time-consuming task because the *graphical user interface* (GUI) had to be programmed, generally using the C programming language. By combining an interactive window design model with a powerful *event-driven* programming language, Visual Basic allows you to create quality, full-featured Windows applications in a relatively short time. See "Learning Event-Driven Programming" later in this chapter for more information on event-driven programming. Because Visual Basic programs can be developed very quickly, it's often referred to as a *Rapid Application Development*, or *RAD*, language.

Visual Basic is based on the popular BASIC programming language. BASIC, which was created by professors Kemeny and Kurtz at Dartmouth College in the early 1960s, was developed as a quick and easy way to learn generalized programming language. The primary purpose of BASIC was to teach programming. In fact, its name is an acronym for Beginner's All-purpose Symbolic Instruction Code. BASIC quickly gained popularity, and gained new features that addressed some of its original shortcomings.

Visual Basic for Applications and Visual Basic 4.0

Office applications have always contained macros to help you customize and automate your document tasks. When first introduced, Word and Access used a version of the BASIC language called WordBasic and AccessBasic, respectively. Excel originally included a formula-based macro language. With the introduction of OLE, however, Microsoft understood that a more robust macro language would be needed to utilize OLE's capabilities. And so, Microsoft introduced Visual Basic for Applications (VBA).

VBA is a derivative of Visual Basic that closely matches it syntactically. *Syntax* is the way you put together the words and phrases a programming language understands into meaningful instructions. VBA was designed to take advantage of the objects Office applications expose (make available to other applications). VBA allows you to access these objects using OLE automation. Using VBA and OLE automation, you can link and embed Excel spreadsheets and charts, Access databases, and WordBasic scripts. Microsoft has stated that eventually, all Office applications will include VBA as their macro programming language. At this time, Excel and Access use VBA.

The VBA language model in general, and the way it uses OLE Automation in particular, proved to be so well implemented that when Microsoft introduced Visual Basic version 4.0 in 1995, it was based on the VBA model. While there are still differences between Visual Basic and Visual Basic for Applications, their basic language structures are the same. For example, creating an Excel worksheet is accomplished the same in both languages. The following code segment shows how you do this, and can be used interchangeably in VB4 and VBA:

```
Set newBook = Workbooks.Add
With newBook
.Title = "1995 Sales"
    .Subject = "Sales"
    .SaveAs filename:="95Sales.xls"
End With
```

Visual Basic and Object-Oriented Programming

Object-oriented programming (OOP) has become very popular in recent years. OOP is based on the idea that instead of having to re-create the same code every time you program, you create reusable objects that can be used again and again. While many languages support OOP principles, not all are considered to be true OOP languages. Languages that are truly object oriented support the ideas of inheritance, polymorphism, abstraction, and encapsulation. While each of these terms may sound foreign, they are not difficult to understand. In the section titled "Understanding Objects" in Chapter 3, we introduced a hypothetical Automobile class. Each OOP concept is described in the following list, using the Automobile class as an example.

- *Encapsulation.* Encapsulation is the idea that objects are self-contained—that they contain the data and procedures that define them. For example, an automobile contains all the parts required to make it, and it knows how to accelerate when you step on the gas pedal.

- *Inheritance.* Inheritance means that objects that are created from other objects will include all the original object's data and procedures. For example, a station wagon, which could be a class derived from the automobile class, still contains tires, and still accelerates when you step on the gas pedal.

- *Abstraction.* Abstraction is the concept that you can ignore levels of details an object's data and procedures contain. For example, when you step on the gas pedal of a car, you don't need to know anything about linkages, fuel injectors, or pistons, you just know that the car will accelerate.

- *Polymorphism.* Polymorphism is the idea that inherited data and procedures in different object classes created from the same base class will operate the same. An object's class describes what type of object it is. All objects of a particular class share the same properties, methods, and collections. For example, even though sports cars and station wagons are different classes, both work the same way.

Visual Basic and VBA are not object oriented in the strictest sense. While they support encapsulation, abstraction, and polymorphism, they don't support inheritance. If you copy a button from one dialog box to another, for example, the button itself is

Introducing Integrated Applications

copied, but the procedures you define for it are not. Because of this, many people say that Visual Basic is object-based. While it's good to know this, it really won't affect your programming.

Learning Event-Driven Programming

Before Windows was introduced, most computer programs used a *linear*, or *procedural* programming approach. *Linear* programming is a style of programming in which the application controls the execution of the code that defines it. An application written linearly starts with the first line of its code, and ends with the last, with few variations in the way the application executes in between.

Because Windows is a GUI-based operating system, this programming model is not well suited to Windows applications. At any given time, a Windows application may offer hundreds of choices to the user. It would be impossible to know what the user of the application would do in what order. For this reason, Windows applications are based on an event-driven model.

Event-Driven Programming

Event-driven programming is a style of programming in which the user controls how your application executes. An event-driven application starts, and then waits for the user to take some action. The action itself defines what code your application executes next. If the user selects an "Open" button, your application executes the code that opens a document. If the user selects "Save," the code to save a document executes.

Windows' Messaging System

Event-driven programming is well suited to Windows, because Windows itself is an event-driven operating system. Windows operates by passing information from the operating system to and from individual applications, and between applications themselves. When you enter information at your keyboard, Windows interprets those keystrokes, and sends a message to the appropriate window, telling it what you typed.

Before RAD languages such as Visual Basic were developed, Windows programs were developed exclusively using traditional languages, mainly the C programming language. These applications revolved around the Windows messaging system. In short, a Windows program started, and then waited in a large loop that read each incoming message, and executed code in response to it. When the message was that the user had chosen to exit the application, the application ended.

In Visual Basic, each object you use in your program has a set of events associated with it. These events correspond to Windows messages. Some standard events include: `Click`, `DoubleClick`, `Change`, `GotFocus`, and `KeyPress`. These events occur when the user clicks on the object, double-clicks on the object, makes the object the active object, or presses a key while the object is the active object. When you write an event-driven application, you write code to respond to these events.

Learning the Visual Basic Interface

Visual Basic includes an *integrated development environment* (IDE) that you use to create applications. The Visual Basic IDE allows you to create windows and add controls to them. There is a properties window that allows you to set the properties of these windows and controls. There are code windows in which you write the code that defines how your application behaves. Figure 4.1 shows each component of the Visual Basic IDE.

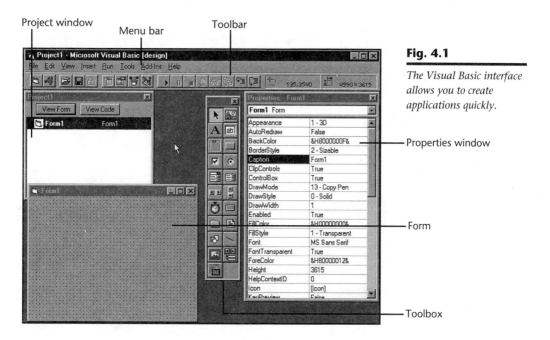

Fig. 4.1

The Visual Basic interface allows you to create applications quickly.

The elements of the Visual Basic IDE include:

- *Menu bar.* Provides access to the functions Visual Basic provides. Table 4.1 lists the Visual Basic menus and their functions.
- *Toolbar.* Gives you one-click access to its most commonly used functions. Table 4.2 lists the buttons on the toolbar.
- *Toolbox.* Provides access to the controls you can place on your forms during the design of your application.
- *Project window.* Displays a list of the files in your project, and allows you to open them.
- *Properties window.* Displays a list of properties for the currently selected object. You can interactively set an object's properties in this window.

Table 4.1 Visual Basic Menus

Menu	Function
File	Provides functions for creating, opening, and saving projects; for adding, removing, and printing files in your project; and for creating an executable file from your project.
Edit	Includes functions for editing the source code and controls in your files, and provides source code search functions.
View	Allows you to view the forms and source code in your project, and the various windows of the Visual Basic IDE.
Insert	Provides functions for inserting new procedures into your source code, and new or existing files into your project.
Run	Includes functions for running your project, and for debugging your source code.
Tools	Provides additional debugging features, the menu editing functions of Visual Basic, access to external OLE objects and custom controls, and access to Visual Basic options you can change.
Add-Ins	Allows you to access third-party add-ins that you have registered.
Help	Provides access to Visual Basic's online help.

Table 4.2 Visual Basic Toolbar Buttons

Button	Name	Function
	New Form	Creates a new form in your project.
	New Module	Creates a new code module in your project.
	Open Project	Opens an existing project.
	Save Project	Saves the project you currently have open.
	Control Lock	Locks the controls on the active form so that you can't accidentally move or resize them.
	Menu Editor	Displays the menu editor for the current form.
	Properties Window	Displays the properties window.
	Object Browser	Displays the Visual Basic object browser window, which gives you information about OLE objects you can access.
	Project Window	Displays the project window.

Button	Name	Function
	Run	Starts the current application, so you can test it.
	Pause	Pauses execution of your running application.
	Stop	Stops the execution of your running application.
	Toggle Breakpoint	Sets a breakpoint on the current source code line, or removes the breakpoint if one already exists.
	Instant Watch	Displays the value of the selected source code object or phrase.
	Active Calls	Displays the list of currently active procedures.
	Single Step	Allows you to execute your application one line at a time.
	Procedure Step	Allows you to execute your application one line at a time, but does not go into each individual procedure that is called.

Learning the Visual Basic Language

Like all programming languages, Visual Basic was designed to understand a particular set of instructions. How you put these instructions together determines how your application will work.

Using Variables

Variables are words you define to hold information while your application is running. Using variables, you can save data you need to use later. All variables have a specific *data type*. A data type determines what type of information the variable will contain, as well as the maximum size or length of the information. When you use a variable, you give it a name to make it easy to remember what information it holds. Table 4.3 lists each Visual Basic data type and its properties.

Table 4.3   Visual Basic Data Types

Data Type	Symbol	Type of Information	Size	Approximate Range
Byte	None	Numbers or single characters	1 byte	0 to 255
Boolean	None	True or False	2 bytes	−1, 0 (True, False)
Integer	%	Whole numbers	2 bytes	−32,768 to 32,767

(continues)

		Table 4.3 Continued		
Data Type	**Symbol**	**Type of Information**	**Size**	**Approximate Range**
Long	&	Whole numbers	4 bytes	-2.15×10^9 to 2.15×10^9
Single	!	Real numbers	4 bytes	-3.40×10^{30} to -1.40×10^{-45}; 1.40×10^{-45} to 3.40×10^{38}
Double	#	Real numbers	8 bytes	-1.80×10^{308} to -4.94×10^{-324}; 4.94×10^{-324} to 1.80×10^{308}
Currency	@	Money formats	8 bytes	-9.22×10^{14} to 9.22×10^{14}
Date	None	Dates	8 bytes	Jan 1, 100 to Dec 31, 9999
Object	None	Object reference	4 bytes	Any object
String	$	Text	Length + 10 bytes	0 to 2×10^9 characters
Variant	None	Any	Depends on data	Depends on the data it contains

You tell Visual Basic what type of data your variable will hold with a variable declaration, using the `Dim` keyword. Variable declarations follow the syntax:

```
Dim VariableName As DataType
```

Since the Variant data type is the default data type in Visual Basic, if you do not specify a data type using `As`, a Variant is assumed.

> **NOTE**
>
> You may wonder why there is a need for all the data types Visual Basic provides, when the Variant data type can assume any type. Because Variants use additional memory to store information, and a conversion is necessary when using them, you can make your program use less memory and run faster by declaring a variable to be a specific data type.

Visual Basic also allows the use of *type-declaration characters*, which are symbols that represent a data type. This is a carry over from earlier versions of BASIC, and is not mentioned in the VB4 documentation. While this may help reduce the amount of typing you do when writing source code, it also makes your code harder to read. It's best to explicitly declare each variable with the `As` keyword, so you and other programmers will be able to follow your source code more easily. In fact, many programmers today use a standard prefixing system, called *Hungarian notation*.

All variables have a *scope*, which determines when the variable is active, and how long it remains in memory. A variable's scope can be local, module-level, or global. When you create a new form, module, or class module in Visual Basic, it is divided into sections with each containing an individual procedure. When a variable is declared within a procedure, it is only available to that procedure. Each form and module will also contain a "declarations" section, which you use to declare variables that you want available throughout the life of the form or module. Variables that are declared within the declarations section of a code file will be available to all procedures in that file. To make a variable available throughout your application, you use the `Public` keyword:

```
Public VariableName As DataType
```

Module-level and local variables lose their values when they fall out of scope. That is to say, when the code file or procedure that the variable is declared in is no longer active, the variable no longer contains the value that was assigned to it. You can make a variable hold its value even while it's out of scope using the `Static` keyword:

```
Static VariableName As DataType
```

Using Declared Constants and Intrinsic Constants

Constants are very similar to variables, in that they use a name to store information. Constants, however, are used to define values that will remain the same throughout your application's execution. Intrinsic constants are defined by the OLE object that they pertain to. Visual Basic itself includes many of them. To use an intrinsic constant, you simply refer to it. You do not need to declare it, since the object already has.

Declared constants are those you create yourself. Like variables, you can declare constants that apply to their own procedure, to an entire source code file, or to your application as a whole. To declare a constant that only applies to a particular procedure or file, you use the following syntax:

```
Const CONSTANTNAME = value
```

Where you place the constant determines its scope. If the constant is placed inside a procedure, it will only apply to their own instances in that procedure. If you place it in the declarations section of a code file, it will apply to all procedures in that file. To declare a constant that applies to your entire application, it must be in the declarations section of a code module, and you must use the `Public` keyword to specify it:

```
Public Const CONSTANTNAME = value
```

Constants serve two major purposes: they make it easier to read and understand your source code by replacing static values with meaningful names, and they make it easier to edit your code when you need to change multiple instances of the same information. Consider the following code segment:

```
sngConvertIt = sngInput * 30 * 1000
```

Nothing in this source code tells what the function does. The static numbers `30` and `1000` do not indicate what they represent. Now, look at the same code, using constants:

```
Const MILLILITERS_PER_OUNCE = 30
Const LITERS_PER_MILLILITERS = .001
sngConvert = sngInput * MILLILITERS_PER_OUNCE * LITERS_PER_MILLILITER
```

It's much easier to read the second example, because the static values have been declared as constants. It's obvious now that the code converts ounces to liters. The second major benefit in using constants is when you use the same static value many times in your code. Suppose your application computes votes by the U.S. House of Representatives. Embedded throughout, maybe in hundreds of places, your code is the total number of Representatives, which was 435 at the beginning of 1996. Now, suppose Congress passes a bill that changes this number. Without a global constant, you would need to change every instance of this number in your code. With a global constant, however, you would simply need to change the constant declaration to reflect the new number of Representatives.

Intrinsic constants work like declared constants, but are defined by the OLE object they apply to. They define names that represent values meaningful to the object. You will need to know these constants before you can use them. Fortunately, in order for an OLE object to use intrinsic constants, it must expose these constants, and you can use an *Object Browser* to examine them. An Object Browser is a specialized application that examines an OLE server and gives you information about the properties, methods, collections, and constants it exposes.

Creating Visual Basic Procedures

Procedures are individual parts of your source code that define the internal and external functions of your program. In Visual Basic, there are three types of procedures: *sub*, *function*, and *property*. Subs are blocks of code that perform a specific function. By separating commonly used blocks of code, you can eliminate writing the same code every time your program needs to perform a function. Functions are similar to subs, in that they are used to perform specific operations. With functions, however, you can pass a value you define back to the code in which you invoked the function, allowing your code to know the result of the function's operation. Property procedures are specialized blocks of statements that define custom properties for the objects you use in your applications.

The methods you use to create subs and functions are very similar, with three exceptions. The first, and most obvious, is that a sub is declared as a sub, and a function is declared as a function. The second exception is that a function is declared as being of a particular data type. This data type is the type of the value that the function will return. Finally, a function will assign itself a value somewhere in the body of the function.

With subs and functions, you can optionally add arguments and that allows the procedure to have access to information it may need. For example, if you create a function that changes the color of an object, the function will need to know what color to change it to. You can pass this information to the function using an argument. Arguments are declared as a variable, but must immediately follow the sub or function name in a sub or function declaration, and be surrounded by parentheses. You can use multiple arguments, if needed. To do this, simply separate the argument declarations with commas, making sure that all of the arguments are within the parentheses.

The following code segments show how you declare subs and functions, and illustrates the differences between them:

A sub declaration is as follows:

```
Private Sub ThisSub(Argument1 As DataType, Argument2 As DataType)
    ' statements that form the body of your sub
End Sub
```

You declare a function like this:

```
Private Function ThisFunc(Argument1 As DataType, Argument2 As DataType) As
➥DataType
    ' statements that form the body of your function
    ThisFunc = value
End Function
```

You can insert a new procedure in your code by entering the declaration directly into the declarations section of a form or code module's code window. You can also use the Visual Basic Insert menu to insert a procedure with a dialog box. To insert a procedure manually, follow these steps:

1. In the project window, select the form or module you want to add a new procedure to, and then click View Code. The code window for the appropriate form or module appears.

2. In the Object combo box of the code window, select the General item.

3. In the Procedure combo box, select the declarations section.

4. Place the cursor on the line in the edit window directly after the last code line (see fig. 4.2).

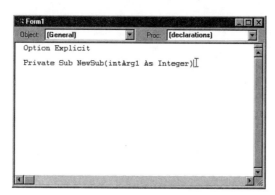

Fig. 4.2

To add a new procedure manually, enter its declaration on the last line of the code window.

   5. Type in the declaration for the sub or function. A new sub or function will be
   added to the module.

To create a new procedure using Visual Basic's Insert menu, follow these steps:

   1. In the project window, select the form or module you want to add a new procedure to, and then click View Code. The code window for the appropriate module will be displayed.

   2. Choose Insert, Procedure from the Visual Basic menu bar. The Insert Procedure
   dialog box appears as shown in figure 4.3.

Fig. 4.3

*You can use the Insert
Procedure dialog box to
add new procedures to
your code.*

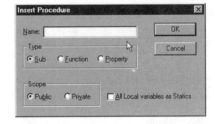

   3. Enter the name of the procedure in the Name text box.

   4. If this procedure will return a value, select the Function option. If not, select the
   Sub option. The third option shown, Property, is discussed later in this chapter.

   5. If you want this procedure to be available to forms and modules other than the
   one you are adding this procedure to, select the Public option. Otherwise, select
   the Private option.

   6. If you need all the variables in this procedure to remember their values, even
   when the procedure is not executing, select the All Local Variables as Statics
   checkbox.

   7. Click OK. The procedure will be added to the module you selected, and displayed in the code window.

Property procedures are different in concept than subs and functions. Whereas subs
and functions can be defined for any task you need to create blocks of code for, property procedures correspond to custom properties you define. Each property gets three
procedures: `Property Let`, `Property Get`, and `Property Set`. `Property Let` procedures define the actions your application performs when the custom property's value
is set. `Property Get` procedures are used to return the value that a property contains.
`Property Set` procedures are used to set a reference to an object. When you create a
custom property, the `Let`, `Set`, and `Get` property procedures are created for you.

Like variables, procedures have a scope. A procedure can be private, in which case it
will only be available to the objects and other procedures defined in the same form or
module. Procedures you declare as public are available throughout your application's
code. While function return values can't be static, the variables inside of subs,

functions, and property procedures can. You can also make all of a procedure's variables static, by declaring the procedure as static. To declare a function, for example, that can be called from any module in your code, and whose variables are static:

```
Public Static Function ThisFunc(arguments) As DataType
```

The body of a procedure can be any valid series of Visual Basic statements. The main purpose of a procedure is to modularize your code to make it easier to read, and to reduce the amount of work you have to do. When you are programming, your application should generally create a sub or function for each set of statements that, together, perform a task. Most importantly, you should create procedures for the most common tasks, to avoid repeating the same code throughout your program. A good example of this is a procedure used to center a form on the screen, as shown in the following code segment. This procedure is often used because there are quite a few times you will want to display a custom dialog box, and have it show up right in the middle of the user's screen. Note the use of the frmThisForm argument, which has been declared as type Form. In addition to the generic Object data type, Visual Basic allows you to declare variables and arguments as specific object types, Form in this case:

```
Public Sub CenterForm(frmThisForm As Form)
    ' center the form on screen
    frmThisForm.Move (Screen.Width - frmThisForm.Width) / 2,
    ➥(Screen.Height - frmThisForm.Height) / 2
Exit Sub
```

Calling Procedures. Once you have created a procedure, you will need to call it to implement it in your source code. Calling a procedure passes control of your code to that procedure. Once the procedure is complete, control returns to the line immediately following the line it was called from. To call a sub procedure, you simply need to name the procedure in your code, followed by any arguments required by the procedure, as shown below:

```
SubName Argument1, Argument2, ..., ArgumentN
```

If the sub procedure is defined in a code module other than the one you are calling it from, however, you need to specify the module it exists in. To call a sub procedure in another code module, you use the following syntax:

```
ModuleName.SubName Argument1, Argument2, ..., ArgumentN
```

Calling function procedures is slightly different. Since functions return a value, you will need somewhere for that returned value to go. Generally, you will assign the returned value to a variable whose data type matches the type the function is defined as. In addition, the argument list must be enclosed in parentheses. The syntax for calling a function procedure is as follows:

```
VariableName = ModuleName.FuncName(Argument1, Argument2, ..., ArgumentN)
```

Positional Arguments. *Arguments* are the parameters that your procedures or objects' methods act upon, or use for additional information to make decisions when performing the tasks they are designed to do. For example, a procedure you write to change the `BackColor` property of any form to any color will require two arguments: the form your procedure will change and the color it will be changed to. Some arguments are required, while others are optional. Objects you use in your application often have methods that require arguments. The `Move` method, for example, requires left and top values. You separate arguments using commas.

Procedure arguments can be specified in two ways: positional and named. Positional arguments must be listed in a specific sequence to determine what values apply to which arguments. When you specify arguments positionally, you must include commas for any optional arguments you do not specify, when you include later arguments. Consider a sub declared as follows:

```
Private MySub (Arg1 As Variant, Arg2 As Variant, Arg3 As Variant)
```

If the three arguments of the `MySub` procedure are optional, and you only want to specify the last one, you would call it like this:

```
MySub , , value
```

Named Arguments. Named arguments, which have been supported in VBA, are new to Visual Basic, being introduced in version 4.0. Named arguments rely on the name you assign to arguments to determine which values apply to them. This requires that the name given to the arguments when the procedure was declared is known. This also eliminates the need to include commas for arguments that are not specified, since the name of each argument is included in the call. To call the same `MySub` procedure shown above using named arguments:

```
MySub Arg3 := value
```

Using Control Structures

Visual Basic, like most modern programming languages, includes control structures to help you build decision-making and iterative processes into your source code. Control structures fall into two groups, decision structures and looping structures. Decision structures test conditions you define, and execute a block of code based on the result of that test. Decision structures include `If` and `Select Case` structures. Looping structures execute the same block of code over and over until conditions you define are met. These structures include `Do` and `For` structures. Visual Basic also supports `While` structures, though they have been largely replaced by the more flexible `Do` structure, and are not discussed here.

If **Structures.** The simplest form of an `If` structure tests a condition to see if it evaluates to True. True is defined as any numeric value that is not zero. If the condition is true, a block of code is executed. If the condition is false, the code block does not execute. The syntax for this `If` form is:

```
If condition Then
     CodeBlock
End if
```

Another form of the `If` structure tests for multiple conditions and executes a separate block of code for each condition. When a test condition is met, the remaining conditions are not tested, so that only a single code block will be executed. The syntax of this form begins similarly to the previous form. You define each subsequent condition using an `ElseIf` statement. You can optionally include a block of code that will be executed if none of the conditions are met using the `Else` statement. The syntax for the `If...Then...Else` structure is:

```
If condition1 Then
    CodeBlock1
ElseIf condition2 Then
    CodeBlock2
    .
    .
    .
ElsIf conditionN Then
    CodeBlockN
Else
    DefaultCodeBlock
End If
```

This `If` form can take any number of `ElseIf` statements. However, as soon as one condition is met, the structure will be exited, and any subsequent conditions won't be tested. As more conditions are added, it can make your code difficult to read. An alternative to using this form of the `If` structure is to use a `Select Case` structure, which can add readability to your code.

***Select Case* Structures.** A `Select Case` structure works similarly to an `If...Then...Else` structure, but uses a different syntax. You can test any number of conditions with a `Select Case` structure, and include a default block of code that executes when none of the conditions are met. Instead of testing each condition individually, however, the `Select Case` structure evaluates a single expression, and then compares that result to a list of possible results you define. The syntax for a `Select Case` structure is as follows:

```
Select Case expression
    Case comparisons1
        CodeBlock1
    Case comparisons2
        CodeBlock2
        .
        .
        .
    Case comparisonsN
        CodeBlockN
    Case Else
        DefaultCodeBlock
End Select
```

The comparisons for each `Case` can be a single value or multiple values. You can specify multiple values by separating the values with commas, or a range of values separated by a dash. You can also test for how a value relates to the test expression using standard math operators and the Is statement. For example, to test for odd numbers below 10, or any number above 10, you would use the following Case statement:

```
Case 1, 3, 5, 7, 9, Is > 10
```

If the test expression matches any of the listed comparison values, the corresponding code block will be executed. Select Case offers a concise format that works best when you have a large number of test conditions. If the same test conditions were applied to an IfThen statement, it would look similar to this:

```
If ((varTest < 10) And ((varTest Mod 2) = 1))) Or (varTest > 10) Then
```

As you can see, Select Case can offer greater readability, and can save you quite a bit of typing.

Do Structures. Do structures allow you to execute a block of code repeatedly until a test condition is met. This is helpful when you want your application to perform a task until a specific event occurs, or until a specific value is reached.

Do structures have two basic forms. The Do Until...Loop form tests for a condition, and then runs a block of code if that condition has not been met. Once the block of code has been executed, the condition is tested again, and the code block is executed again, if the condition has not been met yet. This goes on until the condition is met. The Do...Loop Until form runs the code block first, and then tests the condition. If, during the execution of your Do structure, you need to stop execution of the code block, say when the user presses Esc, you can break out of the loop using the Exit Do statement. The syntax of the Do Until...Loop form is:

```
Do Until condition
     CodeBlock
Loop
```

The syntax for the Do...Loop Until form is as follows:

```
Do
     CodeBlock
Loop Until condition
```

The difference between the two forms is that while the code block in the Do Until...Loop form never executes if the condition is met before the Do structure is executed, the Do...Loop Until form always executes its code block at least once, since the test is not applied until after the code block has run.

For Structures. You use a For structure in your applications to execute a block of code a specific number of times. You don't need to know exactly how many times the For structure will execute, as long as you have a relative number you can refer to. For example, you may want to execute a block of code for every employee in your company. Unfortunately, you can't know when writing your application how many people your company will employ in a month, or a year from now. Using a For loop, you can execute the required code once for every employee. For structures require a test variable be declared. This test variable will be compared to a maximum or minimum value, depending on how you use the For structure, and the code block will be executed until the test variable matches or has exceeded the maximum or minimum value. The syntax of a For structure is:

```
For varTest = StartValue to EndValue Step IncrementValue
    CodeBlock
Next varTest
```

The StartValue parameter shown is the first value you want your test variable to have. Assuming the test variable does not exceed the end value, the For structure will then execute the block of code, and add the increment value specified by the Step parameter to the test variable. This will continue until the test variable exceeds the end value. Step can be any positive or negative number, though by default it is 1. If your For structure will increment the test value by one each time, you don't need to include the Step parameter. It's important to remember that if the end value is greater than the start value, Step must be positive, and if the end value is less than the start value, Step must be negative. If this is not the case, the test value will never exceed the end value, and the For loop will execute endlessly.

Another form of the For structure is For Each. The For Each form executes a block of code once for each item in a collection or array. This form also requires a test variable, and an additional reference to a collection or array, but does not require a start value, end value, or increment values. The start value is always assumed to be the first member of the collection or array, the end value is always assumed to be the last member of the collection or array, and the increment is always 1. The For Each structure's syntax is as follows:

```
For Each varTest In GroupVarName
    CodeBlock
Next varTest
```

As with the Do structure, you can optionally exit a For structure using the Exit For statement.

Learning the Structure of a Visual Basic Application

Visual Basic is a *form-based* language. You develop the user interface for your application by drawing the windows that it includes, called *forms*, interactively. You then write code to define how your application performs. The code you write can either be attached directly to the forms you create, or, when the code applies to more than one form, in separate code *modules*. Each form and module you create is saved in a separate file. The collection of these files used together to create an application is referred to as a *project*.

Traditionally, BASIC is an *interpreted*, rather than a *compiled*, programming language. An interpreted language is one that uses a special file called an interpreter during execution to turn the code you write into *machine code* the computer can understand.

Compiled languages use a compiler to create the machine code before your application starts to execute. Traditionally, interpreted applications execute slower than compiled applications. To minimize this, Visual Basic uses a combination of interpretation and compilation. When you develop your Visual Basic application, you create a *pseudo-code* file, which is an interim step between your source code and machine code. Your application then uses an interpreter to finish the process during execution. Because of this, your application will also require one or more runtime files in order to execute properly.

Creating Forms and Dialog Boxes

The basic graphical component of Visual Basic applications is the form. Forms are the windows that make up your application's interface. Forms are used to display and get information from the user. They contain the text and list boxes, and buttons and pictures that your application uses. Creating a form is the first step you take when building your application. To create a form in Visual Basic, choose Insert, Form from the Visual Basic menus. A new, blank form appears.

Each Visual Basic form has code associated with it. This code defines the behavior of the form and how it interacts with other portions of your application. When you double-click a form or control, the code window for that form appears, as shown in figure 4.4 later in this chapter. This code window consists of three main parts: an object combo box, a procedure combo box, and an edit window. You select which object the code you write will apply to in the Object combo box. You select the name of the procedure you write the code in from the Proc: (Procedure) combo box. You write the code in the edit window. When you create custom sub and function procedures for a form, the procedure is placed under the General object heading. To write code to a particular procedure, follow these steps:

1. In the Project window, select the form or module you want to edit, and click the View Code button. The appropriate code window appears, as shown in figure 4.4.

2. In the code window's Object combo box, select the object you want the code to apply to, or select General for a sub or function you have created.

3. In the Proc: combo box, select the name of the procedure you want to edit. The existing code of that procedure appears in the edit window.

In VBA, the main interface component of your application depends on the Office application you develop your application in. When you develop an application in Access using VBA, you use Access forms, which are very similar to Visual Basic forms, but are designed specifically to interface with Access tables, queries, and reports. Access provides a set of form templates that match the most commonly used types of forms. In addition, you can have Access help you create a form using the Form Wizard. To create a form in Access, follow these steps:

1. Choose Insert, Form from the Access menus, or select the Forms tab on the Database Windows, and then select New. Access displays the New Form dialog box, as shown in figure 4.5.

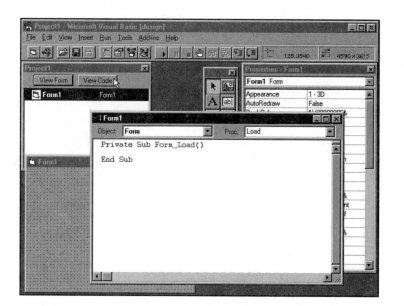

Fig. 4.4

Clicking View Code in the Project window displays the appropriate code window.

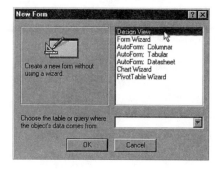

Fig. 4.5

You can select a form template using the New Form dialog box in Access.

2. Select Design View to create a blank form.

   If you want to use one of the Access form templates instead, select the table or query it will be based on, and then select the AutoForm template you want to use.

   Optionally, to use the Access Form Wizard to help you create your form, select the table or query it will be based on, and then select Form Wizard.

3. Click OK. If you selected Design View, a new, blank form appears. If you used an AutoForm template, a new form based on the style you selected appears. If you selected Form Wizard, the Form Wizard dialog box appears, as shown in figure 4.6.

Fig. 4.6

The Access Form Wizard automatically creates a form based on information you give it.

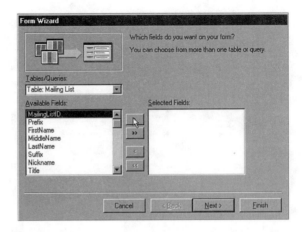

In Excel, you don't create forms, since Excel's workbook window serves as the main window in your application. You can provide a custom interface by including dialog boxes to present and obtain information from your users. Dialog boxes, while not as flexible as the forms found in Visual Basic and Access, offer users a way to input and receive data using the most common windows controls. To create a dialog box, choose Insert, Macro, Dialog from the Excel menu bar.

Inserting Controls

Once you have created a blank form or dialog box, you will need to place controls on it to allow the user to interact with your application. Controls are Windows components that allow the user to enter data, or to present information to the user. Common controls include labels, edit boxes, list boxes, and buttons. In VBA and VB4, which is based on VBA, controls are implemented as OLE objects that conform to the OLE Automation standard. Using OLE Automation, you can access a control's properties, collections, and methods using the Visual Basic programming language. Placing controls on your forms and dialog boxes is accomplished using the same basic steps, whether you're using Visual Basic or VBA found in Access or Excel:

1. Open the form or dialog box you want to place the control on, or create a new form or dialog box.

   TIP

   To create a new form in Visual Basic, choose Insert, Form from the Visual Basic menus. To create a new form in Access, select the Forms tab in the Database Window, and select New. To create a new dialog in Excel, select Insert, Macro, Dialog from the Excel menus.

2. If the toolbox is not displayed, open it. Depending on the application, you can open the toolbox as follows:

   In Visual Basic and Access, choose View, Toolbox.

   In Excel, choose View, Toolbars, and then select Toolbox.

3. In the toolbox, select the type of control you want to place on your form.

4. Click the form, and drag the cursor to draw the control on the form.

Setting Properties. Forms and controls have properties associated with them that allow you to customize the way they appear or interact with the user. Some properties can only be set while you are designing your application (*designtime*). Others can only be set at *runtime*, while your application is running, and you use OLE Automation to set them. You can set most properties at both designtime and runtime.

As you create each form and control, you set designtime properties using the Properties window. In Visual Basic and Access, the Properties window displays a two-column list. The leftmost column lists each property that can be set while you are designing your application. The rightmost column is where you set the value of each property. Some properties will accept any value, limited only by the data type of the property. These you generally enter directly into the right column of the properties window. Others will only accept particular values, called an *enumerated list*, that correspond to defined settings, and you will generally select these via a drop-down list in the right column. Figure 4.7 shows the Visual Basic `ScaleMode` property's drop-down list.

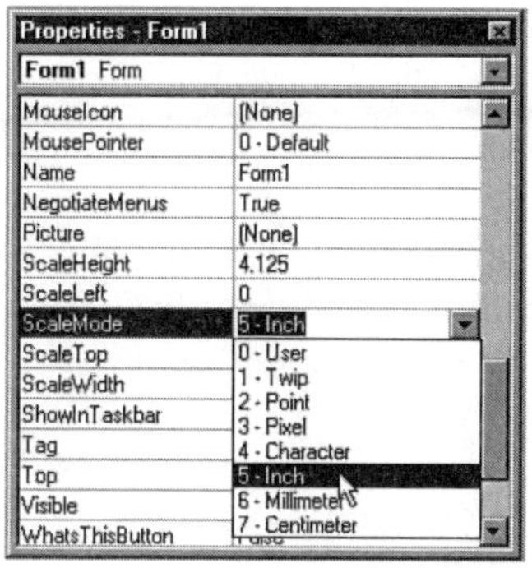

Fig. 4.7

You select a Visual Basic form's `ScaleMode` *property from a drop-down list.*

To set properties at runtime, use OLE Automation. OLE Automation is the standard by which OLE Objects expose their properties, methods, and collections, enabling you to control them programmatically. When setting properties at runtime with Visual Basic, you use an `Object.Property = Value` syntax. For example, to set the `Caption` property of a form named Form1 to "My Form," you would use the following code line:

```
Form1.Caption = "My Form"
```

When a property is an enumerated list property, the object it pertains to will often expose a set of constants to make it easier to set the property. A *constant* is a name that can be used in place of a value to make it easier to remember what each value means. In figure 4.7, you were introduced to a drop-down list that let you set a form's `ScaleMode` property. Each possible value is a number, but Visual Basic includes a name for each so that you will know what effect each value will have on the property. Visual Basic also defines constants that match the possible values of enumerated list properties, so that you can apply this same concept when setting properties at runtime. Often, a programmable OLE object will expose these constants along with its properties. When you set an object's enumerated list property at runtime, you can set it either to the actual value, or the constant defined to represent that value. For example, setting Form1's ScaleMode property to inches, you can use the syntax of either of the following code segments:

```
Form1.ScaleMode = 5
```

or

```
Form1.ScaleMode = vbInches
```

In this example, the constant vbInches is used. Visual Basic defines this constant to be equivalent to 5, which is the enumerated setting of the Inch scale mode.

Calling Methods. Most objects have methods associated with them, which are the predefined actions the object can perform. Many of these methods perform actions that produce visible results. A form's Print method is an example of this. You use the Print method of a form to print a line of text on the form itself. When you want to invoke an object's method, you use the dot separator syntax to refer to it. For example, to print the line "Form printing is fun with Visual Basic!" on Form1, you would use the following syntax:

```
Form1.Print "Form printing is fun with Visual Basic!"
```

Other methods may not produce a visible result, but instead, will return a value to your code. When using this type of method, you generally want to get some information about a particular object, and use it in your application's source code. A good example of this is a form's TextWidth method. The TextWidth method is used to determine how wide a text line will be when it is printed on the form, using the form's current font style and scale mode. When using a method in this fashion, you usually assign the value returned by the method to a variable, so you can refer to it later. To get the width of the text line "Form printing is fun with Visual Basic!" when it is printed on Form1, you would use this syntax:

```
Dim  sngWidth As Single
sngWidth = Form1.TextWidth( "Form printing is fun with Visual Basic!")
```

Accessing Collections. *Collections* are sets of objects contained by a parent object. Since collections may often contain any number of objects, you need some way to refer to an individual object in the collection. With Visual Basic, you can usually refer to a particular member of a collection either with its ordinal index that represents the order it is in the collection, or a key value that represents the name of the object. There are exceptions to this rule, as the objects in some collections can only be referred to by their index. An example of this is the Forms collection of a Visual Basic application. Once you know the index or key of an object in a collection, you can access it by referring to the name in the collection, followed by the index or key in parentheses. Using this technique, you can then refer to the properties, methods, and collections of a collection's individual objects. As an example, Excel's Application object contains a collection of Workbooks, each of which contains a collection of

Worksheets. To change the name of Sheet1 in Book1 in an Excel application object to "MySheet", you would use the following syntax:

```
Workbooks("Book1").Worksheets("Sheet1").Name = "MySheet"
```

> **Caution**
>
> When you delete objects from a collection, you change the index of the object that follows it in the collection. This may affect your source code that refers to the collection's object later. Similarly, when you change an object's key, you cannot refer to that key again, as it will no longer exist.

Responding to Events. In order for your application to be useful, it must respond to the actions the user takes. Earlier in this chapter, you were introduced to the Windows messaging system, which Windows uses to pass information to, and receive information from, applications. When a user interacts with your application, your application is sent a message by Windows to let it know what action was performed. In Visual Basic, you can respond to the messages Windows sends to your application via *events*. Almost all objects in your application will have events associated with them.

Events are implemented in Visual Basic as individual sub procedures. When you create a form or insert a control into your application, the events supported by that object are automatically created. The basic syntax for an event procedure declaration is:

```
Private Sub ObjectName_EventName(arguments)
    CodeBlock
End Sub
```

You don't need to call event procedures. Event procedures are executed when their corresponding event occurs. For example, the TextBox control includes a Change event. This event is executed anytime the text in the TextBox changes. You write code in these event procedures to take action on any events your application needs to respond to. If your application doesn't need to respond to a particular event, you don't need to place any code in it. A good example of using an event procedure to respond to an event is to create an input mask for a TextBox. Suppose you have a text box on your form that should only accept numeric values. You will need to check each keystroke entered by the user to make sure it is a numeral, or a valid numeric separator, such as a comma or period. The best way to do this is to validate each keystroke as the user presses a key. The following code listing demonstrates how to do this using the TextBox's KeyPress event:

```
Private Sub txtNumeric_KeyPress(KeyAscii As Integer)
    Const KEY_0 = 48
    Const KEY_9 = 57
    Const KEY_DECIMAL = 46
    Const KEY_COMMA = 44
    Select Case KeyAscii
        Case KEY_0 To KEY_9, KEY_DECIMAL, KEY_COMMA
            ' we put nothing here, since these are valid keys
```

```
            Case Else
                ' anything else gets discarded
                Beep
                KeyAscii = 0
        End Select
End Sub
```

Writing Visual Basic Modules

Visual Basic *modules* are files that contain source code only. Modules do not include any visual components, only procedures. You can still reference graphical objects in your code, but these objects must be displayed on a form. To create a new module, choose Insert, Module from the Visual Basic menus. A new module will be added to your project and displayed.

Modules are best suited to grouping procedures that can be used in conjunction with many forms. The numeric TextBox mask example used above might be placed in a procedure in module if you have numeric only TextBoxes on more than one form. This eliminates the need to duplicate the code for every TextBox you want to apply a numeric mask to. Instead, you would create a function that examines the user's input, and returns a null character if it is invalid. You call this function in the KeyPress event. This is illustrated in the following code segments:

```
Public Function ValidateKey(intKeyIn As Integer) As Integer
Const KEY_0 = 48
Const KEY_9 = 57
Const KEY_DECIMAL = 46
Const KEY_COMMA = 44

Select Case intKeyIn
Case KEY_0 To KEY_9, KEY_DECIMAL, KEY_COMMA
    ' these are valid, so we return the same value
    ValidateKey = intKeyIn
Case Else
' anything else gets discarded
Beep
ValidateKey = 0
End Select
End Sub

Private Sub txtNumeric_KeywPress(KeyAscii As Integer)
    KeyAscii = ValidateKey(KeyAscii)
End Sub
```

By using code modules and grouping similar procedures into them, you can reduce the amount of code you have to enter, and make your code easier to read and manage.

Writing Class Modules

Class modules are a special type of modules you use to create custom object classes in Visual Basic. You can assign custom properties, collections, and methods to these classes. Once you have created a class, your application can create new objects based on this class. You can also turn this class into an OLE server DLL, which will allow it to be embedded in yours and other applications, so that it can be manipulated via OLE Automation. You do this by creating a new class module, and compiling it by selecting File, Make OLE DLL File from the Visual Basic menus.

Adding Custom Controls and OLE Objects

Visual Basic allows you to add custom controls and insertable OLE objects to your project. This allows you to add the functionality these controls and objects have to your own application seamlessly. You can, for example, add a Word document object to your toolbox, and draw a document directly on your form. This document will have all of the functionality of Word that comes with OLE's embedding capabilities, including in-place activation. In addition, you will be able to control this document object via OLE Automation.

To add a new custom control or OLE object to your application, follow these steps:

1. Choose Tools, References from the Visual Basic menus. The References dialog box appears, as shown in figure 4.8.

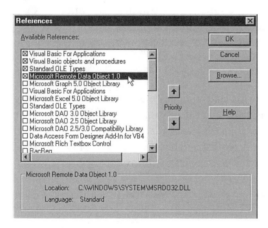

Fig. 4.8

The References dialog box allows you to select OLE servers that you want available to your project.

2. Select the name of the server you want to make available, and make sure there's an X in the corresponding checkbox.

3. Click OK.

4. Choose Tools, Custom Controls from the Visual Basic menus. The Custom Controls dialog box appears, as shown in figure 4.9.

5. Select the name of the control or object you want added to your toolbox, and make sure its checkbox has an X in it.

6. Click OK. The control or object you selected will be added to your toolbox.

Fig. 4.9

The Custom Controls dialog box lets you add controls and insertable objects to your Toolbox.

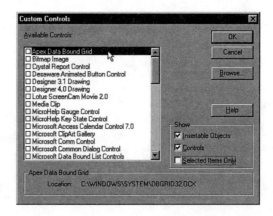

Using Data Access Objects

Visual Basic includes the Access 7.0 database engine, known as the *Joint Engine Technology*, or *Jet*, engine. Visual Basic provides functions to directly work with the data access objects (DAO) that the Jet engine exposes. From Visual Basic you can create and manipulate all of the objects that the Jet engine contains, including databases, tables, queries, and relationships. Since the Jet engine is separated from Access, you don't need to have Access loaded, or even have it installed on the machine your application is running on.

You work with DAOs just as you do any other object. Each DAO includes its own properties, methods, and collections that you can manipulate from within Visual Basic. The base DAO is the DBEngine object. Each DBEngine object contains multiple Workspace objects. A Workspace object is the DAO that defines the user and security parameters of a database system. A workspace has a collection of Database objects you can open and work with. Each Database object contains Table, Query, and Relationship objects. For example, to open and change the name of a table definition named "MyTable" in a database named "MyDB.mdb" to "YourTable", you could use the following code:

```
Dim wksThisWorkspace As Workspace
Dim dbsThisDatabase As Database
Dim tdfThisTableDef As TableDef
' open the default workspace
Set wksThisWorkspace = DBEngine.Workspaces(0)
' open MyDB.mdb
Set dbsThisDatabase = wksThisWorkspace.OpenDatabase("MyDB.mdb")
' open the table def named MyTable
Set tdfThisTableDef = dbsThisDB.TableDef("MyTable")
' change the table def's name
tdfThisTableDef.Name = "YourTable"
```

In addition to the programmatic DAO, Visual Basic has a special set of controls that lets you automatically bind to and work with database objects. These include data controls, which allow you to bind to a particular database and recordset; and bound controls, which let you display and accept input for individual fields. *Bound controls* include text boxes, combo boxes, picture boxes, and labels. To connect a data control to a specific table, follow these steps:

1. Select the Data Control button in the Toolbox.

2. Draw a data control on your form by clicking and dragging the cursor.

3. In the Properties window, enter the name of the database you want to connect to in the `DatabaseName` property.

4. Enter the name of the table or query you want to manipulate in the `RecordSource` property.

5. In the Toolbox, select the type of control best suited for the first field you want to display on your form.

6. Draw the control on your form.

7. In the `DataSource` property of the control, select the name of the Data Control you created in step 2.

8. In the `DataField` property of the control, select the name of the field you want displayed in this control.

9. Repeat steps 5–8 for each field you want to display.

Now, when you run your project, each control bound to the data control will display the value of the field it is assigned to. As you use the data control to navigate through the database, the values of each bound control change accordingly.

Using SQL

With the Jet engine, you can also manipulate databases using *Structured Query Language*, or *SQL*. SQL is a database language that was developed to provide a common query language, regardless of the type of database you are accessing. It includes functions for selecting records, updating records, deleting records, and creating and manipulating tables. With SQL, you send a line of text describing what you want to accomplish to a database, and the database interprets and performs the tasks you set forth.

You can directly send SQL statements that don't return a recordset to a database using the `Execute` method of a `Database` object. The following code example illustrates this by deleting records from an Orders table where the `OrderDate` field is older than December 31, 1994:

```
dbsThisDatabase.Execute "DELETE FROM Orders WHERE OrderDate < #12/31/94#"
```

The Visual Basic data control also recognizes and can use SQL statements. You can use an SQL statement directly in the data control's `RecordSource` property. For example, to change a data control's `RecordSource` to select only the records from a Customers table where the `LastName` field is equal to `"Smith"`:

```
datThisDataControl.RecordSource = "SELECT * FROM Customers WHERE LastName = 'Smith'"
```

From Here...

To learn more using Visual Basic to create integrated applications, refer to these chapters:

- Chapter 3, "Integration Basics," teaches you what OLE and objects are all about.
- Chapter 5, "Programming Application Integration," shows you how to apply Visual Basic to integrated application projects.
- Chapter 17, "Controlling Office Applications with Visual Basic," shows you how to use Visual Basic to manipulate and maintain documents created with Office.
- Chapter 23, "Using Windows APIs," guides you through declaring and implementing Windows 95 API calls, and provides examples of useful API functions.

CHAPTER 5

Programming Application Integration

In Chapter 3, you learned the basics of Microsoft Office applications, including DDE basics, OLE, ODBC, and the other integration interfaces found in the Office suite. In this chapter, you'll take it a step further and learn how these mechanisms work and how to implement them in your applications. The three mechanisms discussed are Dynamic Data Exchange, Object Linking and Embedding (OLE) Automation, and Open Database Connectivity (ODBC).

In this chapter you learn how to

- Establish communications with a DDE server
- Send and retrieve data from Word
- Send and retrieve data from Excel
- Establish communications with an OLE Automation server
- Set properties of an OLE Automation server
- Call methods of an OLE Automation server
- Find information about OLE servers
- Create an ODBC data source for communicating with an ODBC server
- Establish communications with a remote server using ODBC
- Access remote tables with Access

Each of the applications found in the Office suite incorporates one or more of these mechanisms. This chapter covers techniques for implementing the mechanisms into your applications and discusses some of the more technical issues involved when you incorporate these components into your applications.

TIP

This chapter may contain words or terms that you are not familiar with. If you come across a term that you don't know, feel free to consult the glossary of terms found in Appendix C.

Exchanging Data Using DDE

The Windows environment provides numerous mechanisms for communicating with external applications. An *external application* can be defined as one that is outside of the current application you are working with; for example, if you are in Word, examples of external applications would be Excel and Access.

One mechanism for communicating with these external applications is *Dynamic Data Exchange* (*DDE*). The following section defines DDE and some practical uses of this technology. In this section, you learn how to create basic DDE communication sessions, communicate with Excel using DDE, and communicate with Word via DDE.

What is DDE?

The first mechanism developed for interapplication communication was something known as the Clipboard. The *Clipboard* allows you to cut, copy, and paste text from different applications. This mechanism is rather simple and not very robust (in terms of newer technology). The second mechanism developed for Windows is something known as *Dynamic Data Exchange* (*DDE*). Where the Clipboard is limited to the transfer of text, DDE allows you to exchange more complex data. DDE allows Windows applications to send and retrieve data and commands from other external Windows applications.

DDE conversations are carried out by two different types of applications: *DDE clients* and *DDE servers*. DDE clients send commands and data to DDE servers. DDE servers respond to requests for data from DDE clients. First, you'll need a demonstration of the coding techniques for programming DDE clients.

DDE Conversations

DDE communicates with external applications via a mechanism known as a *conversation*. DDE conversations are much like telephone conversations. One application calls another, and if it answers, the two applications can proceed to communicate by sending data and/or commands. The applications found in Office provide a robust set of functions to create DDE conversations.

Initiating a DDE conversation requires three pieces of information: a service name, a topic, and some data items:

- *Service name*. The name of the DDE server that processes the data and commands sent from a DDE client. The service name is in essence the phone number of the application your application wants to have a conversation with. Word for Window's service name is WINWORD; Excel's is EXCEL.

- *Topic*. The subject matter that the server is familiar with and can talk about. Spreadsheet applications talk about spreadsheets, and word processors talk about documents. Usually topics consist of application data file names or a special system topic. Windows and Excel can use either file names or the command word "System" as their topic. The System topic is a general topic that most applications respond to. You will commonly use the System topic to find out what other topics the particular DDE server can manage.

■ *Data items.* The smallest components of a DDE conversation. Data items can consist of raw data or commands to be processed by the DDE server. The data items are essentially the "words" that make up the "sentences" of DDE conversations.

Initiating DDE Client Conversations

The capability to act as a DDE client allows your applications to control other Windows applications. You can extend the capabilities of your applications to provide services such as performing very complex mail merge processes using a word processor, creating a chart with your favorite spreadsheet, or sending documents with your favorite fax software. DDE is a generic communication mechanism found in many Windows applications, not just applications from Microsoft. You can communicate with WinFax Pro, Lotus 1-2-3, WordPerfect for Windows, and many other Windows applications.

All DDE communications begin by initiating a conversation with a DDE server. VBA and WordBasic's mechanism for initiating a DDE conversation is the DDEInitiate() function. This function requires two parameters:

■ The service name of the DDE server

■ The topic to be discussed

Conversations from Excel DDE to Word are initiated as follows:

```
'Attempt to initiate conversation with Word
intChannel = DDEInitiate("Winword", "System")
```

If Word is running, DDEInitiate() returns a value known as a channel. A *channel* is a number representing an area in memory reserved by Windows to conduct the DDE conversation. If Word is not running, the Excel application requesting a conversation is greeted by the dialog box shown in figure 5.1.

Fig. 5.1

This dialog box is displayed by Excel when the DDEInitiate() *function cannot find the requested application.*

Having Excel execute the server application automatically is not desirable in a DDE conversation. What is desired is the ability to see if the DDEInitiate() function succeeded. If the function is not successful in initiating a conversation, the DDE client application should then attempt to manually launch the DDE server and initiate a conversation again.

The first item the DDE client should address is preventing the dialog box (refer to fig. 5.1) from appearing. Excel provides a property that controls the display of messages from DDE. The `Application.DisplayMessages` property allows you to prevent Excel from displaying dialog boxes. The following code illustrates how to turn the DDE error messages off:

```
Application.DisplayMessages = False
```

The client applications now need to deal with the possibility of the server application not being available for a conversation. `DDEInitiate()` returns an error if an attempt to initiate a conversation fails. For more information about functions and return values, see Chapter 4. The following code illustrates how to establish a DDE conversation and what to do if an initiated attempt fails:

```
Function Test()
'Turn message dialogs off
Application.DisplayAlerts = False

    'Attempt to initiate conversation with Word
    intChannel = DDEInitiate("Winword", "System")

    'Check to see if there was an error
    'If so run Word application
    If TypeName(intChannel) = "Error" Then

        ' Run Word
        intNull = Shell("C:\msoffice\winword\winword.exe", 1)

        'Reinitiate conversation
        intChannel = DDEInitiate("Winword", "System")
    End If
End Function
```

Upon initiating a conversation, the DDE client begins sending data and commands to the DDE server.

Sending and Receiving Data with Word. As you just learned, upon establishing a DDE conversation with Word, the client application begins sending data and commands. Sending data and commands requires the use of the channel returned from the `DDEInitiate()` function. The functions used for sending data to a DDE server are `DDEPoke()` and `DDEExecute()`. The function used to retrieve information from a DDE server is `DDERequest()`.

When sending data and commands to Word, use the `DDEExecute()` function. The `DDEExecute()` function requires two parameters:

- The channel you initiated the DDE conversation on
- The command or data you want to send to the DDE server

To send data to the Word servers, the DDE client application uses the following syntax:

```
'Command to send some text to Word
'intNull is a"throwaway variable" The return value will be ignored.
  intNull = DDEExecute(intChannel, "INTEGRATING OFFICE APPLICATIONS SAMPLE")
```

The other data element a DDE client can exchange is a command. This next example illustrates how to send a command to Word using the WordBasic macro language:

```
'Create command string
strCommand = "[fileopen " + Chr(34) + "c:\winword\vfpvsac.doc" + Chr(34) + "]"

' Call open file command
intNull = DDEExecute(intChannel, strCommand)
```

NOTE Take notice of the command syntax the client application sent to Word. Word uses a macro language called *WordBasic* for its DDE conversations. The WordBasic language is very robust. Documentation for the WordBasic language can be found in the Word help files or in the Word Developer's Toolkit.

TIP All functions related to DDE begin with the letters "DDE." Most VBA programming standards dictate using mixed-case VBA keywords. With DDE, it is better to use mixed case after the DDE to make your code more readable.

Retrieving Information from Word Documents. DDE conversations allow client applications to also retrieve information from DDE servers. Visual FoxPro uses the DDERequest() function to retrieve information from DDE servers.

To retrieve information from a Word document, the DDE client first tries to initiate a DDE conversation using the System topic. After establishing a conversation, it then initiates another conversation with the opened document it is going to request information from. The following code illustrates how to initiate a conversation with Word, open a document, and initiate a second channel to that document:

```
'Turn message dialogs off
Application.DisplayAlerts = False

  'Attempt to initiate conversation with Word
  intChannel = DDEInitiate("Winword", "System")

  'Check to see if there was an error
  'If so run Word application
  If TypeName(intChannel) = "Error" Then

        ' Run Word
        intNull = Shell("C:\msoffice\winword\winword.exe", 1)

        'Reinitiate conversation
        intChannel = DDEInitiate("Winword", "System")
  End If
```

```
'Create command string
strCommand = "[fileopen " + Chr(34) + "c:\winword\SAMPLE.DOC" + Chr(34) + "]"

' Call open file command
intNull = DDEExecute(intChannel, strCommand)

'Set up channel to file
intChannel2 = DDEInitiate("Winword", "c:\winword\SAMPLE.DOC")
```

This code initiates a conversation with Word opening the SAMPLE.DOC file when it begins. After initiating a conversation, you can request information from the opened Word document by using the DDERequest() function.

NOTE If you already established a DDE conversation with the System topic, you need to establish a second conversation with Word. This is because a DDE conversation is limited to a single topic. In order to communicate with a document, you need to make sure the topic is the same name as this document.

The DDERequest() function requires two parameters:

- The channel you initiated your DDE conversation on
- The name of the item you want to retrieve from the Word document

You have a few options here. The first item you can return is the contents of a *Word bookmark*. Word has a feature that allows you to jump to a specified point in a document that you have named. This named jump point is known as a bookmark. The syntax for returning a bookmark is as follows:

```
'Retrieve information from bookmark IntroParagraph
strString = DDERequest(intChannel2, "IntroParagraph")
```

This code returns the contents of a bookmark named IntroParagraph.

Another option is to return the entire contents of a Word document. You can do this by specifying a special Word item \doc as the data item you are requesting. The \doc keyword returns the entire text of a Word document. Figure 5.2 demonstrates the following code that returns the entire contents of a Word document:

```
'Retrieve information from entire document
strString = DDERequest(intChannel2, "\doc")
```

The DDERequest function returns an array with the contents of the request. You can evaluate the contents and dimensions of the array using the Ubound and Lbound functions. The Ubound and Lbound functions return the upper and lower bounds of an array. For more information about these functions, consult your VBA documentation.

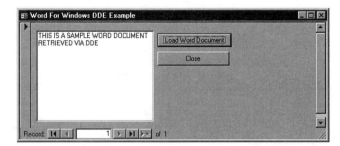

Fig. 5.2

The Access form with contents of a retrieved Word document.

Sending and Receiving Data with Excel. Establishing a DDE conversation with Excel is similar to establishing a conversation with Word. The client application first provides the service name for Excel and then specifies the topic to discuss. Excel also uses the System topic for initiating its DDE conversations. The following code illustrates how to initiate a conversation with Excel:

```
If AppIsRunning("Microsoft Excel") = 0 Then
    Shell "C:\EXCEL\EXCEL.EXE"
    AppActivate "Microsoft Excel", 1
End If

intChannel = DDEInitiate("Excel", "System")
```

Upon establishing a conversation with Excel, it's necessary to establish another connection channel with the worksheet the client application wants to exchange data with. This time, the topic should be the name of the worksheet, rather than the System topic. The following code illustrates establishing a connection with an Excel worksheet:

```
intChannel2 = DDEInitiate("Excel", "Sheet1")
```

Upon establishing a connection with a worksheet, the DDE client begins exchanging data with Excel. Sending data to an Excel worksheet requires the use of the DDEPoke() function.

NOTE You may notice that Word uses the DDEExecute() function to send data while Excel uses DDEPoke(). Because spreadsheets deal with specific data items in specific locations (specific rows and columns), you need to specify where the data will go. Word is freeform, so it doesn't need a specific location.

The DDEPoke() function requires three parameters:

- The channel you established with the Excel worksheet
- The row and column where you want to send data
- Character string representing the data you want to insert into a specified cell location

The following code illustrates how to send a value to a cell located in an Excel worksheet:

```
DDEPoke lnChan2, "R1C1", "Q1"
```

You can also retrieve information from an Excel worksheet using the DDERequest() function. The DDERequest() function requires two parameters:

- The channel you established with the Excel worksheet.
- The row and column designation of the particular cell you want to retrieve. This second parameter has two forms: the row and column location of the data you want to request, and a named location in an Excel worksheet.

The code below illustrates a cell referenced by a cell location, and another cell referenced by name:

```
*-- Reference cell by specific location
strstring$ = DDERequest$(lnChan2, "R1C1")

*-- Reference cell by named region
strString$ = DDERequest$(lnChan2,"SALES_TOTAL")
```

Controlling Excel Using the Excel 4 Macro Language. The second type of data element you can send to Excel comes in the form of Excel's macro language. DDE client applications can programatically control Excel from Word using Excel's built-in macro language. This macro language should not be confused with VBA. DDE client applications need to use the Excel 4 macro language.

 NOTE Another mechanism for communicating with Excel is through OLE Automation. Excel can be used as an OLE Automation server. The next section explains how to use Excel as an OLE Automation server.

Sending commands to Excel requires the use of the DDEExecute() function. The DDEExecute() function requires two parameters:

- The channel the DDE client established with the Excel worksheet
- The command the DDE client wants executed on the DDE server

Sending a command to change a cell to bold in Excel uses the following syntax:

```
DDEExecute lnchan2, "[FORMAT.FONT(,,TRUE)]"
```

The real power of controlling Excel comes with using Excel's macro language to execute a series of commands to perform a specific task. One of these tasks might be to create a chart using Excel's charting tools. Word has no capability to generate a chart naturally from a set of data. Excel provides a very powerful charting tool which would be nice to use from Word. The following code illustrates how to establish a conversation with Excel and use Excel's charting capabilities from the Word macro.

The following code creates a chart using Word as the client and Excel as the charting tool. The chart created by this example is shown in figure 5.3:

```
If AppIsRunning("Microsoft Excel") = 0 Then
   Shell "C:\EXCEL\EXCEL.EXE"
   AppActivate "Microsoft Excel", 1
End If

'Open channel to Excel
intChannel = DDEInitiate("Excel", "System")

'Establish connection to sheet
lnchan2 = DDEInitiate("Excel", "Sheet1")

'-- Send graph range names
DDEPoke lnChan2, "R1C1", "Q1"
DDEPoke lnChan2, "R2C1", "Q2"
DDEPoke lnChan2, "R3C1", "Q3"
DDEPoke lnChan2, "R4C1", "Q4"
DDEPoke lnChan2, "R5C1", "Q5"

'-- Send some sample data
DDEPoke lnChan2, "R1C2", "150"
DDEPoke lnChan2, "R2C2", "250"
DDEPoke lnChan2, "R3C2", "175"
DDEPoke lnChan2, "R4C2", "300"
DDEPoke lnChan2, "R5C2", "350"

'-- Select range to graph
strCommand$ = "[SELECT(" + Chr$(34) + "R1C1:R5C2" + Chr$(34) + ")]"
DDEExecute lnChan2, strCommand$

'-- Create new graph
DDEExecute lnChan2, "[NEW(2,3)]"

'-- Terminate communication
DDETerminate(lnChan2)
```

Introducing Integrated Applications

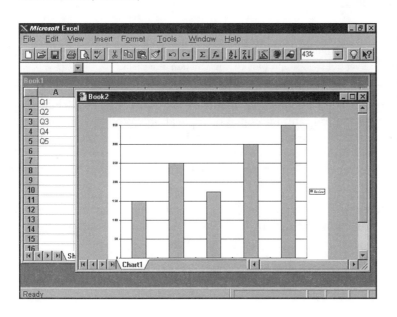

Fig. 5.3

This Excel chart was created using the Excel macro language and an Excel DDE conversation.

Exchanging Data Using OLE Automation

The Windows environment provides numerous mechanisms for communicating with external applications. The next one discussed in this chapter is *OLE Automation*. This section defines what OLE Automation is and shows some practical uses of this technology. In this section, you learn how to establish communications with an OLE Automation server, call methods of OLE Automation servers, and find information about OLE Automation servers.

What is OLE Automation?

OLE is the newest form of interapplication communication in Windows. OLE Automation defines a standardized approach to sending data and commands between dissimilar Windows applications. Examples of dissimilar Windows applications would be Access talking to Word or Access talking to Excel. These applications store and process different types of files and documents. OLE Automation defines a standard API for the communication between these applications.

OLE Automation sessions are performed by two different types of applications: OLE *clients* and OLE *servers*. OLE clients send commands and data to OLE servers. OLE servers respond to requests for data from OLE clients. This section demonstrates the coding techniques for programming OLE clients.

OLE Sessions

OLE's method of communication resides in what is known as *an OLE session*. This session is similar to a conversation in DDE. Your Office application attempts to create a communication session with an OLE server. Upon establishing this session, you can begin sending and receiving data and commands. Office provides a robust set of functions to create OLE sessions.

 NOTE   Creating OLE automation conversations is limited to Access and Excel. Word can act as an OLE server but lacks support for OLE automation as a client.

OLE sessions are created by establishing what is known as an *instance of an application*. Windows allows you to run multiple copies of applications. What this means is that if you want to open two copies of Word, you can do so with no problem. Each copy of Word is known as an *instance*. Whenever you attempt to create an OLE session, Windows runs another copy of the application you are attempting to communicate with.

Creating an instance of an OLE server requires that you know the name of the OLE server you wish to communicate with. Table 5.1 lists the names of various OLE servers.

Table 5.1 OLE Server Names	
Server Name	**Application It Creates**
Word.Basic	Word
Excel.Application	Excel Session
Excel.Chart	Excel Chart
Excel.Sheet	Excel Sheet
SQLOLE.Server	SQL Server DMO Database
SchedulePlus.Application.7	Schedule Plus Object

Creating OLE Automation Sessions

To create an OLE automation session from Excel or Access, you can use either the CreateObject or GetObject functions. CreateObject is used to create a new instance of the OLE sever you wish to communicate with. GetObject allows you to attach your OLE session to an already running session of the OLE server. The following code creates an object session variable and creates an instance of Excel using the CreateObject function:

```
Dim oExcelObject As Object
Set oExcelObject = CreateObject("Excel.Application")
```

The following example demonstrates using GetObject to create a session with an already-running session of Excel:

```
Dim oExcelObject As Object
Set oExcelObject = GetObject(,"Excel.Application")
```

If you take a close look at this code, you'll notice that GetObject has two parameters. The first parameter is optional and specifies the name of an already existing file to open in the OLE session. The second parameter is the name of the OLE Automation server you want to communicate with. VBA does not require that you specify an optional parameter; you simply put the comma where the optional parameter would be and continue your code after the comment.

Upon establishing a conversation with an OLE server, you can begin sending and retrieving data or commands from the OLE server. OLE Automation sessions behave just like Access form controls. You have the ability to read and set properties or call the methods of the OLE server. The following code demonstrates changing properties and sending commands to Excel:

```
Dim oExcelObject As Object
Set oExcelObject = CreateObject("Excel.Application")

'Change visible property to show the server
oExcelObject.Visible = True
```

```
' Set the title of the running session
oExcelObject.Caption = "HELLO WORLD"

'Call add new workbook method of OLE server
oExcelObject.Workbooks.Add
```

In the DDE section of this chapter, you learned how to create graphs with Excel using DDE commands. The following example demonstrates the same action using OLE automation:

```
Dim oMyOBject As Object

  ' We can use either CreateObject or GetObject
  Set oMyOBject = CreateObject("Excel.Application")
  'Set oMyOBject = GetObject(, "Excel.Application")

  ' Show Excel
  oMyOBject.Visible = True

  'Add new workbook
  oMyOBject.Workbooks.Add

  ' Add data to the cells
  oMyOBject.Cells(1, 1) = "Jan"
  oMyOBject.Cells(2, 1) = "Feb"
  oMyOBject.Cells(3, 1) = "Mar"
  oMyOBject.Cells(4, 1) = "Apr"
  oMyOBject.Cells(5, 1) = "May"
  oMyOBject.Cells(6, 1) = "June"

  oMyOBject.Cells(1, 2) = 100
  oMyOBject.Cells(2, 2) = 200
  oMyOBject.Cells(3, 2) = 300
  oMyOBject.Cells(4, 2) = 250
  oMyOBject.Cells(5, 2) = 150
  oMyOBject.Cells(6, 2) = 50

  ' Select range to graph
  oMyOBject.Range("A1:B6").Select

  ' Add new chart
  oMyOBject.Charts.Add
```

This example creates a basic chart from a set of fixed information. Chapter 9 has a more detailed example that sends the contents of an Access query to an Excel chart.

Understanding Object Hierarchies

An important concept to understand when using OLE automation is the object hierarchy of the particular server you are communicating with. OLE servers commonly have a set of different types of objects that you can manipulate—Excel has workbooks, sheets, and charts. These are three different types of objects that you can create and manipulate using automation. Figure 5.4 illustrates some of the hierarchies found in Excel and SQL Server.

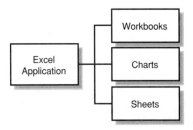

Fig. 5.4

Object hierarchies found in the Excel and SQL Server object models.

Object Browsers

One of the more useful tools for researching OLE servers is something known as an object browser. *Object browsers* are tools that allow you to view the hierarchies, properties, and methods of OLE servers. Whenever you install an application that is an OLE server, it commonly provides information regarding object hierarchies. One of the better object browsers on the market is a tool known as VBA Companion from Apex Software. Figure 5.5 shows an example of the Excel hierarchy.

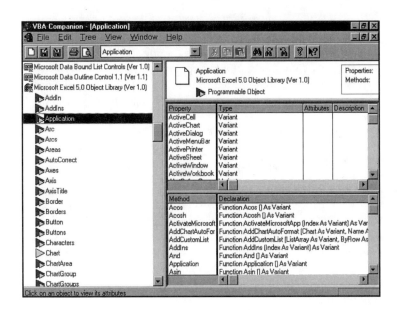

Fig. 5.5

Excel's object hierarchy appears in the VBA Companion Object Browser.

Along with commercially available tools such as VBA Companion, many of the Office applications have built-in browsers. When editing code in Excel, you can activate its browser by selecting View, Object Browser from the Excel menu. Figure 5.6 shows Excel's built-in Object Browser.

Fig. 5.6

The object browser is built into Excel.

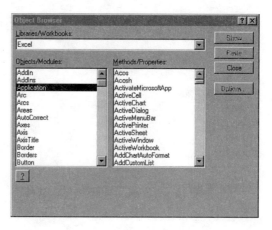

 TIP   If you are going to do any serious development using OLE, these tools are invaluable.

Notice that OLE Automation and DDE take similar approaches to sending data and commands to other applications. OLE Automation provides a more powerful interface because of its capability to check return values from functions, where DDE provides no such mechanism. So why would you want to use DDE? Word doesn't yet allow the creation of OLE Automation conversations from its macros, leaving DDE as the only mechanism for sending data to external applications. Also, some server applications are not always OLE servers. WinFax Pro, a popular fax application, does not yet support OLE Automation; thus, developers are required to use DDE for the transmission of fax information. The generally recommended technique is to use OLE if it is available, and if not, use DDE.

Exchanging Data Using ODBC

Since the inception of Access 1.0, the ability for the user to create client/server applications has been part of the Office repertoire. Access and other Office applications use *Open Database Connectivity (ODBC)* as a mechanism for communicating with external database servers. ODBC is a generic approach to access data from remote servers such as SQL Server, Oracle, and Informix. This section explains how to access data using ODBC. In this section, you learn how to create ODBC data sources for communicating with ODBC servers, establish communication with a remote server, and link remote tables into your Access applications.

Accessing Client/Server Data from Office

Office applications use ODBC as their mechanism for accessing server data. Before you can access data using ODBC, you must configure an ODBC data source. To create an ODBC data source, activate the ODBC Administrator from the Control Panel (see fig. 5.7).

Fig. 5.7

*The ODBC Administrator
icon is found in the
Windows Control Panel.*

ODBC
Administrator icon

Upon activating the ODBC Administrator, the Data Sources dialog box appears (see
fig. 5.8). This dialog box controls the configuration of ODBC data sources. From this
dialog box, you can add new data sources or edit existing ones.

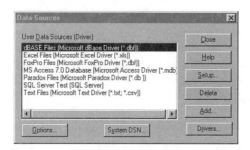

Fig. 5.8

*ODBC Administrator's
Data Sources dialog box
displays available data
sources.*

Click Add from the Data Sources dialog box, and the ODBC Administrator presents a
list of its available drivers. These drivers are programs supplied by the database vendors that can be used to create an ODBC link to their respective databases. Office
ships with SQL Server, Excel, Paradox, Text File, FoxPro, and Access ODBC drivers.

NOTE   If you want to experiment with client/server development but you don't have a server,
Office provides FoxPro and Access drivers. These are formats that Office can export
many different ways allowing you to develop client/server applications immediately.

Configuring ODBC Drivers

After you select a driver, the ODBC Administrator opens a setup screen for the selected driver. The setup screen is responsible for the configuration parameters of an

ODBC driver. This screen controls the specification of the source name and the database connection parameters necessary for an ODBC conversation.

Figure 5.9 demonstrates the ODBC configuration screen for an Access ODBC driver. The name of the data source is Integrating Office NWIND Link. This driver requires that the path of the access database be specified for the connection. Clicking the Select button activates the Windows Open File dialog box, allowing the developer to specify an available Access database.

Fig. 5.9

The ODBC Configuration dialog box appears for the Access driver.

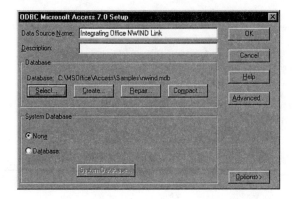

Linking Tables to Access

Once you've created a data source, you can begin accessing data with your Office applications using ODBC. To link an ODBC database to your Access database, choose File, Get External Data, Link Tables from the Access menu. A dialog box similar to the Windows Open File dialog box appears (see fig. 5.10).

Fig. 5.10

This screen shows the Link Table dialog box found in Access.

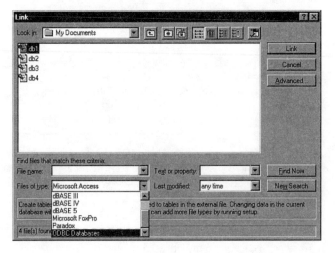

Select the ODBC Databases option from the Files of Type list in the lower-left corner of the dialog box. Upon selecting this option, you are prompted with a list of the available data sources (see fig. 5.11).

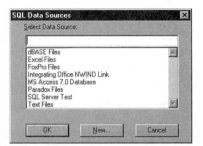

Fig. 5.11

The SQL Data Sources dialog box allows developers to select from available data sources.

This dialog box prompts you to select the data source that is configured to access your database. If your database requires a password, Access prompts you with a server login screen (see fig. 5.12).

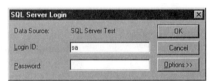

Fig. 5.12

The SQL Server Login dialog box requires a user name and password.

After entering the user name and password for your server, you are prompted with a list of the tables found for that server. The Link Tables dialog box allows you to select the table(s) you want to link to your Access database (see fig. 5.13). The Save Login ID and Password Locally option in this dialog box allows you to save the user name and password in your Access database. This is a convenient option if you don't want to have users entering this information every time this database is accessed.

Fig. 5.13

The Link Tables dialog box allows you to specify which tables to link to your Access database.

> **Caution**
>
> One of the most important aspects of database development is the security of the data. You may want to require that the users of your system provide a user name and password every time they log in. Check with your database administrator before checking this option.

After you've selected the table(s) to link to your Access database, Access places them into the Tables tab of your database (see fig. 5.14). Notice the globe next to your table name. Now you can begin using the server data as though it were an Access table. Figure 5.15 shows the linked database in Datasheet view.

Fig. 5.14

An Access database appears with a linked table noted by a globe icon.

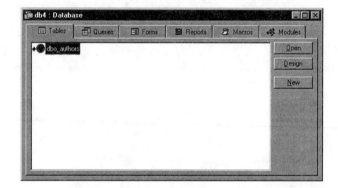

Fig. 5.15

The Linked SQL Server table appears in Datasheet view.

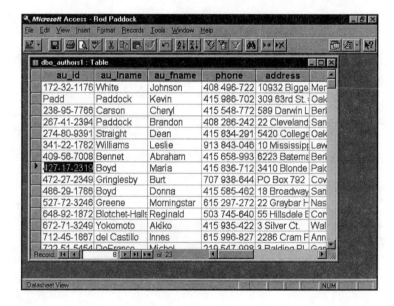

NOTE If you want to be able to update data from Access, make sure the table you are linked to has a Primary Key defined. Contact your database administrator for help with this task.

From Here...

There are many different methods of accessing data within our Office applications. You can use DDE and OLE to send data and commands to different external applications and ODBC to access different types of data. The mechanisms provided by Office allow you to create very complex applications.

The following chapters further illustrate using the tools provided with Office for creating integrated applications:

- Chapter 3, "Integration Basics," discusses the basics of integrating Office applications.

- Chapter 4, "Visual Basic and Visual Basic for Applications," describes how to write Visual Basic code and use the tools found in the VBA environment.

- Chapter 23, "Using Windows APIs," describes how to integrate the power of the Windows API into your applications.

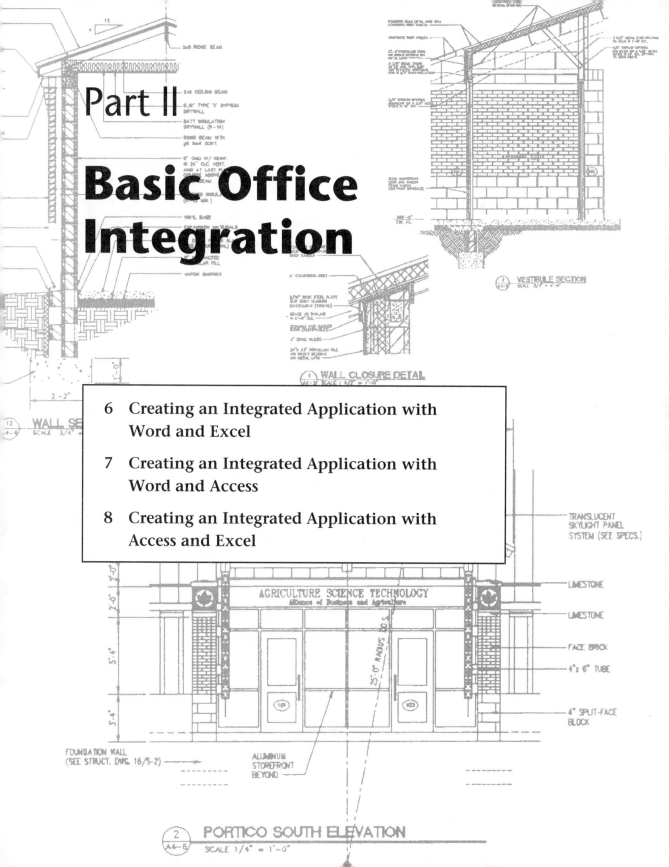

Part II

Basic Office Integration

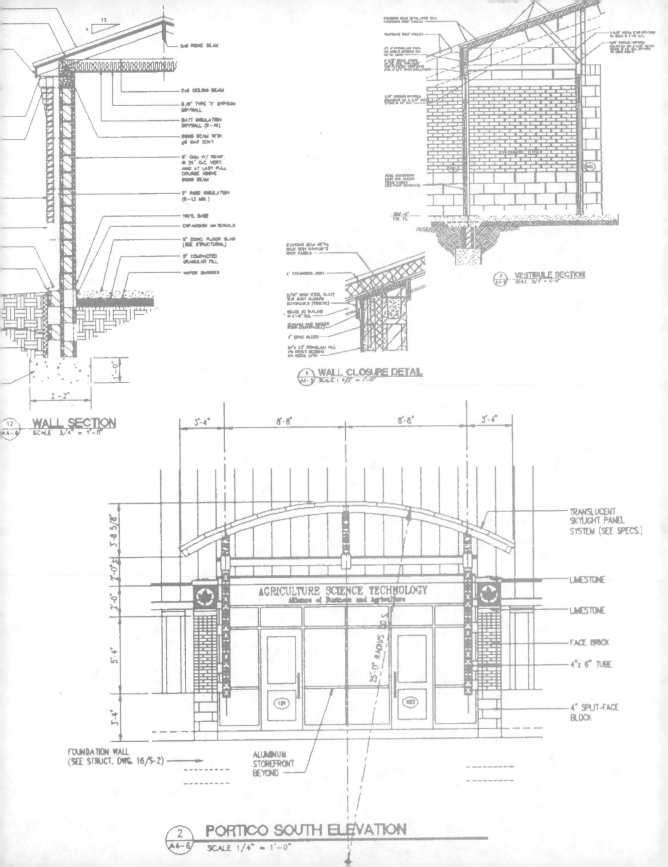

2x8 RIDGE BEAM

2x8 CEILING BEAM

5/8" TYPE "X" GYPSUM
DRYWALL

BATT INSULATION
DRYWALL (R-19)

BOND BEAM WITH
#4 BAR CONT.

6" CMU w/ REINF.
@ 24" O.C. VERT.
AND AT LAST FULL
COURSE ABOVE
BOND BEAM

3" RIGID INSULATION
(R-13 MIN.)

VINYL BASE

EXPANSION MATERIALS

5" CONC. FLOOR SLAB
(SEE STRUCTURAL)

8" COMPACTED
GRANULAR FILL

VAPOR BARRIER

1'-0"

2'-2"

WALL SECTION
SCALE 3/4" = 1'-0"

VESTIBULE SECTION
SCALE 3/4" = 1'-0"

WALL CLOSURE DETAIL
SCALE 1 1/2" = 1'-0"

5'-4" | 8'-8" | 8'-8" | 5'-4"

TRANSLUCENT
SKYLIGHT PANEL
SYSTEM (SEE SPECS.)

LIMESTONE

LIMESTONE

FACE BRICK

4" x 6" TUBE

4" SPLIT-FACE
BLOCK

AGRICULTURE SCIENCE TECHNOLOGY
Alliance of Business and Agriculture

25'-0" RADIUS TO S

101   102

FOUNDATION WALL
(SEE STRUCT. DWG. 16/S-2)

ALUMINUM
STOREFRONT
BEYOND

PORTICO SOUTH ELEVATION
SCALE 1/4" = 1'-0"

CHAPTER 6

Creating an Integrated Application with Word and Excel

6

Now that you have explored the basics of creating integrated applications with Microsoft Office for Windows 95, you can practice what you've learned by developing a simple integrated application using Word and Excel. The example in this chapter guides you through creating a Word mail merge using an Excel worksheet as the data source. You can then enhance your document with more of Office's integration features, such as linking and embedding objects from a variety of other applications. Finally, by using Word's powerful macro language, WordBasic, you can create menu items to easily access your integrated mail merge documents.

In this chapter, you learn how to

- Create a mail merge document integrating Word and Excel
- Link and embed data from other applications in your Word documents
- Use macros to add items to the Word menu bar

Creating a Word Mail Merge Using an Excel Data Source

One of the most common business uses of Word's Mail Merge feature is to send the same letter or document to a variety of clients or customers. Although Word is naturally the preferred application for creating letters, an application such as Excel or Access is more suited for creating and maintaining a customer list. By using Office's integration features, you can take advantage of the strengths of both applications to create the functionality you need. For example, say you just opened your own financial consulting business. You may want to create letters to send to prospects, to thank clients for their business (once you get clients), and perhaps to introduce a new service you plan to provide in the future.

NOTE For more complete instructions on how to use Mail Merge, see *Special Edition Using Microsoft Office for Windows 95* or *Special Edition Using Word for Windows 95*, both published by Que.

Before you can integrate your Word document with data created in another application such as Excel, you must first create a *main document* and a *data source*. In this case, the main document is your basic form letter in Word. The data source is a prospect list you create in Excel.

Creating a Main Document in Word

To create a main document in Word, follow these steps:

NOTE You can choose File, New to open the New dialog box where you can select pre-formatted letter styles. You can also access the Letter Wizard from this dialog box, which provides step-by-step guidance on creating a well-designed letter suited to your needs.

1. Click the New button to create a new document.

2. Write your letter as desired, omitting the name, address, and salutation, but leaving room to insert them (see fig. 6.1).

3. Click the Save button to open the Save As dialog box.

4. Type a name for your letter, such as **Prospect**, in the File Name box.

5. Click Save to close the dialog box.

Fig. 6.1

Create your client prospect letter in Word to merge with data in Excel.

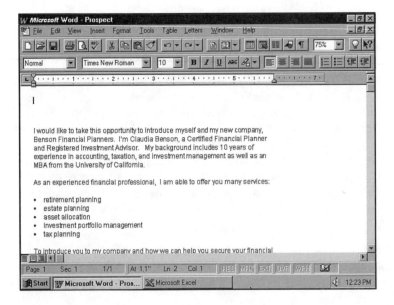

Creating a Data Source in Excel

Before creating your data source in Excel, you need to determine how to use it in Word. For example, you could enter client names in an Excel worksheet column in several ways:

Mr. John Smith

Smith, John

John Smith

There are several problems with these entries, however. The first and third options make sorting by name very difficult. Second, including salutation, first, and last names in one field or column makes creating a mail merge difficult. If you want to write to Dear John or Dear Mr. Smith, it's a lot more difficult to extract the appropriate words from one field than it is to use three separate fields.

TIP

If your list includes addresses in other countries, you may want to take this into consideration when designing your worksheet. For example, you could change zip code to postal code and add a country field.

A preferred structure for use in mail merge is to create separate columns as follows:

Salutation

Last Name

First Name

Company

Title

Address1

Address2

City

State

Zip

NOTE

For more complete instructions on how to create Excel worksheets, see *Special Edition Using Microsoft Office for Windows 95* or *Special Edition Using Excel for Windows 95*, both published by Que.

To create your Excel worksheet, follow these steps:

1. In a blank worksheet, enter the column titles listed previously in row 1.
2. Position the cell pointer in any cell in your column headings.
3. Choose <u>D</u>ata, F<u>o</u>rm to open the Data Form dialog box, illustrated in figure 6.2.

Fig. 6.2

*Using forms simplifies
Excel data entry.*

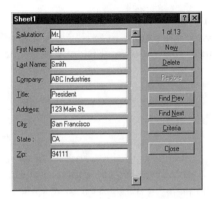

4. To add a new record to the list, click the Ne<u>w</u> button. A new blank form appears.

 TIP   Press Tab to move forward to the next text box. Press Shift+Tab to return to the previous text box.

5. Enter the appropriate data in each text box on the form.

6. When you finish entering data for the record, press Enter to add the new record to the list. Another blank form appears, enabling you to enter another new record.

7. Click the C<u>l</u>ose button to return to the worksheet (see fig. 6.3).

Fig. 6.3

*Create your data source
as an Excel worksheet to
merge with letters in Word.*

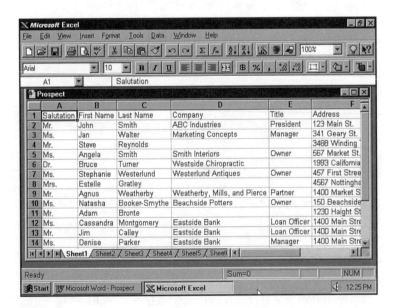

8. Click the Save button to open the Save As dialog box.

9. Type a name for your worksheet, such as **Prospect**, in the File Name box and click Save to save the file and close the dialog box.

Sorting Your Excel Data Source

If you want, you can sort your Excel worksheet before using it as your data source in Word. This saves time if you plan on viewing the data in a sorted order in Excel as well. To sort data in Excel, follow these steps:

Caution

Be sure to select all the data you want to sort. Only the selected columns will sort, causing serious sorting problems if essential columns are omitted.

---

1. Select the data you want to sort.

2. Choose Data, Sort to open the Sort dialog box (see fig. 6.4).

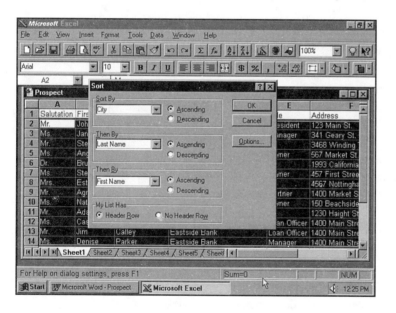

Fig. 6.4

You can sort data in Excel before merging with Word.

3. You can select up to three sort fields. Enter these in the Sort By, Then By, and Then By boxes.

4. Choose to sort in either Ascending or Descending order. Ascending order is the default.

5. In the My List Has area, select either Header Row or No Header Row, so you can avoid sorting your header information.

TIP Click the Options button for more advanced options concerning case-sensitivity, sorting months or days of the week, or sorting orientation (top to bottom or left to right).

6. Click OK to sort.

Merging Your Word Document with the Excel Data Source

To merge the Excel worksheet data into your Word documents, use Word's Mail Merge feature. This book assumes you are already familiar with basic Word features such as Mail Merge, and only discusses this feature as used in this example.

To merge your document with the Excel worksheet, follow these steps:

1. Open your main Word document (in this example, PROSPECT.DOC).

2. Select Tools, Mail Merge to open the Mail Merge Helper.

3. Click the Create button in step 1 and select Form Letters from the drop-down list.

4. Click the Active Window button in the dialog box that appears to use the current open document as your main mail merge document.

5. In step 2, you define your data source—in this case, the Excel worksheet discussed earlier. Click the Get Data button.

6. Choose Open Data Source to access the Open Data Source dialog box, select MS Excel Worksheets from the Files of Type list, and then select your Excel worksheet (Prospect).

7. The Excel dialog box appears. Choose Entire Spreadsheet in the Named or Cell Range list box and click OK.

8. A dialog box tells you that you haven't selected any merge fields. Click the Edit Main Document button to reopen your main document.

TIP When inserting merge fields, be sure to also include the appropriate spaces and punctuation marks required for your address format, such as a space between first and last names, a comma between the city and state fields, and so on.

Insert Merge Field

9. The Mail Merge toolbar now appears in your Word document. Click the Insert Merge Field button to insert the name and address fields in this document. Figure 6.5 illustrates the use of merge fields.

TIP You can also print your letters directly from this document by clicking the Merge to Printer button.

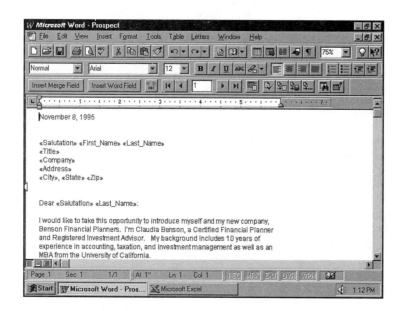

Fig. 6.5

Enter Excel merge fields in the Word document.

> **NOTE** Merge to a new document to view all the mail merge letters you have just created by clicking the Merge to New Document button on the toolbar. To return to your original document, choose File, Close. You can save this new document, but keep in mind it creates a page for every record you have in your data source. Merging a single-page Word document with a 500-record Excel worksheet, for example, would produce a 500-page mail merge.

10. Click the View Merged Data button to preview your mail merge (see fig. 6.6). Click this button again to return to your original view.

11. Click the Save button to save your changes to Prospect.

Selecting Specific Records

So far, the mail merge you have created establishes a new page for every Excel record in the worksheet. This is fine if you want to include everything, but in many cases you'll want to narrow down your list to specific clients or locations.

> **TIP** Click Clear All to remove a filter or sort you've created.

To create a mail merge that includes only specific records, follow these steps:

1. Click the Mail Merge Helper button on the toolbar to return to the Mail Merge Helper.

2. Click the Query Options button in step 3 in the Mail Merge Helper to open the Query Options dialog box.

Fig. 6.6

Your completed mail merge document should look like this.

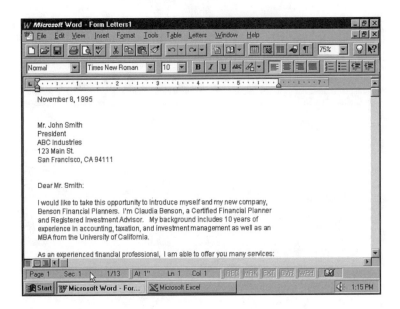

3. Select the Filter Records tab (see fig. 6.7).

Fig. 6.7

Select specific records in the Query Options dialog box.

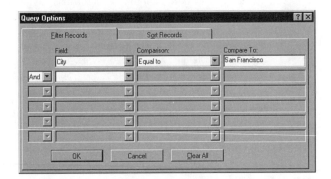

4. Choose the field on which you want to filter in the Field column. In this example, you will filter for all prospects located in San Francisco, so choose the City field.

5. Click Equal To in the Comparison column.

6. Type **San Francisco** in the Compare To column.

7. Select OK to return to the Mail Merge Helper and click Close to exit.

8. Clicking either the Merge to New Document or the View Merged Data button will enable you to verify that only the selected records are now included in your merge.

Sorting Records

To sort records, follow these steps:

1. Click the Mail Merge Helper button on the toolbar to return to the Mail Merge Helper.

2. Click the Query Options button in step 3 in the Mail Merge Helper to open Query Options dialog box, shown in figure 6.8.

 TIP
You can also sort your data in Excel by choosing Data, Sort.

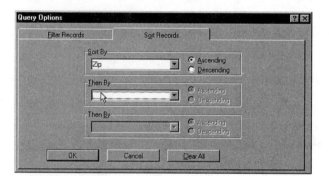

Fig. 6.8

You can sort records in the Query Options dialog box.

3. Select the Sort Records tab.

 TIP
You can sort your data in either Ascending or Descending order, by selecting the appropriate option button.

4. Choose the first field on which you want to sort in the Sort By box. Add additional sort fields in the Then By and Then By boxes. In this example, choose Zip.

5. Select OK to return to the Mail Merge Helper and click Close to exit. Your mail merge document will now be sorted by zip code.

 TIP
If you want to cancel your mail merge for any reason, select the Restore to Normal Word Document option under the Create button in the Mail Merge Helper.

II

Basic Office Integration

Linking and Embedding in Word

Linking and embedding are related tasks that both place data from a source application (in this case, Excel) into a destination application (Word in the examples in this chapter). As is explained in Chapter 3, "Integration Basics," linking places the presentation data and information about where to find the native data into a compound document. Embedding places the presentation data and the native data into the compound document, but provides no link to the data in its source application.

You need to ask yourself several questions before you decide whether to link or embed your information and which method to choose:

- Do you want to be able to edit the Excel data in Word?
- Do you want to simply display the data? If so, do you want it to update in Word every time you update it in Excel?
- Will your source data always be available?

Let's take an example. You want to include a list of all employees in your department in a Word document. The employee list is currently an Excel worksheet that is updated every month as employees join and leave the company. If your document is to reflect employee status as of a particular date (for example, you are referring to employee creation as of January 1996), then you should embed the Excel file so that changes made in February won't appear in January's document. On the other hand, if your Word document will be reused every month to reflect that month's employee status, you should link the Excel file to the Word document so that all changes are updated in Word as well.

Although you can simply copy the data from the Excel worksheet and paste it into the Word document using the Copy and Paste buttons or the Ctrl+C and Ctrl+P commands, this won't enable you to easily update the Excel data should it change.

When you link or embed data from one application to another, you have several choices regarding how to accomplish this task. The Paste Special dialog box, described in more detail in the following section, "Linking and Embedding Excel Data in Word," determines whether your object is embedded (Paste option) or linked (Paste Link option), as well as the format in which this is accomplished. You can link or embed an object in the following ways:

- *Excel Worksheet Object.* Inserts data as a picture, but allows editing as an Excel worksheet.
- *Formatted Text (RTF).* Inserts the text with font and table formatting. Choose this option if you want to convert Excel worksheet data to a Word table.
- *Unformatted Text.* Inserts text without font and table formatting. Essentially, converts Excel worksheet data to regular Word text.
- *Picture.* Inserts data as a picture. Takes up less space and is more suitable to high-speed printing than a bitmap image.

TIP
Picture is a good choice if you plan to send your document by e-mail, because it reduces file size.

- *Bitmap.* Inserts data as a bitmap.
- *Display As Icon.* Displays an icon as the link to the document rather than the document itself. By selecting the icon, you automatically open the linked document. This is available with all options if Paste Link is selected, but only with Microsoft Word Document Object if Paste is selected. Once you check the Display As Icon box, the Change Icon button appears. Select this button to open the Change Icon dialog box (see fig. 6.9). In this dialog box, you can choose any displayed Icon instead of the default, use the Browse button to search for another icon, or change your Caption.

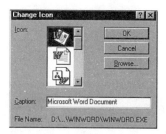

Fig. 6.9

Use the Change Icon dialog box to choose a different icon or enter a new caption.

Linking and Embedding Excel Data in Word

NOTE
If you want to link or embed an entire file rather than just specific data, you can choose Insert, Object as a shortcut. In the Object dialog box, choose the Create from File tab and then enter your file in the File Name box. Select the Link to File or Display as Icon check boxes if desired.

TIP
In addition to Excel worksheet data, you can also link or embed Excel charts in your Word documents.

To embed or link Excel data in Word, follow these steps:

1. Select your desired text in Excel, shown in figure 6.10.
2. Click the Copy button in the Standard toolbar, or press Ctrl+C.
3. Return to Word and place the cursor where you want to place the Excel worksheet data.
4. Choose Edit, Paste Special to open the Paste Special dialog box, shown in figure 6.11.

II

Basic Office Integration

Fig. 6.10

*Select and copy data in
Excel to insert in your
Word document.*

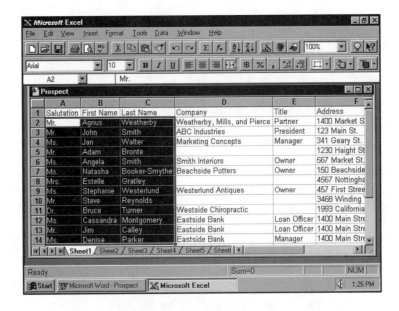

Fig. 6.11

*Determine how you
want to link or embed
the object in the Paste
Special dialog box.*

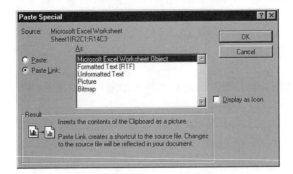

5. Determine whether you want to Paste or Paste Link. In this example, choose Paste Link so the Excel data automatically updates in Word.

6. In the As list box, choose one of the following options: Microsoft Excel Worksheet Object, Formatted Text (RTF), Unformatted Text, Picture, or Bitmap. Select Microsoft Word Document Object for this example.

7. Select the Display As Icon checkbox if desired.

8. Click OK to return to your Word document (see fig. 6.12).

TIP

Choose View, Page Layout to view your linked or embedded object; choose Insert, Frame to move the object.

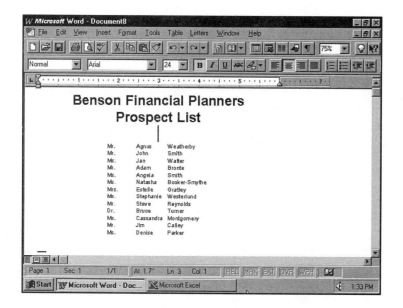

Fig. 6.12

The Excel data is now linked to your Word document.

Basic Office Integration

Inserting a New Object

Although Word is a powerful, sophisticated program with many advanced features, it can't do everything. Sometimes you need the features of another application to create a new object to embed or link into your Word document.

You can create an object in another Office application such as:

PowerPoint	Project
Excel	

Or use one of the many other object types, created in Microsoft's shared applications, such as:

Video Clip	Microsoft Graph
Media Clip	Word Picture
Wave Sound	Drawing
MIDI Sequence	Equation

You can also insert an object created in another compatible commercial product:

VISIO	Harvard Chart XL
CorelDRAW!	Calendar Creator
SPSS	

To create a new object for insertion in a Word document, follow these steps:

1. Choose Insert, Object to open the Object dialog box.

2. Choose the Create New tab.

3. Select the appropriate Object Type from the drop-down list. This list may vary depending on the applications you have installed.

4. Check the Display As Icon box if desired.

5. Click OK. Depending on your object type, you will either open a new application or view new menu options in Word with which to create your inserted information.

6. To return to standard Word, either choose File, Exit if you are in another application, or click outside of your inserted object if you remained in Word.

Updating a Link

 NOTE   If you move or rename a source file, you lose its link. To reconnect, select the link in the Links dialog box, and click Change Source. Choose your new link file in the Change Source dialog box.

If you linked your Excel spreadsheet to your Word document, Word can update the information either automatically or manually. By default, Word updates the link automatically, but you can also choose to manually update the link if you want to control when updates happen (for example, on a specific date). To update a link:

1. Choose Edit, Links to open the Links dialog box (see fig. 6.13).

Fig. 6.13

You can choose to update your link manually in the Links dialog box.

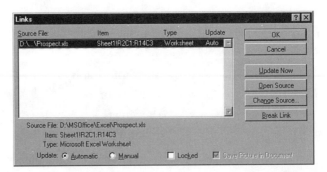

2. Select the link you want to update in the list.

3. Select the Manual option button to manually update all future links.

4. Click OK to close.

 TIP   To prevent a link from being updated, select it and choose the Locked checkbox.

To perform manual updates, do the following:

 TIP You can also manually update a link by selecting the linked object and pressing F9.

1. Choose <u>E</u>dit, <u>L</u>inks to open the Links dialog box.

 TIP To break a link, select it and click the <u>B</u>reak Link button.

2. Select the link you want to update. If you want to update more than one link, press Ctrl while selecting links.

3. Click the <u>U</u>pdate Now button.

4. Select the Close button.

Using Macros To Automate Word Tasks

A *macro* is a series of Word commands that is grouped together as a single command. By using macros, you can:

- Automate repetitive tasks
- Combine a series of commands
- Perform a complicated series of tasks more efficiently

Once you've recorded a macro, you can view its contents in the macro-editing window. Word translates the keystrokes you entered into its macro language, WordBasic. Once you are familiar with WordBasic, you can edit macros in this window, or add additional WordBasic code to create powerful macros that can't be created by recording keystrokes alone.

Recording a Simple Macro

In this example, you want to make retrieving your mail merge documents even easier. To do so, you can make them a menu option. Let's say you initially plan on creating three basic client mail merge letters—Prospect, New Service, and Thank You. You can create a menu item on the menu bar for Letters with Prospect, New Service, and Thank You as options under that menu.

To create a macro that makes selecting one of your mail merge letters a simple menu option, follow these steps:

1. Choose <u>T</u>ools, <u>M</u>acro to open the Macro dialog box.

2. Enter a name for your macro in the <u>M</u>acro Name box. In this example, name your macro **Prospect**, because it will open the Prospect letter.

3. Determine which templates should include your macro in the Macro Available In box. The default, All Active Templates, allows your macro to be accessed from all Word templates active at the time of recording.

4. Include a Description of what your macro does.

5. Click the Record button to access the Record Macro dialog box. The macro name appears in the Record Macro Name box (see fig. 6.14).

Fig. 6.14

You can assign a macro to a toolbar, menu, or short-cut key in the Record Macro dialog box.

6. In the Assign Macro To section, you have the option of assigning your macro to a toolbar, menu, or the keyboard as a shortcut key. In this example, select Menus.

TIP

You can also customize your menus directly by choosing Tools, Customize to open the Customize dialog box.

7. The Customize dialog box appears (see fig. 6.15) with the Menus tab selected. Click the Menu Bar button to open the Menu Bar dialog box, as illustrated in figure 6.16.

Fig. 6.15

The Customize dialog box allows you to assign a macro to a menu.

Fig. 6.16

Define your menu options in the Menu Bar dialog box.

8. In the Name on Menu Bar box, enter the name that you want to appear on your menu bar. If you want to include a hot key, insert the **&** sign before the letter that is to be the hot key. In this case, enter **&Letters**.

>
> **TIP**
> You can also Remove or Rename any selected menu item.

9. Determine where on the menu bar you want this menu to appear. Normally, you want your custom menus to appear after the regular Word menus but before the generic Window and Help menus. To do this, select T&able, then click Add After, followed by Close. You will return to the Customize dialog box. In the Change What Menu, &Letters appears. In the Name on Menu box, &Prospect appears.

10. Click the Add button and then Close. The Macro Record toolbar appears. The Stop and Pause buttons are located on this toolbar.

11. Begin recording your macro by choosing File, Open to display the Open dialog box.

12. Select the Prospect document (in this example, located in the D:\MSOFFICE\ WINWORD\MAIL folder) and click the Open button.

13. Press the Stop button on the Macro Record toolbar to stop recording your macro.

14. You can now choose Letters, Prospect to open the Prospect letter. As you create more merged letters, you can add these to the menu as well.

Assigning Your Macro to the Toolbar.

>
> **NOTE**
> To restore a toolbar to its original settings, choose View, Toolbars to open the Toolbars dialog box. Select the toolbar you want to restore and click the Reset button. In the Reset Toolbar dialog box, indicate the template in which you want to restore the selected toolbar, and then click OK.

>
> **TIP**
> You can also choose Tools, Customize to open the Customize menu if you want to assign an existing macro to a keyboard command.

To assign your macro to the toolbar, follow these steps:

1. In the Record Macro dialog box, click the Toolbars button in the Assign Macro To section. The Customize dialog box opens, with the Toolbars tab selected (see fig. 6.17).

Fig. 6.17

The Customize dialog box offers several options for assigning a macro to the toolbar.

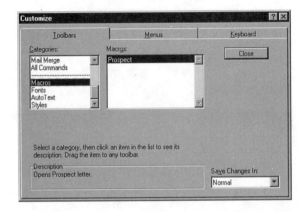

Caution

If you are editing an existing macro, you must select Macro in the Categories list box and your desired macro in the Macros list box.

---

2. Macros appear in the Categories list box, and the macro name you originally entered appears in the adjacent list box. Select the macro name and drag it to the appropriate toolbar.

   The Custom Button dialog box appears (see fig. 6.18), because this macro doesn't already have an assigned button.

Fig. 6.18

Assign your macro to a new toolbar button in the Custom Button dialog box.

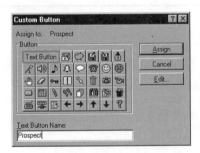

TIP
To edit a button, click Edit to open the Button Editor dialog box. In this dialog box, you can customize the color and shape of your button.

TIP

If you want to create a text button, enter the button name in the Text Button Name box.

3. Select one of the sample buttons in the Button group box and click Assign.

4. Click OK.

Assigning Your Macro to the Keyboard.

TIP

You can also choose Tools, Customize to open the Customize menu if you want to assign an existing macro to a keyboard command.

To assign your macro to the keyboard, follow these steps:

1. In the Record Macro dialog box, click the Keyboard button in the Assign Macro To section. The Customize dialog box opens, with the Keyboard tab selected.

NOTE

If you are editing an existing macro, you must select Macro in the Categories list box and your desired macro in the Macros list box.

Macros appear in the Categories list box, and the macro name you originally entered appears in the Commands list box.

NOTE

If the shortcut key you chose in step 4 already exists, the Currently Assigned To section of the dialog box displays the command to which it already has been assigned. For example, if you enter **Ctrl+C** in the Press New Shortcut Key box, you learn that this shortcut belongs to the EditCopy command. In general, it isn't a good idea to reassign shortcut keys, unless you are sure you won't be using the existing one. Once Currently Assigned To displays [unassigned], you know you have found a shortcut that hasn't yet been assigned to a command.

2. Place the cursor in the Press New Shortcut Key box and enter the keyboard command to which you want to assign this macro.

3. The NORMAL.DOT template defaults in the Save Changes In list box. If you want to save this shortcut only in a specific template, indicate it here.

4. Click the Assign button to assign the shortcut to the macro and then press Close.

Viewing a Macro

To view the WordBasic code that makes your macro perform the series of commands you specified, follow these steps:

1. Choose Tools, Macro to access the Macro dialog box.

2. Select the Macro Name from the drop-down list.

3. Click the Edit button to open the macro-editing window (see fig. 6.19).

Fig. 6.19

You can view and edit a macro in the macro-editing window.

The Macro toolbar

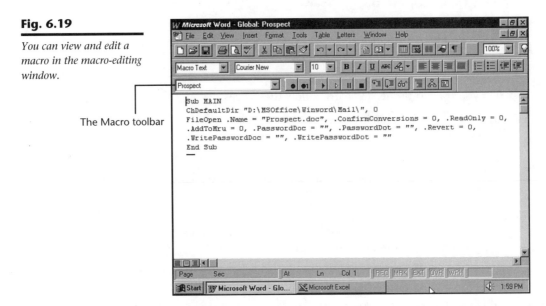

In the macro-editing window, the Macro toolbar appears with the buttons listed in table 6.1. These buttons are used to edit, display, and test macros.

Table 6.1   The Macro Toolbar

Button	Name	Description
Leftmost text box on toolbar	Active Macro	Lists open macros in the macro-editing window.
●	Record	Opens the Record Macro dialog box.
●1	Record Next	Records a singular Word command and inserts it in the open macro.
▶	Start	Runs the macro listed in the Active Macro list box.
▷	Trace	Runs a macro and displays each line of code as it performs it.
❙❙	Continue	Continues to next step.

Button	Name	Description
■	Stop	Stops the macro.
	Step	Runs a macro step-by-step; used for debugging.
	Step Subs	Runs a macro step-by-step through the main subroutine.
	Show Variables	Displays the Macro Variables dialog box.
	Add/Remove REM	Adds or removes a REM instruction; used to temporarily stop a particular macro instruction from running.
	Macro	Opens the Macro dialog box.
	Dialog Editor	Opens the Dialog Editor where you can create a custom dialog box.

Exploring the Use of WordBasic in Macros

> **TIP**
>
> Choose Help, Contents to open Word Help and select Programming with Word for detailed help on the WordBasic macro language.

The macro-editing window displays the following macro:

```
Sub MAIN
ChDefaultDir "D:\MSOffice\Winword\Mail\", 0
FileOpen .Name = "Prospect.doc", .ConfirmConversions = 0, .ReadOnly = 0,
➥.AddToMru = 0, .PasswordDoc = "", .PasswordDot = "", .Revert = 0,
➥.WritePasswordDoc = "", .WritePasswordDot = ""
End Sub
```

Essentially you have created a macro that opens the document D:\MSOFFICE\ WINWORD\MAIL\PROSPECT.DOC. The text that appears in the macro-editing window is a translation of the actions you performed in the WordBasic macro language. The first line Sub MAIN and the last line End Sub begin and end every macro. Sub refers to *subroutine*, which is a part of a larger program. More complex macros can include many subroutines.

A macro contains a series of statements and functions that perform specific tasks. A *statement* performs an action, such as opening a file. A *function* gets information and returns it to the macro to use. Words in a statement that begin with a period are called *arguments,* which serve as qualifiers for the statement and also correspond to Word dialog box options.

Let's examine the two statements and their arguments in the macro shown earlier. ChDefaultDir sets a Word default folder to a specified path and includes two arguments—Path$, which lists the path, and Type, which displays the number that corresponds to the folder, in this case 0, which refers to DOC-PATH.

FileOpen opens a document and includes several arguments:

Argument	Description
.Name	Displays the name of the document to open.
.ConfirmConversions	If 1, opens the Convert File dialog box for files that aren't in Word format.
.ReadOnly	If 1, opens the document in read-only format.
.AddToMenu	If 1, adds file to the list of recently opened files that appears at the end of the File menu.
.PasswordDoc	Displays the password to open document.
.Revert	If 1 and file is currently open, Word doesn't keep unsaved changes and opens new version of the document. If 0, activates the open document.
.WritePasswordDoc	Displays the password to save changes to the document.
.WritePasswordDot	Displays the password to save changes to the template.

This information tells you that this macro opens D:\MSOFFICE\WINWORD\MAIL\ PROSPECT.DOC as a regular Word document requiring no passwords, will activate the document if it's already open, and won't add it to the list of recently opened files.

Editing a Macro

If you want to change any of these arguments, you can do so in the macro-editing window. For example, you could change .AddToMenu from 0 to 1 to add this file to the list files at the end of the File menu. As you can see, an understanding of WordBasic will help you to determine exactly what actions your macros perform and how to edit them for more precise performance.

To make changes to an existing macro, follow these steps:

1. Choose Tools, Macro to access the Macro dialog box.
2. Select the Macro Name from the list box.
3. Click the Edit button to open the macro-editing window.
4. Revise your macro as necessary.
5. Choose File, Save Template.
6. Choose File, Close to close the macro-editing window.

Copying, Deleting, and Renaming Macros

You can use the Organizer dialog box to copy, rename, or delete a macro.

Copying a Macro. To copy or move a macro, follow these steps:

1. Choose Tools, Macro to open the Macro dialog box.

2. Click the Organizer button to open the Organizer dialog box, shown in figure 6.20.

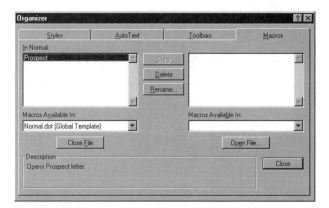

Fig. 6.20

Use the Organizer dialog box to copy, delete, and rename macros.

NOTE If the macro you want is in a template that isn't currently open, click the left Close File button, then click the left Open File button that replaces it. This displays the Open dialog box where you can choose the appropriate template.

3. Select the template that contains the macro you want to copy or move in the left Macros Available In list box.

TIP To select more than one macro, press Shift and then click the first and last macros in the series. If you want to select individual macros, press Ctrl and choose each macro.

4. Choose your macro in the In list box, then click the Copy button to copy the macro to the To box.

5. When you have finished, select Close.

Deleting a Macro. To delete a macro, follow these steps:

1. Choose Tools, Macro to open the Macro dialog box.

2. Click the Organizer button to open the Organizer dialog box.

3. Select the macro you want to delete in the In box.

4. Click the Delete button, and then the Close button to exit.

Renaming a Macro. To rename a macro, follow these steps:

1. Choose Tools, Macro to open the Macro dialog box.
2. Click the Organizer button to open the Organizer dialog box.
3. Select the macro you want to rename in the In box.
4. Click the Rename button to open the Rename dialog box.
5. Enter the new name for your macro in the New Name dialog box.
6. Click the Close button to exit.

Using Word Data in Excel

TIP

You can also insert objects and data from other applications in your Excel worksheets, just as you can in Word.

In addition to using Excel data in Word documents, you can also use Word data in Excel. One of the most common uses of Word data in Excel is the conversion of Word tables to editable Excel worksheet data. To use a Word table in Excel, follow these steps:

TIP

For more detailed instructions, see the section "Linking and Embedding in Word" earlier in this chapter.

1. Select your table in Word.

2. Click the Copy button, or select Ctrl+C.
3. Go to Excel and place the cursor where you want to insert the Word table.
4. Choose Edit, Paste Special to open the Paste Special dialog box.
5. Determine whether you want to Paste or Paste Link. In this case, you want to Paste Link so that changes in Word will reflect in Excel.
6. In the As list box, choose one of the following options: Microsoft Word Document Object, Picture, or Text. In this example, you want to choose Text to convert the table to editable Excel data.
7. Select the Display As Icon checkbox if desired.
8. Click OK to close and return to your Excel worksheet (see fig. 6.21).

You can now use this data in Excel formulas and functions; it also updates should you change your Word table in the future. If you had chosen the Paste option rather than Paste Link, the table data wouldn't update.

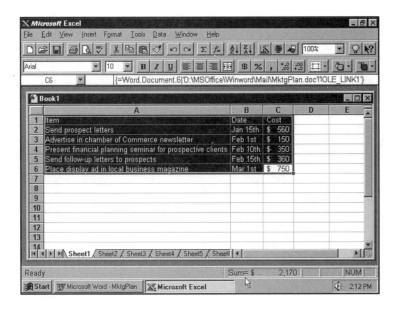

Fig. 6.21

The Word table can now be edited in an Excel worksheet.

From Here...

In this chapter, you learned the basics of integrating Word and Excel as well as how to take advantage of the strengths of each program within an integrated application. To go over the basics again, or delve into more advanced topics, refer to the following chapters:

- Chapter 3, "Integration Basics," provides a basic description of what makes integration work, such as DDE and OLE.

- Chapter 4, "Visual Basic and Visual Basic for Applications," provides a basic introduction to Visual Basic including the use of WordBasic.

- Chapter 10, "Automating Office Integration with Word," illustrates how Word can be used as a component within an integrated environment.

- Chapter 11, "Automating Office Integration with Excel," shows how Excel can be used within an integrated environment.

II

Basic Office Integration

CHAPTER 7

Creating an Integrated Application with Word and Access

In Chapter 6, you learned how to create a basic Word mail merge using an Excel worksheet as a data source. In that example, you created a prospect list in Excel, but this list could also have been created using the relational database, Access. In addition to creating a mail merge, you can also integrate Access and Word in other ways—by publishing the contents of Access tables, queries, reports, and forms in Word as well as by linking and embedding Word documents in Access.

In this chapter, you learn how to

- Create a mail merge document by integrating Word and Access
- Use the Access Mail Merge Wizard
- Publish Access data in Word
- Link and embed Word documents in Access
- Update links

Creating a Word Mail Merge Using an Access Data Source

When using Access as the data source for a Word mail merge, you have two options for creating the merge—Word's Mail Merge Helper and the Access Mail Merge Wizard. Both of these options essentially do the same thing—link a main Word document with an Access data source and allow you to place fields from the data source in the Word document. The main difference is whether you begin the process from Word or Access. If you primarily work in Word, choose the Word Mail Merge Helper; if, however, your main application is in Access, then the Access Mail Merge Wizard will be more convenient. For instructions on how to use the Access Mail Merge Wizard, see the section "Using the Access Mail Merge Wizard" later in this chapter.

The example that follows uses Word's Mail Merge Helper to create your merge. You'll use the same main document, Prospect, that you used in the previous chapter, and merge it with the data in a Mailing List table you'll create in an Access database.

NOTE For complete instructions on how to use Mail Merge, see *Special Edition Using Microsoft Office for Windows 95* or *Special Edition Using Word for Windows 95*, both published by Que.

Creating a Data Source in Access

NOTE For complete instructions on how to create Access databases and tables, see *Special Edition Using Microsoft Office for Windows 95* or *Special Edition Using Access for Windows 95*, both published by Que.

NOTE You can also use the Database Wizard to easily create predesigned databases such as Contact Management, Address Book, Expenses, or Time and Billing. To use this feature, select Database Wizard in the opening Microsoft Access dialog box and choose the Databases tab in the New dialog box.

In the example that follows, you use the Mailing List table in the Benson Financial Planners database as your mail merge data source. This table and the database that contains it can be found on the accompanying CD. If your data source doesn't already exist, you must create it.

To create your mailing list table in Access, follow these steps:

1. Open Access and click the Blank Database option button in the Microsoft Access dialog box that appears.

TIP A *database* can contain tables, forms, reports, queries, macros, and modules.

2. In the File New Database dialog box, enter a name for your database in the File Name text box. In this example, name the database **Benson Financial Planners**.

3. Click the Create button, and the Database dialog box appears.

4. Select the Tables tab and click the New button.

5. In the New Table dialog box, select the Table Wizard option and click OK to open the wizard (see fig. 7.1).

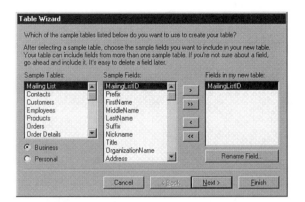

Fig. 7.1

The Table Wizard assists you in creating a new table.

NOTE The Table Wizard contains sample table structures for a variety of tables useful for business such as Contacts, Customers, Orders, Invoices, Time Billed, or Expenses. Using these predesigned table structures can greatly decrease the time it takes for you to create a new application.

6. With the Business option button selected, choose Mailing List in the Sample Tables scrolling list.

TIP You can rename a field by selecting it and clicking the Rename Field button.

7. Click the double right arrow to move all fields to the Fields in My New Table list. Or, select individual fields by highlighting them and clicking the right arrow button.

TIP You can click the Back button to return to the previous step.

8. Click the Next button.

NOTE Object names (for tables, queries, forms, and so on) can be up to 64 characters long and can include spaces. Although this is helpful for making your object names clearer and more precise, it isn't recommended if you plan to use the names in Visual Basic code.

9. Enter a new name for your table in the text box (see fig. 7.2), or accept the default, Mailing List, and click Next.

Basic Office Integration

II

Fig. 7.2

Name your table in this step of the Table Wizard.

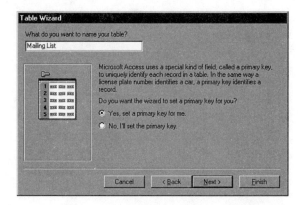

> **TIP**
>
> A *primary key* is a unique identifier for each record in a table.

10. Let Access set the primary key by selecting the Yes, Set a Primary Key For Me option.

11. Click the Next button to continue to the next step of the wizard.

12. You want to enter data directly into the table, so select the Enter Data Directly into the Table option button.

13. Click Finish to begin data entry.

Sorting Your Access Data Source. If you want, you can sort your Access table before using it as your data source in Word. This will save time if you plan on viewing the data in a sorted order in Access as well. To sort data in Access, follow these steps:

1. Open the Mailing List table in the Benson Financial Planners database.

2. Select the Last Name field.

3. Click the Sort Ascending button on the toolbar. Figure 7.3 displays the table sorted by Last Name.

Fig. 7.3

You can sort your Access table before merging it with Word.

	Prefix	First Name	Middle Name	Last Name	Suffix	Nick
▶	Dr.	James		Atterly	M.D.	Jim
	Ms.	Althea	M.	Blackstone		Allie
	Mr.	Adam	J.	Booker		
	Mr.	Jason	E.	Brantley		
	Mrs.	Samantha		Gill		
	Mr.	Bradley		Jonsson	III	Brad
	Ms.	Jennie	Elizabeth	Parker		
	Ms.	Joanne		Smythe		
*						

Mailing List : Table

Record: 1 of 8

Filtering Your Access Data Source. To select only certain records for your mail merge, such as only prospects living in San Francisco, follow these steps:

1. Open the Mailing List table in the Benson Financial Planners database.

2. Select a City field with San Francisco as its entry.

> **TIP**
> To remove the filter, click the Apply Filter button.

3. Click the Filter by Selection button to apply the filter (see fig. 7.4).

	Title	Organization N	Address	City	State	Rec
▶	Partner	Eastside Medic	1400 Market Str	San Francisco	CA	
			12348 Winding	San Francisco	CA	
	Partner	Jonsson, Meyer	1400 Market Str	San Francisco	CA	
	Vice President	Executive Image	1350 California :	San Francisco	CA	
*						

Mailing List : Table

Record: ◄◄ ◄ [1] ► ►I ►* of 4 [Filtered]

Fig. 7.4

Use the Filter by Selection button to easily filter data in your Access tables.

Exporting Your Access Data Source to a Word Mail Merge File. To export the data in your Access table to a Word mail merge file, follow these steps:

1. In the Database window, select the table you want to export and then choose File, Save As/Export.

2. In the Save As dialog box, select the To an External File or Database option and then click OK.

3. Select the directory where you want to export your merge file in the Save In box.

4. In the File Name text box, enter the file name; in the Save As Type text box, select Microsoft Word Merge (see fig. 7.5).

5. Click the Export button to export your file to a Word mail merge format.

> **TIP**
> If you don't want to include all the fields or records in a table in your mail merge, you can create a query to select your desired output and export the query to the mail merge format.

Fig. 7.5

You can export Access tables and queries to a Word mail merge text file.

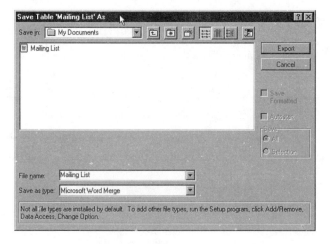

Merging Your Word Document with the Access Data Source

To merge the Access data into your Word document, you use Word's Mail Merge feature. This book assumes you're already familiar with basic Word features such as Mail Merge, and only describes this feature as used in this example.

> **NOTE**
>
> For more information on creating mail merges, refer to Chapter 6, "Creating an Integrated Application with Word and Excel" or see *Special Edition Using Microsoft Office for Windows 95* or *Special Edition Using Word for Windows 95*, both published by Que.

To merge your document with Access data, follow these steps:

1. Open your main Word document entitled Prospect.

2. Choose Tools, Mail Merge to open the Mail Merge Helper, illustrated in figure 7.6.

3. Click the Create button in Step 1 and select Form Letters from the drop-down list.

4. Click the Active Window button in the dialog box that appears to use the current open document as your main mail merge document.

5. In step 2, you define your data source, in this case the Access Table Mailing List. Click the Get Data button.

> **Caution**
>
> If you use an exported text file as your data source, rather than linking to the existing Access table, any updates you later make to the original data source won't reflect in your mail merge.

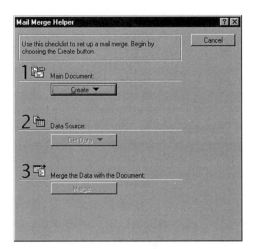

Fig. 7.6

Use the Mail Merge Helper to guide you through the steps required to create a mail merge.

NOTE You can also merge your Word document with a text file that you exported from Access. See the section "Exporting Your Access Data Source to a Word Mail Merge File" for more details on how to do this. Be sure to select Text Files in the Files of Type list in the Open Data Source dialog box when searching for your data source.

6. Choose <u>O</u>pen Data Source to access the Open Data Source dialog box (see fig. 7.7); choose MS Access Databases in the Files of <u>T</u>ype list; select your Access data source, Benson Financial Planners; and click <u>O</u>pen.

7. The Microsoft Access dialog box appears. Select the <u>T</u>ables tab, choose Mailing List, and click OK.

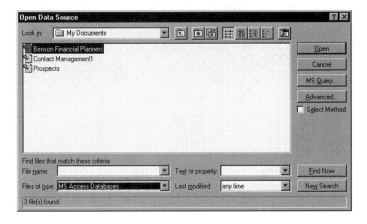

Fig. 7.7

Select your Access data source in the Open Data Source dialog box.

8. A dialog box tells you that you haven't selected any merge fields. Click the Edit <u>M</u>ain Document button to return to your main document.

> When inserting merge fields, be sure to also include the appropriate spaces and punctuation marks required for your address format, such as a space between first and last names, a comma between the city and state fields, and so on.

9. The Mail Merge toolbar now appears in your Word document. Click the Insert Merge Field button to insert the name and address fields in this document.

> You can also print your letters directly from this document by clicking the Merge to Printer button.

> Merge to a new document to view all the mail merge letters you have just created by clicking the Merge to New Document button on the toolbar.
> To return to your original document, select <u>F</u>ile, <u>C</u>lose. You can save this new document, but keep in mind it creates a page for every record you have in your data source. Merging a single-page Word document with a 500-record Access table, for example, would produce a 500-page mail merge.

10. Click the View Merged Data button to preview your mail merge (as shown in fig. 7.8). Click the View Merged Data button again to return to your original view.

11. Click the Save button to save your changes to Prospect.

Fig. 7.8

Your completed mail merge document should look like this.

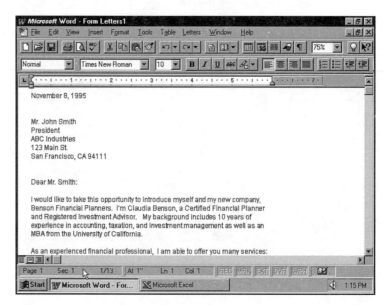

NOTE You can sort or filter your mail merge records. To do so, click the Mail Merge Helper button on the toolbar to return to the Mail Merge Helper. Click the Query Options button under step 3 to open the Query Options dialog box and choose either the Sort Records or Filter Records tab.

NOTE For more information on sorting and filter in a mail merge, see the sections "Sorting Records" and "Selecting Specific Records" in Chapter 6, "Creating an Integrated Application with Word and Excel."

TIP If you want to cancel your mail merge for any reason, select the Restore to Normal Word Document option beneath the Create button in the Mail Merge Helper.

Using the Access Mail Merge Wizard

In addition to creating mail merges using Word's Mail Merge Helper, you can also create a merged application from within Access. Using the Access Mail Merge Wizard, you can merge an Access table or query with a Word document. For example, you can create the exact same mail merge you created in the previous section by following these steps:

1. In the Database window, select the Tables tab and choose the Mailing List table.
2. Click the OfficeLinks button to open the Microsoft Word Mail Merge Wizard.

TIP If you haven't already created a main document in Word, choose the Create a New Document and Then Link the Data To It option in the wizard. Word then opens a blank document.

3. In the Microsoft Word Mail Merge Wizard, select the Link Your Data to an Existing Microsoft Word Document option. The Select Microsoft Word Document dialog box appears.
4. Choose your desired document, in this case the Prospect document, and click Open. Word opens the document and displays the Mail Merge toolbar.
5. Continue to create your mail merge as described in the previous section, "Merging Your Word Document with the Access Data Source."

II

Basic Office Integration

Publishing Access Data in Word

> **TIP**
> You can also output a subform or subreport to an RTF format. For more information on subforms and subreports, see *Special Edition Using Microsoft Access for Windows 95*, published by Que.

In addition to merging Access database information with Word documents, you may also want to publish Access data *in* a Word document. The OfficeLinks feature, Publish It With MS Word, allows you to output Access tables, queries, reports, and forms to an RTF file format in Word. *RTF* stands for *Rich Text Format* and allows you to keep formatting options intact.

To publish the Mailing List table in Word, follow these steps:

1. In the Database window, select the Tables tab and choose the Mailing List table.

2. Select the drop-down arrow next to the OfficeLinks button, and choose Publish It With MS Word from the menu that appears.

3. Access outputs the contents of the table as a Microsoft Word RTF file and places it in the directory where your database is located. Word then opens to display your new document (see fig. 7.9).

Fig. 7.9

You can edit, format, and sort the Access data in a Word RTF file.

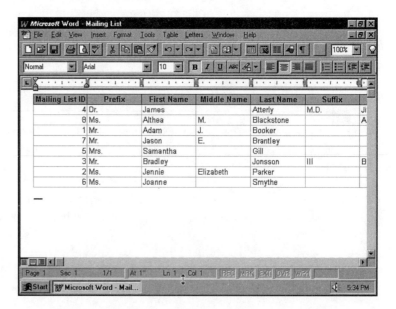

Once your data is in Word, you can sort the table information, convert the table to text, or format it as desired. Note that any changes you make are to the Word document you have created, not to the original Access table. To save the RTF file as a Word document, choose File, Save As to open the Save As dialog box. Choose Word Document as your Save as Type, and click the Save button.

Using a Query to Select Data to Output

If you don't want to output the entire contents of a table, you can select only the records you want to output in the datasheet first. For more complicated filters, you can create a query. You might also want to create a query if you plan on using the same filter over and over again and you will be adding records to your table. Then you can run your query whenever you want, and it will include these new records. For example, you might want to include a list of all your customers in San Francisco in a document you publish every month. You can then output the results of that query every month to an RTF file you include in your Word document.

To do this, follow these steps:

1. In the Database window, select the Queries tab and click the <u>N</u>ew button. The New Query dialog box appears, as shown in figure 7.10.

Fig. 7.10

Select the type of query you want to create in the New Query dialog box.

2. Select Design View in the list of query options and click OK. The Show Table dialog box appears over the query window (see fig. 7.11).

Fig. 7.11

The query window enables you to design sophisticated queries.

3. Select the Mailing List table, click <u>A</u>dd, and then click <u>C</u>lose.

4. All of the fields contained in the Mailing List table appear in the field list in the upper-left portion of the query window. Drag the First Name, Last Name, Title, Organization Name, and City fields from the field list to the Field row in the data pane in the lower portion of the window.

5. In the City field, remove the check in the Show checkbox and enter **San Fran-cisco** as your Criteria. Figure 7.12 illustrates how the query window should appear now.

II

Basic Office Integration

Fig. 7.12

Your query will only select prospects in San Francisco.

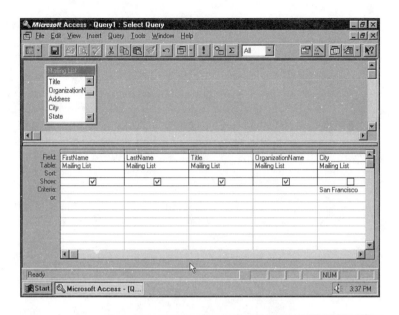

6. Click the Run button to view the results of your query (see fig. 7.13).

Fig. 7.13

You can view the results of your query.

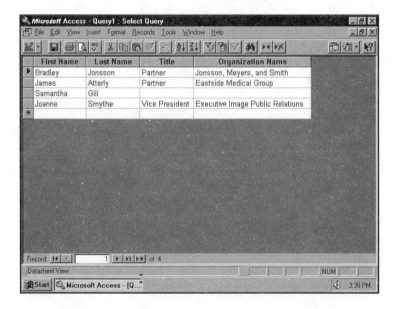

7. Click the Save button to save your query.

You can now select the query in the Database window and use the OfficeLinks feature Publish It With MS Word to output the results of this query to an RTF file format as decribed in the previous section, "Publishing Access Data in Word."

Linking and Embedding Word Data in Access

In addition to using Access data in Word, you can also use Word data in Access. For example, you may want to display a WordArt logo in an Access form or report, or include a link to a Word document in a field in an Access table. You can *link* or *embed* the data using either a *bound* or *unbound object frame*.

Linking and embedding are related tasks that both place data from a source application (in this case, Word) into a destination application (Access in the examples in this chapter). But how they treat this data is very different.

When you link an object, it is updated automatically whenever the source changes. For example, if you link a Word document to an Access table, any changes you make to the document are reflected in Access. Linked information is stored in the source document.

Embedded data is stored in the destination document and is useful when the source document becomes unavailable or is changed, yet these changes aren't desired in the destination. When you embed an object, it doesn't automatically update in the destination document if the source changes. Embedded objects must be edited separately.

With a bound object, the contents of that object are derived from a field in a table. Adding fields in an employee tracking table to store identification photographs, résumés, or other objects created in another application are examples of using bound objects. An unbound object isn't tied to a field in a table. It can be any object that is inserted in an Access form or report, such as a WordArt logo or Excel worksheet data.

Linking and Embedding Bound Objects

To illustrate an example of linking a bound object, let's say you have created a background document on each of your prospects. Because you will primarily use Access to track your mailing list activity, you want to be able to view each prospect's background without opening Word and searching for individual documents. By creating an OLE object field in the Access Mailing List table and linking each background document to its corresponding record, you can easily retrieve background information without leaving Access. To do this, follow these steps:

1. Select the Tables tab, highlight the Mailing List table, and click the Design button. The Mailing List table opens in Design view.

2. Insert a new Field Name called **Background** at the end of the list of field names.

II

Basic Office Integration

> **NOTE**
>
> An *OLE object field* is a field that stores documents, sounds, graphics, or binary data you created in another application, such as Word, Excel, or PowerPoint.

3. Choose OLE Object as the Data Type. Figure 7.14 illustrates how your screen should look.

Fig. 7.14

You can insert a new field in an Access table.

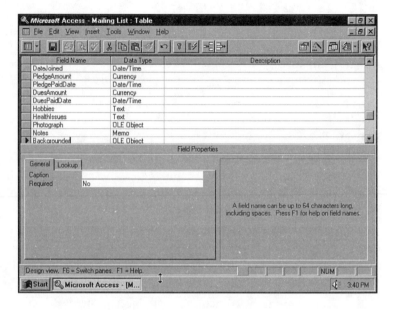

4. Click the Save button to save your table, then click the Datasheet View button to go to Datasheet view.

> **Caution**
>
> You must insert the related object for each specific record in the appropriate field. For example, if you want to link the photograph of each employee to a 20-record employee table, you would need to follow these steps 20 times to link each individual photograph to its corresponding record in the table.

5. With the cursor in the Background field of your first record, choose Insert, Object. The Insert Object dialog box opens.

> **NOTE**
>
> If you haven't already created your Word document, you can do so now by choosing the Create New option in the Insert Object dialog box. Select Microsoft Word Document as your Object Type, and click OK to open Word.

6. Choose the Create from File option and enter the name of your Word document in the File text box.

> **TIP**
>
> You can also use the Browse button to open the Browse dialog box, which can make finding a file in another folder easier.

7. If you want to link the Word document to the Access table, select the Link checkbox. If this box isn't checked, you will embed the document.

> **NOTE**
>
> To display an icon rather than the document itself, choose the Display as Icon checkbox. By selecting the icon, you automatically open the linked document. Once you check the Display As Icon checkbox, the Change Icon button appears. Click this button to open the Change Icon dialog box. In this dialog box, you can choose any displayed Icon instead of the default, use the Browse button to search for another icon, or change your Label.

8. Click OK to close the dialog box.

Placing a Bound Object in a Form. Now that you have created an object field in an Access table, you can display it in a form. To do this, follow these steps:

> **TIP**
>
> You can also place a bound object in a report.

1. Select the Form tab and click the New button. The New Form dialog box opens, as shown in figure 7.15.

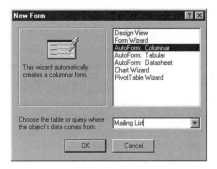

Fig. 7.15

The New Form dialog box offers several alternatives for creating a new form.

2. Choose the AutoForm: Columnar option from the list on the right side of the dialog box.

3. Select the table or query on which you want to base your form. In this example, choose the Mailing List table.

4. Click OK.

The AutoForm Wizard automatically creates and displays a form. The Word document that you linked to the first record appears in the large bound object frame in the lower-right corner of the form (see fig. 7.16).

Fig. 7.16

Your linked field appears in the bound object frame.

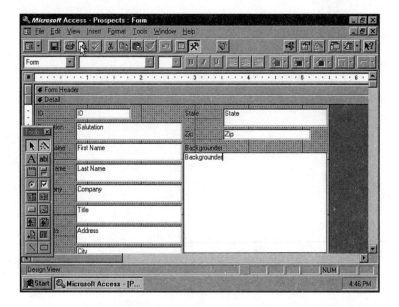

Notice that your Word document isn't entirely visible in the frame. To resolve this problem you can:

■ Change the font size and formatting in Word so your document is legible in the Access form. This works best when you have only a small amount of text to display.

> **TIP**
> SizeMode also has a `Stretch` property which enables you to size an object to fit the control, but this may make the object appear out of proportion.

■ In Access's Form Design view, change the `SizeMode` property from Clip (the default) to Zoom so that the entire Word document appears in the bound object frame. Do this by selecting the frame, right-clicking, and selecting Zoom as the `SizeMode`. You may, however, not be able to read the entire Word document this way because it may be too small.

■ Select the Display as Icon option in the Insert Object dialog box. The document itself won't appear, but you can select the icon to open the Word document.

Inserting a Partial Word Document. In the previous section, you learned how to link or embed entire Word documents into Access tables. You aren't confined to inserting entire documents, however; you can also link or embed selected sections of Word documents. Let's say, for example, that you don't want to include the entire Backgrounder document in the Access table. Instead you only want to link the first paragraph of each prospect's backgrounder. To do this, follow these steps:

1. Open the Background document in Word.
2. Select the first paragraph and click the Copy button.
3. Leaving Word open, switch to Access and select the Background field in the first record of the Prospects table.
4. Choose Edit, Paste Special to open the Paste Special dialog box.
5. Select the Paste Link option button.
6. Choose Microsoft Word Document in the As box.
7. Click OK.

When you create a form based on this table, you can view only the selected text in the Background field.

Linking and Embedding Unbound Objects

Placing a logo in an Access form or report is an example of linking or embedding an unbound object. Let's say you created a logo for your financial planning company using WordArt. You can copy this WordArt logo from Word and place it in an Access form you've created. To do this, follow these steps:

> **NOTE**
> WordArt 2.0 is a shared application that enables you to create special text effects such as borders, shading, or stretch and rotational effects. WordArt creates special text as an object that you can embed in other applications using OLE. To use WordArt in Word, choose Insert, Object and select WordArt 2.0 as the Object Type. WordArt isn't in-cluded in Office's typical installation; you must run Setup again and choose to install it if it doesn't appear in this the Object Type list in the Object dialog box.

1. Open your Word document and select the WordArt logo (see fig. 7.17).
2. Click the Copy button.
3. Switch to Access and open the Design view of the form in which you want to place the logo.
4. Select the Unbound Object Frame button in the toolbar, and drag to the place you want to insert the WordArt object.
5. Right-click the mouse and choose Paste from the shortcut menu that appears.

Access embeds the logo in the form, as shown in figure 7.18.

Fig. 7.17

Select the WordArt logo in Word.

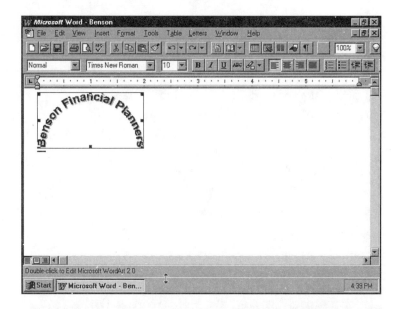

Fig. 7.18

You can embed a WordArt logo in an Access form or report.

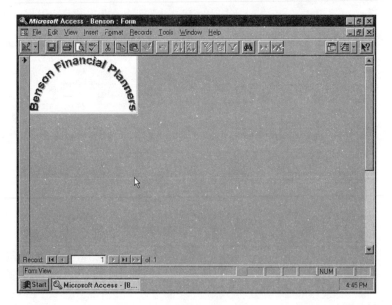

Updating a Link

If you link an Access table and a Word document, you can update the information either automatically or manually in Word or Access (depending on where you initiated the link). By default, the link updates automatically, but you can also choose to manually update the link if you want to control when updates happen (for example, on a specific date). To update a link:

 NOTE If you move or rename a source file, you'll lose its link. To reconnect, select the link in the Links dialog box, and click Change Source. Choose your new link file in the Change Source dialog box.

1. With your object (document, table, or whatever) open, choose Edit, OLE/DDE Links in Access or Edit, Links in Word to open the Links dialog box (see fig. 7.19).

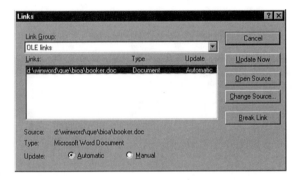

Fig. 7.19

You can choose to update your link manually in the Links dialog box.

2. Select the link you want to update in the list.

3. Select the Manual option button to manually update all future links.

4. Click OK to close.

 TIP In Word, to prevent a link from being updated, select it and choose the Locked checkbox.

 TIP You can also manually update a link by selecting the linked object and pressing F9.

To perform manual updates, do the following:

1. Choose Edit, Links to open the Links dialog box.
2. Select the link you want to update. If you want to update more than one link, press Ctrl while selecting links.
3. Click the Update Now button.
4. Select the Close button.

 TIP
To break a link, select it and click the Break Link button.

From Here...

In this chapter, you learned the basics of integrating Word and Access as well as how to take advantage of the strengths of each program within an integrated application. To go over the basics again, or delve into more advanced topics, refer to the following chapters:

- Chapter 3, "Integration Basics," provides a basic description of what makes integration work, such as DDE and OLE.
- Chapter 6, "Creating an Integrated Application with Word and Excel," covers the use of Word's Mail Merge feature in more detail.
- Chapter 10, "Automating Office Integration with Word," illustrates how Excel can be used as a component within an integrated environment.
- Chapter 12, "Automating Office Integration with Access," shows how Access can be used within an integrated environment.

CHAPTER 8

Creating an Integrated Application with Access and Excel

Access and Excel each have their own individual strengths, and in an integrated application, you can take advantage of this. You may, for example, want to develop your basic application in Access because it's a relational database with a powerful programming language, yet still benefit from the calculation abilities, functions, and formulas Excel offers.

In this chapter, you learn how to

- Use Access data in Excel through Microsoft Query, Excel pivot tables, and Access OfficeLinks
- Use Excel data in Access through the Access Label Wizard and Excel AccessLinks
- Link and embed Access and Excel data

Using Access Data in Excel

NOTE This chapter assumes that you are already familiar with the basic uses and functions of Access and Excel. For more information on these applications, refer to *Special Edition Using Microsoft Office for Windows 95*, *Special Edition Using Excel for Windows 95*, or *Special Edition Using Access 95*, all published by Que.

There are basically four ways you can use Access data in Excel:

- Copy and paste Access datasheet data in Excel
- Use Query to retrieve specific Access data
- Use the Access OfficeLinks feature Analyze It with Excel to output Access tables and queries to Excel
- Retrieve and analyze external Access data with an Excel PivotTable

Copying Access Data and Pasting into Excel

The simplest way to use Access data in Excel is to copy and paste it. Although this is the fastest method, it does have limitations.

To copy the contents of an Access table, form, or query, follow these steps:

> **TIP**
>
> A form opens in Form view. Click the arrow by the Form View button and select Datasheet View from the menu to switch views.

1. Open the table, form, or query you want to copy to Excel by selecting its Datasheet view. To do so, select the appropriate tab in the database window, choose the file, and click <u>O</u>pen.

2. Select the records you want to copy (see fig. 8.1).

Fig. 8.1

Select the data to copy to Excel.

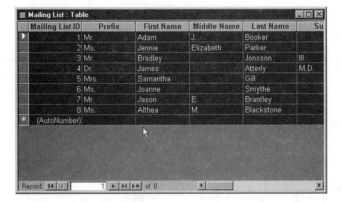

3. Click the Copy button.

4. Switch to Excel.

5. Select the worksheet cell where you want to place the copied data.

6. Click the Paste button. Figure 8.2 displays your copied data.

Fig. 8.2

Your Access data is inserted into an Excel worksheet.

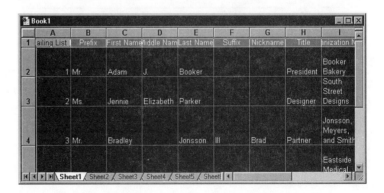

Querying Access Data from Within Excel

 NOTE You can also use Access data in Excel by clicking the OfficeLinks button on the Access toolbar and selecting the Analyze It with Excel option.

Query is an Excel for Windows 95 add-in that allows you to use the Query application. By using Query, you can access not only data from other applications, such as Access, but also sort and filter data, make calculations based on that data, and join data from more than one table.

You can access and retrieve data with the following drivers, which are available in Excel 95:

Access	SQL Server	dBASE
FoxPro	ODBC ODS Gateway	
Paradox	Text	

Installing the Query Add-In. Before you can use Query, you must first load the Query add-in into memory. When you installed Excel, you had the option of installing several add-ins. If you chose to install the add-ins, you can choose Tools, Add-Ins to load Query into memory. If you did not install the add-ins, you must do so before you can use Query. You can do this by clicking Browse and locating the add-in you want to load, or by reinstalling Office 95 with the add-ins selected.

To load Query, follow these steps:

1. Choose Tools, Add-Ins. Figure 8.3 shows the currently installed add-ins.

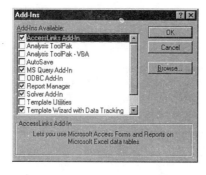

Fig. 8.3

The currently installed add-ins appear in the Add-Ins dialog box.

2. From the list of installed add-ins, select MS Query Add-In.

3. Choose OK or press Enter. The Get External Data command now appears in the Data menu; Query has been installed.

Creating a Query. In Excel, you use Query to retrieve information from an external data source, such as an Access database. Query is, in fact, very similar to Access' query feature. For example, you might have a table in your Access applications called Invoices that tracks all your client invoicing. You want to continue tracking this information in Access, but also use Excel's powers to do some forecasting and financial analysis based on this information. To retrieve all your invoices for clients in San Francisco for the past three months, you could create the query as described in these steps:

 NOTE You can also use the features of Graph, which has much of the same functionality as Excel, to forecast and analyze data. To do so, in Report or Form Design view, choose Insert, Chart to open the Chart Wizard, which guides you through the creation of a graph.

1. Choose Data, Get External Data to open Query. The Select Data Source dialog box appears (see fig. 8.4).

Fig. 8.4

Choose your data source in this dialog box.

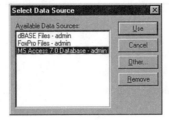

2. From the list of Available Data Sources, select your desired source and click the Use button.

 NOTE If your required data source isn't in the list, you must add it. To do so, select Other to open the ODBC Data Sources dialog box. Click the data source you require, moving it to the Enter Data Source edit box. Click OK to return to the previous dialog box.

 NOTE If you're not able to access the external database you need, be sure that the appropriate ODBC driver is installed. If the data source you want still isn't listed in the ODBC Data Sources dialog box, click New to open the Add Data Source dialog box. Choose one of the ODBC Installed Drivers and click OK.

TIP

You can remove data sources and drivers by selecting them and clicking the Remove button.

3. The Add Tables dialog box appears in the Query window, as shown in figure 8.5. Table 8.1 shows all the buttons available in the Query toolbar.

Fig. 8.5

The Add Tables dialog box enables you to include one or many tables in your query.

Table 8.1   Query Toolbar

Button	Name	Description
New Query	New Query	Creates a new query.
Open Query	Open Query	Opens an existing query.
Save Query	Save Query	Saves a query.
Exit	Exit	Exits query.
SQL	View SQL	Displays SQL (Structured Query Language) statements.
Show/Hide Tables	Show/Hide Tables	Enables you to show or hide the Table pane.
Show/Hide Criteria	Show/Hide Criteria	Enables you to show or hide the Criteria pane.
Add Table(s)	Add Table(s)	Displays the Add Table dialog box.
Criteria Equals	Criteria Equals	Enables you to specify criteria.
Σ	Cycle thru Totals	Cycles through different totals for the selected column.

(continues)

II

Basic Office Integration

Table 8.1 Continued		
Button	**Name**	**Description**
	Sort Ascending	Sorts in the order of A–Z or 0–9.
	Sort Descending	Sorts in the order of Z–A or 9–0.
	Query Now	Runs the query.
	Auto Query	Enables queries to run as you display them.
	Help	Displays context-sensitive help.

4. Select the Invoices table, click <u>A</u>dd, and then click <u>C</u>lose.

5. Drag the * from the field list to the Field row in the lower portion of the window to include all your fields in your query.

6. In the City field, enter **San Francisco** as your Criteria; in the Date field, enter **>07/31/95**. Figure 8.6 illustrates how the query window should appear now.

Fig. 8.6

Your query will only select clients in San Francisco who have been invoiced since 7/31/95.

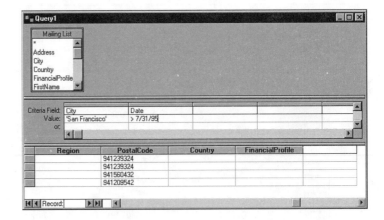

7. Complete your query and then choose <u>F</u>ile, <u>R</u>eturn Data to Microsoft Excel.

8. The Get External Data dialog box appears, illustrated in figure 8.7. Select your desired options, as described in table 8.2.

9. Click OK to return to your Excel worksheet.

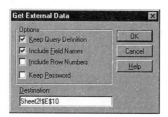

Fig. 8.7

*Save your query in the Get
External Data dialog box.*

Table 8.2   Get External Data Options

Option	Description
Keep Query Definition	Saves the query and enables you to update the result set if the data later changes.
Include Field Names	Includes field names as column headings in Excel.
Include Row Numbers	Includes row numbers as the first column in Excel.
Keep Password	Select to save the password for the external data source. If not selected, you must reenter the password every time you connect to the external data source.
Destination	Enter the cell reference for the upper-left cell in the range in which you want to place the query result set. This option only appears with new queries.
Refresh	Select to update a result set with new data without opening Query. This option appears only when you have already saved a query.
Edit Query	Enables you to edit the existing query by returning to Query. This option only appears when you have already saved the query.

Basic Office Integration

II

Caution

When you refresh your data, any formatting or sorting you have applied will disappear.

Once you've created a query, you can update it if the original data changes. To do so, select a cell in the result set and choose Data, Refresh Data. You can also edit an existing query by selecting a cell in the result set and choosing Data, Get External Data. Select Edit Query in the dialog box, and the existing query opens, enabling you to edit it.

NOTE You can also create a macro that retrieves data in other applications, such as Access, without using Query.

Analyzing Access Data in Excel

The Access OfficeLinks feature, Analyze It with MS Excel, offers another way to use Access data in Excel. It allows you to output Access tables, queries, reports, and forms to an Excel XLS format. To use this feature, follow these steps:

1. In the database window, select the table or query you want to analyze in Excel.

2. Click the drop-down arrow next to the OfficeLinks button and choose Analyze It with MS Excel from the menu. Access outputs the contents of the table or query as an Excel worksheet.

   Excel opens to display your new worksheet (see fig. 8.8).

Fig. 8.8

You can edit, format, and analyze the Access data in an Excel worksheet.

	A	B	C	D	E	F
1	Mailing List ID	Prefix	First Name	Middle Name	Last Name	Suffix
2	1	Mr.	Adam	J.	Booker	
3	2	Ms.	Jennie	Elizabeth	Parker	
4	3	Mr.	Bradley		Jonsson	III
5	4	Dr.	James		Atterly	M.D.
6	5	Mrs.	Samantha		Gill	
7	6	Ms.	Joanne		Smythe	
8	7	Mr.	Jason	E.	Brantley	
9	8	Ms.	Althea	M.	Blackstone	
10						
11						
12						
13						
14						
15						

Once your data is in Excel, you can use all of the features and capabilities of Excel to analyze and make calculations on it.

Sorting Your Access Data. If you want, you can sort an Access table before outputting it to an Excel format. This will save time if you plan on viewing the data in a sorted order in Access as well. To sort data in Access, follow these steps:

1. Select the Tables tab in the Database dialog box and open the table you want to sort.

2. Choose the field on which you want to sort.

3. Click the Sort Ascending or Sort Descending button on the toolbar.

Filtering Your Access Data. To select only certain records to output, such as all records with San Francisco as the City field, follow these steps:

1. Open the table you want to filter by selecting it in the Tables tab and clicking OK.

2. Select a City field with San Francisco as its entry.

NOTE

To remove the filter, click the Apply Filter button.

3. Click the Filter by Selection button to apply the filter (see fig. 8.9).

Organization N	Address	City	State	Region	Postal
Jonsson, Meyer	1400 Market Str	San Francisco	CA		94123-9
Eastside Medic	1400 Market Str	San Francisco	CA		94123-9
	12348 Winding	San Francisco	CA		94156-0
Executive Image	1350 California :	San Francisco	CA		94120-9

Fig. 8.9

Use the Filter by Selection button to easily filter data in your Access tables.

Summa bles

NOTE

For m sing Microsoft Office
for Wir ing Data with Excel,
all pub

Excel includes a uickly and easily
summarize and c ... in Excel list or in an external application,
such as Access. When you want to summarize your data in another way, you only
need to drag and drop fields to create a whole new report, without changing the
structure of the data in your worksheets.

You use the automated PivotTable Wizard to create pivot tables in Excel. The
PivotTable Wizard guides you step-by-step through the process of creating a pivot
table. The PivotTable Wizard prompts you to define the pivot table information by
using the fields defined in a list.

NOTE

Position the cell pointer in a list in your worksheet prior to choosing the PivotTable
command. Excel pastes the range of the list in the Range text box. Click Next if that's
the list you want to use.

Creating a Pivot Table with the PivotTable Wizard

TIP

Don't spend too much time deciding where to place the fields. You can always rearrange the fields after you add the pivot table to your worksheet.

When you create a pivot table from a list, the column titles in the list are used as Row, Column, and Page fields. The data in the columns becomes items in the pivot table. When the data in your list contains numeric items, Excel automatically uses the Sum function to calculate the values in the pivot table. If the data in your list contains text items, Excel uses the Count function to calculate a count of the source items in the pivot table.

To create a pivot table from an Access table, follow these steps:

1. Choose Data, PivotTable. Step 1 of the PivotTable Wizard appears, as shown in figure 8.10.

Fig. 8.10

Specify the data to use for the pivot table in Step 1 of the PivotTable Wizard.

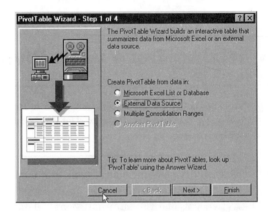

2. Select External Data Source and click the Next button. Step 2 of the PivotTable Wizard appears, as shown in figure 8.11.

Fig. 8.11

Specify the data source in Step 2 of the PivotTable Wizard.

3. Click the Get Data button. The Select Data Source dialog box appears. Choose MS Access 7.0 Database from the Available Data Sources list and click Use.

4. Choose the Access database in the Select Database dialog box and click OK.

5. Query opens. Create a query, following the steps outlined in the previous section "Creating a Query."

6. Choose File, Return Data to Microsoft Excel, then click Next to display Step 3 of the PivotTable Wizard, as shown in figure 8.12.

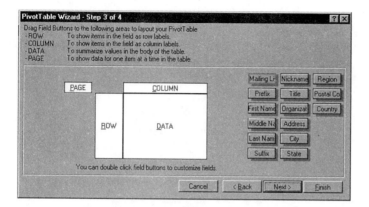

Fig. 8.12

Define the pivot table layout in Step 3 of the PivotTable Wizard.

7. Define the layout of the pivot table by dragging the field names displayed on the right side of the dialog box to the Row, Column, or Page area. Fields placed in the Row area appear in each row in the pivot table. Fields placed in the Column area appear in each column of the pivot table. Fields placed in the Page area filter the data shown in the pivot table.

8. Click Next to display the final step in the PivotTable Wizard (see fig. 8.13).

Fig. 8.13

Specify the location of the pivot table in Step 4 of the PivotTable Wizard.

9. Enter a cell reference in the PivotTable Starting Cell text box. If you leave this text box empty, Excel creates a new worksheet and adds the pivot table to it. In Step 4, you can also create a name for your pivot table in the PivotTable Name box as well as choose from the following options: Grand Totals for Columns, Grand Totals for Rows, Save Data With Table Layout, or AutoFormat Table.

10. Choose Finish. The PivotTable Wizard displays the results in a table on the worksheet (see fig. 8.14).

Basic Office Integration

Fig. 8.14

This pivot table summa-rizes prospects by city.

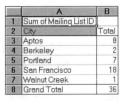

When you add a pivot table to the worksheet, Excel automatically displays the Query and Pivot toolbar. The toolbar contains buttons for the most frequently used pivot table commands (see fig. 8.15). Table 8.3 describes this toolbar in detail.

Fig. 8.15

The Query and Pivot toolbar simplifies working with pivot tables.

Table 8.3	Query and Pivot Toolbar	
Button	**Name**	**Description**
	PivotTable Wizard	Opens the PivotTable Wizard.
	PivotTable Field	Opens the PivotTable Field dialog box.
	Ungroup	Ungroups selected rows or columns.
	Group	Groups selected rows or columns.
	Hide Detail	Summarizes data in current selection.
	Show Detail	Shows data in current selection.
	Show Pages	Copies each page field item to a separate worksheet.
	Refresh Data	Retrieves most recent data.

Editing and Updating a Pivot Table. After you have added a pivot table to your worksheet, you can quickly rearrange the fields in the pivot table to display an en-tirely different view of your data. Each field in the list is represented by a shaded cell in the pivot table. You change the view of the data by dragging the fields to other areas in the pivot table.

Rearranging a Pivot Table. You can rearrange data in a pivot table in several ways:

- To change the data displayed on the current page, click the drop-down arrow displayed in the Page area of the pivot table. A list of items for the current field appears. Select an item from the list to filter the data in the pivot table to display data for that item only.

- To change the data displayed in the columns of the pivot table, drag a Row or Page field to the Column area of the pivot table. When you do, the pivot table displays a columnar view of the data.

- To change the data displayed in the rows of the pivot table, drag a Page or Column field to the Row area of the pivot table. The pivot table displays data in a Row field in each row.

Adding and Removing Fields in a Pivot Table. You can change the data used in a pivot table by adding new fields to the pivot table or by removing fields that you no longer need. When you add a new field to the pivot table or delete an existing field, Excel automatically updates the pivot table.

NOTE
When you add and remove data from a pivot table, the action has no effect on the source data in the list.

To add a field to the pivot table, follow these steps:

1. Position the cell pointer in the area of the pivot table where you want to add a field. To add a field to the Row area, for example, select a cell in the Row area of the pivot table.

2. Click the right mouse button to display the PivotTable shortcut menu and choose Add Row Field.

3. The fields in the list used to generate the pivot table appear in a cascade menu. Select the field you want to add to the pivot table.

Figure 8.16 shows the pivot table after adding an additional field.

	A	B	C
1	Sum of Mailing List ID		
2	State	City	Total
3	CA	Aptos	8
4		Berkeley	2
5		San Francisco	18
6		Walnut Creek	1
7	CA Total		29
8	OR	Portland	7
9	OR Total		7
10	Grand Total		36

Fig. 8.16

The State field is added to the pivot table layout.

You can remove a pivot table field directly from the pivot table in the worksheet. To remove a field, drag it outside the pivot table area. Excel then removes the data from the table.

II

Basic Office Integration

Modifying the Appearance of a Pivot Table

Excel provides special formatting commands for modifying the appearance of a pivot table. When you use these commands, Excel retains the format, even when you reorganize and recalculate the data in the pivot table.

You can change the numeric format of the data displayed in the data area, format an entire pivot table, and rename fields and items in the table.

 NOTE When you update a pivot table, Excel recalculates and reformats the data in the table. Therefore, you should avoid manually formatting the table.

Applying a Numeric Format. To change the numeric formatting in the data area of the pivot table, follow these steps:

1. Select a cell in the pivot table.

 2. Choose <u>D</u>ata, PivotTable F<u>i</u>eld, or click the right mouse button and choose PivotTable Field from the shortcut menu. The PivotTable Field dialog box appears (see fig. 8.17).

Fig. 8.17

The PivotTable Field dialog box offers several options for modifying the appearance of your pivot table.

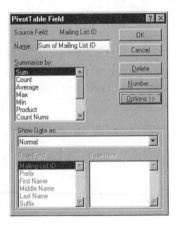

3. Click the <u>N</u>umber button from the PivotTable Field dialog box. The Format Cells dialog box then appears (see fig. 8.18).

4. Select the numeric format you want to apply to the data area from the <u>C</u>ategory list.

5. Choose OK twice to return to the worksheet.

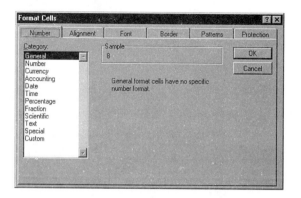

Fig. 8.18

*Change the numeric
format of cells in the
Format Cells dialog box.*

Formatting the Pivot Table. When you create a pivot table and select the
AutoFormat Table checkbox in the PivotTable Wizard, Excel automatically formats the
table for you. To use another format, select a cell in the pivot table and choose Format, AutoFormat. Select the format you want to use from the AutoFormat dialog box,
and choose OK (see fig. 8.19).

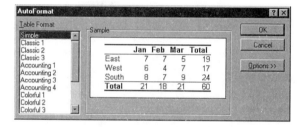

Fig. 8.19

*You can choose from
several predefined formats
in the AutoFormat dialog
box.*

Changing the Calculation Used in a Pivot Table. When the items displayed in the
data area of a pivot table are numeric, Excel automatically uses the Sum function to
summarize the data in the list. When the items are text, Excel uses the Count function
to summarize the text items. You can change the summary function a data field uses
to calculate an average or maximum value, for example. You also can change the
calculation type used in the data area.

To change the summary function the pivot table uses, follow these steps:

1. Select a cell in the data area of the pivot table.
2. Choose Data, PivotTable Field, or click the right mouse button and choose the
   PivotTable Field command from the shortcut menu.
3. In the Summarize By list box, select the function you want to use to summarize
   the data.
4. Choose OK or press Enter.

II

Basic Office Integration

Excel can calculate values used in the data area based on the values of other cells. You can calculate the difference between items in a field, for example, or calculate the items as percentages of the total.

To change the summary type used by the data field in the pivot table, follow these steps:

1. Select a cell in the data area of the pivot table.

2. Choose Data, PivotTable Field, or click the right mouse button and choose the PivotTable Field command.

3. Click the Options button in the PivotTable Field dialog box (see fig. 8.20).

Fig. 8.20

The PivotTable Field dialog box expands to display the summary type options.

4. Click the arrow in the Show Data As drop-down list to display the calculation types available, and choose your desired option.

5. Select the summary method you want to use from the Summarize By list box, and then select the fields and items you want to use.

6. Choose OK or press Enter.

Refreshing Data in a Pivot Table. When you update the data in the source list in your worksheet, you must refresh the pivot table to include the new information. To refresh data in the pivot table, select any cell in the pivot table and choose Data, Refresh Data or click the right mouse button and choose the Refresh Data command from the shortcut menu.

If you add new records to your source list, you must redefine the source range used to create the pivot table by using the PivotTable Wizard.

To extend the source range to include additional records in the pivot table, follow these steps:

1. Select a cell in the pivot table.

2. Choose <u>D</u>ata, <u>P</u>ivotTable, or click the right mouse button and choose the PivotTable command from the shortcut menu. Excel displays Step 3 of the PivotTable Wizard.

3. Click <u>B</u>ack to display Step 2.

4. Respecify the source data range and click <u>F</u>inish. Excel adds the new records to the pivot table.

Creating a Pivot Table in Access

You can also create an Excel pivot table from within Access by using the Access PivotTable Wizard. To do so, follow these steps:

1. Select the Forms tab in the Database dialog box, and click the New button.

2. In the New Form dialog box, select the PivotTable Wizard option.

3. Choose the table or query name in the drop-down list, and click OK. The PivotTable Wizard opens, and you can create a pivot table as outlined in the previous section.

Using Excel Data in Access

To combine Excel data with the relational capabilities as well as form and report design features of Access, you have several options:

- Create labels with the Access Label Wizard
- Import or link your Excel worksheet into Access
- Use the AccessLinks feature in Excel

Using an Excel Worksheet with the Access Label Wizard

In this example, you use the Label Wizard to make mailing labels using the Prospects worksheet you created in Chapter 6. To do this, follow these steps:

1. Open <u>F</u>ile, <u>G</u>et External Data, <u>L</u>ink Tables to open the Link dialog box.

2. Select your file in the dialog box and click the Link button.

 NOTE If your workbook contains more than one worksheet or range, you will be asked to select it first.

3. The Link Spreadsheet Wizard opens (see fig. 8.21). Select the <u>F</u>irst Row Contains Column Headings checkbox, and click <u>N</u>ext to continue.

Fig. 8.21

The Link Spreadsheet Wizard guides you through linking to an Excel worksheet.

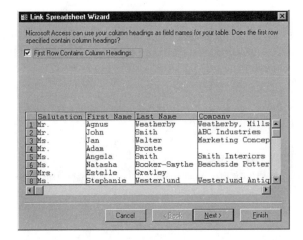

4. Enter the linked table name in the input box and click Finish.

5. In the Database dialog box, choose the Reports tab and click the New button.

6. In the New Report dialog box, choose Label Wizard.

7. Select the table or query from which you want to create labels and click OK.

8. The Label Wizard appears (see fig. 8.22). First, choose the appropriate Unit of Measure—English or Metric, and then the Label Type—Sheet Feed or Continuous.

Fig. 8.22

Design your labels in the Label Wizard.

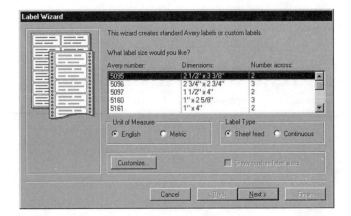

NOTE If the label type you want isn't in the list, you can click the Customize button to open the new Label Size dialog box, where you can create a customized label size.

9. Select the label type and size from the drop-down list, then click <u>N</u>ext.

10. Choose the font name, font size, and font weight from the drop-down lists.

11. Change the text color by clicking the ... button next to the Text color edit box and selecting the appropriate color in the Color dialog box.

> **TIP**
> Click the <u>D</u>efine Custom Colors button to expand the Color dialog box.

12. Select the Italic or Underline checkboxes, if desired, and then click <u>N</u>ext.

13. Choose fields from the Available Fields list and click the right arrow to move them to the Prototype Label list.

> **NOTE**
> Be sure to include all the required spaces and punctuation marks, such as commas, in the Prototype Label list. You can also add any other text that you desire as well.

14. Click <u>N</u>ext and then select fields on which to sort in the Available Fields list. Use the single right arrow to move one field at a time, or the double right arrow to move all fields to the Sort By list.

Figure 8.23 displays your labels.

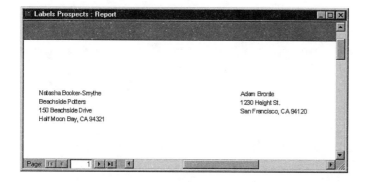

Fig. 8.23

You can view your labels before printing.

Importing Excel Data into Access

To link Excel data to an Access table, choose <u>F</u>ile, <u>G</u>et External Data, <u>L</u>ink Tables to open the Link dialog box. Choose a worksheet to link, click the Link button, and use the Link Spreadsheet Wizard to continue.

You can use the Access Import Spreadsheet Wizard to import Excel data into Access. To do so, follow these steps:

1. In Access, choose File, Get External Data, Import. The Import dialog box opens.

2. In the Files of Type drop-down list, select Microsoft Excel, then enter the workbook name in File Name.

3. Click Import to open the Import Spreadsheet Wizard (see fig. 8.24).

Fig. 8.24

Set up the criteria for importing your Excel worksheet in the Import Spreadsheet Wizard.

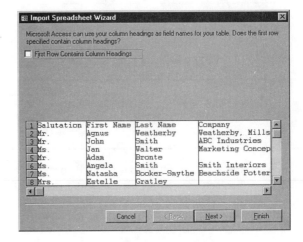

4. Select Show Worksheets or Show Named Ranges, then select your worksheet or range to import. Click Next.

5. Select the First Row Contains Column Headings checkbox if desired, then click Next.

> **TIP**
>
> If you don't want to include a field, select the Do Not Import Field (Skip) checkbox.

6. In Field Options, you can specify a Field Name, Data Type, and Indexed status for each field. Click Next to continue.

7. Choose one of the following options regarding your primary key: Let Access Add Primary Key, Choose My Own Primary Key, or No Primary Key. Select Next.

8. Enter a name in the Import to Table input box, then click Finish.

> **NOTE**
>
> Once you've imported an Excel worksheet into Access, you may want to normalize it. *Normalization* is a process that minimizes data duplication by efficient table design. You can use the Access Table Analyzer Wizard to normalize a table. To do so, select Tools, Analyze, Table and let the wizard guide you through the process.

Using AccessLinks

AccessLinks is an add-in program that allows you to create Access forms, reports, and databases with your Excel data. Before you can use AccessLinks, you must first load its add-in into memory by choosing Tools, Add-Ins. Once AccessLinks is loaded, the Access Form, Access Report, and Convert to Access commands appear in the Data menu.

Creating an Access Form from an Excel Worksheet. To create an Access form from an existing Excel worksheet, follow these steps:

1. Create a worksheet and save it, or open a previously saved worksheet.

2. Choose Data, Access Form to open the Create Microsoft Access Form dialog box, shown in figure 8.25.

Fig. 8.25

Creating an Access form using Excel data is easy with AccessLinks.

3. Choose to place your form in either a New Database or an Existing Database.

4. Enter the name of the database in the edit box. You can use the Browse button to locate a database in another directory.

5. Determine whether your list has a Header Row or No Header Row and then click OK.

   The Access Form Wizard appears (see fig. 8.26). The wizard guides you through form creation—choosing fields, layout, style, and title.

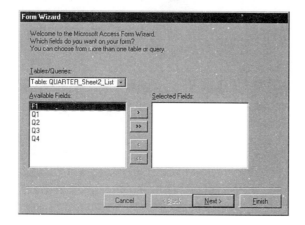

Fig. 8.26

Let the Access Form Wizard design your form.

Once you create an Access form from an Excel worksheet, you can edit it by clicking the View Access Form button.

Creating an Access Report from an Excel Worksheet. To create an Access report from an existing Excel worksheet, follow these steps:

1. Create a worksheet and save it or open a previously saved worksheet.

2. Choose <u>D</u>ata, A<u>c</u>cess Report to open the Create Microsoft Access Report dialog box.

3. Choose to create your form in either a <u>N</u>ew Database or an <u>E</u>xisting Database.

4. Enter the name of the database in the edit box. You can use the <u>B</u>rowse button to locate a database in another directory.

5. Determine whether your list has a Hea<u>d</u>er Row or N<u>o</u> Header Row and then click OK.

   The Access Report Wizard appears (see fig. 8.27). The wizard assists you in creating your report—choosing fields, groupings, sort order, layout, style, and title.

Fig. 8.27

Use the Report Wizard to quickly create a sophisticated report.

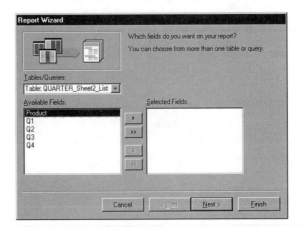

Once you create an Access report from an Excel worksheet, you can view it by selecting the View Access Report button.

Converting an Excel Worksheet to an Access Database. To convert an existing worksheet to an Access database, follow these steps:

1. Create a worksheet and save it or open a previously saved worksheet.

2. Choose <u>D</u>ata, Con<u>v</u>ert to Access to open the Convert to Microsoft Access dialog box.

3. Choose to convert your worksheet to either a <u>N</u>ew Database or an <u>E</u>xisting Database.

4. Enter the name of the database in the edit box. You can use the <u>B</u>rowse button to locate a database in another directory.

5. The Import Spreadsheet Wizard appears, shown in figure 8.28. If you want to include field names on the first row, indicate this in the checkbox.

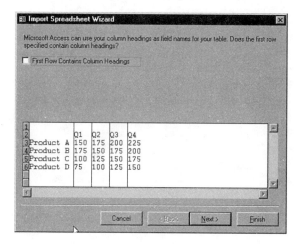

Fig. 8.28

Set up your column headings with the Import Spreadsheet Wizard.

6. Click <u>N</u>ext to move to the next step of the wizard (see fig. 8.29).

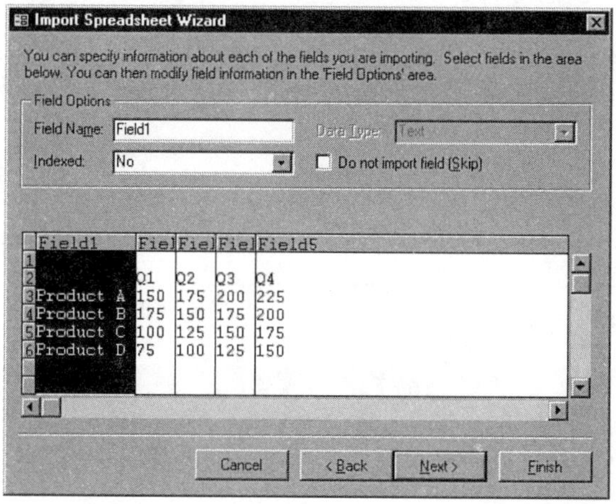

Fig. 8.29

Specify information about your fields in this step.

7. In this step, you can select a Field Na<u>m</u>e for each field, indicate whether or not the field is <u>I</u>ndexed, and choose its Data <u>T</u>ype.

8. Click <u>N</u>ext to continue; indicate a primary key in this step, as shown in figure 8.30.

Fig. 8.30

Indicate your primary key in this step, or let Access choose one for you.

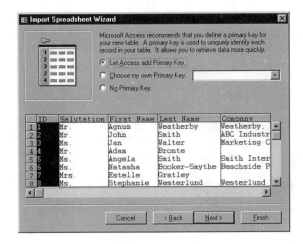

9. Click <u>N</u>ext again to go to the final step. Enter your new table name in the edit box and click <u>F</u>inish.

A dialog box tells you that you've finished importing the Excel file. Once you create an Access table from an Excel worksheet, its location is displayed in the Convert to Microsoft Access box on the original worksheet.

> **Caution**
>
> If you get the warning message A new database cannot be created when you try to create an Access form or report, you may have selected the New Database option in the Create Microsoft Access Form (or Report) dialog box when a database of that name already exists. Instead, select the <u>E</u>xisting Database option, or create a new database name.

Linking and Embedding Excel and Access Objects

TIP   You can also link and embed Access data in Excel, but this is less common.

Linking and embedding are related tasks that both place data from a source application (in this case, Excel) into a destination application (Access in the examples in this chapter). But how they treat this data is very different.

When you *link* an object, it is updated automatically whenever the source changes. For example, if you link an Excel worksheet to an Access table, any changes you make to the worksheet are reflected in Access. Linked information is stored in the source document.

Embedded data is stored in the destination document and is useful when the source document may become unavailable or may be changed, yet these changes aren't desired in the destination. When you embed an object, it doesn't automatically update in the destination document if the source changes. Embedded objects must be edited separately.

With a *bound object*, you store the data in a field in an Access table or query. Adding fields in an employee tracking table to store identification photographs, résumés, or other objects created in another application would be an example of the use of bound objects. An *unbound object* isn't tied to a field in a table or query. It can be any object that inserts an Access form or report, such as a WordArt logo or Excel worksheet data.

Linking and Embedding Objects

To illustrate an example of linking an object, say you created a financial profile worksheet for each of your prospects. Because you will primarily use Access to track your prospect activity, you want to be able to view each prospect's financial profile without opening Excel and searching for individual worksheets. By creating an OLE object field in the Access Mailing List table and linking each financial profile worksheet to its corresponding record, you can easily retrieve information without leaving Access. To do this, follow these steps:

1. Select the Tables tab, highlight the Mailing List table, and click the <u>D</u>esign button.

2. Insert a new Field Name called **Financial Profile** at the end of the list of field names.

> **NOTE** An *OLE Object field* is a field that stores documents, sounds, graphics, or binary data you created in another application, such as Word, Excel, or PowerPoint.

3. Choose OLE Object as the Data Type. Figure 8.31 illustrates how your screen should look.

4. Click the Save button to save your table, then click the Datasheet View button to go to Datasheet view.

5. With the cursor in the Financial Profile field of your first record, choose <u>I</u>nsert, <u>O</u>bject. The Insert Object dialog box opens (see fig. 8.32).

Fig. 8.31

You can insert a new field in an Access table.

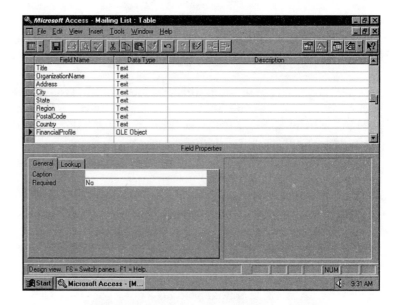

Fig. 8.32

The Insert Object dialog box enables you to link or embed an Excel worksheet into an Access table.

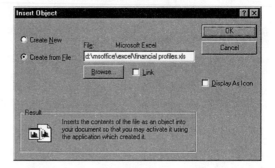

 NOTE   If you haven't already created your Excel worksheet, you can do so now by choosing the Create New option in the Insert Object dialog box. Select Microsoft Excel Worksheet as your Object Type, and click OK to open Excel.

6. Choose the Create From File option, and enter the name of your Excel worksheet in the File input box.

 TIP   You can also click the Browse button to open the Browse dialog box, which can make finding a file in another directory easier.

7. If you want to link the Excel worksheet to the Access table, select the Link checkbox. If this box isn't checked, you will embed the document.

> **NOTE**
> To display an icon rather than the document itself, choose the Display As Icon checkbox. By double-clicking the icon, you automatically open the linked document. Once you check the Display As Icon box, the Change Icon button appears. Click this button to open the Change Icon dialog box. Here you can choose any displayed Icon instead of the default, use the Browse button to search for another icon, or change your Label.

8. Click OK to close the dialog box.

Placing an Object in a Form. Once you have inserted a bound object in an Access table, you can display it in a form.

> **TIP**
> You can also place a bound object in a report.

To do this, follow these steps:

1. Select the Form tab and click the New button. The New Form dialog box opens, displayed in figure 8.33.

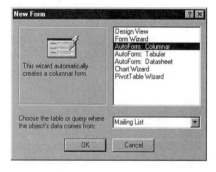

Fig. 8.33

The New Form dialog box offers several alternatives for creating a new form.

2. Choose the AutoForm: Columnar option.
3. Select the table or query on which you want to base your form. In this case, you want to choose the Mailing List table.
4. Click OK.

The AutoForm Wizard automatically creates and displays a form. The Word document that you linked to the first record appears in the large bound object frame in the lower-right corner of the form.

Basic Office Integration

Notice that your Excel worksheet isn't entirely visible in the frame. To resolve this problem, you can:

■ Change the font size and formatting in Excel so that your worksheet is legible in the Access form. This works best when you have only a small amount of text to display.

■ Change the SizeMode property from Clip (the default) to Zoom so that the entire Word document appears in the bound object frame. Do this by selecting the frame, right-clicking and selecting Zoom as the SizeMode. You may not, however, be able to read the Word document this way because it may be too small.

■ Select the Display As Icon option in the Insert Object dialog box. The document itself won't appear, but you can select the icon to open an Excel worksheet.

Inserting a Partial Excel Worksheet. In the previous section, you learned how to link or embed an entire Excel worksheet into Access tables. You aren't confined to inserting an entire worksheet, however; you can also link or embed selected sections of Excel worksheets. For example, you don't want to include the entire Financial Profile worksheet in the Access table. Instead you may only want to link the first section of each prospect's profile, or you may have created one workbook with a separate worksheet for each prospect. To do this, follow these steps:

1. Open the Financial Profile worksheet in Excel.

2. Select the first section and click the Copy button.

3. Leaving Excel open, switch to Access and select the Financial Profile field in the first record of the Mailing List table.

4. Choose Edit, Paste Special to open the Paste Special dialog box (see fig. 8.34).

Fig. 8.34

The Paste Special dialog box enables you to embed or link partial sections of an Excel worksheet.

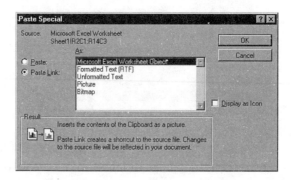

5. Click the Paste Link option button.

6. Choose Microsoft Excel Worksheet Object in the As list box.

7. Click OK.

When you create a form based on this table, you view only the selected text in the Financial Profile field.

Updating a Link

> **NOTE** If you move or rename a source file, you lose its link. To reconnect, select the link in the Links dialog box, and click Cha**n**ge Source. Choose your new link file in the Change Source dialog box.

If you link an Access table and an Excel worksheet, you can update the information automatically or manually in either Excel or Access (depending on where you initiated the link). By default, the link updates automatically, but you can also choose to manually update the link if you want to control when updates happen (for example, on a specific date). To update a link:

1. With your object (document, table, or whatever) open, choose **E**dit, OLE/ DDE Lin**k**s in Access or **E**dit, Lin**k**s in Excel to open the Links dialog box (see fig. 8.35).

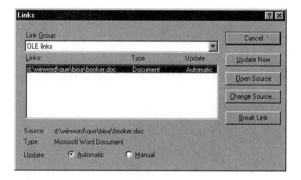

Fig. 8.35

You can choose to update your link manually in the Links dialog box.

2. Select the link you want to update in the list.

3. Click the **M**anual option button to manually update all future links.

4. Click OK to close.

To perform manual updates, do the following:

> **TIP** You can also manually update a link by selecting the linked object and pressing F9.

1. Choose **E**dit **L**inks to open the Links dialog box.

> **TIP** To break a link, select it and click the **B**reak Link button.

2. Select the link you want to update. If you want to update more than one link, press Ctrl while selecting links.

3. Click the <u>U</u>pdate Now button.

4. Select the Close button.

From Here...

In this chapter, you learned the basics of integrating Excel and Access, as well as how to take advantage of the strengths of each program within an integrated application. To go over the basics again, or delve into more advanced topics, refer to the following chapters:

■ Chapter 2, "Windows and Office Capabilities," contains a beyond-the-basics review of the capabilities of Windows and Office, including AccessLinks and Excel pivot tables.

■ Chapter 3, "Integration Basics," provides a basic description of what makes integration work, such as DDE and OLE.

■ Chapter 11, "Automating Office Integration with Excel," illustrates how Excel can be used as a component within an integrated environment.

■ Chapter 12, "Automating Office Integration with Access," shows how Access can be used within an integrated environment.

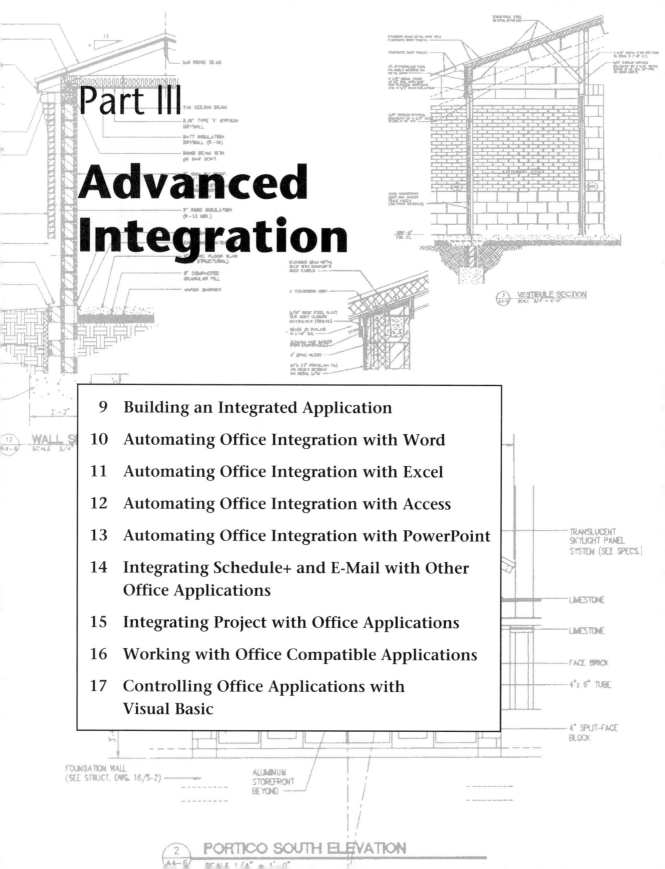

Part III

Advanced Integration

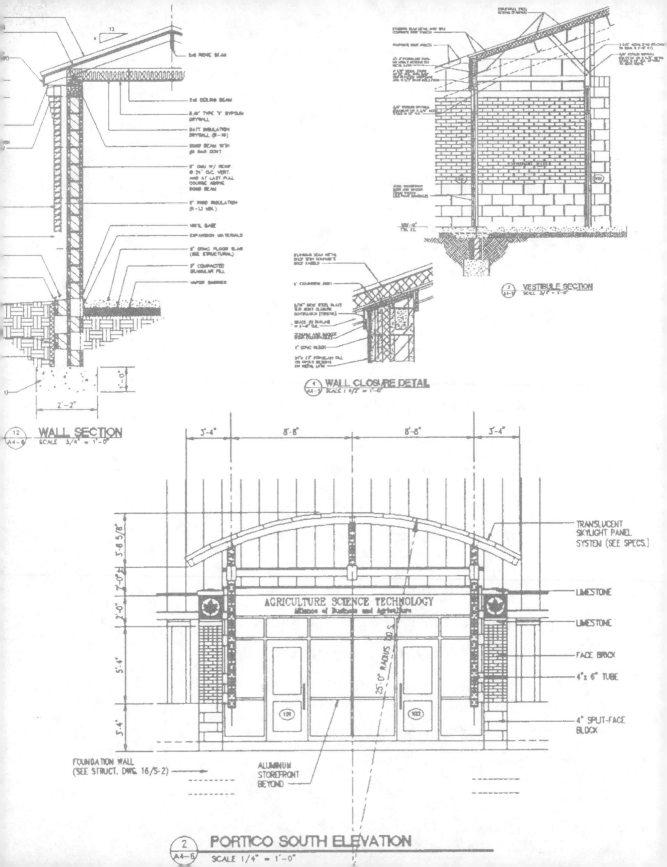

WALL SECTION
SCALE 3/4" = 1'-0"

WALL CLOSURE DETAIL
SCALE 1 1/2" = 1'-0"

VESTIBULE SECTION
SCALE 3/4" = 1'-0"

AGRICULTURE SCIENCE TECHNOLOGY
Alliance of Business and Agriculture

TRANSLUCENT SKYLIGHT PANEL SYSTEM (SEE SPECS.)

LIMESTONE

LIMESTONE

FACE BRICK

4" x 6" TUBE

4" SPLIT-FACE BLOCK

FOUNDATION WALL
(SEE STRUCT. DWG. 16/S-2)

ALUMINUM STOREFRONT BEYOND

25'-0" RADIUS TO S

PORTICO SOUTH ELEVATION
SCALE 1/4" = 1'-0"

CHAPTER 9

Building an Integrated Application

In previous chapters, you learned how to use the features of individual Office applications. Chapters 3 through 5 described the various communication mechanisms that can be used to integrate Office applications. The remaining chapters explore the basic techniques required to integrate these applications. This chapter explains the steps necessary to create fully integrated Office applications.

The depth and complexity of Office applications can vary greatly. In order to successfully develop a quality application, you need to understand methods for analyzing problems and turning them into automated solutions. This chapter focuses on techniques that are useful for developing Office applications.

In this chapter you learn how to

- Distinguish between two different development methodologies
- Implement Rapid Application Development (RAD) while developing Office applications
- Determine the "real" requirements for a system
- Move from a requirements document into analysis
- Recognize the individual strengths of each Office application
- Construct an integrated Office application

Choosing a Development Method

The most important aspect of software development is the method under which the application is developed. It isn't necessarily important which method you choose; it's just important that you have one. Having a development methodology provides you with a standard approach to any problem and guides the development process.

There are two main schools of thought as to which development methodology is the best. These methods are known as the *Waterfall method* and the *Rapid Application Development (RAD) method*. The Waterfall is the older of the two methods, while RAD has become more popular just in the last few years.

The Waterfall Method

The oldest of the two methods is the Waterfall method. Figure 9.1 demonstrates the steps used when developing applications under the Waterfall method.

Fig. 9.1

The Waterfall method proceeds using this sequential set of steps.

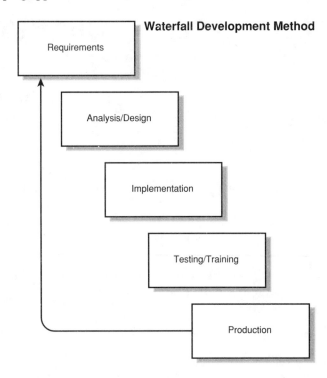

Waterfall Development Method

The steps used in the Waterfall method occur in sequential order. You begin with requirements; from requirements you move to analysis/design; after the analysis and design are completed, you can begin to implement the application; last comes the testing and training, and then the cycle completes. This method requires that you not move to the next step until the prior one is completed. For example, you can't analyze a problem until the requirements of the system have been defined. To better understand this method, you need to understand what is involved in each step and how it relates to the others.

Defining Requirements with the Waterfall Method. The first step of any development project is defining what the system is supposed to do. This is known as the *requirements phase*. The whole purpose of the requirements phase is to define the scope of the development project. The requirements phase is the most important aspect of any individual development project. Without a good set of requirements, the remaining steps of the project have the potential of continuing on with no end in sight.

Commonly, the requirements phase involves interviewing the key people who will be affected by the system you are developing. Some potential people to interview include managers, end users, network managers, executives, and any others who will be affected by the system. The purpose of this phase is to define what all users of a system require in order for the system to be successful. Some questions commonly asked include:

- What are you going to use the system for?
- What are the outputs you need from the system?
- What are the three most important things this system needs to do?
- What type of system does this application need to be run on?

The purpose of these interview questions is to get to the exact requirements of the system. The output of this phase is a *requirements document.* This document guides the remaining steps of the development process.

Analysis/Design with the Waterfall Method. The next step in the Waterfall method is the analysis/design phase. It takes the requirements document and breaks it down into distinct areas and further expands upon the requirements. One of the more common techniques for this phase is to create a set of charts known as *data flow diagrams (DFDs),* as shown in figure 9.2. Data flow diagrams show how data moves through a system.

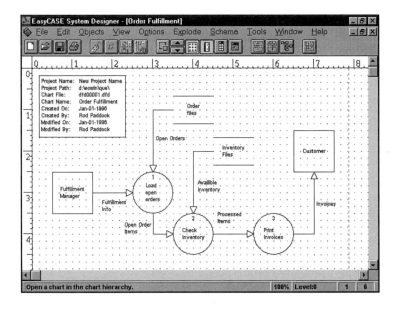

Fig. 9.2

This illustration shows a data flow diagram for an order fulfillment system.

NOTE The program used to create the diagrams for this chapter is EasyCASE from Evergreen Software. This application provides tools for creating many common analysis/design diagrams including DFDs and ERs. Other popular packages for creating analysis/design documents include ERWIN, System Architect, and InfoModeler.

III

Advanced Integration

Another type of diagram created during the analysis/design phase is an *entity-relationship (ER) diagram*. ER diagrams show relationships between different data elements. Figure 9.3 shows an ER diagram for an order entry application.

Fig. 9.3

This entity-relationship diagram depicts the design for an order entry system.

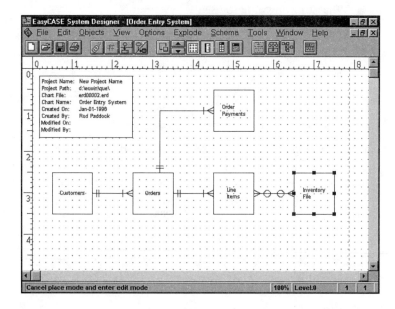

Commonly during the analysis phase, source documents are retrieved and broken down into source elements. *Source documents* potentially include invoices, purchase orders, reports generated by hand or from other systems, manifests, or any other source documents created by the current manual or automated system.

The outputs of the analysis phase include, but are not limited to

- Data flow diagrams.
- Entity-relationship diagrams.
- A data dictionary including data validation information and descriptions. *Data dictionaries* are repositories that store information about your database. Data validations, data descriptions, data types, default values, and business rules are commonly included in a data dictionary.
- Preliminary report and screen designs.

Implementation with the Waterfall Method. After completing the analysis/design phase, you can begin implementing the system with whatever development tools you are using. The *implementation phase* includes the coding and early testing of the system.

Testing and Training with the Waterfall Method. The final step of the Waterfall approach is the testing and training phase of the system. This final step is where the system is put into production. You complete the final integration tests, train the user, and put the system into production.

Repeating the Cycle with the Waterfall Method. Development never ends, so you begin the next development project by repeating the process again. Any changes or updates to the system happen using the same systematic approach defined earlier in this section.

Important Considerations of the Waterfall Method. As you can see, the Waterfall approach provides a systematic method to developing applications. However, there are a few items to consider when using this approach.

The first item to consider is the cost of a mistake in the development process. Studies have shown that no matter the methodology, it can be hundreds of times more costly to fix a bug during production rather than during the analysis/design or requirements phases. This is both an advantage and disadvantage of the Waterfall method. The advantage is that it promotes providing a quality framework for fully completing each step. The disadvantage is that if a mistake is made early and not caught, it can be very costly to fix.

Another item to consider is the amount of time spent during the process of development. Depending upon the complexity of the application, this method of development can take a considerable amount of time before a user ever touches the system. The potential problem with this is that it does not meet the needs of the users. Some complicated development projects can take up to two years before a user ever sees the application. In two years, a lot can change in a company. The business environment can change, and product lines can be added or dropped. The only constant today is change. This requires that systems be developed in a timely and efficient manner, which is sometimes a problem with the Waterfall method. This is where the next methodology comes in.

Rapid Application Development (RAD)

The other development method is Rapid Application Development. RAD is a system of development that gets the user involved in the development process as soon as possible.

The problem with the Waterfall method is that it doesn't involve the user early and often enough. It's a linear approach to development that requires one step be completed prior to another. This means the user is commonly involved in only the early phases of requirements, briefly in the analysis/design steps, and not until somewhere during the implementation phase does the user see any software. Because of the costs involved in the development of software, this may not be adequate. Thus, the rise in the popularity of the RAD method of development is clearly apparent.

The RAD method of development is similar to the Waterfall approach with a few exceptions. The most significant exception is that it removes the requirement that one step be fully completed before the next begins. RAD simply abbreviates the time spent on each step. The main focus behind RAD is to get software into the hands of users as soon as possible. Where the Waterfall approach relies heavily on charts, diagrams, and text, the RAD approach uses the application as the guiding document for development. Where the Waterfall method is a more rigid approach to development, RAD is a looser type of method.

Requirements with the RAD Method. The first phase of the RAD approach is to create a requirements document. As is true of the Waterfall method, the requirements phase of RAD is the most important. RAD is a looser type of development, but it only works well within the framework of a good requirements document.

The big difference between the Waterfall approach and RAD is that RAD does not require that the requirements document be complete prior to proceeding to the next step. The RAD method embraces change and realizes that no requirements document is 100 percent complete. In the RAD approach, you define your requirements until a prototype can be effectively developed. During the development process, you modify this set of requirements depending upon user feedback. The goal of the requirements phase with the RAD method is to get a rough idea of how the system needs to work.

Analysis/Design with the RAD Method. After creating a rough framework of a requirements document, you then proceed to a limited analysis/design phase. Using the RAD development method, this phase is greatly abbreviated. The goal of this step is to quickly define the key data elements that will be created by this application. The main emphasis of this phase is to determine what things comprise the central focus of the system. Using the 80/20 rule, 80 percent of the activity in a system occurs in 20 percent of its functionality. The goal is to determine what this 20 percent is and provide the necessary elements to define it. The outputs of this process are documents identifying these key elements, potentially ER and DFD diagrams, and a set of hand-drawn forms to help guide the implementation phase.

One of the more important characteristics of the RAD method is its refining approach to development. If during the analysis/design phase you find things that may change requirements, you need to return to the requirements document and change them. This is where the RAD method differs from the Waterfall method. The Waterfall method considers the requirements document complete and the analysis must fit within that framework. This is not to say that the requirements of the system are written in stone. You can have a flexible Waterfall method that allows information to travel back up. The difference is that the RAD approach encourages this behavior where the Waterfall method discourages it.

With this refining technique in mind, you can leave elements for definition later in the process. Some of the elements that can be defined later include data integrity rules, data maintenance elements, complete relationship diagrams, and other fully developed documents. The RAD method takes into account that many of these items will come to the surface later in the development process and allows them to be left until later in the development process.

After defining the key elements of the system, you can now proceed to the implementation process.

Prototyping Strategies. There are two schools of thought when it comes to developing prototypes. The first is a method that supports the idea of a "throwaway" prototype. When you develop a prototype under this method, you do so with the knowledge that it will be discarded and redone when the application goes into production development.

The second method is a prototype refinement method. This method considers that the prototype will eventually be the application that goes into production. Thus, the application is developed using the same principles that govern production development. When you begin developing using the RAD method, your strategies will depend greatly on the method you choose. Choose carefully.

Implementation with the RAD Method. After determining the key elements in the analysis/design phase, you can begin the actual development of the system. This is where the greatest amount of effort is focused using the RAD method. With the elements defined in the analysis/design phase, you will proceed to develop the rough framework (or prototype) of a functioning application. The initial goal of this phase is to put a functioning application in front of the user as soon as possible. When developing this prototype, take into account that this is a rough prototype and doesn't need all the bells and whistles found in a fully developed application. The bells and whistles will be added later in the development process.

Some of the areas you need to focus on include

- Developing a menu similar to the one that will be used in the final system
- The creation of the basic forms that will be present in the finished application
- The creation of sample data
- The creation of mock-up reports, preferably pulling from the sample data

Upon completing these basic steps, you present the system to the user. This is where the RAD and Waterfall approaches split. The Waterfall approach would present a completed or nearly completed application to the user. The RAD approach puts a system that is known to be incomplete in front of the user.

Why? The RAD approach takes into account the fact that most users are not capable of understanding DFD, ER, and other computerese diagrams created in a normal analysis/design. Users understand screens. The old adage that "a picture is worth a thousand words" is very true when developing software. A user will immediately tell you what is right or wrong with the system presented to him or her. This is the main goal—you want users to see what the finished product will look like and allow them constant and frequent opportunities to give you feedback.

III

Advanced Integration

Upon presenting the prototype to the users, you need to record any items they feel may be lacking or missing. After recording this information, you return to the development process. This process now consists of further refinement of the requirements, analysis/design, and implementation components. You will proceed to incrementally change the requirements (as determined by user feedback), update your analysis/design documents, and update the actual functionality of the system. During this process, you present new and more refined versions of your software to your users.

Testing and Training with the RAD Method. With the Waterfall approach, you normally have a phase dedicated solely to testing and training. Another advantage of the RAD approach is that the testing and training have already been done during the incremental upgrades to the system. Testing occurs when more and more refined versions of the software are delivered. The training has also occurred as the users have been using the software from the earliest phases of development.

Refinement with the RAD Method. The RAD approach also provides capabilities for the maintenance cycle of development. Where the Waterfall method begins a new development cycle for each modification, the RAD approach has maintenance built right in. Essentially, from day one the RAD approach is a maintenance system. You are constantly refining your system. RAD does not consider a system to ever be complete.

Important Considerations of the RAD Method. The RAD approach can provide great benefits to the successful completion of your projects. However, this comes with its own set of issues.

The first issue is a set of development tools that allow for the quick and rapid development of applications. In the past, the languages used to develop applications consisted primarily of COBOL and BASIC. These languages were not always conducive to changing applications very quickly. It has not been until the last few years that tools like Access, Visual Basic, and Visual FoxPro have provided this ability. Also, with the recent popularity of object-oriented programming tools, it has become possible to develop very robust, functional prototypes from already assembled components.

One of the concerns with the RAD approach is that if there is a problem with the early prototype, users may or may not have the skills to point out system problems. So, if the initial screens do not perform their designated tasks according to an accurate model, the system may be constantly refining an incorrect model.

Besides the two styles of development presented in this chapter, there are probably dozens of other development styles. The important thing is to choose one that works for you and stick with it. You can choose the Waterfall approach, the RAD approach, or a combination of the two. It's important to choose a development method that can fit into your development environment.

TIP For more information on the Waterfall or RAD approaches to development, take a look at the following resources:

Rapid Application Development	*Structured Systems Design*
James Martin	Meiler Page Jones
Macmillan Publishing	Yourdon Press
ISBN 0-02-376775-8	ISBN 0-13-690769-5

Developing an Integrated Office Application

Now that you understand the steps necessary to develop an application, you are ready to begin the development process on your first integrated Office application. The remainder of this chapter takes you through the steps to develop a fully integrated office application.

Receiving the Project Request

Commonly, development begins from a request by a company's management department that needs a system to be developed. That system will assist them in accomplishing their goals. The following sections point out some of the items that usually appear on a systems development request.

High Level Goals. The first set of items on a system request are high level goals. These usually quantify what the users of the systems are looking for. We are going to be looking at the sample requirements for a system called Office Trader. This application is a system that will be used in a sales/marketing type of company. The high level goals for this system are:

- Contact customers on a regular and frequent basis.

- Establish a presence on the Internet.

- Learn more about who the customers are through the use of surveys. Analyze this data and target specific products depending on the analysis of the data.

Detailed Goals. After defining the high level goals of the system, it is common for the request to define the specific components and goals of the system. These specific goals are commonly the modules that need to be developed.

III

Advanced Integration

The detailed goals of the Office Trader application are:

- *Management of Contacts.* We need the ability to manage our contacts in some type of central repository. Some of the information we want to know includes company, title, name, address, city, state, ZIP code, phone number, fax number, birth date, source of lead, product interest, and contact notes. It would be nice if the system would allow multiple product interests per customer.

- *Survey Management.* The system needs the capability to create, record, and analyze the results of customer surveys. Some of the information we want to track includes age group of customer, income group of customer, education level, number of employees in company, total sales for company, number of computers in company, and survey date.

- *Appointment Scheduling.* The system needs the capability to schedule appointments for customer contact. This system needs to schedule appointments and provide reminders for our sales staff to contact our customers.

- *Inventory Management.* The system should provide the capability to maintain our inventory items. Some of the information we would like to provide in this system includes part number, inventory description, price, quantity on hand, product picture, product notes, and product category. If resources and time allow, we would like it if you could retrieve the inventory on hand values from our FoxPro accounting system.

- *Internet Links.* The system should be capable of creating product lists and product pages for our Web site. This means the program needs to be able to export our product lists into HTML pages.

- *Customer Form Letters.* The system needs to be capable of creating and sending form letters to our customers. The user should be allowed to select letters from a list and send them to the printer. The system should fill in the appropriate fields from the specified customer.

- *Reporting System.* The program should be capable of creating reports such as customer lists, customer survey results, customer mailing labels, and any other reports that your analysis uncovers. Keeping with our current environmental programs, we would like to minimize the amount of paper generated from the system. This means we would like to be able to distribute reports via our current e-mail system.

Documenting Project Requirements

From the system request items, you can begin compiling the rough framework of your requirements document. The first step is to determine the mission of your application. Your mission should look something like the following.

The goals of the Office Trader application are to

- Allow for the management of contact information. This information will be used to contact customers on a regular and frequent basis.

- Create tools to aid in the establishment of a presence on the Internet.

- Provide tools that will allow users to learn more about their customers through the use of surveys. This information will be used to target specific products, depending on our analysis of the data.
- Limit the news costs to the company for the development of this application.

After compiling a list of goals for the system, begin breaking down the information provided by the user into a list of necessary features. From the system request, you can determine that the following features are necessary for the system:

1. *Contact Manager.* The contact manager needs to be capable of maintaining a list of contacts. The contact information to be tracked includes but is not limited to:

    Company

    Title

    Address

    City

    State

    ZIP

    Phone

    Fax number

    Source of lead

    Product Interest (would be nice if the system had the capability of allowing multiple interests to be entered)

    Contact notes

    The system should have the capability of sending form letters to customers and scheduling appointments. The system should be capable of loading these form letters and appointments with information from the contact lists.

2. *Survey Management.* The system should be capable of creating and maintaining survey information that will be linked to contact information. This module needs to be linked to an analysis module capable of creating charts. Some of the information to be tracked in the survey includes

    Age group of customer

    Income group of customer

    Education level of customer

    Number of employees in customer's company

    Total sales for customer's company

    Number of computers in customer's company

    Survey date

3. *Inventory Information System.* This system needs to provide the capability to create Internet HTML pages from the information stored in the inventory management system. Some of the information to be tracked by this system includes

Part number	Product picture (image file)
Inventory description	Product notes
Product price	Product category
Quantity on hand	

Also, a desired feature is the capability to pull information from the current FoxPro accounting system.

4. *Other Features.* The system should be able to create reports such as customer lists, labels, and any others found during development. The system should be capable of sending reports via the current e-mail system.

5. *Use of Microsoft Office.* The system will be developed using Microsoft Office. Office is currently installed on all machines throughout the company. This will reduce the need for the purchase of new software and the hassle of installing new software throughout the company.

This is a sample of some of the elements of a requirements document. This document can be quite large depending on the complexity of the system being developed and the level of detail desired for the developers of the system. The next step is to further break down this document into areas that can best use the capabilities of the applications found in the Office suite.

Integration Strengths of Office Applications

After determining the requirements of the system, you need to take a look at how each requirement can be satisfied by the tools found in the Office suite.

When developing an integrated Office application, it's necessary to understand the strengths of each product. When you develop an application, you need to choose the correct tool for the job. The Office suite provides a very robust set of integrated applications, and it's tempting to choose one for all jobs. You need to stay away from the idea that one application can perform all tasks.

The strengths of the applications found in the Office suite can be summarized as follows (see fig. 9.4):

■ *Access* is the database application provided with the Office suite. Access's primary strength is its ability to perform the role of a general purpose development tool. Access provides the tools necessary to maintain large quantities of data and to provide access to other applications' data through the use of OLE, DDE, and ODBC. For the Office Trader application, Access will be used to maintain the customers, surveys, and inventory items. Also, Access will be used to interact with the other components of the Office Trader application.

- *Excel* is the strongest data analysis tool found in Office. Spreadsheets are commonly used for the ad-hoc analysis of data and for the creation of charts. The Office Trader application will use Excel for the analysis of the survey data tracked in the Access databases.

- *Word* will be used in the Office Trader application format and present documents. Word will create and print the form letters that are going to customers.

- *Schedule+* is the scheduling application provided in Office. Schedule+ provides a nice interface for scheduling and maintaining appointments on a regular basis. Schedule+ will be used for scheduling and alerting users of calls they need to make for the Office Trader application.

- *Microsoft Mail* is one of the most overlooked but powerful tools. E-mail is useful for communicating with other users and developers. One feature that is commonly overlooked is its capability to send and receive files in e-mail messages. One of the requirements of the Office Trader application is the capability to disseminate reports electronically.

NOTE Office 95 no longer includes Microsoft Mail. Microsoft Mail is now a native component shipped with Windows 95.

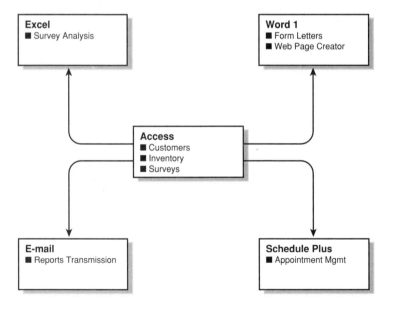

Fig. 9.4

The role and relationship of the Office applications to be used in creating the Office Trader application are shown here.

After determining the requirements of the system and how Office will fit into the development plan, you can begin the analysis/design phase.

III

Advanced Integration

Analyzing and Designing the Application

The next step in the development project is to begin the analysis and design of the system. For our purposes, you will generate a set of simplified DFD and ER diagrams (see figs. 9.5 and 9.6).

Fig. 9.5

This diagram depicts the flow of data within the Office Trader application.

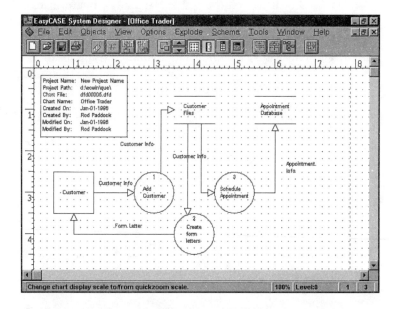

Fig. 9.6

This diagram depicts the relationship between the tables found in the Office Trader Application.

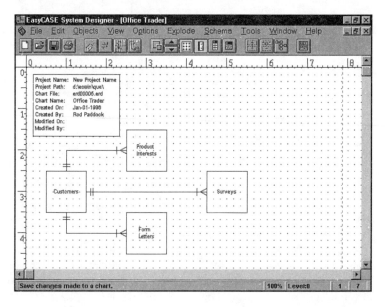

Application Construction

When you have created the requirements document, you can proceed to the analysis/ design phase. It's important to make sure that the requirements document is complete prior to beginning this next step. It may be wise to return the requirements document to the system users for approval before continuing.

Creating the Central Repository. Because Access is the central point of the Office Trader application, it's necessary to begin there. The first step is to create a new database in Access. To create a new database in Access you must do the following:

1. In Access, select Blank Database from the introductory Microsoft Access dialog box and click OK.

2. After creating your new database, you are prompted to enter the name of the new database. For this application call the new database **office_trader**.

Creating the Access Tables. It seems that sometimes the hardest part of developing a database application is simply starting. When developing an application using the RAD method, you will commonly create your tables and forms as quickly as possible. Access provides some very handy tools for creating tables and forms quickly.

You should begin your prototype by first creating your initial table layouts. When you create these tables, your goal is to simply create the basic structure of the tables. You can leave data validation, formatting, and cosmetic items to later in the development process. When using Access, you can create tables using one of two methods. The first is to use the Table Wizard provided with Access. The Table Wizard is a utility that allows developers to create tables from a set of predefined templates. This utility is rather limited and provides few options to select from. The next method is to use the Access Table Designer. Figure 9.7 shows the structure for the customer table to be used in the Office Trader application.

After creating the basic structure of your application's tables, you should begin creating the rough layouts for your forms. You can create the forms using the Form Wizard, or you can create the forms by hand. When developing using the RAD method, you want to produce as much material as you can as quickly as possible. The Form Wizard is a great tool for producing forms under this guideline. Figure 9.8 shows the customer form prototype created using the Form Wizard.

After creating the form for the customer table, you are ready to create the forms for the remaining Office Trader tables. To do this, run the Form Wizard for the remaining tables you defined.

Creating an Access Home Screen. Now, you need to develop a central menuing system. One of the common approaches to developing a menuing system in Access is a home screen form. A *home screen* is a form with buttons on it that can be used to activate the various components of the system. To create a home screen form for the Office Trader application, select the Forms tab of the Office Trader database and click New. For this form, you select Design View from the New Form dialog box and leave the table selector blank.

III

Advanced Integration

Fig. 9.7

Access table designer with Office Trader customer table defined.

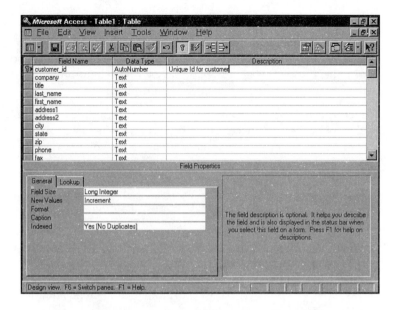

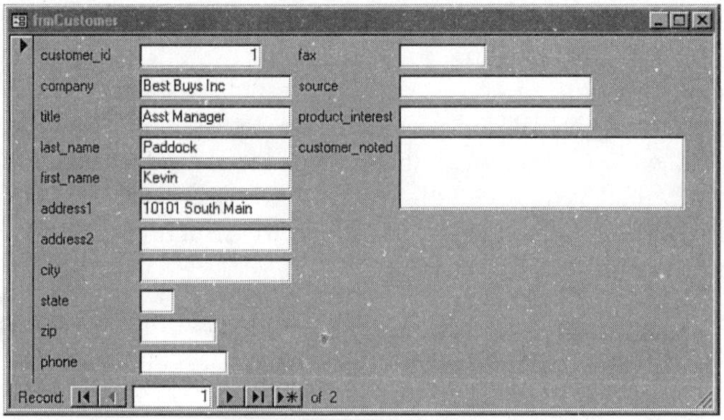

Fig. 9.8

The Form Wizard generated this completed customer form.

Click OK, and the Access Form Designer opens. This tool allows you to create Access forms from the basic components provided by Access. Figure 9.9 shows the Access Form Designer and highlights the components of the Form Designer.

You can begin adding components and modifying this form to perform the tasks needed by the system. The first step is to change the caption shown at the top of the form to represent the name of this system. To change the caption of the form, open the Properties dialog box by either right-clicking the form and selecting Properties from the activated pop-up, or by selecting View, Properties. Select the Format tab and move your cursor to the Caption property. Change the Caption property to **Office Trader Version 1.0**. Figure 9.10 shows the Access properties dialog box with the caption property changed.

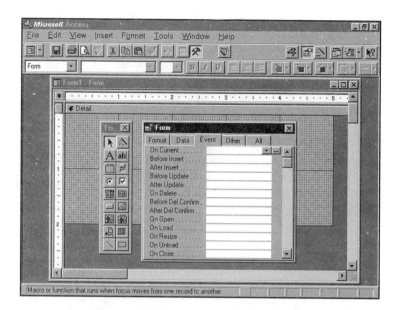

Fig. 9.9

This new Access form is ready for development.

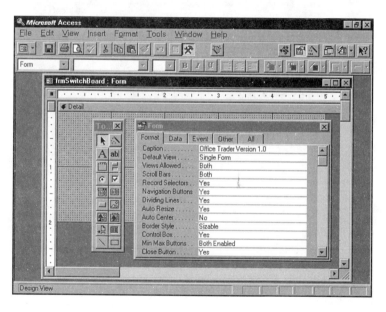

Fig. 9.10

This illustration shows the Access properties dialog box with the caption property changed to "Office Trader Version 1.0."

Now you can begin adding the buttons to the form that will activate the various components of your system. Select the Command Button object from the Form Designer toolbar and highlight the size the button will fill on your form. After adding the button to the form (see fig. 9.11), you need to change the caption of the button to represent the name of the action this button will represent.

III

Advanced Integration

Fig. 9.11

The Customers button has been added to the home screen form.

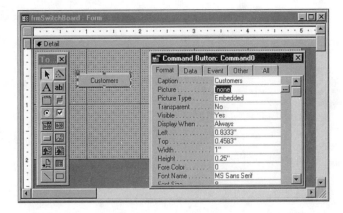

Now you can add the buttons for the survey and inventory modules. Figure 9.12 shows the completed home screen form for the Office Trader application.

Fig. 9.12

The Customers, Inventory, and Surveys buttons have been added to the home screen form.

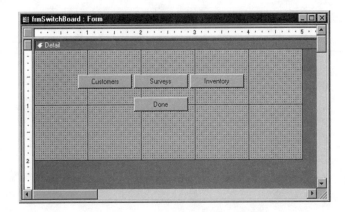

After creating the buttons for your form, you need to make the buttons do something. You do this by linking the click event of the button to a macro. Select the button, and open the properties dialog box by choosing View, Properties. Select the On Click event from the Event tab of the properties dialog box (see fig. 9.13).

Create a macro by clicking the ellipsis button (...) shown next to the On Click field. The Choose Builder dialog box appears and allows you to select one of the code building options. Select Macro Builder.

Access prompts you for a name for the macro you wish to create. Name this macro **mcrOpenCustomer**. Now you can begin specifying the actions this macro is to perform. You specify the actions of a macro by selecting from the list of valid macro actions. Figure 9.14 shows the Access Macro Designer with the list of valid macro actions dropped down. From this list, select the OpenForm action. This action allows you to specify a form to open and the status of that form when it is opened.

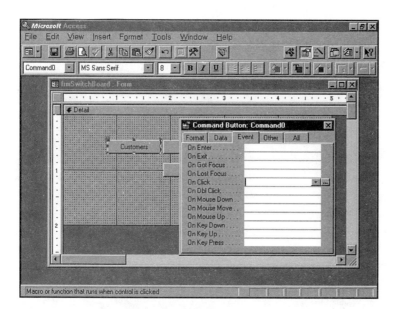

Fig. 9.13

Note the added command button with the On Click Event selected.

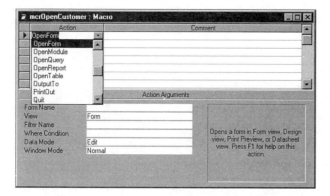

Fig. 9.14

This figure shows the Macro Designer with the macro actions list dropped down.

After selecting the OpenForm action from the Action list, you need to specify which form to open. You do this by specifying the name of the file to open in the Action Arguments section of the Macro Designer. The name of your form goes in the Form Name field. Figure 9.15 shows the Macro Designer with the customer form specified.

Create macros for the inventory and survey forms as well. After completing these macros, you also need to create a macro for closing the home screen form. To do this, select the On Click event from the properties dialog box and create a macro called mcrCloseHomeScreen. This macro needs to call the Close macro action with the object type property set to Form and the object name property set to frmHomeScreen. Figure 9.16 shows the Macro Designer with the correct properties set.

Fig. 9.15

*The macro created will
open the customer form.*

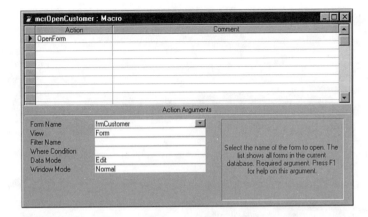

Fig. 9.16

*The Macro Designer has
properties specified to close
the home screen form.*

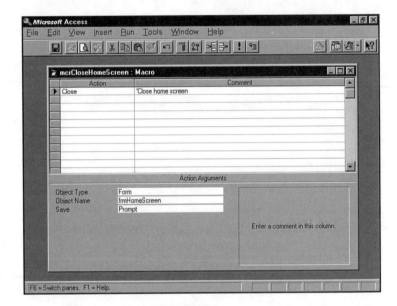

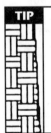
TIP
When developing Access applications, you sometimes have the option of executing
commands with macros or VBA code. Some standards dictate the usage of VBA whenever possible. Where the following example uses macros to open forms, you could
execute the same action using code. The following VBA code is used to open a form:

```
DoCmd.OpenForm "frmCustomer", acNormal, "", "", acEdit, acNormal
```

This code opens the frmCustomer form in allowing edits and as a normal window.

TIP

If you have developed all your applications using macros and want to make the shift to VBA code, Access provides a tool that converts macros to VBA code. You can activate this tool by opening a form and selecting Tools, Macros, Convert Form's Macros to Visual Basic. This will then convert all your macros to VBA code.

If you were using the RAD method of development, you would present the application to your users for evaluation. This is the users' chance to give feedback at the earliest stages of development. After presenting the system to the users, you can begin adding new functionality to your system.

Scheduling Appointments. One of the basic requirements specified is the capability to schedule appointments. To create appointments, you must create a link to the Schedule+ application.

To create a link to Schedule+, you need to create some new components. The first is a new table that will be used to specify data to send to the scheduling application. This table will be called `tblAppointment` and will contain three columns:

- `Appointment_begin_time`
- `Appointment_end_time`
- `Appointment_text`

The appointment `begin` and `end` time fields need to be of the `datetime` data type. The second component is a new form that will be used to send data to the Schedule+ application. This form will provide fields for entering relevant appointment information. It will also have two buttons—a button to create an appointment and a button to close the appointments form.

After creating the form, you need to add some code to the Create Appointment button. Select the On Click event and click the ellipsis button. Select the code builder option. This will take you into the Access code builder screen where you will add the code to create an appointment with Schedule+. To create an appointment from Access, enter the following code.

Listing 9.1 OFFICE_TRADER.MDB. Code for Creating a Schedule+ Appointment

```
'--Dimension Objects for procedure
Dim objObject As Object
Dim objSchedule As Object
Dim objAppointment As Object

'-- Create OLE session
Set objObject = CreateObject("SchedulePlus.Application")

'-- Logon to Schedule+
objObject.Logon
```

(continues)

III

Advanced Integration

Listing 9.1   Continued

```
'-- Set reference to ScheduleLogged Object
Set objSchedule = oleObject.ScheduleLogged

'-- Create new appointment
Set objAppointment = objSchedule.Appointments.New

'-- Set appointment properties
With objAppointment
  .Start = Forms!frmAppointment.appointment_begin_time.Value
  .End = Forms!frmAppointment.appointment_end_time.Value
  .Text = Forms!frmAppointment.appointment_text.Value
End With

'-- Commit appointment
objAppointment.Flush
```

This code establishes a communication session with Schedule+ using the CreateObject function. It logs into Schedule+ and creates a new appointment. For more specific information about creating an appointment with Schedule+, see Chapter 14, "Integrating Schedule+ and E-Mail with Other Office Applications."

Creating Form Letters with Word. Next you must create a link to Word for processing form letters. In order to create a link to Word, you need to create another form. This form contains these three elements:

- A list of available form letters
- A button to create and print a form letter
- A button to close the form

To create the form, select the Form tab from the Office Trader database container and click New. Select Design View from the New Form dialog box. After Access opens the form in Design view, you can begin adding the proper controls to the form.

The first control to be added to the form is a combo box. Select the Combo Box control from the Form Controls toolbox. After selecting this form, click the form. Access then adds the control to the form and opens the properties dialog box. Select the Data tab in the properties dialog box and set the following properties:

- Row Source Type=Value List
- Row Source=Standard Letter;Product Letter;Misc Letter (it is important that this list be delimited with a semicolon)
- Limit to List=Yes

This creates a list with three options that can allow users to specify which form letter to send. Now, add the following code to the new letters button:

Listing 9.2   OFFICE_TRADER.MDB. Code for Creating Form Letters with Word

```
'Create object and link to Word
Dim objWordObject As Object
Set objWordObject = CreateObject("Word.Basic")

'Determine which letter to print depending upon
'Value specified in list box
Dim strLetters As String
strLetters = Forms!frmFormLetters.Combo0.Value

'Process letters depending upon valid selected in list
'Notice that the case structure calls the msgbox command
'Because this is a prototype this is ok. Later we will
'Insert the actual processing code here.
Select Case strLetters

   Case "Standard Letter"
      MsgBox "Standard Letter"

   Case "Product Letter"
      MsgBox "Product Letter"

   Case "Misc Letter"
      MsgBox "Misc Letter"

End Select

' Create a new Word File
objWordObject.FileNew

'Create carriage return value
Dim strCRLF
strCRLF = Chr(10) + Chr(13)

'Insert name of form letter to create
objWordObject.INSERT strLetters & strCRLF

'Insert values from customer table
objWordObject.INSERT Forms!frmCustomer.Last_name.Value & strCRLF
objWordObject.INSERT Forms!frmCustomer.First_name.Value & strCRLF

'Send document to printer
' objWordObject.FilePrint
```

This code establishes a session with Word, creates a new file, and sends the appropriate information to the letter from the currently selected customer. Figures 9.17 and 9.18 show the form letters form and the Word document created by this form.

Fig. 9.17

This is the form used to create form letters with the Form Letters drop-down list displayed.

Fig. 9.18

This is the final output sent to Word from the Access system.

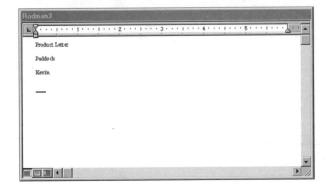

Analyzing Data with Excel. One of the other requirements of the system is the capability to analyze the results of surveys. This analysis will be done using Excel. This is the next component to be developed.

To link this system to Excel, you need to add a new button to the Surveys form. This button will have code that queries the Surveys table and sends the result of that query to an Excel spreadsheet. This function then creates a chart from the data output to the Excel spreadsheet.

The first step is to create a query with the Access query builder that will group some of the data stored in the surveys table. To create a query from an Access table, you need to select the Queries tab in the Office Trader database. Then, click the New button. Select the Design View option from the New Query dialog box and choose the Surveys table from the provided list. The New Query dialog box appears as shown in figure 9.19.

Now, you must select the columns that will be analyzed in this query. Figure 9.20 shows the Designer view with the customer_age field selected and a sum field that will tell how many people fall into specific age groups. Figure 9.21 shows the SQL code that is generated by the Query Designer.

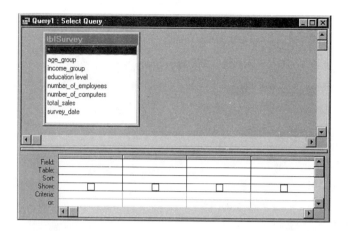

Fig. 9.19

The Access Query Designer will be used to generate a query for analyzing survey results.

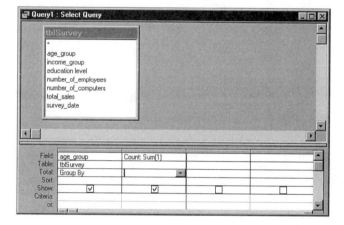

Fig. 9.20

The Access Query Designer shows the criteria specified for the survey analysis query.

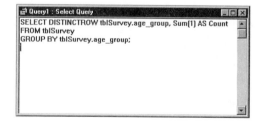

Fig. 9.21

This is the SQL code generated from the options specified in the Query Designer.

III

Advanced Integration

Add the following code to the button you added to the survey form.

Listing 9.3   OFFICE_TRADER.MDB. Code for Sending the Results of an Access Query to Excel

```
Dim objMyObject As Object
 Set objMyObject = CreateObject("Excel.Application")

 'Show Excel
objMyObject.Visible = True

 'Add new workbook
objMyObject.Workbooks.Add


 'Dimension objects for linking to the database
Dim dbTrader As Database
Dim rstSurvey As Recordset

 'Link to the database
Set dbTrader = DBEngine.Workspaces(0).Databases(0)

 'Link to the survey query
Set rstSurvey = dbTrader.OpenRecordset("qrySurvey")

 'Determine if any records are present
If rstSurvey.RecordCount > 0 Then


  'Scan down query file for results
  Do Until rstSurvey.EOF

    'Move record pointer
    rstSurvey.MoveNext

    'Put data in appropriate cell
    If Not rstSurvey.EOF Then
      objMyObject.Cells(rstSurvey!age_group, 2).Value = rstSurvey!Count
    End If
  Loop
End If


  'Add survey data to the cells
  objMyObject.Cells(1, 1).Value = "18-25"
  objMyObject.Cells(2, 1).Value = "26-30"
  objMyObject.Cells(3, 1).Value = "31-40"
  objMyObject.Cells(4, 1).Value = "41-55"
  objMyObject.Cells(5, 1).Value = "55-70"
  objMyObject.Cells(6, 1).Value = "70+"

  ' Select range to graph
  objMyObject.Range("A1:B6").SELECT

  ' Add new chart
objMyObject.Charts.Add
```

This code does the following:

1. Opens the survey query.
2. Creates an Excel communication session.
3. Sends the output of the query to the Excel communication session.
4. Creates a chart of the query results.

This is just a limited example of some of the capabilities of sending data to Excel. Some potential features that could be added include different query criteria, multiple field analysis, and more. You are limited only by the time it takes to develop a new query and send that output to Excel.

Creating Internet Web Pages. One of the most important requirements of this system is the capability to generate Web pages from the inventory files maintained by the system. The Office Trader application uses Word to create these Web pages.

Set up a document that will serve as a template for a Web page. Figure 9.22 shows the Word document that will be used as a template. This document has the basic information that is necessary for a basic Web page. The codes specified in this document are *HyperText Markup Language (HTML) tags*. These tags are used by Web browser programs such as Netscape or Mosaic to display Web pages. Also within this document is a single Word bookmark called `list_start`. *Bookmarks* are defined points within Word documents that you can go to with a macro command.

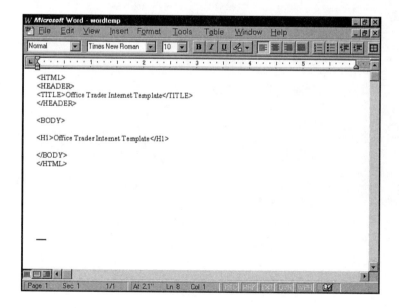

Fig. 9.22

This Web template contains the HTML codes for a basic Web page.

After creating this template file, add a button to the inventory maintenance form. After adding this button, add the following code to the button.

Listing 9.4   OFFICE_TRADER.MDB. Code for Creating Web Pages with Access and Word

```
'Create object and link to Word
Dim objWordObject As Object
Set objWordObject = CreateObject("Word.Basic")

' Open web template
objWordObject.FileOpen "C:\wo\wordtemp.doc"

'Create carriage return value
Dim strCRLF
strCRLF = Chr(10) + Chr(13)

'Dimension objects for linking to the database
Dim dbTrader As DATABASE
Dim rstInventory As Recordset

'Link to the database
Set dbTrader = DBEngine.Workspaces(0).Databases(0)

'Link to the inventory table
Set rstInventory = dbTrader.OpenRecordset("tblInventory")

'Move to the list starting bookmark
objWordObject.EditGoto "List_Start"

'Determine if any records are present
If rstInventory.RecordCount > 0 Then

  'Create placeholder for string creation
  Dim strInsert

  'Scan down inventory file and create entries
  'For each part
  Do Until rstInventory.EOF

    'Create string to insert
    strInsert = rstInventory!part_number & " " & rstInventory!Description & " " & _
    Str(rstInventory!price) & strCRLF

    'Insert text
    objWordObject.INSERT strInsert

    'Move record pointer
    rstInventory.MoveNext
  Loop
End If

'Save HTML form
objWordObject.FileSaveAs "WEBPART.HTM"
```

This code does the following:

1. Creates a link to Word.
2. Opens the Web template file.
3. Opens the inventory table.
4. Scans the inventory table and sends the proper Web codes and text to the Word document.
5. Saves the Web file.

Figures 9.23 and 9.24 show the output of the Web page creator program and the Web page as it will appear on the Internet.

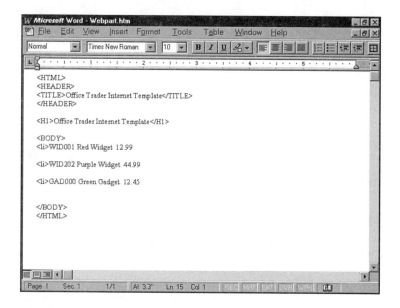

Fig. 9.23

This Word document was created by the Web page creation program.

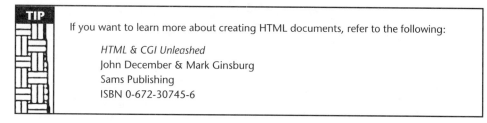

If you want to learn more about creating HTML documents, refer to the following:

HTML & CGI Unleashed
John December & Mark Ginsburg
Sams Publishing
ISBN 0-672-30745-6

Office Trader E-Mail Links. The last feature to be developed is a link to e-mail from the Office Trader application. To do this, you create a new form that will be responsible for sending e-mail. Select the Form tab from the Office Trader database container and click New. Select the Design View option and click OK. Add the controls that will be responsible for creating and sending e-mail messages.

III

Advanced Integration

Fig. 9.24

This Web page was created in Netscape and is shown as it will appear on the Internet.

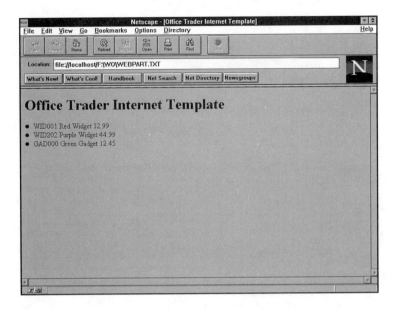

These controls are the MAPI controls that are found in Visual Basic and Visual FoxPro. You can add these controls by choosing Insert, Custom Control. From the Insert OLE Custom Controls dialog box, select the MAPI Session and MAPI Message controls and add them to the form. Figure 9.25 shows the dialog box you use to add custom controls to Access forms.

Fig. 9.25

Use the Insert OLE Custom Controls dialog box to add custom controls to Access forms.

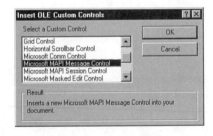

Now, add a button to the form and then place the following code in this button.

Listing 9.5 OFFICE_TRADER.MDB. Code for Creating an E-Mail Message from Access

```
'Get reference to session control
With Forms!frmEmail.ocxSession

    'Set username and password
    .UserName = "VBTEACH"
    .Password = "VBTEACH"
```

```
'Log in to e-mail
.SignOn

'Send session id to message control
Forms!frmEmail.ocxMessage.SessionID = .SessionID

End With

With Forms!frmEmail.ocxMessage

   '-- Create new message
   .Compose

   '-- Set message type (you can set this to an IPC type to prevent
   'users from viewing it in their inboxes.
   .MsgType = ""

   '-- Set message address name
   '-- Format is "MS:HOMER<network>/<server>HOMER/<username>RPAD"
   .RecipAddress = "MS:HOMER/HOMER/RPAD"
   .RecipDisplayName = "MS:HOMER/HOMER/RPAD"

   '-- Set message subject and note text
   .MsgSubject = "HTML TRANSMISSION"

   'OLE message control must have some text
   .MsgNoteText = "ATTACHED HTML FILE "

   '-- Add Attachment Info
   .AttachmentIndex = 0
   .AttachmentPathName = "C:\WO\WEBPART.HTM"
   .AttachmentName = "WEBPART.HTM"

   '-- Send message
   .Send False
End With

'Remember to log out of e-mail
Forms!frmEmail.ocxSession.SignOff
```

This code does the following:

1. Establishes a session with Exchange.

2. Creates a new message.

3. Attaches the Web document created in this example to the e-mail message.

4. Sends the message.

This is just a brief example of what you can do with e-mail in your Office applications. You can transmit data to remote sales offices, send alert messages to system administrators, and disseminate information in a fast and efficient manner.

III

Advanced Integration

From Here...

This chapter has shown that you can develop some very complex and sophisticated applications using the tools provided in the Office suite. You have learned development methodologies that you should consider implementing as soon as your next project.

For more detailed information related to the topics discussed in this chapter, consult these chapters:

- Chapter 3, "Integration Basics," explains the basics of integrating Office applications.
- Chapter 4, "Visual Basic and Visual Basic for Applications," teaches you to write Visual Basic code and use the tools found in VBA.
- Chapter 5, "Programming Application Integration," provides a more in-depth look at communicating with other Office applications.
- Chapter 14, "Integrating Schedule+ and E-Mail with Other Office Applications," looks at the details of integrating Schedule+ and e-mail with Office applications.

CHAPTER 10

Automating Office Integration with Word

Word is a cornerstone of the Office suite, providing the word processing elements of the integrated office environment. Word is also programmable, containing a powerful macro capability that can be used to implement new commands and functions not included in the original program. That programmability can also be accessed from outside of Word, to make it an important part of an integrated application.

This chapter illustrates how Word can be used as a component within an integrated application. The WordBasic macro language cannot manipulate OLE objects in other applications, but must use Dynamic Data Exchange (DDE) to send commands to the other applications. DDE has nowhere near the power and flexibility of manipulating OLE objects, making Word a poor choice for the controller of an integrated application. While Word is not suited to be the controller of such an application, it is a powerful component of an integrated application.

In this chapter, you learn how to

- Embed Word in other applications
- Embed other applications in Word
- Control Word and edit documents using WordBasic
- Control WordBasic using Visual Basic for Applications

Embedding Word or Embedding into Word

When first considering Word as part of an integrated application, you should list what things Word does best, and then consider how that list fits the requirements of your integrated application. The second thing to consider is whether to embed Word into another application, such as Excel, or to embed other applications into Word. What is reasonable? What are the trade-offs?

What Word Does Best

Why use Word? Why not use Excel or some other application? For what tasks is Word best? Consider the following things Word can and can't do:

- Word is best at handling and formatting text.
- Word can do page layout.
- Word displays the contents of a document as sequential pages, as compared to Excel, which displays its documents as a stack of sheets.
- Word has better text editing and search capabilities.
- Word can do forms (documents with fields a user can fill in), but then so can Excel.
- Word can do mail merge documents.
- Word can open and display most picture formats.
- Word can open documents created by other popular applications, such as 1-2-3 worksheets.
- Word cannot be an OLE Automation client.

Word is best at handling and formatting text. This is not unexpected for a word processor. Text handling and formatting are its primary functions. Other Office applications have some simple text-handling capabilities, but they don't have anywhere near the capabilities of Word.

Word does page layout, which is expected in a modern word processing application. In Word, when an object is inserted into a document, the document text flows around the object, filling in any space between the object and the margin of the page. This capability is not available in other Office applications, where any special page layout must be done by hand.

Word displays the contents of a document as sequential pages, as compared to Excel, which displays its documents as a stack of sheets. The way Word displays a document is not necessarily better than that used by Excel—it's just different. On-screen, Word displays a document as one long, scrollable page. When printed, a Word document is a sequential list of pages. Excel displays its documents as a stack of pages, with each page selectable by clicking a tab at the bottom of the page. An integrated application that results in a printed document will usually use Word as the container application, with other applications embedded into it. If you don't intend on printing the document, other layouts may be more appropriate. For example, the tabbed layout of Excel makes it easy to quickly jump from one section of the application to another. The application you choose to embed depends on what you are trying to achieve with your integrated application.

Word has better text editing and search capabilities than most other applications, including the capability to search and replace formatting and format styles. It can also select vertical columns of text (hold down the Alt key while selecting) as well as rows.

The creation of forms is an extra capability of Word. *Forms* are special Word documents that contain fields, where a *field* is a box in the text where a user types specific information. When a form is saved, the contents of the fields can be saved separately from the formatted document that contains them.

Word does mail merge documents, which were originally designed to handle the creation of form letters. A single main document contains fields that are filled from a data document. Each record or paragraph in the data document contains the data needed to fill all the fields in a main document. When printed or displayed on-screen, a merged document is created for each record in the data document.

Word can open and display most picture formats. Most pictures can be opened and directly displayed in a Word document without having to do any special image conversion. Resizing the picture object to fit the current document is done by simply dragging the picture's selection rectangle. This capability is not unique to Word, but becomes special when combined with the capability to wrap text around the object.

Word can open or import and display many different types of document files. Whether it is a word processing document from another word processor, an image file, or a spreadsheet, Word can convert it to a Word document without the benefit of the creating application. Word can also save documents in many foreign file formats.

Word cannot be the controller of an integrated application bound together with OLE Automation. While Word does contain a powerful macro capability, it does not contain the OLE commands necessary to control another application. If OLE Automation is needed for an integrated application, some other program must be used as the controller application. Excel or Visual Basic are good choices for the controller application.

 NOTE Word can control another application using DDE, but DDE is very limited compared to OLE Automation.

Embedding into Word

Other objects are commonly embedded into Word when the final result is a printed document. Excel tables and charts are commonly inserted into a Word document to provide the backup information for a written report. OLE Automation is not usually needed here, because the data in the objects usually remain static once a report is created. That is, you don't use the documents interactively; you insert the new data and view the resulting report.

Embedding into Word is also appropriate when the resulting document should be read sequentially, from beginning to end.

Embedding Word

Embedding Word documents into another OLE application is appropriate when you need to use OLE Automation to control an integrated application, or when you want to view a document differently. For example, if it is more appropriate to randomly access the contents of an integrated application, Excel should be used as the container, and a Word document should be embedded into it. On the other hand, if a document should be read sequentially, then either Word or Excel can be used as the container.

Deciding Whether To Link or Embed

Deciding whether to link or embed a document is primarily determined by where you want the native data stored. Both types of sharing allow the information to be edited in the original program. The decision to link or embed largely depends on what you plan to do with the source file.

Linking Objects

When an object is linked (see fig. 10.1), the native data remains in the source file, and the presentation data is updated whenever the native data changes. When a Word document is embedded into an Excel worksheet, the native data remains in the Word document, and the presentation data is in the worksheet. Should the native data in the Word document be changed, the presentation data in the worksheet is also changed.

Fig. 10.1

Linking objects stores only the presentation data in the container object; the native data stays in the original document.

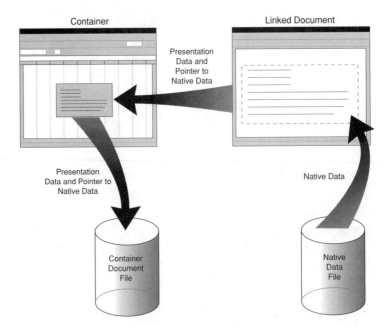

Container

Linked Document

Presentation Data and Pointer to Native Data

Presentation Data and Pointer to Native Data

Native Data

Container Document File

Native Data File

Linking is most useful when you create reports that are periodically updated. By simply updating the native data in the linked documents, the main document is also updated.

NOTE Updating linked objects is either automatic or manual. When automatic updating is set, the presentation data is changed whenever the native data changes. When manual updating is set, linked documents are not updated until the user makes it happen.

Embedding Objects

When an object is embedded into another document (see fig. 10.2), the native data is also stored there, thus disconnecting it from the original document. In this case, if you change the original document, the presentation data does not change.

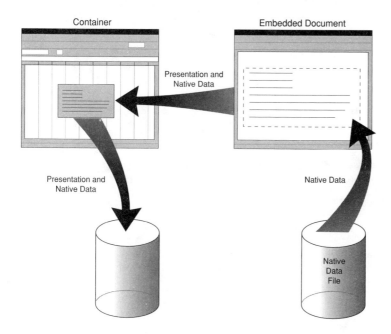

Fig. 10.2

Embedding documents stores the native data in the container object along with the presentation data.

Embedding is most useful when it is difficult or impractical to maintain the links to embedded objects, such as a document that is to be distributed electronically. All of the native data is contained in the container document, so the original data documents do not have to be maintained in order to revise the container document.

Manually Linking and Embedding Word Documents

The most common form of linking and embedding involves manually inserting objects into a document. There is no OLE Automation involved—only the connections between the linked data and the container objects.

III

Advanced Integration

Pasting Word Objects

The simplest method of linking a Word object in another application is to open a document in Word, select the part you want to link or embed, copy it onto the Clipboard, switch to the application and document you want to be the container for the Word document, and choose Edit, Paste Special. A dialog box similar to that shown in figure 10.3 appears, showing you the type of data that is on the Clipboard, and giving you the option to link it.

Fig. 10.3

The Paste Special dialog box shows the linking and embedding options.

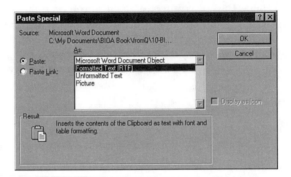

In the As box are the data types currently on the Clipboard. Pasting the Microsoft Word Document Object data type maintains a connection between the data being pasted and the application that knows how to edit it. The other listed data types simply provide the copied data in different formats, without any connection to the application that created them or the file where the native data is stored.

The two option buttons, Paste and Paste Link, control whether the object is embedded or linked. Clicking Paste embeds the object—including the presentation data and the native data—into the container document. Paste Link inserts the presentation data into the container document along with a pointer to the application that created it and the file that contains the native data.

Drag-and-Drop

To use the drag-and-drop method of sharing data between two applications, both applications must be open on the Desktop. Select the data to be embedded, click and drag it to the other application, and drop it where you want it inserted. On smaller monitors, select and drag the object down to the other application's button on the taskbar. When the other application opens, continue dragging back up to where you want the object inserted. To copy data instead of moving it, hold down the Ctrl key while dragging.

NOTE   You don't need to hold down the Ctrl key for the whole operation, just while clicking the object and dropping it.

While easy to do, drag-and-drop embedding is not as consistent as other methods of embedding. When you drag and drop a Word object onto an Excel worksheet, the type of insertion is dependent on what was the active object on the worksheet before you performed the drag and drop. If a cell is active when you perform a drag and drop, only the text of the selection in Word is copied into the cells—no linking or embedding occurs. If any other object—such as a button, graphic element, or text box—is active on the Excel worksheet before the drag and drop, a Word object is embedded into the Excel worksheet.

> **Caution**
>
> When copying data from a Word document to Excel worksheet cells, beware of the 255 character-per-cell limit. Only the first 255 characters of each paragraph are copied to a cell. Characters beyond the 255 character limit are lost.

> **Caution**
>
> Drag-and-drop editing does not always embed a document; in some cases, it can only copy the native data to the container application. For example, dragging a selected paragraph in Word to an Excel worksheet copies the text into a cell instead of embedding a document.

Linking and Embedding with Insert

Most OLE-compliant applications have an Insert, Object command. The Insert, Object command displays a dialog box containing a list of all the insertable objects known to the system. Choose the Create New tab (see fig. 10.4) to embed a new object, or Create from File tab (see fig. 10.5) to embed an existing object. In the Create from File tab, there is an option to link the document. If that option is checked, the file is linked to the container document; otherwise, it is embedded.

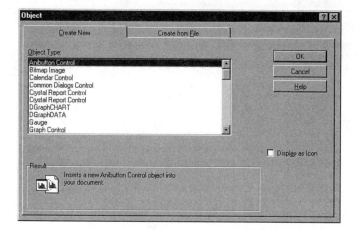

Fig. 10.4

The Create New tab in the Object dialog box allows you to insert a new object into a document.

III

Advanced Integration

Fig. 10.5

The Create from File tab in the Object dialog box allows you to insert an existing object into a document.

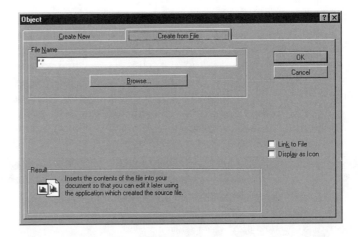

Caution

Unlike the Paste Special or the drag-and-drop methods of embedding—which can embed a selection from a Word document—the Insert, Object, Create from File command always inserts a whole document into the container document.

Editing Embedded Word Objects

To edit a Word object embedded in another application, simply double-click the embedded text. If the object is embedded and the container object supports in-place editing, a Word-like interface appears in the container document for you to edit the Word document (see fig. 10.6). If the object is linked, double-clicking it switches to Word and opens the original document file there.

Fig. 10.6

An embedded Word object is being edited in Excel.

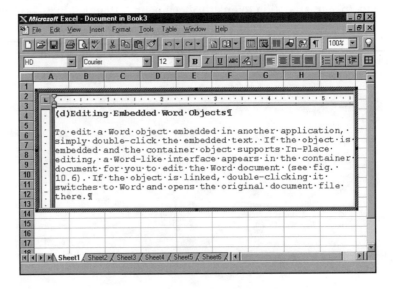

Manually Linking and Embedding Objects in Word

The methods for linking or embedding another application's document into Word are the same as for linking or embedding Word documents into another application's documents. Any OLE server application can be linked or embedded into a Word document—for example, Excel worksheets and graphs.

Linking and Embedding an Excel Worksheet

As one example, consider embedding an Excel worksheet in a Word document. This is a common occurrence when you create reports that involve analysis of numeric data such as financial, marketing, and research reports. If the report is re-created periodically, you should link the worksheet to the document instead of embedding it, to simplify the creation of the next period's report.

To embed an Excel worksheet into a Word document:

   1. Create the worksheet and the text part of the document (see fig. 10.7).

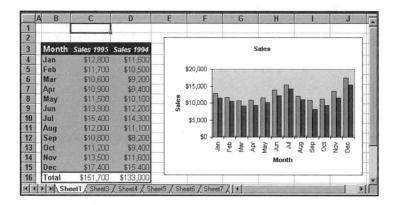

Fig. 10.7

Prepare an Excel worksheet and graph for insertion into a Word document.

   2. Select the table on the worksheet (cells B3:D16) and copy it.

   3. Switch to the Word document, select where you want the table inserted, and choose Edit, Paste Special.

   4. Choose the Microsoft Excel Worksheet Object, click the Paste option, and click OK. The table is now embedded into the document. To link the object instead of embedding it, choose the Paste Link option instead of the Paste option in the Paste Special dialog box.

To position the table and make the text flow around it:

   1. Choose View, Page Layout to switch to Page Layout view if you are not already there.

   2. Select the table.

III

Advanced Integration

3. Choose Insert, Frame; the table is now framed and may be dragged to any position on the page.

Once placed, the existing text on the page flows around the table as shown in figure 10.8.

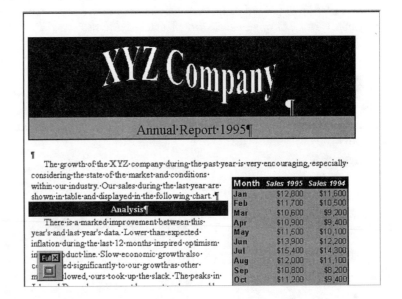

Linking and Embedding an Excel Chart

An Excel chart, such as that shown in figure 10.7, is embedded into a Word document in exactly the same manner as the Excel worksheet. Select and copy the graph, switch to Word, select where you want the graph, choose Edit Paste Special, select the Microsoft Excel Chart Object, click the Paste option, and click OK. The chart is now inserted into the document.

Use the Paste Link option if you want to link the graph instead of embed it. Position the graph by placing a frame around it and dragging the frame to wherever you want the graph to be. The final document is shown in figure 10.9, with the text flowing around the worksheet and graph.

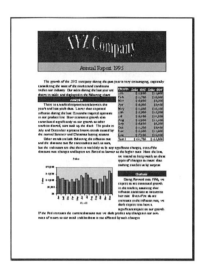

Fig. 10.9

You can embed an Excel worksheet and chart into a Word document.

Using Mini-Applications and Other Objects in Word

Word, Office, and Windows 95 come with several mini-applications that can be embedded into Word, significantly increasing the capability of Word for special situations. The mini-applications consist of such features as WordArt, Graph, and Equation that give extra functionality to the existing Office applications. If any of these mini-applications do not show up in the list displayed when you choose Insert, Object, you probably need to run the Office Setup program again and install the missing parts.

Using WordArt

WordArt is a mini-application for creating artistic shapes with words. WordArt rotates and stretches text, 3D block lettering, shadowing, and text along a curve. The result of the WordArt application is a picture of the text inserted into the Word document. The heading at the top of the document in figure 10.9 was created with WordArt. WordArt objects are inserted by choosing Insert, Object and selecting the Microsoft WordArt 2.0 object.

Using Graph

Graph is a simple charting application with an interface similar to an Excel worksheet. You insert a Microsoft Graph 5.0 object into a document by choosing Insert, Object and selecting the Microsoft Graph 5.0 object. A small worksheet appears for you to insert your data, and a chart appears to display that data. The chart types are similar to those available in Excel, but there is not an extensive list of chart types as there is with Excel, and there are fewer formatting options.

Using Word Picture

A Word Picture is embedded in a Word document by choosing Insert, Object and selecting the Microsoft Word Picture object. The Drawing toolbar appears for you to create your picture. Word Picture is also used to edit a picture inserted by choosing Insert, Picture.

Using Equation

Equation is a variation of the MathType equation formatter. An equation is embedded in a document by choosing Insert, Object and selecting the Microsoft Equation Editor 2.0 object. Equation consists of a series of templates and symbols. The templates create fractions, sub- and superscripts, square roots, and other special symbols and structures of mathematical equations. The symbols, along with the keyboard, make up the rest of an equation. Extremely complex equations, such as that shown in figure 10.10, can be created with Equation.

Fig. 10.10

A complex equation, such as this from solid state physics for the intrinsic carrier density in silicon, can be created with Equation and inserted into a Word document.

$$n_i = \left(4M_c \left(\frac{2\pi m_0 k}{h^2} \right)^3 \right)^{1/2} \left(\frac{m_e^* m_h^*}{m_0} \right)^{3/4} T^{3/2} e^{-E_g/2kT}$$

Using Organization Chart

The Organization Chart mini-application inserts an organization chart template into your document (see fig. 10.11). You then fill in the slots to create an organization chart. As shown in the figure, there are commands on the toolbar to add more co-workers, subordinates, managers, and assistants. You embed an Organization chart by choosing Insert, Object and selecting MS Organization Chart 2.0 from the list of objects.

Using Media Player

Media Player is a mini-application included with Windows 95 for playing audio and video clips (see fig. 10.12). It is embedded into a document by choosing Insert, Object and selecting either the Media Clip, Video Clip, or MIDI Sequence objects. All three objects use the Media Player application, but enable different options and have different icons in a document. Two other options—Wave Sound and CD Audio—are implemented by embedding Media Clip and choosing the media type in the Control Panel. When you choose a particular media type, the icon changes to match the selected media. After selecting a particular media document to play, double-clicking the image or icon plays the sound or video; Alt+double-clicking the image or icon brings up the Control Panel so you can change the media type or file.

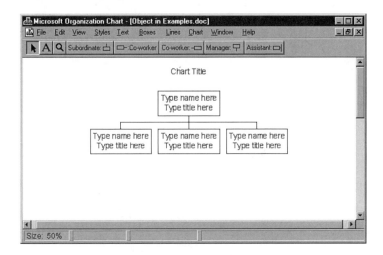

Fig. 10.11

The Organization Chart mini-application shows a blank organization chart template that you can fill in.

Fig. 10.12

The Media Player window controls the playback of multimedia objects.

The Media Clip object uses the Media Player with all its options enabled. With this object, you can choose to play a Windows video clip, CD sound clip, sound file, or MIDI Sequence. When you select a particular media type, the icon changes to match the type.

The Video Clip object uses the Media Player with only the Video for Windows option enabled. This object plays video files stored in the Video for Windows format (AVI). When a video file is loaded, the Video Clip icon is replaced by the starting image in the video file.

III

Advanced Integration

The CD Audio object plays all or part of the audio CD currently in the disk drive. A CD drive and a sound card are required to use this object.

 The Wave Sound object plays wave sound files (WAV). Wave files are usually used for short sounds, such as the beeps, squawks, and trills you hear when you select different options and menus. A sound card is required to use this object.

 The MIDI Sequence object uses the Media Player with only the MIDI Sequence option enabled. With this object, you can choose to play MIDI sequence files (MID). MIDI sequences are used for pieces of music rather than sounds. You must have a compatible sound card in order to play MIDI sequence files.

Using Sound Recorder

 The Sound Recorder is a complementary program to the Media Player, with sound recording, mixing, and playback capabilities (see fig. 10.13).

Fig. 10.13

The Sound Recorder window allows you to create and embed sound files.

Recorded files are stored as wave (WAV) sound files. To embed the sound recorder in a Word document, choose Insert, Annotation. Another way is to run the Sound Recorder directly, then copy and paste it into the Word document. On a Windows 95 system, Sound Recorder is usually started from the \PROGRAMS\ACCESSORIES\ MULTIMEDIA folder on the Start menu.

When Sound Recorder has started up, do the following:

1. Choose Edit, Copy to copy the wave file.
2. Switch to the Word document where you want to insert the sound.
3. Choose Edit, Paste Special.
4. Choose the Wave Sound Object, and click OK.

 To play the currently saved sound, double-click the Sound Recorder icon. To change the sound or record a new one, Alt+double-click the icon to bring up the Sound Recorder Control Panel. To record voice annotations or other sounds, you must have a sound card and a sound source such as a microphone.

Using the Volume and Recording Controls

When using the Sound Recorder or the Media Player, you need to use the Volume Control window to set the recording and playback volume levels (see fig. 10.14). The Volume Control window is accessed from the \PROGRAMS\ACCESSORIES\ MULTIMEDIA folder, or by double-clicking the Speaker icon on the right side of the

Windows taskbar. When preparing to record, choose Options, Properties in the Volume Control window, check the Recording option and click OK. The Volume Control window changes to the Recording Control window shown in figure 10.15. Use the Recording Control window to select the input devices and to set the input volume levels.

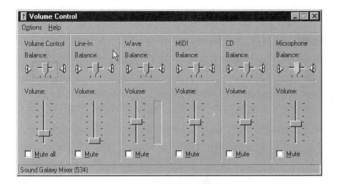

Fig. 10.14

The Volume Control window controls the playback levels for all sounds.

Fig. 10.15

The Recording Control window controls the recording volume levels for all the input devices.

Creating Word Forms

A Word form is an electronic version of a form that can be filled out online. A form contains a protected background of labels and boxes, plus fields to enter data. The labels and boxes describe and delineate the fields, showing the user what to type and where to type it. Thus, these forms are similar to a paper form that you fill out by hand, but these forms are filled out with a computer. They can also be printed and filled out by hand if you are so inclined. The big difference between paper forms and these electronic forms is that the fields have names, and their contents can be accessed electronically after a user has filled one out. The information in the forms can then be saved, sorted, and calculated.

A form is designed by first creating a document template containing all the descriptive text and boxes. You then add fields to the template to contain the information the user types, and then lock and save the template. Users work with the template to create a document which they fill out online.

Creating the Form Template

To create the form template, follow these steps:

1. Start with a new blank template by choosing File, New.

2. Select the Blank Document template, select the Template option and click OK. A new blank template appears on your screen.

3. Choose View, Toolbars, check the Forms toolbar, and click OK. The Forms toolbar appears as shown in figure 10.16, giving you access to the three types of form fields, plus controls to insert a table or frame, set the fields to gray or white, lock the template, and access the field properties.

Fig. 10.16

The Forms toolbar is used to create the fields and tables of an online form.

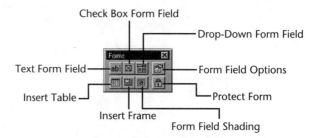

To create the template, type any text on the blank template needed to describe the fields on the form. Use tables and frames to align the text on the template and choose Format, Borders and Shading to create borders around the table cells to better delineate where the fields are. When the form is laid out, insert the cursor where a field is to go and click one of the field buttons on the Forms toolbar. A field is inserted at the cursor.

There are three different form fields you can insert on a Word form (see table 10.1).

Icon	Name	Description
Table 10.1 Three Form Fields Available for Online Forms		
ab|	Text Form Field	A simple, editable text box. Any text can be stored in it, and it can be set to test for the kind of information being typed into it.
⊠	Check Box Form Field	A checkbox for setting options. The checkboxes operate as independent options, so if you want mutually exclusive options, you must add code to the template to uncheck all the other checkboxes when one is checked. Macro procedures will be discussed later in this chapter.
▦	Drop-Down Form Field	A drop-down list of items used to select one of several fixed options.

> **Caution**
>
> Be sure to attach any macros that work with the template to the template file, and not to the global macro file (NORMAL.DOT). Otherwise, if you distribute your template, the people you distribute it to will not get the macros.

For example, figure 10.17 shows a template for a contacts database. The form was created by typing the heading and inserting a two-column by seven-row table. The descriptive information was then typed in the first column, and the two cells in the bottom row were merged into one cell using the Table, Merge Cells command. The Format, Borders and Shading command was used to outline some of the cells. The cursor was then inserted into the right column, next to *Name:* and the Text Form Field button was clicked, inserting a Text form field into the table cell.

Contacts Manager

Name:	
Address:	
City, State:	, CA ◆
Zip:	
Phone ?	☐ Yes
Phone Number:	
Notes:	

Fig. 10.17

The Contacts Manager form template provides a structured way to input contact information.

> **TIP**
>
> When creating a form, you can switch between viewing the field and viewing the field codes by pressing Alt+F9, or use Shift+F9 to change the currently selected field. The field codes tell what kind of a field it is.

Double-clicking the field opens the Text Form Field Options dialog box, shown in figure 10.18. Of the options in that dialog box, the important ones to set are the Bookmark, Fill-in Enabled, and Run Macro On options. The Bookmark text box lists the name of this text form field. It is used to access the field after it has been filled in. In this case, the default name was Text1, which was changed to the more descriptive TextName. The Fill-in Enabled checkbox determines if a user can type in the box when filling out the form. Here, it is checked. The Run Macro On boxes are the place to set a macro to run when the text field gets the focus and when the focus moves elsewhere. In this case, the macro CheckName is set to run when the focus moves away from this field. The CheckName macro was written to prevent the user from typing in the Notes field until he has inserted a name in the Name field. The other text fields on this form are filled out in much the same way.

The field that holds the abbreviation for the state name is a Drop-Down form field. Double-clicking it brings up the Drop-Down Field Options dialog box shown in figure 10.19. The important options to set in this dialog box are the same as for the Text form field, with the addition of the Items in Drop-Down List box. The Items in Drop-Down List box contain the names that appear in the drop-down list. To add a new item to the list, type its name in the Drop-Down Item box and click Add. To move an item, select it in the list and move it with the Move arrows. To delete it, select it and click Remove.

Fig. 10.18

Use the Text Form Field Options dialog box for setting text field options.

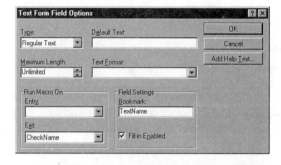

Fig. 10.19

The Drop-Down Form Field Options dialog box sets text field options.

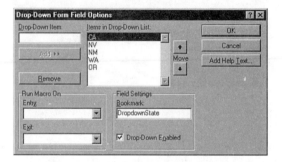

The Phone ? item on the Contacts Manager form (refer to fig. 10.17) is a Check Box form field followed by the text Yes. Double-clicking the checkbox displays the Check Box Form Field Options dialog box shown in figure 10.20. The important options are the same as for the Text form field, with the addition of the Default Value options. Here the checkbox is initially not checked, and the text field below it is disabled. Users cannot type in the Phone Number field unless they have checked the Phone ? checkbox. The CheckIsYes macro in the Run Macro on Exit box takes care of enabling or disabling the phone number field.

Fig. 10.20

The Check Box Form Field Options dialog box sets text field options.

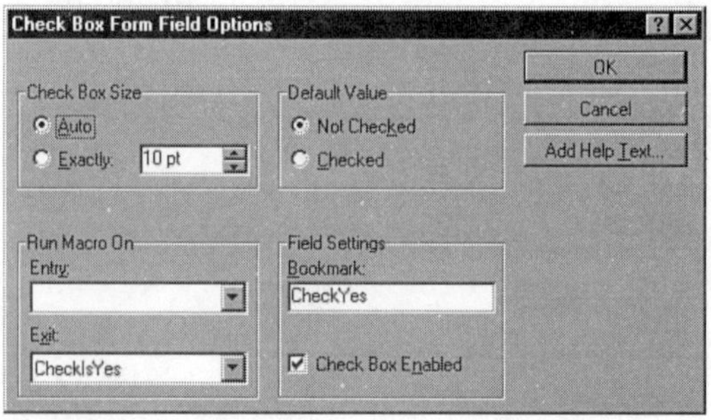

Adding Help to Fields

Help is added to these fields by clicking the Add Help Text button in each of the Options dialog boxes. Clicking the Add Help Text button displays the dialog box shown in figure 10.21. There are two places to add help for a field:

- On the status bar at the bottom of the page.
- In a dialog box that is activated by selecting the field and pressing key F1.

These two help options are set with the two tabs in the Form Field Help Text dialog boxes. To add help, select the tab you want and type the help text into the window.

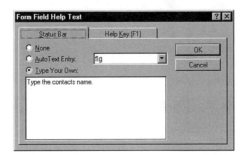

Fig. 10.21

The Form Field Help Text dialog box adds help to a dialog box and to the status bar.

Adding Code to the Form Template

There are two macro procedures attached to this form: the CheckName macro (see listing 10.1) to see that the TextName field has been filled in before the user can insert a note, and the CheckIsYes macro (see listing 10.2) to enable the Phone Number field when the user checks the Yes checkbox. The WordBasic programming language was discussed in Chapter 3 and will be considered again later in the chapter.

Listing 10.1   CONTACTS.DOT;CheckName. Disable Entry into the *TextNotes* Field Until a Name Has Been Typed

```
Sub MAIN
'Enable the Notes field if Name is filled in.
cEnabled = 1
cDisabled = 0
If GetFormResult$("TextName") = "" Then
    EnableFormField "TextNotes", cDisabled
Else
    EnableFormField "TextNotes", cEnabled
End If
End Sub
```

Listing 10.2   CONTACTS.DOT;CheckIsYes. Enable the Phone Field if the Check Box Is Checked

```
Sub MAIN
'Enable the Phone field if the check box is checked.
cEnabled = 1
cDisabled = 0
cChecked = 1
If GetFormResult("CheckYes") = cChecked Then
   EnableFormField "Phone", cEnabled
   EditGoTo .Destination = "Phone"
Else
   EnableFormField "Phone", cEnabled
   EditGoTo .Destination = "Phone"
   ClearFormField
   EnableFormField "Phone", cDisabled
End If
End Sub
```

The CheckName macro defines the constants cEnabled and cDisabled and then tests the contents of the TextName text field with a block If statement. If the TextName field is empty, the EnableFormField function is used to disable the TextNotes field. If it is not empty, EnableFormField is used again to enable the TextNotes field.

The CheckIsYes macro is similar to CheckName, but it first tests the value of the checkbox. For a checkbox, the GetFormResult function returns a 1 if the box is checked, or a 0 if it is not. If the checkbox is checked, the Phone text field is enabled and the focus is moved there. If the checkbox is not checked, the macro enables the Phone text field, selects it, clears its contents, and then disables it. This is to ensure that the field is empty if the checkbox is not checked.

Saving the Form Template

The form template is now ready to use. Click the Form Field Shading button to re-move the shading. Click the Protect Form button on the Forms toolbar and save the template into the TEMPLATES folder. It can now be used by someone to fill out the form.

Caution

The form template must be protected in order to use it. If you don't protect it, clicking the form fields displays the Form Field Options dialog boxes instead of letting you type in the fields.

Using the Form and Saving the Data

To use the form, choose File, New, select the form template, select the document op-tion, and click OK. The form should be displayed on your screen for you to use. Fill in the form by typing the appropriate responses. Use Tab, the arrow keys, or the mouse to switch to different fields. Figure 10.22 shows a filled-in form.

Contacts Manager

Name:	William J. Orvis
Address:	123 Thishereroad St.
City, State:	Livermore, CA
Zip:	94550
Phone ?	☒ Yes
Phone Number:	123-456-7890

Notes: This guy writes books in his spare time.

Fig. 10.22

When complete, the forms for the Contacts database can be filled out by a user.

When you are finished filling in the form, you need to save the information contained in it. If you save the form as a Normal document, all the text on the form—including the fixed labels—is saved with it. That is, the saved form is a copy of what you see on-screen. To save only the data in the fields and none of the other stuff, choose Tools, Options, Save tab, and check Save Data Only for Forms. Now when you save the form, it is saved as a text document containing only the contents of the form fields, separated by commas. When the form shown in figure 10.22 is saved, the file contains the following text (found in CONTACT.TXT):

```
"William J. Orvis","123 Thishereroad St.","Livermore","CA","94550",1,
➥"123-456-7890","This guy writes books in his spare time."
```

On the CD

Caution

Be sure to uncheck Save Data Only for Forms once you are finished. Otherwise, if you save a document that has a single form field in it, only the contents of that field are saved, skipping the rest of the document.

Alternatively, you could write a macro program to copy the values from each of the fields and save them in whatever format you prefer.

Manipulating Documents with WordBasic

While most people realize that Word is a high-powered word processor with more features than anyone ever expects to use, few think of it as a programming environment. Word contains a basic interpreter known as WordBasic. While it's not Visual Basic for Applications, WordBasic is a full-featured Basic programming environment, with extensions to allow it to access and edit the contents of Word documents and to execute Word commands.

Within Word, WordBasic procedures are created on named macro sheets. The procedures are called using the name of the macro sheet. The main procedure is named Main, and is the procedure that is run when the macro is called. The macro sheet may contain other procedures that are called by the Main procedure.

III

Advanced Integration

NOTE   Controlling Word must proceed differently from fully OLE Automation-compliant applications, because Word does not expose its objects the way Excel does. Word exposes only the `Word.Basic` object, which contains the WordBasic language. That language is then used to manipulate Word documents.

Controlling Word with WordBasic

WordBasic is a relatively standard version of the Basic programming language, with special extensions for accessing the contents of a document. The language itself is closer to traditional Basic language, rather than one of the newer object-oriented Basics such as Visual Basic. While not the latest and greatest implementation of Basic technology, it is a completely functional language, capable of controlling Word and editing any document.

NOTE   The functions in WordBasic are documented in the WordBasic online help file. This help file is not installed in the standard installation. To install it, you must do a custom installation and explicitly select it. If you have already installed Word, run Setup again to add the WordBasic help files.

WordBasic has hundreds of functions and statements in more than 40 categories. All of the functions and statements are listed in the online help. Most of the control type statements follow the menu structure used to execute the function manually. For example, the command to make Word open a new document file is `FileOpen`; the command for copying the current selection is `EditCopy`; and so forth.

NOTE   WordBasic procedures with the same names as the built-in commands replace those commands. For example, if you create a procedure named `EditCopy`, that procedure is run whenever you choose the Copy command on the Edit menu.

Using the Macro Recorder

The easiest way to determine what functions are necessary to perform some application level task and to see what the correct syntax is for the WordBasic statements is to turn on the macro recorder and record the task as you perform it. For example, assume you want to create a procedure to perform the following tasks:

1. Create a new document.
2. Open the file CONTACT1.TXT containing the output of the form created previously (or some other file if you don't have that one available).
3. Select the contents of the file.
4. Copy the contents of the file.

5. Switch to the new document.

6. Paste the contents of the Clipboard into the new document.

7. Save the new document as **SUMMARY.DOC**.

8. Close both documents.

To learn what WordBasic statements would be needed to perform these series of steps, record those steps in a macro by following these steps:

1. Start the macro recorder. Choose Tools, Macro, and click the Record button in the Macro dialog box. The Record Macro dialog box appears as shown in figure 10.23.

Fig. 10.23

The Record Macro dialog box allows you to set the name and location for a recorded macro.

2. Type the name **Record1** for the macro. You can also add a description and attach the macro to a menu or toolbar if you want.

3. Click OK to start recording a new macro in the global macro file. The Macro Recorder toolbar appears to stop the recording when you are done.

4. Perform the tasks listed earlier and click the Stop button on the Macro Recorder toolbar.

NOTE When using the Macro Recorder, you cannot use the mouse to select text. You can only use it to choose commands or to scroll the document. To move the insertion point in the text, use the arrow keys; to select text, hold down the Shift key and move the insertion point across the text with the arrow keys.

To see the macro, choose Tools, Macro, select Record1 from the list, and click Edit. Listing 10.3 contains the macro procedure that was recorded. A *procedure* is a series of programming statements that are grouped together to perform some task.

III

Advanced Integration

Listing 10.3 EXAMPLES.DOT:Record1. The Procedure Recorded While Opening Files and Copying Text

```
Sub MAIN
FileNew .Template = "D:\msoffice\Templates\Normal.dot", .NewTemplate = 0
FileOpen .Name = "contact1.txt", .ConfirmConversions = 0, .ReadOnly = 0,
➡.AddToMru = 0, .PasswordDoc = "", .PasswordDot = "", .Revert = 0,
➡.WritePasswordDoc = "", .WritePasswordDot = ""
LineDown 2, 1
EditCopy
WindowList 3
EditPaste
FileSaveAs .Name = "summary.doc", .Format = 0, .LockAnnot = 0, .Password ="",
➡.AddToMru = 1, .WritePassword = "", .RecommendReadOnly = 0, .EmbedFonts = 0,
➡.NativePictureFormat = 0, .FormsData = 0, .SaveAsAOCELetter = 0
FileClose
FileClose
End Sub
```

By examining the listing, you see that `FileNew` is called to create the new document, and then `FileOpen` is called to open the second document. The `LineDown` statement is called to select the text in the first document, then `EditCopy` is called to put it on the Clipboard. The `WindowList` statement is called to switch to the new document, then `EditPaste` is called to paste the contents of the Clipboard there. Finally, `FileSaveAs` is called to save the new document, and `FileClose` is called twice to close the two documents.

Clearly, this procedure isn't general purpose, but is restricted to the exact list of open files and number of lines found in those files that were present when the macro was recorded. Only a few changes are necessary to make it more general so that it can copy any number of lines from a specific file. First, all the options are included for the `FileNew`, `FileOpen`, and `FileSaveAs` statements, even though most of them are set to their default values. All of the options with default values can be removed. The `LineDown` statement used to select the contents of the first document only works on a two-line document. It should be changed to an `EditSelectAll` statement to select everything there.

The `WindowList` statement selects the third item on the current list of open windows. Because you can't always be sure how many open windows there are when you start this macro, you need to save the window name when the document is opened, and then search for the window by name when you need to display it.

To change a recorded macro, or any macro for that matter, simply use the same editing techniques used to edit a Word document. Listing 10.4 contains the revised macro created by editing the recorded macro.

Listing 10.4   EXAMPLES.DOT:Record2. The Revised Recorded Procedure

```
'
' Record2 Macro
' Open files and copy data
'
Sub MAIN
'Create a new document.
FileNew .Template = "D:\msoffice\Templates\Normal.dot", .NewTemplate = 0
'Save its window name.
strNewWindowName$ = WindowName$()
'Open contact1.txt.
FileOpen .Name = "d:\My Documents\BIOA Book\contact1.txt"
'Select everything and copy it.
EditSelectAll
EditCopy
'Find the window number for the new document.
For iintLoop = 1 To CountWindows()
    If WindowName$(iintLoop) = strNewWindowName$ Then
        intWinNum = iintLoop
    EndIf
Next iintLoop
'Activate the new window and paste.
WindowList intWinNum
EditPaste
'Save the new window as summary.doc.
FileSaveAs .Name = "d:\My Documents\BIOA Book\summary.doc"
'Close all files.
FileClose
FileClose
End Sub
```

The first thing you notice in the revised procedure is that it contains lines starting with a single quotation mark. Lines of this type are *comments* that are included to help you remember what it is you are doing in the procedure. Comments have no effect on the execution of the procedure, but considerably improve the readability of the procedure.

After the new document is created, the window name is saved to use later when you need to find it again. While you could save the window number in the window list, that number could change, depending on the name of the next document that is opened.

Next, the CONTACT1.TXT file is opened. All the options but the file name have been removed, and the full path to the file has been inserted. The full path ensures that even if the default directory is changed, the file can still be found. EditSelectAll replaces the LineDown statement to ensure that the whole document is selected, and the contents are copied.

NOTE The path used in this example reflects where the file happened to be on my system. Change it to point to where you have the files stored on your system.

III

Advanced Integration

The next block of code is a For/Next loop that loops over all the open windows looking for the new document created at the beginning of this procedure. When the window is found, its current position in the window list is saved. Following the loop, the `WindowList` statement is used to open the window that was just found, and the `EditPaste` statement is used to paste the information at the end.

The `FileSaveAs` command has had all its options but the file name removed, plus the full path to the file is added to ensure it is written in the correct place. Finally, the two documents are closed.

A useful variation of this procedure would be to add it to the Contacts Database form, and use it to add the new data to the end of a file. A small change to the procedure is needed to make it add the new data to the end of an existing file instead of creating a new file each time. Change the initial `FileNew` command to a `FileOpen` command, then use the `EndOfDocument` statement to move to the end of the document before pasting the new information there.

Moving Around in a Word Document

Now that you can open a document, you need to be able to move around in it to find things. Table 10.2 contains some of the more common cursor movement and selection statements and functions. In addition, there are many find statements that look for everything from words and formats (`GoToNextItem`, `GoToPreviousItem`), to bookmarks (`EditGoto`). You can take your pick of ways to locate things in a document. A complete list of the available statements is in the online help.

Table 10.2 Some of the More Common Move and Select Statements and Functions

Statement	Description
AtEndOfDocument()	True if you are at the end of the document.
AtStartOfDocument()	True if you are at the start of the document.
CharLeft, CharLeft()	Moves the insertion point one character to the left.
CharRight, CharRight()	Moves the insertion point one character to the right.
EditSelectAll	Selects the whole document.
EndOfDocument, EndOfDocument()	Moves to the end of the document.
EndOfLine, EndOfLine()	Moves to the end of the current line.
GetSelEndPos()	Returns the character number of the end of the selection.
GetSelStartPos()	Returns the character number of the beginning of the selection.
GetText$()	Returns text from the document. Not related to the current selection.
GoToNextItem	Moves to next item, where item is Annotation, Endnote, Footnote, Page, Section, or Subdocument.

Statement	Description
GoToPreviousItem	Moves to the previous item, where item is Annotation, Endnote, Footnote, Page, Section, or Subdocument.
Insert	Inserts text at the current position.
LineDown, LineDown()	Moves down one or more lines.
LineUp, LineUp()	Moves up one or more lines.
StartOfDocument, StartOfDocument()	Moves to start of the document.
StartOfLine, StartOfLine()	Moves to beginning of the current line.
VLine	Moves one or more lines vertically.
VPage	Moves one or more pages vertically.
WordLeft, WordLeft()	Moves one word to the left.
WordRight, WordRight()	Moves one word to the right.

NOTE Position in a document is measured in characters from the beginning of the document, with the very beginning of the file being position 0.

TIP If you know where something is going to go, a bookmark is the best method for marking that position. Bookmarks maintain their position relative to the text in a document, unlike the character position that changes as text is added or removed from a document.

Editing Text in a Document

To edit text in a document, you first must select it. Most of the insertion point move commands have a `Select` argument that treats the move as if you were holding down the Shift key while moving the cursor. The effect is to select the text starting from the initial position of the cursor to the current position. Text selection is cumulative, as long as the `Select` argument is True for each move statement. If you know the character positions of the text you want to select, use the `SetSelRange` statement to select it. Other selection commands are listed in the online help.

To insert text at the current insertion point, use the `Insert` statement. `Insert` is the same as typing at the keyboard, and replaces the current selection with the text used as its argument. To get a copy of the text between two character positions, use **GetText$**. To get the text of the current selection, use

GetText$(GetSelStartPos(),GetSelEndPos())

Using the Built-In Dialog Boxes

An important feature of WordBasic is the capability to create dialog boxes. A *dialog box* is a simple way to send a message to the user, or to get information from the user. Dialog boxes are useful in that they can put text on-screen or have the user type something without disturbing the current document. There are two pre-created dialog boxes for you to use: MsgBox and InputBox. The MsgBox function displays a simple message to the user and can return one of up to three button presses (OK, Yes, No, Cancel, Abort, or Retry). Figure 10.24 shows the MsgBox created with the following statements (found in the procedure DisplayDialogs in EXAMPLES.DOT):

```
strMsg$ = "What you are about to do cannot be undone.
➥Do you want to continue?"
strTitle$ = "WARNING"
intOptions = 4 + 48'Yes/No buttons + Attention symbol
intReply = MsgBox(strMsg$, strTitle$, intOptions)
```

The variable `intReply` contains a number that indicates what button was pressed.

Fig. 10.24

A MsgBox dialog box can display the Yes/No reply option.

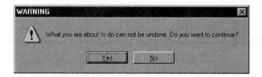

> **TIP**
>
> The MsgBox function can also display text in the status bar by using a negative argument for the button options.

An InputBox is similar to the MsgBox, with the addition of a text box for the user to type a reply, and only provides OK and Cancel buttons. Figure 10.25 shows the InputBox created with the following statements (found in the procedure DisplayDialogs in EXAMPLE.DOT):

```
strPrompt$ = "Please type the file name."
strTitle$ = "File Input Dialog"
strDefault$ = "myfile.doc"
On Error Resume Next
strReply$ = InputBox$(strPrompt$, strTitle$, strDefault$)
If err = 102 Then
    REM The user pressed Cancel
    REM Handle it here.
On Error Goto 0
End If
```

The string `strReply$` contains the text typed by the user. If the user clicks Cancel, the dialog box generates an error. The error is trapped with the On Error statement, which tells the code to continue with the next line. The If statement checks to see if Error 102 has occurred, indicating that the function failed (the user pressed Cancel) and provides a place to do something different when the user presses Cancel. The second On Error statement turns off the error trapping.

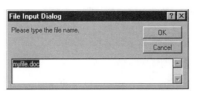

Fig. 10.25

This InputBox dialog box is requesting a file name.

Caution

The operation of the InputBox function appears very similar to that of the same function in Visual Basic, but the operation that occurs when Cancel is pressed is different and must be handled with code differently from the Visual Basic function.

Creating Custom Dialog Boxes

If the built-in dialog boxes don't suit your needs, you can create custom dialog boxes, complete with buttons, lists, pictures, and text boxes. Table 10.3 lists some of the more commonly used statements and functions for creating and using dialog boxes. See the online help for a complete list.

Table 10.3   Dialog Box Statements and Functions

Statement	Description
Begin Dialog..End Dialog	Marks the beginning and end of a dialog box description.
CancelButton	Creates a Cancel button in a dialog box.
CheckBox	Creates a checkbox in a dialog box.
ComboBox	Creates a combo box in a dialog box.
Dialog, Dialog()	Displays the selected dialog box.
DialogEditor	Starts up the Dialog Editor.
DlgFocus, DlgFocus$()	Moves the focus to a specific dialog box item.
DlgListBoxArray, DlgListBoxArray()	Fills a list box with items.
DlgText, DlgText$()	Loads text in a dialog box item.
DlgValue, DlgValue()	Loads a value into a dialog box item.
DropListBox	Adds a drop-down list to a dialog box.
FilePreview	Inserts a file preview window in a dialog box.
GetCurValues	Gets values from a Word dialog box.
GroupBox	Adds a group box.
ListBox	Adds a list box to a dialog box.
OKButton	Adds an OK button to a dialog box.

(continues)

III

Advanced Integration

Table 10.3 Continued	
Statement	**Description**
OptionButton	Adds an option button to a dialog box.
OptionGroup	Creates a series of option buttons in a dialog box.
Picture	Creates a picture in a dialog box.
PushButton	Creates a pushbutton in a dialog box.
Text	Creates a label in a dialog box.
TextBox	Creates a text box in a dialog box.

To create a custom dialog box, you must first define it with a block of code surrounded by the `Begin Dialog` and `End Dialog` statements. Between these two statements, place statements to define the buttons and boxes you want on the custom dialog box. While you can type all of this by hand, it is much simpler to use the Dialog Editor included with Word (see fig. 10.26). To create a dialog box, run the Dialog Editor and draw your interface. Use the Item menu to add items to the dialog box, then drag them to their location. Double-click an item to see and change its properties. One property is `.Field`, which contains the item identifiers (the names of the items) used to access the items in code.

TIP You can start the Dialog Editor from within Word by clicking the Dialog Editor button on the Macro toolbar.

Fig. 10.26

The Dialog Editor included with Word is used to design custom dialog boxes.

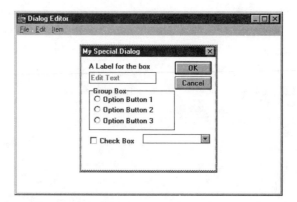

When your dialog box is complete, select the dialog box, copy it, and paste it into a macro. The following dialog box definition is created for the dialog box shown in figure 10.26:

```
Begin Dialog UserDialog 320, 184, "My Special Dialog"
    OKButton 223, 6, 88, 21
```

```
      CancelButton 223, 30, 88, 21
      Text 19, 8, 145, 13, "A Label for the box", .Text1
      TextBox 19, 24, 160, 18, .TextBox1
      GroupBox 19, 48, 204, 69, "Group Box"
      OptionGroup  .OptionGroup2
         OptionButton 29, 60, 148, 16, "Option Button 1", .OptionButton1
         OptionButton 29, 77, 148, 16, "Option Button 2", .OptionButton2
         OptionButton 29, 94, 148, 16, "Option Button 3", .OptionButton3
      CheckBox 21, 126, 111, 16, "Check Box", .CheckBox1
      DropListBox 146, 124, 160, 60, DropListBox1$(), .DropListBox1
   End Dialog
```

TIP

You can also copy a dialog definition and paste it into the Dialog Editor to edit an existing dialog box.

Caution

If a drop-down list is defined to drop down beyond the bottom of the dialog box, you get an `Out of range` error when you run the code to display the dialog box. The Dialog Editor does not test if a drop-down list drops beyond the bottom of the dialog box.

To use the dialog box defined earlier, declare and fill the `strDropListBox1$()` array with items for the drop-down list box, declare the dialog box, define a dialog record variable, and call the `Dialog` function to display the dialog box. Listing 10.5 shows the statements needed to display the custom dialog box, and figure 10.27 shows the dialog box produced by the code.

Listing 10.5   EXAMPLES.DOT:CustomDialog. Define and Display a Custom Dialog Box

On the CD

```
Sub MAIN
'Define an array to hold the items in the drop-down list.
Dim strDropListBox1$(5)
'Fill the array with items for the drop-down list.
strDropListBox1$(0) = "Item 0"
strDropListBox1$(1) = "Item 1"
strDropListBox1$(2) = "Item 2"
strDropListBox1$(3) = "Item 3"
strDropListBox1$(4) = "Item 4"
strDropListBox1$(5) = "Item 5"
'Declare the dialog box
Begin Dialog UserDialog 320, 184, "My Special Dialog"
   KButton 223, 6, 88, 21
   CancelButton 223, 30, 88, 21
   Text 19, 8, 145, 13, "A Label for the box", .Text1
   TextBox 19, 24, 160, 18, .TextBox1
   GroupBox 19, 48, 204, 69, "Group Box"
   OptionGroup  .OptionGroup2
```

III

Advanced Integration

(continues)

Listing 10.5 Continued

```
        OptionButton 29, 60, 148, 16, "Option Button 1", .OptionButton1
        OptionButton 29, 77, 148, 16, "Option Button 2", .OptionButton2
        OptionButton 29, 94, 148, 16, "Option Button 3", .OptionButton3
    CheckBox 21, 126, 111, 16, "Check Box", .CheckBox1
    DropListBox 146, 124, 160, 60, strDropListBox1$(), .DropListBox1
End Dialog
'Define a dialog record.
Dim dlgMyDialog As UserDialog
'Define some constants.
cDisabled = 1
cEnabled = 0
'Disable keyboard interrupts.
DisableInput cDisabled
'Display the dialog box and return the button pressed.
intButton = Dialog(dlgMyDialog)
'Turn keyboard interrupts back on.
DisableInput cEnabled
End Sub
```

Fig. 10.27

The custom dialog box that was produced by running the code in listing 10.5.

Now that you have a dialog box displayed, you need to get access to the fields so you can see what the user typed. The Dialog() function itself returns the number of the button the user pressed to close the dialog box (-1, OK button; 0, Cancel button; 1, first button; and so forth). To access the rest of the items, combine the name of the dialog record with the item identifier in the dialog box definition. The item *identifier* is the last argument on the right—beginning with a dot—for each item. For example, .TextBox1 is the identifier for the text box. To access the contents of the text box, type the following code:

```
strResult$ = dlgMyDialog.TextBox1
```

To access the option buttons, type

```
optionResult = dlgMyDialog.OptionGroup2
```

The variable optionResult receives the number of the selected option button in the group. The buttons are numbered starting with 0 for the first button, 1 for the second, and so forth. Getting the contents of the other items follows in the same manner.

Custom Menus and Toolbars

The menus and toolbars used in Word are customized by choosing Tools, Customize. These objects can also be customized using WordBasic code. The simplest way to do this is to turn on the macro recorder and then make the changes manually. The code generated by the macro recorder can then be edited and combined with a WordBasic program to automatically make the changes.

To change an existing menu command, create a macro with the same name as the command. For example, create a macro named `FileOpen` to replace the File, Open command. If a macro exists in the active or global template with the same name as a built-in command, the macro replaces the built-in command. When you create a macro with the same name as a built-in command, Word automatically inserts code in that macro to execute the original command, which you can modify as needed.

Using Word as an OLE Automation Server

Word can operate as an OLE Automation server, for Word documents embedded in other applications and for remote controlling the Word application itself. WordBasic is the controller language for Word, but is not itself OLE Automation-compliant. Word has a single object called Basic that is OLE Automation-compliant, and can receive commands from other applications. Basic cannot control the application itself, but issues WordBasic commands to do the actual controlling.

> **NOTE**
> While Word can be an OLE Automation client, WordBasic cannot be used as the controller for an OLE Automation client. WordBasic does not have the capability to access OLE Automation objects in other applications. If you want a compound document with the Word format, you must control it by using Visual Basic or VBA.

Accessing the WordBasic Object

To remotely edit Word documents, you must access the Basic object and issue WordBasic commands. This is quite different from other OLE Automation-compliant applications where you directly manipulate the objects (documents) themselves. To access the `Word.Basic` object from Visual Basic for Applications or Visual Basic, you must first declare and create an object variable. There are two ways to do this, depending on where the Word document is that you want to access with Visual Basic. In both cases, you must first declare an object variable to hold the WordBasic object.

```
Dim objWordBasic As Object
```

If you want to start the Word application and open a connection to it, use the `CreateObject()` function to do so.

```
Set objWordBasic = CreateObject("Word.Basic")
```

If you want to use WordBasic to access a Word document embedded in an Excel worksheet, first create another object variable and use the `OLEObjects` collection to find the embedded document and open a connection to it. For example, if the embedded document is named XYZCO.DOC, you would use the following statements to open a connection to the document:

```
Dim objEmbeddedDoc As Object
Set objEmbeddedDoc = ActiveSheet.OLEObjects("xyzco.doc")
```

This opens a connection to the embedded document. WordBasic is in the `Object` property of the embedded document. To access WordBasic, create another object variable to point to it:

```
Set objWordBasic = objEmbeddedDoc.Object.Application.WordBasic
```

 NOTE The name of an embedded Word document is the name that appears in the name box on the Excel worksheet when the object is selected. Most Word documents have the default names `Picture` *n* where *n* is a number.

For Visual Basic, use the `Object` property of the control that the Word document is embedded in to get access to WordBasic, such as

```
Set objWordBasic = MyControl.Object.Application.WordBasic
```

where `MyControl` is some Visual Basic control.

Using WordBasic Statements in Visual Basic for Applications

At this point, you have created a link to the `Word.Basic` object. Now, you can use that link to execute WordBasic commands. Most of the WordBasic statements and functions are available to be executed through the `Word.Basic` object. The statements that are not available are variable declarations (`Dim`), program control structures (`If`, `For`, `While`, `Case`), statements associated with custom dialog boxes, any function that requires an array variable as an argument, and the `FileExit` statement. In any event, you would use the Visual Basic versions of these commands instead of the WordBasic versions.

To execute a WordBasic statement using Visual Basic for Applications, treat the WordBasic statement as a method of the object variable that points to `Word.Basic`. For example, to execute the `FileNew` statement, type the following Visual Basic statement:

```
objWordBasic.FileNew Template := "D:\msoffice\Templates\Normal.dot",
➥NewTemplate := 0
```

where `objWordBasic` is the object variable pointing to the `Word.Basic` object. Note also that the syntax of the named arguments has changed to the Visual Basic for Applications versions, with the period prefix removed and the equals sign replaced with colon equals.

NOTE

WordBasic statements that return a string end in a $. To use them, enclose them in square brackets or leave off the $. Both of the following statements are valid in Visual Basic for Applications:

```
strWinName$ = objWordBasic.[WindowName$](3)

strWinName$ = objWordBasic.WindowName(3)
```

The following three statements have both a version with and without a $. They must be used with brackets so that Word.Basic can determine which of the two versions of each statement to execute.

```
Font$()

GetSystemInfo$()

Language$()
```

NOTE

An embedded object must be activated before you can access it. Use the Activate method of the control the Word document is embedded in to activate the document. For example,

```
MyControl.Activate
```

In Visual Basic 3, setting the Action property of the container control to 7 does the same thing:

```
MyControl.Action = 7
```

NOTE

If you start Word by declaring a Word.Basic object variable, Word will exit when that variable becomes undefined. If Word is already running when the object variable is defined, undefining the variable does not end Word. You can undefine the object variable by setting it equal to Nothing:

```
Set objWordBasic = Nothing
```

Accessing an External Word Document

To control Word external to the OLE controller application, such as Excel, create a WordBasic object and apply the WordBasic commands to it. For example, consider the Record2 macro procedure developed earlier in this chapter that creates a file, opens a file, copies data from one to the other, and then saves the files. The following procedure implements the same procedure but uses Visual Basic for Applications in Excel to control the Word program (see listing 10.6).

III

Advanced Integration

On the CD

Listing 10.6   EXAMPLES.XLS:Record3. Visual Basic for Applications Version of the *Record2* Procedure

```
Option Explicit
'
' Record3 Macro
' Open files and copy data
'
Sub Record3()
Dim objWordBasic As Object
Dim strNewWindowName As String
Dim iintI As Integer
Dim intWinNum As Integer

'Create the Word.Basic object.
Set objWordBasic = CreateObject("Word.Basic")
'Create a new document.
objWordBasic.FileNew Template:="D:\msoffice\Templates\Normal.dot",_
    NewTemplate:=0
'Save its window name.
strNewWindowName = objWordBasic.WindowName$()
'Open contact1.txt.
objWordBasic.FileOpen Name:="d:\My Documents\BIOA Book\contact1.txt"
'Select everything and copy it.
objWordBasic.EditSelectAll
objWordBasic.EditCopy
'Find the window number for the new document.
For iintLoop = 1 To objWordBasic.CountWindows()
    If objWordBasic.[WindowName$](iintLoop) = strNewWindowName Then
        intWinNum = iintLoop
    End If
Next iintLoop
'Activate the new window and paste.
objWordBasic.WindowList intWinNum
objWordBasic.EditPaste
'Save the new window as summary.doc.
objWordBasic.FileSaveAs Name:="d:\My Documents\BIOA Book\summary.doc"
'Close all files.
objWordBasic.FileClose
objWordBasic.FileClose
End Sub
```

To convert a WordBasic macro procedure to a Visual Basic for Applications procedure, follow these steps:

1. Declare and set an object variable such as objWordBasic to point to the Word.Basic object.

2. Insert the object variable container (objWordBasic.) before all WordBasic statements.

3. For statements with named arguments, remove the period before the name and replace the = with :=.

4. Surround any WordBasic statements that end in a $ with square brackets.

5. Insert **Option Explicit** at the top and declare all the variables. Declare string variables without the $ postfix.

Accessing an Embedded Word Document

If you want to edit an embedded document instead of running Word remotely, the methods of coding for OLE Automation are essentially identical. The only differences are the Set statement that creates the object variable pointing to Word.Basic, and the fact that the document is already open for editing. For example, the Visual Basic for Applications procedure in listing 10.7 searches this paragraph embedded in a worksheet for the word Automation and replaces it with the words Remote Control.

> **Listing 10.7 EXAMPLES.XLS:ReplaceIt. Visual Basic for Applications Procedure to Replace Automation with Remote Control in an Embedded Word Document**

On the CD

```
Option Explicit
'
' ReplaceIt
' Search an embedded Word document for Automation and replace it with
' Remote Control.
'
Sub ReplaceIt()
Dim objWordBasic As Object
Dim objEmbeddedDoc As Object
'Create a link to the embedded document.
Set objEmbeddedDoc = ActiveSheet.OLEObjects("Picture 1")
'Create a link to WordBasic through the embedded document.
Set objWordBasic = objEmbeddedDoc.Object.Application.WordBasic
'Activate the embedded document.
objEmbeddedDoc.Activate
'Use WordBasic to move to the beginning of the doucment.
objWordBasic.StartOfDocument
'Find and replace the word Automation.
objWordBasic.EditReplace Find:="Automation",
➥Replace:="Remote Control", WholeWord:=1, ReplaceOne:=1
'Undefine the object variables.
Set objWordBasic = Nothing
Set objEmbeddedDoc = Nothing
'Unactivate the document by activating cell A1.
ActiveSheet.Range("A1").Activate
End Sub
```

This procedure first creates and defines two object variables: objEmbeddedDoc, pointing to the embedded document; and objWordBasic, pointing to the WordBasic object. Next, the embedded document is activated by applying the Activate method to its object variable (not the WordBasic object variable). The procedure then moves the insertion point to the beginning of the document in case it has been changed, and executes the EditReplace statement to find the word Automation and replace it with Remote Control. Figure 10.28 shows the activated document just after this step.

Finally, the procedure undefines the object variable and deactivates the embedded document by selecting cell A1.

Fig. 10.28

A Word document embedded in Excel is automatically edited by a VBA procedure.

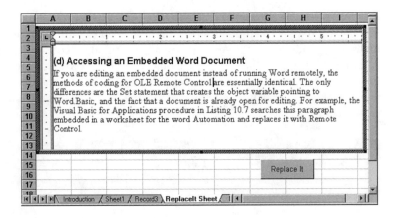

Preparing Macros for Macro Viruses

An unfortunate new development in the Word macro area is the macro virus. A Word *macro virus* is a self-replicating program written in Word.Basic. The number of known word macro viruses has grown from one to five just in the last month and is likely to get worse as time goes on. As a writer of Word.Basic programs, you need to be prepared to protect yourself from these viruses and to work with the anti-virus programs designed to detect and eradicate the viruses.

Operation of Macro Viruses

Macro viruses use the autoexecute macros of Word.Basic to activate themselves. The autoexecute macros are the following:

- *AutoExec*. Executes whenever Word starts if it is in the global macro file.
- *AutoOpen*. Executes when a document is opened.
- *AutoClose*. Executes when a document is closed.
- *AutoExit*. Executes when Word exits.
- *AutoSave*. Executes when a document is saved.

Most macro viruses contain an AutoOpen macro that runs when the infected document is opened and copies the virus code onto the global macro template (NORMAL.DOT). Once there, the virus replaces one or more of the menu commands or uses an autoexecute macro to copy itself onto new documents. For example, it could replace the File, Save command and save itself on the document being saved.

Some of these viruses have payloads that trigger on some event, such as the date. One payload changes the screen colors, while another deletes all the files on your hard drive, making these viruses a serious problem. You don't want your system to be infected with a macro virus and, even worse, you definitely don't want to deliver a macro containing a macro virus to someone else.

Detecting Macro Viruses

There are three ways to scan for a macro virus:

- Use an anti-virus utility.
- Check a document for the virus macros.
- Use the Microsoft Macro Virus Detection macro.

Most current anti-virus utilities have been modified to detect macro viruses in Word documents. You can use these utilities to scan documents in the same way that they are used to scan executable files for viruses.

As macro viruses are made up of Word.Basic macros, you can detect them in a document by checking the list of macros on your system for ones that should not be there. Choose Tools, Macro to examine the available macros and check out any that you don't recognize. Be especially concerned about unknown autoexecute macros or macros that replace menu commands.

Some macro viruses replace the Tools, Macro command, and fix it so that you cannot see the attached macros. If this is the case, use the Organizer to open a document in the background and check for attached macros. There are two ways to open the Organizer dialog box: choose File, Templates or Tools, Macro. In both cases, click the Organizer button in the dialog box that appears. In the Organizer dialog box, you can open a document and view or delete any macros attached to it.

To combat Word macro viruses, Microsoft has made available a detection macro that scans documents as you open them to see if they contain macros. If they do, the detection macro displays a dialog box telling you that the document you are opening contains macros and gives you the option to remove them or open it anyway. The macro is available directly from Microsoft at its Internet site. If you have a Web browser, connect to

http://www.microsoft.com/msoffice

to find the latest version of the macro virus detector. If you don't have Internet access, the macro is available in the Microsoft Word forums on most online services or by calling Microsoft's Product Support Services at 206-462-9673 for Word for Windows, and 206-635-7200 for Word for the Macintosh.

Working with the Detection Macro

A problem with the macro virus detection macros is that they use up some of the special macro names that you might have intended to use in a program. The current version (2) of the detection macro installs the following macros in your global macro file:

```
AutoExit      FileOpen
ShellOpen     InsertVer
```

If you are writing macros that must coexist with the detection macros, you must not use any of these macro names for your macros or they will conflict. If you must use one of these names, you have to edit the protection macro to include your code. Each of the protection macros has a marked place for inserting user code. For example, if you must have a `FileOpen` macro in your program to modify the File, Open command, you need to edit the `ShellOpen` macro and insert your code there. (The `FileOpen` macro simply calls the `ShellOpen` macro which does the actual work.) You must make these modifications in every template that contains a `FileOpen` macro, or the template's command replaces the protection macro whenever a document based on the template is active. Instructions are included with the protection macro for inserting modifications.

Representative Examples of Integrating Word Documents

In this section are several examples of using WordBasic and Visual Basic for Applications to control Word and edit a Word document.

Starting Word in Excel and Passing It the Current Selection

The task here is to have a button in Excel that starts Word with a blank document, inserts the contents of the current selection, and then leaves Word running. All these steps are straightforward, except for the last one. Normally, when Word is run by Excel, it is run hidden in the background and then ended when the Visual Basic for Applications program ends. To get around this problem, make sure Word is already running before connecting to it with OLE Automation.

On the CD

> **Listing 10.8 EXAMPLES.XLS:StartNPass. Visual Basic for Applications Procedure to Replace Automation with Remote Control in an Embedded Word Document**

```
Option Explicit
'
' StartNPass Procedure
' Start Word And Pass It The Current Selection
' leave Word running.
'
Sub StartNPass()
Dim objWordBasic As Object
'Copy the current selection onto the Clipboard.
Selection.Copy
'We want Word to stay running after this procedure ends, so
'make sure it is running before connecting an object variable to it.
'See if Word is running.
On Error Resume Next
AppActivate "Microsoft Word"
If Err Then
    Shell "d:\msoffice\winword\winword", 4
```

```
End If
On Error GoTo 0
Set objWordBasic = CreateObject("Word.Basic")
'Create a new document
objWordBasic.FileNew Template:="D:\msoffice\Templates\Normal.dot",
➥NewTemplate:=0
'Paste the contents of the clipboard as text.
objWordBasic.EditPaste
'Disconnect from Word
Set objWordBasic = Nothing
End Sub
```

Embedding Word with Code

Consider the task of replacing a cell range with an embedded Word document. While that does not seem too difficult to solve, it turns out to not be as easy as it seems. Your first thought would be to do it in the same way that you do it by hand. Select a range, copy it, embed a document, activate it, and paste. Sounds good, right? It even works by hand. However, it does not work in code.

When you copy a range, Excel does not really put it on the Clipboard, but just marks its position. When you paste to another location, it copies from the original marked location. This is done to save time and memory when selecting and moving large objects. When you switch to another application, Excel copies the data onto the Clipboard so it will be there for the other application to use. When you try to use code to embed a copy of a worksheet selection using the steps described in the last paragraph, you never leave Excel, so the data is never actually copied onto the Clipboard and there is nothing to paste in Word.

To make this example work, copy the cells, start an external version of Word, switch to it, and paste the copy of the cells. Now, in the external version of Word, select the image of the cells on the Word document, switch back to the Excel worksheet and embed the copy. By going out of Excel to Word and back into Excel again, you force Excel to put the data on the Clipboard so Word can get it. Listing 10.9 has the Visual Basic for Applications code necessary to do this.

Listing 10.9   EXAMPLES.XLS:StartNPass. Visual Basic for Applications Procedure to Replace *Automation* with *Remote Control* in an Embedded Word Document

```
Option Explicit
'
' StartNReplace Procedure
' Copy the current selection into Word and embed it
' over the selection.
'
Sub StartNReplace()
Dim objWordBasic As Object
Dim objEmbeddedDoc As Object
```

(continues)

Listing 10.9   Continued

```
Dim intSelectionHeight As Integer
Dim intSelectionWidth As Integer
Const cDontSave = 2
'Save the shape of the selection.
intSelectionHeight = Selection.Height
intSelectionWidth = Selection.Width
'Copy the selection.
Selection.Copy
'Open a connection to Word.
Set objWordBasic = CreateObject("Word.Basic")
'Create a new document
objWordBasic.FileNew Template:="D:\msoffice\Templates\Normal.dot",
➥NewTemplate:=0
'Paste the contents of the clipboard.
objWordBasic.EditPaste
'Copy it back onto the clipboard as a Word Document.
objWordBasic.EditSelectAll
objWordBasic.EditCopy
'Delete the document.
objWordBasic.FileClose cDontSave
'Clear the selection on the worksheet.
Selection.Clear
'Embed a Word Document object on the worksheet
Selection.PasteSpecial "Microsoft Word Document Object", False, False
'Get a pointer to it, because it is now the current selection.
Set objEmbeddedDoc = Selection
'Set the shape of the embedded document a little larger than the original.
objEmbeddedDoc.Height = intSelectionHeight
objEmbeddedDoc.Width = intSelectionWidth * 1.05
'Unset the object variables
Set objEmbeddedDoc = Nothing
Set objWordBasic = Nothing
End Sub
```

Embedding a Word Form in Excel

A form generated in Word can be embedded into Excel, and the data from that form can be extracted and stored in a worksheet. As an example, embed the Contacts Manager form created in the "Creating the Form" section earlier in this chapter with its existing procedures into an Excel worksheet:

1. Create a form document from the CONTACTS.DOT template and save it.

2. Link that saved document into Excel. You must link it to the original document instead of embedding it, because the original document has to run in Word itself in order for the embedded macros to run.

3. Create a VBA procedure in Excel to access the form and copy its fields into another worksheet's cells. The procedure then clears the contents of the form.

Listing 10.10 contains the VBA procedure, and listings 10.1 and 10.2 contain the form procedures created previously. Figure 10.29 shows the form embedded in a worksheet, and figure 10.30 shows the worksheet containing the saved data.

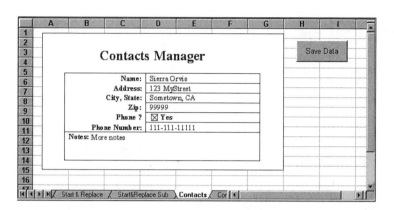

Fig. 10.29

The Contacts Manager form is embedded in an Excel Worksheet.

Fig. 10.30

The data from the Contacts Manager forms is saved in an Excel worksheet.

Listing 10.10   EXAMPLES.XLS:ContactManager. Visual Basic for Applications Procedure to Copy Data from an Embedded Form and Place It into a Worksheet

```
Option Explicit
Option Base 1
'
' ContactManager
' Copy contact info to a worksheet.
'
Sub ContactManager()
Dim objWordBasic As Object
Dim objEmbeddedDoc As Object
Dim strFieldData As String
Dim objNextRow As Object
Dim strFieldNames(8) As String
Dim iintLoop As Integer
'Fill the field names.
strFieldNames(1) = "TextName"
strFieldNames(2) = "TextAddress"
strFieldNames(3) = "TextCity"
```

(continues)

Advanced Integration

III

On the CD

```
  Listing 10.10   Continued
  strFieldNames(4) = "DropDownState"
  strFieldNames(5) = "TextZip"
  strFieldNames(6) = "CheckYes"
  strFieldNames(7) = "Phone"
  strFieldNames(8) = "TextNotes"
  'Create the WordBasic object.
  Set objWordBasic = CreateObject("Word.Basic")
  'Open contacts2.doc.
  objWordBasic.FileOpen Name:="d:\My Documents\BIOA Book\contacts2.doc"
  Set objNextRow = Sheets("ContactData").Range("NextRow")
  'Copy the data from the fields.
  For iintLoop = 1 To 8
     strFieldData = objWordBasic.[GetFormResult$](strFieldNames(iintLoop))
     Sheets("ContactData").Range("A1:H100")
     ➥.Cells(objNextRow.Value, iintLoop).Value = strFieldData
     objWordBasic.SetFormResult strFieldNames(iintLoop), " "
  Next iintLoop
  objWordBasic.FileSave
  objNextRow.Value = objNextRow.Value + 1
  Set objWordBasic = Nothing
  Set objEmbeddedDoc = Nothing
  End Sub
```

The procedure begins by filling an array with the names of the bookmarks used on the Contacts Manager form. These bookmarks are used to access the fields. The procedure then opens connections to the embedded document, the Word.Basic object, and to a cell on the database worksheet named NextRow. NextRow contains the row number to use for the next record of data. Creating an object variable pointing to it simplifies the remaining code in the procedure.

The main work of the procedure is accomplished in the For/Next loop. Within the loop, the first line gets a copy of the contents of a field, the second places that copy on the database worksheet, and the third clears the contents of the field. Following the loop, statements save the document, increment the value of NextRow, and clear the object variables.

Words as Buttons—Hypertext

Hypertext documents are the current standard for help files and other types of informational documents. A hypertext document can be easily implemented in Word using field codes. Consider the NWSLTR.DOC shown in figure 10.31. It has a table of contents that lists the different sections in the document. To make it easy to get to the different sections, change the text in the table of contents to buttons that jump to each section. This is done with GoToButton fields as shown in figure 10.32. The GoToButton field has the following syntax:

```
{GOTOBUTTON bookmark button-text}
```

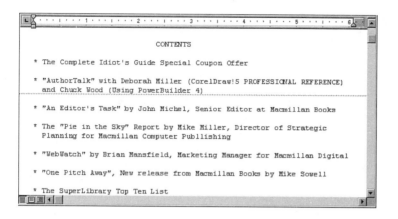

Fig. 10.31

A NWSLTR.DOC file would be much more useful with hypertext links from the table of contents entries to the sections.

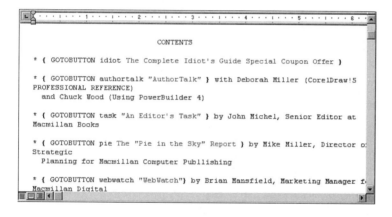

Fig. 10.32

The NWSLTR.DOC file now contains GoToButton *fields inserted in the table of contents.*

The first word following the word GOTOBUTTON is the name of a bookmark to jump to; any following text is used as the button label. To insert these field codes into the document, follow these steps:

1. Place the cursor at the beginning of a line in the table of contents.
2. Choose <u>I</u>nsert, Fi<u>e</u>ld and select the GoToButton field. Press Alt+F9 if the field names are not visible.
3. Place the cursor to the right of the word GOTOBUTTON and type a bookmark name.
4. Select the remainder of the line, and cut and paste it to the right of the bookmark name.
5. Select the text again, choose <u>F</u>ormat, <u>F</u>ont, and change the color to dark green.
6. Scroll down to the beginning of each section and choose <u>E</u>dit, <u>B</u>ookmark to insert the bookmarks inserted in the GoToButton fields. Press Alt+F9 to hide the field codes.
7. To use the buttons, simply double-click them in the table of contents. The document immediately scrolls to the indicated section.

III

Advanced Integration

Scrolling an Embedded Word Document

Scrolling an embedded document under program control is not as simple as it seems. If you have a long document embedded into a worksheet and want to scroll through it using buttons on the worksheet, you run into a slightly perplexing problem. You must activate the document to scroll it, but clicking the worksheet deactivates the document and displays only its top. If you place a button on the worksheet to activate and scroll the document, it is activated and scrolled, but then Excel detects that you clicked the worksheet (the button was on the worksheet) and deactivates the embedded document, scrolling it back up to the top.

You have several options here:

- Activate the document by double-clicking it and then scroll it with the Page Up and Page Down keys. However, you run the risk that your user might accidentally be pressing the Shift key while paging up or down, and at the same time selecting large parts of the document. Pressing any other key deletes the selected part of the document.
- Place each page of the document on a different worksheet. To read it, you just click the worksheet tabs at the bottom.
- Clip off the top of the document and move it to the bottom as you page down and do the reverse when you page up. That way, the top of the document is the page you want to see. This does work, but the screen does a lot of flashing as the document is selected, cut, scrolled, pasted, and deactivated.
- Put the buttons in an Excel custom dialog box. That way, when you click a button, you are clicking the dialog box and not the worksheet.

This last option is shown in the following listing and figures. Figure 10.33 shows the worksheet with the embedded document and an Activate button. Clicking the Activate button runs the `SetupScroll` procedure in listing 10.11. The `SetupScroll` procedure creates the connections to the document and `Word.Basic`, and displays the custom dialog box shown in figure 10.34.

The custom dialog box consists of a spinner named `UpDown` and a Done button. Pressing the arrows on the spinner changes the value of the spinner and runs the `Scroll` procedure in the listing. The `Scroll` procedure scrolls the document up or down, depending on which button you pressed on the spinner. Clicking the Done button runs the `DoneScrolling` procedure that deactivates the embedded document and closes the connections to WordBasic and to the document. The Done button has the `cancel` property set, so it also closes the dialog box.

On the CD

Listing 10.11 EXAMPLE.XLS:ScrollDoc. Visual Basic for Applications Procedure to Scroll an Embedded Document

```
Option Explicit
Dim objWordBasic As Object
Dim objEmbeddedDoc As Object
Dim intSpinnerValue As Integer
```

```
Dim intOldSpinnerValue As Integer
'
' SetupScroll
' Scroll an embedded document.
'
Sub SetUp()
'Create a link to the embedded document.
Set objEmbeddedDoc = ActiveSheet.OLEObjects("EmbeddedDoc")
'Create a link to WordBasic through the embedded document.
Set objWordBasic = objEmbeddedDoc.Object.Application.WordBasic
'Activate the embedded document.
objEmbeddedDoc.Activate
'Show the dialog box.
Sheets("Dialog1").Show
'Initialize intOldSpinnerValue
'Subtract 10000 to make it count down instead of up.
intOldSpinnerValue = 10000 - Sheets("Dialog1").Spinners("UpDown").Value
End Sub
'
' Scroll
' Scroll an embedded document.
'
Sub Scroll()
'Get the current spinner value
intSpinnerValue = 10000 - Sheets("Dialog1").Spinners("UpDown").Value
'See if it has increased or decreased and move up or down a page.
If intSpinnerValue > intOldSpinnerValue Then
    objWordBasic.VPage 1
ElseIf intSpinnerValue < intOldSpinnerValue Then
    objWordBasic.VPage -1
ElseIf intSpinnerValue = 0 Then
    'Reset to page 1 if we get out of sync.
    objWordBasic.EditGoTo "p1"
End If
'Update the value of intOldSpinnerValue.
intOldSpinnerValue = intSpinnerValue
End Sub
'
' DoneScrolling
' Stop scrolling
'
Sub DoneScrolling()
'Unset the object variables.
Set objWordBasic = Nothing
Set objEmbeddedDoc = Nothing
'Unactivate the document by activating cell A1.
ActiveSheet.Range("A1").Activate
End Sub
```

Look at the procedures in a little more detail. First, there are four variables declared at the module level, so they can be used by all three procedures in the module and won't go away when any individual procedure ends. The SetupScroll procedure opens a connection to the embedded document and to WordBasic. It then activates the embedded document, shows the dialog box, and gets the initial value of the spinner. The initial value is set at 10,000, and the value of the spinner is subtracted from 10,000 to reverse the action of the spinner's buttons. This is done to make the document move in the same direction as the arrow points on the spinner.

Fig. 10.33

The Word document is embedded in an Excel worksheet prior to scrolling.

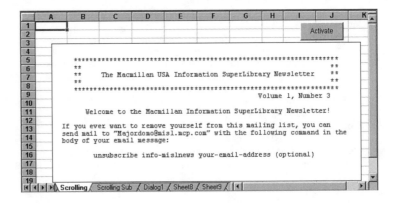

Fig. 10.34

The embedded Word document can be scrolled by using the keys on the custom dialog box.

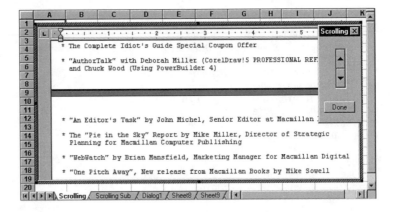

The Scroll procedure is run whenever the spinner is clicked. The procedure gets the current value of the spinner and compares it to the previous value. If the value has increased, the procedure moves forward a page in the document. If the value has decreased, the document is scrolled back a page. If the value reaches 0, the procedure goes directly to page 1. This is to resynchronize the spinner and the displayed page if they get out of sync. The spinner and the displayed page can get out of sync if you click the spinner faster than the code can scroll the pages. Finally, the procedure updates the old value of the spinner and ends.

The DoneScrolling procedure simply disconnects the two object variables and deactivates the embedded document by selecting a worksheet cell.

From Here...

In this chapter, you learned to embed OLE objects in Word documents and to embed Word documents in other OLE applications. You learned to use WordBasic to automate word processing procedures, and to use OLE Automation to access the WordBasic object and remote control Word or to edit embedded Word documents. For more information, refer to the following chapters:

- See Chapter 4, "Visual Basic and Visual Basic for Applications," to learn more about programming in WordBasic. See also the *WordBasic Reference* in the online help for Word and Que's *Special Edition Using Visual Basic 4*.

- See Chapter 6, "Creating an Integrated Application with Word and Excel," and Chapter 11, "Automating Office Integration with Excel," to learn more about integrating Excel and Word.

- See Chapter 17, "Controlling Office Applications with Visual Basic," to learn more about controlling applications using Visual Basic for Applications.

CHAPTER 11

Automating Office Integration with Excel

In this chapter, you expand your application integration skills as you learn about the Excel Object Model and Visual Basic for Applications (VBA). With these tools, you can build integrated applications that automate the features of Excel, Access, Word, PowerPoint, and other Office applications.

Integration with the Excel Object Model and VBA can turn a spreadsheet into a powerhouse of features from word processing, database, graphics, and other applications. As you integrate Excel with the features of other applications, you actually install those features in your Excel workbook. When you install Excel PivotTables and Charts into an Access database, you create a powerful hybrid with both data analysis and database capabilities.

The keys to unlocking the power of application integration are the Excel Object Model and VBA. This chapter provides you with all of the information you need to begin using these tools.

In this chapter, you learn how to

- Understand the Excel Object Model
- Create VBA Procedures
- Control properties and methods with VBA
- Use Excel as a server application
- Use Excel to control Word

Learning the Excel Object Model

All of the features of Excel are available to you through the Excel Object Model. Your investment of time in understanding the Excel Object Model provides you with the keys to unlock Excel's power. If you understand the Object Model for an Excel workbook, you can learn how to write VBA procedures to control all of the properties and methods of the worksheets, charts, and other objects in the workbook.

Each element of Excel is an *object*. Each object has *properties* and *methods* you can reference from VBA. Objects are organized in *collections*. For example, each Excel `Workbook` object contains a collection of worksheets. You can reference a specific worksheet in the `Worksheets` collection as `Worksheets("Sheet1")`.

A *property* is an attribute of an object. For example, `Name` is a property of an Excel worksheet object. You can use VBA to set the name property of a worksheet:

```
Worksheets("Sheet1").Name = "January Sales"
```

A *method* is an action that the object can perform. One action that a worksheet object can perform is the `PrintOut` method. The VBA statement to print a worksheet is

```
Worksheets("Sheet1").PrintOut
```

To control the properties and methods of a specific object, you must use the Object Model *drill down* technique. As an example of drill down, this VBA statement changes the color of a cell:

```
Worksheets("Sheet1").Range("A1").Interior.ColorIndex = 3
```

The cell referenced in this example is in the worksheet named `Sheet1`. The location of the cell is specified by `Range("A1")`. The object that is to be changed is `Interior`. The property to be changed is `ColorIndex`.

The Object Model reference in a VBA statement is easier to understand if you read it from right to left. You would read the previous example as the following:

Assign the value 3 to the `ColorIndex` property of the `Interior` of `Range "A1"` of the worksheet named `Sheet1`.

This statement will change the color of the cell to red. The standard color palette is illustrated in the `ColorIndex` Property help topic.

Understanding Collections and Objects

If you begin by learning about the `Worksheets`, `Charts`, `Dialog Sheets`, and `Modules` collections, you can develop an overall understanding of the Excel Object Model. Table 11.1 describes these objects.

Table 11.1 Worksheets, Charts, Dialog Sheets, and Modules

Object	Description
Worksheet	Each `Worksheet` object includes the cell ranges, PivotTables, embedded charts, pictures, and other objects that appear on worksheets. Table 11.2 describes objects in a worksheet.
Chart	Each chart sheet is a `Chart` object. In addition, each embedded chart on a worksheet is a `Chart` object. From the `Chart` object, you can control all of the properties and methods of the objects of an Excel chart. Table 11.3 lists objects in a chart.

Object	Description
Dialog Sheet	You can use the `DialogSheet` object to reference all the list boxes, edit boxes, and other controls on a custom dialog box. Each custom dialog box is contained on a separate `DialogSheet` in the workbook.
Module	`Module` sheets contain VBA procedures. A workbook can contain multiple `Module` sheets.

One of the main reasons you will be integrating Excel with other applications is to tap into the data analysis features of a worksheet. Worksheets contain `PivotTable`, `Filter`, `Range`, `List`, `Formula`, and other data analysis objects.

In table 11.2 and later in the chapter, you learn more about worksheet objects. After you learn to control worksheet objects with VBA, you can transform your Excel worksheet into a custom information system where VBA automates data analysis.

Table 11.2 Example Worksheet Objects

Object	Description
Range	A selection of one or more cells. You can refer to a `Range` of one cell—`Activesheet.Range("B4")`—or to a block of cells—`Activesheet.Range("B4:E9")`.
PivotTable	Tables of totals that Excel creates with the PivotTable Wizard. A worksheet can contain multiple `PivotTable` objects.
Scenario	Contains input values and parameters for Excel's scenario feature. Each worksheet can contain multiple `Scenario` objects.
Name	References ranges of cells. A `Name` can be defined at the workbook or worksheet level. Workbooks and worksheets may have one or more `Name` objects.
PageSetup	Contains all the header, footer, margin and page printing information for a worksheet.

Excel's charting capabilities are so broad and powerful that you can create thousands of different chart presentations. If you understand the objects within a chart and learn to control them with VBA, you can add the powerful features of Excel charts to other applications.

To help you understand charts, table 11.3 lists some key objects in a chart. Later in the chapter, you learn more by studying example VBA statements that create and modify charts.

III

Advanced Integration

Table 11.3	Example Chart Objects
Object	**Description**
`Range`	A selection of one or more cells. You can refer to a range of one cell—`Activesheet.Range("B4")`—or to a block of cells—`Activesheet.Range("B4:E9")`.
`ChartTitle`	The title displayed at the top of chart.
`Series`	Charts contain multiple `Series` objects, one for each line on a line chart or series of data on another type of chart.
`Chart Group`	Used to format one or more `Series` objects.
`Legend`	Defines the chart legend and contains one or more `LegendEntry` objects.
`Axis`	A 3D chart will have three `Axis` objects. A 2D chart has a category axis and a value axis.

The most important method among all of the chart objects is the `ChartWizard` method. You can use the `ChartWizard` method to create a chart or modify its content. For example, this statement changes the source data range of a chart:

```
Charts("MyChartSheet3").ChartWizard source:= _
    Worksheets("Mysheet2").Range("A3:B17").
```

Drawing objects are tools you can add to worksheets, charts, or dialog sheets. The `DrawingObject` collection is called a *metacollection* because it can contain objects of different types. The `DrawingObject` metacollection contains

- Controls such as list boxes, edit boxes, and buttons
- Lines, arcs, rectangles, and other shapes you can draw
- Text boxes
- Pictures
- Embedded objects such as a chart embedded on a worksheet

If you assign a VBA procedure to a `DrawingObject`, the procedure runs when you click the mouse on the object. For example, a VBA procedure can be assigned to run whenever you click a button or rectangle on the worksheet. You learn more about `DrawingObjects` as you study the VBA examples later in the chapter.

Expanding Your Knowledge with Online Help

The complete details of the Excel Object Model hierarchy are available to you online. The online description of the Object Model is extremely well-organized, and you can use it to explore each element of Excel as you develop VBA procedures. In addition to a diagram of Excel's objects, the online Object Model includes definitions of each object, examples of VBA procedures, and complete lists of all properties and methods.

Unfortunately, Excel's online help system is so extensive that it can be difficult to find and learn to use the online Object Model. To help you master this tool, the following instructions lead you through the process.

To use online help as a reference to the Object Model, follow these steps:

1. Click <u>H</u>elp and choose Microsoft Excel Visual Basic Reference from the Contents tab.

2. Select the Microsoft Excel Object Model. The Microsoft Excel Objects information shown in figure 11.1 appears.

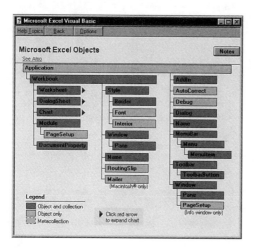

Fig. 11.1

Explore the online Object Model to learn the objects, properties, and methods of Excel.

NOTE The online Object Model is part of Excel's VBA help file. If you cannot find the topic "Microsoft Excel Visual Basic Reference," you may need to add the help file to your installation with the Add/Remove Programs option in the Control Panel.

3. Click the arrow next to the Chart box. The Chart Object Model appears, as shown in figure 11.2.

4. Click the `DataLabel` object to see complete help information about `DataLabel`, as shown in figure 11.3. You can review a list of all the properties and methods that can be used with the `DataLabel` object. The help system includes VBA coding examples.

Creating Your Own Procedures with VBA

If you know how to use Excel's user interface, you can use Excel's macro recorder to develop useful procedures and automate features of your workbooks. You can begin with simple procedures and then add more power to your code with the Excel Object Browser. Before long, you will have increased your understanding of both VBA and the Object Model. This section gets you started by teaching you how to record a simple VBA procedure and then develop it using the Object Browser.

III

Advanced Integration

Fig. 11.2

Drill down into the details of the chart object by clicking the red arrows.

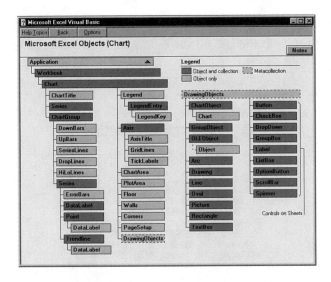

Fig. 11.3

Obtain detailed information about an object by clicking the object's name.

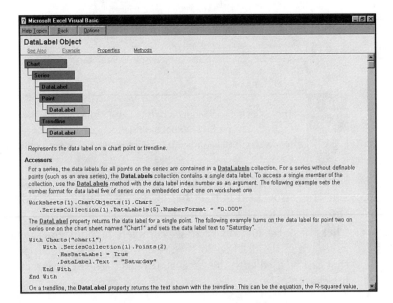

To use the macro recorder to create a VBA procedure for custom page headers, follow these steps:

1. Choose Tools, Record macro, Record New Macro.

2. Enter the name of the macro in the Record Macro dialog box. In this example, the procedure's name is ChangeHeaders.

3. Click the Options button in the Record Macro dialog box and create a menu item for the procedure (see fig. 11.4).

Fig. 11.4

Use the macro recorder to record a VBA procedure and automatically create a module sheet.

4. With the Recorder running, choose File, Page Setup, Header/Footer, and choose Custom Header. Enter the header text **Test Value** in the Header dialog box, shown in figure 11.5.

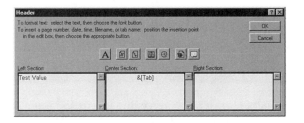

Fig. 11.5

VBA code can be recorded while you use Excel menus, toolbars, and other user interface controls.

5. Click OK to close the Header Setup dialog boxes.

6. Choose Tools, Record Macro, Stop Recording.

Excel creates a module sheet for you with the default name Module1. The recorded code is similar to the following:

```
Sub ChangeHeader()
  With ActiveSheet.PageSetup
    .PrintTitleRows = ""
    .PrintTitleColumns = ""
  End With
  ActiveSheet.PageSetup.PrintArea = ""
  With ActiveSheet.PageSetup
    .LeftHeader = "Test Value"
    .CenterHeader = "&A"
    .RightHeader = ""
    .LeftFooter = ""
    .CenterFooter = "Page &P"
    .RightFooter = ""
    .LeftMargin = Application.InchesToPoints(0.75)
    .RightMargin = Application.InchesToPoints(0.75)
    .TopMargin = Application.InchesToPoints(1)
    .BottomMargin = Application.InchesToPoints(1)
    .HeaderMargin = Application.InchesToPoints(0.5)
    .FooterMargin = Application.InchesToPoints(0.5)
    .PrintHeadings = False
```

III

Advanced Integration

```
            .PrintGridlines = False
            .PrintNotes = False
            .PrintQuality = 600
            .CenterHorizontally = False
            .CenterVertically = False
            .Orientation = xlPortrait
            .Draft = False
            .PaperSize = xlPaperLetter
            .FirstPageNumber = xlAutomatic
            .Order = xlDownThenOver
            .BlackAndWhite = False
            .Zoom = 100
        End With
    End Sub
```

The macro recorder includes all of the many Page Setup values in the recorded code. You can delete all but the lines of code that affect the `LeftHeader` property. Select all but these lines of code and press the Delete key:

```
    Sub ChangeHeader()

        With ActiveSheet.PageSetup
            .LeftHeader = "Test Value"

        End With
    End Sub
```

Every time you choose Tools, Change Header, the procedure inserts the value `Test Value` into the left header area of the active worksheet.

NOTE
You can use `With` and `End With` to make your VBA procedures more efficient and easier to understand. All of the statements between the `With` and `End With` statements can reference the object on the `With` line with just a dot. In the previous example, Excel uses the object on the `With` line to interpret the statement

```
        .LeftHeader = "Test Value" as ActiveSheet.PageSetup.LeftHeader = _
            "Test Value"
```

You now know how to create your own VBA procedure using the macro recorder. With this knowledge, you can create many useful procedures that automate objects in your Excel workbook. If you assign a procedure to a button or menu, you can run the procedure with a click of the mouse.

Now, you can take the next step and learn to compose your own VBA statements. When you have acquired this skill, you can create much more powerful procedures that make decisions and perform other functions that are not available when you use the macro recorder. Begin composing your own VBA statements by modifying a recorded procedure.

In the previous example, you can change the procedure to insert a value from a worksheet cell instead of the constant `Test Value`. To use the Object Browser to help you change the VBA code, follow these steps:

1. Select the text Test Value in the VBA code.

2. Press F2 to display the Object Browse dialog box.

3. Select Excel in the Libraries/Workbooks drop-down list.

4. Select Application in the Objects/Modules list box.

5. Select ActiveSheet in the Methods/Properties list box.

6. Click the Paste button as shown in figure 11.6 to replace Test Value with ActiveSheet in the macro.

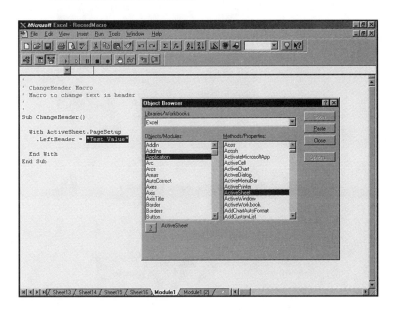

Fig. 11.6

You can use the Object Browser to modify VBA code in a module.

7. Add a dot after ActiveSheet and use the Object Browser to add a Range reference, as shown in figure 11.7.

8. Click the help button in the Object Browser to see VBA Help and an example for using the Range object. As shown in figure 11.7, the help button is identified by a question mark. Figure 11.8 shows the help screens that are available from the Object Browser.

9. Insert the Range reference in the module by using the Object Browser Paste button. Change the cell reference in the Range property to **A1** as shown in figure 11.9.

   The completed procedure shown in figure 11.9 inserts the value of cell A1 in the left portion of the active sheet's header.

10. Add a For Each loop to perform the header change operation on each worksheet in the workbook. Figure 11.10 shows the completed procedure. You can use the Object Browser again as shown in figure 11.10 to learn how to insert the oWorksheet.Activate code line.

III

Advanced Integration

Fig. 11.7

Select the application, object, and method or property in the Object Browser list boxes.

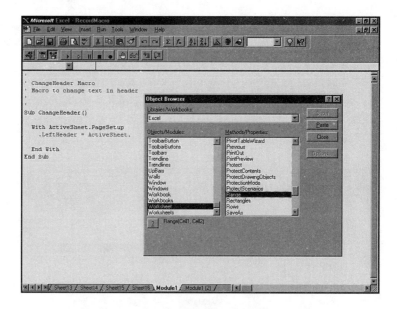

Fig. 11.8

When you press the help (?) button, the Object Browser displays VBA on-line help and example code. You can copy the example code to your module sheet.

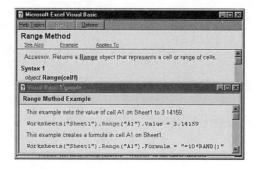

Using VBA To Control Properties and Methods

By now, you have learned to record and modify your own VBA procedures. In addition, you have learned about some of the most useful objects and how to explore the details of the Object Model using Excel's online help.

The next step is to learn more about the methods and properties of the most used objects. By studying the VBA examples in this section, you learn more about the properties and methods of workbooks, worksheets, ranges, PivotTables, charts, and worksheet controls. With this knowledge, you can begin to develop your own VBA procedures.

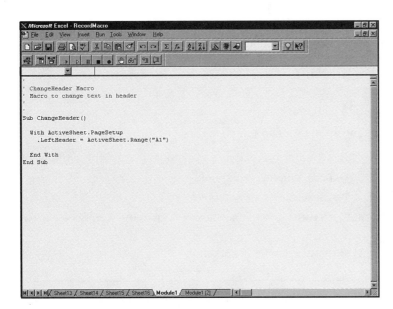

Fig. 11.9

You can develop a complete VBA procedure with the macro recorder and Object Browser.

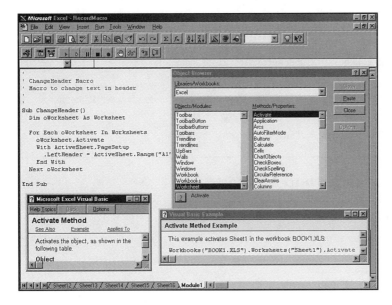

Fig. 11.10

A completed code module is shown with the online help, Visual Basic Example, and Object Browser tools used to help in development.

Workbook Properties and Methods

You can use the name `ActiveWorkbook` to reference the workbook in the active window (the window on top of the other windows). For example, this VBA statement prints the active workbook:

```
ActiveWorkbook.PrintOut
```

When you are referring to an object in the active workbook, you can streamline your VBA code by omitting the workbook reference. Instead of

```
ActiveWorkbook.Worksheets("MySheet").PrintOut
```

you can code

```
Worksheets("MySheet").PrintOut
```

Other examples of workbook properties and methods are:

- *Workbook("MyOtherWB.XLS").Activate*. Puts a workbook in the active window.

- *Workbook("MyWB.XLS").Open*. Opens a workbook.

- *Workbooks("MyWB.XLS").Save*. Saves a workbook.

- *Workbooks("MyWb.XLS").SaveAs name:="NewWBName"*. Saves the workbook with a different name.

- *Workbooks("MyWB.XLS").Close*. Closes a workbook.

> **NOTE**
>
> When your VBA code is in an add-in, it is good practice to use the special object reference names ActiveWorkbook and ThisWorkbook to qualify your references to objects. When you need to refer to an object in the add-in, you should use the name ThisWorkbook. For example, this statement displays a custom dialog sheet stored in the add-in:
>
> ```
> ThisWorkbook.DialogSheets("MyDialog").Show
> ```
>
> When the code in the add-in refers to an object in the active workbook, use the name ActiveWorkbook. For example, this statement in the add-in refers to a worksheet in the workbook that called the add-in:
>
> ```
> ActiveWorkbook.Worksheets("Sheet1").Name
> ```

Worksheet Properties and Methods

You can use the ActiveSheet name to refer to the active worksheet (the worksheet on top). For example, this statement prints the active worksheet in the active workbook:

```
ActiveWorkbook.ActiveSheet.PrintOut
```

Other examples of worksheet properties and methods include:

- *ActiveWorkbook.Worksheets("MySheet7").Activate*. Activates a worksheet.

- *ActiveWorkbook.Worksheets.Add.Name = "MyNewSheet"*. Adds a new worksheet to the active workbook.

- *ActiveWorkbook.Worksheets("MySheet5").Range("F4")*. Refers to cell F4 on worksheet MySheet5.

- *ActiveWorkbook.Worksheets.Count*. Counts the number of worksheets in the active workbook.

- *ActiveWorkbook.ActiveSheet.Copy*. Copies the active sheet.

- *ActiveWorkbook.ActiveSheet.PrintOut*. Prints the `ActiveSheet`.

- *ActiveWorkbook.Worksheets("MySheet").Visible = False*. Hides a worksheet.

- *ActiveWorkbook.ActiveSheet.UsedRange*. Refers to the area of the worksheet that contains data or formats.

- *Activeworkbook.Worksheets("MySheet").name = "NewName"*. Changes the name of the worksheet MySheet.

- *ActiveWorkbook.Worksheets.Onentry = "MyProcedure"*. Runs a VBA procedure named MyProcedure each time you enter data into the worksheet.

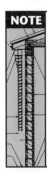

> **NOTE**
>
> You can refer to an object in a collection by using an index. `Worksheets(1)` references the first worksheet in the worksheets collection. VBA provides a `For...Next` control structure to loop through all the objects in a collection. For example, this VBA procedure displays the name of all the worksheets in the active workbook:
>
> ```
> Sub DisplayNames
>     For iintWork = 1 to Worksheets.Count
>     MsgBox Worksheets(iintWork).Name
>     Next iintWork
> End Sub
> ```

Range Properties and Methods

Ranges are selections of one or more cells in a worksheet. This statement selects a single cell range:

```
ActiveSheet.Range("B4").Select
```

Once you have selected the range, you can refer to it as in this example:

```
Selection.Value = "Hello"
```

This statement selects multiple cells:

```
ActiveSheet.Range("A2:F43").Select
```

With multiple cells selected, `Selection.Value = "Hello"` places the value Hello in each of the cells in the range.

Other examples of Range object properties and methods are:

- *ActiveSheet.Columns("B").Select*. Selects an entire column.

- *ActiveSheet.Rows("3").Select*. Selects a row.

- *ActiveSheet.Range("D5").Formula = "=B5 * 1.25"*. Places a formula in cell D5.

- *ActiveSheet.Range("D5").NumberFormat = "0.00"*. Changes the number format of cell D5.

- *ActiveSheet.Range("C4:G7").Copy*. Copies a range of cells.

III

Advanced Integration

- *ActiveSheet.Range("A10").Paste*. Pastes copied cells to a range beginning at A10. If you want to copy values or formats, use the `.PasteSpecial` method instead of `.Paste`.

- *ActiveSheet.Range("A1").CurrentRegion*. Refers to the block of cells with data values starting at cell A1. The selection stops at blank rows or columns, just as it does when you press Ctrl+Shift+* on the worksheet.

- *Activesheet.CurrentRegion.Find(What:="Hello").Delete*. Finds and deletes a value in a range of cells.

- *Activesheet.Range("A3:G6").Name = "MyRange"*. Assigns a name to a range.

- *Range("MyRange").Clear*. Clears the range named MyRange.

- *Range("MyRange").Sort*. Sorts the range.

- *Range("MyRange").AutoFilter*. Creates an AutoFilter for the range.

You can copy a range of data in a procedure with just one line of code. The example VBA that follows copies the range A1:C20 from the active sheet to another worksheet named MyOtherSheet:

```
Sub CopyRange()
    ActiveSheet.Range("A1:C20").Copy_
    Destination:=Worksheets("MyOtherSheet").Range("A1")
End Sub
```

> **NOTE**
>
> A cell seems like it should be an Excel object, but it is not. In the Excel Object Model, a cell is a range object. Ranges with multiple cells contain ranges of single cells. For example, the first cell in the range named MyRange is referenced as
>
> ```
> WorkSheets("MyWorksheet").Range("MyRange").Range("A1")
> ```
>
> The cell location A1 refers to the cell in the first row and column of the range named MyRange, not the first cell in the worksheet.

Referring to Ranges Without Using Select

When working with ranges of cells in Excel's user interface, you often must select the range before initiating an action. For example, when you copy a range of cells, you first make the worksheet active and then select the cells to copy.

The macro recorder records each step you take and creates VBA code for all of the `Select` and `Activate` steps. For example, if you record the process of naming a range, the recorded code includes the following:

- `WorkSheets("MySheet8").Activate`
- `ActiveSheet.Range("A3:G6").Select`
- `Selection.Name = "MyRange"`

With VBA, you don't need to activate or select an object to control its properties and methods. You can eliminate the activate and select statements and shorten the code to one statement:

```
WorkSheets("MySheet8").Range("A3:G6").Name = "MyRange"
```

TIP

It's good practice to avoid `Activate` and `Select` statements in your VBA procedures. Your procedures become more readable and execute more quickly with fewer lines of code.

Referring to Ranges with the *Offset* and *Cells* Methods

You can use the `Offset` method to refer to a cell based on its position relative to another cell. For example, this statement changes the number format of a cell one row below cell B5:

```
WorkSheets("MySheet4").Range("B5").Offset(1).NumberFormat = "**.0"
```

`Offset` can be used with a VBA variable. In the following example, the variable x is set to the value 12, and the `Offset` function sets the variable y equal to the value in the cell 12 rows below cell B5:

```
x = 12
y = WorkSheets("MySheet4").Range("B5").Offset(x).Value
```

You can also use the `Offset` function to refer to cells in a different column. For example, this statement changes the number format of a cell one row below and three columns to the right of cell B5:

```
a = 1
b = 3
WorkSheets("MySheet4").Range("B5").Offset(a,b).NumberFormat = "**.0"
```

The `Cells` method provides another way to use a variable to refer to a cell. For example, if x is 2, then this statement selects the cell in the second row and first column of the range B5:G9:

```
WorkSheets("MySheet4").Range("B5:G9").Cells(x,1).Select
```

You can use the `Cells` method to reference a range with more than one cell. This statement uses the `Cells` method to change the interior color of the cells in the range A1:G10:

```
Range(Cells(1, 1), Cells(7, 10)).Interior.ColorIndex = 5
```

NOTE

Many Excel methods return range objects. For example, `ActiveSheet.Range("A1").EntireColumn` refers to the range A1:A16384. The `Rows` method returns a row within a range. In this example, `ActiveSheet.Range("B3:D6").Rows(2)` refers to the range B4:D4.

Properties and Methods of Worksheet and Dialog Sheet Controls

Excel provides properties and methods to use with list boxes, control buttons, check boxes, option buttons, and other worksheet or dialog box controls.

Examples of properties and methods of a list box include:

- *WorkSheets("MySheet3").ListBoxes(1).AddItem Text:="Widgets"*. Adds an item to the first list box in the worksheet.

- *WorkSheets("MySheet1").ListBoxes(MyProductListBox).RemoveAllItems*. Removes all items from the list box.

- *WorkSheets("MySheet1").ListBoxes(MyProductListBox).ListIndex*. Returns the index number of the item selected.

Each type of control has different properties and methods. For example, this statement turns on an option button:

```
WorkSheets("MySheet1").OptionButtons(1).Type = xlOn
```

NOTE   In the previous example, the value x1On is an intrinsic constant. The statement would produce the same result if you replaced the constant x1On with the value 1. By using intrinsic constants, your code is easier to understand and is protected from any future change in the underlying values of arguments. If Microsoft decides to change the x1On value from 1 to 1.3, code referencing the constant x1On will work properly, while code containing the literal value 1 will have to be modified.

All worksheet controls share the OnAction property. OnAction sets the name of the VBA procedure that is called when the control is clicked. The following VBA procedure is called by the OnAction property of a worksheet button:

```
Sub GoToNewSheet()
    WorkSheets("MySheet").Activate
    Range("A1").Select
End Sub
```

When the button is clicked, Excel activates the worksheet MySheet and selects the range A1.

PivotTable Properties and Methods

PivotTables are tables of totals that Excel creates with the PivotTable Wizard. To create a PivotTable with VBA, you can use the PivotTableWizard method. In this example, a PivotTable is created for a source data range on Sheet1:

```
ActiveSheet.PivotTableWizard SourceType:=xlDatabase, SourceData:= _
    "Sheet1!R11C1:R14C2", TableDestination:="R19C1", TableName:= _
    "PivotTable1"
  ActiveSheet.PivotTables("PivotTable1").AddFields RowFields:="q"
  ActiveSheet.PivotTables("PivotTable1").PivotFields("w").Orientation = _
    xlDataField
```

Once the PivotTable is created, you can reference each of its components. For example, this statement changes the orientation of the "Product" field in the PivotTable named "Pivot Table 1":

```
Worksheets("MySheet19").PivotTables("Pivot Table 1").PivotFields( _
    "Product").Orientation = xlPageField
```

If you assign a variable to an object, you can use the variable to make your VBA code more readable and efficient. Variables assigned to objects are called *object variables*. The Set statement performs the assignment of the variable as shown in this example:

```
Set pvtMyPivot = WorkSheets("MySheet19").PivotTables("Pivot Table 1")
```

Once the object variable is assigned, you can use it just as you would the complete reference to the PivotTable. In these examples, pvtMyPiovt is an object variable assigned to a PivotTable:

- *pvtMyPivot.DataBodyRange.Interior.ColorIndex = 5.* Changes the color of the data area of the PivotTable.

- *pvtMyPivot.DataLabelRange.Interior.ColorIndex = 3.* Changes the color of the data label area of the PivotTable.

- *pvtMyPivot.TableRange1.Autoformat Format:=xlClassic1.* Changes the format of the PivotTable.

- *pvtMyPivot.Refresh.* Refreshes the PivotTable.

- *pvtMyPivot.PageFields(1).CurrentPage = "Widgets".* Selects the item Widgets in the PivotTable page field.

When you need to provide an option to change the appearance of a PivotTable, but want to avoid offering the dozens of options available in the PivotTable Wizard, you can create a VBA procedure like this one that changes the PivotTable automatically:

```
Sub ChangePivot()
    If ActiveSheet.OptionButtons(1).Value = xlOff Then
        ActiveSheet.PivotTables("PivotTable1" _
            ).PivotFields("Location").Orientation = xlHidden
    Else
        ActiveSheet.PivotTables("PivotTable1" _
            ).PivotFields("Location").Orientation = xlRowField
    End If
End Sub
```

The procedure changes the Orientation property of the PivotField named Location. When you click the option buttons, the PivotTable changes from a table of totals by location and division to a table of totals by division. When you click the option buttons again, the table changes back to show totals for both location and division.

In this example, you learned how to create and modify a PivotTable with a VBA procedure. Later in the chapter, you learn how to change the page field of an Excel PivotTable from the value in a list box on an Access form.

III

Advanced Integration

Chart Properties and Methods

You can use the Chart Wizard from VBA to create a new chart or change the properties of an existing chart. In this example, the `ChartWizard` method is used to change the source range of a chart:

```
Charts("MyChartSheet3").ChartWizard source:= _
    Worksheets("Mysheet2").Range("A3:B17").
```

Other examples of chart properties and methods include:

- *Charts("MyChartSheet3").Type = xlColumn.* Changes the chart type of a chart on a chart sheet.

- *WorkSheets("MySheet16").ChartObjects("MyChartObj2").Chart.type = xlBar.* Used for a chart that is embedded in a worksheet.

- *WorkSheets("MySheet16").ChartObjects("MyChartObj2").Chart.Title = "New Title".* Changes a chart's title.

From a button on the chart sheet, you can call a VBA procedure that changes the chart from a line chart to a bar chart. The following procedure changes the `Type` property of the chart from `xlBar` to `xlLine`:

```
Sub ChangeChartType()
  If ActiveChart.Type <> xlBar Then
    ActiveChart.Type = xlBar
  Else
    ActiveChart.Type = xlLine
  End If
End Sub
```

If the chart type is `xlLine`, `xlColumn`, or another type not equal to `xlBar`, the procedure changes the `Type` property to `xlBar`. If the chart is a bar chart, the procedure changes the `Type` property to `xlLine`.

Using VBA To Integrate Applications

You can integrate Excel's data analysis capabilities with other OLE applications. OLE (Object Linking and Embedding) is the glue that permits one application to control another. Access, Word, PowerPoint, and Schedule+ are OLE applications. Microsoft Project, Visio, and Janna Contact Manager are examples of OLE applications outside of the Microsoft Office suite.

With OLE integration, you can create a powerful combination with Access and Excel. Your Access database application can display Excel charts and worksheets. You can use buttons and other controls in Access to control the content and appearance of the Excel object. All of the functions, charts, PivotTables, filters, and other features of Excel become part of your Access application. For more information on integrating Access and Excel, refer to Chapter 8, "Creating an Integrated Application with Access and Excel."

Another powerful combination can be created with Excel and Word. You can use Word to build a report generator into your Excel workbook. With the report generation features of Word, you can publish Excel data with text and document publishing features such as a table of contents. For more information on integrating Word and Excel, refer to Chapter 6, "Creating an Integrated Application with Word and Excel."

When you learn how to integrate OLE applications, you can command many other powerful combinations of applications. You can create a convincing call to action by building a PowerPoint presentation into your Excel workbook. If you combine Excel and Project, data in Excel can automatically update a schedule in Project. You can combine Excel and VB4 to create a state of the art user interface that includes Excel charts and worksheets.

The first step in learning how to integrate OLE applications is to understand the concept of OLE *servers* and *controllers*. The *server* application makes its Object Model available to the *controller* application. The integration examples in this section show you practical ways to use Excel as both a *controller* and *server*:

- In the first example, Access controls the properties and methods of Excel. Excel is the *server* and Access is the *controller*.

- In the second example, Excel controls the properties and methods of Word. In this example, Excel is a *controller* and Word is the *server*.

After you learn the basics of using Excel as an OLE controller and server, you can create powerful combinations of applications on your own.

NOTE

This chapter uses the term *server* to describe an application that supplies information and functions to another, and the term *controller* to describe the application that uses the information and functions. In other documentation, you may find the terms *client*, *destination*, *user*, or *container* employed to identify *controller* applications. You can consider the terms *client*, *destination*, and *user* to have the same meaning.

Container is used to refer to a document that contains an embedded OLE object. The Access database with an embedded Excel worksheet is an OLE Automation controller that is also a container document.

Using Excel as a Server Application

When Excel acts as a server, another application can use VBA to control the Excel Object Model. Once the connection between the applications is complete, all the data analysis and charting features of Excel become available to the other application.

In the example that follows, the PivotTable, charting, and Trendline features of Excel are built into an Access application. From Access, you can change the PivotTable and chart to display a sales projection by product.

The screen shown in figure 11.11 is an Access form that includes these elements:

- An Excel workbook embedded in the Access form. The workbook contains two sheets: a PivotTable and a chart sheet that graphs the values in the PivotTable.
- An Access list box used to select a product to display in the Excel chart.
- An Access command button labeled `Refresh Data`.

Fig. 11.11

The chart shown in the Access form is an embedded Excel chart. The projection line is produced automatically using the TrendLine feature of Excel.

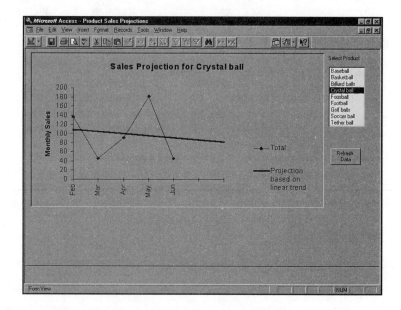

Linking an Access List Box to an Excel PivotTable. This example demonstrates how to use VBA to control an Excel workbook that is embedded in an Access form. When you know how to control an integrated application, you can create an automated user interface that makes it easy to use the combined features of the applications.

In the example shown in figure 11.11, the chart and Trendline automatically adjust to show data for the product you select in the list box. When you click the Refresh Data button in figure 11.11, the Excel workbook reads the Access database and refreshes the data in the PivotTable and chart.

NOTE When integrating applications with VBA, it is helpful to establish a reference from the VBA controller application to the server. After the reference is established, you can use the Object Browser to look up the objects, properties, and methods of the server application. To establish a reference, open a module in the controller application and choose Tools, References. You can then check the server application in the References dialog box or click the Browse button to add the server's object reference file to the list of applications.

The following VBA code runs each time you select an item from the list box. The code is contained in the `cboProduct_Click` procedure in the Access database application.

```
Private Sub cboProduct_Click()

    Dim wkbWork As WorkBook
    Dim pvtSales As PivotTable
    Dim pvfProducts As PivotField

    On Error Resume Next

    Set wkbWork = Me!PivotTable.Object.Parent
    Set pvtSales = wkbWork.WorkSheets("Sheet1").PivotTables(1)
    Set pvfProducts = pvtSales.PageFields(1)
    pvfProducts.CurrentPage =_
        Me!cboProduct.ItemData(Me!cboProduct.ListIndex)

    If Err <> 0 Then
      MsgBox "Cannot set the pivot table to that value", vbExclamation
    End If
End Sub
```

The first three lines of the procedure define variables that are assigned values in the `Set` lines that follow. `WkbWork` is set to the embedded Excel workbook. `PvtSales` is set to the pivot table on `Sheet1` of the workbook `wkbWork`. `PvfProducts` is set to reference the first page field in the PivotTable `pvtSales`.

Setting variables equal to workbooks and PivotTables is standard fare in VBA. What is different in this example is that the VBA procedure that contains the variables is in an Access module. Before Access can control the Excel workbook, it must first establish a connection to the workbook's Excel Object Model.

This line of VBA code establishes a connection to the workbook's Excel Object Model:

```
Set wkbWork = Me!PivotTable.Object.Parent
```

`Me!` is the Access abbreviation for the Access form. `PivotTable` is the name of the Access object frame that contains the Excel workbook. `Me!PivotTable.Object` is the embedded object contained in the object frame. Because this embedded object is an Excel worksheet, you need to add **.Parent** to the statement to change the reference to the workbook.

After the set statement runs, the variable `wkbWork` is set to reference the Excel Object Model of the embedded workbook. You can use `wkbWork` to control all the other objects in the workbook.

When you use the `Object` method to create a connection to the Excel workbook, a copy of the workbook becomes active in your system. If Excel is already open and running, the embedded workbook becomes a hidden workbook in the Excel application. You can investigate this process by switching to Excel and choose <u>W</u>indows, <u>U</u>nhide to examine the embedded workbook.

If Excel is not running when the `Object` method runs, Excel starts as a hidden application. You can see that a hidden version of Excel is running by pressing Ctrl+Alt+Delete to view the Windows Close Program dialog box. You see Excel in the list, but it is not visible on the Windows taskbar.

The next lines of Visual Basic code use the object variable `wkbWork` to set variables equal to the pivot table and the pivot field named `Products`. The following line of code changes the PivotTable's current page value to the item selected in the list box:

```
pvfProducts.CurrentPage = Me!cboProduct.ItemData(Me!cboProduct.ListIndex)
```

`ListIndex` is used to return the name of the product selected in the list box. The `CurrentPage` of the pivot table field is changed to the product name, causing the PivotTable to display a different set of values. The chart and Trendline automatically change to display new values from the PivotTable.

The `If Err <> 0` statement displays an error message if Excel was not able to set the `CurrentPage` property of the `PivotTable` field. This error can result when the list box contains a product that is no longer in the database or PivotTable.

Creating an Access Command Button To Refresh the Excel PivotTable. You can control an embedded Excel workbook with an Access command button. The button enables you to run a VBA procedure that establishes a connection to the workbook's Object Model and makes changes to the workbook. In the following example, a command button is used to refresh the data in the Excel workbook.

To add new data to a PivotTable, you must use the `Refresh` method. The PivotTable in the example is connected to the Access database. When you add new data to the database, you can refresh the PivotTable in order to include the new data.

This VBA code runs when you click the Refresh Data button shown in figure 11.11:

```
Private Sub cmdRefresh_Click()

    Dim wkbWork As Workbook
    Dim pvtSales As PivotTable
    Dim pvfProducts As PivotField

    On Error Resume Next

    Set wkbWork = Me!PivotTable.Object.Parent
    Set pvtSales = wkbWork.Worksheets("Sheet1").PivotTables(1)

    DoCmd.Hourglass hourglasson:=True
```

```
      pvtSales.RefreshTable
      DoCmd.Hourglass hourglasson:=False

      If Err <> 0 Then
        MsgBox "Cannot refresh pivot table data", vbExclamation
      Else
        MsgBox "Data in chart has been refreshed", vbInformation
      End If

  End Sub
```

The first lines of the procedure are the same as those used in procedure for the list box. The difference is that this procedure uses the statement `pvtSales.RefreshTable` to cause the PivotTable to refresh. The `DoCmd.Hourglass` statements set the cursor to an hourglass shape while the refresh operation is in progress.

During refresh, the PivotTable's internal cache of data is updated with any new or changed values from the database.

Using the ORDERENTRY1 Example on the CD-ROM. The example described in the previous section is included in the `ProductSales` form of the ORDERENTRY1.MDB example file on the CD-ROM that accompanies this book. You can use the example Access database application to learn more about using an Excel workbook in an Access application. It contains a full-featured Order Entry application that was created in minutes using the Access Database Wizard.

On the CD

After you study the example, you can create your own example application by following these steps:

1. In Access, choose File, New Database.

2. In the New dialog box that appears, select the Databases tab and choose the Order Entry database template. The Access Database Wizard automatically creates an Order Entry database application for you.

3. Add a new form to the database with the Access PivotTable Wizard.

4. Add a chart to the embedded Excel workbook that contains the PivotTable.

5. Place a list box and command button on the form.

6. Create VBA procedures as described in the earlier sections "Linking an Access List Box to an Excel PivotTable" and "Creating an Access Command Button To Refresh the Excel PivotTable."

With the skills you have learned from this example, you can create powerful combinations of Excel and Access. You can add PivotTables, charts, Trendlines, filtered lists, "what-if" analyses, and all of Excel's built-in functions to your Access application.

Using Excel To Control Word

Excel can be a client and control another application's object model with VBA. When you use Excel as a client, you can include features of other applications in your Excel workbook.

III

Advanced Integration

In the following example, you learn how to enhance an Excel PivotTable with Word's reporting capabilities. One of the most useful features of a PivotTable is *page fields*. You can use page fields to filter the data in the PivotTable. For example, in a PivotTable containing data by location, you can view the data for any one location by creating a page field.

Excel provides a Show Pages feature that produces a copy of the PivotTable for each location. You can print the copies to prepare a report of results by location.

In this example, you learn how to add the power of Word to produce a much more useful report of results by location. The report produced by Word provides these features not available in Excel:

- Multiple PivotTables are printed on each page.
- The first page is a title page.
- A table of contents provides an easy way to look up data in the report.
- Text descriptions can be added with each PivotTable.
- All of Word's headings, footers, formatting and print settings are available to enhance the report.

A copy of the example application is available on the CD-ROM that accompanies this book. With the techniques you learn from the example, you can create integrated Word reports from data in Excel workbooks.

Creating a PivotTable in Excel. The Excel workbook that produces the Word report contains a PivotTable by location. In figure 11.12, you can see that location is a page field.

Fig. 11.12

The PivotTable worksheet contains a button used to call a VBA procedure that automatically prints a report from the PivotTable. The report is printed in Word using templates and Word's automatic Table of Contents feature.

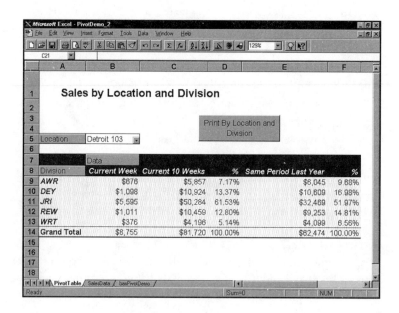

Changing the value of the location page field filters the PivotTable data and shows the sales results for the selected location.

The PivotTable is formatted by choosing F<u>o</u>rmat, <u>A</u>utoformat. When the PivotTable is copied to the Word report, the format is also copied.

The Print By Location and Division button in figure 11.12 runs the VBA procedure described in the next section.

Connecting to Word. The first segment of code establishes a connection to Word:

```
Sub PivotDemo()

    'Define Variables
    Dim wrdbas As Object
    Dim pvtPivotTable As PivotTable
    Dim pvfPivotField As PivotField
    Dim pviPivotItem As PivotItem

    'create connection to Word
    Application.ActivateMicrosoftApp xlMicrosoftWord
    Set wrdbas = CreateObject("Word.Basic")
```

In this example, the `ActivateMicrosoftApp` method causes Word to be the active or top window before the procedure sets a connection to Word. While the procedure is running, you can see the report as it is created in Word. At the completion of the procedure, the Word window remains on top so that you can add text to the report, save the report, and print it from Word. When you close the window containing Word, Excel again becomes the active window.

The `CreateObject` method is used to start Word. The variable `wrdbas` becomes the link to all of the features of Word. With `wrdbas`, you can access Word's Object Model.

Object variables defined with the `Dim` statements are used later in the procedure to reference fields in the PivotTable.

The next segment of code creates a new Word document with the `.filenew` statement. The document is created using a Word template named TABLEDOC.DOT. You can use Word templates to store the formatting for the report. A new document created with the template contains a copy of the formatting.

```
    'use template to make Word active and open new Word document
    With wrdbas
        .filenew ThisWorkbook.Path & "\TableDoc.dot", 0
        .AppRestore
        .AppSize 407, 327
        .AppMove 33, 84
```

The `With` statement is used to automatically add the `wrdbas` prefix to any references that start with . (a period).

The `.AppRestore`, `.AppSize`, and `.AppMove` statements adjust the Word window so that it appears over just a portion of the Excel window. As illustrated in figure 11.13, you can see the report as it is being built in the Word window.

Fig. 11.13

As the report is prepared in Word, it is displayed in a window on top of Excel's window.

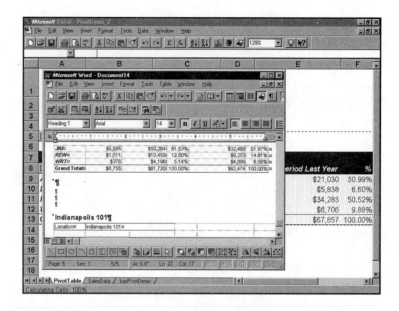

In this example, the template contains bookmarks that mark the locations where titles will be inserted in the Word document. Bookmarks in Word are similar to range names in Excel. You can add a bookmark to a template and use the .EditGoTo statement to insert text or other information at the bookmark.

You can use Word's macro recorder to help construct Word Object Model references. Once you have recorded a WordBasic macro, you can copy it to a VBA module page and modify it so that it works with VBA. WordBasic statements require only slight modifications to become Word Object Model references. Chapter 6 contains more information about using Word's macro recorder.

The next segment of code sets variables equal to the PivotTable and PivotTable page field. These variables are used later to change the page field settings when the PivotTable is copied to the Word report:

```
'find the first page field in the pivot table and assign it to
'pvfPivotField
    Set pvtPivotTable = ActiveSheet.PivotTables(1)
    Set pvfPivotField = pvtPivotTable.PivotFields( _
    pvtPivotTable.PageRange.Range("A1").Value)
```

Next, the procedure uses .EditGoTo to move to the bookmark where the first PivotTable copy is to be printed:

```
'go to bookmark in Word document
    .StartOfDocument
    .editgoto Destination:="StartTables"
```

For each location in the page field, this procedure copies the Excel PivotTable and pastes the copy to Word:

```
'loop through page field items and copy PivotTable to Word document
    For Each pviPivotItem In pvfPivotField.PivotItems
        pviPivotItem.Visible = True
        pvfPivotField.CurrentPage = pviPivotItem.Name
        .insertpara
        .Style "Heading 1"
        .Insert CStr(pvfPivotField.CurrentPage)
        pvtPivotTable.TableRange2.Copy
        .editpaste
        .insertpara
        .insertpara
        .insertpara
    Application.CutCopyMode = False
    Next pviPivotItem
```

This procedure inserts a heading before each PivotTable copy. The headings are used to create the table of contents.

The next lines of code insert the title and subtitle at the bookmark locations.

```
'add titles to Word Document
    .StartOfDocument
    .editgoto Destination:="TitleText"
    .Insert "Sales by Location, Unit and Division"
    .insertpara
    .editgoto Destination:="SubTitleText"
    .Insert "Report Prepared "
    .Insert CStr(Date)
```

In the code that follows, the `.InsertTableOfContents` statement starts Word's automatic indexing features. Word builds a table of contents that includes all text entries in the standard heading styles:

```
' insert Table of Contents
    .InsertPageBreak
    .Insert "Table of Contents"
    .inserttableofcontents
    .StartOfDocument
End With
```

Finally, the procedure sets the object variable `wrdbas` to `Nothing`. This releases any system resources used in making the connection to Word.

```
'free the object variable
    Set wrdbas = Nothing
End Sub
```

The completed Word document is shown in figures 11.14, 11.15, and 11.16.

The title page contains the `Title` and `SubTitle` text collected with the `InputBox` statements. The text is inserted at bookmarks set in the template document.

The table of contents lists each location and a page number that shows where you can find each table in the body of the document.

Fig. 11.14

Page 1 of the Word report contains the title and subtitle entered by the user of the Excel PivotTable workbook.

<u>**Sales by Location, Unit and Division**</u>

<u>**Report Prepared 2/8/96**</u>

Fig. 11.15

Word's Table of Contents feature can be used to automatically add a table of contents to the report. The section headings in the report were inserted using Word's heading 1...n styles which are used to create the table of contents.

<u>**Table of Contents**</u>

ALBANY 101 3
ALBANY 102 3
ALBANY 103 3
CHARLOTTE 101 4
CHARLOTTE 102 4
COLUMBUS 101 4
COLUMBUS 102 5
DETROIT 101 5
DETROIT 102 5
DETROIT 103 6
INDIANAPOLIS 101 6
INDIANAPOLIS 102 7
INDIANAPOLIS 103 7
KNOXVILLE 101 7
KNOXVILLE 103 8

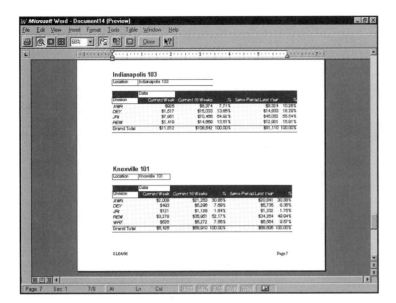

Fig. 11.16

The body of the Word report contains copies of the Excel PivotTable. The VBA procedure creates a copy for each combination of PivotTable page fields.

In this example, you learned how to create a Word report from Excel. You can experiment with the example Excel workbook and Word document template found in the file PIVOTDEMO_2.XLS on the CD-ROM that accompanies this book. The complete procedure is in listing 11.1.

On the CD

Listing 11.1   PIVOTDEMO_2.XLS. PivotDemo Subroutine

```
Option Explicit
Option Base 1

Sub PivotDemo()

  'Define Variables
  Dim wrdbas As Object
  Dim pvtPivotTable As PivotTable
  Dim pvfPivotField As PivotField
  Dim pviPivotItem As PivotItem

  'create connection to Word
  Application.ActivateMicrosoftApp xlMicrosoftWord
  Set wrdbas = CreateObject("Word.Basic")

  'use template to make Word active and open new Word document
  With wrdbas
    .filenew ThisWorkbook.Path & "\TableDoc.dot", 0
    .AppRestore
    .AppSize 407, 327
    .AppMove 33, 84
```

(continues)

III

Advanced Integration

Listing 11.1 Continued

```
      'find the first page field in the pivot table and assign it to
      'pvfPivotField
      Set pvtPivotTable = ActiveSheet.PivotTables(1)
      Set pvfPivotField = pvtPivotTable.PivotFields( _
          pvtPivotTable.PageRange.Range("A1").Value)

      'go to bookmark in Word document
      .StartOfDocument
      .editgoto Destination:="StartTables"

      'loop through page field items and
      'copy PivotTable to Word document
      For Each pviPivotItem In pvfPivotField.PivotItems
        pviPivotItem.Visible = True
        pvfPivotField.CurrentPage = pviPivotItem.Name
        .insertpara
        .Style "Heading 1"
        .Insert CStr(pvfPivotField.CurrentPage)
        pvtPivotTable.TableRange2.Copy
        .editpaste
        .insertpara
        .insertpara
        .insertpara
      Application.CutCopyMode = False
      Next pviPivotItem

      'add titles to Word Document
      .StartOfDocument
      .editgoto Destination:="TitleText"
      .Insert "Sales by Location, Unit and Division"
      .insertpara
      .editgoto Destination:="SubTitleText"
      .Insert "Report Prepared "
      .Insert CStr(Date)

      ' insert Table of Contents
      .InsertPageBreak
      .Insert "Table of Contents"
      .inserttableofcontents
      .StartOfDocument
    End With

    'free the object variable
    Set wrdbas = Nothing
  End Sub
```

In this example, you learn how to prints copies of PivotTables in a Word report.
The example built a table of contents you can use to find data in the report.

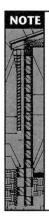

NOTE

You can learn more about using Word as report writer for Excel in the example PIVOTPRINT_8.XLS on the CD-ROM that accompanies this book. PivotToDoc adds these enhancements to the PivotTable reporting example described earlier:

■ Nested PivotTable reports for PivotTables with multiple page fields. The Word report contains subtotal PivotTables and for up to five page fields. The sub-total pivot tables are shown as subheadings in the table of contents.

■ Error checking with error messages displayed in a message box.

■ User input of report title and subtitle using the InputBox method.

■ Ability to select a PivotTable before running the report. This feature is useful if you have more than one PivotTable on a worksheet.

From Here...

In this chapter, you learned about the Excel Object Model and how to use VBA to control the features of Excel. By now you should be comfortable using the Excel macro recorder to create VBA procedures. With the built-in Object Browser and online help for the Object Model, you have the tools you need to begin writing your own VBA procedures.

As you become familiar with using the Excel Object Model, you can leverage your skills by referencing the Object Model from other applications. The Access integration example in this chapter demonstrated how to control an embedded Excel workbook from an Access application.

You can also use the features of other applications from Excel. The Word integration example showed how to use Word as a report writer for Excel.

From here you can continue to sharpen your VBA skills by studying the following chapters:

■ Chapter 4, "Visual Basic and Visual Basic for Applications," enables you to learn by example by reviewing the VBA examples in this chapter.

■ Chapter 10, "Automating Office Integration with Word," describes the Word Object Model. Object models for PowerPoint, Schedule+, and Project are described in Chapters 13–15.

■ Chapter 12, "Automating Office Integration with Access," explains more about the object models for Access.

■ Chapter 16, "Working with Office Compatible Applications." You can learn more about integrating other applications that are not part of the Microsoft family.

■ Chapter 17, "Controlling Office Applications with Visual Basic," shows you how similar VBA is to the Visual Basic 4.0 language.

III

Advanced Integration

CHAPTER 12

Automating Office Integration with Access

Up to this point, this book has focused on Office application capabilities and interactive skills needed to build integrated Office applications. Chapter 2, "Windows and Office Capabilities," introduced you to many of the new features in Access and discussed ways to incorporate Access features into your integrated Office application. In Chapter 3, "Integration Basics," you learned how to link and embed objects (OLE) interactively, drag-and-drop data, and edit OLE objects in-place. As you learned in Chapters 7 and 8, Access integrates smoothly with Word and Excel, making it easy to interactively share data between Office applications.

This chapter builds upon these foundation skills and focuses on the integration features of Access Visual Basic for Applications (VBA). Once you know how to refer to Access objects, you can control the objects in Access and respond to conditions at runtime. Access VBA allows you to communicate with other Office applications to automate many of the data sharing and exchange tasks key to building an integrated Office application. You can write Access VBA code that controls objects in other Office applications, or controls Access objects from other Office applications.

In this chapter, you learn about

- Access object architecture
- Data access object hierarchy
- Object reference approaches
- Object manipulation within Access
- OLE Automation with Access as the client
- OLE Automation with Access as the server

Exploring the Access Object Architecture

By design, the Windows 95 environment revolves around objects—buttons, windows, even text are selectable objects. It comes as no surprise then that Access databases consist of objects. When a user opens an Access database, the Database window lists tables, queries, forms, reports, macros, and modules, all of which are objects. Many objects in Access contain other objects. For example, a form contains controls such as labels, combo boxes, and option buttons. To manipulate Access objects, you need to understand the object hierarchy and terminology.

NOTE This chapter assumes that you are familiar with the concepts covered in Chapter 4, "Visual Basic and Visual Basic for Applications," and Chapter 5, "Programming Application Integration." Basic programming skills such as declaring variables and attaching code to events are not covered in this chapter. If necessary, refer to Chapters 4 and 5 for complete coverage of foundation programming concepts before continuing. This chapter builds on the programming basics and focuses on Access-specific concepts.

Tracing the Data Access Object Hierarchy

The Jet database engine forms the foundation beneath Access that manages data manipulation tasks for Access. In addition to the objects defined by Access (such as forms and controls), the Jet database engine defines objects you can use in VBA to handle data management tasks (such as creating a table or compacting a database). Access organizes the Jet database objects, called *Data Access Objects* (*DAO*), into a hierarchy (see fig. 12.1).

The underlying premise of the hierarchy is that objects can contain other objects. Objects contained by other objects are grouped into collections. In Access VBA, you can work with the collection (such as all fields in a table) instead of writing code for each individual object in the collection. This feature speeds up your programming efforts and makes your code easier to read. Because collections are treated as objects, they have their own methods and properties. An object within a collection is referred to as an *element*. For example, in the Forms collection, a specific form is an element of the Forms collection.

Figure 12.1 shows the top level object in Access is the DBEngine object. DBEngine object represents the Microsoft Jet database engine. The Jet database engine is the data manager component on which Access is built. The Jet engine retrieves data from and stores data in user and system databases. DBEngine contains and controls all other objects in the DAO hierarchy.

You can use the DBEngine object to control the Jet database engine, modify its properties, and perform tasks on temporary objects that aren't elements of collections. For example, you can change the current directory path by setting the SystemDB property of the DBEngine object:

```
DBEngine.SystemDB = "C:\Windows\System\System.mdb"
```

DBEngine CompactDatabase and RepairDatabase methods allow you to compact and repair database files under program control. The following example copies a database named NORTHWIND.MDB, creates a compacted copy named COPY.NEW, and encrypts the database:

```
DBEngine.CompactDatabase "C:\Northwind.mdb", "C:\Copy.mdb","",dbEncrypt
```

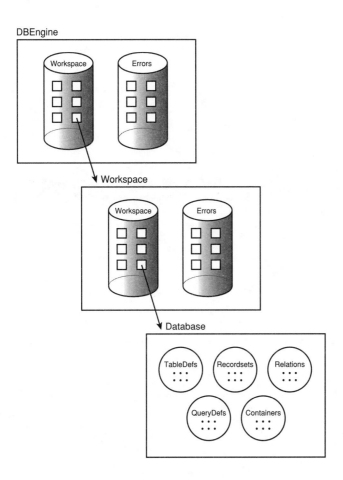

DBEngine

Workspace

Database

Fig. 12.1

The Data Access Object hierarchy allows you to work with object collections and specific objects within a collection.

You can even start a new session from VBA by using the CreateWorkspace method. A session (called a Workspace object in Access VBA) begins when a user logs on and ends when a user logs off. The following example creates a new Workspace object named Restricted and sets its UserName property to "guest":

```
Dim wspRestricted As Workspace
' Create new workspace.
Set wspRestricted = DBEngine.CreateWorkspace("Restricted","guest", "")
```

As you can see in figure 12.1, the DBEngine object contains a Workspace collection and an Errors collection. The Errors collection can be used to get information on data access errors that occur during program execution. See Chapter 19, "Handling the Unexpected," for more information on error trapping and handling.

Within the Workspace object, you find three collections: Databases, Users, and Groups. The Databases collection includes all open databases. When you open an existing database, or create a new one, it is automatically added to the Databases collection. The Users collection contains all current user account information.

The Groups collection contains all current group account information. You can use the User and Group objects to create and manage permissions—what users and groups are allowed to do in a database.

In figure 12.1, you see that the Database object on the bottom contains five collections: TableDefs, Recordsets, Relations, QueryDefs, and Containers. Figure 12.2 further breaks down the Database collection, showing the objects within each DAO collection. Table 12.1 lists and describes the collections and objects found within the Database object.

Table 12.1	Access Database Collections and Objects	
Collection	**Object**	**Description**
Containers	Container	Contains eight predefined Container objects that organize information by object type: Databases, Forms, Modules, Relationships, Reports, Scripts, Tables, and SysRel.
Documents	Document	Information about a saved, predefined object.
Fields	Field	A column that is part of a table, query, index, relation, or recordset.
Indexes	Index	Predefined ordering and uniqueness of values in a table.
Parameters	Parameter	A parameter for a parameter query.
Properties	Property	A built-in or user-defined property. Note that every DAO has a property collection that contains property objects.
QueryDefs	QueryDef	A saved query definition.
Recordsets	Recordset	The records in a table or query.
Relations	Relation	A relationship between fields in tables and queries.
TableDefs	TableDef	A saved table definition.

Referring to Objects

To refer to an object within a collection, you need to know the identifier. An identifier can be the name of the collection that includes the object name or the name of an object whose default collection includes the object name. For example, suppose that an open form named Customer is a member of the Forms collection of open forms. If the Customer form is the first form opened, you could refer to the Customer form using any of the following lines:

```
Forms!Customer
Forms("Customer")
Forms(0)
```

The first syntax version lists the object collection (Forms), an exclamation mark (!), and then the specific object name (Customer). If the object name contains a space or punctuation, or if the object name is a restricted VBA word, syntax rules require the object name be enclosed in square brackets ([ ]).

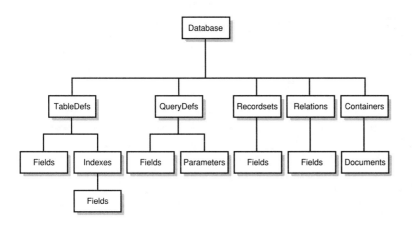

Fig. 12.2

To change the design of a table in VBA, you need to access the TableDef *object.*

The second syntax version lists the object collection (Forms) and then the specific object name enclosed in quotes and then parentheses. If the object name is stored in a string variable, omit the quotes.

The third syntax version lists the object collection (Forms) and then an index number enclosed in parentheses (an example of this version appears later in this chapter). The index number is the ordinal position of an object in a collection. Because the Customer form was the first form opened, it has an index value of zero. You can use this syntax version to loop through all the objects in a collection.

Which syntax version you decide to use depends on the circumstances at runtime and what information you have at runtime. The first two versions document your work better by listing the exact object name to which your code refers. The index version is trickier and may give odd results if the user interferes and opens additional objects without your knowing.

Creating Object Variables

VBA allows you to declare object variables to refer to objects instead of typing out the entire object identifier every time you need to work with that object. Object variables streamline your code and allow you to create generic procedures that work for various types of objects.

NOTE   You can't assign object variables to collections or to the following Access objects: DoCmd, Debug, Module, Screen, or Section. You can assign object variables to any of the Data Access Objects except the DBEngine object (no DAO collections, either).

Object variables follow the same declaration and scoping rules as other variables. You can declare an object variable using the `Dim`, `ReDim`, `Static`, `Private`, or `Public` statements. The `Set` statement associates an object variable with an existing object. The following example declares an object variable named `frm` for a form named `Customer`. The variable `frm` is then used to change the form's `Caption` property to the current date and time:

```
Dim frm As Form
Set frm = Forms!Customer
frm.Caption = Now
```

NOTE Object variables differ from regular variables in one major area. When you assign values to regular variables, the values for each variable are stored in separate memory locations. Object variables refer to actual physical objects in the database or in memory. An object can have more than one object variable, but an object variable can't refer to more than one object. This ensures that the object's properties reflect the most current settings, whether modified by you in code or by the user.

In the `Set` statement, the keyword `New` can be used to create another instance of an object. For example, you may want to view more than one customer at a time. In the following code example, another instance of the Customer form appears, allowing the user to see two customer records at once:

```
Dim frmNewInst As Form_Customer
Set frmNewInst = New form_Customer
frmNewInst.AllowAdditions = False
frmNewInst.Visible = True
colFrmInstances.Add frmNewInst
```

Also, be sure to add the following line to the general declarations section:

```
Dim colFrmInstances as new collection
```

TIP When using the `New` keyword to create another instance of an object, set the `Visible` property to True to see the new instance.

TIP To release memory and system resources when done with an object variable, set the object variable equal to Nothing.

Working with Access Object Collections. The following example shows how to use an object variable for the collection `Control` to clear all the text boxes on the current form. Notice that the use of an index works well here and makes the code portable (generic) to other forms:

```
Sub ClearControls (frmTemp As Form)
  'Declare control and integer variables.
  Dim ctlCurrent As Control, intIndex As Integer
  'Loop through the controls on a form.
  For intIndex = 0 To frmTemp.Count - 1
    Set ctlCurrent = frmTemp(intIndex)
    'If control is a text box, clear it.
    If TypeOf ctlCurrent Is TextBox Then
      ctlCurrent = Null
    EndIf
  Next
End Sub
```

NOTE
When you need to set several properties of the same object or perform several tasks with a single object, consider using the With..End With construct instead of listing each statement separately. Aside from saving you typing time, using With..End With makes your code easier to read. The following example sets several properties of the Form object in one statement:

```
With frmTemp
      .RecordSource = "Products"
      .Caption = "Products Form"
            .ScrollBars = 0
      .NavigationButtons = True
End With
```

Working with DAO Objects and Collections. The next example shows how to use object variables with data access objects and collections. The procedure returns a Database object representing the current database, which is open in the Access window. Next, the procedure creates another database called NEWDB.MDB and saves it to disk. Then it opens an existing database called DB1.MDB. Finally, it enumerates all Database objects in the Databases collection:

```
Sub ReferenceDatabases()
    Dim wsp As Workspace
    Dim dbsCurrent As Database, dbsNew As Database
        Dim dbsAnother As Database, dbs As Database

    ' Return Database object pointing to current database.
    Set dbsCurrent = CurrentDb
    ' Return Workspace object pointing to current workspace.
    Set wsp = DBEngine.Workspaces(0)
    ' Create new Database object.
    Set dbsNew = wsp.CreateDatabase("Newdb.mdb", dbLangGeneral)
            'Open database other than current database.

    Set dbsAnother = wsp.OpenDatabase("db1.mdb")
    ' Enumerate all open databases.
    For Each dbs in wsp.Databases
        Debug.Print dbs.Name
    Next dbs
End Sub
```

Advanced Integration

III

Using Generic Object Properties

As an experienced programmer, you know the value of a good generic routine. A good generic code routine sits in your programming toolbox ready to be used in any programming project with little, if any, modification. It takes longer to develop generic code routines, but you save time in the long run. Access VBA recognizes this need and provides special object properties that you can use in your code to refer generically to objects based on their state. Most of the object properties refer to the currently active object. Several refer to an object based on its relationship as the container of the object or object that previously had focus. Table 12.2 lists these nifty little object properties and describes each one.

Table 12.2   Generic Object Reference Properties

To Refer To A:	Object Class	Property
Control that has focus	Screen	ActiveControl
Form that has focus or contains the control with focus	Screen	ActiveForm
Report that has focus or contains the control with focus	Screen	ActiveReport
Form that contains the code or form associated with the subform control	Form or Subform	Form
Form or report that contains the code	Form or Report	Me
Module of the form or report	Form or Report	Module
The form or report that contains the control	Control	Parent
Control that previously had focus	Screen	PreviousControl
Clone of the form's underlying recordset	Form	RecordsetClone
form or report associated with the subreport control	Report or Subreport	Report
Section of a form or report where the control is located	Control	Section

Working with Screen Properties. The Screen object has properties that you can use to react to conditions at runtime depending on the Screen control that has focus. For example, you can display a message when a user arrives on a specific control to give the user status information. The following code example uses the ActiveControl property of the Screen object to determine if the user has arrived on the CustomerID control. If so, a message box displays stating the status of the customer's account:

```
Sub CheckStatus()
  Dim ctlCurrent As Control
  Set ctlCurrent = Screen.ActiveControl
  If ctlCurrent.Name = "txtCustomerId" Then
    MsgBox "This customer's account status is " & status
  End If
End Sub
```

Working with Form and Report Properties. The Me, Module, and RecordsetClone properties can be used with any form or report. Use the Me property to determine which form or report the code is currently running in. This is especially helpful when building integrated Office applications and when sharing code across various forms and reports. Unlike the ActiveForm and ActiveReport properties, the Me property can refer to a form or report that is not currently active. For example, suppose that you have a Timer event coded on a hidden form or report. Using Me in that code block will always correctly refer to the form or report that contains the Timer event routine, regardless of what form or report the user is currently working on.

The Module property can be used to modify procedures at runtime. You can insert, delete, and edit module code from within your VBA code. The following example inserts a Beep into the form's Open event procedure at runtime:

```
Sub AddBeep()
  Dim strFormOpen As String
  strFormOpen = "Sub Form_Open(Cancel As Integer)" & vbCrLf & "Beep" &
  ➥strCRLF & "End Sub"
  Forms![MyForm].Module.InsertText strFormOpen
End Sub
```

The RecordSetClone property refers to a form's Recordset object specified by the form's RecordSource property. It is a copy of the underlying query or table specified by the form's RecordSource property. If a form is based on a query, for example, referring to the RecordsetClone property is the equivalent of cloning a Recordset object using the same query. If you then apply a filter to the form, the Recordset object reflects the filtering.

NOTE The RecordsetClone property provides access to all the methods and properties that apply to a Recordset object. However, you can't edit or add data. The RecordsetClone property is read-only in all views.

The RecordsetClone property is mainly used when you need to navigate or operate on a form's records independent of the form itself. For example, suppose that you need to use a method such as the FindFirst method that isn't available to be used in a form. You could use the RecordsetClone property to access the underlying data and use the FindFirst method.

III

Advanced Integration

TIP

When using `RecordsetClone`, be sure to synchronize the current record in the `Recordset` object with the form's current record (assign the form's `Bookmark` property to a string variable; then assign the string variable to the `Recordset` object's `Bookmark` property).

The following example uses the `RecordsetClone` property to count the number of records in a form:

```
Sub HowManyRecords()
    Forms!Customer.RecordsetClone.MoveLast
    Msg = "We currently have " & Forms!Orders.RecordsetClone.RecordCount
    Msg = Msg & " customer records.", vbInformation, "Record Count"
    MsgBox Msg
End Sub
```

Working with Control Properties. The `Parent` property of a control refers to the object that contains the control. Usually, a control's container is the `Form` or `Report` object. But a control could be embedded inside another control. For example, an option button's parent is the option group object. The parent of a label control is the control the label is linked to. You can use the `Parent` property to refer to the parent of a control, section, or control that contains other controls. The `Parent` property returns a `Control` object if the parent is a control; it returns a `Form` object or `Report` object if the parent is a form or report.

The `Parent` property can be used to determine which form or report is currently the parent when you have a subform or subreport that has been inserted in multiple forms or reports. For instance, you might insert a CustomerDetail subform into both a form and a report. The following example uses the `Parent` property to refer to the CustomerID field, which is present on the main form and report. You can enter this expression in a bound control on the subform:

```
= Parent![CustomerID]
```

`Form` and `Report` properties are usually used to work with subform and subreport controls. If you need to refer to the form or report that contains your code, use the `Me` property instead. Your code will be easier to read and maintain if you use `Me` (the `Form` and `Report` properties work the same for backward compatibility purposes only).

The `Section` property gives you a way to access the section of a form or report that contains a control. You can use the `Section` property to identify a section of a form or report and use the properties of that section. You can also identify controls by the section of a form or report where the control appears. The `Section` property is an Integer data type value corresponding to a particular section (see table 12.3). If a report has additional group-level sections, the header/footer pairs are numbered consecutively beginning with 9.

Table 12.3 **Section Settings**	
Setting	**Description**
0	Form detail section or report detail section
1	Form or report header section
2	Form or report footer section
3	Form or report page header section
4	Form or report page footer section
5	Group-level 1 header section (reports only)
6	Group-level 1 footer section (reports only)
7	Group-level 2 header section (reports only)
8	Group-level 2 footer section (reports only)

For forms and reports, the Section property is an array of all existing sections in the form or report specified by the section number. For example, Section(0) refers to a form's detail section, and Section(3) refers to a form's header section. You can also refer to a section by name. The following statements both refer to the Visible property of the Detail section of a form named Customer:

```
Forms![Customer].Section(0).Visible
```

```
Forms![Customer].Detail0.Visible
```

At times, you may want to hide or display certain sections of a form or report depending on conditions at runtime. For example, in a Payroll system, you may need to hide the Officers salary details unless the user has the proper security clearances:

```
Forms![Payroll].Section(0).Visible = False
```

The Section property can also be used to determine which section of a form or report contains a specific control. The following example uses the Section property to determine which section contains the CustomerID control:

```
Dim intSectionNumber As Integer
intSectionNumber = Forms![Customer]![CustomerID].Section
```

Using the Object Browser

The *Object Browser* lists the objects in your Access database, in the Access object library, and in the object libraries of other available applications. An *object library* contains information about the types of objects that an application contains (sometimes referred to as a *type library*). Using the Object Browser, you can get help on an object, paste Method or Property code syntax into a module, or locate a specific object type.

To display the Object Browser, open a module in Design view and choose View, Object Browser or press F2. As you can see in figure 12.3, the Object Browser window is divided into four major sections. The Libraries/Databases box allows you to select the library or database in which you want to browse. The Modules/Classes box displays

III

Advanced Integration

the types of objects available in the selected library or database. The Methods/Properties box displays the methods, properties, and data elements defined for the selected object type.

Fig. 12.3

In the Access library, for the Screen *object type,* ActiveForm *is a defined property.*

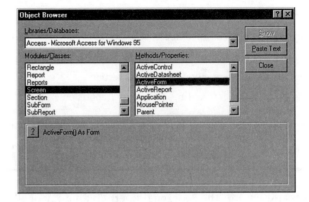

The bottom pane of the Object Browser window displays any applicable syntax (see fig. 12.4). The ? button opens the Help application and displays the Help page on the selected object, method, or property. Use the Show button to view the selected procedure listed in the Methods/Properties box. This feature allows you to use the Object Browser to browse through modules and locate procedures quickly. The Paste Text button inserts the syntax listed in the bottom panel into your program at the current cursor location.

Fig. 12.4

The bottom pane provides the full syntax for the CreateTableDef *method, which can be pasted into a module.*

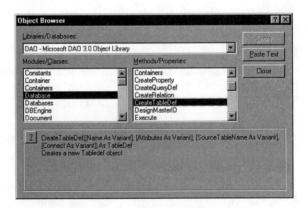

Some applications store their object library in a separate file (for example, the VBA object library resides in the file VAEN232.OLB). The Access databases you create store the object library information with the database, rather than in a separate file. To browse through object libraries, a reference to that application's object library needs to be set.

To set a reference to an application's object library, follow these steps:

1. Choose Tools, References (the References dialog box appears, shown in fig. 12.5).

2. Select the checkboxes for the desired application type libraries.

3. Choose OK.

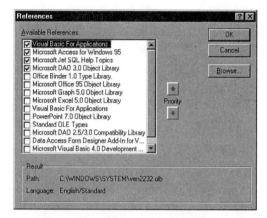

Fig. 12.5

The bottom pane of the References dialog box lists the full path to the selected object library file.

Caution

Being able to access objects and procedures from a variety of object libraries is a powerful programming tool. But you need to make contingency plans for when your application is distributed to other users in different environments. The object library reference relies on the exact path and file name you indicated when you created your application. If the file name changes (as frequently happens when software is updated) or if the location of the file changes, your code will not work. Build in error-handling routines that control what happens when a library database cannot be loaded. If you rely on external libraries, add file name and location checks to your on-going maintenance checklist. (See Chapter 19, "Handling the Unexpected," for more information on error-handling routines.)

By setting a reference to another Access database, you can call the public (not private) functions and procedures listed in that other database. For example, the Northwind sample database includes a module named Utility Functions that contains a function called IsLoaded. You can set a reference to the Northwind sample database from the current database and then call the IsLoaded function just as you would if it were defined within the current database. If the function or procedure being called has the same name as another function or procedure, provide the full dot notation qualifier. All the following statements call the IsLoaded function, but with varying degrees of qualification:

```
' Fully qualified.
[Northwind.mdb].[Utility Functions].IsLoaded("Orders")
```

III

Advanced Integration

```
' Qualified by name of module.
[Utility Functions].IsLoaded("Orders")

' Not qualified.
IsLoaded("Orders")
```

OLE Automation

Object Linking and Embedding (OLE) is a Windows protocol that allows you to integrate information from different applications and present objects from those applications to users in a single compound document. Applications that support OLE expose their objects to other OLE-compliant applications. Using OLE, you can create and manipulate objects in other applications without ever having to start the other application yourself.

OLE Automation is a feature of OLE that allows you to access another application's objects from outside that application. Windows applications that support OLE Automation expose their objects to other OLE applications, such as Access and VBA. You can control another application by accessing its objects and methods. When you use OLE Automation, the attached application's objects and methods become an extension of the VBA language.

For example, Visio 4 supports OLE and exposes many objects such as documents, windows, shapes, and pages. Each Visio object has its own set of methods and properties. Using OLE Automation in Access VBA, you could create a Visio rectangle in the Visio application and then type text into the rectangle:

```
Set MyRect = CurrPage.DrawRectangle(1,1,2,2)
MyRect.Text = "Hello From Access"
```

NOTE Not all Windows 95 applications support the OLE Automation protocol, and of those that do, some only expose a few objects. Project 4.1, for instance, only exposes the `Application` object. Furthermore, some applications only support OLE Automation as a client and don't expose OLE objects to other applications. Before assuming that you can use OLE Automation, check with the vendor to make sure that you have access to the objects you need.

Access, Excel, and Word all support OLE Automation as a server or client. An OLE Automation server application exposes certain objects and allows you to set object properties and use object methods from an external "client" application. The OLE Automation client application provides programming code access to other OLE Automation servers. Access 2.0 is a "client only" OLE Automation application. And, Word only supports OLE Automation as a server. Access 95 supports OLE Automation as both a client and server.

Table 12.4 lists the key Office applications and the OLE Automation objects that each exposes.

Table 12.4 OLE Automation Objects	
Office Application	**OLE Automation Object**
Word for Windows 95	Application Document WordBasic
Excel for Windows 95	Application Chart Worksheet
Access	Application
Project	Application

NOTE

OLE Automation objects can't be linked or embedded. This is because they only exist while your code runs. Users can't access OLE Automation objects interactively. You create them in code, and they cease to exist after your code executes.

Using Access as an OLE Automation Client

In Access, you can use OLE Automation to manipulate objects available only at the Jet database engine level, such as workspaces and users. Using OLE Automation, you can create and manipulate Access objects such as forms and reports to respond to runtime events. Rather than create a procedure that performs a specialized task, you can use OLE Automation to bring an external application that performs that task into your application.

To use objects from another application, the application must be properly registered with Windows 95 (this usually happens when you install applications). In Access, you need to open the References dialog box (choose Tools, References) and check the appropriate object library (see the earlier section, "Using the Object Browser"). After the object library reference is set up, you can use the Object Browser to explore the other application's objects, methods, and properties.

NOTE

Access 95 supports the New keyword for declarations such as Dim, Private, and Set. New can be used to declare the object variable as a new instance of a Visual Basic object or an externally created OLE Automation object. The New keyword can't be used to declare variables of any intrinsic data type and can't be used to declare instances of dependent OLE Automation objects.

Using OLE Automation Functions. Access VBA has two functions that provide access to OLE Automation objects in cases where the library is not available: CreateObject and GetObject. The CreateObject function creates a new object of the specified type.

III

Advanced Integration

The syntax is as follows, where *class* is the name of the object type exposed by the other application. To determine the object type without a library, you need to access the application's documentation:

```
CreateObject(class)
```

> **TIP**
>
> For applications without an object library, use the CreateObject method to access a new object, or the GetObject method to access an existing object.

To create an OLE Automation object, you need to assign the object returned by CreateObject to an object variable. In the following example, the Word application is opened. If Word is already running, a new instance of Word is started. Finally, a WordBasic OLE Automation object is created:

```
Dim objWordBasic As Object
Set objWordBasic = CreateObject("Word.Basic")
```

Once created, you can use the OLE Automation object in your Access VBA code as needed, just as if it was part of Access VBA. The following are some examples of running Word from Access VBA:

```
objWordBasic.Insert "Hello from Access!!"
objWordBasic.FilePrint
objWordBasic.FileSaveAs "C:\TEST.DOC"
```

Caution

Unfortunately, not all applications react the same when you use CreateObject or GetObject. Excel, for example, starts up invisibly. Word starts up visibly. Word closes when its variable is set to Nothing or goes out of scope. Excel closes if it is invisible when its object variable is set to Nothing or goes out of scope.

Furthermore, if an object has registered itself as a single-instance object (for example, the Word.Basic object in Microsoft Word 6.0), only one instance of the object is created, no matter how many times CreateObject is executed.

In addition, with a single-instance object, GetObject always returns the same instance when called with the zero-length string syntax (""), and it causes an error if the path name argument is omitted. You cannot use GetObject to obtain a reference to a class created with Visual Basic.

As with most things in life, nothing teaches like first-hand experience, so proceed with caution and test, debug, and expect the unexpected.

The following example uses OLE Automation to create an Excel worksheet object and access its methods and properties from Access VBA. The UpdateSheet procedure receives income data from an Access table (the AccessIncome variable) and inserts the value on an Excel worksheet (cells 1,1). Using OLE Automation, the Excel worksheet is saved, and the OLE object objSheet is removed from memory (doing so closes Excel):

```
Sub UpdateSheet(AccessIncome As Integer)
Dim objSheet As Object      ' Declare variable to hold the reference.
Set objSheet = CreateObject("excel.sheet")
objSheet.Cells(1,1).Value = AccessIncome
objSheet.SaveAs("NewIncome.xls")
Set objSheet = Nothing
End Sub
```

The `GetObject` function retrieves an OLE Automation object from a file. The syntax is as follows where the *pathname* is the path and name of the object to be retrieved. The *class* argument is optional and specifies the object type:

```
GetObject([pathname][, class])
```

Whereas the `CreateObject` function is used when there is no current instance of the object, the `GetObject` function is used when there is a current instance, or if you want to start the application and have it load a file. Some applications allow you to activate only part of a file by adding an exclamation point (!) to the end of the file name and then following it with a string that identifies the part of the file you want to activate.

> **NOTE**
> If *pathname* is a zero-length string (""), `GetObject` returns a new object instance of the specified type. If the pathname argument is omitted entirely, `GetObject` returns a currently active object of the specified type.

The following example opens the Excel workbook located at C:\EXCEL\INCOME.XLS and enters data from Access (the `AccessIncome` variable) into the first cell. The edited worksheet is saved and then Excel is closed:

```
Sub UpdateSheet(AccessIncome As Integer)
Dim objSheet As Object      ' Declare variable to hold the reference.
Set objSheet = GetObject("c:excel\Income.xls","Excel.Sheet")
objSheet.Cells(1,1).Value = AccessIncome
objSheet.Save
Set objSheet = Nothing
End Sub
```

Using OLE Automation Methods and Properties. After you have created a variable that references an OLE Automation object, you can use the `Object.Property` syntax to set and get object properties and to use object methods. Some applications such as Word don't support methods and properties. Instead, you manipulate objects by using the application's programming language functions and statements. Refer to the server application's documentation.

In the following example, Project and the file WORKPLAN.MPP are opened from Access VBA. The first task for project 1 is then entered into the `ActiveControl` in Access. Finally, Project is closed:

```
Sub RunProject()
  Dim objProject As Object, Task As String
  MsProject.Application.FileOpen Name:="C:\Projects\WorkPlan.MPP"
  Task = MSProject.Application.Projects(1).Tasks(1).Name
```

```
        ActiveControl.Value = Task
        MSProject.Application.FileExit
    End Sub
```

In the next example, Word functions and statements are used to create a new document using the Letter template in Word. The cursor is sent to the Envelope bookmark
in the template; the address from the Customer form is entered; and the document is
printed:

```
    Sub FindText(target As String)
        Dim objWord As Object
        Set objWord = CreateObject("Word.Basic")
        With objWord
          .FileNew "Letter"
          .EditGoTo "Envelope"
          .Insert Forms!Customer.Name & Chr(10)
          .Insert Forms!Customer.Address & Chr(10)
          .Insert Forms!Customer.City & ", "
          .Insert Forms!Customer.State & "   "
          .Insert Forms!Customer.Zip & Chr(10)
          .FilePrint
        End With
    End Sub
```

Using Access as an OLE Automation Server

As you build your integrated Office application, you may find that you need to run
Access from within another Office application. Because Access 95 supports OLE Automation as both a client and a server, you can do so. Access exposes the `Application`
object to provide other applications access to its objects, methods, and properties.
The `Application` object contains the `Forms` collection, the `Reports` collection, the
`DBEngine` object (see the earlier section "Tracing the Data Access Object Hierarchy"),
the `Screen` object, and the `DoCmd` object. By combining `CreateObject`, `GetObject`,
and the Access `Application` object, you can manipulate Access objects and use their
methods and properties from an external application.

In Access, the `Application` object is at the top of the object hierarchy, and all other
objects and collections are members of it. To control Access with OLE Automation,
you can create an instance of the `Application` object and access all other objects and
their properties and methods through it. The following code example creates a new
instance of Access from Excel:

```
    Dim appAccess As Access.Application
    Set appAccess = CreateObject("Access.Application.7")
```

From some applications, such as Visual Basic 4, you can use the `New` keyword to
declare an object variable and point it to a new instance of Access in one step:

```
    Dim appAccess As New Access.Application
```

If you use the `New` keyword to create an instance of Access, that instance will not
become visible until you have called a method or set or returned a property on the

Application object. For example, the following line of code would make the new instance of Access visible and also make it the active application:

```
appAccess.AppActivate
```

Using the DBEngine property of the Application object, you can return a reference to the DBEngine object. Using this reference, you can access all data access objects and collections.

You can also use the Application object to apply methods or property settings to the entire Access application. For example, you can use the SetOption method of the Application object to set database options from Visual Basic:

```
Application.SetOption "Show Status Bar", True
```

For example, Visual Basic is an OLE Automation controller. You can open an Access database from Visual Basic and work with its objects. From Visual Basic, first create a reference to Access. Then create a new instance of the Application object and point an object variable to it, as in the following example:

```
Dim appAccess As Access.Application
Set appAccess = CreateObject("Access.Application.7")
```

After you have created a new instance of the Access Application object, you can open a database or create a new database, using either the OpenCurrentDatabase method or the NewCurrentDatabase method. You can then set the properties of the Application object and call its methods.

To create a new instance of the Access Application object from Excel, you must declare the object variable as type Object:

```
Dim appAccess As Object
Set appAccess = CreateObject("Access.Application.7")
```

You can also manipulate other Access objects through the Application object. For example, using the OpenForm method of the Access DoCmd object, you can open an Access form from within an Excel VBA procedure:

```
appAccess.DoCmd.OpenForm "OrderForm"
```

The following procedure creates a new instance of the Access Application object and opens a new database in the Access Database window. It then creates a new form in that database. This code can be placed in any Visual Basic module of an application that supports OLE Automation as a client (be sure that Microsoft Access 7.0 is checked in the References dialog box).

NOTE An instance of Access closes when the variable pointing to the Application object goes out of scope. To prevent Access from closing when the procedure ends, declare the variable representing the Application object at the module level.

III

Advanced Integration

```
' Declare object variable in Declarations section of module.
Dim appAccess As Access.Application

Sub NewAccessDB()
      ' Declare Database variable and Microsoft Access Form variable.
      Dim dbs As Database, frm As Access.Form

      ' Return instance of Application object.
      Set appAccess = CreateObject("Access.Application.7")
      ' Create new database in Microsoft Access window.
      appAccess.NewCurrentDatabase("Newdb.mdb")
      ' Create new Microsoft Access form in Design view.

      set frm = appAccess.CreateForm
      ' Restore form window.
      appAccess.DoCmd.Restore
End Sub
```

From Here...

This chapter examined how to automate the integration of Access into your Office application. You learned about the Access object architecture and how to use the data access object hierarchy. You directly referenced objects and manipulated objects in Access. Lastly, this chapter showed you how to use OLE Automation with Access as the client and as the server.

If you would like to learn more about integrating Access into your Office application, you can find more information on related topics in the following chapters:

■ Extend the power of Access VBA by using Visual Basic; see Chapter 17, "Controlling Office Applications with Visual Basic."

■ Spend time up front to plan the user interface; see Chapter 18, "Designing the User Interface."

■ Integrated applications need to gracefully handle errors at runtime. See Chapter 19, "Handling the Unexpected."

CHAPTER 13

Automating Office Integration with PowerPoint

Office is a very productive tool for creating and keeping track of your ideas and information. Many users are familiar with gathering information in the form of a Word document or Excel worksheet, maybe even an Access database. But there will be times when you want to visually communicate your ideas and information to people. Microsoft's PowerPoint delivers on this need, offering specialized tools for creating and enhancing slides while maintaining its complete integration with the other Office applications. PowerPoint gives you a number of different ways to deliver your presentations, including on-screen slide shows, 35mm slides, overhead transparencies, and printed material.

In this chapter, you learn to

- Use the integration features included with PowerPoint
- Insert objects from other applications
- Edit and maintain inserted objects
- Use VBA to integrate PowerPoint into an application

Reviewing PowerPoint's Integration Features

Because of Microsoft's continued investment in making Office applications work together seamlessly, PowerPoint supports many of the same Windows 95 integration features as the other Office applications, including the Binder (see Chapter 2, "Windows and Office Capabilities").

In addition, however, PowerPoint has been optimized for working with multimedia objects. While in Word, Excel, and Access documents you use multimedia to enhance the text and data, you build PowerPoint presentations primarily by using multimedia elements, supplementing the multimedia with text only when necessary for clarity. For example, two of PowerPoint's predesigned slide layouts have placeholders for media (video or animation) clips. None of the other Office applications offer a comparable feature.

PowerPoint for Windows 95 offers the following integration features:

■ *OLE*. As with the other Office applications, PowerPoint supports OLE and OLE Automation. OLE enables you to easily insert objects from other applications into PowerPoint, or insert objects from PowerPoint into other applications. As you learned earlier in Chapter 3, "Integration Basics," OLE gives you full access to the source application's tools when you create or edit an object in the container file.

■ *Look and Feel*. As an Office-compatible application, PowerPoint offers the same look and feel as other Office applications. For example, the Standard toolbar in PowerPoint is nearly identical to the Standard toolbar in Word and Excel.

■ *Drag-and-Drop*. Drag-and-drop information to and from PowerPoint to share information between applications.

■ *Write-Up*. This new feature, found only in PowerPoint, automatically sends PowerPoint slides to a Word document, creating a simple way to print, format, and distribute a presentation as a hard copy.

Enhancing PowerPoint with Other Office Applications

In addition to using PowerPoint as a stand-alone application, you can incorporate objects from other Office applications into your presentations. These objects can be from Word, Excel, Access, or many of the additional software tools that are included with Office.

Chapter 3, "Integration Basics," introduced the procedures for using OLE features in Office and the different methods for creating linked and embedded objects. This section, provides an overview of working with objects in PowerPoint to supplement the steps you learned in Chapter 3.

Creating Linked Objects

As you learned, linked objects in PowerPoint are connected via OLE to original source files. This enables PowerPoint to automatically update objects it contains after you update the source information. This form of integration can be particularly useful in business, not only because it saves the time required to retype information, but also because it eliminates errors that may creep in when you're retyping information. Here are just a few situations where you might want to create linked objects in PowerPoint:

■ Part of your business presentation is based on an Excel worksheet that's updated by members of another department and stored on the network. By linking objects in your presentation to the Excel file, you can update those objects daily, so you're always reporting the most current figures.

- You're a sales representative selling several different product lines to companies in widely differing industries. You've got about 10 different PowerPoint presentations tailored for different kinds of clients. Although the presentations are different, many contain similar components. Say that five presentations contain the description for the XYZ product line, but the XYZ description is out of date. In this case, you could create a master document in Word that contains all the information you need for your presentations, and link parts of that master file to different presentations as needed. Then, instead of editing the XYZ information five times in five presentations, you could edit it once in the Word master file and simply update your PowerPoint objects as needed.

- You've created and nicely formatted a Word table with product pricing information. Rather than retype and reformat the information, you paste it as a linked object into PowerPoint. Then, as prices change and you make those changes in the Word table, you can quickly update the PowerPoint object to show the correct pricing.

Figure 13.1 shows inserted, linked objects from both Word and Excel. The source data for each object was copied from the source application by choosing Edit, Copy. Then, by choosing Edit, Paste Special, they were pasted into PowerPoint as linked objects using the Paste Link option button. So, when the source documents change, the objects in this presentation also change to reflect the new data.

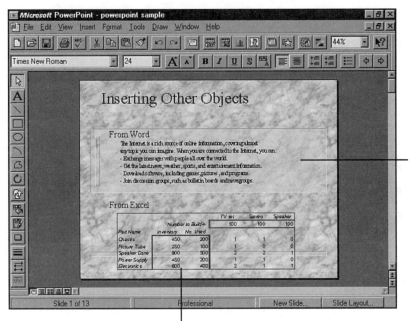

Fig. 13.1

Objects from Word and Excel are easily inserted into a presentation.

This text has been inserted from a Word document.

These cells have been inserted from an Excel worksheet.

You also can create a linked object by choosing Insert, Object. In the Object dialog box, click the Create from File tab. Enter a File Name, including the path, and click Link to File to link the inserted object to the original (source) file. Click OK to finish inserting the object.

Inserting Objects from Other Office Applications

The procedure for inserting objects into PowerPoint is the same as when using Word, Excel, or Access. Unless you create an inserted object from a file, you can't link the information; the inserted, unlinked object merely gives you access to the tools from the source application. As you can see in figure 13.2, the Insert menu looks a bit different in PowerPoint.

Some of the Office applications—Clip Art, Microsoft Word Table, Microsoft Graph, and more—are now located on the Insert menu to save you a step or two in creating these kinds of embedded objects. These object types have not been removed from the Object dialog box (which appears when you choose Insert, Object); instead, because they account for the majority of the objects you insert, Microsoft has made these choices more accessible.

Fig. 13.2

Some of the Office applications are now available directly from the Insert menu.

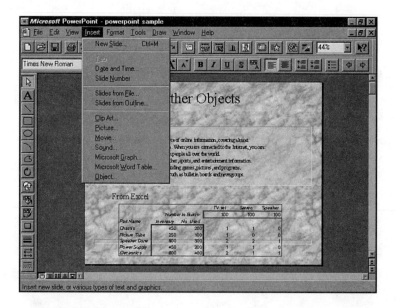

  Two icons on the Standard toolbar provide an easy way for you to insert a Word Table or Excel worksheet onto a slide; Insert Microsoft Word Table and Insert Microsoft Excel Worksheet. Click one of these Insert icons and then drag within the grid to specify the number of cells in the table or worksheet grid (see fig. 13.3). The object appears on the slide, and you can drag and resize it as needed, and then enter the data for it.

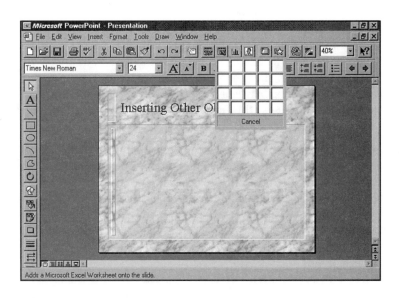

Fig. 13.3

After clicking a Word Table or Excel Worksheet insert icon on the Standard toolbar, then click to choose the number of cells for the object.

Viewing a List of Links

PowerPoint, as well as other Office applications, keeps a list of the objects in each presentation document that are linked to other applications and documents. Choose Edit, Links to display the Links dialog box shown in figure 13.4.

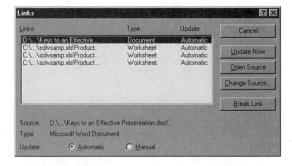

Fig. 13.4

The Links dialog box shows links to the current presentation.

The Links dialog box provides you with a great deal of control over the linked objects. There are four buttons, each giving you a different function in controlling the linked objects:

- *Update Now*. Locates the source file and update its contents in the current presentation.
- *Open Source*. Opens the source file in the source application for editing.
- *Change Source*. Enables you to update the name or location of the source file.
- *Break Link*. Ends the link between the source file and the object; when you break a link and make changes in the source file, the presentation object will no longer reflect those changes.

III

Advanced Integration

Dragging-and-Dropping Objects into PowerPoint

As with all Office applications, PowerPoint supports the Windows 95 drag-and-drop feature. For example, if you prefer to sketch out the text of a presentation in Word you can do so, then select and drag the original (or a copy) of your text into PowerPoint. Dragging-and-dropping between applications inserts the information as an embedded object. So, when you use this feature you can bypass using any menu commands to create the object.

To drag from another OLE-compatible application to PowerPoint, select the information that you want to embed. Press and hold Ctrl (this copies the information rather than moving it to PowerPoint), then drag the object to the taskbar (over the PowerPoint button); continue holding the mouse button until PowerPoint appears, then drag the object into position and release the mouse button. The object appears selected in the presentation, and the tools of the source application appear at the top of the PowerPoint screen.

Editing Objects Inserted into PowerPoint

Once you've inserted an object in a PowerPoint presentation, it's just as simple to edit it as in any other Office application. If an object is embedded, the OLE application usually supports in-place editing and displays its tools within PowerPoint. A linked object opens in the source application that it was created with. Either way, it's easy to edit the object.

Figure 13.5 shows a CorelDRAW! sketch embedded into the PowerPoint presentation. Double-clicking the CorelDRAW! object adds the CorelDRAW! tools to the PowerPoint window (see the toolbars) for editing.

Fig. 13.5

The PowerPoint window has changed to allow the in-place editing of a CorelDRAW! object.

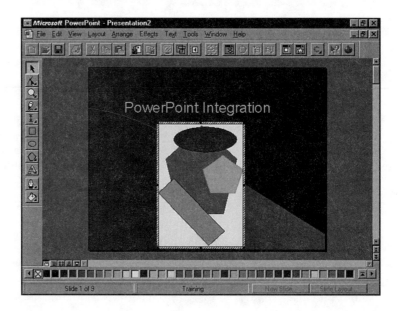

Simply make the changes you want to make, then click outside the linked object or choose File, Exit & Return.

Using WordArt To Enhance Text

One of the supporting applications included with Office is WordArt. WordArt enables you to take normal text and liven it up by applying different effects to it, such as making a phrase take on the shape of a circle or a waving banner. Other programs like CorelDRAW! give you far more options and effects to use when manipulating text. However, WordArt works well for most purposes and saves you the expense of purchasing another program that you may only use in very limited instances.

WordArt adds design flexibility to PowerPoint that may otherwise not have been available. Use WordArt to add emphasis to your message. For example, if you have a slide advising the viewer to Stop Wasting Paper!, you could present that phrase in a WordArt object shaped like a stop sign. Or, in a slide about rising profits, you could present the text in the form of an upward-pointing WordArt arrow. PowerPoint is by nature designed to communicate visually, and WordArt applications like the examples just noted enable you to present text in a more visual format.

Opening WordArt Within PowerPoint

You can only launch WordArt from within one of the Office applications, such as PowerPoint. Choose Insert, Object. In the Insert Object dialog box, scroll down the Object Type list, select Microsoft WordArt 2.0, and click the OK button. WordArt opens and replaces the Standard toolbar with the WordArt toolbar (see fig. 13.6). Simply begin typing to enter the text for the WordArt object; as you type, the text appears in the Enter Your Text Here window.

Using the WordArt Text Effects

The Font Effects drop-down menu is the heart of WordArt. It is responsible for the wild effects that are possible (see fig. 13.7). To display it, click the down arrow beside it on the WordArt menu. The small icons that appear represent the position that the text will appear in once the effect has been applied. Simply click the icon you want to apply the effect. When you're finished applying text effects and other formatting to the WordArt object, exit WordArt and move or size the WordArt object on the slide as needed.

III

Advanced Integration

Fig. 13.6

WordArt replaces the Standard toolbar with its own to enable you to easily manipulate the text.

Font effect

Font style

Sets font to italics

Rotates text vertical

Text alignment

Spacing between characters

Shade of text

Adds shadows behind text

Font size

Sets font to bold

Text preview

Changes the text case

Text entry box

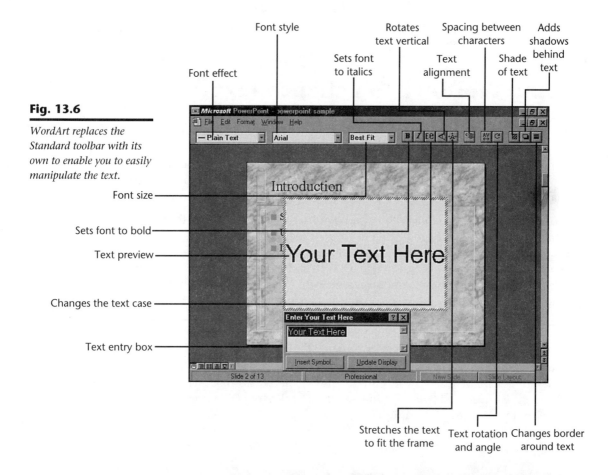

Stretches the text to fit the frame

Text rotation and angle

Changes border around text

Fig. 13.7

Use WordArt's text effects choices to apply eye-catching effects to your text.

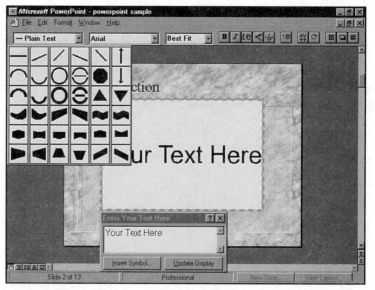

Adding Sound to Presentations

Using sound or MIDI files is another way to enhance your presentation. Any WAV, MID or RMI sound file can be inserted into PowerPoint. In addition, PowerPoint comes with many built-in sound effects for you to use during the slide show.

Inserting Sound or Music

You can add music or sound objects to your slide shows by choosing Insert, Sound. Once you locate and insert the sound file, a small speaker icon appears on the slide. This icon can be positioned anywhere you want on the slide. When the user double-clicks the icon, the sound file begins to play.

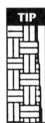

TIP

There are many different sources for obtaining sound files. Just about every online service has areas dedicated to downloadable sounds. For your convenience, Microsoft has included many different types of sounds on the Office 95 CD. You may use these sounds as you want in PowerPoint. Use the Windows 95 Find command to search the CD for all WAV files. This same search method will also help you to locate all the AVI files that you can also use in PowerPoint.

Changing a Sound File's Settings

Once a sound has been inserted into PowerPoint, you can click to select the sound and choose Tools, Animation Settings (or right-click the Sound icon and choose Animation Settings from the shortcut menu) to configure the sound to play (see fig. 13.8). These settings enable you to change when and how a sound is used in a particular slide:

Fig. 13.8

Change the sound settings with the Animation Settings dialog box.

- *Build Options.* Changes when the sound is played. Your choices are: as soon as the slide is shown, when the user clicks to go on, and as each object level appears.

- *Effects*. Enables you to define what visual and auditory effect will be used when displaying the object. Choose from over a dozen built-in sound effects, or specify your own.

- *Play Options*. When a sound is inserted as an icon, specify what characteristics are used when playing the sound. You can even open the OLE-compatible sound application for editing the sound.

 **NOTE**   PowerPoint offers another way to use sound effects in a slide. You can apply a sound effect to any object on the slide. For example, you can select a text box, then open the Animation Settings dialog box. In the Effects section, use the bottom drop-down list to apply a sound that PowerPoint will play back when it "builds" that text box (or other selected object) during the presentation.

Using Write-Up To Prepare Audience Handouts

In addition to users viewing your presentation on-screen, you might also want to prepare a handout they can take with them. PowerPoint makes this simple to do with a feature called Write-Up. Choose Tools, Write-Up and the Write-Up dialog box appears (see fig. 13.9), enabling you to choose one of four layouts for the slides and any associated notes you add. In addition, you can choose whether to link the original PowerPoint presentation contents with the Word document Write-Up creates. If you plan to frequently update the presentation and reprint the Word Write-Up, you should select the Paste Link option button in the Write-Up dialog box. Click OK, and the Write-Up feature opens Word, creates a new document with the layout you specified, and inserts the slides.

Fig. 13.9

Write-Up enables you to select a layout and specify whether to link the original presentation with the Write-Up document.

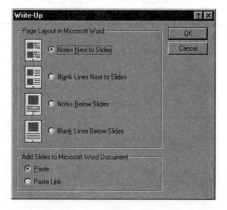

Once it's created in Word, the Write-Up is a normal document, and you should save it like any other file (see fig. 13.10).

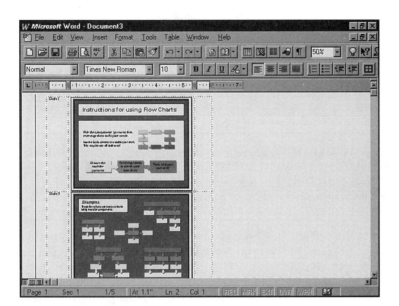

Fig. 13.10

Write-Up created a new Word document with the presentation slides.

Controlling PowerPoint with VBA

PowerPoint doesn't provide a facility for writing and recording macros, as it already provides commands to automate many of the features and objects you might like to automate. Also, there's not a lot of repetition (when you're creating a PowerPoint presentation) that would cry out for a macro. Thus, you can't really write VBA macros within PowerPoint.

However, that doesn't mean you can't use VBA to integrate PowerPoint with other applications. In fact, you can use VBA OLE Automation techniques from a *controller* application (Visual Basic, Excel, Access, or Project) to manipulate PowerPoint, which in such a case is called the *server* application.

You can use VBA, because the latest version of PowerPoint for Windows 95 now follows an object model based on the Excel object model (see Chapter 11, "Automating Office Integration with Excel," to learn more). So, you can use VBA to manipulate a particular PowerPoint object like a slide or text placeholder. And, as for Excel objects, PowerPoint objects have properties that describe them and methods you use with them.

TIP

To learn more about PowerPoint's objects, use the Object Browser. If PowerPoint doesn't appear in the Libraries/Workbooks drop-down list, exit the Object Browser. Choose Tools, References. Select the PowerPoint 7.0 Object Library checkbox, then choose OK. Then, you should be able to access the list of PowerPoint objects in the Object Browser.

III

Advanced Integration

Microsoft intentionally structured PowerPoint using an object model. This moves Office 95 a bit closer to having a programming language that works universally in all its applications. Now, an application that manipulates particular PowerPoint objects should be structured much like any other application. You'll even find that the statements used to control Excel objects and analogous PowerPoint objects tend to be similar.

> **NOTE** To learn more about using VBA to program PowerPoint operations, you can download, expand, and read the document WT1229.EXE from the Microsoft Software Library on CompuServe (type **GO MSL**). To learn even more about using VBA to control PowerPoint, you have to buy the Microsoft Solutions Development Kit from Microsoft.

As alluded to earlier in this section, however, you have to work from within another application to create a program that controls PowerPoint. As the example later in this section shows, for example, you can create a VBA module in Excel and write code that refers to and controls objects in PowerPoint. Generally, the part of your program dealing with PowerPoint needs to start by opening communication with PowerPoint and opening the PowerPoint application. From there, your VBA application can create and manipulate objects; for example, you can create a new presentation, add slides to it, and add objects like text, graphics, and even OLE objects to a slide.

So, how would you integrate PowerPoint in a real-world VBA application? Here are a few ideas:

- You can run an already-created PowerPoint presentation from an Excel or Project document. For example, if you distributed a document describing a budget proposal over a network, you could distribute a PowerPoint presentation file with it. In the Excel workbook, you could create a macro button that would get and display the presentation to provide a "dog and pony show" for viewers who aren't convinced by the raw data.

- Suppose your inside sales or telemarketing force works from an Access database. You could use VBA to give those users a way to display a PowerPoint slide, reminding them of the key points to close a sale or of the key steps for dealing with a complaint, for example. This kind of information wouldn't normally be contained in the database, but it's the kind of customized information that users might need at their fingertips.

- If you want users to be able to create a particular presentation in a particular way (for example, with a consistent background and with a graphic file like a logo placed in a particular location), you could create a Visual Basic front end that launches PowerPoint and kicks off the presentation for the user.

An Example Application Integrating PowerPoint with Excel

Obviously, describing all the particular objects and all the project possibilities for integrating PowerPoint is beyond the scope of this book. However, the following example introduces you to the overall method for integrating PowerPoint via VBA and working with PowerPoint objects. This application copies cells from an Excel worksheet and creates a PowerPoint presentation and slide to display that information. So, for example, if you have monthly sales figures to report and want to distribute them in a nice format, you could create this application and use it over and over; all you have to do is update the Excel information and run the application, which formats the data for you.

To create this example, open a new, blank workbook in Excel, and enter the data listed in table 13.1 (this book's companion CD also offers a file with the sample data). Then save the workbook and name it something like Monthly Sales Update.

On the CD

Table 13.1 Cell Entries for the Example Application

Cell	Entry
A1	Monthly Sales Update by Region
A5	North
A6	South
A7	East
A8	West
B4	Week 1
B5	150000
B6	205000
B7	350000
B8	205000
C4	Week 2
C5	175000
C6	230000
C7	180000
C8	260000
D4	Week 3
D5	198000
D6	230000
D7	300000
D8	350000
E4	Week 4
E5	201000
E6	300000
E7	180000
E8	400000

III

Advanced Integration

Then, use the following steps to build the application:

1. Format the cells the way you want them to appear on the PowerPoint slide. (You want to format them in Excel because the formatting will be copied to the slide as well, and copying the formatting is a bit easier than applying it via VBA.) For example, format cell A1 and the range A4:E8 in a 24-point font. Adjust the column widths so that the data is readable.

2. Choose Tools, Record Macro. From the submenu, choose Record New Macro. In the Macro Name text box of the Record New Macro dialog box, type a name like **MakeSalesUpdateSlide** for the macro. Click OK to start the recording.

3. On the worksheet, drag to select the A4:E8 cell range. Click the Copy icon on the Standard toolbar.

4. Stop the macro by choosing Tools, Record Macro, Stop Recording.

5. Switch to the Module 1 sheet to view the macro you just recorded. This serves as the beginning for the application that creates a PowerPoint slide from the Excel data you just copied.

6. Just below the line that reads Sub MakeSalesUpdateSlide(), enter the declarations for the application. The application needs to manipulate several objects—the PowerPoint application, a new presentation, a slide, and a text frame for the slide title. You need a declaration for each, so enter these declarations:

```
Dim objPPT As Object
Dim objPres As Object
Dim objFirstSlide As Object
Dim objMyFrame As Object
```

7. Add a comment line identifying the two lines you recorded earlier so that this section of the procedure becomes:

```
' Select and copy Excel cells
Range("A4:E8").Select
Selection.Copy
```

At this point, your application should look like figure 13.11.

8. Next, the application needs to open PowerPoint, display the PowerPoint application, and start a presentation. The VBA statements for doing so are pretty straightforward, and resemble the statements for, say, starting Excel and opening a workbook. So, add the following lines to the application, below Selection.Copy:

```
' Open PowerPoint and create a presentation
Set objPPT = CreateObject("PowerPoint.Application.7")
objPPT.AppWindow.Visible = True
Set objPres = objPPT.Presentations.Add
```

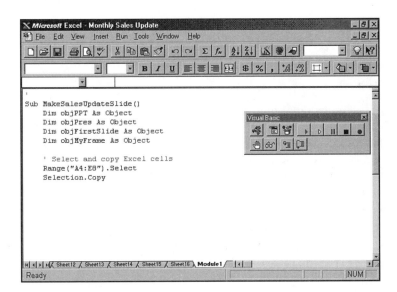

Fig. 13.11

At this point, you've identified the objects the application will manipulate and the procedure you initially recorded.

9. When you start a presentation from within PowerPoint, it generally creates the first slide for you. In contrast, a VBA application must include a statement to add the slide object manually. Add it now, with a comment describing it:

    ```
    ' Add the first slide with a blank layout

    Set objFirstSlide = objPres.Slides.Add(1, ppLayoutBlank)
    ```

    Notice the end of the statement. It tells PowerPoint to add a single slide (1), with a blank layout that has no placeholders for text or graphics (`ppLayoutBlank`). You want a blank layout, because the application pastes the Excel data onto the slide rather than into a placeholder. To learn more about the layouts you can select, refer to WT1229.EXE or the Microsoft Solutions Development Kit, described earlier.

10. Next, you want to create a text placeholder for the slide title and specify its position on the slide. PowerPoint uses *twips* rather than points for such measurements, with each twip being 1/20 of a point. The application should specify three measurements: the distance from the left edge of the slide, the distance from the top edge of the slide, and the width of the text placeholder:

    ```
    ' Add and position a frame for the slide title

    Set objMyFrame = objFirstSlide.Objects.AddTextFrame(2500, 1000,
    ➡15000)
    ```

11. Once the application creates the text placeholder, text can be inserted into the placeholder and formatted. Add the following lines to your application to do so. Notice that to specify a 50 point font, the application must multiply 50 times 20 to give PowerPoint the font size in twips:

```
' Add the text and format it
objMyFrame.Text = "Monthly Sales Update"
objMyFrame.Text.Font.Bold = ppTrue
objMyFrame.Text.Font.Size = 50 * 20
```

12. There wouldn't be much point in copying the Excel data to PowerPoint and presenting it on a blank, undecorated slide. Thus, the application should take advantage of at least one of PowerPoint's design features. In this case, the application can assign a background to the slide (again, see WT1229.EXE or the Microsoft Solutions Development Kit to learn more about the backgrounds you can specify via VBA). Add the following lines to have the application assign a white marble background to the slide:

```
' Add the White Marble slide background
objFirstSlide.Background.Fill.PresetTextured
➥ppPresetTextureWhiteMarble
```

13. To finish the slide, the application needs to paste the Excel information copied at the beginning of the application onto the slide:

```
' Paste the Excel information from the Clipboard
objPPT.ActiveWindow.View.Paste
```

So, the full, finished application should appear as follows:

```
Sub MakeSalesUpdateSlide()
    Dim objPPT As Object
    Dim objPres As Object
    Dim objFirstSlide As Object
    Dim objMyFrame As Object

    ' Select and copy Excel cells
    Range("A4:E8").Select
    Selection.Copy

    ' Open PowerPoint and create a presentation
    Set objPPT = CreateObject("PowerPoint.Application.7")
    objPPT.AppWindow.Visible = True
    Set objPres = objPPT.Presentations.Add

    ' Add the first slide with a blank layout
    Set objFirstSlide = objPres.Slides.Add(1, ppLayoutBlank)

    ' Add and position a frame for the slide title
    Set objMyFrame = objFirstSlide.Objects.AddTextFrame(2500, 1000, 15000)

    ' Add the text and format it
    objMyFrame.Text = "Monthly Sales Update"
    objMyFrame.Text.Font.Bold = ppTrue
    objMyFrame.Text.Font.Size = 50 * 20
```

```
          ' Add the White Marble slide background
          objFirstSlide.Background.Fill.PresetTextured
          ➥ppPresetTextureWhiteMarble

          ' Paste the Excel information from the Clipboard
          objPPT.ActiveWindow.View.Paste
     End Sub
```

14. Save the worksheet file to save your newly-constructed application.

Running the Sample Application

To run the application you just created, go back to the first sheet where you entered the Excel data that you want to place on a slide.

Choose Tools, Macro. In the Macro/Name Reference list in the Macro dialog box, choose the MakeSalesUpdateSlide macro and click the Run button. The application selects your data, launches PowerPoint, and builds the slide on-screen. The resulting slide appears in figure 13.12.

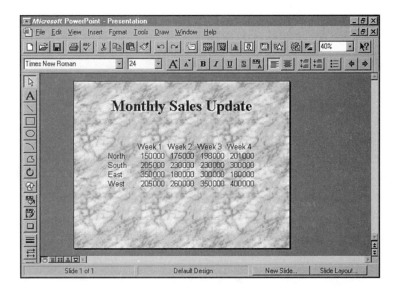

Fig. 13.12

Here's the slide built by the example application.

You can print as many copies of the PowerPoint slide as you need. Be sure to save your workbook to save your application.

> **TIP**
> You can add a macro button to the sheet with the sales data. Attach the MakeSalesUpdateSlide macro to the button. Then, to run the macro and create the sales slide, you can simply click the macro button. See Help in Excel for more about creating macro buttons.

III

Advanced Integration

From Here...

You now have a better understanding of how PowerPoint fits into the Office suite of applications. It's an essential tool for sending your ideas to others in a multimedia format that enhances your message.

Refer to the following chapters for more information pertaining to the topics discussed here:

- Chapter 20, "Creating Custom Menus, Toolbars, and Shortcut Bars," explains how to customize the PowerPoint interface.
- Chapter 22, "Working in a Multimedia Environment," provides guidance about adding multimedia to your Help files.

CHAPTER 14

Integrating Schedule+ and E-Mail with Other Office Applications

In the preceding chapters, you learned about integrating some of the larger applications found in the Office 95 suite. Microsoft Office and Windows 95 have a few other applications that integrate nicely within an Office application. These applications are Schedule+ and Mail (Exchange). This chapter explains methods for integrating these two applications into your Office 95 solutions.

In this chapter, you learn how to

- Create appointments using Schedule+
- Read information from your Schedule+ applications
- Log into e-mail using the MAPI session control
- Retrieve information from e-mail using Microsoft's MAPI message control
- Create e-mail messages using the MAPI message control

Integrating Schedule+

Schedule+, one of the more useful tools found in Office 95, enables you to manage contacts and appointments. In your applications, you may want to provide some method of scheduling appointments or providing automatic notification from your applications on a regularly scheduled basis. This is where using Schedule+ comes in handy. Schedule+ provides a robust OLE object model for communicating with applications such as Excel and Access. This section describes the techniques for communicating with Schedule+ using OLE Automation.

Beginning a Schedule+ Session

The first step in creating a link to Schedule+ is to create an OLE Automation session using the `CreateObject` function and Schedule+'s OLE server name, `SchedulePlus.Application`. The following code demonstrates creating a session from within Access 95:

```
'--Dimension Objects for procedure
Dim oleObject As Object

'-- Create OLE session
Set oleObject = CreateObject("SchedulePlus.Application")

'-- Logon to Schedule+
oleObject.Logon
```

Because Schedule+ is a user-specific application, it requires you to log on after establishing a connection. Logging on provides your application access to the schedule, contacts, and other information that can be stored in Schedule+. Schedule+ provides a method known as Logon for logging on. The following code demonstrates logging on to Schedule+:

```
'--Dimension Objects for procedure
Dim oleObject As Object

'-- Create OLE session
Set oleObject = CreateObject("SchedulePlus.Application")

'-- Logon to Schedule+
oleObject.Logon
```

The default behavior of the Logon method is to log the user on as the last person who logged into Schedule+. Schedule+ enables different users to manage their own schedules. This capability requires that the users log on providing different user names. The object model provided by Schedule+ allows you to log on as a different user by specifying a user name with the Logon method. The following code demonstrates logging on with a user name:

```
'--Dimension Objects for procedure
Dim oleObject As Object

'-- Create OLE session
Set oleObject = CreateObject("SchedulePlus.Application")

'-- Logon to Schedule+
oleObject.Logon "Rod Paddock"
```

Upon logging in, you can begin accessing the objects, properties, and methods provided in Schedule+'s Object Model. Figure 14.1 points out some of these items provided by Schedule+.

Creating an Appointment

One of the features found in Schedule+'s Object Model is the capability to create an appointment. After initiating an OLE session with Schedule+, you can create an appointment by accessing Schedule+'s ScheduleLogged object. The ScheduleLogged object is a child object to the Application object and has a method called New that creates a new appointment. The method for creating an appointment is to do the following:

1. Create an OLE session with Schedule+.
2. Create a reference to the application's ScheduleLogged object.
3. Call the newly referenced object's New method.
4. Set the appointment's properties.
5. Save the appointment by calling the Flush method.

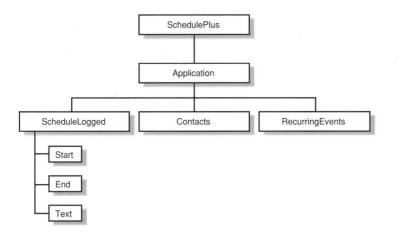

Fig. 14.1

Representation of Schedule+'s Object Model.

The following code demonstrates creating an appointment using Schedule+. The result of this code is shown in figure 14.2.

```
'--Dimension Objects for procedure
Dim oleObject As Object
Dim oleSchedule As Object
Dim oleAppointment As Object

'-- Create OLE session
Set oleObject = CreateObject("SchedulePlus.Application")

'-- Logon to Schedule+
oleObject.Logon

'-- Set reference to ScheduleLogged Object
Set oleSchedule = oleObject.ScheduleLogged

'-- Create new appointment
Set oleAppointment = oleSchedule.Appointments.New

'-- Set appointment properties
With oleAppointment
  .Start = #12/6/95 8:00:00 PM#
  .End = #12/6/95 9:00:00 PM#
  .Text = "Building Office Applications Due"
End With

'-- Commit appointment
oleAppointment.Flush
```

Advanced Integration

III

Fig. 14.2

Schedule+ shows an appointment created by an OLE Automation session.

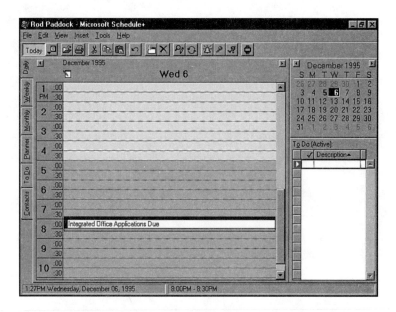

In the previous code, you learned how to create an appointment with Schedule+, and were introduced to some of the properties and methods found in the Schedule+ OLE object hierarchy. Some of the new properties and method include:

- `Start`. The beginning date and time of an appointment. This property has a `datetime` data type.
- `End`. The ending date and time of an appointment. This property has a `datetime` data type.
- `Text`. The text that is shown in the Schedule+ appointment description.
- `Flush`. The Method that saves the appointment into the Schedule+ system.

Reading Information from Schedule+

Along with creating appointments with Schedule+, you can also read information from Schedule+'s contacts, appointments, and other databases. You access information from Schedule+ by navigating up and down a database using Schedule+'s data access methods and properties. To access the contents of a database, you need to do the following:

1. Create an OLE session to Schedule+.
2. Create a reference to the object that you want to extract information from. If you want to pull out schedule information, create a reference to the `ScheduleLogged` object. If you want to extract information from the contacts, create a reference to that object.
3. Scan the database using the `GetRows` and `Skip` methods in conjunction with the `IsEndOfTable` property.

On the CD

The following code demonstrates creating a session with Schedule+ and loading the contents of the schedule into a combo box on an Access 95 form (see fig. 14.3):

```
'--Dimension Objects for procedure
Dim oleObject As Object
Dim oleSchedule As Object


'-- Create OLE session
Set oleObject = CreateObject("SchedulePlus.Application")

'-- Set reference to ScheduleLogged Object
Set oleSchedule = oleObject.ScheduleLogged

FOR intKount = 1 to 1000
  '-- Retrieve info from schedule
  chrText = oleSchedule.GETROWS(1,"Text")

  ' Add item to combo box
  FORMS!FORM1!cboAppoint.Additem(chrText)

    '-- Move to next record
    oleSchedule.Skip

    'Check for End Of Table
    IF oleSchedule.IsEndOfTable THEN
           EXIT
    END IF

NEXT
```

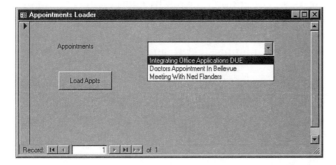

Fig. 14.3

Access the combo box with information loaded from the Schedule+ schedule.

In the previous code, you learned how to extract appointments from a Schedule+ appointments database. This code introduced a number of new terms and methods:

- GetRows. Method that extracts information from the specified object.
- Skip. Method that moves the application down the list of appointments.
- IsEndOfTable. Property that specifies when the last record was reached in the database.

Integrating Microsoft Mail

On occasion, you may find that you want your applications to do the following:

- Alert you of certain conditions.
- Provide an inexpensive protocol for transferring data to and from different sites.
- Distribute information to multiple users with low or no interaction for the user.

Access provides this capability through the use of e-mail with MAPI controls developed by Microsoft. This section demonstrates how to integrate basic e-mail capabilities into your VB applications using the MAPI controls.

NOTE The MAPI OCX controls are available in Visual Basic 4 Professional or Microsoft Visual FoxPro 3. Contact Microsoft for information about these products or purchasing the MAPI OCX controls separately.

Understanding MAPI and TAPI

Whenever you deal with the e-mail systems found in the Office environment, you always come across the terms *MAPI* and *TAPI*. These two terms represent two generic programming interfaces that developers can use to integrate mail and telephony into their applications. To put it simply, MAPI is an interface that can be used to create e-mail messages. TAPI is an interface that stores information about connecting your systems to phone lines using a modem or other telephony equipment. The popularity of these interfaces is growing, allowing you to send mail from applications and store information about your phone system directly on your computer. In this section, you use a set of MAPI controls that can communicate with any MAPI-compliant system.

Logging into E-Mail

The first step to integrating e-mail into your applications is to sign onto e-mail. To create an e-mail application, perform the following steps:

1. Create a new form.
2. Add an OLE session control to a form.
3. Add an OLE message control to a form.
4. Add a button to the form and insert the following code into the click event of that button:

```
FORMS!FORM1.OleSession1.username = "TEST"
FORMS!FORM1.OleSession1.password = "TEST"
FORMS!FROM1.OleSession1.SignOn
```

This logs your user into e-mail using the username TEST and the password TEST. The OLE session control also provides the capability of calling an e-mail login by setting the LOGINUI property.

NOTE The preceding code works fine for Windows 3.x users. For Exchange/Windows 95 users, the `username` property needs to correspond with a Profile setup in your Exchange settings. You also need to specify the option for Exchange to supply the password upon login.

After logging in, you need to assign the `SessionID` property set by the MAPI session control to the MAPI message control you added to your form. The MAPI session control is used to establish communications with the e-mail system and to control access to the messages for a particular e-mail user.

Retrieving Messages from E-Mail

After logging in and setting the Session ID of a message control, you can retrieve information about the messages found in the inbox. The first step is to call the `Fetch` method. The `Fetch` method retrieves messages into the e-mail buffer of the MAPI message control. The following code demonstrates:

- Signing onto e-mail
- Setting the Session ID of a message control
- Calling the `Fetch` method
- Setting the text property of a text object to the number of messages found in the e-mail system

```
With FORMS!Form1.MAPISession1
     .UserName = "ROD"   'Exchange Profile Name
     .Password = "RPAD"
     .SignOn
End With

     'After logging in set the message control
     'Session ID to ID Generated By Session Control
     FORMS!Form1.MAPIMessages1.SessionID = Form1.MAPISession1.SessionID

     'Retrieve messages from e-mail with fetch command
     FORMS!Form1.MAPIMessages1.Fetch

     'Display number of messages
     FORMS!Form1.Text1.TEXT = Str(Form1.MAPIMessages1.MsgCount)
```

Table 14.1 shows some of the properties you can retrieve about e-mail messages.

Table 14.1 Some Properties of E-Mail Messages

Property	Description
Subject	The subject of a particular message.
MsgType	A system- or developer-assigned message type; IPC = system messages that are not viewable in the user's inbox.
MsgNoteText	The text of the message.
MsgDateReceived	The date the message was received.

III

Advanced Integration

Reading a Mailbox

Along with the capability to read a single message, you can navigate through an e-mail session's messages using the `MsgIndex` and `MsgCount` properties. The `MsgCount` property represents the total number of messages retrieved from an e-mail session. The `MsgIndex` property is a zero (0) based property that can be used to navigate from one message to another. The value of `MsgIndex` ranges from 0 to `MsgCount` − 1. The following code loads the `MsgSubject` property from all e-mail messages into a combo box on an Access 95 form.

Creating E-Mail Messages

On the CD

To realize the full potential of the e-mail messaging components provided with Visual Basic, you need to understand how to create e-mail messages. The following code demonstrates the properties and the steps necessary to create and send an e-mail message:

```
With FORMS!Form1.MAPIMessages1

    '-- Create new message
    .Compose

    '-- Set message type (you can set this to an IPC type to prevent
    'users from viewing it in their inboxes.
    .MsgType = ""

    '-- Set message address name
    '-- Format is "MS:HOMER<network>/<server>HOMER/<username>RPAD"
    .RecipAddress = "MS:HOMER/HOMER/RPAD"
    .RecipDisplayName = "MS:HOMER/HOMER/RPAD"

    '-- Set message subject and note text
    .MsgSubject = "TEST MESSAGES 1"

    'OLE message control must have some text
    .MsgNoteText = "HEY MAN THIS IS A MESSAGE "

    '-- Send message
    .Send False
End With
```

The preceding code is the basic set of steps necessary to create an e-mail message. One of the more powerful features of MAPI is its capability to attach files to messages. The next section demonstrates attaching files to e-mail messages.

Attaching Files with MAPI

One of the many capabilities of e-mail is sending and receiving attached files from other applications. The MAPI controls allow you to attach files to your e-mail messages using the `AttachmentIndex`, `AttachmentName`, and `AttachmentPathName` properties. The following code demonstrates how to send an Excel spreadsheet to another user for approval:

```
With FORMS!Form1.MAPIMessages1

  '-- Create new message
  .Compose

  '-- Set message type (you can set this to an IPC type to prevent
  'users from viewing it in their inboxes.
  .MsgType = ""

  '-- Set message address name
  '-- Format is "MS:HOMER<network>/<server>HOMER/<username>RPAD"
  .RecipAddress = "MS:HOMER/HOMER/RPAD"
  .RecipDisplayName = "MS:HOMER/HOMER/RPAD"

  '-- Set message subject and note text
  .MsgSubject = "Expense report 1Q 96"

  'OLE message control must have some text
  .MsgNoteText = "Expense report for approval "

  '-- Add Attachment Info
  .AttachmentIndex = 0
  .AttachmentPathName = "C:\EXCEL\EXPENSE.XLS"
  .AttachmentName = "EXPENSE.XLS"


  '-- Send message
  .Send False
End With
```

On the CD

> **TIP**
>
> The capabilities that you can add to your applications using e-mail are endless. You can create inventory ordering messages when inventories reach critical levels; you can return errors to your IS department when they occur; or you can create a full-fledged network system using e-mail.

From Here...

Office provides many unique features with its assortment of integration possibilities. Communication with other applications expands the operations you can perform with Office and other applications. The following chapters further illustrate using Office's tools for creating integrated applications:

- Chapter 3, "Integration Basics," explains the basics of integrating Office applications.
- Chapter 4, "Visual Basic and Visual Basic for Applications," teaches you how to write Visual Basic code and use the tools found in VBA.
- Chapter 5, "Programming Application Integration," demonstrates how to communicate with other applications using DDE, OLE, and ODBC.

III

Advanced Integration

■ Chapter 23, "Using Windows APIs," describes how to integrate the power of the Windows API into your applications.

■ Appendix B, "Office Resources," lists numerous useful resources for Office developers.

CHAPTER 15

Integrating Project with Office Applications

So far you have been learning about integrating both major and minor Office 95 applications. Project, though not a part of the Standard or Professional Office suite, has a user interface that conforms to Office standards. You can install it in the MSOFFICE folder, and you can integrate it with other Office applications using VBA. This chapter discusses methods for integrating Project for Windows 95 into your Office 95 solutions.

In this chapter you learn how to

- Recognize the Project Object Model
- Manage Project objects
- Program Project using macros and Visual Basic for Applications
- Use Project as both an OLE client and OLE server
- Store Project data in a database
- Use the Mail-enabled components of Project
- Send messages from Project to Schedule+

Project as an Office Application Component

Project for Windows 95 is a special-purpose tool for planning, budgeting, and managing projects. Project data is time-dependent, consisting of tasks broken down step-by-step and spread throughout time. Project for Windows 95 shows these time-dependent tasks in a Gantt Chart. This is a popular way of arranging project tasks on a two-dimensional surface, listing the tasks vertically and time horizontally. Each task then gets beginning and ending coordinates on the chart. In Project, the remaining component of a project—resources—are listed next to the task graphic. For this chapter, the examples reference a sample project taken from the Special Event template that installs with Project, as shown in figure 15.1.

Fig. 15.1

A Gantt Chart shows tasks spread throughout the timespan of a project.

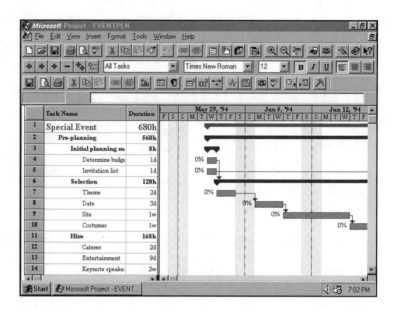

To plan a project, you must divide it up into its major *tasks*, decide on how long each task must take, when the project must start, and what dependencies exist between the tasks. The longest part of the project through time is then called the *critical path*. To budget the project, you list your *resources*, their costs, and assign the resources to tasks. As the project proceeds, you can record the degree of completion and actual time taken. While you can use Project's Gantt Chart to gain an overall perspective, Project provides a Task sheet and Resource sheet for viewing these entities in a grid format. In addition, Project allows you to compare actual versus projected costs for each task.

Project is OLE-compliant; you can embed or link external objects from other Office applications. However, the display of the linked or embedded object depends on where in Project you place it. You cannot embed or link external objects into calculated fields. In order to get Project to use the data from an external application, you must embed or link it into a sheet or table view. It cannot go directly into a Gantt Chart, a Pert Chart (an alternative graphical view of a project), or a Calendar View.

For example, in the Special Event example for this chapter, the resource data is directly linked to an Excel worksheet. The cells containing the data in the Excel worksheet match the cells in the Project Resource sheet, so the standard Paste Special command creates a link with the data.

Project for Windows 95 offers a number of new features not found in Project 4.0. The most significant are:

■ Support for long file names

■ Capability to save and restore from some databases using ODBC

- Support for custom OLE document properties
- Capability to post to Exchange folders using the Mail methods
- Support for the MPX file format

	Resource Name	Initials	Group	Max. Units	Std. Rate	Ovt. Rate	Cost/Use	Accrue At	Ba
1	Marilyn	M		1	$60.00/h	$0.00/h	$0.00	Prorated	St
2	Joe	J		1	$48.00/h	$0.00/h	$0.00	Prorated	St
3	Patty	P		1	$40.00/h	$0.00/h	$0.00	Prorated	St
4	Larry	L		1	$45.00/h	$0.00/h	$0.00	Prorated	St

Fig. 15.2

You can link Project resource data to Excel.

The second item, ODBC support, is very significant. Project is a single-user application that stores its data in a Project-specific format. The ability to save and restore that data from a database adds a limited ability to share Project data with other users in a format that they can query using database tools.

Working with the Project Object Model

Project is a large and complex application, and so, accordingly, is its object model. Like Excel, the Project Object Model has hundreds of available properties and methods. Figure 15.3 shows a diagram of the entire object model.

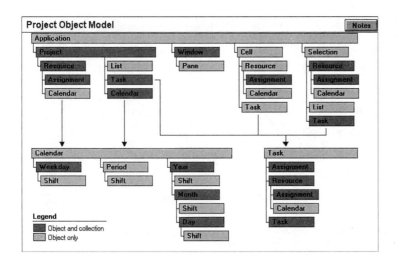

Fig. 15.3

The full Project Object Model shows all Project objects and their relationships.

The model can be simplified by removing the user interface objects and focusing on the Project-specific objects, as shown in figure 15.4.

Notice the shading in each diagram. A lighter shade indicates an *object class*, while the darker shade indicates the *object and collection class*. You can reference object classes individually, because there is always only one instance; whereas with object and collection classes, you can refer to the collection class or a specific object within the class.

Fig. 15.4

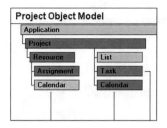

A simplified version of the
Project Object Model can
be easier to follow.

The application object, for example, has light shading and is not a collection, because there can only be one instance of the application—Project—running at a time. The dark shading in the project objects means that you can refer either to the project's collection as a whole, or to an individual project object as part of the collection. For example, to display the name of the Application object from within Project's Immediate window, you can type

```
print Application.Name
```

To find the number of active projects, you can reference the Count property of the Projects collection:

```
print Application.Projects.Count
```

To print a project's name, you can either refer to it as a member of the Projects collection object:

```
print Application.Projects(1).Name
```

or you can refer to the active project individually:

```
print ActiveProject.Name
```

These Project 95 objects correspond to the primary components of any project, namely the tasks, resources, and calendars, as well as any project that is currently active in Project 95. When you combine a project object with one of its properties or methods, you can inspect all the data elements you see when running Project interactively. You can find out more about the methods and properties by using the Object Browser, our next topic.

Using the Object Browser To Explore the Project Object Model

A good way to learn about the Project Object Model is to use Project's Object Browser (see fig. 15.5). You can access the Object Browser in two ways. First, enter the Module Editor view by choosing View, More Views, highlight the Module Editor in the list, and click the Apply button (or you can choose Tools, Macros, and then click the Edit button to edit a macro). In either case, you end up in the Module Editor. From here, the View option on the menu now shows Object Browser (also the F2 function key). A neat way to make the Object Browser more immediately available is to activate the Visual Basic for Applications toolbar to show the Object Browser button.

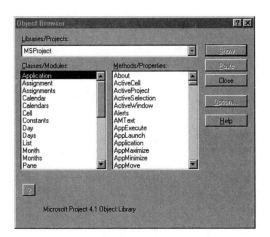

Fig. 15.5

You can use the Project Object Browser to inspect Project objects, properties, and methods.

Once in the Object Browser, a variety of libraries are available, including the GLOBAL collection of modules, and the classes from Project. In the Object Browser, a library can be either a project that contains modules with code (macros), or a library of objects that have methods and properties.

In the Object Browser, you can browse the objects, properties, and methods of other libraries, such as those from Excel and Access, but only if you register them first with Project. To register Excel's libraries in Project, quit the Object Browser and choose Tools, References, check the Microsoft Excel 5.0 Object Library checkbox, and then OK.

For this discussion, choose the MSProject library in the Object Browser, and notice the list of objects in the Classes/Modules list box, and the properties and methods in the Methods/Properties list box. You can explore the object model by choosing an object and selecting either the object or one of its properties or methods. A brief description of the selected item often appears at the bottom of the dialog box, and you can click the ? button in the lower-left corner of the dialog box for help if it is enabled. The ? button is enabled only if the selected property or method is a topic in a related help file.

If you select Application in the Classes/Modules list, notice the extensive number of properties and methods in the Methods/Properties list. For example, select the Project object from the Classes/Modules list and observe the long list of properties and methods. Now select the Projects collection and compare its list of properties and methods. The Projects collection has a much shorter list. Note that one of the properties of the Projects collection is Count. That means you can use the following command to determine the number of active projects in the currently running instance of Project:

```
Set lnCount = Projects.Count
```

III

Advanced Integration

NOTE The `Project` object has many more methods and properties than the `Projects` collection object. Unfortunately, the Object Browser does not automatically make it clear whether a given entry in the <u>M</u>ethods/Properties list is either a method or a property. If the description at the bottom of the dialog box is unclear, you can use the Help system to tell for sure. If you click the <u>?</u> button while focus is on the <u>C</u>lasses/Modules object so that no entry in the <u>M</u>ethods/Properties list is selected, the resulting help screen for that object contains jump words for `Methods` and `Properties` just below the Help Topic title. When you click either jump word, the help system shows you the methods or properties in individual lists. However, you can't print these lists of methods and properties from the help screen.

Now that you've seen some of the Project objects' methods and properties using the Object Browser, it's important to note that each data element in a Project view or table can be accessed via a property. For example, in the Project Gantt Chart view, the Task Name column corresponds to the `Name` property of the `Task` collection object, while each row in the `Task` Name column corresponds to one of the subscripted objects in the Task collection object. This holds throughout Project: each data element seen in a view or table can be accessed through the Project Object Model. You can see a list of the Task Entry View data elements and their corresponding object references in table 15.1. In each object reference, just substitute an actual task subscript for the variable *n*.

Table 15.1 Project Task Entry Data Elements and Corresponding Object References

Data Element	Object Reference
Task Name	`Activeproject.Tasks(n).Name`
Duration	`Activeproject.Tasks(n).Duration`
Start	`Activeproject.Tasks(n).Start`
Finish	`Activeproject.Tasks(n).Finish`
Predecessors	`Activeproject.Tasks(n).Predecessors`
Resource Names	`Activeproject.Tasks(n).Name`
Resource Names	`Activeproject.Tasks(n).ResourceNames`

Accessing Project Objects

You can access all the Project objects using VBA, either within Project or from other Office applications. Within Project, just enter the Module Editor view, and from the menu choose <u>V</u>iew, <u>D</u>ebug Window (or press Ctrl+G). Click the Immediate pane, and type the following to inspect the `Name` property of the `Application` object, for example:

```
print Application.Name
```

To determine the properties of currently active objects, you can use the Active Objects properties listed in table 15.2.

Table 15.2 Active Objects Properties with Contents

Active Objects Property	Contents
ActiveCell	Returns the active cell.
ActivePane	Returns the active pane.
ActiveProject	Returns the active project.
ActiveSelection	Returns the active selection.
ActiveWindow	Returns the active window.

So for example, you can determine the active project by typing

```
print ActiveProject.Name
```

in the Immediate pane.

From other applications outside Project, you need to create a reference to the application object first, and then all the objects, properties, and methods become available. For example, from an Excel macro you can enter:

```
'-- Dimension the objects and variables
Dim oProj         As Object
Dim lnNumRes      As Integer

'-- Create the OLE session
Set oProj = CreateObject("MSProject.Application")

'-- Open the project file
oProj.Application.FileOpen "c:\msoffice\winproj\examples\ch15event.mpp"
```

Hidden Project Object Properties

All Project objects are exposed to you through VBA, but many of the properties are not available to the Project user interface. In other words, they are "hidden" from the user. You can use these hidden properties to store additional data using VBA code. Table 15.3 illustrates some of these hidden properties.

Table 15.3 Hidden Properties in the Project User Interface

Project Object	Hidden Properties
Resources	Text1 through Text5
Tasks	Text1 through Text10
Tasks	Cost1 through Cost3
Tasks	Flag1 through Flag10

III

Advanced Integration

For example, with each resource object in a project, you could store address, phone number, and other information using the Text1 through Text5 properties. To access the Text1 property from within Project, you can enter the following to store some address data:

```
ActiveProject.Resources(1).Text1 = "1234 5th Street"
```

TIP The maximum length for Text fields is 254 characters.

Programming Project Using Visual Basic for Applications

Like Excel, Project has integrated its macro recorder into its VBA interface. You can create procedures using the macro recorder, or you can write your own in the Module Editor.

Using the Macro Recorder

Project's macro recorder captures a sequence of object selection and data entry actions from the user. Project macros are stored in VBA modules. You can store those modules globally in the GLOBAL module, or you can store them with each project. When you store them in the GLOBAL module, they are actually stored in the GLOBAL.MPT file.

When you create a macro, you are creating a VBA procedure, as you see when you edit the macro. The result of recording a macro is VBA code which you can edit using the Module Editor.

When you record a macro, Project makes absolute references to objects, and the resulting code often needs polishing to make it more general. For example, a recorded macro that adds a new resource looks like:

```
' Macro Macro10
' Macro Recorded Mon 12/18/95 by Ron.
Sub Macro10()

    SetResourceField Field:="Name", Value:="Abel"
    SelectResourceField Row:=0, Column:="Initials"
    SelectResourceField Row:=0, Column:="Group"
    SelectResourceField Row:=0, Column:="Max Units"
    SelectResourceField Row:=0, Column:="Standard Rate"
    SetResourceField Field:="Standard Rate", Value:="50"
    SelectResourceField Row:=1, Column:="Standard Rate"

End Sub
```

In VBA, though, you can shorten this by rewriting it and removing references to keystrokes or cell movement:

```
Sub AddResource

    ActiveProject.Resources.Add  Name:="Abel"
    ActiveProject.Resources("Abel").StandardRate = "$50.00/h"

End Sub
```

NOTE Project comes with a set of macros located in the GLOBAL module or library. To inspect them, bring up the Object Browser and choose the GLOBAL library. All macros stored in GLOBAL modules are available to all projects.

To make a macro apply specifically to just one project, choose Tools, Record Macro to bring up the Record Macro dialog box. Then click the Options button, and the same Record Macro dialog box expands showing a number of extra options. Notice the Store Macro In area located in the lower-left part of the dialog box. Click the Current Project File option button to make this macro apply to the current project only.

Customizing Forms, Menus, and Toolbars

You can customize data entry forms and menus for a particular project, and then invoke those forms from within a Project macro. To customize a form, choose Tools, Customize, Forms and then choose a form. To customize a menu, choose Tools, Customize, Menu Bars, and then choose a menu. Any customized form or menu defaults to storage with the GLOBAL module, but you can cause them to be stored in a particular project by using the Organizer. To use customized forms interactively, activate the Custom Forms toolbar.

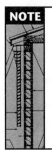

NOTE You can customize the Project menu so that you can go directly to the Module Editor and skip the More Views list. Just choose Tools, Customize, Menu Bars. Then edit the Standard menu. At the bottom of the Views section, insert a new line and give it the Menu Item name of **Module Editor**. In the Command/Macro field, enter the command

```
ViewApply name:="Module Editor", singlePane:=True
```

You may also want to add this command to the Standard No File menu as well.

Creating a Project Application

You can create an application that runs from menu options, and also you can cause your Project application to be automatically invoked whenever the project in question is loaded, just by naming the procedure Auto_Open. By expanding the role that the Auto_Open procedure plays, you can call other procedures and data entry forms.

III

Advanced Integration

For example, to cause a project upon startup to request a user name and then bring up the Task Entry data entry form, you can use the following procedure:

```
'-- Requests a user name upon startup
Sub Auto_Open()

    '-- Get the user name
    lcUserName = InputBox("Enter your first name:")
    ActiveProject.Manager = lcUserName

    '--Activate the Gantt chart
    ViewApply Name:="&Gantt Chart"

    '-- Invoke the task entry form
    Form Name:="Entry"

End Sub
```

Project and OLE Automation

You can use Project both as an OLE Automation client and as a server. In the following sections, you see how you can use OLE Automation to reference Project objects internally and externally.

Project as an OLE Automation Client

In addition to OLE linking and embedding and Project's import and export features, you can also use OLE Automation to store and retrieve data. Suppose you have the following resource data stored in an Excel worksheet, but it's not stored in such a way that it can be linked to Project's resource sheet, as shown in figure 15.6.

Fig. 15.6

Resource data in an Excel worksheet can be linked to Project.

	A	B
1	Marilyn	
2	Joe	
3	Patty	
4	Larry	

You can use the following Project procedure to populate resource names from the above Excel worksheet:

```
'-- Project procedure to retrieve resource names from an Excel worksheet
Sub Retrieve from Excel

    '-- Dimension the object
    Dim objXl As Object

    '-- Open the Excel worksheet
    Set objXl = CreateObject("Excel.Application")
    Workbooks.Open "EventPln.xls"

    '-- Initialize a counter and the worksheet cell variable
    x = 1
    lcRange = "A" & Trim(Str(x))
```

```
'-- Do while there are non-empty cells to load
Do While Not_
    IsEmpty(Activeworkbook.ActiveSheet.Range(lcRange).Value)
    '-- Add a new resource
     ActiveProject.Resources.Add

    '-- Load the name
    Name:=Activeworkbook.ActiveSheet.Range(lcRange).Value

    '-- Increment the counter
    x = x + 1

    '-- Revise the cell reference
    lcRange = "A" & Trim(Str(x))
  Loop

'-- Remove the object
Set objXl = Nothing

End Sub
```

This Project procedure uses Project 95 as an OLE Automation client by instantiating an Excel application object. If Excel is not running, this will create an instance of it which is not visible on the screen. The `Workbooks.Open` method is called to load a worksheet, and then a loop starts that reads a range of cells while they are not empty. For each non-empty cell in column A, starting with row 1, a new resource is added into the current Project 95 project using the `Resources.Add` method. Then the `Resources.Name` property is loaded with the Excel cell value. When the procedure is finished, the Excel application is terminated by removing the Excel object. This procedure will run as a Project macro.

Project as an OLE Automation Server

If you want to retrieve data from a Project resource sheet and put it into an Excel worksheet, you can use a similar procedure—this time from inside Excel:

```
'-- Excel procedure to retrieve resource names from a Project
Sub RetrieveFromProject()

    '-- Dimension the object
    Dim oProj As Object

    '-- Initialize a counter
    Dim lnNumRes As Integer

    '-- Open the Project
    Set oProj = CreateObject("MSProject.Application")
    oProj.Application.FileOpen_
        "c:\msoffice\winproj\examples\ch15event.mpp"

    '-- Get the number of resources
    lnNumRes = oProj.ActiveProject.Resources.Count


    For x = 1 To lnNumRes
        '-- Set the range reference
```

```
                    lcRange = "A" & Trim(Str(x))

                    '-- Put the value into the resource
                    Worksheets(1).Range(lcRange).Value = _
                    oProj.ActiveProject.Resources(x).Name
            Next

                    '-- Get rid of the object
                    Set oProj = Nothing

        End Sub
```

In this Excel procedure, you access Project 95 as an OLE Automation server by instantiating Project in an Excel object. The procedure gets the number of resources from
the Resources collection object and stores the result in a variable. Then it scans the
resource objects one by one, picking up each resource name from the Resources collection class object and copying it to the next worksheet cell. The procedure ends by
removing the Project object.

Project and Databases

Project stores its data in a project-specific format, in files with an MPP extension.
This project-specific format is not multiuser, because only one user can work on a
given project at a time. You can get a degree of multiuser support by saving and re-
storing Project data from an Access database, where many users can access the data
simultaneously. While there are a number of limitations to this storage method, it
gives you a way to share the data for query and other purposes. In the following sections, you learn how to use Project's Database Utility, how the utility communicates
with databases, and specifically how to communicate Project data with an Access
database.

Using the Database Utility

Project 95 comes with a Database Utility (DBU) to load and store project data using a
restricted set of ODBC (Open Database Connectivity) drivers. When you install Project
95, ODBC drivers for dBASE, Excel, FoxPro 2.6, Access 7.0, Paradox, and Text files
will be installed automatically on your computer. However, from this list of drivers,
Project 95 only supports the Access driver for storing and loading projects from a
database. Project 95 also supports Microsoft SQL Server, but it does not supply its
ODBC driver with installation. Project 95 uses only ODBC drivers to communicate
with databases, and has no native database access.

The ODBC interface consists of drivers and data sources. When you first install Project
95, the ODBC drivers are installed into the Windows 95 SYSTEM folder. When you
first access the DBU, it presents you with a Data Sources screen. Each of these data
sources is based on the installed drivers. For each ODBC driver, there can be many
data sources, but the ODBC installation supplies these initial data sources based on
however many drivers you have installed.

These initial data sources do not specify any particular database or storage location. You can make a new data source which does specify a particular database by clicking the New button. You will do this later in this section for Access.

You can access the DBU by choosing Tools, Multiple Projects, or from the Workgroups toolbar. Notice the resulting options Open from Database, Save to Database, and Save to Database As. By choosing these menu options, you can use the DBU to load and store Project 95 data from a database via your installed ODBC drivers. When you use the DBU, you are asked to supply an existing data source name. You can use the DBU to create a new database to store Project data, or create all the necessary tables for storing Project data in an existing database, or use already existing project tables if it finds them.

When the DBU stores your project data, it creates a unique key for the project and uses that key to identify relevant data in the tables. If you save a second project to the same database, the DBU creates a new key name and adds the data for the new project to the same tables. If you save the same project to the database again, the DBU recognizes that the key name is the same and asks you whether you want to overwrite the data.

Also, the DBU requires a unique project name in the tables, beyond its own unique key. It won't let you store more than one project with the same name in the same database.

How Project's DBU Communicates with Databases

Project's DBU uses ODBC drivers to save and restore project data from databases. In order to do this, the target database must support a specified number of data types. Table 15.4 cross-references the project data, their ODBC data types, their corresponding Access data types, and Microsoft SQL Server data types. Currently, Microsoft only supports storing Project 95 data in Access and Microsoft SQL Server databases.

Table 15.4	Project Database Utility Data Types		
Project	**ODBC**	**Access**	**MS SQL Server**
Dates & Time	SQL_TIMESTAMP	Date/Time	datetime
Costs	SQL_DOUBLE	Number - Double	float
Percent	SQL_REAL	Number - Double	real
ID's	SQL_SMALLINT	Number - Integer	smallint
Notes	SQL_LONGVARCHAR	Memo	text
Text	SQL_VARCHAR	Text	varchar

When you save project data to a database, the DBU creates four tables: project, tasks, resources, and resource assignments. The project table contains one record for each project, and the project key is the first field in the table. Each of the other tables references the project key to link back to the project table.

III

Advanced Integration

Limitations of Project 95's Database Utility

There are several limitations concerning Project's Database Utility that you need to keep in mind:

- When you save a project using the Database Utility, only project-specific data is stored. If you want to keep formatting information such as fonts, views, macros, filters, forms, OLE objects, and so on, you must store them in the GLOBAL.MPT file.

- If you load a number of projects from a database and consolidate them, the consolidated project cannot be saved back to the original database.

- The Database Utility uses the Text1–Text4 properties of the project object, so if you save and restore a project using the DBU, you lose any information stored in those properties.

- The Database Utility doesn't store subprojects, only the current project.

- The Database Utility only supports ODBC drivers which permit table creation, read/write access, and the timestamp and varchar datatypes. Therefore, you can't use the Database Utility to save to Excel, xbase tables, or text files.

- Project 4.0 has a native use of the Access 2.0 engine, whereas Project 4.1's Database Utility uses ODBC to store to Access 7.0 and earlier databases. To share project data between 4.0 and 4.1, store data in the Access 2.0 format.

- Project 4.0 creates an Access 2.0 database, whereas Project 4.1's Database Utility doesn't. To store data from Project 4.1 in an Access 2.0 format, you need to create a blank database using Access 2.0.

- You can use Project 4.0's Database Utility to create a blank Access 7.0 database by creating a new data source and clicking the Create button in the Data Source Name dialog box.

- Project 4.1 installs the wrong Access 7.0 ODBC driver. To make sure you have the right ODBC driver, either install Access 7.0 after Project with the Access 95 driver, or reinstall Access 7.0 with just the ODBC driver options changed.

- When the Database Utility creates tables on MS SQL Server, you need to log on with the system administrator's login (**sa**) and password. This enables you to set permissions for any user to have or not have access to the tables.

This list was gleaned from the document "Saving and Retrieving Microsoft Project Data Using the Database Utility" (which you can find as DATABASE.WRI in the WINPROJ folder), as well as trial and error.

Despite these limitations, there is a real advantage to exporting Project data to a database like Access. When you do this, you can provide many users the ability to query the data in a shared fashion. However, given the intricacies of the keys, if you let the users update the data outside of Project, you must make sure they do not violate any unique keys.

One means of protecting Project data stored in an Access database from users would be to create a parallel set of tables in the database which contain a snapshot copy of the Project data. Then you can impose indexing and relations on the copied data and let the users query it rather than the original. Users should make changes to the tables in Project itself.

Communicating Between Project and Access

When you save to an Access database, the DBU uses its ODBC drivers to create the four tables mentioned in the previous section. It can create these tables in an existing Access database, or it can create the database for you.

If you want, you can index the key fields of the Access Project 95 tables. In the Project table, for example, you can create a primary key on the `ProjectKey` field. In the Tasks table, you can create a compound primary key on `ProjectKey` plus `TaskUniqueID` fields. You can then safely draw a one-to-many relationship between the Project's table `ProjectKey` field and the Tasks table.

However, you must be very careful here, because any mistaken primary keys or relations will prevent the DBU from saving Project data. If the DBU accidentally violates any uniqueness conditions based on your primary keys, the update will fail. The safest approach is to leave the Project tables unindexed. That way, the DBU has free reign when updating the data, and you avoid any possible violations of uniqueness on primary keys by the DBU.

Using the Project DBU Methods

Project 95 contains a number of methods located in the Database module by which you can gain programmatic access to the DBU. These methods do not belong to any Project object; instead, they behave more like native macros.

In the following section, you learn how to invoke the DBU methods programmatically, from a macro and a procedure.

Creating a Macro To Save to a Database. When you create a macro to save to or retrieve from a database, the macro recorder assigns one of the DBU methods names as a macro name. For example, to save to a database from a macro and invoke the DBU dialog boxes, you can use

```
MacroName:="SaveToDatabase"
```
or
```
MacroName:="SaveToDatabaseAs"
```

To retrieve from a database, use

```
MacroName:="OpenFromDatabase"
```

These macro names refer to the DBU methods in a way designed to invoke the same dialog boxes the user would see by clicking the toolbar buttons or selecting the menu choices.

Using the DBU Methods in a Procedure. You can inspect the DBU Methods using the Object Browser; what you find are a total of six, as shown in table 15.5.

Table 15.5 Project Database Utility Methods

Project Macro Version	Programmable Version
OpenFromDatabase	OpenFromDatabaseEx
SaveToDatabase	SaveToDatabaseEx
SaveToDatabaseAs	SaveToDatabaseAsEx

When you need full programmatic control over the Open or Save methods, you can use the "Ex" versions. Both the OpenFromDatabaseEx and SaveToDatabaseAsEx can take a number of parameters:

- *Data Source.* The ODBC-named data source.
- *User ID.* (If required by the database.)
- *Password.* (If required by the database.)
- *Driver Parameters.* Specified driver parameters (if required by the database).

When you choose Tools, Multiple Projects, Open From Database, notice that the resulting dialog box asks you for the data source name and then possibly the location of the data. For example, if you choose the data source name MS Access 7.0 Database, you are then prompted to locate the MDB file on disk.

The ODBC dialog boxes only prompt you for locations of databases if you choose the generic data source names that appear in the default list, as shown in figure 15.7.

Fig. 15.7

Project supplies a number of default data sources.

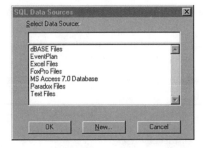

You can make your own data source names that bind the Access ODBC driver and a specific MDB database by clicking New from the SQL Data Sources dialog box. Then choose an ODBC driver (Microsoft Access Driver), and type your new data source name in the ODBC Microsoft Access 7.0 Setup dialog box, as shown in figure 15.8.

Click the Select button to link this new data source name with a specific database. You no longer have to tell ODBC where the database is located.

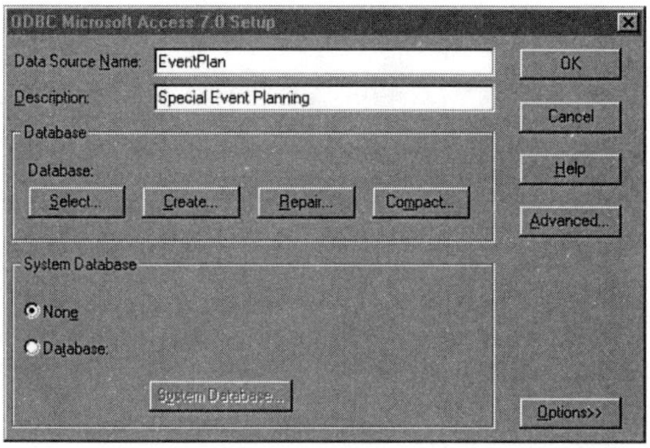

Fig. 15.8

You can create a new Access data source using the ODBC Microsoft Access 7.0 Setup dialog box.

The following example assumes you make a new data source called EventPlan, which links the Access 7.0 ODBC driver to the EVENTPLN.MDB file. Then you can use the OpenDataBaseEx command as follows:

```
'-- Project procedure to retrieve project data from an Access database
Sub RetriveFromDatabase()

    OpenFromDatabaseEx "EventPln", "", "", "", "Special Event Plan", False

End Sub
```

There are two Save commands because the first, SaveToDatabaseEx, just performs a save to a previously opened database. The second version, SaveToDatabaseAsEx, takes the same parameters just mentioned. If any of the parameters fail, you can receive an ODBC error message or a dialog box requesting the missing information.

Integrating Project with Other Office Applications

In addition to the standard Office 95 components, Project 95 can also communicate with other Office applications like Mail and Schedule+. For each of these products, Project 95 contains methods and macros to assist you in communicating with them programmatically.

Using Mail-Enabled Components of Project

You can send a Project 95 project to someone by choosing File, Send. However, Project 95 has a more interesting interface with Mail which lets you use Mail to send e-mail to your resources and receive e-mail answers from them. As they respond, your project data can be selectively updated automatically.

III

Advanced Integration

To send e-mail to your resources, their resource names must match their Mail display names. If your resources have Windows 95 on their desktop, they automatically have the workgroup message-handling interface which provides a special prompt for resource data.

TIP

To test the Mail features of Project 95, just make yourself a resource and send workgroup messages to yourself. Then when you log into e-mail, you'll be able to respond to the e-mail messages and update your project.

NOTE

If you have users that are not running Windows 95 or Windows NT, you can't send and receive formatted Project e-mail with them. Microsoft Product Support Services distributes a special disk called the "Microsoft Project 95 Workgroup Message Handler for Users Running Windows 3.x," #WP1250. The disk contains the Project 95 message-handling software for Windows 3.x users running Lotus cc:Mail, Lotus Notes Mail 3.3, Microsoft Mail, or Microsoft Exchange.

You can see the workgroup options when you choose <u>T</u>ools, <u>W</u>orkgroup, and the TeamAssign, Team<u>U</u>pdate, or Team<u>S</u>tatus options. You can use <u>T</u>eamAssign to query a resource on whether it can accept a task. Once accepted, you can use TeamUpdate to get your resource to state how much time it has spent to date on a task. Finally, the Team<u>S</u>tatus notifies users about changes in its task status.

NOTE

The Project 95 <u>T</u>eamAssign, Team<u>U</u>pdate, and Team<u>S</u>tatus menu choices replace Project 4.0's Send <u>T</u>ask Request and Send Task <u>U</u>pdates choices.

Project comes with a set of built-in Mail application methods, by which you can initiate and control a mail session. These methods belong to the `Application` object:

- `MailLogon`
- `MailRoutingSlip`
- `MailSendProjectMail`
- `MailSendScheduleNote`
- `MailLogoff`
- `MailSend`
- `MailUpdateProject`

Use of these methods is fairly straightforward. They attach to the `Application` object, so to log into a mail session, for example, you just issue the method, followed by user name, password, and a logical indicating whether to download messages:

```
Application.MailLogon <resource/email name>, "1234", True
```

The resource and e-mail name must be the same for this command to work.

Logging off is performed without any passwords:

```
Application.MailLogoff
```

You can establish a Mail routing slip for the current project by using the `MailRoutingSlip` method.

You can send Mail using the `MailSend` method, but the more interesting `MailSendProjectMail` method allows you to send Mail messages in which the recipients can return information about their tasks. This assumes you have already established an e-mail address for each resource, and that the Mail name is the same as the resource name. To send Project mail, you decide on what tasks you want your recipients to give information about, and then supply them in the method call. You can also use the `MailUpdateProject` method to gather updates from e-mail and update the current project.

Using either of these methods assumes that other MAPI information is available; they cannot be executed without code to read Project mail. You can see this by looking at the use of the `MailUpdateProject` method in the `AcceptAllUpdates` macro in the GLOBAL Mail Utilities module. To view this macro, choose <u>T</u>ools, <u>M</u>acros, select `AcceptAllUpdates` in the list, and then click the <u>E</u>dit button.

What this macro does is log onto an e-mail session and check all pending e-mail messages, looking for those with a Project message type. Whenever a message of the correct type is found, the macro reads the e-mail message using its `MAPIReadMail` function. If the message has not already been updated, the macro opens up the attached data file and checks for a Project signature type. If the attachment has the correct signature, the macro then checks the session type of the data file to make sure it is a reply to an assignment or status request. If it is, the macro sends a message to the user asking whether he or she wants to accept updates from the sender of the mail message. If the user agrees, the macro issues the command

```
MailUpdateProject DataFile:=MyFiles(0).PathName
```

where `MyFiles(0).PathName` is the pathed filename of the e-mail attachment containing the update information.

After the update is done, the macro asks the user whether to delete the message from the user's inbox. If the user says yes, the macro marks a flag for deletion, and if not, the macro marks the e-mail message as already updated using the `MAPISaveMail` function. The macro then looks for the next message using its `MAPIFindNext` function. The prior message gets deleted, if the delete flag is true. If there was only one message, the attached file is also deleted from disk. At this point, if there is another message, the macro repeats its processing. This continues until all messages have been read and updated, at which point the macro logs off e-mail.

As you can see, you need to read or write e-mails using the MAPI API calls in order to use the `MailSendProjectMail` and `MailUpdateProject` methods. They cannot be run from the Immediate pane.

> **NOTE** Project also provides two `Application` properties for Mail. You can tell whether a Mail session is underway by accessing the `MailSession` property. You can also determine whether the current Mail system is MAPI-compatible, or what version of Mail it is, by inspecting the `MailSystem` property.

In addition, the `MailSendScheduleNote` method sends a note to a resource. It corresponds to the Send Schedule Note dialog box that you reach by choosing <u>T</u>ools, <u>W</u>orkgroup, Send Sc<u>h</u>edule Note. This function sends a message to a resource and/or a project manager, attaching either the entire project or a bitmap of the selected task.

Setting a Reminder in Schedule+ from Project

You can also set a reminder in Schedule+ from Project by using the `SchedulePlusReminderSet` method. This method also belongs to the application object, and only takes two parameters—start and leadtime. This method corresponds to the Schedule+ Reminders dialog box that you can find by choosing <u>T</u>ools, <u>W</u>orkgroup, Set <u>R</u>eminder.

From Here...

Project is a special-purpose tool that integrates well with Office, primarily because of its OLE capabilities and Visual Basic for Applications commands. You can easily integrate Project with major and minor Office applications to share and update your project data.

For more information about topics described in this chapter, see the following:

- Chapter 3, "Integration Basics," for a discussion of the basic strategies for integrating Office applications.

- Chapter 4, "Visual Basic and Visual Basic for Applications," for technical details of Visual Basic for Applications.

- Chapter 5, "Programming Application Integration," for information about OLE and ODBC.

- Chapter 11, "Automating Office Integration with Excel," for information about Excel macros and VBA in Excel.

- Appendix B, "Office Resources," for a comprehensive list of developer tools and documents.

CHAPTER 16

Working with Office Compatible Applications

Office provides a means to integrate many different types of objects into a single document. However, there are times when you want objects beyond those provided by Microsoft products. Any application that supports OLE Automation can be used to extend your integrated application. While you can share data between applications using DDE, it's the in-place activation capability provided by OLE and OLE Automation that facilitate integrated documents.

To illustrate some of these capabilities, examples of non-Microsoft applications were selected that complement functionality provided by Microsoft products.

In this chapter you learn how to

- Use the Office Compatible program
- Use Office compatible applications to extend your development environment
- Use applications that are not Office compatible to extend your development environment
- Use Visio to add sophisticated drawings to your applications
- Integrate Janna Contact 95, a Personal Information Manager (PIM), into your applications
- Use Statistica to add advanced statistical and graphing functionality to your applications
- Use CorelDRAW! to add advanced graphics to your application

Does Microsoft Office Satisfy All Your Needs?

Office is a powerful suite of desktop applications and, at the same time, a powerful development platform for creating custom business solutions.

Three technologies make Office a compelling solutions platform:

- Office is composed of powerful applications, each of which exposes its functionality as a programmable OLE object.
- Office applications have total support for OLE.
- Office applications use common programming languages—mostly variations of Basic.

NOTE   See Chapter 1 for basic features of Office applications.

These technologies work together and allow the developer to create business solutions in less time and with less code. Additionally, the resultant application is based upon software—Office—that users are already familiar with.

If Office products meet all your needs for supplying documents, analysis, and graphics business solutions, you may not need to consider any other software. On the other hand, if there are times when you want functionality that is not supplied by Office or other software from Microsoft, you will want to look at software from other vendors.

NOTE   As with any development effort, you must define your needs before defining a solution. That means, itemize the functionality that you want. Then identify and get any software that supports that functionality.

One of the key design goals for a Windows application has always been consistency. One of the main benefits of learning to use Windows applications is consistency in how to accomplish tasks. Once you learn how to edit data or save your work, the same, or similar, commands work in all Office products. Office version 4.0 moved a long way toward standardizing the interface for all Office components. Office 95 now moves even closer to the goal of having a common interface and command structure for all Office products.

NOTE   Implementing OLE technology into a product demands a consistent interface. The OLE technology of in-place activation and in-place editing virtually demands that common menu interfaces exist across applications. For example, if you have an Excel worksheet inside a Word document and double-click the worksheet, you activate Excel, and the Word main window menus change to Excel menus.

In an attempt to address consistency between applications from various suppliers, Microsoft has instituted the Office Compatible program.

Understanding Office Compatible Applications

The Office Compatible program is designed to encourage the consistent adoption of frequently used Office features within all products—both from Microsoft itself and outside vendors. Research by Microsoft has shown that the adoption of Office Compatible consistency features will cause the following:

- Increase ease-of-use
- Reduce training costs
- Increase user productivity

Microsoft's Office Compatible program provides information and tools to software vendors to help them create Office compatible products with the overall goal of benefiting Office users.

Two major types of Office compatible applications are identified by the Office Compatible guidelines:

- *Stand-alone applications.* Applications that can be started whether Office is running or not.
- *Host-Required applications.* Applications that can only be used from within their Office host. Many of these products add buttons to the Office product toolbar and/or modify the host menu structure.

 NOTE For more information about Office compatibility and Office compatible products, refer to Appendix A, "Office 95 Compatible Products."

Of course, some products will have attributes of both stand-alone applications and host-required applications. Both Visio and Janna Contact 95 can run as stand-alone applications. Additionally, they add buttons and menu commands to Office products so that you can readily access the power and features of the application. For such applications, it might be more appropriate to call them *host-based* rather that *host-required*. Host-based would mean applications that can use a host as opposed to those which require a host.

What is an Office Compatible Application?

You will see the Office Compatible logo displayed on products that have been certified to be Office compatible. A vendor who wants to have their product certified as Office compatible must submit their products for testing by VeriTest, a third-party test company. VeriTest determines whether the product conforms to Microsoft guidelines for toolbars, menus, and accelerator keys. In addition, Office 95 Compatible products must pass Windows 95 compatibility testing.

III

Advanced Integration

An Office compatible application must also include a special Help topic that does the following:

■ Describes the Office Compatible program

■ Documents differences (if any) in the application's version of the Office compatible features

■ Explains how to use the product with Office and its component applications

Figure 16.1 shows the Office Compatible help window from Janna Contact 95.

Fig. 16.1

Janna Contact 95 describes its Office compatible features in a Help window.

NOTE

If you are a vendor and want to obtain the right to use the Office Compatible logo, you must join the Office Compatible program and ensure that your application meets the basic Office compatible features of standard Office menus, accelerator keys, and toolbars.

Information about joining the Office Compatible program can be found on the Microsoft TechNet CD or obtained from Microsoft.

For information regarding the testing of your Office compatible application, contact:

Office Compatible Logo Administrator
VeriTest, Inc.
3420 Ocean Park Blvd., Suite 2030
Santa Monica, CA 90405

310-450-0062 (voice)
310-399-1760 (fax)

VeriTest's Office Compatible testing fee is $600 U.S. ($800 U.S. for non-English language products). VeriTest also performs testing for the "Designed For Windows 95" compatibility program.

Products that pass VeriTest's tests receive the right to display the Office Compatible logo on their box and in their advertising.

> **Caution**
>
> You must be aware that an application may be certified as Office Compatible and still not smoothly integrate into your environment. You must evaluate the functionality of each application to ascertain the usefulness of that functionality to you.

Partly Compatible Applications

There are many applications that support many of the Office compatible features but for one reason or another are not certified. Some vendors may not want to spend the money so that their products can be called Office compatible. Perhaps their applications have special needs that require deviation from Office standards. In certain cases, Microsoft will grant a waiver to a company for such deviations. Of course, some vendors that support integration may disagree with the Office Compatible program goals.

You will have to evaluate any product to ascertain if the product meets your need. Some excellent products have not been engineered to be integrated with Office. Others have added OLE capability in a newer version.

NOTE In general, if you are developing an application, it's wise to follow the Office Compatible program guidelines. The consistent interface and commands will help greatly—even if you are developing a game.

Windows and the Windows interface has become the de facto standard for PC applications. It's easier to go with the flow than to fight the current.

Using Visio

Visio from Visio Corporation is a Windows drawing program that features a drag-and-drop user interface. Drawing components (called *shapes*) are dragged from a shape palette (called a *stencil*) and dropped on the Visio drawing surface. Once the object has been dropped on the drawing, it can be repositioned, resized, rotated, and modified in a number of ways.

Visio was the first, and still is a primary, non-Microsoft contributor to the Office environment. Visio and Visual Basic 3.0 were the first products to fully support OLE. You can use VB or VBA to control Visio and, by doing so, can create just about anything that can be drawn, and then integrate the drawing into an Office application.

Visio 4.0 is Office compatible. When you install Visio, you get a dialog box as shown in figure 16.2 asking if you want a Visio icon installed on your Word and Excel toolbars.

Fig. 16.2

The Visio Installation asks you if you want to install a Visio icon on the Office toolbars.

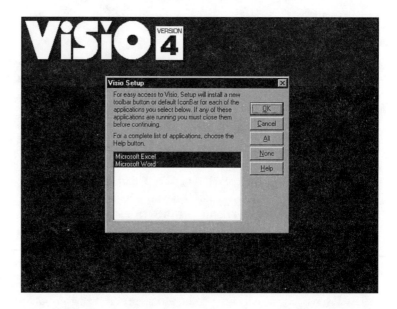

When you select the OK button, the Visio icon is installed on the Standard toolbar. Figure 16.3 shows the Visio icon on the Word toolbar.

Visio icon

Fig. 16.3

The Word toolbar shows the Visio icon.

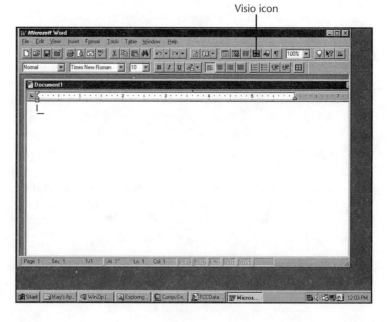

As an OLE server, Visio exposes many OLE objects for manipulation by OLE controllers. Visio does not include a programming language of its own. However, Visio is easily programmed using VB or VBA. Figure 16.4 shows the Visio environment with a drawing designed to illustrate a view of a project plan that cannot be created directly from Project.

Toolbar

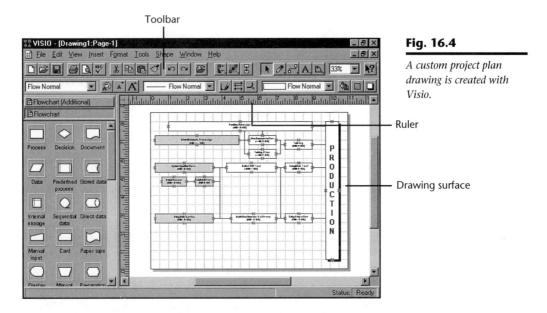

Fig. 16.4

A custom project plan drawing is created with Visio.

Ruler

Drawing surface

Visio includes a large number of tools for manipulating a drawing and its components. You can add text, color, lines, boxes, and other geometric shapes to a drawing. Shapes may be resized, rotated, stretched, and manipulated in a number of ways. The drawing surface is scalable to fit almost any size drawing.

Understanding Visio's Editions and Supplementary Products

TIP

Visio 3.0 included a standard version and Visio Express. Visio Express was designed as a lightweight version that could only be used with Office 4.x applications. Visio Express is not available for Office 95.

Visio 4.0 is expressly designed for use with Windows 95 and Windows NT 3.51. However, it still supports Windows 3.1. Visio Version 4.0 is produced in two versions.

Visio 4.0—For Normal Business Drawings. Visio 4.0 is an easy-to-use tool for creating a variety of business drawings, including project timelines, organizational charts, network diagrams, office layouts, quality management diagrams, geographic maps, and more. There are Visio 4.0 diagramming wizards to assist in the creation of organizational charts, timelines, and page layouts.

Visio Technical 4.0—For Professional Technical Drawings. Visio Technical 4.0 includes all the functionality in Visio 4.0 and adds the capability to create technical drawings, including electrical schematics and facility management drawings. Visio Technical 4.0 allows technical professionals, such as architects, designers, and engineers, to create and share drawings and technical schematics. Visio Technical 4.0 can be used to share drawings between CAD and non-CAD users and can import drawings created by AutoCAD. Visio Technical 4.0 adds some 2,000 technical SmartShapes to the shapes included with Visio 4.0.

TIP
Visio Technical is a new product that seems to be targeted to the high-end user who may have selected a CAD software package in the past.

Visio Add-Ons. Visio offers several sets of predesigned shapes, called *SmartShapes*, that you can purchase. You can get shapes for things like a chemistry set from which you can create drawings of molecules or a calendar maker for creating calendars in various layouts and styles.

Complementing Office with Visio

Visio installs itself in Word and Excel. When you click the Visio toolbar icon in Word, you see a view like figure 16.5.

Fig. 16.5

Create a new Visio drawing in Word using OLE in-place activation.

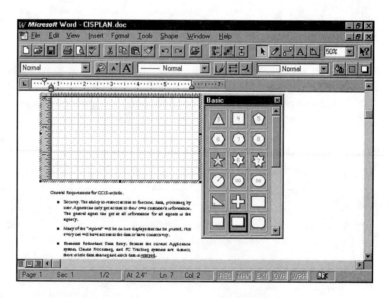

As you can see, the toolbar has become the Visio toolbar; the menus, as appropriate, have become Visio menus, and you have the Visio drawing surface and selected stencil.

NOTE

When you create the drawing, you can only open one stencil. If you need to use a second stencil, choose <u>V</u>iew, <u>O</u>pen in Visio. Then you can add more stencils.

This results because when opening an OLE object, the File menu is not replaced. The Stencils function is on the File menu in Visio. It might have been better to place the Stencils function under the View menu in Visio.

After you complete your drawing, return to Word and continue to work. If you need to edit the drawing, click it. You will see the sizing handle appear and a message in the status bar `Double-click to Edit VISIO 4.0 Drawing`. Double-clicking activates Visio for in-place editing.

Inserting a Visio drawing in an Excel worksheet works exactly the same. For all Office products, including PowerPoint and Access, you can choose <u>I</u>nsert, <u>O</u>bject and then pick VISIO 4.0 drawing from the list of insertable objects. The toolbar icons in Word and Excel are shortcuts for this process.

In all Office products, a Visio drawing is encapsulated in an unbound object frame.

Visio as an OLE Automation Server

Visio is object-based and exposes its drawing shapes, environment, and other Visio components as objects that are controllable from other applications via OLE Automation.

Visio objects exhibit *encapsulation*, which means that each Visio shape contains the following:

- *Properties*. Data that describes the appearance, position, size, and other attributes of the shape.
- *Methods*. Used to control and manipulate the object.

As with other OLE Automation servers, most of your work automating Visio involves learning the object hierarchies and the properties and methods of the Visio drawing objects and environment. The VBA commands to manipulate Visio are straightforward and are the same commands used with any OLE Automation object. Therefore, you don't have to learn a new language in order to use Visio as an OLE Automation server regardless of the automation controller (VB4, Excel, and so on) used. Each of the tasks required to create a drawing, complete with shapes and their properties, is handled in Visual Basic.

Visio exposes a wide range of objects for OLE Automation. Table 16.1 identifies some of the objects that are most useful in programming Visio.

III

Advanced Integration

Table 16.1 Visio Programming Objects	
Object and Collections	**Description**
Application	The Visio application itself.
Cell	Belongs to a Shape or Style object and represents a property of the shape or style. The data that describes a shape is stored in a *shape sheet* as a series of rows and columns of cells. A single cell contains properties such as the width, height, and X and Y coordinates of the shape as it appears within a drawing.
Characters	Represents the text contained in a shape. The Text property of the Characters object is used to set or retrieve the value.
Connect, Connects	The Connect object represents the connection between two shapes in a drawing. Connects is the collection of all connect objects. The GlueTo method connects two objects.
Document, Documents	An individual document (which may contain a number of Page objects), stencil, or template. Documents is the collection of all Document objects.
Master, Masters	An individual shape or master in a stencil. To create an instance of a master in a drawing, use the Drop method of a Page object for the drawing. Masters is the collection of Master objects in a stencil.
Page, Pages	An individual drawing page in a document. The ActivePage property returns or sets the active drawing page. Pages is the collection of drawing page objects in a document.
Shape, Shapes	The Shape object can represent any object on the drawing. Generally, the Shape object is identified with an index into the Shapes collection.
Style, Styles	A Style object represents a style defined in a document and defines some combination of line, fill, and text attributes. A Style object is contained in the Styles collection of a Document object.

TIP
If you don't have Visio Technical, you can still get the Visio object reference by downloading it from the Visio CompuServe forum and typing **GO VISIO**; then search for PROGREF.ZIP in Library 8.

Visio is controlled much like any OLE server using OLE Automation tasks such as creating a new drawing page, opening a stencil containing the shapes you want to use, dropping shapes on the drawing, and reading or setting the values of the cells in a shape sheet. The majority of this chapter describes how each of these tasks is implemented in VB code.

Interfacing with Visio. All OLE clients must follow these steps to use Visio:

1. Attach to a running instance of Visio, or start a new instance.
2. Add a new drawing page to the Visio `Documents` collection.
3. Establish an object variable to the drawing page.
4. Set the drawing page parameters.
5. Open a stencil and acquire handles to that stencil and its collection of shapes.
6. Drop and position shapes on the drawing page.
7. Draw other needed objects on the drawing page.

The following procedures are generic VBA functions that can be used in VB4, Access, Excel, and Project. There will be some access routines for getting data that is specific to each platform.

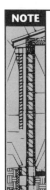

NOTE

Through the use of VBA, VB4, Access, Excel, and Project, all use the same OLE Automation commands to interface with Visio and other OLE servers.

The interface routines presented here work in these OLE clients. There are some idiosyncrasies in the various versions of VBA, and you must watch out for any discrepancy.

For example, in VB4, you can use the `Err` object. This is not available in Excel. Also, VB generally handles type conversion. In Excel, you must explicitly convert every value to have the correct type. VB4 supports default properties; Excel does not.

One specific point of difference is subtraction of two variables of Date datatype. VB4 gives the number of days between the two dates. Excel gives an error.

NOTE

All of these procedures are identified as `Private`, which means that the procedure cannot be accessed from another module in either VB4 or Excel. In general, a procedure should be `Private` unless there is an expressed need to make it `Public`.

Listing 16.1 shows the code to initialize the Visio application. This code uses the `GetObject` function to see if Visio is already running. If `Visio.Application` cannot be found, a trappable error is returned by the `GetObject` function call, and `CreateObject` is used to start Visio. If `Visio.Application` has been properly registered, there will be no error, and the desired stencil is loaded.

Listing 16.1 DOVISIO.FRM. Setting Up the Visio Application

```
Private Sub SetUpVisio()
  Dim objStencil  As Object
  On Error Resume Next

  'GetObject attaches to Visio, if running.
  'If this command generates an error,
```

On the CD

III

Advanced Integration

(continues)

Listing 16.1   Continued

```
'CreateObject creates a new instance of Visio.

Set appVisio = GetObject(, visApi)

If Err > 0 Then
  Err = 0
  Set appVisio = CreateObject(visApi)
  If Err > 0 Then
    Exit Sub
  End If
End If

On Error GoTo 0
'Add the Basic Shapes stencil .
Set objStencil = appVisio.Documents.Open("Basic Shapes.VSS")
End Sub
```

NOTE

These procedures use constants defined in the Visio supplied file VISCONST.BAS which contains Visio constants for Visual Basic. For example, the constant visApi contains the string Visio.Application.

This procedure, along with VB4 project that uses these routines, are on your CD. In addition, an Excel workbook, PROJMGT1.XLS, also uses these same procedures to generate the same Visio drawing.

When using VB4, add VISCONST.BAS to the project. When using Excel 95, you have to import the file into a Module sheet. You cannot share files between VB4 and Excel 95.

The code in listing 16.2 will set up the drawing page in Landscape mode.

Listing 16.2   DOVISIO.FRM. Setting Up the Drawing Page

```
Private Sub SetUpPage(alScale As Long)
  'Set page object to active page
  '"ThePage" is a Visio reference
  'to the current drawing page
  Set objPage = appVisio.ActivePage.Shapes("ThePage")

  'Set up page parameters for drawing
  objPage.cells("DrawingSizeType") = visStandard
  objPage.cells("DrawingScaleType") = visScaleCustom
  objPage.cells("DrawingScale") = 1
  objPage.cells("PageScale") = 1 / alScale
  objPage.cells("PageWidth") = alScale * 11
  objPage.cells("PageHeight") = alScale * 8.5
  objPage.cells("ShdwOffsetX") = 0.125
  objPage.cells("ShdwOffsetY") = -0.125
  objPage.cells("GridDensity") = visGridFine
  objPage.cells("RulerDensity") = visRulerNormal
End Sub
```

`objPage` is an object variable to reference the current drawing surface. It is assigned to a special Visio Shape that represents the current drawing page:

```
Set objPage = appVisio.ActivePage.Shapes("ThePage")
```

`ThePage` is used by Visio to reference the active drawing page in the `Documents` collection. `ThePage` is itself, a shape.

In the previous code, `DrawingSizeType` defines the page's size and scale. A value of `visStandard(2)` indicates to use a standard 8.5×11-inch sheet of paper.

For the `DrawingScaleType` parameter a value of `visScaleCustom(3)` means that you intend to define your own scale using `DrawingScale` and `PageScale`.

The `DrawingScale` and `PageScale` settings determine how many divisions per measurement unit will be used by Visio. In this case, the `DrawingScale` is 1 for a one-to-one correlation, and `PageScale` is set to the width of the data.

The `PageWidth` and `PageHeight` settings tell Visio how to present the page on the screen by using the width of data, passed in as the argument `alScale` and multiplying by the desired page width and height.

Dropping a Shape onto a Visio Page. Listing 16.3 will drop a given shape at specified X, Y coordinates and then rotate it as desired.

Listing 16.3 DOVISIO.FRM. Drop a Shape onto a Visio Page

On the CD

```
Private Sub DropObject(sShape As String, _
    dX As Double, dY As Double, dAngle As Double)
    'sShape = Shape name
    'dX and dY are the X and Y coordinate for shape
    'dAngle determins the rotation of the object
    Dim objMaster As Object
    Dim objShape As Object

    'Activate Visio.
    AppActivate "VISIO" ' Technical"
    'Note: Add "Technical" to work with Visio Technical.
    'AppActivate "VISIO Technical"

    'Use sShape to assign objMaster to the correct shape
    ' Note: sShape is the name of the object in stencil
    Set objMaster = objMasters(CStr(sShape))

    'Set objShape to the shape object being dropped on drawing.
    Set objShape = objPage.Drop(objMaster, dX, dY)
    'Then rotate objShape as indicated by dAngle
    objShape.cells("Angle") = dAngle

    'Destroy object variables
    Set objMaster = Nothing
    Set objShape = Nothing
End Sub
```

The variables objMaster and objShape represent the shapes being added to the drawing. The AppActivate statement is used to bring Visio to the top of the screen so that you can see the automation in action.

The following line assigns the object variable that will be used to represent the shape to the mStr parameter passed into DropObject:

```
Set objMaster = objMasters(CStr(sShape))
```

sShape is the name of the object to be dropped at location dX and dY. This must be a valid shape on your stencil, or you will get an error. dX and dY are in inches, while dAngle is in radians. These are the default measurement units for Visio.

> **TIP**
>
> You can change the measurement units for the drawing when you set up the drawing page.

The shape is finally dropped on the Visio page with the following statement:

```
Set objShape = objPage.Drop(objMaster, dX, dY)
```

objShape is assigned to the value returned by the Drop method so that the handle to the object dropped on the page is available for use by the cells method to rotate the object:

```
objShape.Cells("Angle") = Angle
```

Drawing on a Visio Page. Listing 16.4 illustrates drawing the diagram on the Visio page. This routine calls the SetUpPage routine to create a new page and GetData. The GetData routine is specific to the server being used. You can see specific examples on the CD.

On the CD

Listing 16.4   DOVISIO.FRM. Drawing on the Visio Page

```
Private Sub DoDrawing(dMinDate As Date, dMaxDate As Date, alTasks As Integer)
    Dim objDocuments As Object
    Dim objDocument As Object
    Dim objPages As Object
    Dim objPage As Object
    Dim objShape As Object
    Dim lScale As Long
    Dim ctr As Integer
    Dim X1 As Double, Y1 As Double, X2 As Double, Y2 As Double
    Dim dStart As Date, dEnd As Date, sDescription As String
    Const DELTAX = 3, DELTAY = 15
    Const PAGEWIDTH = 264 - DELTAX * 2, PAGEHEIGHT = 204 - DELTAY * 2
    lScale = DateValue(dMaxDate) - DateValue(dMinDate)
```

```
'Set up object references
Set objDocuments = appVisio.Documents
Set objDocument = objDocuments.Add("")
SetUpPage
Set objPages = objDocument.pages
Set objPage = objPages(1)

For ctr = 1 To 13
  'Draw a rectangle, set its text,
  'and format it with a style
  GetData ctr, dStart, dEnd, sDescription
  X1 = DateValue(dStart) - dMinDate
  X2 = X1 + (DateValue(dEnd) - DateValue(dStart))
  X1 = X1 * (PAGEWIDTH / CDbl(lScale)) + DELTAX
  X2 = X2 * (PAGEWIDTH / CDbl(lScale))
  Y1 = PAGEHEIGHT / 14 * (15 - ctr)
  Y2 = Y1 + 15
  Set objShape = objPage.DrawRectangle(X1, Y1, X2, Y2)
  'objShape.TextStyle = "Arial 24pt. centered"
  objShape.Text = sDescription & vbCrLf _
  & "(" & dStart & " - " & dEnd & ")"
Next
'Save the drawing and quit Visio
objDocument.SaveAs "d:\PPlan.vsd"
appVisio.Quit
Set appVisio = Nothing

End Sub
```

The statement

```
Set objShape = objPage.DrawRectangle(X1, Y1, X2, Y2)
```

will draw a rectangle on the page at the specified coordinates. The handle to the object is returned as objShape so that the statement

```
objShape.Text = sDescription & vbCrLf & "(" & dStart & " - " & dEnd & ")"
```

can write text into the shape.

Caution

Be careful with some functions across different VBA dialects. In VB4, you can subtract two date datatypes and get the number of days between the two dates. In Excel, you get an error. In this case, the CDbl function was used to convert the date to a double precision value so that the arithmetic works.

Figure 16.6 shows the Visio drawing generated from these procedures.

Fig. 16.6

The Visio Project plan drawing is generated by the VB4 project or the Excel VBA macro.

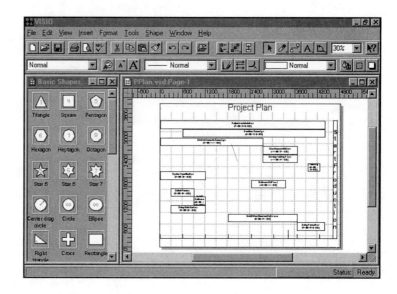

Finding Out More About Visio

For information about using Visio for custom development solutions, see "Developing Visio Solutions." This comes with Visio Technical but must be purchased separately if you have the standard edition.

TIP

If you don't have a copy of Visio yet, get Visio Technical. It's a much better value. In general, it is a bad idea to not buy the high-end version of a product when it's available.

NOTE

You can find information, including Visio product updates, on CompuServe (type **GO VISIO**).

For information on Visio, contact:

> Visio Corporation
> 520 Pike Street, Suite 1800
> Seattle, Washington 98109
> (206) 521-4500.

Using Janna Contact 95

Janna Contact 95 is the only certified Office Compatible Personal Information Manager (PIM). Janna Contact 95 was totally redesigned to be a 32-bit Windows 95, Windows NT 3.51, and Office 95 compatible application. Janna Contact 95 (JC95) is written in VB4 and has smooth integration with many Office products, providing access to information stored in its database. This means that you can access and update the information from within JC95 directly without opening the host application.

JC95 provides both contact and document management services. JC95 provides the ability to store Word documents, faxes, Excel worksheets, PowerPoint presentations, voice notes, and even full-motion video notes associated directly with your contact. The Janna Contact 95 Installation Wizard enables you to create a Word macro that installs a Janna Contact icon on the Word toolbar. This icon makes it easy to embed JC95 OLE fields anywhere in a Word document or template. *Embedded OLE fields* means that you can automatically address and personalize letters for a user or a complete group of contacts. Figure 16.7 shows the Janna Contact 95 icon on the Word toolbar.

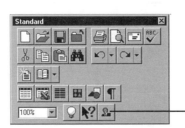

Janna Contact 95 icon

Fig. 16.7

The Janna Contact 95 icon on the Word floating toolbar.

JC95 uses the Access 95/Jet 3.0 database format for storing its data. Because JC95 is designed for Windows 95 and written in VB4, it has the latest OLE technology available. It supports all the Windows 95 requirements, including drag-and-drop editing between applications and right-mouse support.

There are four types of information that JC95 stores by default (see fig. 16.8):

- *Contact.* A person or company for which you want to store information. This can include an unlimited number of addresses, telephone numbers, contact types, categories, and custom fields with which you can define information that you want to capture.

- *Document.* Information associated with a contact. A document can be any information—notes, word processing document, worksheet, graphics, video—that you want to keep with that client.

- *Action Item.* A scheduled activity for yourself or another JC95 user. Action items appear in the schedule as well as the contact's *information log*—a history of activity for that contact. Action items can also appear in Schedule+. If you have a presentation action, you can store your PowerPoint presentation with the action.

- *E-mail.* Mail messages from Exchange or other MAPI 1.0-compliant applications can be sent, read, responded to, and stored with the contact.

NOTE
Janna Contact 95 does not directly interface with online services such as CompuServe. However, Exchange can be configured to access CompuServe and Internet services.

Fig. 16.8

The Janna Contact 95 application appears with the Contact and Document windows open.

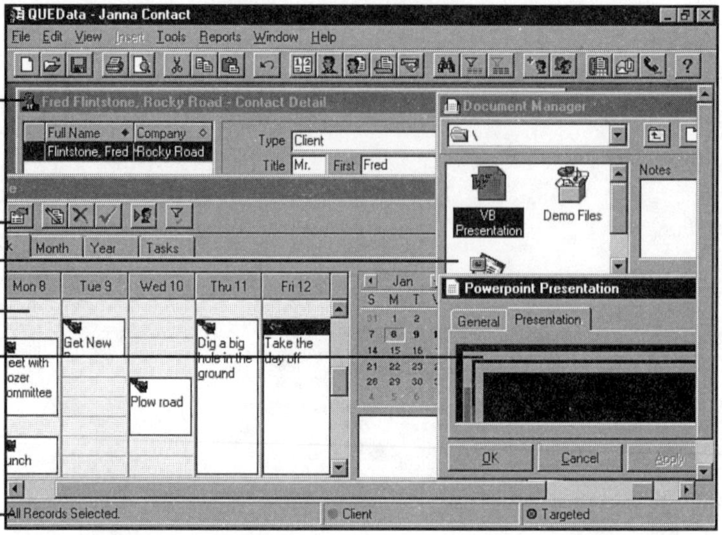

Contact Detail
Toolbar
Document Manager
Schedule
Document Detail
Status bar

Complementing Office with Janna Contact 95

The reason why so many PIMs have been developed and why so many of them have become shelfware is that there are always things that the PIM user wants to do that the product can't. So, why talk about Janna Contact 95?

Janna Contact 95 was constructed to smoothly integrate with Office 95. JC95 installs an icon on the Word toolbar and installs macros in the NORMAL.DOT template. These macros will allow you to read information from your contact database and immediately insert it into a Word document. Figure 16.9 shows the Word dialog box that the Word macro fills with JC95 fields; here, you can easily select information that you want to insert into a Word document.

NOTE
The JC95 Word macro uses OLE fields in Word to read data from the JC95 database and insert that data into the Word document.

For example, listing 16.5 shows the commands to initiate a conversation with JC95 and to insert a JC95 database field linked to a Word field reference.

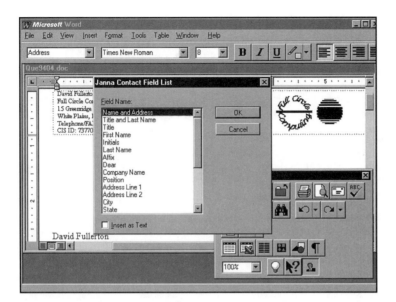

Fig. 16.9

The Word dialog box displays available JC95 fields you can use to insert Janna Contact 95 information into a Word document.

Listing 16.5   Inserting Janna Contact 95 Information Using Word Fields

```
channel = DDEInitiate("JCWIN95", "SYSTEM")
FileName1$ =  DDERequest$(channel, "DBPath")
InsertField .Field = "LINK JCOBJS.JLinkData.3 " + Chr$(34) + \
"DDEADDRLabel(0)" + Chr$(34) + " " + Chr$(34) + "Addr0" + Chr$(34) + " \a \t"
WW2_Insert Chr$(13)
```

This code was taken from the Word macro installed by JC95. The first two lines use DDE to get the location of the current database. The third line then inserts an OLE hot link to the Janna Contact field selected. *Hot links* are used so that you can easily update the document if information changes, or create a batch of letters for a group of contacts.

Caution

In order for Word to communicate with JC95, Janna Contact must be running and have an open database. DDEInitiate starts JC95 if it is not running.

TIP

To find a list of the fields that you can embed, open the InsertJCFieldLink macro in Word. All fields are listed there and displayed in the Word dialog box.

You can use the same technique to access JC95 data from Excel. For example, you might create a macro in Excel to read information from your Contact database using the links provided by Janna. Listing 16.6 illustrates how to use links from Excel to JC95 which will insert a JC95 database field linked to the active cell.

Listing 16.6   Inserting Janna Contact 95 Field Information into Excel

```
Sub GetJannaInformation()
Dim strPath As String
Dim strTemp As String
' Full path including computer
strPath = "\\dcf\c\Program Files\Janna Contact\FCCData\"
' Insert appropriate field name
strTemp = "=JCOBJS40.JLinkData.4¦" & strPath & _
"FCCData.JCD!'!Last Name'"
ActiveCell.FormulaR1C1 = strTemp
End Sub
Sub GetJannaInformationUsingDDE()
Dim strTemp As String
' Insert the appropriate DDE link field
strTemp = "=JCWIN95!system!'DDEADDRLabel(0)'"
ActiveCell.FormulaR1C1 = strTemp
End Sub
```

GetJannaInformation is a procedure that inserts an OLE link into the ActiveCell. GetJannaInformationUsingDDE is a procedure that inserts a DDE link into the ActiveCell.

Caution

Janna Contact 95 did not expose its objects for use as OLE Automation objects by other applications. It provided OLE field links and DDE field links that can be used. The only documented field link information is included in the InsertJCFieldLink macro that's installed in Word when JC95 is installed.

Additionally, only the active record is accessible.

Integrating Janna Contact 95 into an Office Application

Janna Contact 95 was designed to integrate smoothly into the Office environment. One of the more interesting things you can do with JC95 is use the Document Management function for organizing all information regarding a contact or a project. For example, suppose you are giving a presentation at a conference. You can:

- Enter the conference chairperson as a contact.
- Use the information about the conference in the information log.
- Enter the dates for the conference and the dates you need to have materials to the conference chair in the schedule.

- Enter all target dates for working on the conference materials into the schedule.
- Prepare the handout notes in Word and store the document linked to the contact.
- Prepare the PowerPoint presentation and store the presentation linked to the contact.
- Prepare your pictures with CorelDRAW! and store the images linked to the contact.
- Prepare code and database examples and link the files to the contact.
- E-mail the required documents and samples to the conference chair for preparation of the handout materials.

This will organize all your objects needed for the conference in one place. You can open any of the objects from JC95 by double-clicking the object from the Document Manager.

You can organize all your notes and documents by contact and easily find information. If you scan in images, these can be associated with a contact. If you use voice recording, these voice notes can be linked to the contact.

> **NOTE**
> Janna Contact 95 did not expose its objects for use as OLE Automation objects by other applications. To expose a VB4 object, you must set the object's properties of `Public = True` and `Instancing = Creatable, Multiuse`. Janna indicated that objects would be exposed in the future.

Finding Out More About Janna Contact 95

Currently, Janna Contact 95 is available at an introductory price of $99, and it has a competitive upgrade offer.

If you would like to try JC95 out, a demonstration version is available on CompuServe (type **GO JANNA**). Additionally, Janna posts incremental updates in this forum as new features are added and bugs fixed.

> **NOTE**
> If you are using Word for Windows 95, you need to get the updated JC95 macros from the Janna forum on CompuServe.

For information on Janna Contact 95, contact:

Janna Systems, Inc.
3080 Yonge St., Suite 6060
Toronto, Ontario M4N 3N1, Canada
(416) 483-7711

III

Advanced Integration

Using Statistica

Statistica is a very powerful data analysis application that incorporates ease-of-use with powerful functionality. Statistica is not certified Office Compatible. However, it is a program that can be used in concert with Office applications because of its support for OLE and DDE.

> **NOTE**
>
> Statistica does not fully support OLE and OLE Automation in the current release. Statistica version 5 does support in-place activation, which makes it useful for creating integrated applications. StatSoft has indicated that OLE Automation and complete support for OLE will be included in a future version of Statistica.

When you start Statistica, you see the STATISTICA Module Switcher dialog box as shown in figure 16.10.

Fig. 16.10

The Statistica Module Switcher dialog box enables you to select the desired Statistica function.

From this dialog box, you have access to all the facilities in Statistica. Statistica allows you to perform any number of analysis of data you might collect. For example, figure 16.11 illustrates three types of graphs from the same data. There are both problems and benefits from using various presentation formats. The benefit of statistical presentation of data is that you can focus a presentation so that the point you are trying to make is highlighted. However, when you focus analysis in one direction, you may miss something else in the data.

> **Caution**
>
> Statistics and their interpretation can be very dangerous. It's very easy to get caught up in the presentation and overlook some analysis that may result in a different conclusion. Presentation can be used to focus the reader to a specific point of view or direct attention from a point that may be less favorable.
>
> Data doesn't lie. However, the results of statistical analysis of data can be such that the whole truth is not told or, perhaps, even found.

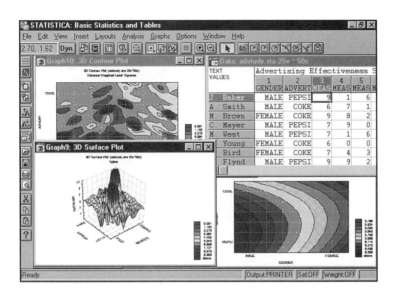

Fig. 16.11

Statistica can graph statistical data in three different presentation graphs styles.

Complementing Office with Statistica

Statistica uses both an OLE client and an OLE server. As a server, you choose Insert, Object and then select Statistica from the list. For example, if you want to include a Statistica graph in your PowerPoint presentation, you see a display that looks similar to figure 16.12.

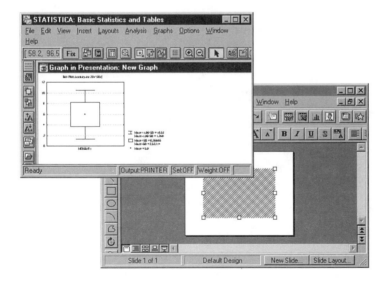

Fig. 16.12

You can prepare a Statistica graph as an embedded object for a PowerPoint presentation.

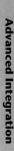

III

Advanced Integration

In the Statistica server, you open your data and prepare the graph. Then when you return to PowerPoint, the graph is ready to present.

On the other side, you can include information from another application in your Statistica graphic.

Integrating Statistica into an Office Application

Statistica can be called from client Office applications to create new statistical graphs or diagrams using the Object command on the Insert menu in the client application. In the Object dialog box, select New and then select Statistica from the list of available OLE-compatible applications. Statistica will open in the Server mode and automatically create a blank graph window. This window can be used to create a new graph, combination of graphs, or other artwork to be inserted as an OLE object to the client application. When you exit Statistica, you will see the Statistica object in the client application window.

In addition, you can also paste Statistica graphs in other applications, creating links from that application to Statistica graph files.

You can also use Statistica as an OLE client in that you can embed an object within a Statistica graph.

NOTE Statistica can act simultaneously as a server and client in that compound graphs can be created consisting of Statistica graphic objects which can contain and can be contained by other OLE servers and clients. Such objects can be edited or updated using the standard OLE conventions of double-clicking or choosing Edit, Object. Some procedures and graphs in Statistica automatically generate compound graphs.

Statistica is extensible through two sources that are included with Statistica:

- *Statistica Command Language (SCL)*. A language used to automate repetitive functions.

- *Statistica Basic*. A variation of the standard Basic language targeted specifically to Statistica.

You can build SCL functions or scripts that include Statistica Basic procedures. In addition, any SCL command or script can be called from an Office application using DDExecute functionality. For example, listing 16.7 is a sample Excel procedure that executes the Statistica SCL command DESC VARS=ALL. This procedure requires that STA_RUN, the Statistica run module, be running or that the Statistica directory be in your path.

Listing 16.7   Excel VBA Macro to Execute a Statistica SCL Function

```
Sub XL_Statistica()
  Dim hChannel As Integer
  Dim sCommand As String
```

```
    sCommand = "DESC CARS=ALL"
    hChannel = DDEInitiate(STA_RUN", "SYSTEM")
    DDEExecute hChannel, sCommand
    DDETerminate hChannel
End Sub
```

At the moment, using DDE is the only way to directly feed Excel or Access data into Statistica.

NOTE

Of course, there is another alternative for the creative application developer in interfacing with Statistica or other applications—SendKeys functionality from VBA. SendKeys can be used with many applications because you are controlling the application by emulating typing keystrokes targeted at the application. The application does not know that the keystrokes did not come from a physical device. The application simply responds to the apparent interrupt. This was the basis of the macro recorder from Windows 3.11 and earlier.

Finding Out More About Statistica

Statistica ships with 10 disks and a massive six-volume set of reference materials which guide you through using Statistica. More than other software, Statistica requires that you have a good understanding of statistics and know what you want to accomplish.

For information on Statistica, contact:

StatSoft
2300 E. 14th St.
Tulsa, OK 74104-4442
(918) 749-1119

Using CorelDRAW!

CorelDRAW! is a very powerful graphics application that incorporates ease-of-use with powerful functionality. CorelDRAW! is not certified Office Compatible. It's a program that can be used in concert with Office because of its support for OLE.

CorelDRAW! 6 is invaluable for the instance that you need more than the standard pictures that you can create with Paintbrush. CorelDRAW! actually consists of several programs along with several utilities and libraries of pictures and other artwork:

- *CorelDRAW!*. A premium drawing tool for illustration and page layout.
- *CorelDream 3D*. A tool for 3D modeling and rendering.
- *Corel Motion 3D*. For creating 3D animation.
- *Corel Photo-Paint*. For editing photographs and creating bitmaps.
- *Corel Presents*. For creating business and multimedia presentations.

III

Advanced Integration

Understanding the CorelDRAW! Versions

CorelDRAW! is available in a variety of versions. Each version with a higher number contains all the functionality of each lower version. The following list identifies the CorelDRAW! software packages available for Windows 3.x and Windows 95:

- CorelDRAW! 3 is an entry-level graphics package designed to get you started creating your own graphics. CorelDRAW! 3 is often included with hardware as an enticement for you to upgrade to another version.

- CorelDRAW! 4 includes the graphics of CorelDRAW! 3 and adds functionality for OCR and scanning support, color separation, animation, and advanced presentation capability.

- CorelDRAW! 5 is the high-end program with enormous capability. It comes with four CDs of data. In addition to the power of CorelDRAW 4, it adds Ventura for desktop publishing capability. To use CorelDRAW! 5 with Windows 95, you need to obtain a patch from Corel.

- CorelDRAW! 6 is an integrated suite of native 32-bit applications designed for the 32-bit Windows 95 environment. While it includes five fully featured applications that encompass all the functionality that is in CorelDRAW! 5, except for Ventura 5, CorelDRAW! 6 is much more than a rewrite of the 16-bit applications.

In addition, there are UNIX and OS/2 versions of CorelDRAW!. Corel also offers many other products, all of which are oriented toward graphics and desktop publishing. Corel also offers some products for the Macintosh environment.

Complementing Office with CorelDRAW!

CorelDRAW! can be used as both an OLE client and an OLE server. As a server, choose Insert, Object and then select CorelDRAW! from the list. For example, if you want to include a CorelDRAW! drawing in your PowerPoint presentation, you see a display similar to the one shown in figure 16.13.

You can also include Office objects in a CorelDRAW! illustration creating compound documents.

Integrating CorelDRAW! into an Office Application

CorelDRAW! and all the various related products are primarily used for the graphic presentation quality. Some of the things you can do with CorelDRAW! might include:

- Create a corporate logo for printing on your Word correspondence and Access reports. This can especially look great if you have a color printer.

- Create a great looking watermark for your Word documents.

- Embellish your presentation with easy-to-create graphic images.

- Create a fancy invoice from a Word layout using information from the Access database, where you track time and billing rate information, and insert the name and address from your Janna Contact 95 system.

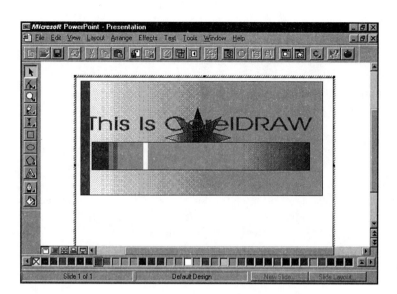

Fig. 16.13

*Insert a CorelDRAW!
drawing as an OLE
Automation object
in a PowerPoint
presentation.*

Finding Out More About CorelDRAW!

Corel provides support for CorelDRAW! in the Corel Applications 1 forum on CompuServe. You can also find updates to the product in this forum.

For information on CorelDRAW!, contact:

> Corel Corporation
> 1600 Carling Ave.
> Ottawa, Ontario CANADA K1Z 8R7
> (613) 728-8200

From Here...

It's difficult to find software or even a suite of software products that does everything that you want to do. This chapter explored some non-Microsoft products that can be used to complement Office 95 products with functionality that expands upon that provided by Microsoft. There are many other products that meet the criteria imposed that the product must be OLE compliant and, preferably, have OLE Automation. The most flexibility is obtained when a product can be both an OLE client and an OLE server as well as supporting OLE Automation. Exposed type libraries greatly facilitate use in an integrated solution.

This chapter explored a drawing package (Visio), a PIM (Janna Contact 95), a statistical and graphing package (Statistica), and a graphics package (CorelDRAW!). Each of these packages has functionality that is not included in Office 95. Such functionality extends the total capability of your integrated application.

III

Advanced Integration

You must define your requirements. Then, evaluate the available software and determine which, if any, meets all or part of your needs. If software meets only part of your need, ask the question, "Can this software be extended or complemented to create a total solution?" The answer is that all software can be used if you let your imagination loose. The easy ones to deal with use OLE and OLE Automation. Others may support the older DDE protocol. At last resort, you can use the SendKeys function from VBA to control an application.

- For information on using VB4 and VBA, see Chapter 4, "Visual Basic and Visual Basic for Applications"; Chapter 5, "Programming Application Integration"; and Chapter 17, "Controlling Office Application with Visual Basic."

- For information on integrating non-Office products with Office products, see Chapter 14, "Integrating Schedule+ and E-Mail with Other Office Applications," and Chapter 15, "Integrating Project with Office Applications."

- See Appendix A, "Office 95 Compatible Applications," for a list of software products that are compatible with Office.

CHAPTER 17

Controlling Office Applications with Visual Basic

In Chapter 4, you learned the history of Visual Basic, including the relationship between Visual Basic 4 (VB4) and Visual Basic for Applications 2 (VBA2). In this chapter, we leverage off your understanding of VBA and provide you with a working knowledge of Visual Basic. After a brief overview of the features in Visual Basic, I'll cover the foundation concepts and basic language tools you need to program in VB. Then, I'll discuss how to use Object Linking and Embedding (OLE) to control Office applications.

In this chapter, you learn

- What VB4 can do and when to use Visual Basic
- How to integrate VB4 with other programs
- How to program in VB
- What VB4 OLE can accomplish
- How to use OLE Automation

What is Visual Basic?

Visual Basic is a full-featured, high-level programming language that enables you to create Windows applications quickly and easily. The word *visual* refers to the way in which you "program" the user interface. Rather than writing lines and lines of code to display a screen element, you drag and drop buttons, text boxes, scroll bars, and other screen objects to graphically build the user interface. Each object comes with a predefined set of properties and behaviors which you can customize to meet your needs. The word *basic* refers to the programming language that you use to manipulate the objects and pull your application together. Visual Basic is a modern form of the Beginner's All-Purpose Symbolic Instruction Code (BASIC) programming language developed in the early 1960s. See Chapter 4, "Visual Basic and Visual Basic for Applications," for more information.

What Can Visual Basic Do?

You can use VB to create simple, single-task oriented programs such as a clock or a sophisticated, full-featured Windows 95 application which provides the user with word processing, database, and spreadsheet tools. Using VB, you develop custom applications that:

- Have the Windows 95 user interface look and feel (complete with dialog boxes, buttons, scroll bars, and pop-up context-sensitive menus)
- Read, write, and create text, database, and binary files
- Incorporate multimedia features such as sound, graphics, and video
- Print sophisticated reports using installed Windows 95 printers
- Communicate using installed Windows 95 modems and faxes (such as e-mail, Internet, and broadcasting faxes)
- Integrate with Office applications such as Word, Excel, and Access

Key Features of Visual Basic 4

Visual Basic 4 is tightly integrated into Windows 95. Not only can you use Visual Basic to create custom stand-alone applications, but you can now use Visual Basic 4 to create fully integrated applications. That is, VB4 allows you to build custom applications that incorporate other applications (such as Word and Excel) objects and Windows 95 into one well-orchestrated custom application.

You can create 32-bit applications that look and feel like Windows 95. VB4 supports the 32-bit Application Program Interface (API) for Windows 95 and Windows NT. Furthermore, because VB4 uses the new Windows 95 memory model, you are no longer limited by the constraints of the Windows 3.1 memory model. For example, text strings are no longer limited to 65,535 characters (the limit is almost a billion characters). VB4 also provides improved implementation of multimedia graphics, video, and sound.

The Visual Basic for Applications version 2 (VBA2) macro language is now included in VB4. This allows you to create and reuse code across the Microsoft applications that support VBA2, such as Excel, Access, and Project. If you need to use a VBA2 routine in your VB4 application, you can just cut and paste the VBA2 code into VB4. However, probably the most important feature that the inclusion of VBA2 gives you is the ability to program embedded VBA-compliant applications directly in VB4. This is accomplished via OLE automation, which you learn about later in this chapter in the section "Using OLE Automation."

If you have been using Visual Basic version 3.0, you will be happy to know that VB3 is a subset of VB4, so most of your existing code will work without modification. However, you can update your existing VB3 code to take advantage of some of the new features available in VB4. One key difference between the versions is the adoption of OLE custom controls (sometimes called *OCX*) in place of VBX controls.

Integrating Visual Basic and Visual Basic for Applications

Visual Basic for Applications version 2 (VBA2) is a subset of Visual Basic 4 (VB4). The entire VBA2 language is included in VB4, which facilitates the integration of Office applications and speeds development by allowing you to reuse code.

VBA2 functions as a macro language which supports the Host-Required application's interface tools. VBA2 does not provide a form window or controls toolbar. Instead, you use the Host-Required application's tools to create the user interface. For example, in Access 95, you would use Access to create a form design and toolbar, but would rely on VBA2 to automate the form and buttons. This helps you maintain a consistent look with the Host-Required application.

VB4 and VBA2 share many of the same language components—sub, function, and properties. The differences are subtle, so the learning curve is short. One key difference between the two languages is that VBA2 relies more heavily on the traditional procedure-driven programming, whereas VB4 relies more on event-driven, object-oriented programming.

When you are trying to decide whether to program in VB4 or VBA2, consider the following issues:

■ In order to execute a VBA2 program, the Host-Required application must be running. VB4 programs can be compiled into separate stand-alone applications.

■ VB4 provides you with more powerful user interface tools such as the capability to create more effective dialog boxes.

■ VBA2 allows you to attach only one procedure to an event in a control. VB4 allows you to attach multiple procedures to any of the events for each control.

■ VB4 allows you to use and create powerful custom controls.

■ VB4 allows you to add any OLE object that is in the Windows 95 Registry to your VB toolbox and create OLE Dynamic Link Libraries (DLLs) based on class modules.

NOTE
A *dynamic link library* (DLL) is an executable code module for Windows that can be loaded on demand and linked at runtime.

A *class* defines the properties and behaviors of an object. An *object* is derived from its class. You can think of an object's class as similar to the pattern a dressmaker uses to make a dress. The pattern is the class; the dress is the object. All objects of a given class have the same properties and behavior, but contain different data in their variables (such as a color property setting, or procedure attached to an event).

In addition to using DLL files created by others, VB4 enables you to create your own OLE DLL files. VB4 also enables you to create new classes of objects. The code is referred to as a *class module*. You can use the class modules to create new objects.

III

Advanced Integration

■ Programs written in VB4 for Windows 95 run (in general) unchanged under Windows NT 3.51. Programs written in VBA2 run (in general) under any platform supported by the Host-Required application (such as Macintosh and Windows NT).

In summary, if you need to develop a program which controls a Host-Required application such as Access, you probably should use VBA2. However, if you need to create an integrated program that controls several applications or if you need features only found in VB4, you can use VB4 with or without VBA2 code sections.

NOTE

Compiling is the process by which a programming language translates the programming code which you wrote into an executable format. In VB4, the compile process creates a stand-alone EXE file. You don't need VB4 to run the EXE file.

In VBA2, the compile process converts your VBA code into an executable format for the Host-Required application. The compiled code is stored in the application file (a workbook for Excel; a database for Access). In order to execute your VBA program, you need the Host-Required application (such as Excel or Access) open and the file (such as XLS or MDB) which contains your code.

Choosing a Visual Basic Edition

Visual Basic 4.0 comes in three editions. The most basic edition, Standard, includes control tools (such as windows, buttons, and menu items), the Visual Basic 4.0 language, the Visual Basic for Applications version 2.0 language, an editor, a debugger, and a compiler. The Standard edition comes with a printed *Programmer's Guide*, plus online help. Using the Standard edition, you can create powerful 32-bit programs.

The Professional edition contains all the features of the Standard edition plus the following:

■ Capability to create 16-bit and 32-bit applications

■ Tools to build applications that support OLE Automation

■ Capability to create your own OLE DLLs

■ Capability to develop add-ins that extend Visual Basic

■ Crystal Reports tool

■ Hotspot Editor (create and edit hypergraphics)

■ Printed Language Reference, Professional Features book, and the Crystal Reports for Visual Basic User's Manual

■ Tools that provide better data access to the new Jet Engine 3.0

■ Help File Editor (create and compile custom help files)

■ Additional online help references (API Text Viewer, Win31SDK, and so on)

NOTE

For more information on the Application Program Interface (API), see Chapter 23, "Using Windows APIs."

The Enterprise edition adds features that assist in client/server development and tools to facilitate team development in Visual Basic. The additional features in the Enterprise edition include

- Automation Manager (client/server remote automation)
- Component Manager
- Tools to assist in database management
- Microsoft Visual SourceSafe version control system
- Printed copies of *Building Client/Server Applications with Visual Basic,* and the *SourceSafe User's Guide*

NOTE

This chapter is written about the Professional Edition of Visual Basic 4. If you have the Enterprise Edition, all examples and issues discussed apply to your edition also. However, if you have the Standard Edition, you won't be able to perform many of the OLE Automation examples in this chapter.

Using VB with C

From within VB, you can call any external library function or procedure that has been compiled in DLL format. All you need to do is declare the call in VB. Then, you can use the C function or procedure in your code as needed. DLLs written in C can also be used for routines which need to be optimized for speed. In addition, you can create your own OLE controls in C and use them in your VB program.

Integrating VB with the Windows API and SDK

The *Windows Application Programming Interface* (API) is a set of functions and procedures used to program Windows. In general, VB4 is so powerful that you'll rarely need to use the Windows API. However, you may need to use the Windows API to access an area of the screen outside of a VB window.

As with using C functions and procedures, you only need to declare the API function or procedure in your VB program in order to use it. To make this process easier, VB4 ships with a special program called the API Text Viewer. *API Text Viewer* allows you to browse through Declares, Constants, and Types that are included in any text file or Jet database that contains API information. You can copy these items onto the Clipboard, and then paste them into your Visual Basic code.

III

Advanced Integration

TIP

API declarations use C-type variables, and some alterations are necessary to use them within VB.

The Windows API contains hundreds of function and procedure calls. To help you work with the API, Microsoft publishes the *Software Development Kit* (*SDK*). If you will be using the API, you should get a copy.

NOTE

The 32-bit APIs differ from the old 16-bit APIs. The Professional and Enterprise editions of VB include a help file for the 16-bit APIs, but not the 32-bit APIs.

In order to take advantage of the performance improvements in Windows 95, you need to start creating 32-bit applications. This means using the 32-bit APIs and using OLE controls instead of the old 16-bit VBX controls.

Exploring Visual Basic

In this section, I introduce you to the Visual Basic 4 environment. If you have used an earlier version of Visual Basic, you may want to just skim this section to get a feel for the new features and tools.

When you install Visual Basic, the Setup program allows you to place the VB programs in an existing program group on the Start menu, or create a new program group. Alternatively, you can create a shortcut to Visual Basic or run the Visual Basic executable file VB32.EXE.

TIP

For quick access, add a new toolbar for VB to your Office Shortcut Bar.

Starting Visual Basic

To start Visual Basic from the default Windows 95 Start menu, follow these steps:

1. Click Start on the taskbar.
2. Choose Programs and then the Visual Basic 4.0 group.
3. Choose Visual Basic 4.0.

Identifying the Components of the VB Environment

When Visual Basic loads (see fig. 17.1), the five main components of the programming environment appear on your screen. The Microsoft Visual Basic window contains the menu bar and toolbar. The toolbar provides quick access to commonly used commands. The *Toolbox* contains tools that you can use to place controls on a form. The *Form window* is the interface for your application that you can customize by adding controls, pictures, and graphics. The *Project window* lists the forms and modules in the current project. In VB, a *project* is another name for an application. VB keeps track of all files that have to do with a specific project. The *Properties window* lists the property settings for the selected form or control. A *property* is a characteristic of an object such as color, size, or name.

In addition to the five main components, VB provides other tools to assist you. The *Object Browser* lists the objects available for your project and lets you access your code. You can use the Object Browser to explore objects in VB and other applications (lists the methods and properties for those objects, and lets you paste code procedures into your code).

Fig. 17.1

The Visual Basic environment consists of five basic screen components.

VB also provides context menus that contain shortcuts to frequently performed actions (similar to the shortcut menus found in Windows 95). To view a context menu, right-click an object.

Fig. 17.2

Most objects in VB have a context menu (shortcut menu).

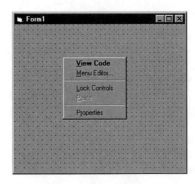

Getting Help

Many say that information is the gold of our world these days. If so, VB4 is a gold mine. Visual Basic 4 comes with many sources of information on VB4. With the Professional and Enterprise editions, all of the VB documentation is available online by choosing Help, Visual Basic Books OnLine. In Books OnLine, you can access topics via an index, table of contents, or by searching for keywords. Another option on the Help menu is Learning Microsoft Visual Basic which takes an online tutorial approach to teaching.

The Visual Basic Help application provides sections on what's new in VB4, numerous How To topics, a program language reference, data access topics, and reference information by function. Help also lists information on how to get technical support. Help provides access to the Microsoft Knowledge Base (MSKB) included in the Professional version of VB. The *MSKB* is a collection of more than 56,000 articles, technical support Q&As, bug lists, fix lists, documentation errata, drivers, and sample code documents. To really keep up-to-date on VB, you might want to subscribe to the MSKB on a monthly or quarterly basis.

In addition to the standard help file, online documentation, and tutorial, VB provides extensive supplemental help files. Table 17.1 lists and briefly describes the additional help files that come with VB4.

TIP Use the Object Browser to get information on objects, their properties, and values; tour object libraries; and determine available constants.

Table 17.1   Supplemental Help Files

Help File	Edition	Description
Biblio	Standard	Sample application which illustrates techniques for browsing database files.
Data Manager	Standard	Application which allows you to create Jet database files, attach or map to other database formats.

Help File	Edition	Description
Product Support Services	Standard	Contact information on various Microsoft product support areas.
Samples	Standard	Lists and describes sample applications.
Setup Wizard	Standard	Helps you create a setup routine for your VB application. Note that this application is tailored to VB developers and limited in scope. Use the GUI Setup Tool in the Windows SDK to create a more robust setup program.
Custom Control Reference	Professional	Lists and describes the custom controls.
Crystal Reports	Professional	Complete reference guide to Crystal Reports.
Hotspot Editor	Professional	Allows you to create and edit hypergraphics. *Hotspots* are regions of a graphic associated with an action (by which you can attach code).
ODBC Installation	Professional	General information on ODBC driver installation.
SQL Server ODBC	Professional	General information on Driver SQL ODBC drivers.
VisData	Professional	Help file for a sample application on data access.
APILOD.TXT	Professional	Describes how to use the API Text Viewer.
LABELS.TXT	Professional	Contains information about mailing labels (descriptions and dimensions of numerous Avery labels).
VB4DLL.TXT	Professional	Contains information on developing DLLs to use with VB.
WIN32API.TXT	Professional	Lists the symbolic constants for 32-bit versions of Windows API functions.
WIN31API.TXT	Professional	Lists the procedure, type, and constant declarations for 16-bit versions of Windows API functions.
WINMMSYS.TXT	Professional	Lists the procedure, type, and constant declarations for Windows 3.1 multimedia API functions.

Creating Your First VB Program

One of the key features of VB is that it empowers the programmer by taking the drudgery out of programming, and allows the programmer to quickly create a Windows 95 program. In this section, you experience the full life cycle of developing a VB application by building a simple VB program.

Most VB programmers agree that developing a VB application is a 1-2-3 process:

1. Create the user interface.
2. Set the properties.
3. Write the code.

Creating the user interface involves drawing the window and placing user interface objects such as buttons, boxes, and labels. The visual feature of VB allows you to see what the end user sees as you develop. You can adjust the size, placement, and type of each user interface object, moving them around as needed to create the appropriate effect. No difficult programming is needed for this step. In VB, the user interface objects that you draw and place on a form are called *controls*. See Chapter 18, "Designing the User Interface," for more information about designing and VBA.

The next step is to set the properties of the controls you have drawn. *Properties* are characteristics of the object such as color, font, and border style. All controls come with some default property settings which may or may not meet your needs. You can change the default settings as you need to. Some properties can be set in the Design screen, while others can only be set at runtime. See the section "Setting Properties" later in this chapter.

> **TIP**
> If you need several of the same controls and you want them all to have the same properties (look, size, and so on), create one and make copies as needed.

The last step is to write any code needed to automate controls or tasks. In VB, code executes in response to events. For example, a VB routine attached to a button runs only when the user presses the button. This is what is meant by *event-driven programming* (covered in more detail later in the section "Writing Code").

The following sections take you through these three steps while creating a simple VB program.

Managing Projects

Each VB application you create may consist of many files such as forms, custom controls, program code, class definitions, and resource files (see table 17.2). Managing these files can be overwhelming. To help you keep track of these files, VB creates a project file which lists the project files by name and location. Although you may store program files in various locations, it is much easier to manage a project if you store the files in one location. In Windows 95 terms, that means creating a new folder for each project. When you finish developing your application, VB compiles your project into an executable (EXE) file based on the files listed in the PROJECT file.

Table 17.2 VB Project Files

File Type	Extension	Description
Form Module	FRM	The form window, controls, and code associated with the form and controls.
Custom Control	OCX or VBX	Custom controls usually shared across projects and stored in a Windows directory.
Standard Module	BAS	Program code for the project.

File Type	Extension	Description
Class Module	CLS	Class definition for the project.
Resource File	RES	Data for the project (such as text, bitmaps, sound files, and so on).
Project File	VBP or MAK	Index of all project files listing the file names and path locations.

To create your first application, you will create a project folder named My First VB Application.

Creating the Interface

The basic VB program that you'll create is a Date/Time application. When the user clicks a button, the program displays the current date and time. Figure 17.3 shows what your completed Date/Time application will look like.

On the CD

Fig. 17.3

The completed Date/Time application.

When you first start Visual Basic, the Form1 window appears in the center of your screen. This is the window in which you create the user interface. VB refers to windows as *forms*. Forms come with certain predefined properties such as a title bar, minimize/maximize buttons, close button, border, and menu icon. The area inside the form with a grid of dots is where you place controls to build your user interface. The grid helps you align controls, but disappears at runtime.

> **TIP**
> Choose Tools, Options and select the Environment tab to adjust the default width and height of the grid as needed.

You use the Visual Basic Toolbox to add controls to a form (see fig. 17.4). The Toolbox displays the standard VB controls plus any custom controls and insertable objects you have added. By default, VB displays *ToolTips* (brief descriptions of each tool) when you place your pointer over a tool button. For a detailed description of each tool, search Help for Toolbox topic. To add a control to a form, click the desired control tool and drag in the form to draw the control.

Fig. 17.4

The Visual Basic Toolbox provides many different types of controls.

 TIP Double-click the desired control tool to place a default-sized control in the form.

Start placing controls on the form to create the Date/Time application. First, you need a control which will allow you to display the time and date, but not allow the user to change the time or date. Because the Textbox control allows the user to edit data, use the Label tool. Draw a label control to resemble the label in figure 17.5. Next, you need a button object that the user can click to update the date and time display. Draw a button control to resemble the button in figure 17.5.

Fig. 17.5

This is the form design so far with a label control and a command button.

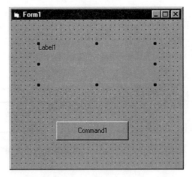

Setting Properties

The second step in creating a VB application is to set the properties. *Properties* are the characteristics of an object such as the form object or control object. The object Form1, for instance, has properties such as caption, color, visibility, screen position, and border style. A *label control* would have a different set of properties, such as font size and type. Each object has a set of properties that reflects the type of data normally associated with the object.

As you select the form or a control object, notice that the properties listed in the Properties window change to match the specific object selected (see fig. 17.6). You can view and edit properties in the Properties window. Each object can have different properties. For example, you could have one blue button, one red button, and one white button. The property settings are stored with the object. So, if you move or copy the object, all the property settings stay with the object.

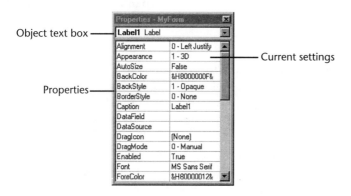

Fig. 17.6

To select an object, either click it or select it from the Object text box.

Do the following to set some properties for your Time/Date application:

1. Change the caption for the Form window from Form1 to **Date/Time**.
2. Change the name of the Form window from Form1 to **frmDateTime**.
3. Change the form's height and width to 3,000 pixels.
4. Use the mouse to adjust the size and location of the label and button objects to better fit the new form size. Notice that each object's height and width properties change to reflect the new size.
5. Change the name of the label control from Label1 to **lblDateTime**.
6. Change the name of the button control from Command1 to **cmdDateTime**.
7. Change the caption of the label control from Label1 to **Click Update**.
8. Change the caption of the button control from Command1 to **Update**.

NOTE

In general, you only need to change the name of objects that you will refer to in code. Otherwise, using the default names is perfectly fine.

The object naming rules in VB are very straightforward:

- 40 or less characters
- Characters must be letters, numbers, or an underscore (_)
- Names must begin with a letter
- Names cannot be restricted keywords

In addition to these rules, you should follow the object naming conventions outlined in Appendix B. Using these naming conventions makes it easier for VB programmers to read and understand code written by other VB programmers.

At this point, you could run the project, but it wouldn't do much because you haven't written any code yet.

Writing Code

The third step in creating a VB application is to write the code. Objects such as forms and controls come with some predefined, built-in behavior. A button, for instance, moves in and out when clicked. You don't need to program that basic behavior; it comes with the button. But, to make the button do something such as print a report or display the time, you need to write the VB code and assign the code to that object.

Code is written in the Code window. To view the Code window, double-click the control, or select the control and press F7 (see fig. 17.7). The Code window consists of an Object list box, a Procedure list box, and a code pane. The Object list box automatically displays the name of the current object. You can select another object to work with from the Object text box, rather than going back to the Form window. The Procedure list box displays the name of the default event procedure for that object type. For example, a command button's default event procedure is the click event. The code listed in the click event procedure executes whenever the command button is clicked. If you want to work with a different event for the selected object, choose one from the Procedure (Proc) list box.

TIP

To view all the procedures in a module at once, choose Tools, Options, select the Editor tab, and check Full Module View.

Fig. 17.7

The Code window opens with the Sub..End Sub *procedure construct already filled in for you.*

Program your Update button in the Date/Time application. Set the label control's caption property equal to the Now function whenever the Update button is clicked. Your code for the click event procedure should look like this:

```
Private Sub cmdDateTime_Click()
    lblDateTime.Caption = Now
End Sub
```

Note that VB uses dot notation to refer to an object's property. Also, values on the right side of the equal sign are assigned to the item on the left side. The value returned by the function Now is assigned to the property Caption of the object lblDateTime.

Close the Code window and press F5 to run your first VB application. Click the Update button to display the current time and date. When finished, close the Date/Time window to return to VB Design mode.

NOTE VB has to be up and running in order for you to run your new application, since you have not yet created an executable file (EXE). Once you create the executable file, you no longer need VB in order to run the application.

Saving Project Files

To save your project files, select the desired Form, Code, Class, or Resource window and choose File, Save, or Save File As and specify the desired name/location. To save all of a project's files, choose File, Save Project or Save Project As and specify the desired name/location.

To save your first VB application, do the following:

1. Click the Form window.

2. Choose File, Save File As.

3. Specify the desired folder location.

4. Specify the desired file name such as DATETIME.FRM.

5. Click OK.

6. Choose File, Save Project As.

7. Specify the desired folder location.

8. Specify the desired file name such as DATETIME.VBP.

9. Click OK.

Compiling a Project

Once you complete the design process (creating the user interface, setting properties, and writing code), and you have tested your application (removing all bugs), you are ready to compile your application. The compilation process creates a stand-alone executable (EXE) file that runs in Windows without requiring the user to have Visual Basic:

1. Choose File, Make EXE.

2. Specify the desired folder location and file name.

3. Click OK.

NOTE In addition to the EXE compiled program, users who don't have VB installed will need some other files. The VB40032.DLL for 32-bit applications and VB40016.DLL for 16-bit applications must be copied to the WINDOWS\SYSTEM directory (it is permissible to distribute these files as part of your VB application). Any OCX or VBX custom control files must also be copied to the WINDOWS\SYSTEM directory. Other files necessary for runtime execution are listed in the SWDEPEND.INI file in your WINDOWS directory.

TIP The Setup Wizard locates all the files you need to distribute your application's EXE file and helps you build an install routine.

Compile the Date/Time application, close Visual Basic, and use the Windows 95 Start menu option Run to execute the program.

Programming in VB

Now that you have some experience creating a VB application, this section explores the components of the VB language and discusses event-driven programming and program control. By now you may have noticed how similar VB is to the VBA language that you've been working with throughout most of this book. Because many of these language components are the same, I briefly review similar components here and refer you back to Chapter 4, "Visual Basic and Visual Basic for Applications," for detailed explanations. Of course, you may prefer to use that great VB Help system to get online documentation on a language component. The online documentation gives you a description of each item, its syntax, and programming examples that you can cut and paste into your code.

NOTE The most this chapter can hope to do is enlighten you on the power of VB and provide a basic working knowledge of how to program in VB. For more in-depth coverage, refer to Que's *Using Visual Basic 4.0, Visual Basic 4 Programming By Example, Visual Basic 4 Expert Solutions, Visual Basic 4 Unleashed* (SAMS Publishing), and *Optimizing Visual Basic 4.0*.

Exploring VB Language Components

Table 17.3 lists the VB4 language components. Think of these components as the building blocks of your program code. Whereas the user-interface tools (forms and controls) communicate with the user, the VB language components do something with the results of that communication. An analogy could be made to a stereo. The front panel of buttons and display give and get information from the user, but it's the components behind the panel that perform the tasks.

Table 17.3 VB4 Language Components	
Component	**Description**
Variable	A named place in memory for storing data that can change during program execution.
Constant	A named place in memory for storing data that does not change during program execution.
Intrinsic Constant	A constant that is predefined in a programming language or application. The prefix indicates the type of object library the constant came from. For example, `vbTileVertical` is from VB, `dbAppendOnly` is from Access and, `xlDialogBorder` is from Excel.
Array	A group of variables with the same name and a unique index value. VB4 supports fixed and dynamic arrays.
Data Type	A definition of a data element. In VB4, the default data type is `Variant`. For a complete list of data types, search Help for the Comparison of Data Types topic.
Control Structure	A programming construct that helps you control program flow. VB4 has the following: if..then..elseif..end if, select case..case else..end case, do until, do while, while..end, for..next, exit, and loop.
Declaration	A statement that assigns an identifying name to a variable or constant (in the case of a variable, it also defines the data type), or defines other user-defined code elements. In VB4: Dim, Redim, Type..end type, and Const.
Procedure	A programming construct that defines a routine or subroutine. In VB4: `sub..end sub`, `Function..end function`, and `property..end property`. VB4 also comes with many predefined functions such as `ASC()`, `LTrim()`, and `UCase()` which you can use in your code.
Scoping statement	Key words that control the visibility (availability) of variables and procedures. In VB4: static, private, and public. Scope is also controlled by where the declaration is made.

(continues)

Table 17.3 Continued	
Component	**Description**
Method	A procedure that is part of an object. Methods only act on the object to which they are attached. As with properties, dot notation is used to call a method for an object (*object.method*).
Property	A characteristic of an object such as color, size, or value.
Statement	VB4 keywords which perform tasks such as `Beep`, `FileCopy`, and `Get`.
Operator	A symbol, character, or sequence of characters that performs arithmetic, comparison, or logical calculation such as +, Or, and >=.

Working with Modules

Visual Basic supports a modular approach to programming. For each programming project, you can have three types of modules. The most popular module is the Form module (FRM). Each Form module contains the code and user interface components to be a stand-alone application. Or, you may have several forms in your application, in which case you would have several Form module files.

As the number of forms in your application grows, you may find that you are repeating code routines in each form. Instead of repeating the code routines, you can create a Standard module (BAS) that acts as a code library. All the forms in your application can then access the common routines stored in the Standard module.

The last type of module you can create in VB4 is the class module (CLS). *Class modules* are used to define classes that are new to Visual Basic. You might think of Class modules as blueprints that tell VB what the new object class looks like and how it behaves. Each Class module defines one class. The procedures in a Class module are the methods of the new class, and the variables and property procedures are the properties of the new class. Class modules look just like Form modules, except that they are not visible at runtime. The addition of Class modules to VB4 brings more Object Oriented Programming (OOP) capability to VB.

Working with Procedures

The modular programming approach is further supported by program units called *procedures*. VB has two basic types of procedures you can use to organize your code into manageable modules:

- Event procedures
- General procedures

In the Date/Time application created in the last section, you placed your code in an event procedure. An *event procedure* executes when a specific event occurs in a program. VB objects come with predefined event procedures to which you can attach your own code.

A general procedure executes only when called (use in an executing code line).
In VB4, you can create three types of general procedures: sub, function, and property.
A subprocedure can be sent arguments and can make changes to those arguments.
The basic syntax of a subprocedure is as follows:

```
Subprocedurename()
     ...your code...
End Sub
```

Here is an example of a simple subprocedure that calculates the sales tax on a product:

```
Sub SalesTax(Cost,Tax)
     Const TaxRate = .0725
     Tax = Cost * TaxRate
End Sub
```

The calling program passes down to this procedure the cost of the item. This sub-procedure declares a constant called TaxRate and assigns the value .0725 to the constant. The second line computes the sales tax. The tax is then passed back to the calling program via the second argument, Tax.

A *function procedure* is similar to a subprocedure, except that the function's name returns a value (it *must* return a value). Functions are sometimes referred to as *user-defined functions* (UDF). The basic syntax of a function procedure is as follows:

```
Function functionname()
     ...your code...
End Function
```

Here is the previous subprocedure example rewritten as a function. Notice that the Tax argument is no longer needed. Instead, the name of the function holds the result of the calculation.

```
Function SalesTax(Cost)
     Const TaxRate = .0725
     SalesTax = Cost * TaxRate
End Function
```

Functions differ from subprocedures in three ways:

- Functions must return a value.
- Functions have a type, just like variables.
- Functions can be called by listing the function name and arguments on the right side of a statement or expression assignment.

This next example uses a function procedure to perform a calculation (converting Fahrenheit to centigrade) for a subprocedure. The subprocedure displays a dialog box prompting the user to enter the temperature in Fahrenheit. After a quick check to make sure the user entered a number, the function is called and the answer is displayed in a message box.

On the CD

Advanced Integration

```
Function ConvertToCent(fTemp) As Variant
     ConvertToCent = (Val(fTemp)-32)*5/9
End Function

Sub TempInCent()
     fTemp = InputBox("What is the temperature in Fahrenheit?")
     If fTemp = "" Then Exit Sub
     cTemp = ConvertToCent(fTemp)
     MsgBox fTemp & " F degrees equals "  & cTemp & "C degrees."
end Sub
```

The last type of procedure is called a *property procedure*, which is used to create and manipulate custom properties. New properties created in a property procedure belong to the module containing the procedure. In VB4, three types of property procedures exist:

- Property Let sets the value of a property.
- Property Get returns the value of a property.
- Property Set sets a reference to an object.

In the following example, a property procedure is used to set the PenColor property for a drawing package by calling the Property Let procedure with the statement PenColor() = "Red":

```
Dim CurrentColor As Integer
Const BLACK = 0, RED = 1, GREEN = 2, BLUE = 3

' Set the pen color property for a Drawing package.
' The module-level variable CurrentColor is set to
' a numeric value that identifies the color used for drawing.
Property Let PenColor(ColorName As String)
     Select Case ColorName          ' Check color name string.
          Case "Red"
               CurrentColor = RED       ' Assign value for Red.
          Case "Green"
               CurrentColor = GREEN     ' Assign value for Green.
          Case "Blue"
               CurrentColor = BLUE      ' Assign value for Blue.
          Case Else
               CurrentColor = BLACK     ' Assign default value.

     End Select
End Property
```

Using Visual Basic and OLE

In Chapter 3, you explored Object Linking and Embedding (OLE), a Windows protocol that allows you to create compound documents (documents which contain data from more than one application). In this section, you learn how Visual Basic implements OLE version 2.0.

VB4 changes some of the terminology used to describe OLE. The following table summarizes the old and new OLE terms.

Old Visual Basic 3 Term	New Visual Basic 4 Term
Source Application or Server	Object Application
Destination Application or Client	Controlling Application
OLE Client Control object	OLE Container Control

Applications that support OLE make available (expose) many different objects to other applications that support OLE. For example, Excel exposes worksheet, macrosheet, cell, cell range, and chart objects. Other applications can then use these objects and make them available to their users without reinventing the wheel.

How OLE Works in VB4

The name "Object Linking *and* Embedding" really is a misnomer. The name should be "Object Linking *or* Embedding," because you can either link *or* embed objects. Which method you select depends on the following:

- Where you want to store the data
- Whether you want other applications to have access to the data
- Whether your application has file size limitations

Figure 17.8 illustrates the differences between a linked OLE object and an embedded OLE object. In the Controlling Application, an OLE Container Control object has been drawn on a form. With an OLE Link, the OLE Container Control is just a placeholder which lists the name and location of the Object Application and presentation data (an image of the data). At runtime, the user can double-click this placeholder to start the Object Application and edit the native data. In an OLE link, the data is stored in the Object Application. This allows other OLE compliant applications to also access the data. Data stored in an Object Application can have many OLE links to other applications.

On the other hand, with an embedded OLE object, the data is stored in the Controlling Application along with the application name. Because the data is stored in the Controlling Application, no other OLE-compliant applications can access the data. This can be very beneficial in situations where you want to make sure that users only use your application to edit and maintain the data.

TIP
If you don't need to see the embedded object, reduce the file size by selecting the Display As Icon property.

III

Advanced Integration

Fig. 17.8

Consider the differences between linking and embedding before creating your OLE object.

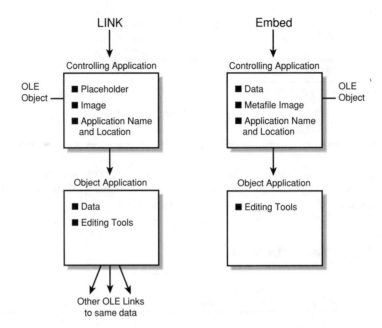

What Can VB4 OLE Do?

In Visual Basic 4, several new OLE 2.0 features have been added:

- Class Modules
- OLE Automation
- Create OLE Servers

Support for class modules allows you to create any kind of OLE object. A *class* is a definition of an object type—as in a blueprint or format of how the object looks and behaves. OLE Automation is separate from OLE. OLE Automation defines how applications share code, and how applications can be controlled by other applications. Not all applications support OLE Automation, but those that do expose certain objects and development tools.

Also new in VB4 is the capability to create an OLE Server (only available in Professional and Enterprise editions). An *OLE Server* is an application that exposes its objects to other applications. You can create your own OLE Server and decide which objects (classes) to expose and which applications can use them.

TIP
VB4 allows you to create object applications that supply object libraries in the EXE file format only. You can't create object applications in dynamic link library (DLL) format.

Furthermore, you can't create an OLE Container Control (OCX) by using VB4. Instead, use a programming language such as C++ to do this.

Creating OLE Objects

In VB4, there are three ways to create an OLE object:

- Use a Container Control
- Use an Insertable Object
- Use VB code

Using Container Controls. The Container Control tool in the Toolbox allows you to create an embedded or linked OLE object interactively. The steps involved and issues are the same as was covered in the section "What is OLE?" in Chapter 4. OLE objects thus created have properties which you can set interactively in the Properties window, or through code. If you linked the object, you probably want to use the Update method to refresh the data every time the application runs:

```
object.update
```

This is needed because with links, other applications may change the data when your application is not running. At runtime, the user can double-click the OLE object to edit data and then choose File, Save to save their changes. The OLE-linked object automatically reflects the changed data (the update is automatic).

You are more apt to use VB code when working with embedded objects. Edits to embedded OLE objects aren't saved automatically. Instead, your code must use the SaveToFile method to save the changes:

```
object.savetofile filenumber
```

The argument, filenumber, refers to an open binary file. You can also use the ReadFromFile method to load saved data into an OLE object:

```
object.ReadFromFile filenumber
```

NOTE In order to insert an object into an OLE Container Control, the object must be properly registered in the Windows 95 Registry. Only the registered objects appear in the Insert Object dialog box. To verify registration, you can run REGEDIT.EXE and search the registration database for the object name.

Inserting OLE Objects. A new feature in VB4 is using registered OLE Servers instead of an OLE Container Control to embed data (only embed, not link). In the Custom Controls dialog box (get there by choosing Tools, Custom Controls), check the Insertable Objects option. This will list the applications registered with Windows 95 that support OLE and the document types they support. For example, Excel makes available Chart, Worksheet, and Graph. Word makes available Document, Picture, and WordArt. VB4 allows you to add these objects to your Toolbox. You no longer need to write code to provide the functionality of these objects. Just click the tool in the Toolbox and draw the fully functional embedded object. For example, if you added the Graph tool to your VB4 Toolbox, dropping the Graph object on your form gives your application a fully functional, embedded Graph object without writing any code.

III

Advanced Integration

Creating OLE Objects in Code. The CreateEmbed and CreateLink methods are used to create OLE Container objects at runtime. In addition, you could display the Paste Special dialog box by using the PasteSpecialDlg method, or use the InsertObjeDlg method to display the Insert Object dialog box. Once the container object has been created, you can use the DoVerb method to open the object for editing and set various properties such as size, display type, and focus. For a complete list of methods, properties, and events associated with the OLE Container Control object, search Help for the OLE Container topic.

NOTE VB4 supports the old VB3 Action property to create OLE Container objects at runtime for backwards compatibility.

TIP Use VB constants to quickly set OLE Container properties. Search Help for a list under the Constants, OLE Container topic.

In the following example, an OLE Container object for linking is created. Then, a With..End With construct is used to set properties for the OLE Container:

```
MyOLE.CreateLink = "C:\excel\Budget.XLS"
With MyOLE
    .DisplayType = vbOLEDisplayContent
    .Top = 140
    .Left = 140
    .Height = 2500
    .Width = 6000
    .SizeMode = vbOLESizeZoom
End With
```

Using OLE Automation

OLE Automation is an exciting new feature in VB4. OLE Automation gives you access (from within code) to the object application's menus and commands. Applications that support OLE Automation expose their objects to other OLE 2.0 applications such as Excel and Access. You can control another application by accessing its objects and methods. When you use OLE Automation, the attached application's objects and methods become an extension of the Visual Basic language.

For example, Visio supports OLE 2.0 and exposes many objects such as documents, windows, shapes, and pages. Each Visio object has its own set of methods and properties. Using OLE automation in VB, you could create a Visio rectangle in the Visio application, and then type text into the rectangle:

```
Set MyRect = CurrPage.DrawRectangle(1,1,2,2)
MyRect.Text = "Hello From VB4"
```

Not all Windows applications support the OLE Automation protocol, and of those that do, some only expose a few objects. Furthermore, some applications only support OLE 2.0 as a client and expose no OLE Automation objects. For example, you can run Word from VB using OLE Automation, but you can't run other OLE-compliant applications from WordBasic.

> **NOTE** OLE 2.0 does not allow you to share objects across a network. This feature is planned for a future release of OLE.

Working with OLE Automation Objects

The functions `CreateObject` and `GetObject` are used to access OLE automation objects. The `CreateObject` function creates a new object of the class you specify. The class is the name of the object type exposed by the other application. The following example creates an Excel worksheet OLE Automation object. The object class is `Excel.Sheet`:

```
CreateObject("Excel.Sheet")
```

When you need to work with an existing f   the `GetObject` function. The following example retrieves an OLE Automation   You can optionally follow the file pathname with a com   the class   is omitted, VB uses the default object class f   is the default for Excel):

```
GetObject("C:\Excel\Budget.XLS")
```

In order to work with an OLE Automati   ly to with an object name that you can use to refer to   a variable name.   to this by declaring the object name in a `Dim` state   and after   the `Set`   to assign the reference. For example:

```
Sub MyOLEDemo()
        Dim NewOLE As Object
        Set NewOLE = CreateObje
```

> **NOTE** Applications react differently wh
> instance, starts up invisibly by
> when its variable is set to `Noth`
> when its object variable is set to `Nothing` or go
> you can handle these situations by setting properties and using meth

Once the OLE Automation object is created, you can issue commands from VB4 that belong to the other application. In the following example, a new OLE Automation object is created called `MyWord`. The VB4 procedure then issues WordBasic commands to run Word from VB4.

```
Sub OLEAutoDemo()
      Dim MyWord As Object
      Set MyWord = CreateObject("Word.Basic")
      With MyWord
            .FileNew
            .Bold
            .FontSize 24
            .CenterPara
            .Insert "Hello from VB4."
            .FilePrintDefault
            .FileSaveAs "C:\VB4\OLEDemo.doc"
      End With
      MyWord.Quit
      Set MyWord = Nothing
End Sub
```

Examine the OLEAutoDemo() procedure. The first line declares an object variable named MyWord. The next line creates an OLE Automation object for Word Basic. This opens the Word application visibly on-screen. The With..End With construct uses OLE Automation to create a new Word document, set the font to bold at 24 point, center the text, and type in the characters Hello from VB4. The FilePrintDefault is a Word Basic command that prints the current document using the default print settings. The FileSaveAs Word Basic command saves the new document as OLEDEMO. DOC in the VB4 folder. The last two lines are important and should not be overlooked. The Quit method closes the Word application (no need to keep Word open in memory if you are done with it). The Set statement releases the MyWord object variable from memory by setting it equal to Nothing.

From Here...

The best way to learn more about VB4 is to start using it to automate your Office projects. Think of VB4 as the glue to hold your Office applications together, and the communication medium that allows you to interact better with Windows 95 and between the Office applications. To learn more about using VB4 with VBA and the other Office applications, see the following chapters:

- Chapter 18, "Designing the User Interface," shows you how to create clearer, easier-to-use screens that have the standard Windows 95 look and feel.

- Chapter 19, "Handling the Unexpected," covers error trapping, error avoidance, and error recovery using VB and VBA.

- Chapter 20, "Creating Custom Menus, Toolbars, and Shortcut Bars," shows how to provide users with menus, toolbars, and shortcut bars that are appropriate for the application you are designing.

- Chapter 21, "Providing Help for Users," shows you how to create your own help system that integrates well with the Windows 95 help system.

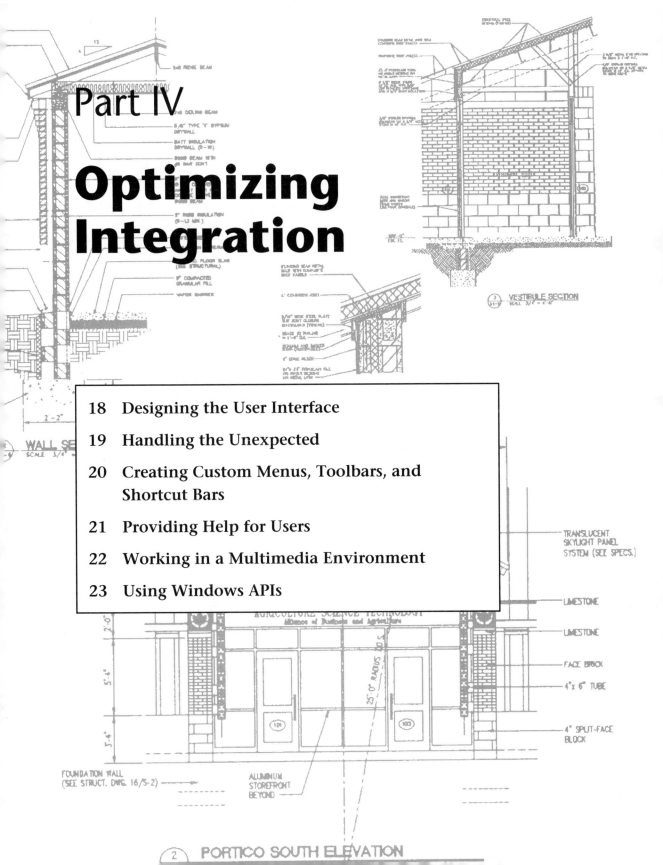

Part IV

Optimizing Integration

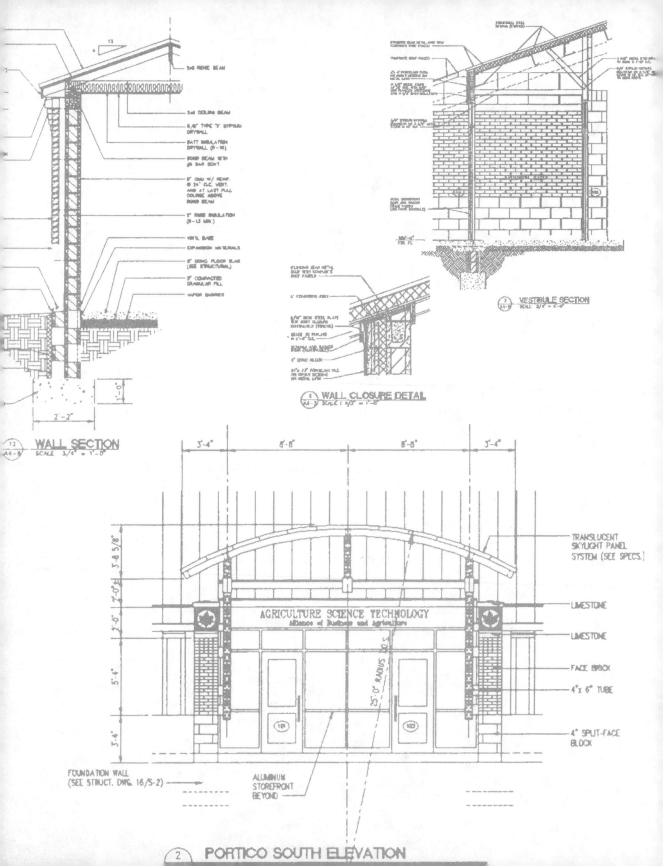

WALL SECTION
SCALE 3/4" = 1'-0"

WALL CLOSURE DETAIL
SCALE 1/2" = 1'-0"

VESTIBULE SECTION
SCALE 3/4" = 1'-0"

TRANSLUCENT
SKYLIGHT PANEL
SYSTEM (SEE SPECS.)

LIMESTONE

LIMESTONE

FACE BRICK

4" x 6" TUBE

4" SPLIT-FACE
BLOCK

AGRICULTURE SCIENCE TECHNOLOGY
Alliance of Business and Agriculture

FOUNDATION WALL
(SEE STRUCT. DWG. 16/S-2)

ALUMINUM
STOREFRONT
BEYOND

PORTICO SOUTH ELEVATION

CHAPTER 18

Designing the User Interface

In 1985 (four years after IBM introduced the IBM PC), Microsoft released a new software application called Windows, which promised to make the user's job easier. The success of Microsoft Windows over the past decade can be directly attributed to the user interface guidelines that Microsoft built into the Windows graphical user interface (GUI). As a result, programmers from various software houses were able to develop applications that had a common interface.

Software developed before Windows usually had different interfaces, although they all did many things the same. For example, they all had a menu from which the user could open or print a file. But instead of the common File, Open and File, Print commands that we have today, users had to pick through a Utilities menu to find the print command, and use the View menu to load a document. In another application, that same user may have had to use the F10 key to even see the menu and then use Alt+key combinations to invoke commands.

Windows rescued the user from the whims of various program development teams and set down some ground rules. In this chapter, we explore the ground rules in Windows 95, apply the principles of user interface design to the Office 95 applications, and review common issues as you begin to build your integrated Office application.

In this chapter, you learn how to

- Plan the user interface
- Select and place controls
- Incorporate built-in dialog boxes
- Handle special display issues

Planning the User Interface

When a client calls or a department in your company calls to request that a project be automated, the end user knows exactly what the user interface should look like—a large toaster with one button. The user puts in the data, pushes the button, and in a reasonable amount of time, out pops the finished project. Your job is to build the toaster into your integrated Office application, or conversely educate the user on how the extra buttons actually make the project work faster.

Accuracy and speed are important elements of building any application, but the user interface is the most important element. In fact, a poorly designed user interface can result in inaccurate data being entered, confused users, and features which simply do not work on all monitors. Taking time up front, before you program, to plan out the user interface elements and design a consistent user interface supports the accuracy and speed of your application.

In the following sections, I review the principles of user interface design that Microsoft and Windows 95 developers follow, explore the design elements available in Office applications, and outline an approach to designing an integrated Office application's user interface.

Principles of User Interface Design

When designing Windows 95-based applications, you need to be aware of certain principles of user interface design that Windows 95 developers follow. These principles provide the foundation of user interface design. Most of the principles come from Microsoft and form the foundation concepts of the Windows 95 interface design. Although you may come across other lists or establish your own "principles" as you go along, this list will provide you with a good starting point. Each of the following sections will describe one of the principles.

 NOTE For a complete and thorough coverage of Microsoft's guidelines for designing a user interface for Windows 95 and Windows NT 3.51-based applications, refer to *Windows Interface Guidelines for Software Design* published by Microsoft (ISBN 1-55615-679-0).

User Control. The user should be in control of the application, not the application in control of the user. You can see this principle at work in Windows 95 and Office 95 applications. Consider who determines the font, printer to be used, file name, and color attributes. In Windows 95 and Office 95 applications, users can customize the user interface to meet their needs and preferences by setting properties and options. The user decides when to initiate automated tasks such as updating files, editing records, or sorting data. Furthermore, applications avoid "trapping" the user into a modal dialog box without a Cancel option (*modal* means the user is restricted to that dialog box). The user is always in control.

In figure 18.1, you can see how the Windows 95 interface puts the user in control. The taskbar, the Desktop icons, the Office Shortcut Bar—these automated features lie ready for the user and can be customized to meet individual needs.

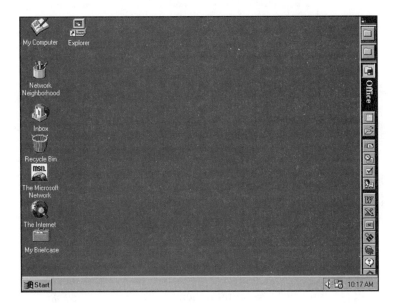

Fig. 18.1

From the moment Windows 95 loads, the user is in control.

Directness. The user should be able to directly access application elements or invoke commands, and not have to pick through menu trees or type cryptic commands. For example, in Windows you can use the mouse to select an object to work with, or click a button to invoke a command. Allowing users to directly manipulate (move, copy, or cut) objects puts the user in control and more closely reflects the real world. Programs that require the user to use cryptic key combinations or multiple menu commands are more difficult to learn and use. Figure 18.2 shows how in Excel the direct manipulation feature allows users to select a range of cells for transfer purposes and as a side benefit, provides automatic calculation of the range (SUM, in this case).

NOTE The object-based design of Windows 95 and Office 95 supports user control and directness. Users can select objects, move objects by dragging-and-dropping, and customize objects by setting object properties. By providing users with objects that closely reflect the real world, users recognize the object and immediately know what the object does. For example, instead of providing users with a generic rectangular button that says Record, put a picture of a microphone on the button and display the word Record as a balloon tip.

Fig. 18.2

Users need to directly manipulate objects.

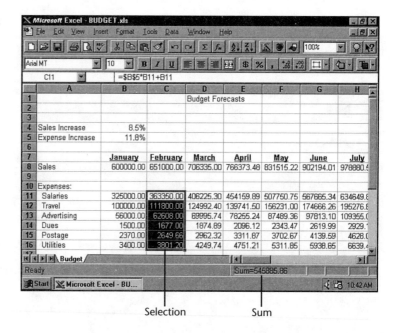

Consistency. Applications should share a common interface whenever possible. In Windows 95 and Office 95, features such as common menus, common dialog boxes, and common toolbars help the user reduce the learning curve across applications. Once a user has learned how to open a file in Word, the user knows how to open a file in Excel, Access, PowerPoint, and Schedule+. The steps are the same across all Office applications. Whether the user uses the menu (File, Open), the Start menu (Start, Open Office Document), or the toolbar, the user interface, dialog box, and file browsing features are the same. Be consistent within an application, across applications, and with Windows 95 itself. Consistency can be found in the appearance and functionality of the Open/Save As dialog box in Windows 95 and across Office applications (see fig. 18.3).

Fig. 18.3

A consistent user interface reduces the user's learning curve.

Clarity. Applications should have a clear, concise user interface. This principle applies to the visual elements, the wording used, and the functionality of an application. Visually, the screen should be free of clutter. The application elements should be simply displayed and clearly visible. The purpose of the application features should be easily understood. If a menu command is named Archive, a button which performs the same action should also be named Archive. In a dialog box, the title that appears should be consistent with the menu or button name that displayed the dialog box. Help text should be indexed by that name and provide clear, unambiguous assistance to the user on how and when to use that command.

Other modules of your application should use the same term to describe the same action. Whenever possible, use the same terms as Windows and Office use to reduce the learning curve (this supports consistency and clarity principles).

You can help users by disclosing information at the appropriate time. By reducing the information being displayed, users can focus better on the task at hand. In figure 18.4, the Options dialog box clarifies settings for the user by dividing the various options into tabbed pages and within a page using boxes and lines to organize common items.

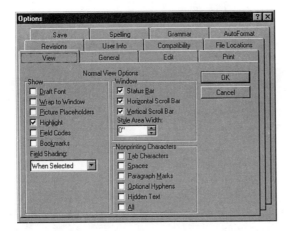

Fig. 18.4

Be sure the options available are clearly conveyed to the user.

Aesthetics. Applications should be visually appealing, without sacrificing any of the other design principles. Graphical layout, color, texture, and special effects must combine well to provide a polished user interface. Avoid colors or patterns which distract users. A poor choice of colors or patterns can annoy users and result in incorrect or missed data entry.

TIP

Involve a desktop publishing or graphics design professional in your project to improve the aesthetics of your user interface.

Feedback. Applications should provide the user with feedback for user actions. In trying to make applications more closely reflect the real world, this principle provides users with a "seventh sense." When users click an object, the object gets focus, and the program lets the user know by changing the color of the object, displaying a cursor, or drawing a thick border around the object. Other examples of providing feedback include playing a sound file, changing the pointer from an arrow to a pencil to indicate that the user selected Edit mode, and changing the title of a window or dialog box to indicate the user's action. In Access (see fig. 18.5), users are given feedback as to the table name (title bar), the current record, and the total number of records. The record selector icon changes to let users know if the record is locked, newly inserted, being edited, or currently viewed.

Table name

Fig. 18.5

Give users feedback on the status and results of their actions.

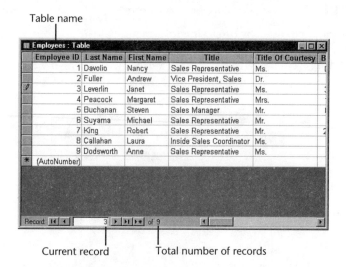

Current record   Total number of records

If you need to let the user know something but it isn't important enough to interrupt the user's work by displaying a message dialog box, use a flashing taskbar button to notify the user of a pending message.

If a programmed process takes several seconds to occur, give the user some visual indication of the progress. For example, in Access you can use the SysCmd() function to display a progress meter in the status bar. By giving the user feedback while your program works on a task, the user knows the computer is working OK (and hasn't run into a problem).

Forgiveness. Applications should protect the user from mistakes as much as possible, anticipate the mistakes, and provide the user with friendly remedies. To err is human, and programs should allow for the human error factor and help the user in these situations. For example, the Undo feature in Office applications allows users to reverse accidental deletions, format changes, or other actions. The interface should allow users to explore and experiment with features, without causing irreversible damage to the data. Error-handling routines should be written into the application to catch and explain errors to the user in an understandable way. Error messages should never degrade or blame the user, but instead help the user remedy the situation and avoid future errors. The Troubleshooter Help feature in Windows 95 (see fig. 18.6) is a perfect example of a user interface which "forgives."

Fig. 18.6

Provide users with graceful ways to handle problems and errors.

User Awareness. Applications should be aware of the strengths and limitations of users. Know your audience as well as you know your programming tools. If the audience consists of a department of engineers who are comfortable with technical jargon and specialized procedures, your user interface should reflect that audience. The user interface would be demeaning to the engineers if you babysat them through a process or failed to use the jargon that they use.

On the other hand, if the application audience turns over routinely, has little or no experience in the tasks at hand, and isn't familiar with the jargon, your user interface must guide the user along, document the process, and use the appropriate wording. Don't overlook automation opportunities such as performing small calculations for the user, linking to another application, or using fax or e-mail capabilities. Watch the user use the system. If, after entering invoice information, the user always needs to print, have the print automatically happen unless the user chooses *not* to print. Figure 18.7 shows how Excel supports user awareness by automatically filling in field values in a list (called the Auto Complete feature).

Fig. 18.7

When you know your users, it's easier to provide the right automation tools.

Fitting into the Development Cycle

The user design principles are all fine and good, but you need to fit them into your overall development cycle (see fig. 18.8). In the object-based world of building integrated Office applications, the development cycle is dynamic. You will find that you may be planning one module of your application as you test another module. Involving end users in the planning and testing phases helps you build a better user interface.

Fig. 18.8

The Application Development Cycle is not static.

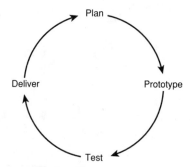

Planning. It's extremely important that you plan all aspects of your application *before* the first code statement is written. Although some single step tasks may seem self-explanatory, automating tasks across tables, documents, forms, and reports is a substantial undertaking. Schedule an adequate amount of time to properly plan the features, functionality, integration, and user interface of your application. Planning usually consists of three steps:

1. Information gathering
2. Needs analysis
3. Design statement

Before you start creating tables, linking worksheets, and designing forms, you need to define the information that's needed, the tasks that must be automated, and the people who will use the application. As you gather this information and begin to define what the users need, you'll start to design the user interface. For example, the existing paper forms that users have been using to manually calculate or record a transaction may become the form you use in Access to gather and report on that same transaction.

The information gathered in the planning stage becomes the basis for the design statement. A *design statement* lists the goals of the application, the people involved, responsibilities, budgets, deadlines, and system specifications. A design statement may include:

- Goals of the application
- Users (application audience)
- Time/cost budget
- Approvals
- Sample data to be used for testing
- Users available as "experts" during development
- Users available for testing
- Task and data specifications
- User and system documentation specifications

Every application project should have a design statement which is updated and modified as needed during the project. Think of the design statement as a road map for the application development. The design statement insures that everyone involved (users and developers) understands the design specifications, due dates, and responsibilities.

Prototype. A *prototype* is a working model of the application. In the object-based world of building integrated Office applications, you don't need to create a prototype of the entire application all at once. Instead, prototypes are developed for modules or sections of an application. And better yet, the time invested into most prototypes can be directly channeled into developing the final module. For example, you may take an existing paper form and spend time in Visual Basic to recreate the form. This is your prototype of that user interface element of your application. You can take that to the users and get feedback on how to improve the form's look and appearance on-screen. The time you invested in Visual Basic to create the form is not wasted and speeds your final development. Once the layout of the interface is finalized, you can set properties and write the code that ties the user interface together. If possible, involve end users as you prototype—from layout, to properties, to code.

Testing and Debugging. In reality, testing and debugging is an on-going process. Every time you add a line of code or link a new module, you will be testing and debugging your own work. In addition to this self-review, you should arrange for someone else on the development team to test and debug your work. Then, if possible, arrange for users to test forms, worksheets, links, reports, and queries with real data (not live data) as you complete each module. In addition to testing your code, you get valuable feedback from users on the user interface and the logical steps required to complete the task at hand.

Delivery. Once your application is tested and debugged, you are ready to deliver the applications to the users. The delivery phase consists of compiling, duplicating, distributing, documenting, and maintaining your application. A good delivery phase ends with getting user feedback, which leads to planning the next version of your application.

Exploring Design Elements

The Office 95 environment provides you with many different design elements that you can use in creating your user interface. The variety is almost overwhelming. Consider the core elements available in each of the Office products:

- Documents
- Worksheets
- Tables (Datasheets)
- Forms
- Dialog boxes

- Windows
- Query forms
- Reports
- Presentation slides
- Multimedia effects (graphics, sound, video)

In Word, you have all the various types of documents possible. In Excel, you can create worksheets, charts, graphs, dialog boxes, windows, buttons, and forms. In Access, you can create datasheets, forms, dialog boxes, windows, queries, reports, and controls such as buttons. Using PowerPoint, you can incorporate presentation slides and animation effects. In VBA, you have the ability to create custom menus, automate toolbars, and so on. In VB, you can code in OLE Automation to run Access from within Excel. Determining which Office application to use for each task, and how best to integrate the various design elements must be determined early in the planning stage of a development project.

> **TIP**
> The trick is to know which user interface element to use, and when to use that particular element.

Converting to a Windows 95 Interface

Converting an existing Windows 3.x-designed application to a Windows 95 interface presents you with many opportunities to improve the user interface. From an application design standpoint, Windows 95 is a more data-oriented design than Windows 3.x. This data-oriented approach may cause you to rethink your application's user interface and program design. Windows 3.x has a more application-oriented design. In Windows 3.x, users start applications, and through the applications, access their data. In Windows 95, users access data, and the tools (applications) to work with that kind of data automatically become available. This data-oriented approach can be seen in the Start menu's Documents command, the Office Shortcut Bar's Open a

Document button, OLE, and Microsoft Binder. The user focuses on the data, and the applications provide the necessary viewing and editing tools.

As you redesign your Windows 3.x interface, consider the new Windows 95 user interface aspects described in the following sections.

Title Bar. The title bar now has a title bar icon, text, and standard window buttons (minimize, full screen, and close). Figure 18.9 illustrates the new title bar and window appearance.

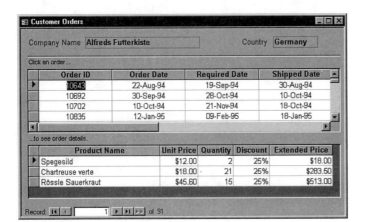

Fig. 18.9

This title bar displays a Form icon, the Form name, and the standard window control icons.

Right-Click. The right mouse button is used to display shortcut menus called pop-up menus (see fig. 18.10). *Pop-up menus* appear at the pointer's location and are context-sensitive to the current object. You can populate pop-up menus with common object-oriented tasks, such as opening the object, cut/copy/paste, renaming, and setting object properties.

Fig. 18.10

This pop-up menu in Excel provides users with easy access to common cell-oriented tasks.

Property Sheets. *Property sheets* is the new term to describe the entire property dialog box. Within the Properties sheet, sets of common properties are tabbed and called property pages. Figure 18.11 shows the property sheet for the Windows 95 Desktop.

Fig. 18.11

*Properties sheets organize
common items onto tabbed
pages.*

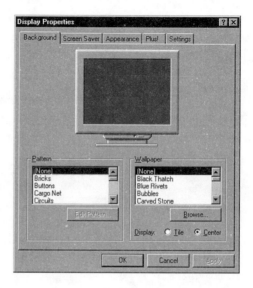

Help System. The Help system in Windows 95 has changed the user interface in a
number of ways. First, you'll want to consider the use of the "What's This?" toolbar
button (see fig. 18.12), menu command, and title bar button. Tooltips provide an
easy way to give users context-sensitive help. For example, in Access, by setting the
ControlTip text property, you can produce Tooltips to help identify controls on a
form. Within the Help system itself, tabbed pages include Contents, Index, and the
new Find page. You may also want to provide an Answer Wizard feature (consistent
with the Office applications).

Fig. 18.12

*Use the "What's This?"
feature to provide users with
context sensitive help.*

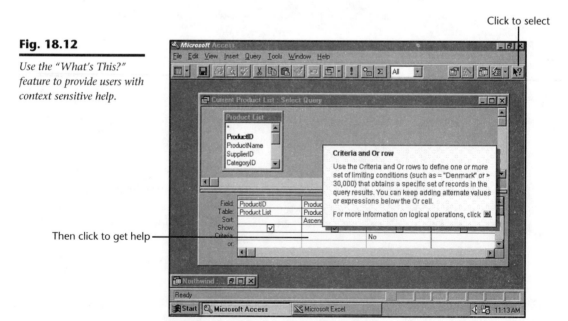

Drag-and-Drop. The default drag-and-drop operation uses the left mouse button to directly transfer objects. The default transfer method is a Move, but you can redefine the default drag-and-drop in the destination object to be something else, such as Print, Send To, or Copy. Depending on the application being used, the non-default drag-and-drop uses the right mouse button to transfer objects and displays a pop-up menu at the destination, asking the user to define the transfer type (Move, Copy, Link, and so on). Which user interface you decide on depends on your users and the task at hand.

OLE Embedding and Linking. Be aware of how OLE objects are now registered in Windows 95 and the new options available for Office applications. New powerful tools such as OLE Automation and the capability of creating your own OLE servers should be considered in your overall application design.

New Controls

Office applications, VBA, and VB support many new controls which you should incorporate into your Windows 95 user interface. You can use these new controls to enhance your application. Many of the new controls have been added to support the Windows 95 GUI. Others help you incorporate the principles of user interface design into your application.

Navigation and Selection. Menus are now *sticky*—as the user moves the pointer over the menu, the selection bar moves with the pointer. A single click selects the currently highlighted menu command. Shortcut keys and text selection is basically unchanged.

Window Management. Minimized windows now appear on the taskbar. The management of parent and child windows is different. When you minimize a child window, it now appears as a small title bar at the bottom of the parent window (inside the parent window). Figure 18.13 shows minimized application windows on the taskbar, an open parent window, and a minimized child window. Depending on the application's purpose, you may prefer to use a project-based window design (as done for Access databases), a workbook design (as done for Excel worksheets), or a workspace design (as done for Binder documents).

Registry Database. The Windows 95 Registry database is the hub of Windows 95 application integration. Whereas your existing Windows 3.x application relied on various INI files, AUTOEXEC.BAT, and CONFIG.SYS files for configuration settings, Windows 95 applications look to only one file, the Registry database (see fig. 18.14). Your application must work within the Registry database to properly store information for your application (such as user settings and application's state), define path information, register file extensions, enable printing, and use OLE.

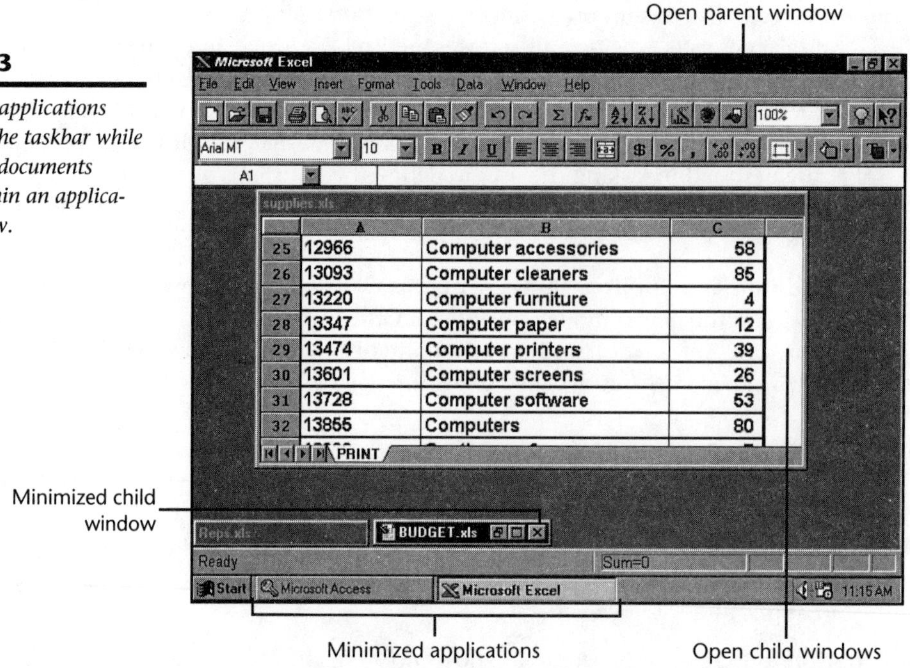

Fig. 18.13

Minimized applications appear on the taskbar while minimized documents appear within an application window.

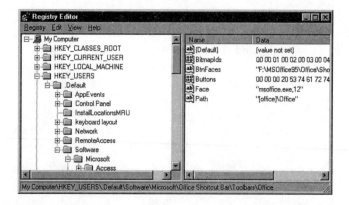

Open parent window

Minimized child window

Minimized applications

Open child windows

Fig. 18.14

Use the Registry Editor to view the Registration database.

Installing. Redesign your installation program to use the folder and file metaphor, provide users with access to the program via the Start menu, and follow new conventions such as Typical and Custom setup options. If your application will be distributed on a CD or Flash card (ROM card), consider supporting the AutoPlay feature of Windows 95 (the program automatically runs when the CD or Flash card is inserted).

Plug and Play. Support for Plug and Play is built into Windows 95, so you really don't need to change your existing application except to anticipate equipment changes during operation. For example, a user may change a PC card or dock a portable while your program is running. Your program processes should continue uninterrupted, or if using the hardware that has been removed, gracefully recover and prompt the user to reinsert the needed equipment.

Recycle Bin. Consider supporting the Recycle Bin feature in your application for deleted files. The SHFileOperation function (see the Win32 Software Development Kit (SDK) for more information) lets you write the deleted files to a temporary directory so the user can reclaim files from the Recycle Bin if needed.

Visual Design. As you work with Windows 95 and Office 95 applications, you'll notice many nuances in the visual design. The shading and size of buttons is slightly different. The coloring and appearance of controls, windows, and icons is different. Try to conform the visual design of your dialog boxes, windows, and controls to this new look and feel.

Giving the User Control

Controls are graphic objects that represent the properties or operations of other objects. Some controls allow the user to view and edit information; other controls execute actions. Across the Office applications, in VB4 and VBA2, Microsoft makes many controls available to you. You can use these controls to build your user interface—keeping the user in control of the application and supporting the various user interface principles described in the prior sections.

In the following sections, you examine each of the foundation controls that you can use in designing the user interface of your integrated Office application.

TIP

Microsoft provides detailed information about the appearance of user interface elements such as menus and buttons in several articles about Office compatibility on the Developer Network CD (October 1995).

Buttons

Buttons perform actions. In the Windows 95 user interface, you have three kinds of buttons to choose from: command buttons, option buttons, and checkboxes. A *command button* (sometimes called a *pushbutton*) is usually rectangular and has a label (text and/or graphic). When the user chooses the command button, the coded action programmed into the button executes. For example, clicking the Print button on the toolbar in Word immediately prints the current document. Command buttons have default behavior that gives the button a "pushed-in" appearance. The button commonly pushes in and pops out when selected.

> **TIP**
> When a command button requires additional information, let the user know with an ellipsis (...).

> **TIP**
> If using a command button to display a pop-up menu, use an arrow to indicate multiple selections.

Option buttons (also called radio buttons) are used to give the user mutually exclusive choices. In a group of option buttons, only one option button can be selected at any one time. The option button is usually a round circle (a dot inside the circle indicates selection) with a text label. In Access, in addition to the option button control, you'll notice a toggle button control which creates an on/off button (the on value appears as a depressed button).

Checkboxes are used to give the user multiple choices. In a group of checkboxes, the user can select all that apply. A checkbox is square (a checkmark or X indicates selection) with a text label.

> **TIP**
> Consider changing the text label of checkboxes in code at runtime to communicate the current settings to the user.

For all buttons, provide keyboard access. Assign access keys to buttons. Define Tab and arrow keys to allow the user to navigate among the selections. Consider providing shortcut keys to automatically set checkboxes or make common selections for the user.

Boxes

Boxes display information in a structured way to the user, allow the user to select information, and/or gets information from the user. Boxes come in many different forms, each serves a unique purpose. The simplest is a plain *text label* (also called *static text field*). Use text labels to describe other controls or provide information for the user. Many controls come with a text label component by default. This is how you can provide keyboard access to the control for which the label is associated. A colon is usually placed at the end of the text label to indicate to the user that the label describes the following control.

> **TIP**
> Screen review utilities often look for the colon at the end of a text label to locate text label and data controls.

A *group box* (called an Option Group in Access or Frame in VB) is a border which encloses a group of controls. Group boxes can optionally have a label that describes the contents. Use a group box to organize controls—such as radio buttons—into easily understood groups.

A *text box* (called an edit box in Excel) allows the user to edit and enter data. The default behavior of a text box allows the user to insert and delete data. You can set the font properties for the text box, provide text wrapping, and make the contents read-only. Your program can limit the number of characters or type of characters permitted. You can even perform data entry validation and formatting. For example, a text box that gathers phone number data could be validated as numbers only, and formatted for the user with dashes in the appropriate places.

> **TIP**
> For data entry intensive applications, consider automatically exiting a field that is limited in characters—such as a date—to speed the user's work.

A *list box* provides the user with a list of values from which to select. The user cannot edit the contents of a list box, and usually selects only one item from the list. Alternatively, the list box can be programmed to allow the user to select multiple items. The items in the list could be data or graphics. Only list available items. The list is usually sorted into an appropriate order (such as alphabetical, or in ascending value order). By default, list boxes do not have text labels. If the list box needs a label, create a text label.

> **TIP**
> If a control such as a list box is disabled, be sure to also disable the appearance of any text label you created for the control (for example, by graying out).

List boxes take more time to design and code, but provide users with an efficient method of locating and selecting data. For example, in Excel, you can link the list box to a range of cells and let the user select from the list rather than typing in commonly used data. The length of the list box control should be long enough to display the average width of an item. At the very least, users need to be able to distinguish between the items in a list. Weigh the benefits of providing a horizontal scroll bar against the reduced number of items visible. Single selection list boxes usually show three to eight items at a time and provide a vertical scroll bar.

> **TIP**
> Rather than making users type information, consider using list boxes and drop-down list boxes where users can select from a list of choices.

A *drop-down list box* displays as a single item text box with a down arrow. When the user clicks the down arrow, the list box opens, and a list of values appears. Use drop-down list boxes when you need to conserve screen space and reduce clutter.

To help the user navigate the list box, match keyboard entries to the list. For example, if a user types the letter T, scroll the list to the first item starting with the letter T. Not only does the list box scroll to the first matching entry, but it also selects the match.

Combo boxes (called Combination List-Edit in Excel) work similar to list boxes but also enable the user to enter data in a text box which appears above the list box. The user can type in an entry or choose one from the list. As the user types data into the text box, the list box scrolls to the first match found. If the user selects an item from the list box, the item appears in the text box.

Drop-Down Combo Boxes (called *Combination Drop-Down Edit* in Excel) provide combo boxes which open and close like a drop-down list box, but allow data entry. As with drop-down list boxes, use the drop-down combo box when you need to conserve screen space or reduce screen clutter.

Controlling Views

A *list view* (only available in the VB4 toolbox) control is similar to a list box, but displays a collection of items with an icon and a label. The list views in My Computer and Explorer are good examples. In your application, you can alter the list display to appear as:

- Full-sized icon with label below where the user can drag the icon (<u>V</u>iew, <u>L</u>arge Icons)

- Small icon with label to the right where the user can drag the icon (<u>V</u>iew, <u>Sm</u>all Icons)

- Small icon with label to the right in a sorted list (<u>V</u>iew, <u>L</u>ist)

- Small icon with label to the right in a sorted list, followed by additional columns of information your application supplies (<u>V</u>iew, <u>D</u>etails)

A *tree view* (only available in the VB4 toolbox) control is a special list box control that displays the hierarchical relationship of the items being listed. The drive and folder tree that appears in the left pane of the Explorer window and the Device Manager page of the Systems Properties sheet use Tree View as the user interface.

> **NOTE**
> VB4 provides several "special-purpose" controls that help you build your user interface for popular views such as listing files, selecting drives, and navigating directories. These standard controls include DriveListBox, DirListBox, and FileList Box.

Scroll Bars (available in Excel and VB4) display horizontal or vertical scrolling controls that you can use to move display contents. Disable the scroll bar arrows when the user scrolls the information to the beginning or end. Don't use a scroll bar to set or adjust values; instead, use a spin box or slider control.

The *Spin Box* control (called Spinner in Excel and SpinButton in VB4) is essentially a text box control which has up and down buttons and displays a circular list of specific values. When the user clicks the up or down button, the value displayed in the text box changes to the next value. Users can type a text value into the text box or use the buttons.

NOTE VB4 provides the Outrider SpinButton as a custom control which you can add to your Toolbox using the files SPIN16.OCX or SPIN32.OCX. In addition to these, VB4 comes with two special controls—HScrollBar and VScrollBar—which allow the user to select a value from within a range of values. Consider using HScrollBar and VScrollBar to indicate the speed or quantity of something, such as a volume control or time elapsed.

TIP Consider using a progress or gauge control during an install or other lengthy routine to let the user know the progress.

A *slider control* (only available in the VB4 Toolbox) is usually provided to allow the user to adjust a value from within a range of values, such as for brightness or volume. A slider control is a window containing a slider and optional tick marks. You can move the slider by dragging it, clicking the mouse to either side of the slider, or by using the keyboard.

Caution

In VB4, custom controls exist as separate files with either a VBX or OCX filename extension. Custom controls with the OCX filename extension take advantage of OLE technology. Custom controls with the VBX filename extension use older technology and are found in applications written with earlier versions of Visual Basic. You can use VBX custom controls with the 16-bit version of Visual Basic. You can't use VBX controls with the 32-bit version of Visual Basic.

The OCX controls can be used in both 16-bit and 32-bit versions of Visual Basic. Be sure to use the 16-bit version of the OCX controls with the 16-bit version of Visual Basic, and 32-bit version of the OCX controls with the 32-bit version of Visual Basic. For example, use the SPIN16.OCX with the 16-bit version of VB, and the SPIN32.OCX with the 32-bit version of VB.

A *progress indicator* control (available only in VB4 as a custom control named ProgressBar found in the COMCTL32.OCX file) shows the progress of a lengthy operation by filling a rectangle with chunks from left to right. The progress indicator functions like the Gauge control, but without the same precision. The ProgressBar control is a 32-bit custom control that can only run on Windows 95 and Windows NT 3.51 or higher. Additionally, the ProgressBar control is part of a group of custom controls that are found in the COMCTL32.OCX file. To use the ProgressBar control in your application, you must add the COMCTL32.OCX file to the project.

NOTE

Many of the custom controls provided with VB4 are 32-bit and only run on Windows 95 and Windows NT 3.51 or higher. For example, the Slider and ProgressBar controls are part of a group of custom controls that are found in the COMCTL32.OCX file provided with VB4. To use these controls in your application, you must add the COMCTL32.OCX file to the project. When distributing your application, your install routine must copy the COMCT32.OCX file to the user's Windows SYSTEM folder.

Controlling Images

No Windows 95-based application interface would be complete without images. You can display graphs and charts to graphically represent data, use pictures to quickly convey a message (you've heard the old adage, "a picture is worth a thousand words"), and use drawing tools such as lines and shapes to focus a user's attention on the task at hand.

 A *line* control adds a straight line, wherever you need one. Use lines to connect topics, separate sections, or emphasize text or objects.

  The *Shape* controls (*Rectangle* and *Ellipse,* or *Shape* in VB4) allow you to draw rectangles, squares, ellipses, or circle shapes. Use shapes to group similar controls together, add visual appeal to a graphic, or add emphasis to an important item.

 The *Image* control displays bitmaps, icons, or metafiles and acts as a command button when clicked. In addition to the Image control, VB4 provides a PictureBox control which displays bitmaps, icons or metafiles and acts as a visual container for other controls. By default, the PictureBox control clips a graphic if the control isn't large enough to display the entire image, whereas image controls automatically change size to fit the picture loaded into it. The downside of the Image control is that it has fewer properties, methods, and events than picture boxes and can't act as a container.

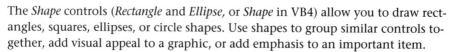

TIP

 If you don't need the extra functionality of a PictureBox control, use an Image control. Image controls use fewer system resources and repaint the screen faster.

Linking and Embedding Data

 All the Office applications support Object Linking and Embedding (OLE). Through code you can invoke and control OLE, and control the access users have to OLE. In building forms and dialog boxes, you can use OLE controls to create a frame in which you can display OLE objects. In Access, two special controls allow you to build OLE into your user interface. The *Bound Object* control allows you to display an OLE object that is stored in the database. The *Unbound Object* control allows you to display pictures, graphs, and other OLE objects that are not stored in the database.

In VB4, a standard OLE container control and several database connection controls are available for you to use in building your user interface. The *Data* control connects to an existing database and displays information from the database for you. The *DBCombo* control connects to an existing database and displays information in a combo box format with special data access capabilities built-in. The *DBList* control does the same as the DBCombo, but in a list box format.

Using Built-In Dialog Boxes

Why reinvent the wheel? When you plan the user interface for your application, don't overlook the built-in dialog boxes and windows that are available. Using built-in interfaces saves you time, reduces the testing burden, and provides users with a common, familiar interface. By using VBA in Excel and Access and VB4 across all applications, you can access and provide users with the standard Windows 95 Open, Save As, Print, Find/Replace, and Font dialog boxes. Even better, you can customize these dialog boxes to only permit the user to see a certain type of file, or preset file types or find criteria. In this section, you examine the common dialog boxes and explore customizing them for your needs.

Displaying Messages

Message boxes are windows that provide the user with pertinent information. Your user interface should take a practical approach to messages. Don't bother the user with unnecessary information, poorly written or vague messages, or use messages as a crutch (as in placing information in a message box which should be in a Help screen or on the form itself).

The title bar of a message box should reflect the object to which the message pertains. For example, a message saying that the printer needs paper would be best entitled `Printer` or `Printer Problem`. Message boxes usually display an icon which quickly conveys to the user the message type. Table 18.1 lists the symbols and describes the message box types.

	Table 18.1 Message Box Types	
Icon	**Type**	**Description**
ⓘ	Information	Provides the user with information, but offers the user no choices. The user acknowledges the message by clicking an OK button or closing the message box.
⚠	Warning	Informs the user of a condition which requires an action from the user before preceding. Buttons provide the user with choices such as Yes, No, or Cancel.
⊗	Critical	Informs the user of a serious problem that requires immediate intervention or correction before the program can continue. Buttons provide the user with choices such as Retry or Abort.

> **NOTE**
>
> The question mark icon used in Windows 3.x is no longer used in the Windows 95 user interface. The question mark was found to have confused users who associated the question mark with the "What's This?" question mark feature. Instead, use the exclamation mark icon to display a Warning message box, with the message phrased as a question if applicable.

VBA and VB support a `MsgBox` function which displays a standard message box. Constants such as `vbYesNo`, `vbCritical`, and `vbOKOnly` can be used in your code to customize how the built-in message box appears and behaves. For a complete list of message box constants in VBA or VB4, search Help for the MsgBox Function topic. In the following example, a `MsgBox` function is used to display a critical message in a dialog box with Yes and No buttons.

```
Msg = "Are you sure you want to delete?"   ' Define message.
Style = vbYesNo + vbCritical + vbDefaultButton2   ' Define buttons.
Title = "Customer Record:" + LastName      ' Define title.
Help = "Customer.HLP"      ' Define help file.
Ctxt = 1000        ' Define topic context.
Response = MsgBox(Msg, Style, Title, Help, Ctxt) ' Display message.
If Response = vbYES Then   ' User chose Yes button.
   MyString = "Yes"        ' Perform some action...
Else       ' User chose No button.
   MyString = "No" ' Perform some action...
End If
```

Getting Input

The `InputBox` function works similarly to the `MsgBox` function, except no special icons need to appear. The `InputBox` function displays a prompt in a dialog box, waits for the user to enter data or select a button, and then returns the contents of the text box and button selected. The buttons are limited to an OK and a Cancel button. For a full description of the `InputBox` syntax, search Help for the InputBox Function topic.

In the following example, a VB4 procedure asks the user to enter the program name to be executed. The `InputBox` function passes the user's choice to the `Shell` function, which then opens a normal window with focus (vbNormalFocus) and runs the requested application. This procedure is attached to the click event of a menu item called `mnuFileRun`.

```
Sub mnuFileRun_Click()
Message = "Enter name of application to run:"      ' Set prompt.
Title = "Run"      ' Set title.
Default = "c:\windows\calc.exe"    ' Set default.
' Display message, title, and default value.
RetVal = Shell(InputBox(Message, Title, Default), vbNormalFocus)
End Sub
```

Managing Files

Providing users with the standard Windows File Open, File Save, and File Save As dialog boxes shortens the user's learning curve and builds confidence in using your application. The commands and controls differ between VBA and VB4, so let's review them separately.

In VBA, you can use the `GetOpenFilename`, `GetSaveAsFilename`, and `GetSaveFilename` methods to display the corresponding built-in dialog boxes. For the specific syntax of each, search the Excel Help file for the method name. The methods work on the application object and allow you to customize the dialog box by specifying parameters such as the file type, drive, or folder to display by default.

In the following Excel VBA example, a File Open dialog box is displayed to show text files. The selected file name is returned from the `GetOpenFilename` method and displayed in a message box.

```
fileToOpen = Application.GetOpenFilename("Text Files (*.txt), *.txt")
If fileToOpen <> False Then
    MsgBox "Open " & fileToOpen
End If
```

In VB4, you have choices. You can display and customize default dialog boxes in code, or use a custom control at design time. The COMDLG32.OCX file is a custom control that comes with VB4 and provides you with a CommonDialog Box control in your Toolbox. The CommonDialog control provides a standard set of dialog boxes for operations such as opening, saving, and printing files or selecting colors and fonts.

Caution

In order to use the CommonDialog control, the Windows dynamic link library which contains the common dialog boxes, COMMDLG.DLL must be in the Windows SYSTEM directory.

As with other custom controls, you need to add the COMDLG16.OCX or COMDLG32.OCX file to the project. And, users need the OCX file installed in their Windows SYSTEM directory.

Also, when using the CommonDialog control, keep in mind that you can't specify where the dialog box appears.

You create dialog boxes for your application by adding the CommonDialog control to a form and setting its properties. The type of dialog box displayed is determined by the methods of the control. At runtime, a dialog box appears when the appropriate method is invoked; at designtime, the CommonDialog control is displayed as a non-sizeable icon on a form.

The following VB4 example uses the CommonDialog control and the ShowColor, ShowFont, ShowHelp, ShowOpen, ShowPrinter, and ShowSave methods to display the common dialog boxes. The form contains a command button, an option button (index property set to 0), and a CommonDialog control. The code is attached to the Declarations section of the form. When the form is run, you can select the type of dialog box (from the option button) and click the command button to see the common dialog box. Figure 18.15 shows the VB form with the Open dialog box selected.

On the CD

```
Private Sub Form_Paint ()
    Static FlagFormPainted As Integer
    ' When form is painting for first time
    If FlagFormPainted <> True Then
            For i = 1 To 5
                    Load Option1(i) 'Add five option buttons to array.
                    Option1(i).Top = Option1(i - 1).Top + 350
                    Option1(i).Visible = True
            Next i
            Option1(0).Caption = "Open"       'Put caption on buttons.
            Option1(1).Caption = "Save"
            Option1(2).Caption = "Color"
            Option1(3).Caption = "Font"
            Option1(4).Caption = "Printer"
            Option1(5).Caption = "Help"
            Command1.Caption = "Show Dlg"   ' Label command button.
            FlagFormPainted = True  ' Form is done painting.
    End If
End Sub

Private Sub Command1_Click ()
    If Option1(0).Value Then          ' If Open option button selected,
            CommonDialog1.ShowOpen  ' display Open common dialog box.
    ElseIf Option1(1).Value Then     ' Or,
            CommonDialog1.ShowSave  ' display Save common dialog box.
    ElseIf Option1(2).Value Then     ' Or,
            CommonDialog1.ShowColor ' display Color common dialog box.
    ElseIf Option1(3).Value Then     ' Or,
            CommonDialog1.Flags = cdlCFBoth
            CommonDialog1.ShowFont  ' Display Font common dialog box.
    ElseIf Option1(4).Value Then     ' Or,
            CommonDialog1.ShowPrinter        ' display Printer dialog box.
    ElseIf Option1(5).Value Then     ' Or,
            CommonDialog1.HelpFile = "VB.HLP"
            CommonDialog1.HelpCommand = cdlHelpContents
            CommonDialog1.ShowHelp  ' Display VB Help.
            End If
    End Sub
```

Fig. 18.15

By using the VB4 CommonDialog control, you can easily incorporate common dialog boxes into your application.

Handling Display Issues

The variety and quality of screens that will display your application impacts how you design your user interface. If you design your application on a 19-inch monitor, but some users only have 15-inch monitors, part of your screen display may be cut off, or graphics could be incorrectly drawn. The screen resolution, video memory, and graphics display all play a part in how your application will look. Pay particular attention to the use of color. Forms developed using a 256-color monitor will look very different on a 16-color monitor. Portable computers such as laptops present their own display issues often with reduced screen size and color differences.

> **TIP**
>
> When developing the user interface, use a computer with the most common type of video display and speed.

If the speed of display is an issue, consider reducing the number of graphics, using labels instead of text boxes, and keeping data on disk until needed. Forms display more quickly if kept in memory. You could hide a form instead of unloading it and then reloading the form. Also, in a VB4 application, use image controls for graphics instead of picture controls. The picture controls are actual windows that use significant system resources.

> **NOTE**
>
> In general, you should develop your applications for a standard 640 × 480 VGA screen, unless you know for a fact that all users have a higher definition screen resolution, or you are prepared to incorporate a means for the applications to adapt to the definition of each user's screen.

Also consider any disabilities in your user group. Avoid relying solely on sound in cases where users may be hearing impaired. Visual disabilities such as color blindness may make it difficult for such users to distinguish between objects. Use color as an enhancement, and use lines and borders to separate objects. Other disabilities can be handled, too, but you need to know about them and plan for them in your user interface design.

From Here...

This chapter examined the Windows 95 user interface and discussed user interface design issues. You learned about the principles of user interface design and how to apply them in your application. The design elements and controls available to you in the Office applications and VB4 were reviewed. Lastly, this chapter looked at the display issues and provided some guidelines on how to handle display issues.

If you want to learn more about designing the user interface, you can find more information on related topics in the following chapters:

- The better you know Windows 95 and the Office applications, the easier it will be to build a powerful integrated Office application; see Chapter 2, "Windows and Office Capabilities."

- Every application needs menus and toolbars in the user interface design; see Chapter 20, "Creating Custom Menus, Toolbars, and Shortcut Bars."

- Never underestimate the power of a good Help system in your user interface; see Chapter 21, "Providing Help for Users."

CHAPTER 19

Handling the Unexpected

Developing a software application is challenging and rewarding, but it can also be frustrating, especially when you can't determine why your code isn't working as expected. Users are equally frustrated when unexpected errors or problems occur while trying to use applications. Every programmer—from the beginner to the expert—makes mistakes when writing programs. By testing programs before they are delivered, you try to test all avenues a user may take, but repeating the conditions of all users is impossible.

As a VBA and VB4 programmer, you can build in certain safeties to gracefully handle unexpected errors, spruce up your error-trapping routines, and test for common causes of program errors.

In this chapter, you learn how to

- Identify error types
- Review debugging resources
- Develop a testing and debugging strategy
- Handle runtime errors
- Write error-handling routines

Finding Errors

Program errors (also affectionately referred to as *bugs*) usually fall into one of the following categories:

- Syntax
- Compiler
- Runtime
- Logic

Syntax errors result from typos, misspelling keywords, or omitting punctuation (such as missing a comma in an argument list). Most of the syntax errors are caught by the editor, which interactively detects syntax errors as you enter a line of code (provided you have Syntax Checking turned on; see the section "Syntax Checking" on the next page).

Compiler errors result when you attempt to run a procedure. Visual Basic begins to compile the code and checks to make sure the decision-making constructs, loops, declarations, and so on are correct. If VBA finds any discrepancies, an Error dialog box appears, and your code does not compile.

Runtime errors result when Visual Basic actually executes a line of code that fails. For example, a runtime error may occur because a file name doesn't exist at runtime or an expression has evaluated to an invalid value, such as division by zero.

Logic errors result when the program code you wrote doesn't perform the way you intended the code to work. Flaws in logic are the hardest program errors to find. For example, perhaps you performed multiplication instead of division. The code is syntactically correct, compiles, and runs without error, but the result is incorrect.

Debugging Resources

VBA and VB4 provide many debugging tools to help you locate and correct program errors. You will recognize most of these tools from your prior programming experience. I'll review each of them briefly before launching into error-trapping and handling routines. For a more in-depth discussion of the built-in debugger in VBA and VB4, refer to the online help (in VB4, choose Help, Learning Visual Basic, Debugging Your Application, or in VBA, search Help for the How to Use the Debug Window topic). Here's a list of the debugging tools:

- Syntax checker
- Break mode
- Breakpoints
- Immediate code execution

- Watch expressions
- Instant watch
- Stepping
- Calls

TIP

Although this section focuses on the features of the Debugger in VB/VBA, the languages themselves provide a few useful debugging tools. Consider inserting temporary MsgBox statements into your code to help you better understand what's going on. Also, consider inserting temporary SysCmd functions that display informative messages in the status bar.

Syntax Checking. A built-in syntax checker reviews your code as you type, when you compile, and when you run a program. If an error is found, Visual Basic highlights the code line that contains the error and displays a message describing the error. To enable syntax checking while you type, follow these steps:

1. Choose Tools, Options.
2. In Excel VBA, select the Module General tab and check the Display Syntax Errors check box.

   In Access VBA, select the Module tab and check the Auto Syntax Check option.

   In VB4, select the Environment tab and check the Auto Syntax Check option.
3. Click OK.

> **NOTE**
>
> A good programming habit to get into is to add the statement `Option Explicit` at the beginning of every module. Doing so forces you to explicitly declare all variables in that module. Otherwise, all undeclared variables will be `Variant`, unless the default type is specified with a `Deftype` statement.
>
> But the real advantage of using `Option Explicit` is that when you misspell a variable name, the compiler catches it for you! Moreover, explicitly declaring variables avoids confusion in determining the scope of a variable and makes your code easier to read and maintain.
>
> When using the `Option Explicit` statement, make sure it appears in a module before any statements that declare variables or define constants. Use the `Dim`, `Private`, `Public`, `ReDim`, or `Static` statements to explicitly declare all variables.

Entering Break Mode. Use Break mode to stop program execution, but leave the current variable and property settings in memory. Break mode lets you be a church mouse in your own program. You can examine the values of variables, change values, run other code, and determine which line of code runs next. At any point, you can continue execution. In VB4, you have the added benefit of being able to edit code and continue.

If you suspect a section of your program contains an error, you can set a breakpoint at that line. When the program runs, execution stops before executing the line which contains the breakpoint. Alternatively, you can run the program and press Ctrl+Break at any time to enter Break mode. Break points are automatically cleared and removed from your code when you exit.

> **TIP**
>
> If you need to keep a breakpoint saved in code during testing, use the `Stop` statement. Just be sure to remove all `Stop` statements before delivering the application.

To set a breakpoint, follow these steps:

1. Move the insertion point to the line of code where you want execution to stop before executing and enter Break mode.

2. Click the Breakpoint button on the toolbar, or press F9.

To clear a breakpoint, follow these steps:

1. Move the insertion point to the line of code that contains the breakpoint.

2. Click the Breakpoint button on the toolbar, or press F9.

Navigating the Debug Window. When program execution halts and enters Break mode, the Debug window appears (previously called the Immediate window). Figure 19.1 illustrates the VBA Debug window for an Excel program. Access VBA has a similar-looking Debug window. Figure 19.2 illustrates the VB4 Debug window for a Visual Basic 4 program called Calc (one of the sample programs that comes with VB4).

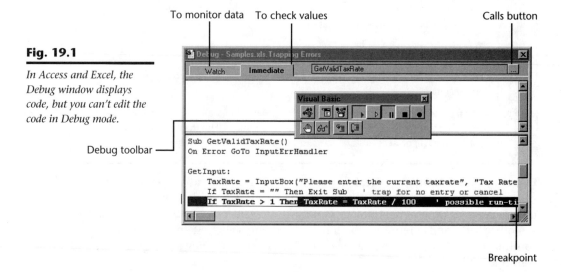

Fig. 19.1

In Access and Excel, the Debug window displays code, but you can't edit the code in Debug mode.

The VB4 Debug environment is much different than working in VBA Excel or Access. The first thing you'll notice is that you have so many windows open. In VB4, you should arrange your windows so you can see the Code window, the Debug window, and the Run window. The edit and continue feature of VB4 allows you to modify code in the Code window and continue running the program.

By default, the Debug window opens with the Immediate pane active. Choose <u>T</u>ools, <u>A</u>dd Watch to specify variables, properties, or expressions that you want to track. Once watch points have been defined, the Watch pane section of the Debug window appears (see fig. 19.3).

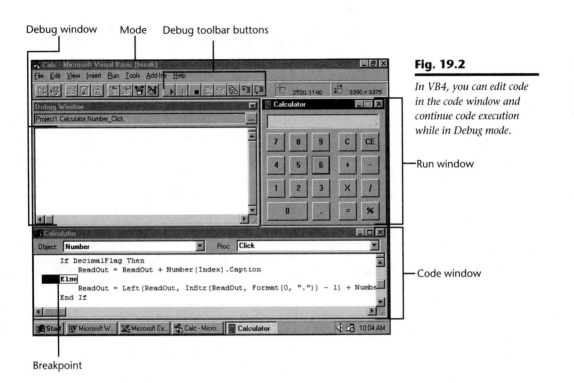

Fig. 19.2

In VB4, you can edit code in the code window and continue code execution while in Debug mode.

Debug window   Mode   Debug toolbar buttons

Run window

Code window

Breakpoint

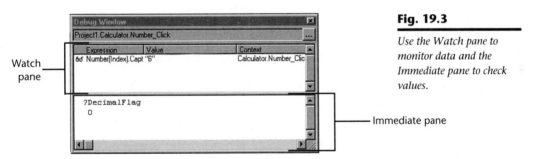

Fig. 19.3

Use the Watch pane to monitor data and the Immediate pane to check values.

Watch pane

Immediate pane

Executing Immediately. The Immediate pane allows you to execute a code statement and send the results to the next line in the Immediate pane. You can use the Immediate pane to test procedures, evaluate expressions, determine property values, or assign new values while still in Debug mode. The Print method of the Debug object displays results in the Immediate pane. You can include debug.print statements in your application code when debugging to enter Break mode and display a value in the Immediate pane. To save on typing, you can use the shorthand question mark (?) instead of the Print method in the Immediate pane.

> **Caution**
>
> In VBA, you need to remove all debug.print statements before delivering your application.
>
> In VB4, the compiler automatically removes debug.print statements. However, any function calls as arguments to debug.print are not removed. Be sure to comment out or remove these statements before delivering your application.

> **TIP**
>
> To reexecute a statement in the Immediate pane, move the insertion point back to that statement and press Enter.

The examples in table 19.1 show how to get and set values in the Immediate pane.

Table 19.1   Using the Immediate Pane

Type in the Immediate Pane	Result Displayed in Immediate Pane
Print TaxRate	.08
? TaxRate	.08
TaxRate =	.10
? TaxRate	.10
? Form1.BackColor	-2147483633
Form1.BackColor = vbRed	
?Form1.BackColor	255

> **TIP**
>
> To quickly determine the description of an error number, type **error** followed by the error number in the Immediate pane (for example: **error 58**).

Setting Watch Expressions. When you need to monitor the value of an expression, property, or variable, set up a watch expression in the Watch pane. As code executes, any change in value is reflected in the Watch pane. Watch expressions can be any valid VB4 or VBA (respectively) expression such as variable names, properties, and functions. The Watch pane displays the expression, value, and context.

To add watch expressions, follow these steps:

1. Choose Tools, Add Watch. VBA and VB4 display a similar Add Watch dialog box (see fig. 19.4).

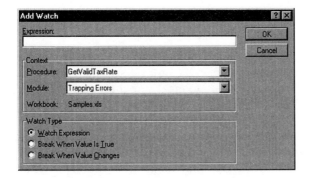

Fig. 19.4

Enter a variable, property, function call, or other valid expression in the Expression text box.

2. Enter the expression to be monitored in the Expression text box.

3. If you have variables with the same name but different scope, or if you want to speed up evaluation by restricting the scope, set the scope of the variables to watch in the Context option group. Select the appropriate Procedure or Module to indicate scope.

4. In the Watch Type option group, select Watch Expression (only appears when Break mode occurs), Break When Value Is True (automatically enters Break mode when expression evaluates to True), or Break When Value Changes (automatically enters Break mode when expression changes).

5. Click OK.

Using Instant Watch. Use the Instant Watch feature when you need to check a value, but not monitor its value throughout the entire procedure or program. To access Instant Watch, you need to be in Break mode. To display the Instant Watch dialog box, follow these steps:

1. Enter Break mode.

2. Select an expression in the Code window.

3. Choose Tools, Instant Watch, or click the Instant Watch button on the toolbar. The Instant Watch dialog box appears (see fig. 19.5).

Fig. 19.5

The Instant Watch dialog box displays the expression you selected and its current value.

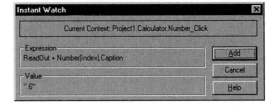

4. If you want to add the expression to the Watch pane, Click <u>A</u>dd.

5. Close the dialog box when done.

Stepping Through Code. One of the most useful techniques for debugging a program is to step through the code one statement at a time. Stepping through the code allows you to see how the program flows and to make sure that control constructs, variables, and procedure calls execute properly. VB4 and VBA provide two ways to execute code one statement at a time: Step Into and Step Over. Step Into executes every line of code in this procedure and any procedures called by this procedure, one line at a time. Step Over executes every line of code in this procedure, but executes calls to other procedures as a single step (not line-by-line). Use the Step Over method when you are sure that the procedures being called do not cause program errors.

To step through code, follow these steps:

1. Enter Break mode.

2. Choose <u>R</u>un, Step <u>I</u>nto, or click the Step Into toolbar button.

3. Repeat step 2 as needed to execute the next lines of code.

To step through the current procedure, but over procedure calls, follow these steps:

1. Enter Break mode.

2. Choose <u>R</u>un, Step <u>O</u>ver, or click the Step Over toolbar button.

3. Repeat step 2 as needed to execute the next lines of code.

> **TIP**
>
> In VB4, choose <u>R</u>un, Step To <u>C</u>ursor to quickly execute code up to the insertion point in the Code window and then reenter Break mode.

> **NOTE**
>
> If you accidentally step into a lengthy procedure you'd rather step over, set a breakpoint at the end of the procedure and resume execution. Visual Basic will reenter Break mode, and you can continue debugging using the Step Over feature.

Using Calls. The Calls feature allows you to view a list of your program's currently active procedure calls during Break mode. This feature helps you trace the program execution flow and narrow down the possible locations of logic errors. To view a list of currently active procedure calls, choose <u>T</u>ools, <u>C</u>alls, or click the Calls button (see fig. 19.6).

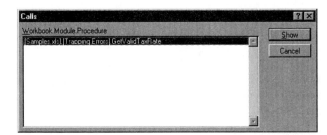

Fig. 19.6

The Calls dialog box displays a list of active procedure calls.

TIP
Click the Show button in the Calls dialog box to view the statement which calls the selected procedure.

Developing a Testing and Debugging Strategy

Here are some suggestions on how to avoid programming errors and tips on how to find the errors. Although not a finite list, it may give you some ideas on what you can do to produce more polished programs:

- Use comments to document your work. This helps you and others better understand the purpose of each procedure and speed your debugging task.

- Use Option Explicit to avoid misspelling control and variable names.

- Document your code as you go, including event procedures and property settings. When you change code, document why the change was made and the variables or other procedures affected by that change.

- When testing, try to use real data (not live data) and real users. Be sure test data covers the value extremes, positives and negatives, division by zero, and mid-range values.

- Keep a log of problems found, who fixed them, and which version of the program contains the fix.

- Test the program on various computers representative of the final user installation.

Handling Runtime Errors

An important part of creating a professionally designed application is handling errors gracefully. This means that when the users of your application encounter errors, your program handles the error without terminating the program, losing data, or displaying cryptic error messages. Anticipating common runtime errors and protecting against them is a necessary programming strategy.

Here is a list of common runtime errors:

- Reading beyond the end of a file
- Writing to a floppy drive that does not have a disk inserted
- Writing to a drive that is full
- Division by zero
- Numeric overflow
- Incorrect data type entered by user

For those errors that you can't anticipate, you should include an error-handling routine that still performs basic tasks such as closing any open files (potentially saving data that would otherwise be lost).

When Visual Basic encounters a runtime error, execution halts and a dialog box appears with a message describing the error. At this point, the user can stop execution, view the Debug window, go to the module, continue execution (provided the error was resolved in the Debugger), or get help on the error.

When an error occurs, the error handler gets control of the user's program. It gets the error number from the system and checks for an error trap in the user's program. If an error trap is found, control passes to the program's error handler. If no error handler is found, the VBA error handler displays the standard Error dialog box.

To process errors, you need:

- An *error handler*—code that handles the error.
- An *error trap*—a statement that turns on the error trap, and identifies the error-handler routine.
- A statement that resumes program execution, or if the error handler can't recover from the error, exits the application.

NOTE Although various If..Then and Select Case statements could be used throughout your code to handle runtime errors in each procedure, doing so would not be very efficient. Writing a separate error-handling routine that handles all errors reduces the lines of code needed and centralizes this task into a more manageable unit.

Setting the Trap

The On Error statement enables Visual Basic's built-in error trapping mechanism. The basic syntax of On Error is as follows:

```
On Error GoTo line
```

The line argument specifies the line number or line label that identifies where the error-handling routine starts. The line must be in the same procedure as the On Error statement. Once the On Error trap is set, Visual Basic passes control of any runtime errors to the error-handling line.

The On Error statement has two other syntax forms.

```
On Error Resume Next
```

This form of the On Error statement specifies that when a runtime error occurs, control should be passed to the next statement. In other words, the line that caused the error is skipped and execution continues on the next line.

```
On Error GoTo 0
```

The third syntax form lists the error-handling line number as zero. The effect of this form is to disable all error handlers in the current procedure.

 NOTE Note that the error-handling routine is not a separate Sub or Function procedure. Instead, it is a block of code identified by a line label or line number.

Here is an example that shows how the error trap is set, and the flow of program control:

```
Sub CheckFile()
    Dim Filename As String
    'Set Trap
    On Error GoTo ErrorHandler
    'Ask user for file name.
    Filename = InputBox("Enter file name.")
    If (Dir(filename)<>"") Then
        MsgBox "Found" & Filename
    Else
        MsgBox "Couldn't find" & Filename
    End If
    Exit Sub            'End of proc.

ErrorHandler:
    ...     'Code to process errors,
            'and resume execution.
End Sub
```

Handling Errors

The error-handling routine begins with the line label or line number listed in the On Error statement, followed by a colon. Error-handling routines usually use a decision-making construct such as Select Case to test for different errors and then processes each error.

Visual Basic assigns error numbers to each error that you can trap. Use the Err function to determine the error number that has occurred. For a complete list of error codes and their messages, search the Visual Basic Reference Help file for the Trappable Errors topic. You can also trap for and handle Excel cell errors. For a list of cell errors, search the Visual Basic Reference Help file for the Errors: Cells Containing topic and Cell Error Values show topics.

> **TIP**
>
> Set up your own user-defined constants for error numbers to make code easier to read and maintain (for example, `errFileNotFound` for error number 53).

Exiting the Error Handler

Once an error is trapped and processed, you need to exit the error handler. An error-handler routine can end with an `Exit Sub`, `Exit Function`, `Resume`, or `Error` statement, as shown in table 19.2.

Table 19.2 Statements to Exit the Error Handler	
Statement	**Description**
`Exit Sub`	Disables the error trap and returns control to the procedure that called the procedure with the error.
`Exit Function`	Disables the error trap and returns control to the procedure that called the procedure that had the error.
`Resume`	Reenables the error trap and returns control to the current procedure.
`Resume Next`	Reenables the error trap and returns control to the statement following the statement that caused the error.
`Resume line`	Reenables the error trap and returns control to the line label or line number specified. Line must be in the same procedure as the error handler.
`Error errorNumber`	Simulates the error number specified, causing control to return to the VBA error handler.

> **TIP**
>
> If you can't process the error, pass control back to VBA by issuing the statement `Error Err`.

On the CD

In the following example, the error handler routine checks for the missing disk or an unavailable device and prompts the user accordingly:

```
Sub CheckFile()
  Dim Filename As String
  'Set Trap
  On Error GoTo ErrorHandler
  'Ask user for file name.
  Filename = InputBox("Enter file name.")
  If (Dir(filename)<>"") Then
     MsgBox "Found" & Filename
  Else
     MsgBox "Couldn't find" & Filename
  End If
  Exit Sub          'End of proc.
```

```
ErrorHandler:
  Select Case Err
    Case 76
          MsgBox "Insert a disk and press enter."
                Resume
    Case 68
          MsgBox "Device Unavailable"
    Case Else
          Error Err
  End Select
End Sub
```

Trapping Excel Errors

To detect Excel cell value errors, use the CVErr() function. This function takes as an argument the Excel constant which represents the error number. In the following example, the IsError() function is used on the active cell to determine if certain Excel cell errors occurred and processes the error:

```
If IsError(ActiveCell.Value) Then
    Select Case ActiveCell.Value
        Case CVErr(xlErrName)
           MsgBox "Invalid name."
        Case CVErr(xlErrValue)
           MsgBox "Invalid value."
        Case CVErr(xlErrDiv0)
           MsgBox "Division by zero."
    End Select
End If
```

Trapping User Interruptions

Another common error trap needed is handling user interruptions of the running procedure; for example, stopping the user from pressing Ctrl+Break during program execution. To trap for user interruptions, set the EnableCancelKey property of the Application object to one of the values listed in table 19.3.

Table 19.3   Values for Trapping User Interruptions

Value of *EnableCancelKey* Property	Description
xlDisabled	Disables the Cancel key.
xlInterrupt	Enables the Cancel key and allows the user to interrupt the currently executing procedure.
xlErrorHandler	Passes control to the error handler specified by an On Error Go To statement. Trap for error code 18 to handle the user's action.

NOTE   Exercise care when using xlDisabled, because there is no way to stop a runaway loop other than turning the computer off.

In the following code example, the Cancel key is disabled:

```
Application.EnableCancelKey = xlDisabled
```

Creating User-Defined Errors

Visual Basic allows you to set up your own system of error numbers and error messages. You can use any of the unused error numbers to create your own custom error messages. Error numbers can range from 1 to 65,535, but Visual Basic currently only uses the first few thousand. Since future versions of Visual Basic will probably use more of the lower numbers, begin custom error numbering at a higher number, such as 50,000.

```
Error 50000
```

TIP   Use custom error messages to make other error handlers in other parts of your application aware of the error, without processing the real error number.

Use the Error statement to generate your own, user-defined errors by supplying the desired custom error code. Then, in your error-handling routine, process the custom error.

TIP   Use constants to define custom errors. This makes your code easier to read and maintain.

Causing an Error

You can also use the Error and Err statements to cause a built-in error to occur, or change the error that did occur to another error. The Err statement sets the value that the Err function returns.

```
Error 71   'Simulates "Disk Not Ready" error

Err = 71   'Sets the error value to 71
```

Understanding the Chain of Traps

Only one error handler is active at any time in a single procedure. However, because procedures can call other procedures and each called procedure can have its own error-handling routine, it's possible for more than one error handler to be active. The active calling chain is the list of active procedures in the order that they were called to reach the currently executing procedure. This is referred to as the *Calls list.*

The error handler first looks to the currently executing procedure for an error handler. If none is found, Visual Basic looks in the procedure that called the active procedure. This continues up the calling chain until an error handler is found. If no error handler is found, Visual Basic processes the error and displays the appropriate error dialog box.

The way Visual Basic looks for error handlers in a chain of procedures allows you to handle the general errors once at the top of the calling chain, rather than repeating code in each called procedure. In the procedures low on the calling chain, you can place special purpose error handlers which do not apply to other procedures in the calling chain.

In the Error Trap Calling Chain illustration (see fig. 19.7), the active call chains are A-B, A-C-D, and A-E-F-G. Errors occurring in Procedure A or B are handled by the Main error trap. Errors occurring in Procedure G are first passed to Trap 4 in G. If Trap 4 cannot handle the error, Visual Basic passes the error up the procedure call chain until another error trap is found. Thus, Procedure E, Trap 3 gets the error next. If E cannot handle the error, Visual Basic passes the error up to Procedure A. If no error traps can handle the error, Visual Basic displays the Error dialog box.

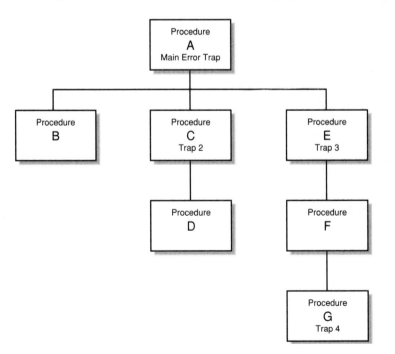

Fig. 19.7

Understanding the calling chain helps you write error-handling routines.

Centralizing Error Handling

Centralizing error handling code into one procedure reduces code size, speeds programming efforts, and makes future maintenance easier. A serious limitation of VBA error handling is that the error-handing routine must reside in the same procedure as the On Error statement. Many other programming languages allow the error-handling routine to be in a separate procedure.

There is, however, a way to better centralize the error-handling code in VBA. You can centralize much of your program's primary error handling by creating a main error-handling function that tells a procedure how to process an error. Other procedures call the error-handling function and take action based on the returned value. This of course requires that each procedure still have its own error handler structure.

NOTE The centralized approach to error handling moves a large volume of code repetition within each error handler to a centralized function. It does not replace or remove the error handler section.

Also notice that Resume statements can only appear within the procedure that contains an On Error statement.

```
Sub Main()
Dim filename As String
'Set the trap.
On Error GoTo ErrorHandler

'Ask the user for file name.
filename = InputBox("Enter file name.", _
    "On Error Demo")
If (Dir(filename) <> "") Then
    MsgBox "Found " & Filename
Else
    MsgBox "Couldn't find " & Filename
End If
Exit Sub

ErrorHandler:
    TypeOfError = CentralErr(Err)
    Select Case TypeOfError
        Case 1
            Resume
        Case 2
            'any other special error handling.
    End Select
End Sub
```

...continued on next page...

```
'Central error handling function.
Function CentralErr(ErrNum) As Integer
  Select Case ErrNum
        Case 76      ' "DiskNotReady" error.
            MsgBox "Insert a disk and press enter."
            ErrorType = 1
        Case 68      ' Device not available.
            MsgBox "Device Unavailable"
        Case Else
            Error Err ' Pass back to VBA.
  End Select
  CentralErr = ErrorType
End Function
```

From Here...

In this chapter, you learned how to avoid, anticipate, and handle errors in your applications. You learned the difference between syntax, compiler, runtime, and logic errors. We reviewed the debugging tools provided in Visual Basic and Visual Basic for Applications. You learned how to trap an error, and how to handle the error at runtime. This chapter also discussed advanced error-handling techniques such as centralized error handling and working with a chain of error traps.

If you want to learn more about handling program errors, you can find more information on related topics in the following chapters:

- A fully integrated Office application will most probably use OLE Automation to perform some tasks, which presents a unique set of errors to handle; see Chapters 10–12 which cover automating integration in Word, Excel, and Access VBA. Also see Chapter 17, "Controlling Office Applications with Visual Basic."

- Help systems have their own errors to be handled; see Chapter 21, "Providing Help for Users."

- When working with the Windows APIs, you encounter special error-handling issues; see Chapter 23, "Using Windows APIs."

CHAPTER 20

Creating Custom Menus, Toolbars, and Shortcut Bars

The graphical nature of Windows 95 and Office 95 gives you many options for communicating with the user. Menus and toolbars are the most popular way to provide users with access to the features of an application. The Office applications provide you with the ability to use the existing application menus and toolbars, modify the existing menus and toolbars to create your own custom menus and toolbars (interactively in some cases), or develop completely new menus and toolbars from scratch. You explore how you can incorporate custom menus and toolbars into your integrated office application.

In this chapter, you learn how to

- Review the command interface options and standards
- Modify built-in menus and toolbars
- Create custom menus and toolbars
- Manipulate menus and toolbars in code

Putting the User in Command

The Windows 95 interface provides many interactive components that you can use in your application to carry out commands. Menus and toolbars are the key user interface components used to provide the user with access to commands in an application.

Commands are the features or actions that your program automates for the user. For example, you may provide a search feature that displays a customer's record based on a customer ID or phone number. The user interface element that you use to provide access to this feature may be in the menu, on the toolbar, or incorporated into a field control (in response to a data entry event). Or, you may choose to provide the user with multiple access in all three places.

Menus (historically the core of an application) are no longer the only way to communicate with the user. Toolbars, button controls, and automatically invoking a command in response to an event offer you other user interface options.

Before you delve into the specifics of creating custom menus and toolbars, you should learn what user interface command options and Windows 95 menu and toolbar standards are available to you.

NOTE

Nothing holds an application together like a common user interface. As described in Chapter 18, "Designing the User Interface," consistency across applications and within an application reduces the user's learning curve. Consistent user interfaces also make your job of creating and maintaining an application easier. In Office 95, you can see how Microsoft has applied the common user interface principle to its own application menus and toolbars. For example, the Edit, Find menu command appears in Word, Excel, Access, and PowerPoint with the shortcut key combination Ctrl+F. The Find command is one example of how Microsoft applies the common user interface principle to Office 95. In all the applications within Office 95, the Find command works the same, can be found in the same place in the menu, and has the same keyboard shortcut and toolbar icon. Furthermore, the toolbar icon that performs the Edit, Find command looks the same across all applications (it looks like a pair of binoculars). As you begin to plan the menus and toolbars for your integrated office application, remember to be consistent within your application, and consistent with Windows 95 and Office 95 wherever possible.

Providing Menus

A menu lists the application commands available to users. In a way, menus provide users with a road map to the application features. Users can browse through the menu, review the commands available, and then decide which one they want to invoke. Menus are a historical user interface component that users expect to see and have access to.

In the Windows 95 environment, menus come in several varieties, each having a standard user interface appearance and behavior:

- A *menu bar* is a menu displayed horizontally across the top of the application window, directly below the title bar (see fig. 20.1).
- The menu bar consists of words called *menu titles*. Each menu title provides access to a drop-down menu.
- A *drop-down menu* consists of *menu items*. When the user selects a menu title, the menu displays the drop-down menu associated with that title.
- As the user drags the pointer over the menu items, the highlight bar moves to indicate the current choice. When the user clicks a menu item, the command associated with that menu item executes.
- If the menu item displays another submenu, it is called a *cascading menu*.

Menus items give users visual clues as to their purpose. A triangular arrow usually appears in the menu item to visually indicate that the menu item displays a cascading menu. Another visual clue used in menu items is the ellipsis (...) to indicate that the menu item needs further information before a command can be executed. For example, the F̲ormat, F̲ont command displays a dialog box of options rather than immediately performing an action. On the menu, three dots follow the F̲ont menu item text to let the user know that additional information is needed.

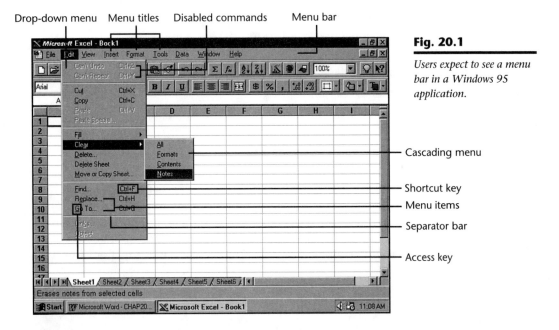

Fig. 20.1

Users expect to see a menu bar in a Windows 95 application.

TIP

Disable and gray out unavailable menu items rather than remove the menu item.

Other standard features of a Windows 95 menu bar include access keys to provide keyboard access to the menu, gray menu items to indicate unavailable commands, and graphics such as check marks and bullets to indicate selected features (toggle on/off). In addition, users expect to see:

■ Menu bars that conform to the Windows 95 and Office 95 standards.

■ F̲ile, E̲dit, V̲iew, W̲indow, and H̲elp menu titles wherever applicable.

■ On those drop-down menus, certain common commands such as P̲rint on the F̲ile menu, and C̲opy on the E̲dit menu.

TIP

Use separator lines to group common menu items together.

Here are some guidelines on defining menu items:

- Use the same text and access keys as Windows 95 and Office 95 whenever possible.
- Menu items can be text, graphics, or a combination of the two.
- Use unique item names within a menu.
- Keep the wording down to one or two words.
- Provide unique access keys.
- To determine upper- and lowercase, use book title capitalization rules.
- Use a consistent and clear font.
- Display shortcut keys next to menu item text and left align at the first tab position after the longest menu item text.
- List primary menu items first, followed by less frequently used commands (follow Windows 95 and Office 95 ordering whenever possible).

Another type of menu in Windows 95 is the *shortcut menu* (sometimes referred to as a *pop-up menu*). Shortcut menus appear at the pointer's current location and list commands relevant to the current object or current context (see fig. 20.2). Right-clicking an object displays the shortcut menu. Otherwise, shortcut menus appear and act the same as drop-down menus. Consider providing shortcut menus in situations where the user repeatedly chooses commands.

Fig. 20.2

Right-clicking a cell in Excel displays a context-sensitive shortcut menu.

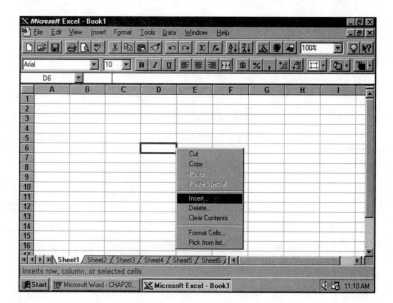

Providing Toolbars

In DOS-based or other linear programs, the menu is the core of the system. Users need to know the menu system in order to use the application. In graphical

Windows-based applications, users rely less on menus and more on objects such as buttons to activate commands when needed. Instead of hiding features in a menu tree, features are displayed in the context that they apply. For example, the Drawing toolbar appears by default in Word when the user creates or starts to work on a drawing object. User interface techniques such as ToolTips describe each button, and the What's This? feature provides context-sensitive help for each button.

Windows users have come to expect toolbars in applications. They provide easy access to commonly used commands. A *toolbar* is a panel that contains command button controls. Toolbars sometimes take on different shapes and names depending on their purpose. Some specialized toolbars include the following (see fig. 20.3):

- Toolbox
- Ruler
- Ribbon
- Palette

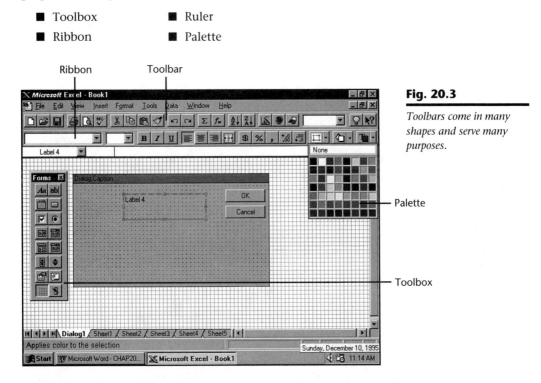

Ribbon   Toolbar

Fig. 20.3

Toolbars come in many shapes and serve many purposes.

Palette

Toolbox

Typically, toolbar buttons display a graphic called an *icon*, support keyboard access through shortcut keys or access keys, and display descriptive text as a ToolTip (preferred) or status bar text. You may optionally allow the user to move and reposition the toolbar. Buttons which are not available usually appear gray and are disabled. When buttons toggle a feature on and off, on is depicted as a pushed-in, sunken look. As with menus, custom toolbars should be consistent in appearance and behavior with Windows 95 and Office 95 whenever possible.

Automatically Invoking Commands

In some cases, you may prefer to automatically respond to a user's action and launch a command for the user. For example, suppose that in a video rental store, the clerk always prints the rental invoice for the customer to sign. Rather than making the clerk choose File, Print, Current Page or click the Print Current Page button, you could always print the rental invoice when the clerk finishes entering data. Similarly, you could track the progress of a task and present the user with a suggested command at the appropriate moment. A reminder to back up or update data would be examples of context-sensitive suggested commands. The "behind-the-scenes" backup and save features of Word allow the user to decide when automatic commands are completed.

As you build your application menus and toolbars, look for opportunities to attach a command to an event. Better yet, give the user the option (Tools, Options) to have certain commands automatically invoked in response to events, or only manually invoked.

Using the Office Shortcut Bar

A new feature in Office 95 is the Office Shortcut Bar (see fig. 20.4), which more than replaces the Office Manager toolbar. The Office Shortcut Bar runs as a separate application that provides easy access to programs and files. The Shortcut Bar appears as a toolbar which you can display along any border of the Desktop, or as a free-floating toolbox. The Office Shortcut Bar contains a collection of toolbars which you can customize, display, or hide. And each of these toolbars contains buttons which you can customize, display, or hide.

Fig. 20.4

The Office Shortcut Bar acts as a launchpad for programs and files.

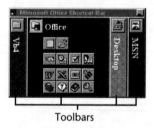

Toolbars

When planning your integrated Office application, consider creating a custom Office Shortcut toolbar to provide users with quick and easy access to your programs, their files, and common commands.

Customizing Menus

When creating custom menus for an integrated Office application, you need to plan the menu system and then decide on whether to use an interactive menu builder and/or create the menus from scratch in code. In several of the individual Office applications (Word, Excel, and Access) and in Visual Basic 4 (VB4), Microsoft provides interactive menu building editors to help you modify the existing built-in application menus and create your own custom menus. Although creating a menu from scratch in code gives you greater control, the interactive menu editors speed your development work and, by allowing you to see the "big picture," help you to better organize your menus.

Planning the Menu System

As always when planning, finalize the design on paper before starting to create the menu interactively or through code. When you begin to design the menu system for your application, consider the following issues:

- Is a menu the best way to provide this feature to the user? Would a dialog box or button be better?
- Can existing Office application menus be used, or do you need to build new custom menus from scratch?
- What are the menu titles?
- What features go on each pull-down menu?
- Are cascading menus needed?
- Can shortcut menus be used? If so, which menu items go on the shortcut menus?
- Will more than one program need to use the menu?
- How will the menus be integrated across applications?
- What menu building tools should be used?

Customizing Word Menus Interactively

Word provides an interactive method of customizing built-in menus and creating custom menus. You can change the organization, position, and content of default Word menus. To do so, follow these steps:

1. Choose Tools, Customize, or right-click the toolbar and choose Customize. The Customize dialog box appears.
2. Select the Menus tab (see fig. 20.5).
3. Select the category that contains the command you want to use.
4. In the Commands list, select the desired command.
5. To assign a command to another menu, select the menu name from the Change What Menu drop-down list box.
6. To change the position, select the position you want from the Position on Menu drop-down list box. (Select Auto if you want Word to position the menu item for you.)
7. To change the name of the menu item or the shortcut key, edit the text in the Name on Menu text box. Put an ampersand (**&**) before the key you want to designate as the shortcut key.

Fig. 20.5

Use the Menus tab of the Customize dialog box to modify existing menus and add new menus.

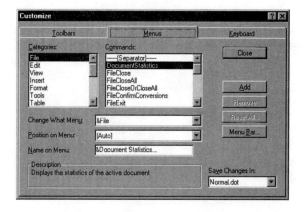

8. In the Save Changes In drop-down list, select the template in which you want to save the customized menu.

9. Click the Add button to add the selected command to the menu.

10. Click the Close button when you complete your changes.

In addition to modifying the built-in menus, you can add your own custom menus to Word's built-in menu bar. You could, for example, create a custom menu which lists the integrated Office reports that your programming automates for the user. To create custom menus in Word, follow these steps:

1. Choose Tools, Customize, or right-click the toolbar and choose Customize. The Customize dialog box appears.

2. Select the Menus tab.

3. Click the Menu Bar button. The Menu Bar dialog box appears (see fig. 20.6).

Fig. 20.6

By using the Menu Bar dialog box, you can add a new menu bar title.

4. In the Name on Menu Bar text box, type the name of the menu title. To assign a shortcut key, type an ampersand (&) in front of the letter you want underlined.

5. Select a position from the Position on Menu Bar list. The menu item appears before the item selected.

6. Click the Add button. The new menu title appears in the Change What Menu drop-down list box. Assign commands or macros as needed to populate the new drop-down menu.

TIP

If you accidentally save the changes to the incorrect template, choose Reset All to restore the default menus.

Customizing Excel Menus Interactively

In order to interactively customize Excel menus, you need to be in Module mode, on a module sheet. In Module mode, the Tools menu lists the Menu Editor as a menu item. The Menu Editor is an interactive program you can use to:

- Add or delete commands from built-in Excel menus
- Replace existing menu commands with your own commands
- Create custom menus
- Delete menus
- Attach custom menus to any built-in menu bar

NOTE

If you only want to add a few items to an existing menu, consider using the Menu Item on Tools Menu option in the Macro dialog box. Of course, to make a macro available all the time, store the macro in the Personal Macro Workbook (PERSONAL. XLS).

When you use the Menu Editor, keep in mind that the customized menus are stored in the current workbook. When you close this workbook, Excel reverts to the default menus. If you want the customized menu to always appear, use the Personal Macro Workbook (PERSONAL.XLS). For more information about the Personal Macro Workbook, search Excel's Help system for that topic.

To modify built-in Excel menus using the Menu Editor, follow these steps:

1. Switch to a module sheet.

2. Choose Tools, Menu Editor. The Menu Editor dialog box appears (see fig. 20.7).

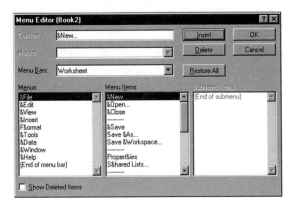

Fig. 20.7

Assign VBA procedures to menu and submenu items using the Menu Editor.

3. In the Menu **B**ars drop-down list box, select the desired built-in menu system.

4. In the M**e**nus list, select the menu to which you want to add a new menu bar item.

5. In the Menu I**t**ems list, select the name of the menu item before which you want to insert a new menu item. Or, if working on a submenu, select the name in the S**u**bmenu Items list before which you want to insert a new submenu item.

6. Click **I**nsert.

7. In the **C**aption text box, enter a name for the menu item. Use an ampersand (**&**) before the letter in the name that you want to designate as the access key.

8. In the **M**acro box, type or select a procedure name to execute when the user chooses this menu item. If the procedure resides in another workbook, provide the workbook name followed by an exclamation mark (!). For example:

   personal.xls!GetData

9. Repeat steps as needed to add more menu items.

10. Choose OK to save the customized menu.

TIP

To create a separator bar, type a single hyphen instead of a caption.

TIP

To edit an existing menu item, first delete the menu item, then add it back with your revisions.

To create custom menus for your application using the Menu Editor, follow these steps:

1. Open the Menu Editor.

2. In the Menu **B**ars list, select any one of the menu bars to clear the other selection areas.

3. Click the **I**nsert button. The **C**aption text box is enabled, and a blank menu is created.

4. In the **C**aption text box, enter a name for the new menu.

5. In the M**e**nus list box, select the [End of menu bar] item and click **I**nsert.

6. Enter the text for the menu bar item **C**aption.

7. In the Menu I**t**ems list box, select the [End of menu] item and click **I**nsert.

8. Enter the text for the menu item **C**aption and any **M**acro.

9. In the S**u**bmenu Items list box, select the [End of submenu] item and click **I**nsert.

10. Enter the text for the menu item **C**aption and any **M**acro.

11. Repeat steps 5–10 as needed to build the custom menu.

12. Choose OK to save the custom menu.

Customizing Access Menus Interactively

In Access, the Menu Builder is used to interactively customize the built-in Access menus, or create custom menus. By using the Menu Builder, you can create custom menus that replace the built-in menus in a form or report. Or, you can create a global menu bar that replaces the built-in menus in all Access windows (except in forms or reports that have their own custom menu bar).

NOTE If you want menu items to carry out actions other than the DoMenuItem, RunMacro, or RunCode actions, you must edit the macros created by the Menu Builder, or create them from scratch.

TIP To switch between built-in menu bars and a custom menu bar, press Ctrl+F11.

To create a custom menu bar for a form or report using the Menu Builder, follow these steps:

1. Switch to Form or Report Design view and open the form or report's property sheet.

2. In the property sheet, select the Other tab.

3. Click the MenuBar property and then click the Build button to the right of the property box. The Menu Builder wizards load, and prompt you to select a template from which to create the new menu (see fig. 20.8).

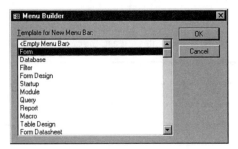

Fig. 20.8

Use a built-in Access menu as a template to speed your custom menu work.

4. In the Template for New Menu Bar box, select one of the built-in Access menus or <Empty Menu Bar> and choose OK. The Menu Builder dialog box appears (see fig. 20.9).

5. If working with built-in menu template, in the lower half of the window select a menu title, menu item, or submenu item to modify. Modify the Caption, Action, Argument(s), and Status Bar Text as needed.

6. If working on an empty menu bar, enter a Caption, Action, Argument(s), and Status Bar Text as desired, then click Next to add the menu item, and start working on the next item.

Fig. 20.9

The Access Menu Builder allows you to modify built-in Access menus, or create custom menus from blank templates.

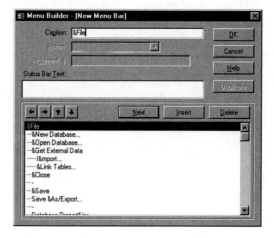

7. Use the buttons in the middle to indent or move the items shown in the lower half of the window.

8. If you need to delete a menu title, menu item, or submenu item, select the item and then click Delete.

9. Choose OK when finished, and save the form or report to save the customized menu.

NOTE The lower half of the Menu Builder window displays a menu as an indented list. The position of a menu caption in this list determines whether it's a menu title, menu item, or submenu item. Flush-left captions are menu titles. One level indent indicates the drop-down menu items. The second level indent indicates cascading submenus. A caption that only has one hyphen (-) indicates a separator bar.

TIP To make a copy of a custom menu bar, click Duplicate.

TIP If you haven't created all the procedures for your menu yet, create a temporary procedure that just displays a message box with the text `Menu choice not available yet`. This way, you can create your menu structure now and fill in the appropriate procedure names as they are completed.

To create a global menu bar that appears when a database or application opens, follow these steps:

1. Choose <u>T</u>ools, Star<u>t</u>up. The Startup dialog box appears (see fig. 20.10).

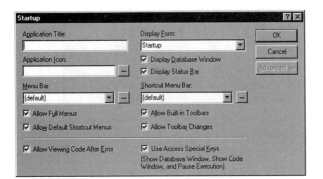

Fig. 20.10

Define global menus for a database using the Startup dialog box.

2. In the <u>M</u>enu Bar drop-down list box, select the name of a menu bar macro.

3. To create a custom menu bar using the Menu Builder, click the Build button next to the Menu Bar box.

4. Choose OK.

TIP

To prevent keyboard access to the built-in menu bars, click the <u>A</u>dvanced button and deselect the Use Access Special <u>K</u>eys checkbox.

Using the Visual Basic 4 Menu Editor

VB4 provides an interactive method of creating custom menus, too. The Menu Editor that comes with all three editions of VB4 allows you to build custom menus quickly and easily. Menus created with the Menu Editor are visible at design time, but no events are generated until you write code.

To create a menu bar using the VB4 Menu Editor, follow these steps:

1. Open the project and form for which you want to create a menu bar.

2. Choose <u>T</u>ools, <u>M</u>enu Editor. The Menu Editor window appears (see fig. 20.11).

3. In the <u>C</u>aption text box, type the menu item caption as you want it to appear on the menu bar. Type an ampersand (**&**) before the letter you want to specify as the access key. Type a single hyphen (-) to create a separator bar instead of a menu caption.

4. In the <u>N</u>ame text box, type a control name to refer to the menu item in code. This name can be identical to the caption.

5. Use the left and right arrows to change the level of a menu item (from a higher level to a lower level, or vice versa). VB4 supports up to four levels of submenus.

6. Use the up and down arrows to change the position of a menu item (up or down in the list box).

Fig. 20.11

The Menu Editor window in VB4 closely resembles the Access Menu Builder window.

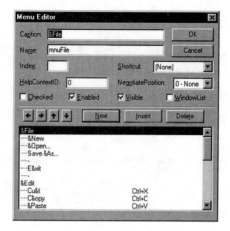

7. Click <u>N</u>ext to move to the next line and add another item to the menu.

8. Click <u>I</u>nsert to add a line before the currently selected line.

9. Click <u>D</u>elete to delete the currently selected line.

10. Repeat steps as needed to build the custom menu.

11. Choose OK when finished, and save the form to save your custom menu.

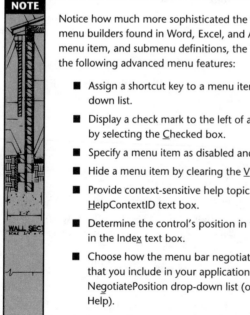

NOTE

Notice how much more sophisticated the VB4 Menu Editor is than the interactive menu builders found in Word, Excel, and Access. In addition to the basic menu title, menu item, and submenu definitions, the VB4 Menu Editor also allows you to define the following advanced menu features:

■ Assign a shortcut key to a menu item by selecting a key from the <u>S</u>hortcut drop-down list.

■ Display a check mark to the left of a menu item to indicate the item is activated by selecting the <u>C</u>hecked box.

■ Specify a menu item as disabled and grayed by clearing the <u>E</u>nabled box.

■ Hide a menu item by clearing the <u>V</u>isible box.

■ Provide context-sensitive help topics by entering a unique number in the <u>H</u>elpContextID text box.

■ Determine the control's position in the menu control array by typing a number in the Inde<u>x</u> text box.

■ Choose how the menu bar negotiates menu items from active applications that you include in your application through OLE by selecting a value from the NegotiatePosition drop-down list (only valid for menu titles such as File, Edit, or Help).

Creating Menus in Code

Just as the interactive methods of creating custom menus differ across Office applications, the coding methods differ across Office programming languages. In this section, you look at the basic menu creation commands in WordBasic, VBA, and VB4. Keep in mind that menus created interactively with one of the menu editors can be manipulated in code. For example, you can designate or change the global menu bar in a VBA procedure by setting the `MenuBar` property of the `Application` object.

Programming Menus in WordBasic

WordBasic provides many commands that allow you to customize existing built-in menus and create custom menus in code. The main menu manipulation commands are `ToolsCustomizeMenuBar`, `ToolsCustomizeMenus`, `MenuText$()`, `MenuItemText$()`, and `MenuItemMacro$()`.

The `ToolsCustomizeMenuBar` statement allows you to add, remove, or rename menu titles on the menu bar. The syntax provides arguments (see table 20.1) that you can use to customize built-in menus via code.

Table 20.1	*ToolsCustomizeMenuBar* Arguments
Argument	**Description**
Context	Specifies where a menu is stored. A zero or omitted context indicates the Normal template; 1 indicates the active template.
Position	Specifies where to add a new menu. Zero indicates the first, leftmost position; 1 the second; and so on. Use **-1** to indicate the rightmost position.
MenuType	Specifies which menu bar to modify. Zero or omitted indicates when a document is open; 1 indicates when no document is open.
MenuText	Specifies the menu caption.
Add	Adds the new menu specified in .MenuText.
Remove	Removes the specified menu.
Rename	Renames the specified menu.

In the following example, a new menu title named <u>R</u>eports is added to the right of the Help menu:

```
ToolsCustomizeMenuBar .MenuText = "&Reports", .Add, .Position = -1
```

The `ToolsCustomizeMenus` statement gives you access to the <u>M</u>enus tab of the Customize dialog box through code. Table 20.2 lists the syntax arguments available.

Table 20.2 *ToolsCustomizeMenus* Arguments	
Argument	**Description**
MenuType	Specifies the type of menu. Zero or omitted indicates an open document menu bar; 1 indicates no document open; 2 indicates shortcut menus.
Position	Specifies where to add a new menu. -1 or omitted automatically determines the position; -2 indicates the bottom; 1, 2, 3, and so on indicates the first, second, third, and so on item.
Category	Specifies the type of item to be assigned. 1 or omitted indicates Built-in commands; 2, Macros; 3, Fonts; 4, AutoText entries; 5, Styles.
Name	Specifies the caption name. Use **(Separator)** to add or remove a separator bar.
Menu	Specifies the Change What Menu list box menu name to be modified.
AddBelow	Specifies the name of the menu item after which you want to add a new item.
MenuText	Specifies the menu item caption.
Rename	Renames the specified menu item.
Add	Adds the specified menu item.
Remove	Removes the specified menu item.
ResetAll	Restores all default menus (reverses any changes made with ToolsCustomizeMenuBar and ToolsCustomizeMenus).
CommandValue	Specifies value of command specified in .Name, if any.
Context	Specifies where to save the modified menu. Zero or omitted indicates the Normal template; 1 specifies the active template.

The following example adds the macro GetData to the File menu. The menu item for this macro is Import, which appears immediately after Send. Because .AddBelow is specified, .Position is not required.

```
ToolsCustomizeMenus .Category = 2, .Name = "GetData", \
        .MenuType = 0, .Menu = "File", .MenuText = "&Import", \
        .AddBelow = "Send", .Context = 0, .Add
```

The other WordBasic menu commands return information about a current menu. MenuText$() returns the name of a shortcut menu or menu on the menu bar. MenuItemText$() returns the menu text associated with a macro or built-in command assigned to a menu. MenuItemMacro$() returns the name of the macro or built-in command associated with a menu item. Use these commands to determine the status of menus that you don't have control over.

TIP

For more information on the syntax and arguments, search Word's help system for the command names.

Programming Menus in VBA

Although the Excel and Access interactive menu editors make menu system creation easier, the interactive menu editors limit what you can do. For example, using an interactive menu editor, you can't

- Display menu item attributes, such as check marks
- Disable menu items at runtime in response to an event
- Change menus dynamically at runtime

Creating a menu in VBA consists of the following tasks:

- Add a new menu bar
- Add menu bar items
- Add commands to the menu
- Add submenus
- Display the new menu bar

The first step is to create the menu object which will contain your custom menu items. Use the Add method of the MenuBars object collection to create a new menu. The basic syntax is as follows, where *menuName* is the string value which names the menu:

```
MenuBars.Add menuName
```

Once the menu bar has been added, you can add menu titles. Use the Add method for the Menus object collection to define each of the menu titles on the menu bar. The syntax of this Add method has several parameters:

```
Menus.Add(Caption, [before], [restore])
```

The *Caption* is a string value which names the menu title. The optional before parameter specifies to insert this menu title prior to the named existing menu title. The optional restore parameter is set to True to restore any previously deleted built-in menu commands.

With the menu bar and menu title defined, you can now begin to build the drop-down menu of menu items. The MenuItems object collection has its own rendition of an Add method with the following syntax:

```
MenuItems.Add(caption,onAction,[shortCutKey],[before],[restore])
```

Only the *Caption* and *onAction* arguments must be provided; the remaining arguments are optional. The *Caption* is a string value that names the menu item. The *onAction* argument indicates the name of the procedure that executes when the user chooses this menu item. The shortCutKey argument applies only to Macintosh systems. The optional before and restore arguments work the same as in the Menus Add method.

If you need to build cascading submenus, use the `AddMenu` method of the `MenuItems` collection. The syntax is similar to the `Add` method, and only the caption argument is required:

```
MenuItems.AddMenu(caption, [before], [restore])
```

The `Activate` method of the `MenuBars` collection is used to display a menu. The syntax is as follows, where the *menuName* is the name of the menu bar:

```
MenuBars("menuName").Activate
```

You can also use the `Activate` method to display built-in menus. The following line displays the Excel built-in Worksheet menu:

```
MenuBars(xlWorksheet).Activate
```

The following example creates a menu bar, adds two menu bar commands, and populates both with several menu items:

```
Sub CreateMenu()
    MenuBars.Add Name:="Main"
    MenuBars("Main").Menus.Add Caption:="Orders"
    MenuBars("Main").Menus.Add Caption:="Financial"

    'Now define the menu items on Orders
    MenuBars("Main").Menus("Orders").MenuItems.Add _
        Caption:="Get Orders", _
        OnAction:="GetOrders"
    MenuBars("Main").Menus("Orders").MenuItems.Add _
        Caption:="Print", _
        OnAction:="PrintPage"

    'Now define the menu items on Financial
    MenuBars("Main").Menus("Financial").MenuItems.Add _
        Caption:="Calculate Pay", _
        OnAction:="CalcPay"
    MenuBars("Main").Menus("Financial").MenuItems.Add _
        Caption:="Annuity", _
        OnAction:="Investor"

    'Now display the custom menu named Main.
    Application.MenuBars("Main").Activate
End Sub
```

Several other VBA menu-related methods are handy. You can use the `Reset` method to restore a built-in menu bar and all of its menu items. To remove a menu from memory (always a good idea when you're done using a custom menu), use the `Delete` method. You can also use the `Delete` method to delete a specific menu item. The `Enabled` property can be used to enable (=`True`) or disable (=`False`) menu items and control accessibility of menus at runtime. In the following example, the Import menu option is temporarily disabled:

```
MenuBars("Connect").Menus("&File").MenuItems("&Import").Enabled = False
```

Similarly, you can change the `Checked` property of a menu item at runtime to reflect the status of a menu item as selected or not. In this example, the Import menu item is checked (=True):

```
MenuBars("Connect").Menus("&File").MenuItems("&Import").Checked = True
```

Programming VB4 Menus

In VB4, the tedious process of creating the menu system structure is performed by the Menu Editor. When you close the Menu Editor, VB4 applies all changes to the last form you selected. The menu you created is available at design time, but selecting a menu at design time opens the code window for that menu's `Click` event rather than executing any event code. This is where you automate your menu items. Figure 20.12 shows the `Click` event for the Settings, Font Sizes menu item. This code example is from the TEXTEDIT.VBP sample application that comes with VB4 (located in \SAMPLES\MENUS).

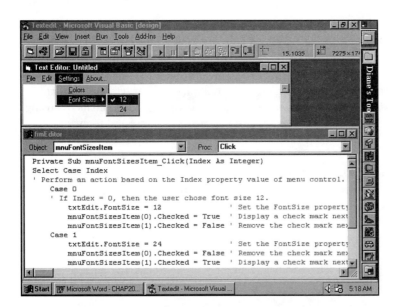

Fig. 20.12

In VB4, you add code to each menu item event.

Notice in figure 20.12 that an index is used to determine if font size 12 or 24 was chosen. When this menu item was created in the Menu Editor, a unique index value was entered into the Index property box. Furthermore, the object name `mnuFontSizesItem` was entered into the Name property box for both menu items. Assigning index values to menu items that share the same object name creates a menu control array. A *menu control array* is a set of menu items on the same menu that share the same name and event procedures.

Menu control arrays simplify code by allowing you to use common code blocks for multiple menu items. You can also use a control array to dynamically add or delete menu items in the array at runtime (use Load and Unload). Note, however, that at runtime you cannot remove commands created at designtime.

To add or delete menu items in a control array at runtime:

1. Create a menu control array.

2. Open the code window by double-clicking a control or the form itself.

3. Go to the event or procedure where you want to load or unload members of the control array, and write code within that procedure to load or unload the items at runtime.

Menus created at design time can be changed at runtime by changing property values. As with VBA, you can display check marks, enable/disable menu items, change the menu item caption, and make menu items invisible. The following code lines provide examples of setting properties at runtime:

```
mnuFontSizesItem(0).Checked = True
mnuFontSizesItem(1).Caption = "Font Size 24"
mnuFontSizesItem(0).Visible = False
mnuFontSizesItem(1).Enabled = True
```

Creating Custom Toolbars

The methods of creating custom toolbars across the Office applications are much more consistent than creating custom menus. Each application provides an interactive method of modifying the built-in toolbars and creating custom toolbars. By using WordBasic, VBA, and VB4, you can automate the toolbars and respond to events at runtime.

Customizing Toolbars Interactively

You can customize any of the built-in toolbars to better meet your needs. Modifying the existing toolbars to meet your application's needs helps you maintain consistency and speeds your application development.

To customize a built-in toolbar, follow these steps:

1. Choose View, Toolbars. The Toolbars dialog box appears (see fig. 20.13).

Fig. 20.13

The Toolbars dialog box enables you to customize the view and contents of toolbars.

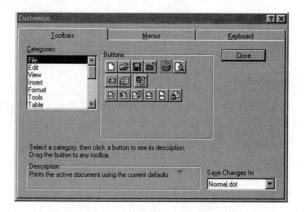

TIP To quickly customize toolbars, right-click a blank area of any toolbar and select Customize from the shortcut menu.

2. Click the Customize button. The Customize dialog box appears. In PowerPoint and Access, this is called the Customize Toolbars dialog box.

3. To add items to a built-in toolbar, click the category that contains the buttons or other items you want to add.

4. Drag the buttons or items you want from the Buttons section to the toolbar.

5. To remove items from the toolbar, drag the buttons or items off the toolbar.

6. To move buttons or items, drag them to a new location on the same toolbar or to a different toolbar.

7. Click Close to close the Customize dialog box.

In addition to modifying the default toolbars of Office applications, you can create custom toolbars that contain built-in buttons, or buttons which launch procedures.

To create a custom toolbar, follow these steps:

1. Display the Toolbars dialog box.

2. In Excel, enter a name for the toolbar in the Toolbar Name text box (doing so enables the New button), and click the New button.

   In Access and PowerPoint, click the New button to display the New Toolbar dialog box. Type a name for the toolbar in the Toolbar Name text box and choose OK.

   In Word, click the New button to display the New Toolbar dialog box. Type a name for the toolbar in the Toolbar Name text box. Select the template in which you want to store the toolbar from the Make Toolbar Available To drop-down list and choose OK.

   The Customize dialog box appears, along with the new (empty) toolbar.

3. Select the category that contains the buttons or other items you want to add to the new toolbar.

4. Drag the buttons or items you want from the Buttons section to the new toolbar.

5. Repeat steps 3 and 4 until you fill your custom toolbar with the features you want (the toolbar expands to accommodate your selections).

6. Click the Close button to close the Customize dialog box.

Programming Toolbars

WordBasic, VBA, and VB4 provide many commands that allow you to manipulate toolbar buttons and toolbars at runtime. Although it's easiest to create the basic toolbar interactively, the statements and commands allow you to respond to events at runtime and modify the toolbars to reflect runtime conditions.

Working in WordBasic. In WordBasic, you can add, delete, and move buttons on a toolbar using the AddButton, MoveButton, and DeleteButton statements, respectively. In the following example, the button at position 11 on the Formatting toolbar is replaced with button image 80. The built-in command assigned to the button is Color, which requires that an additional value be specified (in this case, 2 for the color blue):

```
DeleteButton "Formatting", 11, 0
AddButton "Formatting", 11, 1, "Color", 80, 0, "2"
```

WordBasic also provides code access to button images. You can use ChooseButtonImage, EditButtonImage, PasteButtonImage, and CopyButtonImage to manipulate button images at runtime. For the exact sytax and list of built-in button images, search Help for the topic **Toolbar Button Images and Numbers**. The following example changes the image on the Stop button on the Macro toolbar to button image 50:

```
ChooseButtonImage .Face = 50, .Button = 9, .Context = 0, \
        .Toolbar = "Macro"
```

You can even create a new toolbar in WordBasic by using the NewToolbar statement. The syntax of NewToolbar takes two basic arguments:

```
NewToolbar .Name = text [, .Context = number]
```

The .Name argument specifies a name for the new toolbar (spaces are allowed). The .Context argument specifies the template in which you want to store the toolbar. If .Context is set to zero or omitted, the toolbar is stored in the Normal template, and the toolbar always appears in the Toolbars dialog box (View menu). If .Context is set to 1, the toolbar is stored in the active template, and the toolbar only appears in the Toolbars dialog box when the template is active.

Working in VBA. In VBA, you use Toolbar objects and collections to create and manipulate toolbars. Using VBA you can

- Create new toolbars
- Add buttons to toolbars
- Hide, move, and delete toolbar buttons
- Reset toolbars

To create a new toolbar in VBA code, use the Add method of the Toolbars object collection. The syntax is as follows, where *toolbarName* is a string that is used to refer to the toolbar:

```
Toolbars.Add toolbarName
```

Use the Add method of the ToolbarButtons object to add buttons to an existing toolbar. The syntax of this Add method is as follows:

```
ToolbarButtons.Add(button,before,onAction,pushed,enabled)
```

The *button* argument is a numeric or string value that represents the name of the button. The optional `before` argument indicates which button to insert the new button before (if not listed, the new button is added at the end of the toolbar). The `onAction` argument specifies the name of the procedure to execute when the button is clicked. The `pushed` argument is a Boolean value that indicates that the button is pushed in (True) or popped out (False, the default setting). `Enabled` is a Boolean value that indicates whether the button is available (True, the default setting) or not available (False).

To display the toolbar, set the `Visible` property of the toolbar to True:

```
Toolbars(toolbarName).Visible = True
```

 TIP
To change the ToolTips for a button, change the text of the `Name` property.

The following example creates a new toolbar named Reports and adds a button to import data:

```
'Create the toolbar object.
tlbReport = "Reports"
Toolbars.Add tlbReport
'Add a button
Toolbars(tlbReport).ToolbarButtons.Add _
    button:= 225, _
    before:= 1, _
    onAction:= "ImportProc"
'Display the toolbar.
Toolbars(tlbReport).Visible = True
```

By using VBA, you can control many aspects of built-in and custom toolbars at runtime:

- Set the toolbar size and position
- Change the appearance of buttons
- Delete and reset toolbars

Use the `Height`, `Width`, and `Position` properties to determine and control the size and location of the toolbar. Height and Row values are measured in points from the top-left corner of the application window. The `Position` property can be set to any of the following Excel constants: `xlTop`, `xlBottom`, `xlRight`, `xlLeft`, or `xlFloating`. Here are some examples:

```
Toolbar.Height = 10
Toolbar.Width = 40
Toolbar.Position = xlFloating
```

To change the appearance of buttons, use one of the following methods/properties:

Method/Property	Description
Edit	A method that displays the Button Image Editor.
CopyFace	A method that copies the bitmap image from a toolbar button to the Clipboard.
PasteFace	A method that copies a bitmap image from the Clipboard to a toolbar button.
BuiltInFace	A property that, when set to True, removes any custom image and displays the default built-in image on the button.
LargeButtons	A property of the Application object that, when set to True, displays larger sized toolbar buttons.

You can use the Delete method to delete an entire custom toolbar or to remove specific buttons. In the following example, the second button is deleted from the Reports toolbar:

```
Toolbars("Reports").ToolbarButtons(2).Delete
```

Use the Reset method of the Toolbars collection to restore built-in toolbars. In the following example, the Standard toolbar in Excel is restored to the default settings:

```
Toolbars("Standard").Reset
```

Working in VB4. In VB4, you create toolbars manually by placing a picture box on the MDI form. The width of the picture box automatically stretches to fill the width of the form's internal area. Inside the picture box, you can then populate the picture box with any controls (such as buttons) that you want to appear on the toolbar. Set control properties such as Picture and Enabled. Then attach code to the button's click event (such as a procedure call). As in VBA, you can change toolbars at runtime by setting properties and using toolbar methods.

Alternatively, you can use the Toolbar control (a custom control found in COMCTL32.OCX) to create and maintain toolbars. The Toolbar control allows you to create toolbars by adding Button objects to a Buttons collection; each Button object can have optional text and/or an image, supplied by an associated ImageList control. For each Button object, you can specify text with the Caption property, and an image with the Image property. At design time, you can add Button objects to the control with the Toolbar Control Properties dialog box. At runtime, you can add or remove buttons from the Buttons collection using Add and Remove methods.

NOTE   The Toolbar control is a 32-bit custom control that can only run on 32-bit systems such as Windows 95 and Windows NT version 3.51 or higher. To use the Toolbar control in your application, you must add the COMCTL32.OCX file to the project. When distributing your application, install the COMCTL32.OCX file in the user's Windows SYSTEM directory.

To program the toolbar, the `ButtonClick` event allows individual `Button` objects to respond to the user's actions. You can also determine the behavior and appearance of each `Button` object by using the `Style` property. You can place another control on a toolbar by assigning a `Button` object the PlaceHolder style. Double-clicking a toolbar at runtime invokes the Customize Toolbar dialog box, which allows the user to hide, display, or rearrange toolbar buttons. To enable or disable the dialog box, use the `AllowCustomize` property. You can also invoke the Customize Toolbar dialog box by using the `Customize` method. If you want to save and restore the state of a toolbar, or allow the user to do so, two methods are provided: `SaveToolbar` and `RestoreToolbar`. The `Change` event, generated when a toolbar is altered, is typically used to invoke the `SaveToolbar` method.

A real time-saver is the `ToolTipText` descriptions of each `Button` object. To display ToolTips, the `ShowTips` property must be set to True. Note that when buttons are selected in the Customize Toolbar dialog box, the text entered into the `Description` property appears (not the ToolTips text). For more information on the Toolbar control, search the VB4 Help system for the topic **Toolbar Control**.

From Here...

This chapter examined how the graphical nature of Windows 95 and Office 95 governs the user interface design of your integrated Office application. You learned how to put the user in command by providing menus, toolbars, and shortcuts. You customized the existing menu and toolbar systems in the Office 95 applications. You also learned how to program custom menus and toolbars.

If you would like to learn more about creating custom menus and toolbars, you can find more information on related topics in the following chapters:

- The better you know Windows 95 and the Office applications, the easier it will be to build a powerful integrated Office application; see Chapter 2, "Windows and Office Capabilities."

- In addition to menus and toolbars, Office applications need to have a consistent user interface in other areas; see Chapter 18, "Designing the User Interface."

- Providing users with a Help system reduces the number of support calls you'll have to answer; see Chapter 21, "Providing Help for Users."

Providing Help for Users

The main purpose of any Windows 95 Help system is to give users quick access to specific information. In many of the commercial software applications being developed for Windows 95, an online help system has replaced some or all of the volumes of hard copy documentation that used to come in the box. It presents the information to the users on-screen, instead of in a printed manual.

Help files offer several advantages over hard copy documentation. Help files are in a compact electronic format. They typically contain links between different topics; jumping among these on-screen topics is generally faster than flipping through the pages of a software manual. Unlike a hard copy document, help files can also contain audio, video, and graphic objects that enhance and reinforce what the user is learning.

By using some simple tools, you can take advantage of Windows 95 help capabilities and create online Help for any Office application you develop. Including your own help file will give your application a more professional look and feel. At the same time, you give the user a robust and specific resource for information about your custom application. In addition, the help file is likely to be superior to—and less expensive to distribute than—any hard copy manual you could create.

This chapter introduces you to the new Windows 95 Help system features that have transformed Help into a more complete system for providing information to users. Because the Microsoft Office suite of applications fully supports the Windows 95 Help system features, creating online help files for your Office applications will reduce the hard copy documentation and technical support you'll need to provide to end users. As you read on, you learn how simple it is to integrate Help into your Office applications.

In this chapter, you learn about

- The anatomy of a Help file
- Creating and organizing a Help file
- The different tools available for creating Help files
- Using RoboHELP, a third-party product, to create a Help file
- Integrating Help files into Office Applications

Introducing Windows 95 Help

Online help systems provide a simple and effective way for users to obtain help about the software they are using. Today, online help systems are vastly different from their simple-text ancestors.

Even in Windows 3.1x, the online Help system was *context-sensitive*, and it still is in Windows 95. Context-sensitive help means that the user can receive help directly based on the context of the feature or dialog box presently on-screen. To access context-sensitive help, users click a button in the active window or press a special key such as F1 (or even a special keystroke combination like Shift+F1). Then, Help opens to the topic that directly relates to the operation at hand. No searching or guessing—Windows presents the correct information to the user with one keypress or mouse click.

Help in Windows 95 is context-sensitive, but provides even more features and more types of help. In addition to navigating through the Help Contents, users can view an index and even search through the entire Help file for a specific word or phrase. See the next section, "Using Windows 95 Enhanced Help Capabilities," for more about new Help features.

What does all this mean for you as a developer? Perhaps the most significant lesson is that users will become increasingly accustomed to seeking help on-screen rather than on paper. While you may not be able to incorporate all the Windows 95 Help features in the Office applications you create, users will come to expect some kind of customized online help. Thus, you can and should incorporate online help in applications you create whenever possible.

Using Windows 95 Enhanced Help Capabilities

Windows 95 Help offers many improvements over Help from previous Windows versions. The most visible enhancement, of course, is the way the Windows 95 Help applications look when you run them. For example, figures 21.1 and 21.2 compare the Help Contents window for Windows for Workgroups (Windows 3.1x) and the Help Contents tab for Windows 95.

In addition to the changes in the way Help looks in Windows 95, the Help system has been enhanced in a number of other ways. These major enhancements make Windows 95 Help more useful than ever for end users:

- *More ways to access Help.* In addition to accessing Help through Help menus and pressing F1, in Windows 95, Help is available directly from the Start menu.

- *Contents improvements.* In the Windows 95 Contents tab, the user can expand and collapse subject areas preceded by book icons to navigate to specific topics. This is very similar to the way users can navigate through folders in the Windows 95 Explorer. The Windows 3.1x Help Contents page, in contrast, only displays a limited number of topics and serves more as an opening screen. The Windows 95 Help Contents tab enables the reader to find the desired subject much more quickly.

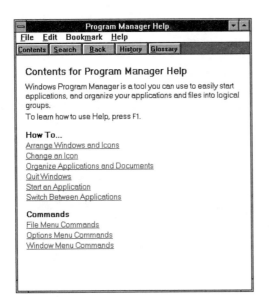

Fig. 21.1

A Help Contents window when designed to run on Windows 3.1.

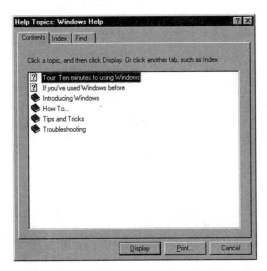

Fig. 21.2

A Help Contents tab when designed to run on Windows 95.

■ *Tabbed pages.* Gone are the Windows 3.1x Help Contents and Search buttons. In Windows 95 Help, they are replaced with Contents, Index, and Find tabbed pages. Many dialog boxes in Windows 95 now include the new tabbed pages. These tabs make switching between pages of settings as simple as clicking on the tab.

■ *Options menu.* This replaces the History button from Windows 3.1x Help, and adds many new features to Windows 95 Help, such as the capability to adjust the font size used in the Help window. (These features are covered in detail later in this chapter.) This menu is only available in a topic window, not from the Help Topics window.

- *Jump buttons and shortcuts.* To jump from topic to topic in Help, you now click well-defined buttons rather than search for highlighted words. Some buttons embedded in Help files are shortcuts that can launch other applications (like Paint) or open a dialog box (such as a properties sheet).

- *Improved searching on the Find tab.* The Windows 95 Find tab provides several ways for you to narrow your search for a particular topic (and therefore find the help you need more quickly). For example, unlike the Search feature in Windows 3.1x Help, the Find tab lets you specify whether Help should also find terms that are similar to the terms you specify.

- *Dialog box Help.* Many applications developed in the last few years display a shortcut menu of options when you right-click an on-screen element. Similarly, in Windows 95, you can right-click dialog box items to display pop-up Help with information about that dialog box option. (Right-clicking in some applications may display a <u>W</u>hat's This? command that you need to click to display the pop-up Help.) Most dialog boxes also offer a question mark button in the upper-right corner. Clicking this icon followed by clicking a feature in the dialog box also displays a pop-up Help window.

- *Multimedia.* In addition to the text Help Windows 3.1x users are familiar with, Help files in Windows 95 can include graphic, sound, and video files.

- *Full text formatting.* In Windows 95, you can format Help file contents using just about every font, size, color, and style available. (Under earlier versions of Windows, you were limited in the formatting you could use.)

Online Help Files

If you decide that your application warrants the creation of an online help system, your first step in creating one is to understand what an online help file is. A Help file is actually just a compiled program. Just as in many other programming languages, to create a Help file, you develop source code which a compiler program uses to create an executable program file that your computer understands. Compiled Help files have the HLP file name extension.

Most Help files are launched from within a Windows application (such as any Office application), but they don't have to be. A Windows Help file behaves just like a normal executable (EXE) application. To start a Help file to display the online help it contains on-screen, you can double-click the file name or icon anywhere in Windows.

In reality, Help files only *behave* like real programs. They are actually controlled by a program called WINHLP32.EXE. When you double-click to start the Help (HLP) file or use a command that launches Help from an application, WINHLP32.EXE launches first and in turn opens the HLP file. When you launch a Windows 3.1x Help file, the WINHELP.EXE program opens first. WINHELP.EXE is provided with Windows 95 to maintain backwards compatibility with Windows 3.1x.

Because Help files can be started from anywhere in Windows, you may want to include more than one Help file with your application. For example, you could include one Help file that a user can call from within an application and another as a stand-alone program. This stand-alone Help file could offer some additional reference material or troubleshooting hints. You may even want to create a Help file that contains your application's release notes (version number, planned improvements, and so on).

In Windows 95, the icons representing Help files are easy to distinguish from other files. For Windows 3.1x Help files, the default icon is a white page with a yellow question mark. For Windows 95 Help files, the default icon is a three-dimensional purple book with a yellow question mark on it (see fig. 21.3).

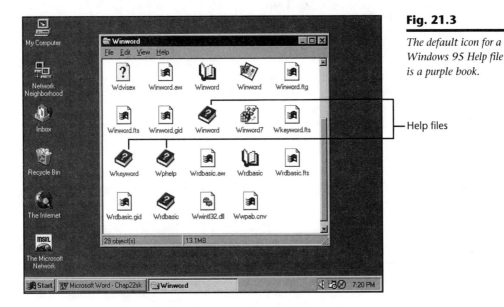

Fig. 21.3

The default icon for a Windows 95 Help file is a purple book.

Help files

Windows 3.1x and Windows 95 Help File Compatibility

The Windows 95 Help system is completely backwards-compatible. Any Help file written for previous versions of Windows will work in Windows 95. However, Windows 95 Help files compiled with the new HCW.EXE Help compiler do not work in previous versions of Windows. You can still use older Help compilers (HCP.EXE, HC31.EXE, and HC.EXE) to create Help files for use with Windows 95; however, you won't be able to include the new Windows 95 features in those Help files.

Deciding What Kind of Help To Provide

Even a basic Help file greatly enhances an application's usability and professional appearance. However, creating a full-blown Help application using many of the advanced Help features may not be necessary in every situation. Let your common sense guide you in deciding how much help to provide for your users, and consider factors like those described next.

For starters, always keep your intended audience in mind. What's the typical user's level of experience—novice, intermediate, or advanced? If the typical user isn't familiar with Windows 95 applications, you may need to include step-by-step instructions for all the features of your application. On the other hand, more advanced end users may need only reference material, such as information about the formulas used in an Excel application.

You should also consider time and resources in planning to provide online help. Creating even a simple Help file does take time, and it's not necessarily realistic to believe that you'll have time to create online help every time you create an application. If you have the time to include the help in the application, by all means do so. However, if you're under severe time pressure, you may have to complete the application first and later provide Help in hard-copy form.

Finally, the complexity of the application should also drive your decision about how much help to include, and what form it should take. For example, for simple applications, users may only need installation information. In such a case where the user's information need is limited, another option is to include a text (TXT) Help file on the disk with your application. Many commercial applications include such a file, typically named README.TXT or README.1ST. Keep in mind that text files provide no formatting capabilities (fonts, styles, colors, and so on). Text files do work, but are not very pretty. If you find yourself in a bind and just don't have the time to create a Help file or if the user only needs a limited amount of information, use your word processor to create a Help file, making sure to save it in plain-text format rather than in the word processor format.

TIP

As you create the application, simultaneously collect the information you need for the Help file. Then, when you complete your application, you should only need to compile the Help file.

Understanding the Anatomy of a Windows 95 Help Application

When you open the Help file for Windows 95, you'll notice three tabs (see fig. 21.4): Contents, Index, and Find. Each of the three tabs enables you to use a different technique to access Help information. Since the Help files you'll be creating will take advantage of many of the same features contained in Windows 95 Help, it pays to take the time to review and understand Help file features and how they interrelate. This knowledge is vital as you begin planning and developing your own Help files. The following sections introduce you to the primary Help features and how they work.

Fig. 21.4

The three tabs provide different ways to find the Help information.

Listing the Contents

The Contents tab displays the contents of the Help file in a graphical tree. You'll learn later in this chapter how to create your own Contents page, but to do so, you need to understand how to navigate through one. Closed purple book icons indicate a branch holding Help *topics*. Double-clicking a closed book icon changes it to an open book icon and displays the topics it contains (see fig. 21.5). There can be additional books holding more topics located within each book. A user can continue double-clicking to open books until the desired topic page is displayed in the list.

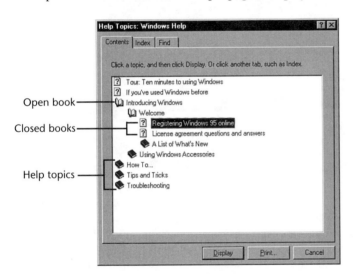

Open book

Closed books

Help topics

Fig. 21.5

The Contents tab enables users to navigate to a Help topic by double-clicking through the hierarchy of book icons.

An icon that looks like a page with a blue question mark represents a Help topic, which is analogous to a page from the open book. Each topic (page) contains information on a specific section or element of a program. Double-clicking a topic icon, or selecting it by clicking it and then clicking Display, opens a window with the topic text.

NOTE The Contents tab information is actually contained in a file that is compiled and kept separate from the main Help file. The Contents tab file has a CNT extension, and if located in the same directory as the Help file, it will be used automatically. The icon for a CNT file is an open, three-dimensional, purple book.

Using the Index

The Index tab works exactly the same way as the Search button does in Windows 3.1x Help. Clicking the Index tab moves it to the front of the window and places the insertion point in the first text box (see fig. 21.6). Type in the word or phrase to search for. As you enter each letter, the bottom list dynamically changes to display a list of topics that match the character(s) you have entered. Once you locate the topic you want to view, you can either double-click the topic in the lower list, or click it once and then click the Display button.

Fig. 21.6

The Index tab lets you search for a specific topic.

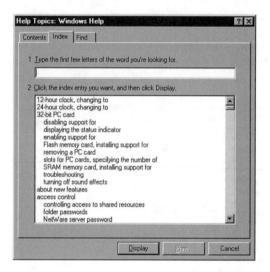

Finding Information

The Find tab enables you to search for any word or phrase in a Help topic name. This differs from the Windows 3.1x Help Index search, which only searches through the first word of each topic. The first time you click the Find tab in any Help file, the Find Setup Wizard dialog box opens (see fig. 21.7). It offers options to determine how you will be using the Find tab. Selecting Minimize Database Size means that Find will search through a list of just the major topics in the Help file. Selecting Maximize Search Capabilities creates a database (it takes a few minutes) that lets you use the Find tab to

■ Search for topics that don't have titles (like pop ups)

■ Search for complete phrases

■ Match phrases as you type in characters

■ Mark topics, enabling you to search for additional related information

Fig. 21.7

Selecting the Find tab for the first time will let you choose the search method.

TIP

The Options button on the Find tab offers settings Help uses when searching through the Help file. For example, you can change *when* Help begins to search for the words you type in. By default, Help will search through the Help file as you type the words in. You can tell Help to wait until you click the Find Now button to begin the search.

Selecting Customize Search Capabilities lets you pick and choose which of the previous Maximize options to enable. No matter which option you choose from the first wizard screen, work through the wizard by specifying options and then clicking the Next button.

Then, when you click the Finish button, Help automatically generates a database using the selected criteria. Help stores the database file in the same folder the Help file was launched from. The database filename extensions are GID and FTS. Once the database has been created, the Find tab is displayed (see fig. 21.8). Type the word or phrase to search for in the first text box. The other options change to match the character(s) typed. Clicking words in the middle text box narrows the search and changes the list of topics in the bottom list. To view a topic, click it in the bottom list box and click the Display button.

Understanding Help Topics

As mentioned earlier, a Help topic contains a specific portion of information in the Help file (see fig. 21.9). If the window isn't large enough to display the full text of the topic, a scroll bar appears along the right side of the topic window. Notice that the Help topic window offers buttons at the top to enable you to return to the main Help Topics window, and more.

Clicking some buttons in the topic text opens a secondary window in front of the topic window, displaying additional information (see fig. 21.10). *Secondary windows* provide even more specific information than the main window does. The text is normally short and to the point. It's easy to tell a secondary window apart from the main window, as the secondary window does not have the three command buttons at the top.

Fig. 21.8

The Find tab lets you search for a specific word or phrase in a Help file.

Fig. 21.9

The Help topic is like a page in a book, offering a specific portion of information.

Finally, when you click a green term with a dotted underline in a Help topic window, a pop-up description appears. This pop up is simply a box; it doesn't have any window features or buttons.

Options Button

When you click the Options button in a Help topic window, a menu providing many useful functions appears. Depending on how the Help file is created, some or all of the functions described in table 21.1 may be available.

Fig. 21.10

Secondary windows contain very specific information on a topic.

Table 21.1	Functions Available in the Options Menu
Menu Item	**Description**
Annotate	Enables the user to add notes and comments to the current topic. When a topic has annotations added, a small paper clip icon appears in its upper-left corner.
Copy	To copy a specific portion of the topic window text, highlight the text you want to copy (just as in a word processor), then choose Options, Copy.
Print Topic	Prints the entire topic. However, the contents of any related topics or pop ups will not be printed.
Font	You can change the size of the font used to display the text in the topic window by choosing Small, Medium, or Large. This will change the font size in the entire Help file display, not just in that topic.
Keep Help on Top	Help windows always appear on top of any other open windows. Even if you click a window behind it, the Help window stays on top. This is useful for simultaneously following the step-by-step directions given in a Help file, and working in an application.
Use System Colors	Changes the Help system display colors to the color scheme set in the Control Panel.

TIP

Right-clicking anywhere in a topic window displays a shortcut menu offering the same commands that are on the Options menu.

Working with Help File Navigational Tools

The following features, many of which were touched on in the preceding section, are the heart and soul of any Windows 95 Help file you create. They are the navigational tools you will incorporate in your Help application to enable the user to find the information. You include these tools within each Help topic window, giving the user many different ways to maneuver to other areas of the Help file. In essence, you will be creating *hypertext links*. Each link points to another area of the Help file; selecting a link enables the user to move directly to that area of the Help file (in a non-linear method). Read the next several paragraphs to learn more about these navigational tools.

Jumping Among Topics

A *jump tool* does just what it says. Clicking it "jumps" the user from one topic to another. In a compiled help file, a jump can be indicated by green text that has a solid underline (this is typical in Windows 3.1x Help files). The Help for Windows 95 offers three-dimensional buttons for the jumps (see fig. 21.11).

Fig. 21.11

Clicking a three-dimensional button or green text with a solid underline displays another topic.

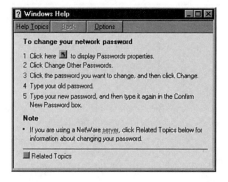

Understanding Pop Ups

A *pop up* is also self-explanatory. Clicking pop-up text, which is green with a dotted underline, pops up a second window in front of the first displaying even more specific information (see fig. 21.12). Pop ups work like a light switch. The text you click to display a pop up is the on switch. Once displayed, clicking anywhere will turn the pop up off.

Helping with Hotspots

A *hotspot* is a predefined area of a graphic image included in a Help file. Clicking a hotspot can activate either a jump or a pop up. As the user moves the mouse pointer around the graphic, the mouse pointer changes to a hand to indicate when a hotspot area is directly under the pointer. If the user clicks there, the hotspot will be activated.

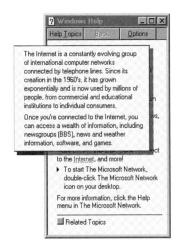

Fig. 21.12

Clicking text with a dotted underline pops up a small Help window.

Hotspots are very useful when used in an illustration or diagram graphic included in Help. For example, in the main Help Topics screen of Windows 95 Help, you could click the If You've Used Windows Before topic in the Contents tab to display a Help window that includes a graphic of the Windows Desktop. Clicking that Desktop image displays a pop-up message.

Graphic images that contain hotspots are called *hypergraphics*. A program called SHED.EXE can be used to create a hypergraphic. SHED.EXE lets you define hotspots in a BMP graphic and convert it into a format that the Help system can recognize. SHED.EXE displays the BMP graphic and lets you draw boxes on it as you would draw on a picture in a painting program. These boxes become the hotspots and can be sized and positioned as needed anywhere on the graphic. There is also no limit to the amount of hotspots a single graphic can contain. When you finish, SHED.EXE saves the hotspot graphic with a file extension of SHG. (SHED.EXE is available in the **WINSDK** forum on CompuServe as well as most other online services.)

Using Shortcuts

Shortcut buttons are new to Windows 95 Help. Each shortcut button in a Help topic has a small curved arrow. Clicking a shortcut button activates a specific command in the application or launches another program. In the example shown in figure 21.13, clicking the shortcut button opens the Multimedia Properties sheet. Shortcuts in Help files save both the user and the creator of the Help file many unnecessary steps. The user gets to perform an action immediately, rather than first reading about the steps, trying to remember them, then performing the required steps. You as the creator of the Help file do not have to write the steps to tell the reader how to get to the location the shortcut represents.

Fig. 21.13

Clicking the shortcut button takes the user to a specific part of a program or launches another program.

Shortcut button

Multimedia in Help Files

In previous years, Help in computer programs was nothing more than a text file users could open in a text editor and read. Since the introduction and acceptance of Windows, Help files have evolved into a key component of any Windows program. They assist, and in many cases visually guide, the user through using the program. For example, "screen cameras" programs record screen movements—mouse actions, menu selections, and everything else that happens on-screen—and save the sequence in an AVI file that can be replayed from within a Help file. Now with Windows 95 and the added support for the inclusion of these multimedia files and others, Help and guidance for the user has reached a new and exciting level.

Any multimedia object can be incorporated into a Help file to enhance and improve upon its capability to teach. Sounds, video, animation, and even still graphics and pictures are all part of multimedia and, when used, can create a more comprehensive learning experience.

The multimedia objects become part of the Help file, so you won't have to send a plethora of files along with each Help application. With Windows 95 help, the capability to play back the multimedia files is now part of the Windows 95 system. (In contrast, Windows 3.1x requires that the user have other special applications to play back sounds, video, and so on.) This ensures that the user will have the ability to play the multimedia Help without difficulty.

 TIP

Because multimedia files can be quite large, I recommend keeping them short to minimize their size. If the Help file is too large, it won't be practical to distribute with your application. While video is great, you may want to stick to short audio files. Audio is very effective, and the Help file size will be controllable.

Chapter 22, "Working in a Multimedia Environment," covers using multimedia objects within Office. These same objects can also be included in your Help files. Use that chapter as a more detailed guide to the different multimedia sources available to you.

Different Ways To Create Help Files

When you go through the Help development process and compile the Help file, the final product is a file with an HLP extension. No matter what development program you use, it compiles a number of source files together to create the HLP file. There are a number of ways to create the source files, and this is where things get a bit complicated.

At a minimum, you need the following tools to create a Help application:

- A word processor or text editor that saves files in Rich Text Format (RTF). RTF is the only format that the Microsoft Help Compiler can understand.
- The Help Compiler Workshop (HCW.EXE). This Microsoft program creates Help files. HCW.EXE takes all the source files and compiles them into a Help file with an HLP extension.

Unfortunately, HCW.EXE does not come free with Windows 95. It's included in the Microsoft Developer's Network (MSDN) Level 2 subscription and the Windows Software Development Kit (SDK). MSDN is a program that, for a charge, Microsoft provides you with documentation and software to assist in the creation of software for the Microsoft family of operating systems. In many cases, it's also included with Help authoring software like Blue Sky's software RoboHELP (covered later in this chapter). You should contact Microsoft at (800) 759-5474 for more information about MSDN and other products and services.

Using Word To Create Source Information

Because this is a book about Office, we must touch on how to use Word in the Help creation process. You can use Word to write Help file source information and save it as an RTF file. The Help compiler then turns the RTF into the HLP Help application file.

But wait—don't begin just yet. Using Word by itself to create an RTF file for the Help compiler is a very complicated process. You'll be pulling your hair out if you begin using this method. When you use Word as a Help authoring tool, you have to include numerous special control characters in the file to guide the Help Compiler along. Learning what these control characters mean is almost like learning another programming language, and it's a huge waste of time. You can accomplish the same tasks with third-party Help authoring software in a fraction of the time.

Included with the Microsoft Help Compiler Workshop program is a Help file called HCW.HLP. If you feel daring, you can try to use this Help file to guide you through the process of using Word by itself to create Help file source information. HCW.HLP does cover what you need to know, but only briefly.

Using Third-Party Help Content Software: A Better Way

Using third-party software is a much more practical and more productive way to develop the source information for your Help application. You still need to create the

RTF file, but the software hides all the difficult steps for you and adds tools to make special coding easy. There are many different public domain and shareware utilities available for creating help files. These are available on just about all of the online services and on the Internet. All the programs have different interfaces and features, but they do the same thing—create Help files. You can try many of them and decide which one suits your needs the best. Here are a couple of examples:

- Software Description: HELLLP!

   http://mindlink.net/ed_guy/helllp.html

- Software Description: HWA/WinHelp

   CompuServe

Some commercial applications provide tools that let you author Help file source information; many of these also include a Help Compiler. Later in this chapter, you'll learn more about RoboHELP, a program that you use with Word to create Help files.

Designing the Help Source Information

The most difficult and important step in the process of creating a Help file comes even before you turn on the computer. Spending some time and energy thinking through and carefully designing a Help file will save you hours, if not days, of work when you begin. But don't get discouraged; it's really not hard. In the following sections, you walk through the process of planning, gathering, organizing, and polishing the text and other elements for your online help application.

Gathering the Information

The first step in designing your Help file is to gather the information and source files you want to include in the Help file. By deciding now what to include, you're less likely to forget something later on. If you forget something, you can add it at any time. However, the further along the Help file progresses, the more difficult it becomes to add on. Because you'll be using an editor or word processor, adding text to an already existing topic is easy—you just add it. But adding a new topic could be a little more difficult. It all depends on where it is and how it's connected to other topics in the Help file. Adding a topic in the middle of the Help development process creates more of an organizational issue than an operational one. It's important to group topics together in some type of logical order. If you don't, you may forget where you placed a topic, and always be searching for it.

What you need to gather also depends on the complexity of your application. If you've created a simple dialog box to prompt the user to enter some information, you may only have a one-page Help file that includes a paragraph of text. Or, you may have created a very sophisticated application with the need for hundreds of pages, including reference material with graphics. Either way, there are files and information that must be collected.

You need to gather the following information and source files during this phase:

- *Background information from other sources.* For example, if you want the Help file to describe the formulas in a sophisticated spreadsheet application, you need to have them handy.

- *Graphics.* You need the electronic files (usually BMP files) for the graphics you want to include in Help. These may include company logos, photos, or illustrations.

- *Graphics that will have hotspots.* Clicking a hotspot can activate either a jump or a pop up. See "Helping with Hotspots" earlier in this chapter to learn more.

- *Multimedia elements.* Again, you need the electronic files for any sounds, video, screen cameras, or other multimedia elements you want to include in Help. In some cases, you may need to develop multimedia elements as you write or *script* the Help text. These elements need to be tightly integrated with the contents of the Help file. For example, you don't want Help to play a sound file offering verbal instructions that contradict the written instructions in the Help Topic text.

Storing the Source Material

File organization is important whenever you create end-user applications, and the same is true when you're creating a Help application. Create a separate project folder for each Help file you create. If you are writing a large Help application, the list of source files, such as graphic files and multimedia files, may become large. If you create an RTF file with a word processor to create the Help text, be sure to save the file in the Help file project folder, as well.

Mapping Out What You Want To Cover

After you gather some of the resource files and information you'll need, you should create a complete outline. It really should be a map that establishes everything to include in the Help file, how the information is to be divided, and the primary path(s) that will be between individual chunks of information (windows). Begin at the top of your application (the first screen the user will see), and work your way through to the end. Wherever you can, note where pop ups, graphics, hotspots, and other special elements will appear. The major topics on this map will eventually become the list of information for the Contents page. The map should resemble a family tree or a *hierarchy* (a directory list in Windows 95 is an example of a hierarchy). Figure 21.14 shows an example of a map (outline) for a small Help application.

NOTE While your outline may resemble a family tree in structure and will establish the primary flow of information, this doesn't prevent you from adding as many jumps as you want in the topics. This is an important concept, so don't forget to add in your jumps, pop ups, and more!

Fig. 21.14

This is an example drawing of a map (outline) for a small Help application.

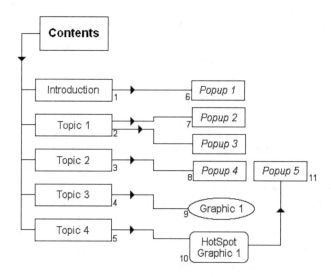

Your map should reflect the order in which the reader uses the application you're writing the Help for. For example, if the user needs to start using your application by creating a new file from a particular template, your first Help topic under Contents should explain how to create the new file with that template.

I suggest creating screen prints of all the windows (press the Print Screen key) and dialog boxes (press Alt+Print Screen) in your application. After you press Print Screen or Alt+Print Screen, you need to immediately print that screen (as creating another screen print wipes out the one that's presently in the Clipboard). To print a screen, choose Edit, Paste to paste it from the Clipboard into a Word file, then print the page with that image. To create the screen prints, you also can use a third-party capture utility such as Collage Complete for Windows or HiJaak.

After you print each screen print, lay them all out on your floor. Position the screen prints in a hierarchy mimicking the order in which the user will access and use the features depicted in the printouts. Then draw your map based on what you see, numbering topics in the order they will appear in the Help file.

There are some conventions to keep in mind while developing your Help outline. These are elements that are commonly included in Help files from commercial software companies, or guidelines that will give you an idea of how to divide the information more effectively. In any case, following some of these conventions will enable you to create Help files that will have a structure that's familiar to, and more helpful for, your users:

■ *What's New.* This is an important Help topic to include at the top of your Help system if you are creating a new version of an existing application. People like to know what's new first, so they can go directly to a new feature. If this is the first version, you may want to rename this section "Features."

- *About....* Introduce your application, give the version number, and tell the users what the application does. You may also want to tell them how they can get in touch with you (or maybe not).

- *Feature topic pages.* These constitute the heart of the Help file. There should be a topic for each main feature of your application. A good rule of thumb is to create, at a minimum, a topic page for every dialog box the user can access in the application. Most users will not complain about having too much information at their disposal. Don't get carried away, though. Limit each topic page to about two or three screens in length. Try to base each topic on an action, not a feature. For example, "Creating a New File" is a stronger, more useful topic than "The File New Command."

- *Pop ups.* Keep these short and to the point. They should contain specific and detailed information, such as the definition for a term.

- *Troubleshooting.* Use these to offer information about how the user can work around problems.

- *Other help and resources.* If you are providing multiple Help files with an application or have suggestions about other applications the reader may want to obtain, be sure to document these in Help.

Writing Understandable Text

The text you include in your Help file is the most important ingredient for providing the help a user needs. That text must be clear, accurate, easy to read, and concise. Remember, the user is accessing the Help file because he or she doesn't understand something, so don't make too many assumptions about what the user should know, nor render any criticism.

As you begin writing the text for your Help application in your word processor or Help application development software, keep your audience in mind. Are they beginners, power users, or somewhere in the middle? You should write your Help file text to whomever your target audience is. If they are beginners, don't use very complicated or technical words, and be sure to include pop-up definitions whenever you think they may be needed. If the users are advanced, don't explain basic things like how to use a mouse.

Although this book isn't a Writing 101 primer, there are a few tips you can use to improve the quality of the text you create for your Help files:

- Make sure topic headings are active, clear, and descriptive.

- Keep your sentences relatively short. Longer sentences are more difficult to read and understand.

- Limit paragraphs to a few sentences. When in doubt, start a new paragraph.

- When you can, break processes into numbered steps. Steps break an operation into manageable parts that the reader can digest one at a time.

- Similarly, use bulleted lists to highlight key points.

- Don't hesitate to include tips, notes, and warnings where they apply and when you have room.

- Adjust the amount of text as needed to allow for graphics and other elements. For example, if you want to include a large graphic on a topic page, cut back on the amount of text.

- Make sure the text you write is consistent with the information offered in graphics and multimedia elements. Conflicting information will confuse your users.

- Finally, "beta test" your text if you can. Have an end user in your target audience use the Help text to work with a beta version of the main application. Your tester will provide useful information about what works and what doesn't in your Help text.

Assigning Context Numbers

Context numbers enable you to make your Help system context-sensitive, so that, for example, clicking a particular button in the application directly displays a particular Help topic (bypassing the Help Contents screen).

Let's say that a Product Identification dialog box requires the user to enter a product identification number (PIN). However, the user needs to choose from more than one PIN. You use context numbers and create links from the application to call particular Help topics. The user can click the Help button in the Product Identification dialog box to display the Product Identification Help topic, which explains what PIN to enter. This is done by assigning each topic page a reference (context) number.

To call a Help topic from within the main application, you assign the Help topic's context number and the Help file name to the button in the application. Then, when the user clicks the button, your application knows which Help file to open and which topic to display.

As you create your Help map and develop the text, you should assign context numbers to each topic page and other elements like pop ups. The subscript characters beside the map items in figure 21.14 shown previously illustrate how context numbers might be assigned in a particular Help file.

TIP

It's important to keep a list of all your context numbers and what topic you have assigned them to. I recommend beginning at number 100 and adding one for each topic page. I also recommend using Excel to keep track of these numbers. Using a spreadsheet is a fast and easy way to make sure mistakes are not made.

Using RoboHELP To Create a Help File

As noted earlier in this chapter, there are many software tools available to author and compile Help files; so many, in fact, that it's only possible in the scope of this book to talk about just one of them. Blue Sky Software's RoboHELP 95 is one of the more popular Help authoring tools because it integrates itself into Word 95. Word has excellent editing capabilities, and RoboHELP takes full advantage of them. Once you've installed RoboHELP, you can display a custom toolbar that makes the RoboHELP features available in Word.

 NOTE   If you can't find RoboHELP 95 in your local computer store or through a computer catalog, contact Blue Sky Software Corporation, 7777 Fay Avenue, Suite 201, La Jolla, CA 92037; (619)459-6365; Internet: **http://www.blue-sky.com**.

This section doesn't present a step-by-step tutorial for using RoboHELP. In fact, RoboHELP offers hundreds of features for fine-tuning the Help files you create, so covering them all would be impossible in a single chapter. There are literally hundreds of additional features available, including the ability to create macros that perform all kinds of automated tasks for the user. The possibilities are limitless. Instead, the following sections provide an example meant to give you an idea of what is involved in creating a Help file using Help authoring tools. In the following example, assume that RoboHELP has been installed and Word has been opened. You would begin looking at the Word screen with a blank document open.

Creating a New Help Project

Choose File, New. Under the General tab, select RoboHELP, and then click OK. A new Help project document is created, and as shown in figure 21.15, RoboHELP prompts you for some information. Enter the Title of the Help project and the File Name to use when it's saved, then click OK.

The Word file then holds all the source code for your Help file application. You should use Word to save your project periodically as you develop it. Don't forget to save the file as an RTF (Rich Text Format) file.

 NOTE   The help source file must be saved in RTF format. If it's not, the Help Compiler will not be able to compile it into a Help file.

Creating the First Topic

In the RoboHELP Tool palette on the right side of the Word screen, click the top-left Topic button on the toolbar to create a new topic. When you do, the dialog box shown in figure 21.16 appears. Enter the first topic name you defined in your outline map, then click OK. RoboHELP creates the topic in the document, so you can enter the first text for it.

Fig. 21.15

RoboHELP creates a new Help project document for you and prompts you to enter some information.

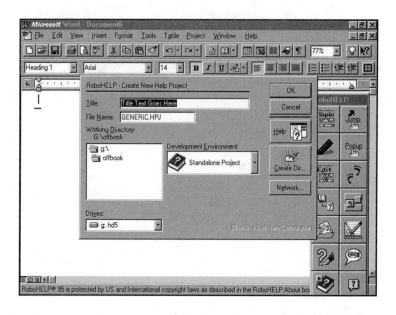

Repeat the process for each topic you want to create. Remember to follow your outline carefully.

Fig. 21.16

The Insert New Help Topic dialog box lets you specify some of the settings to use.

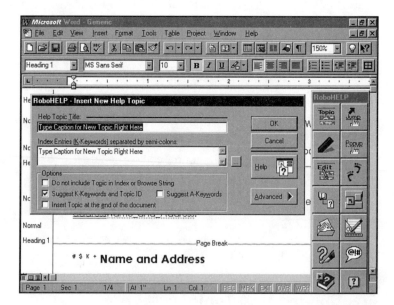

Creating a Jump to Another Topic

After you've created the topics for your Help file, you can make a jump from any character, word, or phrase. Most often, you'll jump the reader from the highlighted jump

IV

word or phrase to another topic page in Help. (Before you can jump to another topic, you need to create the topic in your Help file.)

First, highlight the text you would like to make into a jump. Then click the Jump button on the toolbar to open the Create Hypertext Jump to Help Topic dialog box (see fig. 21.17). From the list box at the bottom of the dialog box, select the help topic to jump to. If you want the reader to be able to click a graphic to jump to the new Help topic, click the Graphic button in the dialog box and specify the name of the graphic file to use (you should have already placed it in your Help project folder).

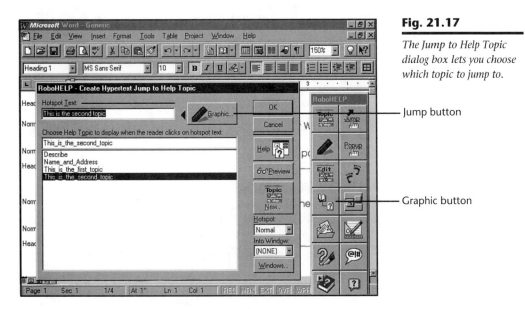

Fig. 21.17

The Jump to Help Topic dialog box lets you choose which topic to jump to.

Jump button

Graphic button

Click OK to finish creating the jump. The jump text is now highlighted in green and has a solid double underline. This formatting identifies the text that users can click to jump to another topic (see fig. 21.18).

> **NOTE** Once the Help file is compiled, green jump text has a single solid underline.

Creating a Pop Up

A pop up works like a jump; when you click the pop-up text, Help displays the specified small pop-up Help box rather than another Help topic window.

First highlight the text you want to be able to click to display a pop up. Then click the Pop-up button on the tool palette to open the Create Popup dialog box. You can enter the text to display in the pop-up box in the New Popup tab. However, if you click the Existing Topic tab (see fig. 21.19), you can select an already-created topic to pop up. In either case, click the OK button to finish creating the pop up.

Fig. 21.18

Green text and a solid double underline identify a jump.

Clicking this text in the compiled Help file jumps the reader to another topic.

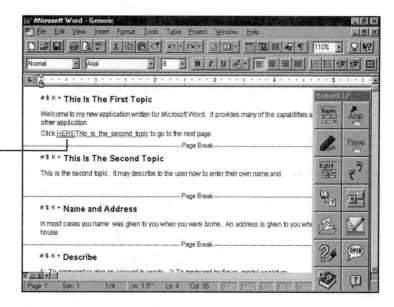

Pop-up button

Fig. 21.19

The Create Popup dialog box lets you choose which topic to pop up.

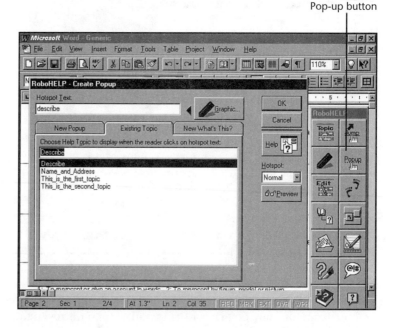

After you click OK, the pop-up trigger text turns green and a has a solid single underline. This formatting identifies the text you click to display the pop-up box (see fig. 21.20).

NOTE Once the Help file is compiled, text you click to display a pop-up box is green text and has a dotted underline.

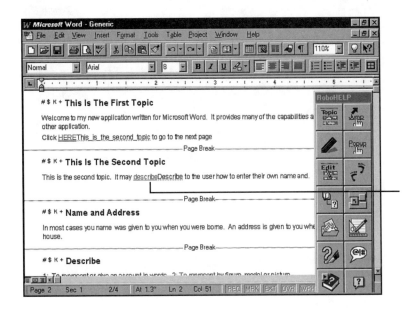

Fig. 21.20

Green text with a solid single underline identifies a pop up.

Clicking this text in the compiled Help file will display a pop-up box.

Compiling the Help Project

You are ready to compile your Help file. Click the Make Project button on the Tool palette (button with a question mark and pen on it). The Make Project dialog box opens. It enables you to change some of the default settings for compiling, but in this case, there's no need for changes to the default settings. Click the Make button at the top of the dialog box to compile the Help file (see fig. 21.21). RoboHELP compiles the Help file and gives it the name you specified when you first created the Help file project. When complete, you can click the Run button in the dialog box to open the compiled help project.

Running the Compiled Help File from RoboHELP

As you learned earlier in the chapter, you can run a Help file in Windows by double-clicking its file name or icon. You can run the newly compiled Help file from within RoboHELP, as well, to take a look at it. To do so, click the Run Project button (the book icon with a right arrow) on the RoboHELP toolbar. Your Help file opens on-screen.

Creating a Windows 95 Contents Tab with RoboHELP

New to the Windows 95 Help system is the Contents tab. It displays the Help file topics in a tree-like graphical hierarchy. The Contents page should group the topics you listed in your Help file outline map into categories. RoboHELP provides a utility called the Contents Tab Composer, which enables you to graphically design and create the Contents tab.

Fig. 21.21

Many of the default compile settings can be changed in the Make Project dialog box.

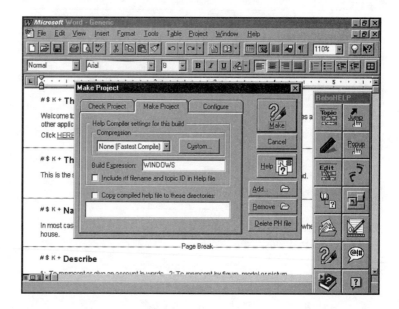

To begin, open the Help file RTF source code file (or the appropriate DOC file) in Word. Then click the Add Contents button on the RoboHELP toolbar to open the Contents Tab Composer, shown in figure 21.22.

There are two distinct sides to the Composer window. On the left are the Help topics that are available to be included in a contents category (inserted into a book). You'll use the pane on the right to graphically lay out the books and topics. In the example shown in figure 21.22, no book has been created yet.

First, you would create some books (groups of topics) to insert the topics into. Clicking the leftmost toolbar button (it's the button with the open book on it) opens the New Book dialog box. In the dialog box, enter the name of each book you want to add. Then, to add topics to a Contents category, drag any topic from the list at the left on top of the book that you want to add the topic to. When you finish dragging, the Contents Tab Composer adds the topic to that book, as shown in figure 21.23.

The final step is to compile the Contents file by simply clicking the Compile button in the toolbar. Compiling takes the help source files and packs them together to create a single HLP file.

The compiler creates a new file with the CNT extension. As long as this file is in the same directory as the main HLP Help file, the Contents tab will be displayed.

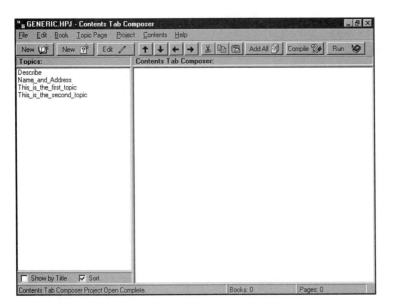

Fig. 21.22

The Contents Tab Composer enables you to design the Contents Tab.

Fig. 21.23

The topics from the list at the left have been dragged into the books on the right.

NOTE A simple Contents tab makes your application much more professional looking. However, a Contents tab is not necessary. If none exists, the Help file opens to the Index tab. In this case, a warning may appear that reads `Unable to open the file C:\path`; this means the Help file is looking for the CNT file and can't find it. This is OK, it's just a warning. Click the OK button, and the Help file will work fine. There just won't be a Contents page.

Accessing Help Files from Within Your Office Applications

Your Help file is now complete. You have spent many hours planning and creating the Help file to make life as easy as possible for the users of your application. You may be saying, "So now what?" Before the user can access the Help from the Office application it accompanies, you need to make the application aware of the Help files' existence. This process is different for each application in Office, but is simple no matter which one you use.

Word and Excel applications access the Help file using macros. In Access, you can enter the Help file name and context numbers directly through Properties sheets. In the rest of this section, I have explained the particular process for Word, Excel, and Access.

From Within Excel

To run a Help file from an Excel application, use a macro. To do so, you must include a line of code to open a Help file (an example follows this paragraph) in the macro. The `Application.Help` command specifies the Help file name. In the following sample code, the Help file name is GENERIC.HLP. You can include the entire path to the Help file, if you like. If no path is entered, Excel assumes the Help file is located in the same directory as your application. The number after the quotes is the context number for the topic that will be displayed. Attach the finished macro to a macro button or object in your Excel application, or assign it to a particular event. After you do so, selecting that button or object will launch your Help file and display the topic or information associated with the context number you've specified in the macro.

```
Application.Help "C:\GENERIC.HLP", 113
```

You can create additional macros to call the Help file. In each one, change the context number to point to the appropriate topic page.

From Within Access

Access makes it easy to incorporate custom Help files into your databases and integrated applications. When creating a form or report, you can display a Properties sheet where you can enter the Help file information. In the Form or Report Designer, choose View, Properties. Select the All tab. Scroll down until you see Help File and Help Context Id.

In the Help File property field, enter the complete path and name for the Help file. In the Help Context Id property field, enter the context number for the Help topic you would like to open when you request help by pressing F1 from the form or report (see fig. 21.24).

Fig. 21.24

The Form properties sheet lets you enter a Help File Name and Help Context Id to access when the user presses the F1 key.

From Within Word

As in Excel, in Word you use a macro to call a Help file. The macro must contain lines of code resembling the example ones that follow this paragraph. The helpfile$ command specifies the Help file name. In the following sample code, the Help file name is GENERIC.HLP. You can include the entire path to the Help file name, if you like. If no path is entered, Word assumes the Help file is located in the same directory as your application.

```
Declare Function WinHelpA Lib "USER32"(hWnd As Integer, lpHelpFile \
    As String, wCmd As Integer, dwData As String) As Integer
Declare Function GetActiveWindow Lib "USER32"() As Integer

Sub MAIN
    hWnd = GetActiveWindow
    helpFile$ = "C:\GENERIC.HLP"
    wCmd = 261            'The decimal value for HELP_PARTIALKEY
    keyWord$ = "This is the second topic"
    success = WinHelpA(hWnd, helpFile$, wCmd, keyWord$)
    If success = 0 Then MsgBox "Could not start Windows Help"
End Sub
```

Word deals with context-sensitive help a little differently than Excel and Access do. In Excel and Access, you used the context number for a topic from the Help file to call that topic page. In Word, you need to use the actual topic name as the reference. In the preceding sample code, the line keyWord$ = "This is the second topic" will display the topic named This is the second topic after the GENERIC.HLP application is launched.

NOTE The exact topic name—with correct spaces, special characters, and capitalization—must be entered between the quotes. If the name does not match the topic exactly, the keyWord$ variable will place it in the first field on the Help Index tab.

As in Excel, you can create numerous macros in your Word application to call specific Help topics. And, you can attach those macros to buttons and other objects.

From Here...

You now have a better understanding of the options available to you for integrating Help files into your Office applications. The following chapters offer even more information you can apply to improve your Help application files:

■ Refer to Chapter 18, "Designing the User Interface," for information about keeping your application's look and feel consistent. This information also applies to Help files.

■ For more about adding multimedia to your Help files, refer to Chapter 22, "Working in a Multimedia Environment."

CHAPTER 22

Working in a Multimedia Environment

Multimedia—combining text, sound, full-motion video, animation, graphics, and MIDI sound—isn't new to computers. In fact, multimedia and its various components have been around for years. But only within the last year has multimedia become one of the most talked about buzzwords in computing, particularly with regard to applications. Multimedia in a document or application can quickly deliver a message to the user that might otherwise take thousands of written words. And, because multimedia provides more sensory stimulation via enhanced sights, sounds, and motions, it makes information more memorable. These capabilities have created a huge demand for multimedia in documents and applications, even in more "business-oriented" products like Office.

Until the last few years, hardware and software barriers prevented many developers from adding multimedia impact to applications. The average DOS-based system lacked the power to handle multimedia, because most systems didn't have enough RAM, lacked a sound card or CD-ROM, or used Windows 3.1x (which wasn't completely multimedia-friendly and often required extra software to run multimedia elements like video clips). As the demand for multimedia grew, the hardware and software it required plummeted in price and became more integrated, so that most entry-level computer systems sold today include full support for multimedia. And, many users now can afford to upgrade older computers, adding CD-ROM drives and sound cards (which often include add-on multimedia software) to take advantage of multimedia software.

Now that more and more users have access to multimedia software and hardware, it's a good time to take advantage of what multimedia has to offer. Additionally, with the release of Windows 95 and Office 95, including multimedia in your Office documents and applications is easier than ever.

In this chapter, you learn about

- The advantages of multimedia in Office 95
- Multimedia hardware requirements and how they affect application users
- Creating and obtaining multimedia source files

■ Developing your own multimedia objects

■ Using multimedia in Office applications

Introducing Multimedia Improvements

As noted at the start of this chapter, multimedia applications combine text, graphics, sound, full-motion video, MIDI sound, and animation. Microsoft has added significant support for multimedia applications and the types of files and objects used to create them in both Windows 95 and Office 95. For starters, Windows 95 includes more of the applications needed to play (and even create, in some cases) different kinds of multimedia files. One of the key applications is Media Player, which plays AVI animation/video files, WAV sound files, MIDI sound, and CD audio tracks.

Also, with the built-in OLE support in Windows 95 and Office 95, you can update most multimedia files from right within Office. For example, once you insert or embed a multimedia object in your document or application, full editing controls for the multimedia object are available to users from within the Office application. So, double-clicking a BMP picture file inserted in a Word document displays a toolbar of graphic editing tools on the left and the Color toolbar at the bottom of the Word screen.

Next, because Windows 95 and Office 95 now provide full 32-bit operation, you see significant performance gains when you include multimedia in your documents or applications. For example, Windows 95 can display larger and smoother digital video images because the 32-bit operating system reads the data from the hard disk, decompresses each video frame, and then writes it to the screen much more quickly than the 16-bit Windows 3.1x could.

Other improvements are much less visible to end users. Microsoft improved the interface to many devices including the file system (VFAT), CD-ROM drives, and the system cache.

Reviewing Multimedia Hardware Requirements

When you include multimedia objects in Office documents and applications for other users, it's important to know what hardware the target users have. This is crucial to delivering an effective multimedia document or presentation. If the target users' computers are not capable of properly displaying your document or application, any multimedia that you have included will detract from the overall effect instead of enhancing it. For example, if you are sending a document to someone using a 16MHz 80386 system, you generally shouldn't include large video files. An 80386, and even some lower-end 486 models, display video very slowly, making the user's viewing experience somewhat painful. In such a case, you could consider smaller video clips or, preferably, audio. Audio files are much smaller than video files and require less processor overhead.

To assist end users and developers in determining what hardware (and software, in some cases) should be used for multimedia, an industry-wide discussion and debate took place. In the aftermath of the debate, multimedia specifications were created and dubbed *MPC* for Multimedia Personal Computer. MPC specifications set minimum standards for the power and capabilities that a computer needs to be multimedia capable. Users refer to MPC standards when purchasing a multimedia computer (or hardware upgrades). And, developers also can use the standards to ensure that multimedia applications don't require more juice than the average multimedia system offers.

Today, there are three levels of MPC specifications: MPC1, MPC2, and MPC3. Table 22.1 outlines the three levels of MPC specifications. In reality, MPC1- and MPC2-compliant computers are no longer practical if a user runs sophisticated multimedia applications. To use the mainstream software found in any computer store, MPC3 is actually the "low-end" hardware requirement. Some multimedia software even requires more power than specified by MPC3.

NOTE The MPC Hardware Specifications were designed to put a label on a specific hardware configuration. Your computer does not have to meet all of the specifications; rather, use it as a guide. The closer your hardware is to the specifications, the better its performance will be.

Table 22.1   MPC Hardware Specification Chart

Hardware Description	MPC1 Specifications	MPC2 Specifications	MPC3 Specifications
CPU type	386SX	486SX	Pentium
CPU speed	16MHz	25MHz	75MHz
System memory	2M RAM	4M RAM	8M RAM
Hard drive	30M	160M	540M
Modem	Not required	Not required	14.4 baud
Monitor	VGA	VGA 640×480	VGA 640×480 (video playback)
Video card	256 colors	65,535 colors	65,535 colors
Printer type	Not required	Not required	Color
CD-ROM speed	150K/sec	300K/sec	600K/sec
Joystick	Required	Required	Flight Stick type
Sound card	8-bit	16-bit	16-bit/wavetable
Scanner	Not required	Not required	24-bit color
Video digitizer	Not required	Not required	Full-screen capture

As you develop Office applications and documents that require multimedia elements, be aware of whether the majority of the users you're designing the application for have MPC1-, MPC2-, or MPC3-equipped computers, and adjust the complexity of your application accordingly. Also, it may sound obvious, but to develop MPC3-level applications and multimedia elements, you need to have an MPC3 system yourself.

Understanding the Files That Make Multimedia Work

You can think of text, audio, video/animation, graphics, and MIDI as *categories* of multimedia files. Within each of these categories, there are many different types of file formats, many of which Office directly supports. As for other kinds of files, Windows identifies each multimedia file format with a specific icon and filename extension (BMP, PCX, AVI, WAV, and so on).

There are no guidelines for which file format to use when. However, each of the formats within each category behaves differently and has different characteristics. These characteristics are generally what determine when one format is better than another for your particular application. The characteristics of a multimedia file or object include on-screen size, length, and quality. These characteristics, in addition to a file's type and the application used to create the file or object, directly impact how much disk space the file or object requires. The larger, longer, and higher in quality the multimedia file is, the more space it takes up on a hard disk and in RAM. For example, a 20-second audio file may only be 150K in size, but a 20-second video file can be 3M because video files include more "information" than audio files.

It's important to be aware of the size of the multimedia files you are using. You won't be able to include a 3M video file if your document or application is being distributed on a floppy disk; it won't fit! Or, for example, there's no point in using extra disk space for a high-quality sound file if end users for the application only have MPC1 machines with 8-bit sound. So, be selective when choosing what type of file to use.

The following sections provide more detail about the types of files within each multimedia category, so you can make intelligent decisions in choosing which type of file to use in a particular situation.

Using Text with Multimedia

It would not be realistic to think that sound, video, and graphics files can tell the whole story by themselves. PowerPoint multimedia presentations and applications still need text, so you should consider this during your planning. In Word, Excel, or Access, use multimedia files to enhance the already existing document, spreadsheet, or database information. In these kinds of documents, multimedia is the icing on the cake. PowerPoint documents, on the other hand, rely much more heavily on multimedia files, particularly graphical charts, to present content. In PowerPoint, text often serves as more of an enhancement in the form of bullets, titles, and small informational paragraphs.

The more creative you are with the text that you use, the more impact your document or application will have. Selectively take advantage of the many different built-in fonts, styles, colors, and sizes (using too many different fonts and styles will detract from the document). This will add flair, making it easier and more interesting to view your document. The section "WordArt" later in this chapter describes how the WordArt application (which comes with Office) provides one option for creating interesting text effects.

TIP

When writing text, always keep the target audience in mind. If the audience is highly skilled in the topic you are discussing, don't include too much beginner-level material or fluff. Once you have identified the audience, write the text to that skill level, and let the multimedia elements do the rest.

Adding Visual Flair with Graphic Images

Still images are a vital part of the multimedia picture. There are two kinds of still images: those created using a computer, and real photographs that have been digitized. While these graphics do not themselves constitute multimedia, they add interest by serving as a backdrop, illustrating a particular point, or being used as an icon or area to click. Graphic images are sometimes called *clip art*. For example, Microsoft has included a CLIPART folder that contains a collection of clip art images on the Office CD-ROM.

Graphics generally are the easiest type of multimedia component to include in your documents or applications. You can often add them to a document by choosing Insert Picture. They take up the least amount of hard disk space, making it easy to manipulate them from within Office. The Office applications support many different types of graphic file formats. The BMP format is the most commonly used Windows format, with just about every application supporting it. However, there are other formats that are common and available as well, so you may need to use image editing software like Adobe Photoshop (described later in this chapter), Corel PhotoPaint, Collage Complete for Windows, and so on to convert an image to the type you need. The following are types of graphics files that are widely available today:

- *Windows Bitmap (BMP).* Originally designed by Microsoft for use with Windows. There is no file size limit for BMP images, and the format supports a color depth of 1-bit to 24-bit. Because this format stores images as a series of *bits*, or colored dots, increasing the size of one of these images can degrade its quality and make it look "jaggy."

- *Windows Metafile (WMF).* Stores an image as a series of functions. When the metafile is opened, each function is played back. Metafiles are excellent for transferring images between applications, because they allow scaling without any loss of quality. They are generally used for low-resolution clip art. The clip-art images that come with Office are in Windows Metafile format.

- *PaintBrush (PCX).* Established by Zsoft for its PC Paintbrush software, PCX is also supported in the Windows PaintBrush and Windows 95 Paint programs. PCX files are also bitmap images, so increasing their on-screen size can degrade their appearance.

- *Joint Photographic Experts Group, or JPEG (JPG).* Using compression, changes the way data is stored (to save disk space), discarding the extra data that isn't necessary for the display of the image. Because it discards data, once an image has been compressed (saved), it won't have the same quality as the original. When saving a JPEG image, you can choose a quality setting for the compression. A trade-off exists between the image quality and the amount of compression you choose. For example, an image compressed using Excellent compression is not compressed as much as an image compressed using the Fair compression option. Generally, images compressed using the Excellent option have compression ratios between 5:1 and 15:1. Opening a JPEG image automatically decompresses it for viewing. You may need to convert JPEG files to another type before using them in Office.

- *CompuServe Graphics Interchange Format (GIF).* Commonly used to upload documents to online services (including the Internet) and between different operating systems. Like JPEG, GIF is a compressed format, designed to minimize the time it takes to transfer a file. Like JPEG files, you may need to convert GIF files before using them in Office.

- *Tagged-Image File Format (TIF).* Frequently used to exchange documents between non-compatible applications and computer platforms. The TIF format supports LZW compression, which is the same compression used by GIF format. Like compressed and bitmapped images, resizing a TIF image affects how attractive it looks on-screen.

- *Kodak Photo CD (PCD).* Developed as a method for converting images from regular photographic negatives to a digital format stored on CD-ROM. Most image editing software now enables you to convert PCD files to those in other formats.

- *Encapsulated PostScript (EPS).* Conforms to the Adobe PostScript language format and is supported by most illustration and page layout programs. EPS images are fully scalable, meaning you can resize them without any significant loss in quality.

- *Macintosh PICT (PCT).* Primarily used on the Macintosh computer system. It is an excellent format for transferring raster images between applications.

Due to their characteristics, the file size for each of the graphic image formats varies greatly. You should keep relative file sizes in mind when designing your multimedia application. If you want to conserve disk space and image quality is a secondary issue, or if your users' systems have older monitors with a lower resolution, choose files with a more compact file size.

In contrast, if you want to pull out all the stops and display the most dazzling images you can, use a format that yields greater quality but takes up more disk space. Table 22.2 compares the size difference the same example picture—a screen capture of the Windows 95 Desktop—can have in different formats. The example picture's attributes are 640×480, 72 dpi (dots per inch), and 8-bits (256 colors). The file size was rounded up to the nearest kilobyte.

TIP

The graphics you distribute should be the same amount of colors that the target computer can display. For example, if a graphic is 24-bit (millions of colors) and the target computer can only display 256, the image may be distorted.

Table 22.2   File Sizes for Images Saved in Various Graphic Formats

Name	Extension	Size
Windows Bitmap (256 Colors)	BMP	307K
Windows Bitmap (24-bit)	BMP	900K
Graphics Interchange Format	GIF	14K
Encapsulated PostScript	EPS	2,600K
Paintbrush	PCX	48K
Tagged-Image File Format	TIF	309K
Joint Photographic Experts Group	JPG	28K (Excellent Compression) 131K (Least Compression)

Sound and MIDI

Next to graphic images, including sound files in your Office documents or applications is a very practical option. Sound files take up much less disk space than video or animation files, yet are very effective in passing along information. While sound can be an additional component in a video file, it can also be used by itself. The sounds you can use may include brief sounds to highlight an event, music to enhance meaning, or even a recording of your own voice explaining a fact or calculation.

To digitize sound (record it) using your computer, you need additional hardware, namely a sound card. *Sound cards* get sound into and out of a computer. Today, 16-bit sound cards are mainstream, but 8-bit sound cards are still out there in some users' systems. Again, this is something to keep in mind when creating your own sound files. A sound file may sound great on your computer with a 16-bit sound card, but the target user's computer may only have an 8-bit card. The sound may not sound the same on both! Windows 95 includes the Sound Recorder application, which you can use to record and then save or embed WAV sound files.

Some sounds cards include support for MIDI (Musical Instrument Digital Interface). *MIDI* is a programming language by which your computer can control a musical instrument that has the proper MIDI connectors on it, or a "virtual" musical instrument within a computer. The computer can record the actions of the instrument exactly as they are played by the musician. Then, the computer will use the instrument just as the musician did, playing the recorded notes. MIDI files are significantly smaller than digitized audio, because MIDI only records the actions of the instrument and not the sound the instrument makes.

Many sound cards use FM synthesis to create the sound. *Oscillators* produce tones that are mixed together to give the audience an approximation of the instrument being played. FM synthesis works fine with games and other applications whose primary output is for entertainment. Newer sound cards use a new technology called *Wavetable sound*, where an actual "sample" of a musical instrument is stored in ROM. This sample is then used to produce the instrument's sound. MIDI and other digital music applications require a Wavetable that contains the actual sounds of the musical instruments. FM synthesis uses an approximation created by synthesizing frequencies.

The largest contributing factor in the size of a digitized sound file is the sampling rate used when recording. Different frequency settings change the quality of the recording. Select the setting that best matches the quality you want to deliver to the audience. Remember, the higher the rate, the larger the file size will be. Most sound cards allow three different settings:

- *11KHz.* The quality of the human voice.
- *22KHz.* Equal to sound quality heard from an AM radio.
- *44KHz.* As good as the sound quality from an audio CD.

Most sound cards include three main connectors that you use to record and work with sound. If you plan to do a lot of work with sound, you may need to use the following three types of input jacks or connectors:

- *Microphone input.* Accepts input from a microphone. Many sound cards include a microphone. You use the mic and this connector to digitize your voice into the computer, or record sounds. This hardware setup can also take advantage of voice recognition software.
- *Line input.* A connection that accepts input from an audio device such as a CD player, cassette deck, or any other device that provides a line output.
- *Audio output.* Connects to speakers. Obviously, the better the quality speaker, the better the output sounds. The speakers should match the quality of the sound card. A high-end sound card deserves high-end speakers.

Video and Animation

Adding video and computer animation will have the greatest impact on your audience. Just as with television, moving pictures and sound are capable of telling a story that will not easily fit on paper. *Multimedia video clips* are digitized computer "movies" captured from a television or similar source such as a VCR, video camera, or laser disc. To capture video and save it in digital format on disk, your computer has to have a video capture board, sometimes called a *video digitizer* or *video grabber*, and the accompanying software. After installing the video capture board, you connect it to the source to record from, then record and save the video clip, usually as an AVI file.

On the other hand, *animation files* are generally created with a computer using drawn images and animation software. Computer animation also can be saved in an AVI file format. A vast amount of software is available for creating computer animation, each with a different set of features, output quality, and price.

One of the strongest new features of Windows 95 is its capability to easily play AVI files without the need to install any additional software. Although Windows 95 and Office 95 applications can play back any AVI clip, if the clip includes audio, users need a sound card and speakers to play it back. There are other video formats available, but AVI files are the most widely used and recognized. If you want to use video or animation in another format such as FLC, FLI, QTW (QuickTime for Windows), or MPG (MPEG), end users may need special software to play back those files.

Double-clicking any AVI icon or file name plays the file in a window (see fig. 22.1).

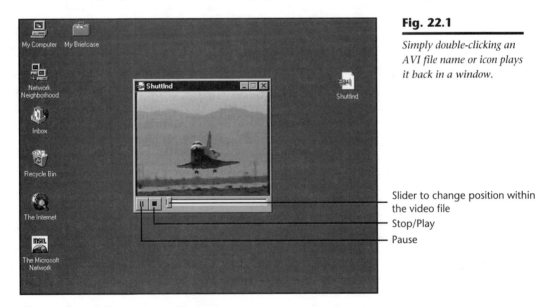

Fig. 22.1

Simply double-clicking an AVI file name or icon plays it back in a window.

Slider to change position within the video file

Stop/Play

Pause

The playback window has two buttons for controlling the playback of the video: Pause and Stop/Play (Play and Stop are the same button). The slider control displays a particular "frame" or position in the video file. As the video is playing, the slider automatically moves to indicate the current playback position. The maximize button is disabled because video files are always shown in the resolution they were recorded in. However, you can manually resize the window to any size you want, even full screen

(640×480). The size of the playback window can also be changed for all AVI files that are played. To do this, open the Multimedia Control Panel and select the Video tab. Keep in mind that the larger the window, the more system resources (and time) it will take to play back.

Video is just as easy to integrate into your Office documents or applications as sound, but video takes up much more space on your hard disk. Compression is key to minimizing the video file size. For example, for a window size of 320×240, uncompressed video takes up approximately 207M a minute. The same window size with minimal compression only takes up 27M a minute. With maximum compression, this video file takes up only 9M—quite a difference! These numbers vary based on the software and hardware combination you use.

> **NOTE**
>
> MPEG (*Moving Pictures Experts Group*) is a video and audio compression standard developed by the ISO (the International Standards Organization). MPEG compresses files by predicting the motion from frame to frame. MPEG looks for a close match to each block in a previous or future frame. When a match is found, its block is dropped, saving that amount of space in the file.
>
> MPEG compression achieves a 6:1 compression ratio, saving a significant amount of space. There is no discernible difference in the before-and-after video/audio file. Just about all video capture hardware supports the MPEG compression scheme.

In addition to compression, two other factors determine the file size of a video or animation: the *video window size*, and the *playback rate* or *frame rate*. A larger video window provides greater visual impact, but creates a larger and possibly slower video file. This means that as the video window size increases, a faster PC would be required to play back these files smoothly. The playback rate or frame rate is measured in *frames per second* (*fps*). Showing more frames or images per second to make the video appear more fluid requires more information, and thus more disk space to hold the file. Tables 22.3 and 22.4 shed more light on which video window sizes and frame rates are appropriate for particular situations.

> **NOTE**
>
> 640×480 video and animation is considered full-frame because it's the closest resolution to a regular television.

Table 22.3 Video Window Size Choices and Uses

Size (In Pixels)	Usage
320×240	Large and practical for many multimedia applications, even though it's not "full-screen."
240×180	For playback on slower computers, this may be a good size. It's smaller than 320×240, but large enough to be effective.

Size (In Pixels)	Usage
160×120	Generally, the smallest video window size you should use; video windows that are much smaller are difficult to see and less effective.

Table 22.4 Video Frame Rate Choices and Uses

Rate (Frame per Second)	Usage
10 fps	Use when low data rates are required.
15 fps	Standard setting for most multimedia applications.
24 fps	The frame rate that theaters use to show motion pictures.
25 fps	PAL broadcast television frame rate.
30 fps	NTSC broadcast television frame rate.

Finding or Creating Your Own Multimedia Files

Once you have decided to include multimedia in your Office documents or applications, the next step is to get or develop the files to include. Over the past year, your options have grown exponentially, due to the average consumer's increased demand for multimedia, which has driven new developments for just about every type of multimedia product.

While Windows 95 has built-in support for multimedia, it does not have all the special hardware and software from third-party companies necessary to create multimedia files. Creating complex sounds, video, animation, or graphics isn't difficult; it just takes the right software and accessories.

This section gives you a sampling of some of the software and hardware solutions you can choose from to obtain or create multimedia files. These are by no means your only alternatives, because there are so many resources out there. But this overview of available solutions should get you started in finding material to include in your Office applications and documents.

Finding Already-Created Files

There is an alternative to creating multimedia files yourself, especially if you're short on the needed hardware, software, or artistic capabilities. You can purchase premade multimedia libraries, usually on CD-ROM, to provide enough space for numerous files. These libraries usually consist of a set of files grouped by category. For example, you can get a CD-ROM with video and audio files about space exploration or of famous speeches. You can get a collection of business or health and fitness clip-art images. Or, you can find goofy sound files to use. Figure 22.2 shows an example of a Photo CD image from one of the early Corel Professional Photos CD-ROMs, converted to BMP format and used in a Word document.

Fig. 22.2

The image enlivening this Word document is from Corel.

Here are the best places to find multimedia files and collections:

- *Peruse a computer catalog or shop a computer store.* Most of them sell collections of various kinds of multimedia files. Collections are also often advertised in magazines. For example, Corel, ClickArt, and PhotoDisk all sell collections of images on CD. Check out ads in computing magazines—especially those targeted toward graphic designers and multimedia developers—to learn more about what's out there.

- *Check out everything that comes with the software you have.* Many applications, especially ones dealing with presentation graphics, not only include clip-art collections but also sample sound and video clips.

- *Go online.* CompuServe, America Online, the Internet, and other electronic gathering places offer numerous example files in various formats for downloading. One company is even licensing stock digitized images via **http://www. weststock.com**.

Caution

There are two things to keep in mind when using multimedia files from other sources. First, make sure the material isn't copyrighted or that you've licensed it and have the ability to use it as needed. Second, make sure the files you get are in the file format that you need, or that you have the software you need to convert them to the right formats.

Creating Files with the Built-In Windows 95 Applications

Microsoft's intention was to make Windows 95 the premiere multimedia operating system. To accomplish this, most multimedia devices are now controlled directly through Windows by using Plug-and-Play, and by integrating hundreds of hardware and software device drivers. A Multimedia Control Panel applet was created to centrally control all of these devices (see fig. 22.3). Every element of multimedia in Windows 95 is controlled through this property sheet.

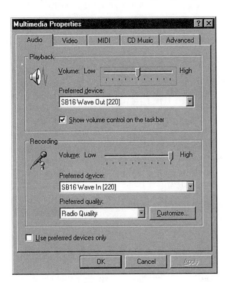

Fig. 22.3

The Multimedia Properties sheet holds all the multimedia settings in Windows 95.

In addition to the multimedia hardware support in Windows 95, there are a number of software utilities available for creating and managing multimedia files. These software utilities are each identified and explained in the following sections.

>
> **TIP**
> You don't need to use the built-in utilities (Sound Recorder, Media Player, Paint); ease of use is their biggest draw. Whatever hardware you purchase will also include software that, in general, will be more powerful and include more features than the built-in Windows 95 software.

Using the Built-In Sound Recorder. The Sound Recorder application (see fig. 22.4) records sound clips taken from the input of a sound card. This input can be from either the microphone, an audio CD in your CD-ROM drive, or from the line input (that is, if you have another sound device attached to the line input connection on the sound card). Once your sound hardware is installed and configured properly through Windows 95, Sound Recorder recognizes the presence of the card and enables you to record with Sound Recorder. To open Sound Recorder, click the Start button and choose Programs, Accessories, Multimedia, and select Sound Recorder.

Fig. 22.4

Use the built-in Sound Recorder to record and play back WAV files.

The Sound Recorder's buttons behave just like those on a real audio tape recorder; they are Seek to Start, Seek to End, Play, Stop, and Record. To create a sound file:

1. If you're planning to record from a CD or other device, cue it up to the appropriate starting position.

2. Click the Record button.

3. Start the audio to record or speak into the microphone.

4. Click the Stop button.

5. Open the File menu and choose the Save command.

6. In the Save As dialog box, specify a File Name, then click Save.

The right side of the window displays the length in seconds of the open audio file. The time noted on the left side indicates the present position of the timing slider. For more advanced editing features, you need to use Media Player, covered in the next section.

> **TIP**
>
> Sound Recorder enables you to perform some simple effects to the open file, like increasing and decreasing the volume and speed of playback. These changes and others are available on its Edit and Effects menus. There is no Undo in the Edit menu, so any changes you make are permanent and cannot be undone.

Controlling Multimedia Playback with Media Player. The Media Player application is not required to play multimedia files in Windows 95 and Office 95; Microsoft Video for Windows is built into Windows 95 and controls all the video playback. However, Media Player is required if you want to edit multimedia files with the following file formats: AVI, MD3, CMR, PRP, LIT, WAV, MID, RMI, and CD Audio. To open Sound Recorder, click the Start button and choose Programs, Accessories, Multimedia, and select Media Player.

> **TIP**
>
> Keep in mind that unless you record CD Audio sound from a CD and save it in a separate file in a new format such as WAV, end users need to have the CD in the CD-ROM drive to play back the sound. Without the CD, Windows tells the user the selected multimedia device is not ready or is not found.

Media Player behaves just like a VCR to control media files (see fig. 22.5). Start by selecting the type of file to play from the <u>D</u>evice menu. Open the file you want. Then, you can "tag" the beginning and ending of a part of the media file and only copy that section out. This lets you choose exactly what portion of the file to paste into Office. (You learn more about the specifics of inserting multimedia objects later in "Inserting Multimedia Component Files into Office Applications.") Once you place a multimedia object in an Office application or document, Media Player is automatically opened when you choose to edit the object. The Media Player controls appear in the menu bar of the Office application.

Fig. 22.5

The built-in Media Player allows the playback of AVI video files as well as other file formats.

Creating and Editing Images with Paint. Microsoft Paint lets you create and edit both simple or complex BMP and PCX graphics. (Click Start and choose <u>P</u>rograms, Accessories, and click Paint to start this program.) Most of the normal graphic editing tools are available in Paint, which is a 32-bit application. Paint is a simple painting program, compared to most third-party painting programs like Corel PhotoPaint or Adobe PhotoShop, which offer many more features, expandability, and easy-to-use interfaces. These programs also include a slew of special effects and filters that Paint doesn't. Paint does work just fine for many simple drawings, charts, and so on.

NOTE

Painting and drawing programs are different and are designed to perform different tasks. Windows 95 Paint is a painting program, and like all other painting programs, it deals with bitmap graphics. Drawing programs like Adobe Illustrator and CorelDRAW! are *vector-based,* which means that each object on the screen can be changed and edited individually. In contrast, painting programs behave like a painter's canvas; once there is paint on the canvas, it can't be removed, but new paint can be placed over it. On a computer, the paint can be removed, but one pixel at a time.

Vector-based images also are scalable. For example, you can insert a vector-based graphic into Word, then expand its size without limitation. When printed, the image looks perfect. Unfortunately, the larger you scale bitmap images, the choppier they look.

So, which one should you use? It depends. You probably want to use painting programs to create images for PowerPoint presentations for on-screen display, and use drawing programs when creating images for printed Word and Excel documents. But there is no rule here—use what suits your needs and looks the best.

The Paint toolbar offers 16 basic tools that help you create or edit pictures easily (see fig. 22.6). These tools work almost exactly like their real-life counterparts. That is, click the Circle tool, then drag on-screen to draw a circle.

Fig. 22.6

Paint is an image-painting program included with Windows 95.

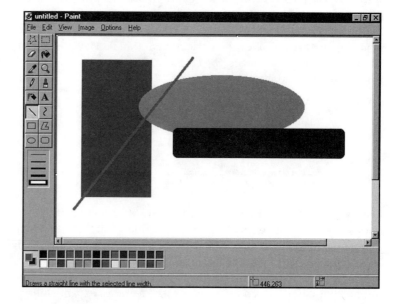

Using the Built-In Office Capabilities

In addition to the applications that come with Windows 95, Office also includes a few applications and features to enable you to create objects that you embed in files. Though the specifics of creating embedded objects are covered in more detail later in the chapter, some of the applications previewed next are used primarily for creating embedded objects rather than stand-alone files.

Drawing Tools. Word, Excel, and PowerPoint offer a Drawing toolbar (see fig. 22.7) with many of the same kinds of basic drawing tools you saw in Windows Paint. Once in Drawing mode, you draw directly on the document that is currently open. Just as with Paint, these tools are fine, but very basic. You get much more functionality, features and effects with third-party drawing tools.

In Word and Excel, it's easy to access the Drawing toolbar by clicking the Drawing button in the Standard toolbar. In PowerPoint, drawing tools appear by default at the left side of the screen.

WordArt. Office includes a program called WordArt that lets you apply different effects to text. By applying these effects, you can take what would normally be ordinary text and manipulate it to create eye-catching text (see fig. 22.8).

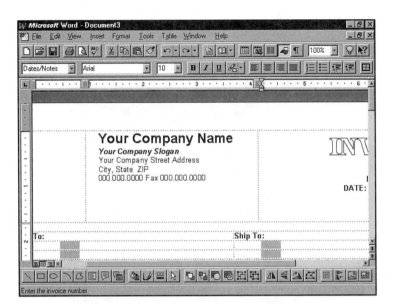

Fig. 22.7

Word, Excel, and PowerPoint provide some basic drawing tools.

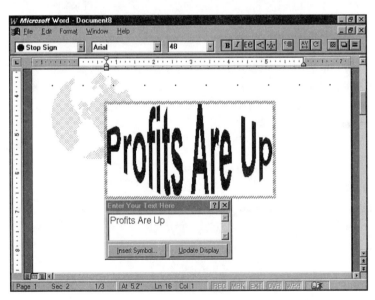

Fig. 22.8

WordArt lets you apply different effects to text.

WordArt can only be launched from within one of the Office applications by inserting an embedded WordArt object. Once opened, the standard toolbars are replaced with the WordArt toolbar. Use WordArt to change the characteristics of the text you are editing. Some of these characteristics include effect, font style, alignment, font size, rotation, and so on.

ClipArt Gallery. ClipArt Gallery, also launched from within Office applications, is a catalog of clip art that is available for you to insert into Office documents (see fig. 22.9). The left side of the dialog box displays the categories of clip art; the right side displays thumbnail previews of the images.

Fig. 22.9

ClipArt Gallery indexes clip art on your computer for easy insertion into documents.

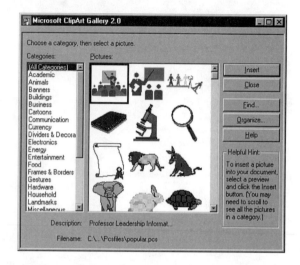

When you find the image you want to use, select it, then click the Insert button. It is pasted into the document where your insertion point was.

You can add additional images to the gallery with the Organize button. Gallery can read the following image formats:

PC Paintbrush	JPEG
Tagged Image File Format	Windows Metafile
WordPerfect Graphics	Macintosh PICT
Encapsulated Postscript	TARGA
Computer Graphics Metafile	CorelDRAW!
HO Graphics Language	CompuServe GIF
Kodak Photo CD	AutoCAD Format 2-D
Micrografx Designer/Draw	Clip Art gallery packages

Once selected, you can assign a new image to one of the categories for easy retrieval.

Microsoft Graph. In addition to still or moving images, a chart or graph is a very effective way to visualize data. A chart or graph takes ordinary data and visually displays it for the user. Because it's easier for someone to see your data visually, don't rule out using a graph.

When you insert a Graph object, a new (default) graph is inserted into the document (see fig. 22.10). In the foreground, a spreadsheet-like window opens with some fake data in it. You edit this data to create your graph. As you do so, the on-screen graph changes to accurately represent your data. Then, use the Graph toolbar on top to modify the way the graph looks.

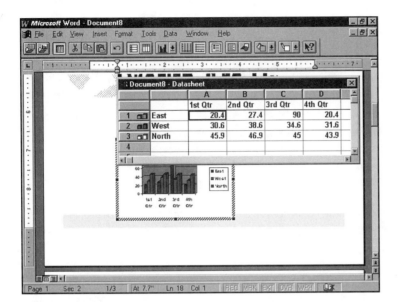

Fig. 22.10

Graph provides an effective way to visualize otherwise meaningless numbers.

Using Graph to create an embedded graph in a Word document can be much more convenient than embedding part of an Excel worksheet, especially if you only have a limited amount of data, if you have not already entered the data in a worksheet, or if your target users may not have the Excel application installed.

Using Third-Party Hardware and Software To Create Multimedia Components

Unfortunately, not every type of multimedia software is shipped with Windows 95. And, as noted earlier in the chapter, creating some kinds of multimedia files (such as video captures) requires specialized hardware. It would be impossible for Windows to cover all the possibilities due to the wide variety of hardware models available.

Each company's hardware comes with specialized software from the hardware manufacturer that best exploits all the hardware's features. To make the most of a particular sound card, it's best to use the software applications that come with the sound card to create and work with various types of sound files. Next, you review some examples of the types of multimedia software that come with hardware or are generally available; keep in mind that these are simply examples, and hundreds of other programs are available.

Contact each manufacturer of the hardware/software described in this and the following sections for pricing and information on their complete line of products, or check out computer catalogs and stores. Check the product documentation to learn how to perform specific operations. If you've recently purchased or will soon purchase new sound or video hardware, or plan to create increasingly sophisticated multimedia component files, by all means review the software that comes with a given piece of hardware and shop around extensively.

Exploring Video Capture with Reveal Video Artist. Video Artist is a software and hardware product that accepts input from any source: VCR, camcorder, laser disk player or anything that generates a composite video signal. The video is then compressed using the Motion JPEG (MPEG) standard and stored on your hard disk. Video Artist has both composite and SVHS inputs and can capture video at 320×240 at up to 30 fps.

Exploiting Sound with the Creative Labs Sound Blaster Card. Creative Labs has an entire line of sound cards available. The Sound Blaster product line features CD-quality and 8-bit or 16-bit stereo sound cards. Some of the Sound Blaster cards include an IDE or SCSI interface for a CD-ROM drive, which provides an effective way to add two devices through a single expansion slot. Because of its early leadership and prevalence, Sound Blaster is the industry standard sound card, meaning that applications such as multimedia games are programmed specifically to be compatible with Sound Blaster. Therefore, any sound card you purchase should be Sound Blaster compatible.

The Sound Blaster AWE32 is a Creative Labs high-end sound card which includes newer technologies to provide better sound, including Wavetable support. All sound cards include the Creative Mixer software, which enables you to control all the inputs and outputs available (see fig. 22.11), so you can change sound recording and playback levels as needed.

Fig. 22.11

The Volume Control allows all sound card settings to be controlled from within Windows 95.

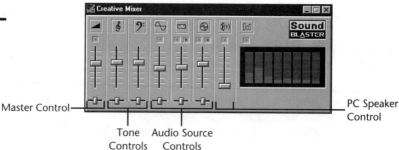

Master Control

Tone Controls   Audio Source Controls

PC Speaker Control

Sound Blaster cards also come with the EnsembleMIDI application for playing back MIDI files, EnsembleCD for playing back CDs, and EnsembleWAV (which can play back multiple WAV sounds, let you record sounds, and synchronize recording with MIDI and CD playback). Sound Blaster cards also come with Creative Wave Studio, which enables you to record sounds from a microphone, CD, or other input source and save it as a WAV file; it also enables you to apply a variety of effects such as reversing and echoing, convert formats (stereo to mono), and more.

Manipulating Bitmap Graphics with Adobe Photoshop. Working with graphic images is often referred to as *photo manipulation* or *image editing*. There are many software choices in this category; however, Adobe Photoshop is the unofficial standard.

Adobe Photoshop lets you create original artwork and retouch scanned images. Photoshop is a high-end professional product designed for processing and enhancing images. There are many extremely powerful and flexible built-in tools, including color correction, retouching, dodging and burning, saturating color, masking and lighting effects, as well as many others (see fig. 22.12).

Fig. 22.12

Adobe Photoshop is one of many software applications that enable you to manipulate graphic images.

Other Sources and Combinations

Finally, there are other ways to gather information that aren't completely do-it-yourself or combine traditional and cutting-edge methods. Here are just a few more ideas for getting the multimedia files you need:

- *Photo CD snapshots.* Many companies in your area can take your 35mm negatives and slides (even ones from professional photo shoots) and put them on a CD in Kodak Photo CD format. This is a cost-effective alternative if you need digitized images and don't have access to a scanner, or need higher resolution than your scanner offers.

- *Scanners.* If you have only a few small images to scan (say, for icons in applications or small logos), many printing companies will scan the images and put them on disk for you.

- *Farm it out.* If you're anywhere near a major city and have some budget dollars available, you should be able to find professionals who have the facilities and expertise to generate top-quality sound, video, and graphics files for a relatively reasonable price.

  For example, if you need a 30-second video clip and don't want to spend two days buying and setting up a video capture card, struggling to capture a quality image, and editing the image, you could hire a graphics/multimedia company to do it for you. To find such a company if you're not familiar with any, look under Computers, Graphics, or Multimedia in the Yellow Pages. This approach is definitely worth the expense if your schedule is busy, if you plan to use the file in multiple documents or applications, or if top-quality results are a must.

Planning Multimedia Use in Office Applications

By using multimedia in your Office documents or applications, you can quickly convey a message to your audience that a skilled writer may need thousands of words to describe. However, you should be selective in choosing the multimedia you will use, keeping the content focused on the message and not the multimedia. Now that you've reviewed the hardware, software, and kinds of files that make up typical multimedia documents and applications, it's time to get down to business.

The planning stage in the multimedia presentation process is the most important. It defines how the final material will look and be delivered to the audience. By jumping right in and creating the presentation, application, or document, you may neglect to include some important information. It's always more difficult to add elements at the end than in the beginning.

Mapping Out the Topics

In many cases, you can think of multimedia as an electronic brochure. It delivers your message to someone with a certain look and feel. Just as you need to lay out how the brochure will look, you need to lay out how the on-screen image will look.

First make a list of what information you are trying to convey to the user. Define the points you want to make and build the presentation backwards from there to suit the audience. This is, in many ways, just like object-oriented programming. Design the front end first, and work backwards from there.

Now create another list. List what you want the experience to be like for the user—shocking, sad, happy, and so on. Match the multimedia content to the type of experience you want to deliver.

Defining Your Audience

By defining who the audience members are, you can design a superior, more focused multimedia document. Use multimedia to enhance the text, demonstrating points and not entire ideas or steps. The following questions are designed to make you think about who the user is. Once you answer them, you will have a clear focus as to who they are and how you should design the document, presentation, or multimedia files:

■ *Who is the person that will be viewing your document?* This person can be anyone—a school teacher, an executive, a teenager, even an entire family. Tailor the files directly for the audience member; for example, you typically don't want to include business jargon in files tailored for teenagers.

- *What is the material your multimedia files address?* Is the material of a technical nature, entertainment, instructional, sales, or what? The type of information you are presenting is also very important.

- *How well does the audience know the material you are discussing?* They may be an expert, a beginner, or anywhere in between. They could be an executive in a company or a new hire. Determine the audience's knowledge of the subject matter to assist you in determining what level to deliver the information.

- *What is the users' level of computer experience?* Determine how long they have been using computers. Your users could range from novices to power users. With this knowledge, you can more effectively design what users see.

TIP

If you don't know who the user will be, always assume the lowest level of knowledge. Never assume the user is an expert and doesn't need much information. Too much information is better than not enough!

Considering the Target User's Computer

Be aware of the type and specifications of the computer systems most audience members will use. Where, when, and how the document will be displayed all impact the final quality. Will it be shown in an office, retail store, trade show, or museum? Differences between your computer and the target computer—such as the speed, amount of memory, free hard disk space, monitor size, display resolution, and display color depth—can all impact the final quality of the multimedia files. If possible, view your completed document or application on the target computer to ensure a quality presentation.

The computer screen is very different from a printed page. When designing an on-screen presentation with PowerPoint in particular, think of the monitor as a television set. Because text is not easy to read on a monitor, avoid completely covering the screen with information. Take advantage of bullets to highlight important points, and avoid using small fonts and hard-to-read styles.

Determining How To Deliver Files to End Users

It's very important to be aware of how you are going to transport the files from your computer to the target computer. Keep in mind that end users need some files used to create embedded objects and many of the other files you use in your multimedia documents and applications. Thus, if you create a multimedia application that calls for a particular file, you need to make sure to provide a copy of that file when you distribute the application.

If you have included many multimedia files, the presentation could be 20M (or much larger). You could use a removable media drive like SyQuest or Bernoulli, or the files can be compressed and spanned across many floppies. The files also could be sent electronically, but if the modems available are not high speed, the transmission time may be unacceptable. Recordable CD-ROM is now becoming commonplace. Lower prices and new models will make this the medium of choice in the coming months due to an over 600M storage capacity.

In either case, file transport is something you should keep in mind when designing the multimedia document, presentation, or application. If the target computer does not have a removable media drive and you don't want to send 10 floppies, then the amount of multimedia you include should be kept to a minimum.

Inserting Multimedia Component Files into Office Applications

Once you have either created or obtained the multimedia objects, you are ready to use them in Office. Because Office 95 supports drag-and-drop, OLE and DDE, you have a number of options for inserting these objects into Office. With each method—a simple copy and paste, drag-and-drop, OLE object—the object behaves differently after being inserted. The choice is yours.

Because there are so many kinds of objects (and therefore, so many different ways to insert them), this section merely provides an overview for creating objects with different methods. To some degree, the kinds of objects you can create will be affected by the applications installed on your computer.

Finding the Right Spot Before Inserting

Before you can insert a multimedia file into Office, you need to decide where it will be placed. Placement is the key to successfully delivering your message to the audience. Give some thought to positioning rather than plucking your decision out of thin air. The multimedia file should not interrupt the flow of the rest of the document.

Inserting Multimedia OLE Objects

Depending on which of the following methods you use, the inserted object will behave differently. An item inserted into Office also will appear differently to the user depending on the type of object it is. How the object looks depends on what type of object it is.

An object can either be inserted to display the first frame of its contents, or appear as an icon. For example, a sound file has no visible contents, so the Speaker icon is displayed.

Pasting a Multimedia Object. The simplest method to add a multimedia object to an application is good old cut and paste. You copy the object from one application—choosing Edit, Copy and Edit, Paste—into another with no strings attached. The object becomes part of the document you have pasted it into. While this is simple, it does not provide any of the advanced linking and embedding capabilities available in Office.

IV

Instead of selecting Paste, you can select Paste Special. Then, if the object was cut or copied from an OLE-compliant application, the Paste Link option button is available (not dimmed). Selecting Paste Link in this case links the pasted object to the original file.

Drag-and-Drop. One of the new and exciting features of Office 95 is the capability to drag and drop objects between Office and other OLE-compatible applications. Generally, when you drag the object, you are cutting it from the source document and embedding it into the target document.

TIP

When dragging an object from one application to another, it's not always necessary to drag the object from window to window. With OLE-supported applications, you can drag the object over the program's button on the taskbar. The program will then open, and you can drag up and release the mouse button. This inserts the object with one click of the mouse.

Using the Insert Menu. The Insert menu is by far the most powerful way of inserting multimedia objects into Office (see fig. 22.13). The two choices available on the Insert menu when working with multimedia files are Picture and Object. Selecting Picture enables you to pick from the available image files on your system. Selecting Object lets you create new objects from other applications. They can be original objects that you create using the tools from the application, or inserted objects based on existing files. For either type of object, you create an OLE link to the source application, which enables you to edit the object from within Office.

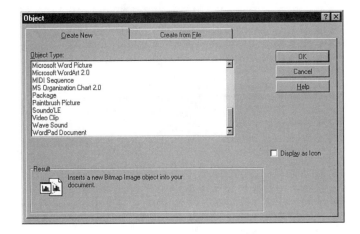

Fig. 22.13

Inserting objects from other applications is simple—just select Object from the Insert menu.

To play an embedded multimedia sound or video object, double-click the icon for it in the client (target) application.

Editing Embedded Files

Once they're inserted into an Office application, you can edit multimedia objects just like any other file. OLE-compatible files can be edited by right-clicking them, then selecting <u>E</u>dit from the shortcut menu. If the file is an image, by default selecting <u>E</u>dit or <u>O</u>pen displays Windows Paint tools or the tools from the application used to create the image. If it was linked or embedded, the application it was created with opens within Office for in-place editing. The icons and images can be resized just as any other object would be.

Creating File Packages Using Object Packager

The Object Packager is included with Windows 95. It enables you to embed an object into Office (or any other application) that is not OLE-compliant. What you are actually doing is taking a file or command and making it look appealing by adding a nice icon for it in the document. You can assign the package an icon, change its description, or even assign it a command that will be carried out when activated by the user.

For example, you can include a text file in your document or an INI file that you need to distribute. By bringing the file into Object Packager, you can change its icon and give it a meaningful name.

To create a package, choose <u>I</u>nsert, <u>O</u>bject. Choose Package from the <u>O</u>bject Type list in the Object dialog box. You see the Object Packager window shown in figure 22.14. Click Appearance on the left side of the window, then click the Insert <u>I</u>con button. Choose the icon you want to use to represent the file in your document using the dialog box that appears. Click the Content side of the Object Packager window, then choose <u>F</u>ile, <u>I</u>mport to add the file you want the package to contain. Then exit Object Packager.

Fig. 22.14

Object Packager allows a non-OLE-compliant file to be embedded into a document.

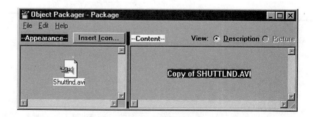

TIP

Object Packager supports Windows 95 shortcuts. So, if you want your package to launch another application or open another file in a separate window outside the current Office application, insert the shortcut or EXE file in the Content side of the package.

Experiencing Multimedia in Office Applications

Finally, you are ready to show the audience your masterpiece. Each of the different types of multimedia files (as well as other types of files) identify themselves with a different icon.

When images are inserted, the actual image is displayed. Video files display only the first frame in the video. This gives users a preview of what they will see when the file is run. Audio files display themselves as an icon. As in figure 22.15, you should place a caption under the multimedia file to identify what it contains.

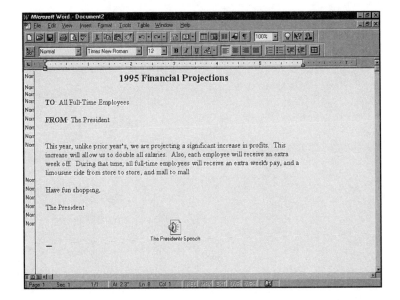

Fig. 22.15

Double-click the speaker to play the audio file.

When you are ready to view a multimedia file, just double-click it, and the file begins playing.

From Here...

You now have a better foundation for using multimedia with Office. Refer to the following chapters for more information pertaining to the topics discussed:

- Chapter 3, "Integration Basics," teaches the basic concepts of integration and what makes it work.

- Chapter 13, "Automating Office Integration with PowerPoint," provides more detailed information of the use of WordArt.

- For more information about other Office-compatible applications, refer to Chapter 16, "Working with Office Compatible Applications."

■ Multimedia files can also be used in help files. For more information, see Chapter 21, "Providing Help for Users."

■ Appendix A, "Office 95 Compatible Products," includes a list of the products that are certified as Office compatible.

CHAPTER 23

Using Windows APIs

Microsoft Office offers a vast array of tools for users and developers to build integrated office applications. There are functions and methods to perform almost every task you want to include in your application.

However, there will be times when you find that even Office applications do not provide you with built-in functions to carry out a specific task—for example, a function to provide you with a list of all open applications on your computer, or a means for you to close down the open application of your choice. Maybe you would like the ability to play music in the background when your Office application executes, or to know the amount of free space on your disk drive at the touch of a button. In such cases, you can turn to the Windows API for quick and efficient solutions. Because the Windows API uses functions written in C or C++, you find that these routines process extremely fast and provide rapid results.

In this chapter, you learn how to

- Make calls to the Windows API from within your Office applications
- Use the Window API functions to obtain information about your computer system
- Display a list of open applications using the Windows API routines
- Use the Multimedia API calls to manipulate sound and video
- Make considerations when programming with the Windows APIs

Introducing the Windows API

The API in Windows API stands *for Application Programming Interface*. Windows 95 is a 32-bit operating system that exposes a number of functions and procedures to the application programmer. Typically, a C or C++ programmer would use these routines to write applications. Every aspect of an application—from the design of its windows, to mouse and keyboard handling, to memory management—is performed through these Windows API routines.

TIP

There are more than 1,000 routines included in the Windows API. You, as an Office developer, do not need all these routines. However, by knowing how to tap into the power of Windows API, you can make your applications run faster and achieve tasks that may not be possible by using the Office software built-in functions.

The routines available under the Windows API are powerful, fast, and—incidentally—free. They come with Windows 95, and all users who operate your Office application under Windows 95 are guaranteed to have them on their systems.

The Windows API routines reside in Dynamic Link Libraries (DLLs) accompanying the Windows 95 operating system. In the next section, you learn how to access these DLLs and the routines within them. Before that, you should understand when to use the Windows API and when not to.

When To Use the Windows API

When you are building integrated Office applications, use all the built-in functions within those applications. When you need to perform a specific task for which you cannot find a built-in function or method, explore the Windows API and use its functionality.

For example, when you are working with Visual Basic for Applications, if you want to programmatically set the focus in your application to a particular object on your screen—a command button, or a list box—you can do one of two things:

- Use the Windows API routine `SetFocus`
- Use the built-in VBA method `Object.SetFocus`

In this case, use the second option—it is easier and less prone to problems.

However, if you want to set the focus in your application to a particular object on another application's screen—such as Notepad—use the first option. It's the only way you can set the focus to the Notepad application.

Using the Windows API is not for the weak-hearted. Calling the routines within the Windows API requires an understanding of how data is passed to and from your application and the API DLL. If you pass arguments incorrectly, you encounter an application error. Because this error is generated by your call to an external DLL, you cannot trap it like other internal errors. Your application will crash, and you will lose data. This chapter provides you with a blow-by-blow account of how to use the Windows API and should help you prevent such errors.

How To Use the API Functions

When you write a function in your application, you declare the function and its arguments and then write the code that is executed when the function is called. At another place in your code, you make a call to the function, passing the correct parameters in the right order. If you pass the wrong parameters or if they are in the wrong order, you receive a runtime error.

Similarly, when you make a call to an API routine, you need to pass the correct parameters in the right order. When you make a call to an API routine, you are placing a number of parameter values at a location in memory called the *stack*. Your API function then executes using the values that you provide. This API function reads the values from the stack and executes its code using those values. If the API function returns a value, it places the return value at another location in memory from where your program can access it.

In order to call an API function, you must therefore perform the following steps:

1. Identify the file containing the API routine, which is usually a DLL. This is described in the next section.
2. Create a `Declare` statement for the API. You learn more about this step later in "Declaring a DLL Routine."
3. Call the function with valid parameters matching your `Declare` statement. Learn more about this step later in "Passing Arguments to a DLL."

Using Dynamic Link Libraries

All Windows API functions reside in DLLs. These are typically files with a DLL or an EXE extension. Conceptually, a *DLL* is a collection of procedures and functions placed inside a Windows recognizable file. Multiple procedures or functions can exist within a DLL. Each procedure or function is similar to the procedure or function that you create within your Office application.

The more than 1,000 API calls in Windows 95 reside in executables and DLLs found in the WINDOWS folder—USER32.DLL, GDI32.DLL, and one of the following KERNEL files: KRNL286.EXE, KRNL386.EXE, or KERNEL32.DLL.

The KERNEL files hold functions responsible for core Windows operations: managing memory, multitasking, and handling virtual memory.

GDI32.DLL contains functions that handle output to devices: the screen, printer, memory blocks, and so on. All drawing functions reside in this DLL.

The USER32.DLL contains functions related to the Windows environment: managing windows, menus, cursors, timers, and so on.

In addition to these core DLLs, you can call functions within any Windows DLL that resides on your computer.

Declaring a DLL Routine

When you are ready to use a routine available in an external DLL file, you first need to `Declare` the routine so that your application will know the following:

■ The name you will be using for the routine

- Where to find the routine—that is, in what DLL file
- The name of the routine within the DLL file, if not the same as the name you are using
- What arguments the routine requires and their data types
- What data type the function returns

When using Basic (Access Basic, VB or VBA, and WordBasic), the keyword `Declare` is the way you indicate to your application that an external function or subroutine is present within a DLL. For example, if you want to know the number of milliseconds that have elapsed since Windows was started, you can use the Windows API function `GetTickCount`. Declare the function as follows:

```
Declare Function GetTickCount Lib "Kernel32" () As Long
```

In this code line, `GetTickCount` is the name of the API function. It is found within the external DLL `KERNEL32.DLL`. It has no arguments, and it returns a long integer data type. This declaration tells your Office application that if the programmer makes a call to a function called `GetTickCount` anywhere in the application, the routine `GetTickCount` within the external DLL `KERNEL32.DLL` needs to be run. So, if you declare the function as shown earlier, then in your application when you need to make a call to the function, you would need to call it as follows:

```
lSomeLongVariable = GetTickCount()
```

Your Office application would look at the name of the routine (`GetTickCount`), and jump over to KERNEL32.DLL to make the call and return whatever the routine returns.

The complete syntax for declaring a subroutine or function is as follows:

```
[Public ¦ Private ] Declare Sub SubName Lib "Libname" _
  [Alias "Aliasname" ][([Arglist])]
[Public ¦ Private ] Declare Function FunctionName Lib "Libname" _
  [Alias "Aliasname" ] [([Arglist])][As type]
```

The `Declare` statement has the following components as described in table 23.1.

Table 23.1 The *Declare* Statement Components

Component	Description
Public	Indicates that this routine is available to all procedures in all modules.
Private	Indicates that this routine is available to procedures in the current module only. A procedure in a different module within your application will not be able to access it.
Declare	The Basic keyword indicating that this is a declaration of a routine within an external DLL.

Component	Description
SubName/FunctionName	The Name of the subroutine or function within the external DLL. If the Alias keyword is used, it could be any valid routine name which you can use in your code. Otherwise, it refers to the name of the routine as found within the DLL.
Lib	The Basic keyword indicating the external library that contains the routine.
Libname	The external DLL name.
Alias	The Basic keyword that indicates that Sub/Function component used in the previous code is a user-defined name. The real name for the routine within the DLL is defined by the next Aliasname component.
AliasName	The case-sensitive name for the routine within the DLL. If the routine within the DLL does not have a name, this refers to an *ordinal* number within the DLL that points to the routine you need.
Arglist	A list of arguments as required by the routine.
As type	For a function within the DLL, indicates what kind of data is returned by the routine.

As a different example, look at how you would use all of the previous Declare statement components in your code. When you want to give a simple beep to your user—maybe just to alert the user about something—you can use the Windows API function called Beep:

```
Declare Function AlertBeep Lib "Kernel32" Alias "Beep" _
    (ByVal dwFreq As Long, ByVal dwDuration As Long) As Long
```

This declaration tells your Office application that the programmer wants to use a function called AlertBeep which resides within the external DLL KERNEL32.DLL. Within that DLL, its name is actually Beep. This function has two arguments—both long integers—and it returns a long integer. Note that I changed the name of the function from Beep to AlertBeep by using the Alias clause. This is very important, as you discover in the next section.

The Declare statement is usually placed at the very beginning of a module, usually following the global type and constant declarations. If you make your declarations Public, you need to declare the routine only once in your application. If you are using Excel, it is better to group all your Public Windows API declarations within one separate module—maybe even called ApiDeclarations. If you are using Word, place all your Windows API declarations at the beginning before any macro code. That way, you can easily find them if you ever need to make modifications later on.

IV

Optimizing Integration

Using the *Alias* Keyword Often

Probably, the most useful of components of the `Declare` statement explained earlier is the `Alias` keyword. The `Alias` keyword always has the associated `AliasName` component following it.

What the `Alias` keyword does is map the name you provide under the `SubName`/ `FunctionName` component of the component of the `Declare` statement to the `AliasName` component, which is the real name of the routine.

Remember the example in the previous section where you declared the Windows API function `GetTickCount`? You used its original name in the `Declare` statement. However, you could also have declared the same function as follows:

```
Declare Function apiTimer Lib "Kernel32" Alias _
"GetTickCount" () As Long
```

Now, your Office application does not know of the existence of a function called `GetTickCount`. It only knows that there exists a function called `apiTimer` that returns a long. Internally, it knows that the function `apiTimer` maps to the function `GetTickCount` within the external DLL KERNEL32.DLL. So in your application, you need to make the call as follows:

```
lSomeLongVariable = apiTimer()
```

Now, why would you want to go through all the trouble of using a new name, via the `Alias` keyword? You would need to do so for a number of reasons:

- The Windows API function name may clash with an Office application reserved name, public variable, or constant. For example, there is a Windows API routine called `SetFocus` that enables a particular window or control to obtain the current user focus. However, `SetFocus` cannot be used as-is, because there is already a reserved word `SetFocus` within Basic. Hence, a declaration such as the one given here generates an error:

  ```
  Declare Function SetFocus Lib "user32" _
      (ByVal hWnd As Long) As Long
  ```

  You need to use the `Alias` keyword to provide a new name for your function that does not clash. You can, instead, use the following declaration:

  ```
  Declare Function apiSetFocus Lib "user32" _
  Alias "SetFocus" _
  (ByVal hWnd As Long) As Long
  ```

  Within your application, now use `apiSetFocus` instead of `SetFocus` to call the Windows API routine.

- The Windows API function name may not be a valid Basic name. For example, the Windows API routine used to open a disk file, `_lopen`, begins with an underscore, which is not a valid function name in Basic code. Therefore, you need to modify the declaration using the `Alias` keyword and provide a valid function name.

■ The Windows API function may not have a name at all! Some DLLs use just numbers instead of names to indicate routines. For example, a DLL could have a function which is internally marked as the number 123 and which returns a long integer. The number 123 that refers to the function is called an *ordinal number*. In order to call a function such as this, you need to supply a valid function name and refer to the number 123 as follows:

```
Declare Function apiFunction Lib "DLLName" _
    Alias "#123" ()As Long
```

In Windows, if # is the first character within the AliasName component of the Declare statement, all characters that follow must indicate the ordinal number of the function. Within your application, you can refer to the function by typing **apiFunction** as its name.

■ The Windows API function is case-sensitive. In the 32-bit world of Windows 95, Windows API routine names are case-sensitive. This means that a routine called GetTickCount will not be the same as a routine called Gettickcount. If you made a mistake in declaring the routine name's case, and if you have made about 20 calls to that routine, when you need to change the name, you have to change the name in more than 20 different locations in your programs.

Instead, *always* use the Alias keyword. Within the quoted string of AliasName, refer to the function name with its correct case. Then it does not matter what case you use to call your function within your application. For example, if you have declared the Windows API routine GetTickCount as apiTimer, then within your application, you don't encounter an error if you make any of the following calls:

```
lSomeLongVariable = apiTimer()
lSomeLongVariable = APITimer()
lSomeLongVariable = apiTIMER()
```

And you can forget about the case-sensitivity of API names when writing code: as long as you spelled and typed the function name correctly in the AliasName string, the function is mapped back to the correct function automatically.

Passing Arguments to a DLL

Like in any other subroutine or function within Basic code, you need to pass arguments (if any are required) to the routines and functions within a DLL.

Caution

Because VBA cannot verify whether the number and type of arguments you declare for a function residing in an external DLL are correct, it ignores them, compiles cleanly, and allows you to run the program. VBA just takes it as you give it, and if the function fails because of incorrect arguments, you encounter a General Protection Fault (GPF), causing your program to hang up and lose data. The only remedy is to make sure you are passing the correct arguments and to save your work often. In fact, to prevent code loss, you should always save before running your application.

By default, Basic passes all its arguments by reference. That is, when you pass an argument to a function, what is actually passed is a 32-bit pointer to the address where the data is stored. This is alright for most DLL functions, but some C functions require you to pass arguments by value—a copy of the argument is passed to the function. In such cases, you can use the ByVal keyword.

Passing strings to functions inside a DLL is perhaps the most frustrating and confusing area to the Office programmer. The reason for this is that Basic handles strings in a manner different from C or C++. Without going into the details of what these differences are (which is beyond the scope of this book), remember that to avoid problems, when a DLL function is expecting a string, pass the string explicitly by value using the ByVal keyword.

When you pass strings to a DLL function and expect the function to modify your string and have it passed back to you, you need to take special precautions. For example, if you want to obtain the text of a window's title in your string variable, you need to pass to the DLL the name of your variable in memory. Because the DLL is writing the text of the window's title to your string variable in memory, if you do not make your string variable big enough to hold the entire window title text, the DLL attempts to write to a portion of the memory that is beyond what your variable points to—overwriting other portions in memory when it runs out of space. This could lead to unpredictable results. The remedy is to make sure that the string that you are passing the DLL to is sufficiently large enough to fit any value you expect the DLL to return.

NOTE As a general rule of thumb, when you are passing strings to a DLL routine, expecting it to return a value back to you within that string variable, pre-initialize the string to be sufficiently large. One good way is to pre-initialize it with about 255 null values by using the string$ function:

```
sVariable = string$(255,0)
```

Now that you have an overview of using API functions, go ahead and put some useful API routines to work in your applications.

Putting APIs to Use in Your Applications

The following examples demonstrate how you can use the Windows API in your Office applications. Most of these examples are either in WordBasic or Excel VBA. In either case, the methodology of incorporating the Windows API code into your application is the same.

Using APIs in Excel

In this chapter, you find a number of Excel VBA code samples. For each sample, the steps involved to incorporate the code into your application is the same. Follow these steps to add Windows API use in your applications:

1. In Excel, choose Insert, Macro, Module. A blank Module1 sheet appears.
2. Choose Edit, Sheet, Rename, or double-click the sheet name tab at the bottom of your screen. The Rename Sheet dialog box appears (see fig. 23.1).

Fig. 23.1

Use the Rename Sheet dialog box to provide a name to your module.

3. Type a meaningful module name. For example, type **ApiCalls** to indicate that this module will hold API declarations. Select OK. The sheet name now changes to the name you typed in.
4. Type in the declarations for your API calls as required. In the examples that follow, this is usually presented at the very beginning.
5. Return to Sheet1 by clicking its tab.
6. If you need to create command buttons or other objects on your screen, make sure that your Forms toolbar is visible. To do so, choose View, Toolbars and make sure the Forms toolbar has a check mark next to it.
7. Create appropriate command buttons or lists as your examples indicate, by clicking once on the corresponding object on the Forms toolbar and then dragging and sizing the object on-screen.
8. When you create a new object, the Assign Macro dialog box appears (see fig. 23.2).

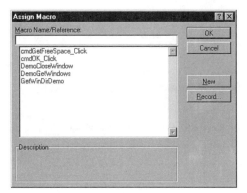

Fig. 23.2

Use the Assign Macro dialog box to create a new macro to assign to the object on-screen.

9. If you do not want to use the default names for command buttons and lists, you can select Cancel in the Assign Macro dialog box. Assign a new name to the object by clicking its name in the pane above the worksheet grid, and typing in the new name. Remember to press Enter after typing in a new name.

IV

Optimizing Integration

10. To assign a new macro to your object, right-click the object and select Assign Macro.... The same Assign Macro dialog box appears. Choose <u>N</u>ew. Excel automatically creates a new macro subroutine based on the name of your object. You can now type the Basic code that is triggered by the object.

To run the code associated with an object (such as a command button), just click the button.

Using APIs in Word

The WordBasic code samples in this chapter can be incorporated into your applications by following a few easy steps. Follow these steps to add Windows API in your applications:

1. In Word, choose <u>T</u>ools, <u>M</u>acro. The Macro dialog box appears. Type in the name of your macro, and choose Cr<u>e</u>ate (see fig. 23.3).

Fig. 23.3

Use the Macro dialog box to create a new macro.

2. When Word presents a blank macro sheet with the `Sub Main` - `End Sub` block, move your cursor to the top of the sheet and add a few empty lines above the `Sub Main` line.

3. Type in the declarations for your API calls as required. In the examples that follow, this is usually presented at the very beginning.

4. Type in the code for your macro within the `Sub Main` - `End Sub` block.

5. To run the macro, again choose <u>T</u>ools, <u>M</u>acro. In the Macro dialog box, select the name of the macro to run and choose <u>R</u>un.

Now look at some useful API routines.

Getting Information About Your System

Frequently, you will need to obtain information about your system from within your application. This is especially true if you are developing an application that will be

used on other people's machines, and they may have set up their machines differently. The Windows API includes many routines that let you obtain information
about the current system.

Obtaining the Windows Folder Name. The Windows API routine
`GetWindowsDirectory` is useful to find out what the name is of the folder from
where Windows 95 is being run. If a user had selected default installation, it would
most probably be C:\WINDOWS. However, you may find users, such as me, who
have installed Windows 95 in a separate C:\WIN95 folder. And if your application
is trying to find a list of files in the WINDOWS folder, you cannot hard code the
name of the folder as C:\WINDOWS in your application. In such cases, you can use
the `GetWindowsDirectory` API routine.

> **TIP**
>
> Under Windows 3.x, files were stored in directories and subdirectories. Windows 95
> calls these directories and subdirectories *folders* and *subfolders*. Although the Windows
> 95 terminology has changed, the Windows API functions still refer to these folders
> as directories to maintain continuity with the older Windows 3.x API functions. Just
> remember—folders and directories are the same thing!

The declaration of the `GetWindowsDirectory` API routine is as follows:

```
Declare Function GetWindowsDirectory Lib "Kernel32.dll"  \
        (lpBuffer$ , nSize As Long) Alias  \
        "GetWindowsDirectoryA" As Long
```

> **TIP**
>
> In Excel VBA, use the underscore character (_) as a line continuation character to break
> long lines of code. This makes code easy to read, without scrolling off to the right of
> your code window. In WordBasic, however, you have to use the backslash character (\)
> as the line continuation character.

The following code demonstrates how you can obtain the current Windows folder
name. In this routine, you simply display a message box with the name of the current
Windows folder, as shown in figure 23.4. You could use this information construc-
tively in your applications.

Fig. 23.4

`WinAPI.Dot` Macro
`DemoGetWindowsDirectory`
*displays a message box
with the name of the
Windows folder on it.*

Listing 23.1 WINAPI.DOT. The *DemoGetWindowsDirectory* Routine Displays the Current Windows Folder

```
Declare Function GetWindowsDirectory Lib "Kernel32.dll"(lpBuffer$ \
    , nSize As Long) Alias "GetWindowsDirectoryA" As Long
'
' GetWindowsDirectory Routine
'
Sub MAIN
' ----- Pre-initialize our string with null characters.
sWinDir$ = String$(255, 0)
' ----- Get the Windows Folder
x = GetWindowsDirectory(sWinDir$, Len(sWinDir$))
' ----- Did we get back any information?
If x > 0 Then
    sWinDir$ = Left$(sWinDir$, x)
Else
    sWinDir$ = ""
End If
MsgBox "Windows Folder  = " + sWinDir$, \
"DemoGetWindowsDirectory", 64


End Sub
```

Obtaining the Amount of Free Disk Space. Another useful API routine is the GetDiskFreeSpace routine. This routine lets you know the amount of free space in your system drive.

The declaration for GetDiskFreeSpace is much longer than any API routine you have encountered so far, but it is easy to implement:

```
Declare Function GetDiskFreeSpace Lib "Kernel32" Alias  _
    "GetDiskFreeSpaceA" (ByVal lpRootPathName As String, _
    lpSectorsPerCluster As Long, lpBytesPerSector As Long, _
    lpNumberOfFreeClusters As Long, lpTtoalNumberOfClusters As Long) _
    As Long
```

The following table explains the different arguments for this API routine.

Argument	Description
lpRootPathName	String describing the root path for the drive you need to check. Use **a:**, **b:**, **c:** and so on for drives A, B and C, respectively.
lpSectorsPerCluster	Long integer that returns the number of sectors per cluster on the disk. Use zero.
lpBytesPerSector	Long integer that returns the number of bytes per sector on the disk. Use zero.
LpNumberOfFreeClusters	Long integer that returns the number of free clusters. Use zero.
LpTotalNumberOfClusters	Long integer pointing to total number of clusters on disk. Use zero.

To obtain the total bytes of free space on drive C, make a call to the previous API routine passing **c:** as the lpRootPathName argument, and then multiply the numbers returned in the arguments:

```
lpNumberOfFreeClusters * lpSectorsPerCluster * lpBytesPerSector
```

The following code demonstrates how to obtain the free disk space from drive C, shown in figure 23.5.

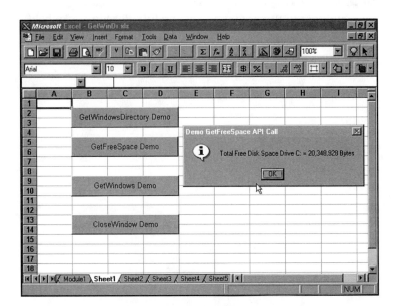

Fig. 23.5

cmdGetFreeSpace_Click event associated with button on Sheet1 displays amount of free disk space on drive C.

Listing 23.2   GETWINDR.XLS. The *cmdGetFreeSpace_Click* Routine

```
Sub cmdGetFreeSpace_Click()
    Dim L As Long
    Dim sPath As String
    sPath = "c:\"
    Dim lpSectorsPerCluster As Long
    Dim lpBytesPerSector As Long
    Dim lpNumberOfFreeClusters As Long
    Dim lpTtoalNumberOfClusters As Long

    L = GetDiskFreeSpace(sPath, lpSectorsPerCluster, _
        lpBytesPerSector, lpNumberOfFreeClusters, _
        lpTtoalNumberOfClusters)

    MsgBox "Total Free Disk Space Drive C: = " & _
        Format$((lpBytesPerSector * lpSectorsPerCluster * _
        lpNumberOfFreeClusters), "#,##0") & _
        " Bytes", 64, "Demo GetFreeSpace API Call"

End Sub
```

NOTE Of course, if you are using WordBasic, you do not need to use the Windows API to obtain the free disk space. Use the built-in function GetSystemInfo$ as follows:

```
' ----- NO api required. Use built-in function
MsgBox "Disk Space Free on Drive C: = " + GetSystemInfo$(26)
```

Obtaining a List of All Drives Existing on Your System. If you wanted to get a list of all drives available on your (or your user's) computer, a useful API routine can help you. The API function GetLogicalDriveStrings returns a list of available drives on the system.

The declaration for the GetLogicalDriveStrings routine is as follows:

```
Declare Function GetLogicalDriveStrings Lib "Kernel32" _
Alias "GetLogicalDriveStringsA" _
(ByVal nBufferLength As Long, _
ByVal lpBuffer As String) As Long
```

In the declaration above, lpBuffer is a string variable, and nBufferLength is its size.

The following code demonstrates how to obtain a list of available drives on your system, shown in figure 23.6.

Fig. 23.6

GetDriveList *routine associated with button on Sheet1 displays a list of available drives on the system.*

Listing 23.3   GETWINDR.XLS. The *GetDriveList* Routine

```
Sub GetDriveList()
    Dim sTmp As String
    Dim L As Long
    Dim i As Integer
    Dim sEndln As String

    sEndln = Chr$(13) & Chr$(10)

    ' ----- initialize our string with nulls
    sTmp = String$(255, 0)

    L = GetLogicalDriveStrings(Len(sTmp), sTmp)

    If L > 0 Then
        ' ----- we received a null
        ' ----- separated list of drives
```

```
' ----- parse it out for presentation
sTmp = Left$(sTmp, L)
For i = 1 To L
    ' ----- replace each occurrence of
    ' ----- \{null} with Carriage Return
    ' ----- and Line Feed.
    If Mid$(sTmp, i, 1) = Chr$(0) Then
        Mid$(sTmp, i, 1) = Chr$(10)
    End If
    If Mid$(sTmp, i, 1) = "\" Then
        Mid$(sTmp, i, 1) = Chr$(13)
    End If
Next i
MsgBox "The following Drives are " & _
sEndln & "available on your Computer System : " & _
sEndln & sTmp, 64, "Demo GetDriveList"
End If

End Sub
```

Handling and Controlling Windows

In Windows, every window has an identifying number (known as a *handle*) associated with it. This handle identifies the window and the application associated with it. Once a window is created, it is assigned a handle. This handle remains associated with a window until it is closed (destroyed by Windows). You can use a number of Windows API routines that use the window handle to identify and manipulate windows. Take a look at a few of them.

Obtaining a Handle to the Current Window. The GetActiveWindow function can be used to retrieve the handle of the currently active window which is the top-level window that has the input focus.

You would declare the GetActiveWindow function as follows:

```
Declare Function GetActiveWindow Lib "User" () As Integer
```

Within your code, you would make your call. The following code retrieves the handle of an Access application, assuming that Access is open and running:

```
Dim hWindow As Integer
On Error Resume Next
Err = 0
AppActivate "Microsoft Access"
If Err <> 0 Then
    MsgBox "Microsoft Access not found"
Else
    hWindow = GetActiveWindow()
    MsgBox "Microsoft window handle = " & Str$(hWindow)
End If
```

Obtaining the Text of a Window's Title. Once you obtain the handle of any window, you can find out the text on the title of the window using the GetWindowText API routine.

Declare the `GetWindowText` API routine as follows:

```
Declare Function GetWindowText Lib "user32" _
Alias "GetWindowTextA" (ByVal hWnd As Long, _
ByVal lpString As String, ByVal cch As Long) _
As Long
```

The following table explains the various arguments in the previous API call.

Argument	Description
hWnd	The handle of the window you want to query.
lpString	A string variable that returns the text of the window's title. Remember to pass the string pre-initialized to nulls and make it wide enough to hold the title text—255 characters is a safe number.
Cch	A long integer that tells the API routine how large you have made the string lpString. Use the Len() function to pass the length of the string.

For example, the following code displays the title of the current window:

```
Dim sTmp as string
Dim hWnd as long
Dim L as long
' ----- get the current window handle
hWnd = GetActiveWindow()
' ----- Pre-initialize the string
sTmp = string$(255,0)
' ----- Call the API
L = GetWindowText(hWnd, sTmp, len(sTmp))
' ----- Did we get back anything?
If L > 0 then
    msgbox "Window Title = " & Left$(sTmp,L)
end if
```

You can make use of the API routines you've learned up until now in the next section to obtain something very useful—a list of all *open windows*—application windows that are visible on your system either in a minimized, maximized, or normal state. This is explained in the next section.

Obtaining a List of All Open Windows. As learned in the previous section, you can get a handle to the current window. And from the handle, you can obtain the title text of the window. If it were possible to walk through the list of all open windows, obtaining each one's handle and each one's title text, you could generate a list of all open windows. You can do this with the help of another API routine, `GetWindow`.

The `GetWindow` API routine to useful to obtain the handle of a specific window, which has a particular relationship with another window whose handle you already know (the source window). Windows can be from different applications, in which case they are all sibling windows to each other. Multiple windows can also occur within each application, in which case there might be a parent-child relationship between windows.

For example, in Word, each document window is a child of the main Word window. And the Word window is a sibling window to the Excel window, if both Word and Excel are running on your computer. We can walk down a list of all sibling windows to obtain a list of open applications, or even walk down a list of parent-child windows to obtain a list of all windows within a single application. In either case, you can use the GetWindow API routine.

To declare the GetWindow function, use the following:

```
Declare Function GetWindow Lib "user32" _
(ByVal hWnd As Long, ByVal wCmd As Long) As Long
```

The following table describes the arguments for this routine:

Argument	Description
hWnd	The handle of the source window, which you obtained— maybe by using GetActiveWindow API call.
wCmd	Long integer that indicates the relationship between the source window and the window you want. The valid values for wCmd are: ■ GW_HWNDFIRST (0). Finds the first sibling window, or the first top-level window. ■ GW_HWNDLAST (1). Finds the last sibling window, or the last top-level window. ■ GW_HWNDNEXT (2). Finds the next sibling window. ■ GW_HWNDPREV (3). Finds the previous sibling window. ■ GW_OWNER (4). Finds the owner (usually the parent) window. ■ GW_CHILD (5). Finds the child window.

The GetWindow API returns a valid handle or zero if no further window exists.

Using the above information, the following code displays a list of all open windows in your system. To run the code, open the file GETWINDR.XLS and click the GetWindows Demo button. Before you click the button, make sure you have a lot of applications (such as WordPad, Calculator, Paint, Word, and PowerPoint) open on your system. Then you can see a list, similar to the one shown in figure 23.7.

Fig. 23.7

DemoGetWindows *routine*
associated with button on
Sheet1 displays list of open
windows in the system.

The following code lists the API declarations used by the DemoGetWindows routine and its associated GetWinText routine.

Listing 23.4   GETWINDR.XLS. The API Declarations Used by
***DemoGetWindows* and Its Associated *GetWinText* Routines**

```
Declare Function GetActiveWindow Lib "user32" () As Long
Declare Function GetWindow Lib "user32" _
(ByVal hWnd As Long, ByVal wCmd As Long) As Long

Declare Function GetWindowText Lib "user32" _
Alias "GetWindowTextA" (ByVal hWnd As Long, _
ByVal lpString As String, ByVal cch As Long) _
As Long

Declare Function IsWindowVisible Lib "user32" _
  (ByVal hWnd As Long) As Long
```

The code for the DemoGetWindows routine and its associated GetWinText routine is given in listing 23.5.

Listing 23.5   GETWINDR.XLS. The *DemoGetWindows* Routine and Its
Associated *GetWinText* Routine

```
'
' DemoGetWindows : Demo for GetWindow API routine
'
Sub DemoGetWindows()
    Dim sMsg As String
    Dim sWinText As String
    Dim hWnd As Long
    Dim sEndLn As String

    sEndLn = Chr$(13) & Chr$(10)

    ' ----- get first window handle
    hWnd = GetActiveWindow()
    Do While hWnd > 0

        ' ----- display only if window is visible
        If IsWindowVisible(hWnd) Then

            ' ----- get window title text
            sWinText = GetWinText(hWnd)
```

```
            ' ----- and add it to our message string
            If sWinText <> "" Then sMsg = sMsg & sEndLn & sWinText
        End If
        ' ----- get next window handle
        hWnd = GetWindow(hWnd, GW_HWNDNEXT)
    Loop

    If sMsg <> "" Then
        sMsg = "List of open windows:" & sEndLn & sMsg
        MsgBox sMsg, 64, "Demo List Windows"
    End If

End Sub
'
' GetWinText : returns the text of a given window's title
'
Function GetWinText(ByVal hWnd As Long) As String
    Dim sTmp As String
    Dim L As Long

    ' ----- initialize our string with nulls
    sTmp = String$(255, 0)

    ' ----- call the API routine
    L = GetWindowText(hWnd, sTmp, Len(sTmp))

    ' ----- Did we get back anything ?
    If L > 0 Then
        GetWinText = Left$(sTmp, L)
    Else
        GetWinText = ""
    End If

End Function
```

NOTE

In the previous `DemoGetWindows` routine, notice a new API being used—
`IsWindowVisible`. This routine simply accepts the handle of a window, and
returns true or false if the window is visible or not. Because Windows on your system
may have a number of invisible windows—especially if you are running System Agent
or other background tasks—you don't want to obtain the title of a window that is not
visible. Hence, use the `IsWindowVisible` API call to weed out the windows that are not
visible. Try removing this filter and see what windows you come up with—it might be
very interesting.

Closing a Specific Window Chosen by the User. Once you obtain a list of all open
windows, you can provide a means for users to choose and close down any window
they want. The resources are thus freed up, if that is a problem. You can modify the
`DemoGetWindows` routine shown earlier to present the list of windows in a list box instead of in a message box, allowing the user to choose one.

You can then use the API routine `FindWindow` to find the window the user has chosen,
and then proceed to close the window by using the `SendMessage` API function.

The `FindWindow` API routine enables you to find the handle of a window whose title text you know, or whose window class name you know. The declaration for `FindWindow` API is as follows:

```
Declare Function FindWindow Lib "user32" _
Alias "FindWindowA" (ByVal lpClassName As Any, _
ByVal lpWindowName As Any) As Long
```

The following table describes the two arguments for `FindWindow` API call.

Argument	Description
lpClassname	Refers to the window class name with which the window was registered when it was created. Use the string name if you know it, otherwise use zero as a long integer.
LpWindowName	Refers to the window title text. Use the string text if you know it, otherwise use zero as a long integer.

For example, if a string variable `sWinText` holds the title text of the window you want, you can obtain the handle of the window into a variable, say `hWnd`, by using the following call:

```
hWnd = FindWindow(0&, sWinText)
```

NOTE

You are sending zero as a long integer in the place of the `lpClassname` argument, which you do not know. Do not use the keyword `null` to send a null string. Do not use the `""` null string, either.

Once you find the window you want, you can close it by sending it a `WM_CLOSE` message using the `SendMessage` API routine. The `SendMessage` API routine is declared as follows:

```
Declare Function SendMessage Lib "user32" _
Alias "SendMessageA" (ByVal hWnd As Long, _
ByVal wMsg As Long, ByVal wParam As Long, _
lParam As Long) As Long
```

The following table describes the arguments for `SendMessage` API call.

Argument	Description
hWnd	Handle of the window to receive the message.
wMsg	Message ID. Numerous message IDs are available in Windows, each of which performs a specific task.
wParam	Long integer parameter that depends on the specific message.
lParam	Long integer parameter that depends on the specific message.

The SendMessage API is probably the most often-used API call of all—because all processing in Windows is done through the means of passing of messages between objects. The entire description of the valid values for wParam and lParam are beyond the scope of this chapter and this book. However, for our purposes, you are interested in a message to close down a window. The message ID for this is the constant WM_CLOSE, and wParam and lParam do not contain any values, hence you should pass zeroes as long integers to your call.

> **Caution**
>
> Although SendMessage is one of the most often-used API calls, it is probably also the most dangerous one in terms of crashing your application. If the argument parameters are not passed correctly or are not of the valid type, unpredictable results can occur. Hence, exercise great caution in using this API call in your programs. Save your work frequently, especially before making your API call.

To close the specific window, therefore, make the following call (assuming that hWnd contains the handle of the window you want to close):

```
Dim L as long
const WM_CLOSE = &H10
L = SendMessage(hWnd, WM_CLOSE, 0&,0&)
if L = 0 then MsgBox "Window Closed Successfully"
```

The following demo describes how you can allow your user to choose a window to close from a list of available ones (see fig. 23.8). As you can see, it uses the DemoCloseWindow routine code and follows up by using the FindWindow and SendMessage API calls (see figs. 23.9 and 23.10).

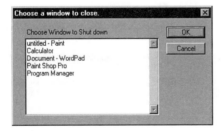

Fig. 23.8

DemoCloseWindow *routine associated with button on Sheet1 displays list of open windows in the system, allowing the user to select one to close. A custom dialog sheet is populated by this routine.*

Listing 23.6 GETWINDR.XLS. The *DemoCloseWindow* Routine

```
'
' DemoCloseWindow
'
Sub DemoCloseWindow()
 Dim sMsg As String
    Dim sWinText As String
    Dim hWnd As Long

    DialogSheets("dlgCloseWindow"). _
    ListBoxes("lstWindows").RemoveAllItems

    ' ----- get first window handle
    hWnd = GetActiveWindow()
    ' ----- do not list our window, so we cannot close ourselves
    hWnd = GetWindow(hWnd, GW_HWNDNEXT)
    Do While hWnd > 0

        ' ----- display only if window is visible
        If IsWindowVisible(hWnd) Then

            ' ----- get window title text
            sWinText = GetWinText(hWnd)
            ' ----- and add it to our dialog box list
            If sWinText <> "" Then
                DialogSheets("dlgCloseWindow"). _
                ListBoxes("lstWindows").AddItem Text:=sWinText
            End If
        End If
        ' ----- get next window handle
        hWnd = GetWindow(hWnd, GW_HWNDNEXT)
    Loop

    ' ----- display our dialog
    DialogSheets("dlgCloseWindow").Show
End Sub
```

Fig. 23.9

DemoCloseWindow
*dialog box asks for
confirmation before
closing a window.*

Listing 23.7   GETWINDR.XLS. The *cmdOK_Click* Routine Associated with the OK Button on the Dialog Sheet Displayed in Figure 23.9

```
'
' cmdOK_Click Macro
'
'
Sub cmdOK_Click()
    Dim hWnd As Long
    Dim sWinText As String
    Dim iLIndex As Integer
    Dim sEndln As String

    sEndln = Chr$(13) & Chr$(10)

    iLIndex = DialogSheets("dlgCloseWindow"). _
    ListBoxes("lstWindows").ListIndex
    sWinText = DialogSheets("dlgCloseWindow"). _
    ListBoxes("lstWindows").List(iLIndex)

    If MsgBox("Are you sure you wish to close the following window:" _
        & EndLn & sWinText, vbYesNo + vbQuestion, _
        "Demo CloseWindows ") = vbNo Then
            Exit Sub
    End If

    ' ----- Find the handle of our window
    hWnd = FindWindow(0&, sWinText)

    If hWnd > 0 Then
        ' ----- Issue a WM_CLOSE message
        L = SendMessage(hWnd, WM_CLOSE, 0&, 0&)
    End If
    If L = 0 Then
        MsgBox "Window : " & sWinText & _
        " Successfully closed.", 64, _
        "Demo CloseWindows "
    End If

End Sub
```

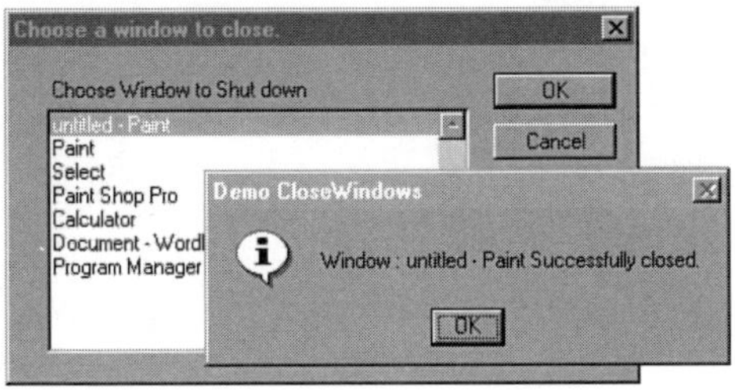

Fig. 23.10

Following success-ful closure, the DemoCloseWindows *dialog box informs the user.*

Playing Multimedia Files in Your Applications

Windows provides you with a set of rich multimedia functions through the Windows Multimedia System built into Windows. With these multimedia functions, you can manipulate sound, graphics, and video.

The functions that provide multimedia Windows API are present in the WINMM.DLL file. And, like any other API call, you can declare and use these functions. The entire gamut of multimedia functions available and their usage is too large for the scope of this chapter. You will, however, learn how to use sound, video, and multimedia text in your applications.

Using Sound. Using sound within your application can provide pizzazz. The simplest way to add sound is the Beep statement in BASIC. However, if you want to provide professional quality sound, you need to be able to play sound files (for example wave audio files that have a WAV extension). To do so, you can use the mciExecute API function:

```
Declare Function mciExecute Lib "winmm.dll"\
    ( lpstrCommand as String) As Long
```

Then in your application, you can have the following code to play the WAV file TADA.WAV:

BASIC Code:
```
Dim x as integer
x = mciExecute("play c:\windows\tada.wav")
```

WordBasic Code:
```
x = mciExecute(play c:\windows\tada.wav")
```

You can test the code only if you have a multimedia PC (or at least have a sound card installed and configured under Windows).

Playing Sound—A Word Example. The following WordBasic code populates a list box on-screen with all WAV files found in the WINDOWS folder and then plays the one selected. This code describes the use of two Windows API commands: GetWindowsDirectory and mciExecute. In addition, it also shows how you can populate a list box in a custom dialog box with a list of files on your drive.

When this macro is run, Word displays the dialog box shown in figure 23.11.

Fig. 23.11

WinAPI.Dot Macro DemoPlaySound *displays a list of available WAV files for the user to select. When the user clicks OK, the selected WAV file is played.*

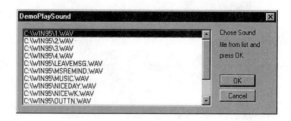

Listing 23.8   WINAPI.DOT. The *DemoPlaySound* Routine that Plays a Selected WAV File

```
Declare Function mciExecute Lib "winmm.dll"(lpstrCommand \
As String) As Long
Declare Function GetWindowsDirectory Lib "Kernel32.dll"(lpBuffer$ \
, nSize As Long) Alias "GetWindowsDirectoryA" As Long
Sub MAIN

' ----- Get the Windows Directory
sWinDir$ = String$(255, 0)
x = GetWindowsDirectory(sWinDir$, Len(sWinDir$))
sWinDir$ = Left$(sWinDir$, x)
If Right$(sWinDir$, 1) <> "\" Then sWinDir$ = sWinDir$ + "\"

' ----- Populate our list with WAV files from c:\win95 folder
temp$ = Files$(sWinDir$ + "*.wav")
count = - 1
While temp$ <> ""
     count = count + 1
     temp$ = Files$()
Wend
If count > - 1 Then
     Dim list$(count)
     list$(0) = Files$(sWinDir$ + "*.wav")
     For i = 1 To count
          list$(i) = Files$()
     Next i
     ' and sort it
     SortArray list$()

     Begin Dialog UserDialog 612, 144, "DemoPlaySound"
        ListBox 10, 11, 449, 122, List$(), .ListBox1
        OKButton 479, 82, 88, 21
        CancelButton 479, 106, 88, 21
        Text 479, 9, 101, 13, "Chose Sound", .Text1
        Text 479, 28, 121, 13, "file from list and", .Text2
        Text 479, 47, 69, 13, "press OK", .Text3
     End Dialog

     Dim MyDlg As UserDialog

     GetCurValues MyDlg
     x = Dialog(MyDlg)
     If x = - 1 Then
        x = mciExecute("play " + List$(MyDlg.ListBox1))
     End If

Else
   MsgBox "No WAV files in Windows Directory, " + \
   "Please copy some to Windows Directory and try again."

End If
End Sub
```

Playing Sound Continuously—An Excel Example. If you want to have a WAV file playing in the background continuously as your application proceeds with its tasks, you can use the sndPlaySound API function, provided you have the waveform audio device driver installed.

```
Declare Function sndPlaySound Lib "winmm.dll" _
    Alias "sndPlaySoundA" _(ByVal lpszSoundName As Any, _
    ByVal uFlags As Long) As Long
```

The arguments for this function are as follows:

Argument	Description
lpszSoundName	Name of the sound as defined under the section [sounds] in the System Registry. Or, the name of a WAV file. Examples of sound names found in the System Registry are: SystemAsterisk, SystemDefault, SystemStart, SystemExit. If no matching name is found in the System Registry, the function assumes it is the name of a WAV file and proceeds to play the WAV file.
Uflags	Options for playing sound. The valid values for uFlags are as follows:

- SND_SYNC (&H0). The function plays the sound and then returns.

- SND_ASYNC(&H1). The function starts playing the sound and immediately returns. The sound continues to play in the background. To stop the sound from playing, call the function again by passing Null as the file name.

- SND_NODEFAULT (&H2). If the function does not find the file name, it does not play anything.

- SND_MEMORY (&H4). The file name does not point to a file on disk but rather points to an in-memory image of the waveform sound.

- SND_LOOP (&H8). Used along with SND_ASYNC to keep playing the wave file continuously in a loop until canceled by a call to the same function with Null as the file name.

- SND_NOSTOP (&H10). If another sound is currently being played, do not interrupt it; return immediately instead.

To see this API in action, run Excel and open the PLAYSOUND.XLS file from the accompanying CD-ROM. You see the sheet shown in figure 23.12.

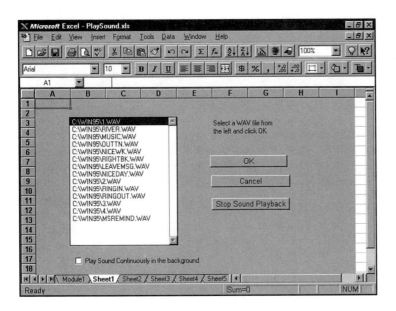

Fig. 23.12

When the Excel file is opened, the Auto_Open macro presents the first sheet with a list box populated with WAV files found in the WINDOWS95 folder.

When you choose a WAV file and click OK, you can hear the WAV file being played once. If you select the Play Sound Continuously in the Background checkbox and then click OK, your WAV file plays over and over again. Even if you quit Excel, the sound file continues to play endlessly in a loop. To stop the sound, click the Stop Sound Playback button.

The following is a list of controls on Sheet1 and the macros they are assigned to.

Control	Name	Associated with Macro
Sheet	Sheet1	Auto_Open Macro. Populates list box.
List box	lstWavFiles	None
Button	cmdOK	cmdOK_Click
Button	cmdCancel	cmdCancel_Click
Button	cmdStopSound	cmdStopSound_Click
Checkbox	chkPlayBack	None

Listing 23.9 PLAYSOUND.XLS. The *Auto_Open* Macro

```
'
' Auto_Open
'
'
Sub Auto_Open()
    Dim x As Integer
    x = DemoPlaySound()
End Sub
```

Listing 23.10 PLAYSOUND.XLS. The *Module1* Code

```
' API declarations
'
'
Declare Function GetWindowsDirectory Lib "Kernel32" _
  Alias "GetWindowsDirectoryA" (ByVal lpBuffer As String, _
  ByVal nSize As Long) As Long
Declare Function sndPlaySound Lib "winmm.dll" Alias "sndPlaySoundA" _
(ByVal lpszSoundName As Any, ByVal uFlags As Long) As Long
'
' Function DemoPlaySound : Main Routine in this XLS
'
'
Function DemoPlaySound()
    Dim sWinDir As String

    ' ----- Get the Windows Directory
    sWinDir = GetWinDir()
    ' ----- And massage it
    If Right$(sWinDir, 1) <> "\" Then sWinDir = sWinDir & "\"

    ' ----- Populate the listbox on screen with all file names
    PopulateList sWinDir

    ' ----- Make sure the checkbox is not checked
    Worksheets("Sheet1").CheckBoxes("chkPlayBack").Value = 0

    ' ----- And go to top left corner
    Application.Goto reference:=Worksheets("Sheet1").Range("A1"), _
    scroll:=True


End Function
'
' Function GetWinDir : Returns the Windows Directory
'
'
Function GetWinDir() As String
    Dim sTmp As String
    Dim L As Long

    sTmp = String$(255, 0)
    L = GetWindowsDirectory(sTmp, Len(sTmp))
    If L > 0 Then
        GetWinDir = Left$(sTmp, L)
    Else
        GetWinDir = ""
    End If
End Function
'
' Routine PopulateList : Populates ListBox in Sheet1
' with WAV file names
'
'
Sub PopulateList(ByVal sWinDir As String)
    On Error Resume Next
```

```
    Dim sTmp As String

    Worksheets("Sheet1").ListBoxes("lstWavFiles").RemoveAllItems
    sTmp = Dir$(sWinDir & "*.WAV")
    Do While sTmp <> ""
      Worksheets("Sheet1").ListBoxes("lstWavFiles").AddItem _
          Text:=sWinDir & sTmp

  sTmp = Dir$()
    Loop
If Worksheets("Sheet1").ListBoxes("lstWavFiles").ListCount _
    > 0 Then
Worksheets("Sheet1").ListBoxes("lstWavFiles").ListIndex = 1
    End If
End Sub
```

Listing 23.11   PLAYSOUND.XLS. The Macros Associated with the OK, Cancel, and StopSound Buttons

```
'
' cmdCancel_Click Macro
'
'

Sub cmdCancel_Click()
    Workbooks.Close
End Sub
'
' cmdOK_Click Macro
'
'

Sub cmdOK_Click()
    Dim x As Integer
    Dim iLIndex As Integer
    Dim lFlags As Long

    iLIndex = Worksheets("Sheet1").ListBoxes("lstWavFiles").ListIndex
    If Worksheets("Sheet1").CheckBoxes("chkPlayBack").Value = 1 Then
        lFlags = &h1 Or &h8
    Else
        lFlags = &h1
    End If

    If iLIndex > 0 Then
        x = sndPlaySound(Trim$(Worksheets("Sheet1")._
          ListBoxes("lstWavFiles").List(iLIndex)), _lFlags)
    End If
End Sub
```

Using Video. In order to run AVI files, you need to have software such as Video for Windows (Microsoft) or QuickTime for Windows (Apple) loaded on your machine. This software comes in runtime versions and is available from numerous bulletin board services and on CompuServe. It provides an extension for Windows that enables applications to play video clips.

You can play an AVI file in your VB application by using the same `mciExecute` command you saw earlier in the section "Using Sound."

```
Declare Function mciExecute Lib "MMSystem" _
    (ByVal lpString as String) as Integer
```

And, in your application, you can call this function to play an AVI file:

```
Dim x as integer
x = mciExecute("play MyAVI.AVI")
```

This code causes Windows to open a new window, title it with the name of the AVI file, and play it. When the file is finished playing, the window is automatically closed.

From Here...

In this chapter, you have had a small introduction to using Windows API in your Office applications. The entire range of API routines available is big enough to fill an entire book. As you use more and more API routines, you will learn how they can be used efficiently in your programs. The key to using the API routines is practice. Learn to pass the parameters the right way, use the API routines to provide functionality in your programs that Office applications do not, and soon you will be developing applications that your users will marvel at, and your colleagues will be wondering how you managed to do *that* using Office.

You should review the material available in the following chapters of this book to round up your knowledge:

- Chapter 3, "Integration Basics," and Chapter 5, "Programming Application Integration," provide more information on using OLE automation, DLLs, and the Windows API.

- Chapter 4, "Visual Basic and Visual Basic for Applications," shows you how to code in Visual Basic for Applications.

- Chapter 10, "Automating Office Integration with Word," provides more information on programming with WordBasic.

- Chapter 11, "Automating Office Integration with Excel," teaches you about Excel-specific programming with VBA.

- Chapter 22, "Working in a Multimedia Environment," provides more information on using multimedia in your Office applications.

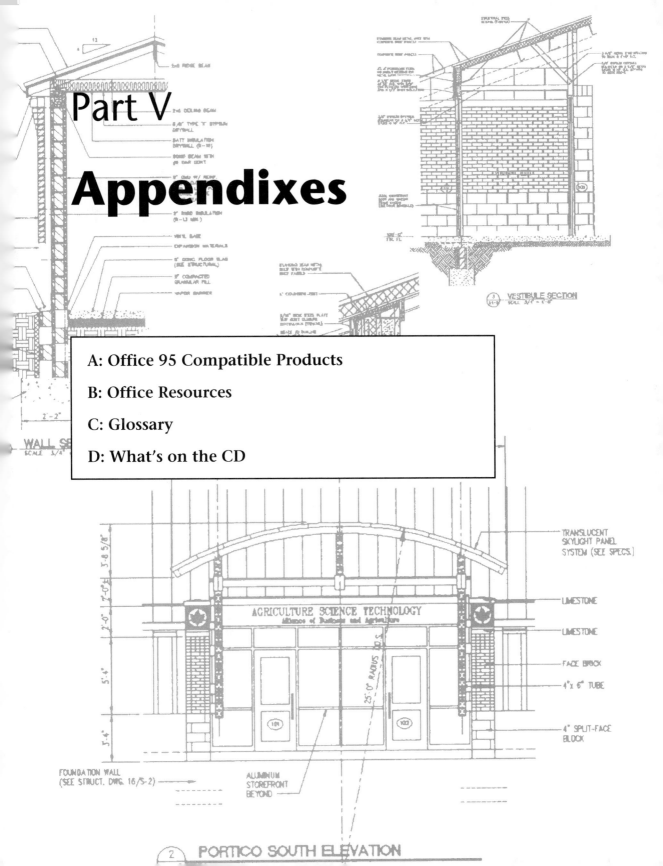

Part V

Appendixes

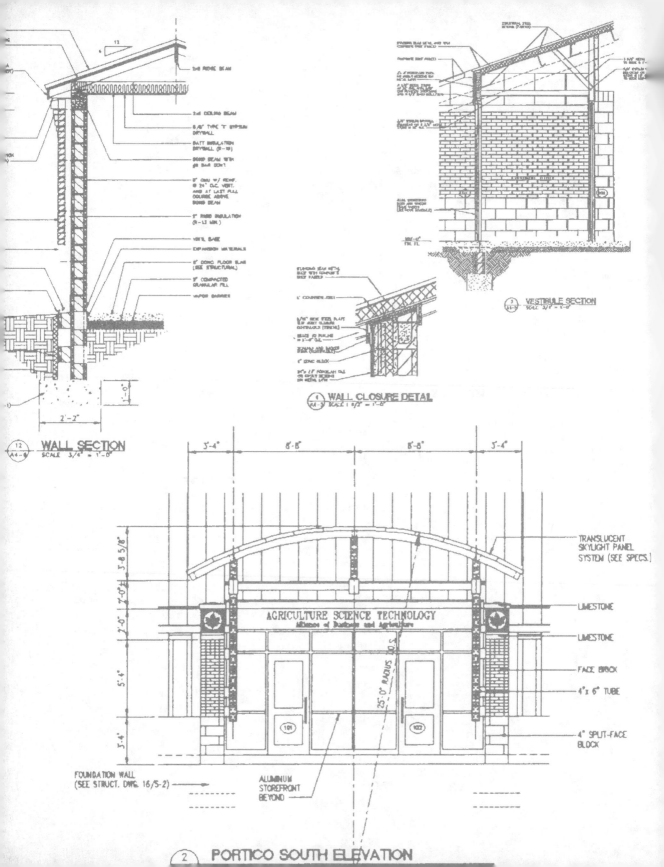

2 ½x8 PRIME BEAM

2x8 CEILING BEAM

5/8" TYPE 'X' GYPSUM DRYWALL

BATT INSULATION DRYWALL (R-19)

BOND BEAM WITH #4 BAR CONT

8" CMU w/ REINF. @ 24" O.C. VERT. AND AT LAST FULL COURSE ABOVE BOND BEAM

3" RIGID INSULATION (R-13 MIN.)

VINYL BASE

EXPANSION MATERIALS

6" CONC FLOOR SLAB (SEE STRUCTURAL)

3" COMPACTED GRANULAR FILL

VAPOR BARRIER

2'-2" 1'-0"

12 / A4-6   WALL SECTION
SCALE 3/4" = 1'-0"

3 / A4-6   VESTIBULE SECTION
SCALE 3/8" = 1'-0"

4 / A4-6   WALL CLOSURE DETAIL
SCALE 1 1/2" = 1'-0"

5'-4"   8'-8"   8'-8"   5'-4"

3'-8 5/8" 7'-0"± 2'-0" 5'-4" 5'-4"

TRANSLUCENT SKYLIGHT PANEL SYSTEM (SEE SPECS.)

AGRICULTURE SCIENCE TECHNOLOGY
Alliance of Business and Agriculture

LIMESTONE

LIMESTONE

FACE BRICK

4"x 6" TUBE

25'-0" RADIUS TO S.

4" SPLIT-FACE BLOCK

101   102

FOUNDATION WALL (SEE STRUCT. DWG. 16/S-2)

ALUMINUM STOREFRONT BEYOND

2   PORTICO SOUTH ELEVATION

Office 95 Compatible Products

One of the major advantages to companies using Microsoft Office is its consistent and common user interface. When Office first appeared on the market in 1991, it was merely a marketing plan of combining applications into a suite for a lower price. After an explosion in sales, Microsoft realized that the applications in its suite should have a more common look and feel across the applications in the suite. So with version 4.3 released in 1993, Office began to have a more common interface across its application suite. This trend continues with the release of Office 95.

What this means to Office users is that when they see the Office Compatible logo on an application, that application has been developed with these guidelines in mind. Additionally, the application has also been certified as Office compatible.

In this appendix, you learn about

- The guidelines developers follow when developing Office compatible applications
- How developers receive the Office Compatible logo
- Which applications have received the Office 95 logo

Guidelines for Office 95 Compatible Applications

According to Microsoft, there are three main benefits to using Office. The benefits can be found in a document called "Testing Guidelines for the Microsoft Office Compatible 95 Program," which can be obtained from Microsoft. The benefits are:

- Increase in the ease of use (particularly when products are used to create cross-application solutions)
- Reduction in training costs
- Generally increased user productivity

These benefits come from one source—a common user interface. When you learn to use one application—Excel for instance—you learn how to open, print, and save files. When you go to Word or PowerPoint, you follow the same patterns for opening, printing, and saving files. You don't need to relearn how to open, save, and print files across different applications. Can you remember the key combinations in your favorite DOS applications? The only commonality among DOS applications is their lack of consistency. You had to relearn how to open, print, and save a file for each application. Can you remember the keys to save a file in WordPerfect or Lotus 1-2-3?

What To Expect from Office 95 Compatible Applications

Whenever you purchase an application that has the Office 95 Compatibility logo, you can expect a certain number of standard features and behaviors from that application. The first thing to expect is that it will conform to the Windows 95 guidelines, and that it has been tested and certified to follow the guidelines put forth in the compatibility logo requirements.

However, there are many applications that do a fine job of following the Windows 95 standards that may not ever receive certification. Some that come to mind include CorelDRAW!, Lotus 1-2-3 for Windows, and WordPerfect for Windows. Many of these applications may have the Windows 95 Compatibility logo but not the Office 95 Compatibility logo. Why? In the case of the Lotus and WordPerfect applications, they are competitors to the Office 95 suite and would probably not apply for certification. The others, like CorelDRAW!, might differ slightly from the standard and not have the logo.

Does the logo mean that an application is good or the lack of the logo mean that the application is of lower quality? In both cases, the answer is uncertain. The best thing for you to do is to evaluate products on a case-by-case basis depending on your needs. There are relatively few Office 95 certified applications at this point, but many would fit the criteria of an Office 95 compatible application. These criteria are discussed in the following sections.

Office 95 Compatibility Requirements

A benefit that a common user interface provides to companies is that their training costs are optimized by using applications that follow the same interface guidelines. The following sections illustrate the requirements for receiving an Office 95 Compatible logo and give you some ideas for your applications.

In order to receive an Office 95 Compatible logo, applications must conform to the following guidelines:

- Windows 95 compatible
- Follow the respective guidelines for its product category

These guidelines are further described in the sections that follow.

Windows 95 Compatibility

The first requirement for Office 95 certification is compatibility with Windows 95. Some of the basic requirements for Windows 95 compatibility are:

- The application must support long file names and follow Universal Naming Conventions
- The application must be 32-bit
- All UI elements must conform to the Windows 95 Style Guidelines

Product Categories

When choosing an Office compatible application, you should be aware of the different categories. Office compatible applications fall into two major categories: *stand-alone* and *host-based*. These two categories are described in the following sections.

Stand-Alone Office Compatible Applications. The first major category of applications falls under the name stand-alone Office compatible applications. This means the application runs on its own, not requiring any of the Office products to be present. These stand-alone applications fall under two subcategories:

- File-based applications
- Non-file based applications

File-based applications deal with the creating, saving, and printing of files. A good example of a file-based application is a graphics package such as Micrografx Designer. A *non-file based application* would be something like a communication or connectivity package such as Q-Modem or Rumba. These applications do not handle files, thereby falling into the non-file based category.

Host-Required Office Compatible Applications. The second major category of applications falls under the name host-required Office compatible applications, with the following subcategories:

- Add-ins (Add-ons)
- Hosted OLE 2.0 servers
- Content products

This category of applications requires that a stand-alone Office compatible application be present in order to work. These applications cannot be executed from the Windows Explorer—only from another Office application. Examples of this type of application include Graph and Query. These programs can only be executed from within another application, thus falling into the host-required category.

Category Guidelines

An Office compatible application must follow the guidelines for its particular category. The focus of these category requirements centers primarily around menus and toolbars and how these application components interact with other applications. The guidelines list features that must be present in an application, and criteria for each feature. The criteria for a feature are divided into three categories:

- *Mandatory*. The feature must be present no matter what.
- *If Supported*. If this feature is supported by the application, it must conform to Office guidelines.
- *Design Adaptation*. An Office feature can be adapted to a particular application's metaphor. In the instance of a connectivity package, you can replace the New File option with New Connection.

Mandatory Requirements. The majority of the requirements found in the Office 95 guidelines center around mandatory requirements for an application. The minimum requirements for a file-based Office application are:

- Windows 95 compatibility.
- A Standard toolbar with ToolTips, large format buttons, small format buttons, and black-and-white buttons.
- A menu bar with a minimum of File, Edit, and Help menus.
- The File menu must have most of the common menu pads such as New, Open, Close, Save, and Save As.
- The Edit menu must have Cut, Copy, and Paste capabilities.
- The Help menu must have a Help topics option and an Office Compatible Help Topic.

If Supported and Design Adaptive Requirements. In the previous section, you learned some of the minimum requirements for a file-based Office application. These requirements change when the application is a non-file based application. The differences between the two categories involve the menu requirements. Depending on the application, the majority of the File menu bar options become If Supported. This means if the feature is relevant to the application, then the feature must follow the appropriate Office 95 guidelines.

This section provided a summary of some key requirements. For further information regarding these guidelines, consult the "Testing Guidelines for the Microsoft Office Compatible 95 Program" document available from Microsoft.

How a Product Receives the Office 95 Logo

In order to receive the Office 95 Compatibility logo, an application must be submitted for testing. The company that performs this testing is named VeriTest, and it charges $600 for English-based applications and $800 for non-English-based applications. This company also certifies Windows 95 applications. VeriTest is an independent company that receives no compensation from Microsoft. It only certifies whether an application follows guidelines or not.

For more information about Office 95 compatibility requirements and compatible applications, contact Microsoft at one the following sources:

Internet	**logo@microsoft.com**
Faxback system	206-635-2222
Voice mail	206-936-2880
Snail mail	Microsoft Office Compatible Program One Microsoft Way Redmond, WA 98052

Currently Certified Office 95 Applications

As of this writing, only a few applications exist that have received the Office 95 Compatibility logo. Table A.1 represents a list of some of the currently certified applications.

Table A.1 Office 95 Compatible Applications

Product/Vendor/Phone	Description
Add-A Barcode/32 Version 1.0 Wallace Computer Services 800-491-6815	Utility for printing bar codes
MASTER.DG Mugg Software 800-606-6815	Project management utility
OfficeBlox AlphaBlox 716-229-2924	Note editor, calculator, and list management utilities
Microsoft Publisher for Windows 95 Microsoft Corp. 800-426-9400	Desktop publishing program
Microsoft Small Business Pack for Microsoft Office Microsoft Corp. 800-426-9400	Business enhancement applications

(continues)

V

Appendixes

Table A.1 Continued	
Product/Vendor/Phone	**Description**
ABC Graphics Suite Micrografx 800-371-7783	Graphics editing programs
Smartsketch 95 FutureWave Software 800-619-6193	Graphics editing program
Numera Visual Cadd 2.0 Numera Software Corp. 800-956-2233	Computer-aided design program
Visio 4.0 Visio Corporation 800-24VISIO	Charting tool
Janna Contact 95 Janna Systems, Inc. 800-268-6107	Contact management program

For a current list of Office 95 compatible applications, call Microsoft at 800-426-9400.

Office Resources

When developing Office applications it's always important to know where to turn for ideas and techniques. This appendix provides a comprehensive list of resources available to Office developers.

Books

A good resource for Office developers is the many books available from various publishers. This list encompasses many of the best books available to Office developers.

Special Edition Using Microsoft Office for Windows 95
Que
Authors: Rick and Patty Winter
ISBN: 0-7897-0146-4
Cost: $34.99

Word Developers Kit
Microsoft Press
Author: Microsoft Press
ISBN: 1-55615-681-2
Cost: $39.95

Special Edition Using Word for Windows 95
Que
Author: Ron Person
ISBN: 0-7897-0084-0
Cost: $34.99

Microsoft Windows 95 Resource Kit
Microsoft Press
Author: Microsoft Press
ISBN: 1-55615-681-2
Cost: $49.95

Building Windows 95 Applications with Visual Basic
Que
Author: Ronald Martinsen
ISBN: 0-7897-0209-6
Cost: $39.99

Access for Windows Bible
IDG Books
Authors: Cary Prague and Michael Irwin
ISBN: 1-56884-493-X
Cost: $39.99

Special Edition Using Excel for Windows 95
Que
Author: Ron Person
ISBN: 0-7897-0112-X
Cost: $34.99

Special Edition Using ODBC 2.0
Que
Author: Robert Gryphon
ISBN: 0-7897-0015-8
Cost: $49.95

Excel For Windows 95 Bible
IDG Books
Author: John Walkenbach
ISBN: 1-56884-495-6
Cost: $39.99

Excel/Visual Basic Programmers Guide
Microsoft Press
Author: Microsoft Press
ISBN: 1-55615-819-X
Cost: $24.95

Visual Basic Programmer's Guide to the Windows API
Ziff-Davis Press
Author: Daniel Appleman
ISBN: 1-56276-073-4
Cost: $34.95

OLE Developer's Guide
SAMS Publishing
Author: Lawrence Harris
ISBN: 0-672-30755-3
Cost: $49.99

Inside ODBC
Microsoft Press
Author: Kyle Geiger
ISBN:1-55615-815-7
Cost: $39.95

Inside OLE
Microsoft Press
Author: Kraig Brockschmidt
ISBN: 1-55615-843-2
Cost: $49.95

Training

There are many available sources of training for Access developers. Most specialize in specific components of the Office suites. Some of the larger training companies are listed here:

Application Developers Training Company

7151 Metro Blvd, Suite 175

Minneapolis, MN 55439

1-800-578-2062

Area of training: National

Softbite International

33 N. Addison Rd. #206

P.O. Box 1401

Addison, IL 60101

1-708-833-0029

Area of training: National

Publications

Another resource for Office developers is trade publications. Trade publications are frequently updated and often have good techniques for development. Subscription prices are the annual subscription rates and are subject to change.

Access/Visual Basic Advisor

Advisor Publications

P.O. Box 469013

Escondido, CA 92046

1-800-336-6060

Cost: $29.99

Visual Basic Programmer's Journal

P.O. Box 58871

Boulder, CO 80321

1-415-833-7100

Cost: $27.95

Smart Access

Pinnacle Publishing

18000 72nd Ave., Suite #217

Kent, WA 98032

1-800-788-1900

Cost: $99.00

Utilities and Developer Tools

When developing Office applications, you may need to use utilities other than those native to Office. These applications are useful for extending the functionality of your Office applications:

Visual Basic version 4.0

Microsoft

Cost: $149–$1,000/Est.

VBA Companion

Apex Software

Cost: $80/Est.

Visual FoxPro version 3.0

Microsoft

Cost: $99–$400/Est.

The Online World

One of the better resources for developers is the online world. Developers commonly share ideas and help solve each other's problems in the many online forums.

CompuServe

1-800-848-8199

GO MSACCESS

GO MSBASIC

GO MSEXCEL

GO MSWORD

GO MSOFFICE

America Online

1-800-827-6364

PDV (PC Development Forum)

VB (Visual Basic Resource Center)

APPS (PC Applications Forum)

DATABASE (Database Resource Center)

Internet

http://www.microsoft.com/devonly (Microsoft Developers Page)

http://www. protosource.com/vbr/vbr-home.htm (Visual Basic Resource Page)

APPENDIX C

Glossary

The words and abbreviations listed in this glossary are those that are frequently used throughout this book. The definitions given here apply to the context of Windows 95 and applications that run in the Windows 95 environment.

Action An operation performed on an OLE object. In Visual Basic, you can use the Action property to specify the operation to perform on an OLE object. Examples of actions are creating an embedded object and creating a linked object.

Activate To make an object available for interaction with a user. The most common interaction is to edit a text or graphics object. When a sound or video object is activated, a user can play it. See *Object*.

API See *Application Programming Interface*.

Application A computer program used for a particular kind of work, such as word processing or database management. This term is used interchangeably with "program."

Application Programming Interface (API) A set of functions that can be called from an application to provide a related set of services. See *Windows API*.

Array A list of data values that are all of the same type. The size of a fixed array remains constant, whereas the size of a dynamic array may change during program execution.

BASIC See *Beginners' All-Purpose Symbolic Instruction Code*.

Beginners' All-Purpose Symbolic Instruction Code (BASIC) A programming language introduced in the mid-1960s that has evolved into Visual Basic and Visual Basic for Applications. See *Visual Basic* and *Visual Basic for Applications*.

BIFF   See *Binary Interchange File Format.*

Binary Interchange File Format (BIFF)   Spreadsheet file format for data and charts. Introduced by Microsoft in Excel version 2.2.

Bitmap   A file format in which an image is represented by individual bits.

Bitmap Graphic   A graphic object that is represented by the colors of individual pixels. Compare with *Vector Graphic.*

Bound Control   A control object that is linked to a data source. For example, a bound text box control in an Access form is linked to a field in a table. Compare with *Unbound Control.*

Button   A small rectangular object in a Windows screen that, when the user points to it and clicks a mouse button, causes some action to occur. Office applications have toolbars that contain preprogrammed buttons. Some applications allow creation of custom buttons that may be placed in a toolbar or elsewhere on-screen.

Client   An application that accepts embedded or linked objects. A system component that requests services from one or more servers. A computer or workstation that uses data provided by a server or relies on a server to provide services such as printing. See *Server.*

Client/Server Network   Two or more interconnected computers where one computer (sometimes more than one) acts primarily as a server and other computers act as clients.

Clipboard   A temporary storage location used by Windows to transfer data between documents and between applications on a single computer. Typically, you transfer data to the Clipboard by using an application's Copy or Cut command, and then you insert data from the Clipboard by using the application's Paste command. You can use the Clipboard Viewer to view the contents of the Clipboard.

Clipbook   An extension of the Clipboard in Windows that allows transfer of data between computers that are interconnected in a Windows for Workgroups environment.

Code   Statements written in a specific programming language or syntax.

Collection   A group of related objects in a single container.

Command Center   See *Home Screen.*

Compound Document   A document that contains embedded or linked data that was created in other applications. A Word document, for example, may contain a chart created in Excel.

Constant   An item of data that remains unchanged during the execution of a program. Compare with *Variable*. See *Intrinsic Constant*.

Construct   A way of controlling execution flow in a program. The IF construct, for example, allows a program to execute certain code if a specific condition is true, or alternative code is the condition is not true. Also known as a *Control Structure*.

Container   An object that contains other objects. A container may contain other containers. The contained objects may be linked or embedded. See *Object*, *Link*, and *Embed*.

Control   An object on-screen that a user can manipulate to perform an action. Buttons, text boxes, list boxes, and combo boxes are examples of controls.

Control Structure   See *Construct*.

Controlling Application   An application which contains VBA or other code that controls one or more other applications. A controlling application is a client; controlled applications are servers.

Conversation   The process of communicating between applications. Used particularly when referring to Dynamic Data Exchange (DDE). See *Dynamic Data Exchange*.

DAO   See *Data Access Object*.

Data   One or more items of information such as text, graphics, sound, or anything else that can be represented digitally. To be grammatically correct, a single item of information is a *datum*; multiple items are *data*. Although *data* is plural, it usually refers to a related set of information as *data*, and is regarded as singular. For example, most people write "the downloaded data *is* in ASCII format." It seems awkward to write "the downloaded data *are* in ASCII format."

Data Access Object (DAO)   An object defined by the JET database engine. Data access objects can represent objects that are used to organize and manipulate data in code.

Data Dictionary   A definition of all the data contained in a database.

Data Type   A definition or description of an element of data such as in a variable. Common data types are Currency, Integer, Number, String, and Variant.

Database An ordered collection of data that can be manipulated under computer control, together with the means to sort, display, and print that data. The data is stored in one or more tables. See *Table*.

DDE See *Dynamic Data Exchange*.

Declaration A statement that assigns an identifying name to a constant or variable. In the case of a variable, a declaration also defines the data type.

Destination An application that initiates a DDE conversation. Often, the initiating application requests data from a source; it is, therefore, the destination for the data.

Device-Independent Bitmap (DIB) A file format in which graphic images can be stored without regard for the type of monitor on which the image will be displayed or printer on which it will be printed.

Dialog Box A special window displayed by an application in which a user can make choices or supply information.

DIB See *Device-Independent Bitmap*.

DLL See *Dynamic Link Library*.

Document Whatever you create with an application, including information you type, edit, view, or save. A document may be a business report, picture, or letter, and is stored as a file on a disk.

Drag and Drop The capability, provided by OLE, to drag an object from one place to another within a document, from one document to another, or onto an icon representing a resource such as a printer or mailbox.

Drill Down To reveal progressively more detail in a document. For example, a user may be able to click a chart to reveal a summary of the data on which the chart depends, and then click an item of data to see the basic data from which that item is assembled.

Dynamic Data Exchange (DDE) The form of interprocess communication (IPC) used by Windows to support exchange of commands and data between two applications running simultaneously. In Windows 3.1, this capability is enhanced with OLE.

Dynamic Link Library (DLL) An executable code module for Windows that can be loaded on demand and linked at runtime, and then unloaded when the code is no longer needed.

EIS See *Enterprise Information System*.

Embed   To use OLE to place an object's presentation data and its native data in a document. An embedded object can usually be edited directly from within the document. Contrast with *Link*. See *Link, Presentation Data,* and *Native Data*.

Enterprise   Any organization, institution, or company.

Enterprise Information System (EIS)   An application that allows users in an enterprise (or organization) to work with various kinds of enterprise-wide data.

Event   Something that happens within a system. Events may be caused internally or externally. An example of an internal event is a timer reaching a predetermined value. External events include the user clicking a mouse button or pressing a key.

Event-driven Application   An application that primarily operates by responding to events.

Expose   To make an object accessible to OLE Automation. Excel exposes hundreds of objects, whereas Word exposes only one. An exposed object is also known as an *OLE Component*.

Expression   A combination of constants, variables, keywords, and operators that, when evaluated, result in a number, object, or string.

Field   A type of information stored in a database table. See *Table*. In some applications (Word, for example) an instruction that controls how specific data is inserted into a document. In forms, such as those created in Word, the space provided for users to insert data.

File   A collection of information that has been given a name and can be stored on a disk. This information can be a document or an application.

Flat-file Database   A database in which a single table contains all the data. As opposed to a relational database, in which two or more linked tables contain the data.

Form   A window that displays information and provides a way for users to communicate with an application. Also an on-screen representation of a form (or blank) on which users provide information.

Formula   In Excel, the contents of a worksheet cell. Compare with *Value*.

Freeze   To keep the data in one pane of a worksheet window stationary while data in another pane scrolls.

Function   A command that returns a result. In Visual Basic, a function is a type of procedure.

Global   See *Scope*.

Handle   Identifying number associated with every window in Windows. The handle identifies the window and the application associated with it.

Help Compiler   A utility that creates a Help file from text in Rich Text Format.

Help File   A file that displays on-screen information about an application. Help file names have an HLP extension.

Home Screen   The screen that appears when a user starts an application. The home screen usually has buttons or other design elements the user can choose from to branch to specific parts of the application. Also known as the *Command Center* or *Switchboard*.

Hypertext   Text, such as in a Help file, that is linked to related text. A user can click an item of text to move immediately to the linked text.

Icon   Graphical representation of an element in Windows, such as a disk drive, application, embedded or linked object, or document.

In-Place Activation   The ability to activate an embedded object within the application in which it is embedded, as opposed to manually opening the application in which the embedded application was created. In-place activation allows you to hear an embedded sound object, see an embedded video object, and edit an embedded text object. Editing an embedded text object is also known as in-place editing or visual editing.

In-Place Editing   See *In-Place Activation*.

Indexed Sequential Access Method (ISAM)   A method of minimizing the time required to locate records in a database. Databases that employ this method are known as *ISAM databases*. dBASE, FoxPro, and Paradox are examples of ISAM databases.

Information Systems (IS)   A department within an organization responsible for the support of computer networks and computer users. Sometimes known as *Management Information Systems* (MIS).

Instance   A program running or an object in existence. By starting Excel, one instance of Excel exists; with that instance existing, starting Excel again results in a second instance of Excel.

Integrated Application   An application that combines the capabilities of two or more separate applications.

Interprocess Communication (IPC)   Exchanging information between tasks or processes.

Intrinsic Constant   A constant that is defined within an application or a programming language. Access and Excel, for example, contain intrinsic constants that can be used within Visual Basic for Applications code to define many aspects of code execution.

IPC   See *Interprocess Communication.*

IS   See *Information Systems.*

ISAM   See *Indexed Sequential Access Method.*

JET   See *Joint Engine Technology Database Engine.*

Joint Engine Technology (JET) Database Engine   The database engine component of Access, also included with Visual Basic. JET controls access to data objects. JET consists of a set of DLLs. See *Dynamic Link Library.*

Keyword   A word or symbol that has a specific meaning within a programming language and cannot be used for any other purpose by programmers.

Link   To place an object's presentation data and a reference to its native data in a document. Some applications let you choose to place a reference to the presentation data as well as a reference to the native data, in order to minimize the size of the document. Contrast with Embed. See *Embed, Presentation Data,* and *Native Data.*

Local   See *Scope.*

Macro   A stored sequence of program statements that an application can execute to perform one or more operations. Some applications—Excel, Project, and Word for example—allow you to record a sequence of actions as a macro so you can subsequently repeat those actions automatically. In Access, macros allow you to automate tasks by selecting from predefined instructions.

Mailbox   The storage for a user's messages provided in an e-mail server.

MAPI   See *Messaging Application Programming Interface*.

Messaging Application Programming Interface (MAPI)   A standard set of functions that allows Windows applications to access messaging services in a consistent manner.

Metafile   A file that contains or defines other files. Many operating systems use metafiles to contain directory information about other files on a given storage device. A Windows metafile (WMF) can contain pictures in vector graphics and raster graphics formats as well as text.

Method   An action defined within an object. A worksheet range object in Excel, for example, has such methods as `Clear`, `Copy`, `Delete`, and so on.

MIME (Multipurpose Internet Mail Extensions)   An extension to Internet mail that allows for the inclusion of nontextual data, such as video and audio, in e-mail.

MIS   See *Information Systems (IS)*.

Module   A collection of declarations and procedures which together execute a task.

Native Data   One of the two types of data OLE associates with an object. Native data is all the information needed by an application to edit the object. See also *Presentation Data*.

Nested Object   An object embedded or linked into another object. OLE allows more than one level of nesting. See *Object*.

Network   Two or more interconnected computers that can communicate with each other. See *Client/Server Network* and *Peer-to-Peer Network*.

Object   Any piece of information created using a Windows application. Also, data contained in a compound document. For example, a single cell, a range of cells, or an entire worksheet can be embedded as an object in a word processing file. Any data can be an object if it is created in a Windows application that uses OLE. Objects can have properties and methods. Objects can also respond to events. See *Compound Document*, *Property*, *Method*, and *Event*.

Object Handler   A dynamic link library for an OLE server application. This DLL acts as an intermediary between the client and the server applications. For example, to improve performance when it's necessary to redraw an object in the window of the client application.

Object Library   File that defines objects available in an application. Object library file names have the extension OLB.

Object Linking and Embedding (OLE)   Windows compound document protocol that uses objects to achieve integration between applications. The client application creates the document; the server application creates an object within the document. A way to transfer and share information between applications. An enhancement to DDE protocol that allows you to embed or link data created in one application into a document created in another application, and subsequently edit that data in the original application without leaving the compound document.

Object Model   A definition of the objects available in an application, and the manner in which those objects are interrelated. An object model is often represented graphically.

ODBC   See *Open Database Connectivity*.

OEM Text   The text characters (alpha, numeric, and symbols) that can be displayed and printed by DOS-based applications without the use of supplementary font utilities.

OLE   See *Object Linking and Embedding*.

OLE Automation   A capability of OLE that allows one application to control objects within other applications. For example, OLE Automation allows control of Word's WordBasic object from Excel without human intervention. Users can create sets of instructions, such as macros, that work across applications.

OLE Component   An object exposed by an application and, therefore, accessible by way of OLE Automation.

Open Database Connectivity (ODBC)   A method of providing standard and consistent access to data stored in a variety of database formats.

Operator   A symbol, character, or sequence of characters specifying an operation on one or more elements. Arithmetic operators include + (add), – (subtract), * (multiply), and / (divide). Logical operators include AND, OR, and NOT. The & (concatenate) character is the only generally used string operator.

Package   In a compound document, an embedded icon that contains an object, a file or part of a file, or a command.

Pane   A part of a window. In Excel, you can show two or four separate parts of a worksheet in individual panes.

V

Appendixes

Peer-to-Peer Network   Two or more interconnected computers in which any or all can be servers and clients.

Picture   A graphics object in Windows metafile format.

Pixel   The smallest element that can be displayed on a monitor, or the smallest dot that can be printed. Pixel is derived from Picture Element, which is sometimes abbreviated to PEL.

Presentation Data   One of the two types of data OLE associates with an object. Presentation data is the information needed to render an object on a display device. See also *Native Data.*

Primary Key   A unique identifier for a record in a database table.

Procedure   A sequence of statements that performs a single task. Visual Basic has two kinds of procedures: *subprocedures* perform a task without returning a value; *functions* perform a task and return a value.

Property   A characteristic of an object that can be accessed from outside that object. Different types of objects have different properties. A worksheet cell object, for example, has such properties as Value, Color, Font, and so on. A read/write property is one whose value can be read and set. A read-only property is one whose value can only be read. See *Object.*

Protocol   A set of rules that determines how applications communicate. Depending on the type of communication, a protocol may deal only with software issues, as in the case of DDE. Other protocols, such as those used in networking and internetworking, cover a wide range of software and hardware issues.

Query   A means of obtaining selected data from the data stored in one or more database tables. The selected data may be displayed in a form, printed in a report, or used internally within the database. See *Form, Report,* and *Structured Query Language.*

RAD   See *Rapid Application Development.*

Rapid Application Development (RAD)   An interative technique for developing applications. When using RAD, a developer designs, develops, and tests an application in increasing levels of detail and complexity, involving typical users at each stage.

RDBMS   See *Relational Database Management System.*

Read-Only Property See *Property*.

Read/Write Property See *Property*.

Registration Database The REG.DAT file that provides the information used by the Windows File Manager and Print Manager to support drag and drop and other actions. Also used by OLE applications to find file types and OLE capabilities for embedded objects. In the Windows 95 environment, the Registration Database is replaced by the Registry. See *Registry*.

Registry A database used in the Windows 95 environment to store information about a computer's configuration, including applications installed on the computer.

Relational Database Strictly speaking, a database that supports the Relational Database model (see *Relational Database System*). Commonly used to refer to any database that contains two or more linked tables.

Relational Database System A database system that supports the model proposed by E. F. Codd in 1969. The word "relational" refers to Codd's concept of a table as a related set of information. A database that supports relations between tables is not necessarily a relational database.

Relational Database Management System (RDBMS) An application that manages access to multiple data tables with relationships between the columns of data in those tables.

Report Data generated by an application, usually a database application, that is intended to be printed, although it may also be displayed.

Resource A part of a computer system or network that an application or process can use. Resources include disk drives, printers, modems, and mailboxes.

Return To provide a value. When a function executes, it returns a value to the program that caused execution of the function.

RFT-DCA A file format created by IBM. DCA (Document Content Architecture) has two formats: RFT-DCA (Revisable-Form Text) can be edited, while FFT-DCA (Final-Form Text) cannot be edited.

Rich Text Format (RTF) A file format, adapted from DCA (Document Content Architecture), created by Microsoft. Rich Text Format can handle text and graphics and supports the ANSI, IBM PC, and Macintosh character sets.

RTF See *Rich Text Format*.

Scope   The program modules to which a variable is available. A variable that has local scope is available only in the program module in which it is defined. A variable that has global scope is available in all program modules.

Server   Application whose objects can be embedded or linked into other documents. A computer that is part of a network and provides services to other computers (clients) on the network. A file server gives clients access to files; a print server gives clients access to printers.

Source   An application that responds to a destination application during a DDE conversation. Often the initiating application requests data from a source; it is, therefore, the source for the data.

Splash Screen   A graphic image that appears on-screen while an application is being loaded from disk.

SQL   See *Structured Query Language*.

Statement   A command that causes an action such as controlling the flow of a program or making a calculation.

Structured Query Language (SQL)   A language used in querying, updating, and managing relational databases.

Subprocedure   A procedure that does not return a value. Subprocedures are often referred to simply as procedures. Compare with *Function*.

Switchboard   See *Home Screen*.

Tab   One of several labels displayed at the top edge of a dialog box. A specific section of a dialog box can be displayed by clicking the appropriate tab.

Table   The component of a database in which data is stored. A database may contain one or more tables, each of which contains data about a similar set of items. The data about each item is contained in a record. Within a table, all records have identical fields that contain the detailed information about each item. For example, a table that contains data about books has one record for each book; individual fields in each record contain such detailed data as the book's title, author's name, publisher's name, publication date, and price. A text document created by a word processor can also contain data in tabular form, which is known as a table.

TAPI   See *Telephony Application Programming Interface*.

Telephony Application Programming Interface (TAPI) A standard set of functions that allows Windows applications to access telephonic services in a consistent manner.

Tool An element of functionality that is readily available to users of an application. In Windows applications, tools are activated by clicking buttons in a toolbar or toolbox. Typical tools allow easy selection of type styles and sizes, and creation of graphics elements. See *Toolbar* and *Toolbox*.

Toolbar A column, row, or array of buttons, usually displayed near the top of a Windows screen, that provides quick access to an application's basic facilities.

Toolbox A column, row, or array of buttons that provides quick access to an application's facilities. Buttons in a toolbox usually provide access to more advanced facilities than those available in a toolbar.

Topic The primary unit of information in a Windows Help file. A topic is a self-contained body of text and graphics.

Unbound Control A control object that is not linked to data. For example, an unbound text box control in an Access form is not linked to a data source in a table field. Compare with *Bound Control*.

UUEncode A program that lets you send binary data through e-mail.

Value In Excel, the entry displayed in a worksheet cell. The value displayed in a cell is the result of evaluating the formula in that cell.

Variable An item of data that can change during the execution of a program. Each variable has a unique name. Compare with *Constant*.

Vector Graphic A graphic object in which elements are represented mathematically. Compare with *Bitmap Graphic*.

Visual Basic A programming environment for development of Windows applications. Indirectly based on BASIC. See *BASIC*.

Visual Basic for Applications A macro language, based on Visual Basic, used in Access, Excel, Project, and other Windows applications.

Visual Editing The capability of OLE that allows users to double-click an object embedded within a compound document and interact with the object right there, without switching to a different application or window. See *In-Place Activation*.

Waterfall Development A technique of application development in which all aspects of the application are completely defined before any development work starts, all development is completed before comprehensive testing starts, and comprehensive testing is completed before the application is released to users.

Windows API A set of functions built into the Windows environment which may be called from Windows applications.

Windows Open Services Architecture (WOSA) A system-level interface for connecting front-end applications with back-end services

Workgroup Two or more computers that communicate with each other under control of Windows for Workgroups.

Workstation A computer, usually a powerful computer, that people use to work on tasks. As opposed to a server.

WOSA See *Windows Open Services Architecture*.

Zoom To display images at greater or lesser magnification on-screen. In some cases, *zoom* refers to the capability to display more details.

What's on the CD

This book has provided an in-depth look at techniques you can use to maximize Office's operating efficiency. To help even further, the CD that comes with this book offers shareware and freeware programs and other add-ons, in addition to the data files for the examples shown in this book. This appendix explains how to install the free software available on the CD, as well as provides a brief description of the products included on the CD.

Installing the Software

The CD provides a convenient Installer program that you can use to install the various software programs on the disc as you need them. The Installer launches automatically the first time you insert the CD in your CD-ROM drive. The following sections describe how to run the Installer the first time you use it and for subsequent installs.

> **Caution**
>
> The first time you run the Installer from the CD, it copies some new and updated system files to your hard disk. Then, it asks you to reboot your system. Therefore, you should always save your work and close open applications before inserting the CD to ensure you don't lose any in-progress work.

Installing the First Time

The steps detailed here walk you through the process of using the CD the first time. The CD takes advantage of Windows 95 autorun capabilities, meaning it launches automatically when you insert it in the drive. Thus, save any work you have in progress and close any open applications, and then follow these steps:

1. Insert the CD in your CD-ROM drive. The Installer launches automatically.
2. At the Welcome dialog box, click OK to continue. (Or click Cancel if you don't want to copy the system files and reboot your system.)

3. The Installer informs you that it's copying files to your system. When it finishes, you can receive either one of two messages, depending upon your system.

   The Installer might ask you whether you want to reboot your system (you must do so in order to be able to use the Installer to install software from the CD); click OK. The system reboots. If the Installer doesn't restart automatically, double-click the icon for the CD drive in the My Computer window.

   Alternatively, the installer might inform you that the setup is complete and that the Que Software Guide will start; click OK to continue.

4. The Building Integrated Office Applications installation screen appears. It offers six tabs, which organize the shareware on the CD into categories:

Office Utilities	Visual Basic Custom Controls
Windows 95 Utilities	Miscellaneous
Graphics	Example Files

   Click a tab to display the software you can install from that category.

5. Scroll through the list that appears on the tab, if needed, to display the name of the software you want to install. Click to select the software to install.

6. (Optional) Click the View Application Information button to take a look at the README information included with the application's Install files created by the software's author(s). After reading the information, click OK to close the Program Information screen.

7. Click Install Application to tell the installer to install the selected application.

8. Click OK on the Welcome screen to proceed with the installation. The README information appears on-screen.

9. Click OK to close the Read Me window and continue with the installation.

10. In the Select Destination Directory window that appears, select the appropriate install drive and directory, then click OK.

11. At the Make Backups? dialog box, click Yes to have the installer create backup copies of any files that may be changed by the program being installed. If you choose Yes, select the backup directory in the dialog box that appears, then click OK.

    The application installs. Repeat steps 5–12 to install other applications from the CD.

12. Click Exit to close the Installer window and complete the installation.

Using the Installer Again

After you've used the CD Installer the first time, the system files that are necessary for it to run exist on your system. If, however, you want to use the CD again to install additional applications, there are one of two methods available:

■ If the CD isn't already in your CD-ROM drive, insert it. The autorun application on the CD starts, and the Installer loads, presenting you with the tabs categorizing the software available on the CD. Then you can repeat steps 4–14 presented in the previous section.

■ If you've already run the Installer and the CD is still in your CD-ROM drive, you can restart the Installer by double-clicking its icon in the My Computer window, or by clicking the Start menu and choosing Programs, Que, Building Integrated Office Applications, Building Integrated Office Applications.

TIP

You can uninstall the Building Integrated Office Applications Installer files or run installed shareware from the CD by choosing Start, Que, Building Integrated Office Applications, then choosing the option that you want. Some of the shareware programs also offer uninstall options via this method.

Examples and Source Code from the Book

Throughout this book, you've seen numerous examples to customize Office and build solutions to streamline Office operations. The CD offers the example and source code files used in creating the applications and other solutions discussed in this book. You can install the example and source code files using the Data Files tab in the CD Installer application. Simply click that tab, select the chapter for which you want to view the example/source code files, then click the Install Application button.

Shareware and Add-Ons

The CD that accompanies this book offers a variety of shareware and freeware programs, VB controls, and add-ons that can help you further customize Office and applications. To make it easier to find what you're looking for, the list is broken up into categories that correspond with the category tabs in the CD installer application.

NOTE

Most of the applications included on the CD are shareware products. Don't forget to register any products you plan to use regularly. See the Help or README information that accompanies each application for registration information.

Office Utilities

On the Office Utilities page of the CD Installer, you find these choices:

■ *Access ELF.* Places Analyze and Query buttons to the Access Database toolbar. The Analyze button generates a natural language interface for the current database. Clicking the Query button enables you to create plain-English queries.

V

Appendixes

NOTE This application cannot be directly installed from the application Installer, because it comes bundled as a ZIP file. The application installer only allows you to view the installation instructions. You must browse the CD and unzip the files yourself, following the directions in the README file.

- *Formtool*. Offers a palette of special tools for moving, widening, or deepening Access form controls in pixel increments.

- *Internet Assistant for Word*. Enables you to use Word for Windows to create hypertext markup language (HTML) documents to be published on the World Wide Web. Internet Assistant can convert document files to HTML; it also provides a template for creating new HTML files.

- *OfficeCab 1.1*. Provides a substitute for the Find File dialog box in Word, Excel, and PowerPoint. It lists all files by name and title in a folder, and enables you to search and filter by title or file name.

- *Powerpoint Backgrounds*. Created by Stuart Kippelman, the BMP images in this collection using Corel Photo-Paint 6.0 and Adobe PhotoShop 3.0, can be used with any software that supports the BMP format. To use an image as a custom presentation background in PowerPoint, choose Format, Custom Background, then choose the desired image.

- *Units & Volumes Excel Add-In v1.1*. Load this Excel 5 add-in module with the Add-In Manager. The Units & Volumes add-in offers specialized functions for converting measurements. For example, you can convert a value in a cell from grams to pounds. Units & Volumes 17 unit conversion functions cover everything from Acceleration to Volumetric Flow (more than 240 common units supported). The six-volume functions calculate partial volumes for different tank geometries. Engineers, in particular, will find this add-in useful.

- *Microsoft Word Macro Virus Protection Tool*. Designed to detect macro viruses, such as the Concept virus, that infect Word documents. The Tool installs a set of protective macros in the NORMAL.DOT template which detect suspicious Word files and alert you to the potential risk of opening files with macros. It gives you the option of opening a file without executing any macros the file contains, thereby ensuring that no viruses are transmitted. The Tool also can be used to scan your hard disk for Word files that contain the Concept virus.

Windows 95 Utilities

If you're looking for tools to work more effectively in Windows 95, consider these items on the Windows 95 Utilities page of the CD Installer:

- *CabWiz v2.00*. Lists the compressed contents of a Microsoft installation cabinet file(s) from a folder on any drive. You can save the list—which shows file names, registered file types, size in bytes, and location in the cabinet—to a text file.

- *Hex Workshop v2.10*. Eliminates some of the pain of editing files and disks in hex. Insert, delete, cut, copy, and paste hex. With Hex Workshop, you can go to, find, and replace hex characters, compare files, and perform checksum calculations. This latest version offers a Base Converter (convert between hex, decimal, and binary) and a Hex Calculator.

■ *Somar ACTS v1.7.* Using your system's modem, dials into the National Institute of Standards and Technology (NIST) or United States Naval Observatory (USNO) time source to set the internal clock of your computer.

■ *WinImage 2.20 for Windows 95.* Enables you to create and manage disk images. A *disk image* is a file that contains all the data from a floppy disk, including files, FAT, boot sector, and directories. Like the DOS `diskcopy` command, WinImage creates an exact copy of the disk contents. WinImage disk images can be copied to a hard drive, floppy drive, network drive, or other media. Once it's on the hard disk, for example, the image can be used to create multiple copies on floppy disk. Individual files can be added to or extracted from an image. WinImage can simultaneously format a floppy disk and copy an image to the floppy disk, a fast and easy way to create floppy disk copies.

WinImage also can use image files created with other disk copy programs, including DiskDupe, DCF (Disk Copy Fast), OS/2 2.x and DR DOS 6 diskimage, and DF (Disk Image File Utility).

■ *WinZip 95.* Enables you to zip and unzip compressed ZIP archive files on the Windows 95 Desktop. WinZip enables you to handle several common Internet file formats (TAR, gzip, and UNIX compress) in addition to ZIP files, supports Windows 95 long file names, and more. WinZip 95's point-and-click, drag-and-drop interface provides for painless viewing, running, extracting, adding, deleting, and testing files in archives. It interfaces with other programs to handle ARJ, LZH, and ARC files, and interfaces with most virus scanners.

Graphics

If you work extensively with graphics files in Windows 95, the following applications listed on the Graphics page of the CD Installer could save you time:

■ *PolyView Version 2.21 by Polybytes.* Enables you to view, convert, and print BMP, GIF, JPEG, Kodak Photo CD, PNG, and TIFF graphics files.

■ *SmartDraw 95.* Creates diagrams, flow charts, flyers, posters, maps, invitations, and other business graphics. It lets you create drawings by dragging-and-dropping shapes into place. SmartDraw also offers a collection of SmartDrawings clip art images and prebuilt design styles to help you set the palette and more for a drawing. SmartDraw works with programs that support OLE, including the Office applications.

■ *SnapShot/32.* SnapShot/32 enables you to capture your screen display under Windows 95 and NT. SnapShot/32 lets you save captured screen images in the BMP, GIF, and JPEG formats (even progressive JPEGs for use on the World Wide Web). You can set up HotKeys to automatically capture parts of the screen. SnapShot/32 can automatically save files and increment file names, and offers other features including easy printing and drag-and-drop file opening.

VB Custom Controls

Shared resources and examples can make any programmer more effective and efficient. The VB Custom Controls tab of the CD Installer offers these resources for programmers developing for Windows 95 and Office:

> **NOTE** Some of the VB control installers enable you to choose between VBX, OCX-16, and OCX-32 formats.

- *Alarm Custom Control.* Lets you set multiple alarms (events) at the time(s) you specify or at specified intervals. This control can be useful when you're writing a PIM, and enables you to schedule events to happen at various times. ALARM1.VBX can tell you when the date has changed or be used to remove all current alarms and set new ones. ALARM1.VBX is compatible with VB 2.0 and above.

- *BmpLst Custom Control.* Lets you create a list box displaying bitmap pictures. The bitmaps can be placed above, below, to the right, or to the left of the list text.

- *DDD FX '95 Professional Toolkit.* Enables you to add special design effects to your Visual Basic applications via easy-to-use BAS modules holding VBA source code, which means no VBX, OCX, or external DLL files are required. Improve your application's look by adding faded forms with gradient colors; 3D appearance on meters, spin buttons, frames, and more; enhanced checkboxes and options buttons; and exploding forms.

- *DFInfo Custom Control.* Lets your VB apps read and modify file information, including date, time, size, and so on (DBINFO2.VBX). You can access information about the computer's drives through another set of properties. It's compatible with VB 2.0 and up.

- *FM Drop Custom Control.* Displays notification when a file has been dragged-and-dropped from the Windows File Manager (FMDROP1.VBX).

- *Formatted Label Custom Control.* A bound label control that lets you format the text within it using different fonts and colors, multiple paragraphs, paragraph formatting, and so on (FLABEL1.VBX).

- *HiTime Custom Control.* Fires timer events nearly every millisecond, as opposed to every 55 milliseconds (18.2 times per second) with the normal Visual Basic Timer control. Use this control just like the default Timer control that comes with Visual Basic. The rate at which HiTime can trigger timer events depends on the speed of your machine: 500 ticks per second for a 486DX2/66s, and 1000 ticks per second for 66MHz Pentiums.

- *INICon Custom Control.* Simplifies INI file access, supporting both WIN.INI and private INI file access without API calls (INICON3.VBX).

- *LED Custom Control.* Enables you to define 3D effects and colors. If you need LED-like display (such as when you need an on/off indicator for items such as modem lights), use the LED custom control.

- *Menu Event Notification (MenuEv) Custom Control.* After placing MenuEv on your form, it immediately provides menu selection notification. In other words, it indicates when the user has selected a menu item. Useful for status bar-style help; MenuEv even automatically updates another control with the selected menu item's text. The events give you the text of the menu item selected.

- *MsStat Custom Control.* Displays a multi-element status bar on the bottom of your form (MSSTAT1.VBX). It automatically handles the Num Lock, Caps Lock, Scroll Lock, and Insert key indicators. With MsStat, you can include times/dates in International and programmer-defined formats on the status bar. Use the Item properties to define the elements in the control.

- *NED 32-bit Image OCX 1.21 Custom Control.* Enables display and printing of various types of image files, including those in the TIFF, BMP, DIB, GIF, JPEG, and Kodak Photo CD formats. Use this 32-bit Windows OLE custom control with any host programming environment or application that supports 32-bit OCX controls. OLE version 2.02 or higher is required.

- *NED 16-bit VUMeter OCX 1.1 Custom Control.* A 16-bit OLE 2.0 OCX control that presents a needle gauge control similar to ones on stereo equipment. When you use the VUMeter control in a finished application, the VUMeter Control DLL (VUMeter.OCX) must be installed with the application. There are properties to adjust the behavior and appearance of the control, such as choosing horizontal or vertical orientation, setting the colors for various parts of the control, and adding 3D effects like bevels. Setting low and high limits (with values from 0–32,767) will cause an event to be sent to your application when either the high or low occurs.

- *NED 16-bit VUGauge OCX 1.1 Custom Control.* A 16-bit OLE 2.0 OCX control that presents a needle gauge control like one on the dashboard of a car. When you use VUGuage in an application, VUGUAGE.OCX must be installed on the user's computer. Use VUGuage's properties to specify one of four orientations, set colors, add 3D borders, and the like. Setting low and high limits (with values from 0–32,767) will cause an event to be sent to your application when either the high or low occurs.

- *NED 16-bit Gauge OCX 1.1 Custom Control.* Enables you to add a gauge similar to ones on industrial process control equipment. It's a 16-bit OLE 2.0 custom control. Make sure NEDGUAGE.OCX is installed on the user's system if you use this control in an application. Properties let you specify one of four orientations, set control colors, and add 3D borders and bevels. Low and high limits with values from 0–32,767 can be set.

- *NED 16-bit Knob OCX 1.1 Custom Control.* Enables you to add a needle gauge control to your application using KNOB.OCX, a 16-bit OLE 2.0 custom control. Properties let you specify one of four orientations, set control colors, and add 3D borders and bevels. Low and high limits with values from 0–32,767 can be set.

- *PerCnt Custom Control.* Displays a percentage bar on your form for status reporting (PERCNT2.VBX). You can specify the 3D effects, fonts, and colors that appear on the bar.

■ *PicBtn Custom Control.* Creates a command button that has both text and a picture on it using PICBTN1.VBX. You control the picture scaling and placement with regard to the text, which may be multiline.

■ *Probe Custom Control.* Enables you to examine and modify other controls' properties at runtime using PROBE1.VBX. Probe lists the properties of a specified control so you can adjust the properties that are only available at runtime using an easy interface. Use Probe as a debugging tool or include it with your project during beta tests. In a final product, Probe can be a useful diagnostic tool.

■ *Project Mapper v2.0 for VB 4.* Scans through your entire project and neatly organizes the project components with its subcomponents (example: Forms with Procedures, Declarations, and so on) in a hierarchical structure. This enables you to have a clear understanding of the structure of your project.

■ *SoundX Custom Control.* Provides Soundex and Metaphone algorithms, which convert words or names to codes that represent how they "sound." Use this control in applications where users may need to find names they may not know how to spell in a database.

■ *Tips Custom Control.* Enables users to display a Microsoft-style ToolTip by pausing the mouse pointer over a control. No extra code is required; adjust Tips by setting the Tag properties.

■ *Tip of the Day version 2.0.* Visual Basic "plug-in" form and code module that enables you to add a Tip of the Day screen to your application. This module contains 100 percent source code and does not require any VBX files. To use Tip of the Day, just add its files to your project. Also included is TipEdit, which enables you to create and edit the TOD file that adds tips to your application.

■ *ToolTips 95 Pro version 3.0.* ToolTips "plug-in" code module for VB that enables you to add yellow pop-up tips to describe toolbar buttons you add into your applications. To display the tip, the user simply needs to move the mouse pointer over the button. This version of ToolTips eliminates the need for any VBX or DLL files that add ToolTips, and is pure VB source code—it takes up less than 7K.

■ *Wizard Wand 2.0.* Builds and generates skeletal screen and navigation code for wizards in applications. After the three seconds or so it takes for Wizard Wand to generate the basic code, you can (and generally should) add greater functionality by editing the code.

■ *ZipInf Custom Control.* ZIPINF1.VBX gives you information about the content (directory) of a ZIP file, which can be useful when an application needs to perform File Manager replacement, search a drive, and so on. ZipInf does not compress or decompress data.

Miscellaneous

If nothing you've read about so far fills your needs of the moment, check out these packages on the Miscellaneous page of the CD installer application:

- *AMF Daily Planner & Personal Information Manager v5.1.* PIM and scheduler that lets you plan your time with an easy drag-and-drop interface. It offers a perpetual calendar and planner to the year 9000. Use the Rolodex-style phone book to store up to 30,000 entries which you can use to dial your phone, fax documents, and address business letters. Edit, save, and print text files, reports, schedules, envelopes, and labels. For added convenience, AMF Daily Planner & Personal Information Manager can create printed pages in the FiloFax format.

> **NOTE** The Installer only installs the setup files onto the drive; you need to run the setup routine.

- *Forms Nexus for Windows.* Offers professionally designed standard office forms for use in businesses of all sizes. Simply select the form you want and fill in the blanks. No form design is required. The Forms Nexus forms offer sophisticated, elegant, and highly professional business designs. All needed mathematical formulas are built-in on necessary cells in each form, including calculations, line-item totals, discounts, column subtotals and totals, shipping, sales tax (if any), and so on. Most forms enable you to compile a list of recipients from which you can later select names. Where applicable, forms are designed to show the recipient's name and address through a standard No. 10 window envelope.

- *Visual Help Pro 3.1.* Offered by Visual Help, an intuitive drag-and-drop interface for creating online help systems in Windows. In addition to creating Help files for applications, you can use Visual Help to present other documents online, such as procedure manuals, company databases, multimedia presentations, information guides, README files, shared network information, electronic books, and online tests.

- *Windows HLP to RTF/HPJ Converter.* Converts Windows HLP files from Windows 3.1x, Windows 95, and Windows NT 3.51 to RTF (Rich Text Format) for use in other documents.

- *x-Fone4 Network Phone Directory System.* Enables you to easily track and maintain contact names and numbers by creating a phone directory on a network with this product. You can add custom fields and prompts, sort by any field, and more. Users can set up colors, fonts, toolbars, and other display features. Many administration and setup features are built-in, including user management, security, reindexing, and so on.

- *x-Forum4 Network Message Forum System.* Creates a public message system on a network. You can establish up to 99 different message forums, with unlimited messages per forum. Forums can be interactive or read-only, with interactive forums offering subject threading, message creation, and message replies. Administration features make user and forum management easy.

- *x-Out4 for Windows Network.* If you need to know when the members of your group are in or out of the office and/or on or off the network, Extensions Software Corporation's X-Out4 for Windows Network offers a budget-conscious solution. Though it's easy to use and maintain, the numerous x-OUT4 Network In-Out System features provide complete status tracking of employees and network users. Among other things, it can display in, out, and in-but-unavailable status; real names versus network login names; and user comments and user contacts. Administrators can benefit from the built-in activity log (audit trail), error log, in-out setup, and user management features, among others.

Index

X-Y-Z

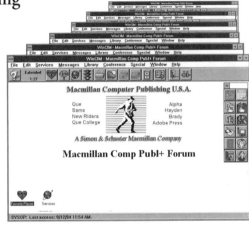

Building Integrated Office Applications CD-ROM

In addition to all the source code and examples from the book, the *Building Integrated Office Applications* CD-ROM contains a number of Que's recommended shareware and freeware programs, utilities, and add-ons, to help you further customize your integrated Office applications:

- **Office utilities** that enhance the power and performance of your applications.
- **Windows 95 utilities** for optimizing the operating system.
- **Graphics tools** that put expanded graphics capabilities at your fingertips.
- **VB custom controls** that simplify procedures and provide preprogrammed, drop-in Visual Basic Objects.
- **Additional shareware packages** that further enhance your Office application environment.

See Appendix D, "What's on the CD," for a complete listing and description of the CD-ROM contents. For installation instructions, see "Using the Installer Again," in Appendix D.

Licensing Agreement

By opening this package, you are agreeing to be bound by the following:

This software is copyrighted and all rights reserved by the publisher and its licensers. You are licensed to use this software on a single computer. You may copy the software for backup or archival purposes only. Making copies of the software for any other purpose is a violation of United States copyright laws. THIS SOFTWARE IS SOLD AS IS, WITHOUT WARRANTY OF ANY KIND, EITHER EXPRESSED OR IMPLIED, INCLUDING BUT NOT LIMITED TO THE IMPLIED WARRANTIES OF MERCHANTABILITY AND FITNESS FOR A PARTICULAR PURPOSE. Neither the publisher nor its dealers and distributors nor its licensers assume any liability for any alleged or actual damages arising from the use of this software. (Some states do not allow exclusion of implied warranties, so the exclusion may not apply to you.)

The entire contents of this disc and the compilation of the software are copyrighted and protected by United States copyright laws. The individual programs on the disc are copyrighted by the authors or owners of each program. Each program has its own use permissions and limitations. To use each program, you must follow the individual requirements and restrictions detailed for each. Do not use a program if you do not agree to follow its licensing agreement.

Microsoft's Internet Assistant was reproduced by Macmillan Computer Publishing on the accompanying CD-ROM under a special arrangement with Microsoft Corporation. For this reason, Macmillan Computer Publishing is responsible for the product warranty and for support. If your CD-ROM is defective, please return it to Macmillan Computer Publishing, which will arrange for its replacement. PLEASE DO NOT RETURN IT TO MICROSOFT CORPORATION. Any product support will be provided, if at all, by Macmillan Computer Publishing. PLEASE DO NOT CONTACT MICROSOFT CORPORATION FOR PRODUCT SUPPORT. End users of this Microsoft program shall not be considered registered owners of a Microsoft product and, therefore, shall not be eligible for upgrades, promotions, or other benefits available to registered owners of Microsoft products.